THE VITALITY OF KARAMOJONG RELIGION

How long can a traditional religion survive the impact of world religions, state hegemony and globalization? The 'Karamoja problem' is one that has perplexed colonial and independent governments alike. Now Karamojong notoriety for armed cattle raiding has attracted the attention of the UN and USAID since the proliferation of small arms in the pastoralist belt across Africa from Sudan to stateless Somalia is deemed a threat to world security. The consequences are ethnocidal, but what makes African peoples stand out against state and global governance?

The traditional African religion of the Karamojong, despite the multiple external influences of the twentieth century and earlier, has remained at the heart of their culture as it has changed through time. Drawing on oral accounts and the language itself, as well as his extensive experience of living and working in the region, Knighton avoids Western perspectivism to highlight the successful reassertion of African beliefs and values over repeated attempts by interventionists to replace or subvert them. Knighton argues that the religious aspect of Karamojong culture, with its persistent faith dimension, is one of the key factors that have enabled them to maintain their amazing degree of religious, political and military autonomy in the postmodern world. Using historical and anthropological approaches, the real continuities within the culture and the reasons for the mysterious vitality of Karamojong religion are explored.

VITALITY OF INDIGENOUS RELIGIONS SERIES

Series Editors

Graham Harvey, Open University, UK
Lawrence Martin, University of Wisconsin, Eau Claire, USA
Tabona Shoko, University of Zimbabwe, Zimbabwe

Ashgate's *Vitality of Indigenous Religions* series offers an exciting new cluster of research monographs, drawing together volumes from leading international scholars across a wide range of disciplinary perspectives. Indigenous religions are vital and empowering for many thousands of indigenous peoples globally, and dialogue with, and consideration of, these diverse religious life-ways promise to challenge and refine the methodologies of a number of academic disciplines, while greatly enhancing understandings of the world.

This series explores the development of contemporary indigenous religions from traditional, ancestral precursors, but the characteristic contribution of the series is its focus on their living and current manifestations. Devoted to the contemporary expression, experience and understanding of particular indigenous peoples and their religions, books address key issues which include the sacredness of land, exile from lands, diasporic survival and diversification, the indigenization of Christianity and other missionary religions, sacred language, and re-vitalization movements. Proving of particular value to academics, graduates, postgraduates and higher level undergraduate readers worldwide, this series holds obvious attraction to scholars of Native American studies, Maori studies and African studies and offers invaluable contributions to religious studies, sociology, anthropology, geography and other related subject areas.

OTHER TITLES IN THE SERIES

Maya Identities and the Violence of Place
Borders Bleed
Charles D. Thompson, Jr.
ISBN 0 7546 1377 1

Sacred Landscapes and Cultural Politics
Planting a Tree
Edited by Philip P. Arnold and Ann Grodzins Gold
ISBN 0 7546 1569 3

Korean Shamanism
The Cultural Paradox
Chongho Kim
ISBN 0 7546 3184 2 (hbk)
ISBN 0 7546 3185 0 (pbk)

The Vitality of Karamojong Religion

Dying Tradition or Living Faith?

BEN KNIGHTON
Oxford Centre for Mission Studies, UK

LONDON AND NEW YORK

First published 2005 by Ashgate Publishing

2 Park Square, Milton Park, Abingdon, Oxon OX14 4RN
711 Third Avenue, New York, NY 10017, USA

Routledge is an imprint of the Taylor & Francis Group, an informa business

First issued in paperback 2017

Copyright © Ben Knighton 2005

The author has asserted his moral rights under the Copyright, Designs and Patents Act, 1988, to be identified as the author of this work.

All rights reserved. No part of this book may be reprinted or reproduced or utilised in any form or by any electronic, mechanical, or other means, now known or hereafter invented, including photocopying and recording, or in any information storage or retrieval system, without permission in writing from the publishers.

Notice:
Product or corporate names may be trademarks or registered trademarks, and are used only for identification and explanation without intent to infringe.

British Library Cataloguing in Publication Data
Knighton, Ben
 Karamojong traditional religion : dying tradition or living
 Faith?. – (Vitality of indigenous religions)
 1. Karamojong (African people) – Religion
 I. Title
 299.6'85

Library of Congress Cataloging-in-Publication Data
Knighton, Ben.
 Karamojong traditional religion : dying tradition or living faith? / Ben Knighton.
   p.cm. – (Vitality of indigenous religions series)
 Includes bibliographical references (p.).

 1. Karamojong (African people) – Religion. 2. Uganda – Karamoja Province – Religion.
 I. Title. II. Vitality of indigenous religions series.

BL2480.K37K65 2003
299'.685–dc21   2003041780

ISBN 978-0-7546-0383-2 (hbk)
ISBN 978-1-138-24624-9 (pbk)

To

Wanja,

Rachel, Charis and Joel

Contents

List of Maps, Photographs, Figures and Tables   ix
Abbreviations   xi
Foreword   xiii
Acknowledgements   xv

1   The Challenges of Circumscribing the Other   1
2   The Series of Human Settlements in Karamoja   35
3   The Colonization of Karamoja and Christian Incursion   57
4   Spirit and Society   77
5   Religion and Social Control   103
6   The Constitution of the Assembly, the Paradigm for Time   133
7   Sacral Leaders and Sacramental Representation   177
8   Mediation and Revelation   209
9   Enduring Vitality and its Challengers   239

Bibliography   263
Index   329

Maps, Photographs, Figures and Tables

Maps

1.1	Average annual rainfall map of Karamoja	21
1.2	The present political units of Karamoja	25

Photographs

1.1	Lobel volcanic plug, Najie	2
1.2	Interviewing under a tree at Lotim, Nadodosó	15
4.1	Teko and brother processing around the clan homesteads of his betrothed before making a bridewealth payment	96
5.1	Herders in the cattle-camp	118
6.1	Lotuko (he of the zebra): the ox to be speared at initiation	165
7.1	The *Agat* litany: praying for a baby to be implanted in the womb	204
8.1	Drinking the blood and sucking out the marrow at an ox-sacrifice	212
9.1	*Akidung Amuro*: cutting the joint of the hind legs of the sacrifice	244
9.2	Women's healing session, Kaabong	254

Figures

2.1	The linguistic classification of Ngakaramojong	39
2.2	Ethnic relationships around Karamoja	52

Tables

1.1	Average annual rainfall at various centres in Karamoja	20
6.1	Karimojong age-classes	139
6.2	Jie age-classes	150
6.3	Dodosó age-classes	152

Abbreviations

ADC	Assistant District Commissioner
BCMS	Bible Churchmen's Missionary Society
CMG	Companion of (the Order of) St Michael and St George
CMS	Church Missionary Society
C-N	Chari-Nile
CO	Colonial Office
Col.	Colonel
COU	Church of Uganda
CS	Central Sudanic
DC	District Commissioner
Dep.	Deputy
EC	Eastern Cushitic
EN	Eastern Nilotic
EP	Eastern Province, Uganda
ES	Eastern Sudanic
FO	Foreign Office
HQ	Headquarters
I	Itunga
KAR	King's African Rifles
KNA	Kenya National Archives
L(ieu)t.	Lieutenant
lit.	literally
MC	Military Cross
MM	*Missionary Messenger*, the BCMS magazine
MP	Member of Parliament
NC	Northern Cushitic
NP	Northern Province, Uganda
N-S	Nilo-Saharan
OC	Officer Commanding
O-M	Ongamo-Maa
P-	Proto-language/ethnic group
PC	Provincial Commissioner
RA	Royal Artillery
RC	Roman Catholic
RE	Royal Engineers
RGS	Royal Geographical Society
Sec.	Secretary
SIM	Sudan Interior Mission

SN	Southern Nilotic
T	Tunga
UN	United Nations
USAID	United States Aid
VF	Verona Father(s)
WN	Western Nilotic

Foreword

Many scholars have contrasted 'tradition' and 'history'. Among the Bakongo, Wyatt MacGaffey (1970) told us long ago, 'tradition' is what offers each household its place in the grand narrative of the expansion of the founding clans, while 'history' is the hard-eyed account of how one's next-door neighbours are really descended from slaves. Other scholars, myself among them, have tried to emancipate a dynamic history from the fetters of invented and static tradition (Ranger 1993). Jan Vansina (1990) has offered a history of political tradition and Jane Guyer (1996) has described 'traditions of invention', both in equatorial Africa.

Now Ben Knighton offers his own perspective on the debate. In his study of Karamoja he does not oppose history and tradition but insists on both. History is hard to come by in Karamoja and has to be constructed largely from linguistic evidence. When it has been so constructed, however, an extraordinarily dynamic pattern of movement and cultural interaction emerges. Knighton argues that Karamojong 'culture' has emerged out of all this dynamism but that once established it proved extraordinarily resilient and resistant to external change. 'The traditional cultures of the present communities,' he writes, 'only date from the 1830s when different ethnic groups and customs were irrevocably amalgamated.' Thereafter 'the traditional cultures' were maintained 'through their religion' so 'subtle and adept at responding to the vicissitudes of historical change'. Without this 'their culture would have fragmented in the face of [imperial] state power'.

Indeed the third term in Knighton's book is religion/ritual. Linguistic evidence for historical change shows both great continuities and great transformations of religious ideas and ritual practices. The Karamoja environment is expressed in religious symbol and ritual. But Karamojong religion is not a mere product of the environment. 'It is in the field of religious ideas', writes Knighton, 'that human freedom is at its highest.' Religion in Karamoja is an amalgam of offices, ideas and rituals from different sources, operating partly in tension and partly in harmony with each other.

Knighton writes about the constant tensions within the Karamojong age-set system in terms of 'salvation history' – the archetypal fear expressed in myth of the young men going off to their cattle camps and never returning, leaving the elders to wither away, and the repetitive salvation expressed in the herders' return. The fact that such secessions and schisms have not happened often is, he says, 'a testament to religious means for resolving socio-political tensions'.

The interaction of religion, environment and society is often described poetically in this book:

The Creator not only brings the rain, but is so closely associated with it that he would be the rain were he not also transcending it ... If the river in spate represents the tempestuousness of lesser spirits, divinity transcends them by bringing his people through the raging waters to protect them in their land against their enemies.

Writing of holy places, Knighton says that 'the sacred grove is crying out for someone to perform a sacrifice there'. Writing of women's rites he speaks of 'the welcome sense of the numinous'.

This book is a discussion of tradition and history which, unlike most others, regularly offers that welcome sense of the numinous.

Terence Ranger
Professor Emeritus, St Antony's College, University of Oxford

Acknowledgements

Nothing would have been written here, but for my memorable time in Karamoja, whose peoples, particularly in the church, made me welcome and continued to tolerate my Mzungu's preoccupation with 'work' (*etic*), when Uganda was ravaged by genocide and civil war. I am therefore most indebted to the Bishop and Diocese of Karamoja, and to my long-suffering colleagues in Kotido, the long-termers being Paul Smith (who supplied the rainfall chart and map) and Eunice, Nick Jewitt, Martin Wamianala, Rose Moding, Caroline Oceng, and Dick and Rosie Stockley, who also provided hospitality in Kampala. Jim Rowland, with his long experience of Karamoja with his wife Jean and family, taught me his love of the Karamojong and their ways. In return the Jie have retained so much love for 'Nakijim' that they include him in their stories, and want him to return to assist with agriculture. He has read and commented on a number of pieces in preparation for this. On my return visits my old friends, David Modo, Revd Andrew Emoru, Revd James Nasak and Revd Nebbi Lopul, arranged accommodation and hospitality for me as well as encouragement and help in my fieldwork. My old colleague, Paulo Longok, afforded me much time and accompanied me on many of my visits. I am grateful to all my informants without whom this book could not haven been written, but especially to the late Alifayo Nacam, whose home I visited every time I went to Kaceri, and to Samuel Locero, who later adopted me into his family.

It has been a privilege to be able to reconstruct, chiefly by correspondence, the select band of expatriates who have lived and worked in Karamoja, some of whom have given up their time in order to let me pick their brains. Among former government officers are John Wilson, Revd Douglas Durand, Robert Leach, the late Sandy Field who sadly flew into Mount Kenya while I was living on a paradisiac foothill in St Andrew's College, Kabare, and Christopher Powell-Cotton, who also gave me a personal tour of the Powell-Cotton Museum, Quex Park, Kent. Another of their number is Prof. James Barber, who, as the foremost authority on the colonial history of Karamoja, gave me access to source material, and arranged a series of seminars in Durham on 'Imperial History'. Among Roman Catholic missionaries I have had much sympathetic help from the late Fr. Bruno Novelli MCCJ and Fr. Mario Cisternino of the Anthropology Department in the University of Milan.

I am also indebted to the library staffs of Partnership House, the British Library, the Royal Geographical Society, SIM Archives, the Missionari Comboniani, Rome, Rhodes House, Oxford, and the Universities of Durham and Birmingham. Further research and the writing of this book has been done while being immersed in the administration and supervision of research in the Oxford Centre for Mission Studies, whose members have become increasingly fascinated by enthusiasm for all things Karamojong.

Those who diminished pertinent sources must be negatively acknowledged: the Luftwaffe for destroying BCMS records up to 1940, retiring Protectorate officers who burned Moroto Archives, and the thief who stole two years' worth of slides in Durham.

Partial funding of my research expenses should be credited to the repeated generosity of the Spalding Trust, and latterly the Archbishop's Council and the Mabledon Trust. Time was allowed by my employer, the Oxford Centre for Mission Studies.

My interest in anthropology was sparked by the late Dr John Beattie, and furthered by Prof. Philip Gulliver and in Oxford by Prof. Wendy James' Northeast Africa Seminar, but taking the risk to start writing at length on Karamoja was due to the advice, accumulated wisdom, trust, patience and continual encouragement of my supervisor, Professor E.D.A. Hulmes for the duration of my doctorate. This work partly fulfils the urging of my examiners, Dr Sigvard von Sicard and Prof. James Barber. Since then I have benefited much from the friendly advice and criticism of Prof. John Lonsdale, Prof. John Lamphear and Prof. Terry Ranger who read the first draft, and also from the friendship of Prof. Peter Clarke. The intellectual failings, or other defects and inaccuracies of this thesis remain, of course, the author's.

St Swithin's Day 2004

Chapter 1

The Challenges of Circumscribing the Other

Sitting under a tree with barely enough shade from the dry-season sun, a small group of older men were talking with me outside their traditional homesteads. The discussion turned to *ngipian* (singular, *ekipye*), generally translated as spirits, although lightning is a particular form that they or their occurrence take. '*Ekipye* can arrest someone at the dam' and the only way out of being stuck there at the dam is to sacrifice. Looking to the north, where hills of rock jutted out of the plain, one was selected for attention by a man only eight years older than myself. 'If you climb Lobel Hill, there is no return without sacrifice' (J31). Gesturing to the north at the volcanic plug, he gave a serious warning. 'Because of *ekipye*, if you point your spear or gun at Lobel, you are pulled.' It was explained that this irreverent action to the spirit of that huge blancmange-shaped lump of rock would, of necessity, result in the offender being drawn to the hill to meet his fate. It was no joking matter, and no jokes were attempted. The efficacy of cause and consequence was not in the least disputed. It was simply the way things are. Nor are the effects limited to Karamojong.

Referring to the westernmost volcanic plug in Karamoja, Rwot at Alerek, Lokori Komol Namuya related how some British landed on top with a helicopter in the 1980s. They fell sick and died for their temerity, it was remembered, corroborating the habitual experience of the locals. The Karamojong cannot even make a corral near this rock, for the corral will be opened mysteriously in the night. The bare rock has its own spritely domestic beasts, and lost livestock may be translated there to this spirit-order of creation. The mysterious properties of the rock are not regularly tested by the Karamojong, for none of these physically brave people dare to scale it for fear of being 'beaten or taken up' by the spirit (J31). After all look what happened to the British, whose technological bravura did not save them! Whatever else may be happening around the world, Karamoja remains a place of enchantment, however uncongenial a fact that may be for modern missionary or postmodern scholar.

1 Tradition and Imagination

Traditions do exist in Africa as elsewhere. Despite the colonial experiment, or new attractions and conditions, there are always some that persist almost to the point of perversity. Further, new traditions are constructed through the collective choices of the people involved, even when the originating event has not been replicated.

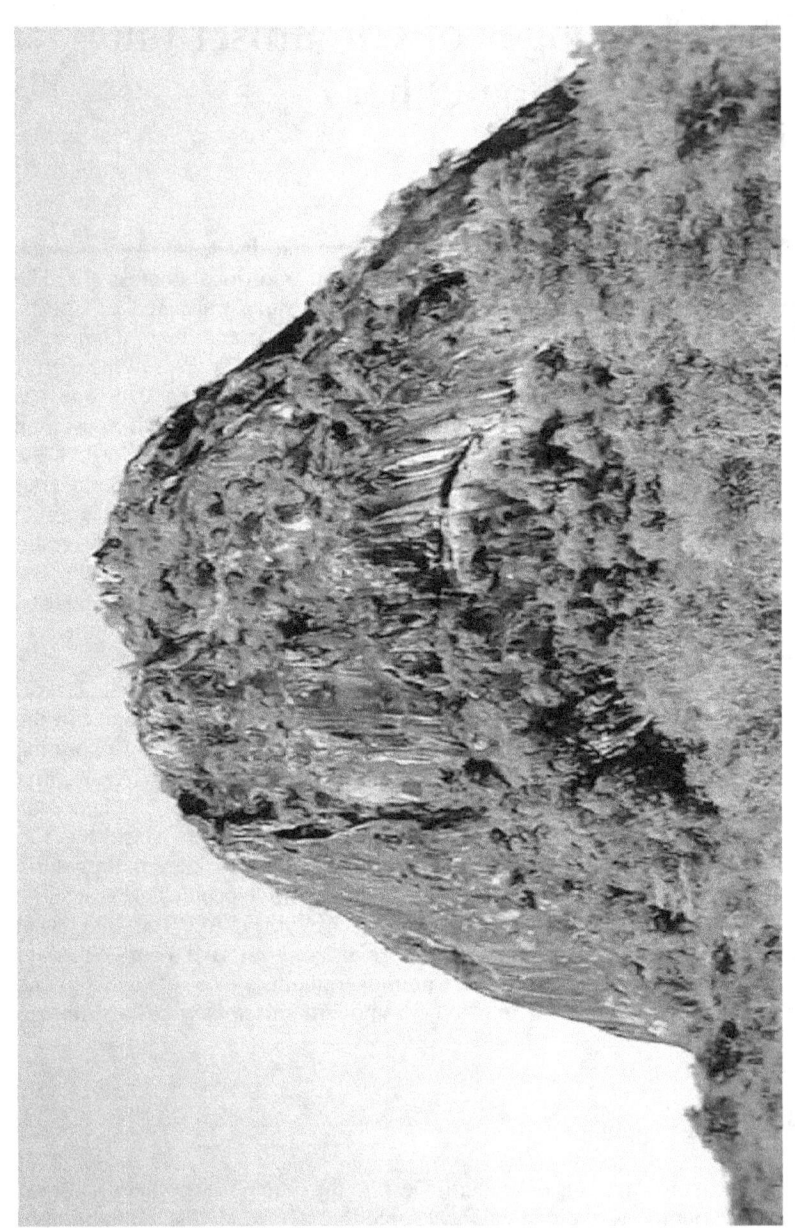

Source: Ben Knighton
Photograph 1.1 Lobel volcanic plug, Najie

Tradition has to be owned and valued, if only in nostalgia. It is difficult to impose tradition. Traditions are held dear when people feel they have participated in initiating, maintaining, modulating or reforming them. Some traditions may be élitist, but then they are the traditions of the élite; the customs belong to them. If the masses voluntarily participate, then perhaps they own the élite! The most peculiar feature can be appropriated for a tradition and events intended only to be one-off can be instituted as a regular part of a calendar.

Traditions therefore emerge or die primarily through collective choice, which is why examining them frequently reveals significant features about the people who maintain them. Thus the term, 'traditional', has valuable import, and is more pertinent than 'indigenous', which relates to a place and puts the stress on origin. 'Traditional' also has a distinguished academic pedigree, being used by Max Weber (Mills, Gerth and Weber 1991) to describe one of three pure types of social activity: rational, traditional and charismatic, although these are attacked as essentialist. For Weber traditional leadership venerates the past and values loyalty and solidarity, characteristic of conservative societies that resist change. The danger when applying this typology to African societies, which Weber never studied, is that the observer is led into mistakenly thinking that traditional societies are necessarily changeless. Just how conservative and how much social change happens will be a special focus of this book, with no presumption that the Karamojong will be an example of the pure type.

Nowadays some courage is needed to depict a traditional African religion.[1] Can it fit the terms of postmodern philosophy? If not, is it the account of the religion or the philosophy that needs to be revised? To update Evans-Pritchard (1965:15), some explanation of the absurdity seems to be required, for instance of the modern gun being thought to be subject to the compelling power of what appears as an old-fashioned nature-spirit. Reviving the use of 'traditional' after the *Invention of Tradition* (Hobsbawm and Ranger 1984) has exposed it carries three dangers. Firstly it risks participating in another round of the Eurocentric invention of Africa (Mudimbe 1988;1995). Secondly not only has African tradition itself recently been seen to be part of what colonial rulers and their hireling anthropologists imagined for 'their' peoples, but also the concept of 'traditional' is being challenged by that of 'indigenous'.[2] Thirdly the nature of religion is contested at least as much as ever

---

[1] Despite the barrage of criticism, the term 'traditional' is remarkably and unavoidably persistent, especially in African discourse. Recent testimony is provided by the African Studies conference held at St Mary's College, University of Durham, 5–7.04: 'Traditional Accountability and Modern Governance in Africa'.

[2] Harvey (2000:9) sees ambiguity in the traditional referring to the primitive and static, not just the authentic and deep-rooted, yet it is a term commonly used in postcolonial Africa, while it is peoples in Australasia and America, continuing in a more marginal position, who have borne the old term 'indigenous'. Outside of these contexts, it is most unclear what is not indigenous when they are the majority of religions and happen everywhere (ibid.:4), while traditional religion contrasts nicely with new religious movements and permits gradation. Weber distinguished world religions from traditional religions by the documentation and intellectualization of cultural principles, which are then socialized into the ideas and actions of believers (Meyer 1996:199).

(Eck 2000), and whether it is possible to talk of a discrete religion in regard to African ways of life is a further issue.

The concept of Africa, even when it was the 'unknown continent', was undoubtedly a European concept, but those who inhabit it want to contest the identity that has been imposed upon them, or sometimes to select from the various types that are on offer. From the romantic to the derogatory, from the cosmopolitan to the racist, Africas have been invented and are being imagined by many. Yet a portrait of all of Africa is not being painted here. The aim is to understand and articulate one small corner of a vast and varied continent without grandiose claims that this speaks for the rest. Neither is the opposite Adullamite reaction present, that this small corner is isolated from Africa and the rest of the world so needs no setting in wider movements. Yet it will not be claimed that the Karamojong are typical in their response to world trends such as globalization, nor even that they are typical of 'traditional' Africa, for even here, their commonalities tend to be with nomadic pastoralist peoples of Africa,[3] not with an essence that defines the continent. It is their ability to resist easy categorization in more general theory that makes them such a fascinating subject for study. Thus, they are not being used as an exemplar of some fashionable line of funded inquiry, but are being depicted for who they are in their own right, so bringing to bear academic insight in the service of their truest representation (Knighton forthcoming).

It must be acknowledged that all representations run short of the complexity of reality, and that what, at best, can be laid between the two covers of a book will be an interpretation, and one that will modify others and then find a reaction in others to come. As an historian of religion Mircea Eliade (1959b:91) thought that he acted 'as a hermeneutist'. A long process of wrestling with contradictory interpretations and aggregation is necessary, drawing on multiple sources and the work of others, where that has been carefully done. Both function and meaning must emerge (Clarke 1988:822). How is the interpretation to be justified? Perhaps, as the late John V. Taylor (1963) found 'the Primal Vision' in his sympathetic study of the Baganda, it is because the vision of the Karamojong way of life is disclosed now at length. There is no intention here to employ Taylor's category of 'primal religion', but rather to show, remorselessly, not romantically, and not idealistically, the factors at work in the enduring vitality of a traditional religion.

2 Invention versus Appropriation

There are two major trends still in fashion today in African studies, yet they must clash before long. On the one hand there is the emphasis on the invention of tradition in Africa (Ranger 1983; 1993a; 1993b; 1998). Colonial rule created maps, defined ethnic groups when they realized the errors in the hastily drawn state

---

[3] Despite the heavy reliance on pastoralist values involved, no revival of Herskovits' (1926) 'cattle complex' is sought here, for it claims to explain far too large a 'culture-area' embracing the whole eastern side of the continent almost irrespective of distinct environments and histories.

boundaries, and manufactured a typology of tribes which even exchanged the ethnic identity of the colonized. The official codification of customary law could certainly be motivated by the desire of colonial governments to find convenient methods of social control (Lonsdale 1992a:209; Maxwell 1999:37). In any case the *mores* of a twentieth-century representation of the nineteenth century, frequently seen as timeless, could hardly reconstruct the past as it was, but conveniently gloss it. On the other hand, there is the great emphasis on the appropriation by Africans of whatever the invading white man had to bring: his religion, his politics, his education. Ranger (1995:248) finds, in Zimbabwe, that 'religious ideas offered a particular effective way for rural Africans to act upon their world'. Women are likewise seen to be subverting the strategies of men. In fact, those to whom power is attributed should better be seen as fellow-actors in the complex games that relate various interest groups, who compete and ally according to a multitude of factors, as has been found in the history of Buganda.

> The social forces that combined and conflicted to shape Africa's history before the colonial period continued to be formative under European rule. More than that, the answer lies in seeing the colonial state as a part of African life right from the outset. Colonial administration did not write the history of their choosing: the colonial state did not develop in a manner determined by local officials, a metropole, or the world economy. On the contrary, it emerged in a contingent manner. Its officials (who, of course, were divided among themselves) were subject to the same conflicts and contradictions to which the people they ruled were subject. Africa's colonial history was driven by forces rooted in the precolonial era, but were refashioned as colonial officials reacted to circumstances they encountered and introduced and as different groups of Africans did the same. (McKnight 2000:84f)

These two trends of thought, invention and appropriation, pose a contradiction. If colonial rulers were so compromised, almost impotent to direct change over against African appropriation, if colonial history is so predicated by precolonial history, how could they invent anything sustainable? If there are traditions, whether old or new, from internal sources or appropriations, it must be anonymous Africans who founded them. Alternatively, if modernization inserted Africa into the world economy, breaking down tribal discipline and authority, how could any traditions persist at all, whether invented by Europeans or imagined by Africans?

The ambiguity is heightened by the use of the term 'African agency' (Lonsdale 2000a). What is meant to be emphasized by its usage is African activity and initiative, but the most common use of 'agent' and 'agency' in English is in legal, political and economic aspects where it always refers to activity for and accountable to another, the principal. Hence there used to be a chasm of subservience between, say, the missionary and the mission-agent the former might employ (Newman 2001). The formal relationship does not prevent the mission-agent from appropriating the dominant narrative to other ends, as Keswick Holiness spirituality was appropriated as an anti-clerical fellowship by the East African Revival. Yet the researcher has to be alive to the possibility that African agency may according to collective choice adopt, to a surprising and apparently dysfunctional extent, the religious ideas and practices of others. There are likely to be conditioning factors, perhaps pressure, even persecution, to convert, but it is in the field of religious ideas that human freedom is at its highest. Thus the African response needs to be carefully observed as to the extent to which Africans adopt, adapt or reject alternative religious traits.

3   Implicitness

The complexity of life on earth cannot be presented in one undifferentiated lump, so selection of the mass of phenomena will firstly be determined on the basis of pertinence to the more religious issues. Again, in the attempt to yield consonance with the alien, it is important that explanatory accounts will employ concepts not simply belonging to one academic discipline or another, 'but will reflect as well the concepts of the agents he studies' (Clarke and Byrne 1993:45). Many of the factors germane to the description of African religion are transcendental[4] or implicit in the academic traditions involved, rather than explicit. Similarly, the implicit inevitably plays a vital rôle in religion.

In traditional African religion it is conceivable that the implicit has wider importance, because of the emphasis on ritual, custom and behaviour rather than on mythology, doctrine and belief, though it would be a mistake to suppose that a mental or intellectual side is lacking. There is undoubtedly a difference between oral and written ways of maintaining and multiplying knowledge, and oral memory skills are likely to be better honed than literate ones (Goody 1987:290). 'The implicit is the foundation of social intercourse' (Douglas 1975:5). Implicit knowledge here is taken, following Fardon's scheme (1990:5), to include tacit knowledge,[5] assumed in a certain paradigm, and doxic knowledge, those cultural frames beyond proof or disproof that shape the self-evident experience of the world. It may be 'under your nose', so too obvious to state normally, but forms the presuppositions on which situated communication regularly takes place, or 'couldn't be otherwise' as a direct reflex of the way things incomprehensibly are. With all human life, not least in regard to technology in the West, there is a disparity between people's capacity to get on with life and their ability to articulate what is happening or why. Furthermore the unconscious and unreflective should not just be predicated on African peoples.

The implicit nature of traditional African religion is one feature that has avoided any direct attack by contemporary scholars. Wendy James (1988:4) writes of 'an

---

[4] The Kantian distinction between transcendental and transcendent is maintained throughout. The former term refers to the filters and formers continually present in the human mind, which give added value to the input of sensation and empirical observation, so must be subjected to rigorous critique. The transcendent is unknowable according to Kant, because it has no connection to sensation, but lies utterly beyond it.

[5] Thomas Kuhn (1970) and Michael Polanyi (1967) emphasize tacit knowledge as the basis for a paradigm or framework for knowing in Western thought. Culture can be seen as a cognitive framework relating awareness and activity or as providing a paradigm at a certain level for thought. In attending to explicit thought, awareness is lost of the tacit knowledge that makes the explicit plausible.

archive, below the level of the explicit statements', and of the 'fundamental levels of silent knowledge' in Uduk divination.

> You cannot so easily accept or reject the advocacy of the ebony oracle because in itself it stands for no dogma. In silence, it is attuned to the implicit assumptions of the proper balance within a person. It reveals the workings of the vulnerable inner person, relations between people, relations between the living and the dead, relations between people and the world of the wild. These matters [are] elusive, 'open-textured', and adaptable. (James 1988:6)[6]

The elusive quality of the significance of religious practices results in the religious aspect not being addressed first by researchers, except in a superficial way. Initial fieldwork is unlikely to accumulate sufficient material to nail the elusive and penetrate the implicit. James might respond here that it is only the elusive which is to be found, yet the presence of contingency and uncertainty in any aspect of life does not evacuate regularity and continual conjunction. The longstanding position is that beliefs are not articulated so much as remaining implicit, there being no defined doctrines, no systematic theologies, no assertive claims to the truth as such, no factional disputes on matters of belief, and no missionary activity (Platvoet 1993). Shaw (1990:349) refers to 'peoples whose understanding of the world and of themselves are [sic] expressed primarily in implicit rather than explicit forms'. Even Ruel writes of cosmology implicit in the custom and ritual of the East African Bantu (1997:77). Implicitness appears as an unavoidable concept in folk religion.

However it should not be deduced that nothing is explicit. Namuya (J31) articulated some activity of the spirits; perhaps he would not do so to every enquiry, for the religious often do not cast their pearls before swine, but explicit he was. Terence Ranger (2001) has gently upbraided the masterly John Peel (2000) for not giving enough cosmology. Caveats about belief, and the need to distinguish belief according to the whole context, have long been made, but the 'element of rationality is still always there ... the beliefs are always coherent' (Evans-Pritchard 1965:7,29). Yet, inevitably in postmodernity, the very idea of belief has been questioned, or relegated to Western Christian faith. 'In anthropology there is a move away from whole systems of belief ... to the study of religion in practice ... Belief is not a neutral term but a post-Reformation idea' (James 2000b). The term 'God', and even its surrogates 'divinity' and 'deity', are subjected to suspicion to the extent they become virtually unusable. Ruel (1997:17), whose book replaces 'the notion of belief with that of ritual', attempts a similar deconstruction on belief and sacrifice.[7]

---

[6] In emphasizing the relational nature of African religion (and social science), James remains true to the tradition of anthropology of religion set by Evans-Pritchard (1965:111f) for the Institute of Social and Cultural Anthropology in the University of Oxford. It is no accident that it is the strengths of the social sciences in analysing kinship and social structure that are commended for the study of religion, but this should be seen as a limitation of this kind of social science, not of religion.

[7] Ruel (1997:34n) could have cited Lienhardt's (1961) reported irrelevance of belief to the Dinka, but fails to do so in support of his argument. James (2000b) finds that sacrifice is 'too much carried over from the theocentric meanings of the Old Testament, having more to

> I wished especially to demonstrate that Kuria religion was not a supernatural speculation but implied a view of the world that could be understood in straightforward empirical terms, and that their ritual had a validity of its own. (Ruel 1997:5)

Belief is not merely, let alone chiefly, a matter of esoteric doctrine but an irreplaceable dimension of human being in the face of a less than amenable environment. The pastoralists believe that, despite the drought, they will find a way to contest harsh reality and survive, 'only by moving subjunctively, by making what was not, but almost was, into what actually now is' (Carrithers 1992:70). The ability to conceive of an existence different from that facing them, and to direct thought and action accordingly is inherent to humanity, not just its Western expression. Thus invention, or rather, creative response, happens not primarily through the trickery of alien rulers, but by the belief and behaviour of those concerned to construct and determine their future.

It has been asserted that 'no statement about a religion is valid unless it can be acknowledged by that religion's believers' (Smith 1959:42), but considering a religion's believers can debate eternally among themselves the validity of its statements, this would appear too hard a test. However it is not one that has been shirked, for preliminary findings and indeed my 1990 thesis as a whole have been broached with certain Karamojong, so that their feedback is part of a 20-year engagement with their traditional religion. Conversely faith in social science is dismissive of interpreting behaviour according to the participants' explanations (Evans-Pritchard 1965:18; Clarke and Byrne 1993:48). There would be as little justification for restricting the study of religion to the statements of believers as in taking licence to put words in their mouth. 'When anthropologists go beyond what informants say, as they must if only to translate, there is a generous choice of levels to which to attribute the discrepancies between the anthropological account and interpretative practices' (Fardon 1990:8). It is worth going through Fardon's levels to show where this account intends to go beyond the data.

Mis-stated Knowledge

By repute the Karamojong are a straightforward people, and ordinarily their words can be taken at face value in terms of veracity. However there is one significant issue that regularly gives rise to a great deal of obfuscation, cattle-raiding. Its authorization and legitimacy have been the subjects of unwelcome government inquisition for 80 years. Karamojong lack of explicitness on this point has misled those who are more concerned with their own programmes than with the people's disapproved priorities. Thus external interventions have not been fully effective in either transforming or dislocating the culture. Karamojong allowing outsiders to mislead themselves has done much to preserve local freedom.

---

do with social and life processes'. Meaning should be understood in the context of the latter, but to detach them *a priori* from any concept of divinity might be a strange imposition on Africa.

Understated Knowledge

Given that the Karamojong have a traditional religion and not a world religion with scriptures, doctrines and teachers, it is likely that a relatively large proportion of knowledge is implicit, to be discovered as latent in the rituals and in their interconnection with other aspects of the culture. An internal, holistic understanding of history and culture will be necessary before articulating religious understanding, which, on Karamojong lips, is expressed typically in few and terse statements. Their youth, not yet having been enculturated into the elder's wisdom, have little or nothing abstract to say, leaving this as a prime area in which the outside scholar can contribute by setting out the implicit. Informants do not give systematic accounts, but these may be put together from verbal and non-verbal evidence to explain how Karamojong do understand and act accordingly with a persistence that has usually baffled observers over the last century. It may require doctoral research to begin to make the implicit explicit. Having dwelt in a mud hut in Karamoja from January 1984 to April 1986, completing a thesis, and returning for short fieldwork visits 12, 14 and 16 years after the first stint, it was most instructive to be able to ask questions that opened up lengthy and fruitful areas for discussion that had not been possible without the implicit understanding which is the foundation of anthropological research. When the informant declares, 'I had not thought of that, but now you have said it, that is just how it is', one is gratified by the effort of research into the implicit. 'You have entered a deep secret of the Karamojong. Many, even Karamojong, would not have understood. They have not dug the reality of the culture.' (P4)

Unstable Knowledge

What is mysterious or inscrutable is difficult for anyone to state. The nature of charismatic features such as Karamojong prophecy and dreams will always be difficult to state, and is capable of the most speculative interpretation.

Unknowable Generative Schema

Marx, Freud, Levi-Strauss and Foucault posit rules that people follow quite obliviously, and propose methods of revealing those rules, putatively leading to the illumination and emancipation of the ignorant. This appears no different from considering the Karamojong as being under the theological rules of sin, death and law itself. In the light of the Christian gospel, they could be redeemed from this bondage. To suppose *a priori* the presence of unknown internal rules, for which there are normative responses prescribed by an outsider, goes beyond the analysis of what is, attempting to determine the history of people before it even has been made.

Unknowable Comparative Schema

The acute, informed observer may detect absences and contradictions unnoticeable to the insider. This frequently may be the case, when knowledge of widely dispersed institutions can be compared, for instance when examining East African age-class systems. It is not difficult through methodical analysis of Karamojong lexemes to discover obvious etymologies of which Ngakaramojong speakers are quite unaware. To give another example, when Loumo (P12) says, the 'Jie and the Pokot are one', he has no awareness of the classificatory distinction of Eastern and Southern Nilotes, even if he is alert to the linguistic difference. In fact his own Pian territorial section is closer to the Pokot, because of intermarriage and other exchange relationships. Yet academic knowledge may serve to highlight his meaning rather than what appears as his mistake: Jie and Pokot are both perennial enemies to the Pian.

Unthought Consequences

Some consequences of holding to certain notions or categorizations may be unknown to informants. This is tantamount to saying that they have an unscientific view of causation. At this point the interpreter would be advised to retain some humility. Even if Karamojong religion has been absorbed into the collective unconscious of the culture through the accumulation of past wisdom, it remains attuned to their environment, and boffins jump in to identify and intervene at their, or more likely Karamojong, peril. For instance restricted grazing proved to have worse ecological effects than the traditional system. Unmasking 'superstition' will have its own consequences.

Validated Knowledge

To an extent Cantwell Smith's unreasonable test of verification, that any account of a religion must be validated by its members, has been passed, but by no means for every finding.[8] Arriving in the south of Karamoja by public transport, the first person (P2) to whom I talked had read the copy of my thesis, which I had left in Moroto on the previous trip. He was happy with its thrust, though the caveat is that the average Karamojong does not read. Speaking for his circle, Emoru (P3) enthused soon after meeting again: 'We were amazed that someone who was not born here could write all these things, some that we did not know.' As with Dyson-Hudson (1966) and Lamphear (1976b), I am now, through my categorization and interpretation, in danger of inventing Karamojong tradition. Yet these writings will have little deterministic value, when the oral culture continues to predominate, and transmission is more implicit than explicit.

---

[8] Karamojong students at Makerere may dispute this, but then they have élitist agendas, born of the very investment to educate them so high, to be spokesmen for the development of Karamoja. 'Some of those lies you were telling were told to us when we were still young,' David Pulkol, director-general of the External Security Organization, told Karimojong opinion leaders (*New Vision*, 12.6.02). Of course there is contestation of interpretations, but what is argued here is that they lie mainly along internal–external polarity in viewing the culture, with the external view only recognizing developmental ends as real or valid that, despite a Christian veneer, tend to be more materialistic.

4 Approaches and Sources

Environment is a peculiarly significant factor for Karamoja as will gradually become apparent, and though it is an avenue for arriving at religion (Ranger 1999b), it is too broad and well travelled in rather different directions to be the most penetrating route here. Thus three main avenues will be selected to cross the same landscape but via the less mapped routes:

History

Hegel and Trevor-Roper were not alone in supposing that Africa had no history. Until the imperial history of James Barber (1968), time-consciousness regarding Karamoja was minimal. Expatriates in Karamoja could perceive no movement in the history of the Karamojong, beyond a moderately recent and seamless transition from Stone Age to Iron Age. The common observation was that the Karamojong had not changed for millennia, as Wilson (1985:163) exemplifies: 'to enter Karamoja circa 1953 was to enter an area in which time had virtually stopped a thousand years in the past'. Gulliver (1955:105) considered that, before the British, there was a 'timeless structure' which contains no historical highlights! 'If a factor is of significance for the understanding of a society under review, it should surely emerge during intensive field research', and history did not emerge from Gulliver's eight months of fieldwork. As if in reaction to such a strong belief, Gulliver's anthropology later took a thoroughly historical turn (19.6.90 Letter). 'Then, in functionalist fashion, I assumed that history was unimportant and unobtainable and so did not try hard to obtain it.' The reputation of intensive field research was redeemed by Lamphear. Not only did his 16 months in Karamoja and Turkana produce extremely valuable material, but his composition of the traditional history of the Jie, which I distributed in Kotido, almost became the scripture of their salvation history. As virtually all of Lamphear's (1972a) informants have now died, his work must remain as an indispensable primary source for any history of the Karamojong in the last half-millennium. However oral research is not the only historical method.

Documentary evidence on Karamoja is almost entirely absent before 1899; indeed, there are grounds for certainty that there is no extant text written in Karamoja before that year. Though the archaeology carried out there yields sporadic data on some previous peoples and humanoids in Karamoja, it does little to advance understanding of the Karamojong as relatively late and nomadic arrivals. Its limitations to reconstruct the past of all these needs to be recognized, even if a new wave of fieldwork were to be done. Termites, hyenas, desiccating wind, bleaching sun and torrential rain, as well as the lifestyles of the peoples themselves, which consumed as much as possible, all mean there are few material objects left to examine. There are pottery sherds, those minority of skeletons that were buried, and grinding stones. Rarely there may be artefacts such as obsidian knives and clay pipes. All organic material is eaten by someone or something and all iron rusts away or is reused. Do then such people have any history beyond what they can remember with all too little chronological precision? The answer must be positive, and in the lack of more usual methods others must be recruited to fill the gap.

It is important to leave behind 'the perceived immobility of myth and cosmology as capsules out of time' (Lovell 1996:121):

> Historical processes in the study of religious phenomena have been highly neglected in the anthropological accounts of African religion, which have often been considered as immutable, homogeneous entities in an ahistorical present.[9] The difficulty in reconstructing the histories of people without a literate tradition has been branded as an excuse for the lack of serious scholarship in this domain. Only since colonization has there been a flow of records sufficient to contribute any notion of a history of African religion.
>
> Existing historical accounts have concentrated on problems of conversion, or on the transition from 'naturalistic' practices to monotheistic belief. As this has corresponded with a transformation in social organisation towards state-based structures, a bias in scholarship has been inevitable. (Lovell 1996:120)

The paucity of documents, and early memories of oral history there recorded, is all part of the 'Karamoja problem'. Yet it also allows memory to counter any bias towards state-based structures and to find monotheism without the state. As the consequences of assuming that Africans have no significant history are so deleterious for Western and African self-understanding, this account must err on the side holding that provisional history is better than nothing, for a study of historiography shows that all history is provisional. When more avenues for research can be opened up in the long term, then the history can be rewritten, but in the meantime to deny a people their history is no less than intellectual grave-robbery.

Joseph Greenberg (1970:2) found that word resemblances in a large number of languages as plausible outcomes of a single ancestral form are of very great evidential power in excluding either chance or loanwords as explanations. The genealogy of African languages he put together is the whole basis for understanding their interrelationship today. Moreover, genealogies give a highly significant idea of history and identity. Extrapolating from the regularities of language change, glottochronology has even attempted to give dates to the formation of new language groups. In any case the likely geographical centres of origin of language families can be identified by isolating the loanwords absorbed from other peoples in spatial movement over time. Hence the names of the largest phyla are Nilo-Saharan (N-S), Afro-Asiatic and Niger-Congo. Assuming the language gives representative expression to the culture, then the origins of the dominant linguistic influence can easily be identified.[10] Further, dominance in language normally results from other dominances as peoples encounter one another, military, political, social, legal, technological or religious. Some strangers are absorbed successfully precisely because they have expertise or power in one or more of these aspects, in which case they will at least contribute loanwords to the larger group. People and their lives cannot be separated from their language, which always leaves its traces in the change and mix of history.

---

[9] Ranger had been drawing attention to this for over a quarter of a century beforehand. The concepts of primitive and primal religion both imply unchanging continuity (Ranger 1988:864).

[10] Deep reconstruction had already been begun with other languages (*New Scientist*, 16.6.90: 46)

Since no language is invented overnight, but has substantial analytical similarity with a long forgotten ancestral proto-language, it can be seen that existing languages, when read in a comparative scheme, are themselves bearers not only of the people's present culture, but also of their history. If the majority of a Nilo-Saharan's language terms regarding root crops are loanwords from Niger-Congo, then this is a good indication that their agricultural technology was also borrowed, prompting a search for physical contact with a Bantu people at some time in history. A word either goes back to the ancestral language, or other words in the same language, or is borrowed from another language. 'Behind each type of word-history lie different human histories' (Ehret 1972:45). Abstract concepts are also given linguistic expression, and some of these, such as father and mother, denote the most fundamental of human relationships and are keywords in the framework of any language. Thus explicit beliefs at least are also borne by words, if with changing meaning, through the flux of history. 'The key to understanding the system of these beliefs was the semantic system underlying the people's religious vocabulary' (ibid.:45). Thus indications of religious history can be accumulated.[11]

Compared with archaeology in Africa at present, so many more indications can then be raised about non-material items or material items that cannot survive the centuries. However, Christopher Ehret's identification of proto-languages with particular archaeological sites can be hotly contested by archaeologists (Blench and MacDonald 2000), though he has received some archaeological support for the Nilo-Saharan domestication of cattle (Wendorf and Schild 1994). Ehret also has seriously annoyed the longstanding proponent of oral history for West Africa, Jan Vansina,[12] who has accused him of being 'cavalier in his attitude towards evidence' and intolerably arrogant (Vansina 1999:471). Such are the barricades between disciplines. Linguistics does attempt a detailed historical construction without concrete agents and events, while revealing the thinking of the anonymous actors. However, although contextual information is needed, the approach is not so far removed from the study of mass movements in history. Social history too does not necessitate named characters, but these are a boon in order to perceive human activity and not just impersonal forces.

Coming into the range of living memory is wonderful. It makes for hours sitting with 'those who know' about the past. No interviews can take place where others are all excluded, for frequently there is no option but to sit in an open place. Buildings may not be in sight. Children may crowd round until talking and listening become difficult. Firm responses have to be employed to stop the occasion becoming too chaotic for speech. Yet among those who come to listen are more informed and articulate people. Hearing the subject, they too want to contribute, although when interviewed they may wilt under the pressure of the questions searching for location in time or place. The promise of Lamphear's oral history was not fulfilled as events were seldom remembered according to age-class. Only one elder suddenly stopped cooperating, when he demanded food. He had become entangled in saying that he could remember Colonel Macdonald who was only in

---

[11] For a much fuller survey of the contributions of linguistics in Africa see Nurse (1997).

[12] Ehret (1998) contains several refutations of Vansina's findings on Bantu history.

Karamoja many years before the informant was born. Memory is social here, not just personal, but he was unable to recall surrounding events. He moved away, but soon positioned his stool so as to be able to listen well.

Having known people in all parts of Karamoja since 1984, it was easy to move from one renowned contact to another, or, if one could not be found, to interview people as they were. Given prior knowledge and appreciation of their culture and history, it was always possible to find an issue of common interest they wished to explore. Of the 68 informants interviewed in Uganda between 1998 and 2002 several were known personally from 1984 and helped to identify and gain access to others not previously known who were acknowledged as authorities in the traditional religion. Since interviewing under men's trees attracted attention, others who showed they could contribute were also interviewed to give a good cross-section of men aged 37 to 92, all at least in the process of marriage. Karamojong informants were normally asked to name their territorial section, subsection, their generation-set and age-set, their clan and their age.

Informants identified strongly with what can only be called tribe, so initials are used to mark their index number (see the Bibliography). Despite wives coming from a different background or men having mothers from afar, categorization is only difficult with two informants. One was from Nyakwai and later absorbed into Jie society, being listed under the former. Another had a Jiot father and a Tesot mother. He completed secondary school education and kept apart from the traditional life. Since he bore a Tesot name, he was categorized as Tesot. Names of informants have not been generally revealed, for they were not all asked in advance whether they wanted to have them written in a book, and it is quite conceivable that, if they were, they might receive some unwelcome attention.

Of Karamojong informants (Dodosǒ, Jie and Pian) 64 per cent gave European-derived Christian names that were given them at baptism by Roman Catholic or Anglican clergy, which is not exceptional. One had a Muslim name, while three of them were Anglican clergy, who had diverse attitudes to Karamojong traditions. Care was taken to sift out any small tendency to Christian reconstruction or abolition of traditional religion. Only 9 per cent of informants were women, though women were observed in various rites. It is much more difficult for a man to interview Karamojong women, especially if he is not known to them, and even then a husband may step in to answer on her behalf. There is certainly room for more research on women's issues and the recording of women's voices, but as public religion is primarily the affair of initiated men, a good cross-section of those qualified to speak about it were interviewed as well as the 15 per cent of the male informants who were not initiated; their age was around 44 with the oldest at 60. Only two informants were much under 30 years of age and they yielded little on traditional religion. From 1989, various colonial officers and missionaries were interviewed and others contributed in correspondence. However their information has largely been ignored and none has been cited here, apart from where their letters are named in the text.

Culture

Culture is a major category that has been overused and abused in the last decade.

Source: Ben Knighton

Photograph 1.2   Interviewing under a tree at Lotim, Nadodosŏ

The effects of globalization (Knighton 2001b) have emphasized doubts about the boundaries of societies. Sociology on the Weberian model has assumed that these are provided by the nation-state, but the boundaries have thinned. Not only were these always a poor definition of African cultures, but now the accelerating urbanization and mobility of Africans have confuted simplistic ethnic models (Featherstone 1995; Jameson and Miyoshi 1998; Staden 1998). The temptation of a global agenda is to see cultures all the more 'as superficially different representations of one abstract culture, human culture' (Sebeok 1987:165). Hence the rise of cultural studies focussing human difference merely on the symbolic representations of art and media. This just repeats the élitist conception of culture as a quality that distinguishes from the masses, derived from European class-consciousness and ethnocentrism. Though it would be a mistake to return to ideas of discrete and bounded cultures, it has been glocalization that has occurred more than homogenization (Robertson 1992; 1994). Rather than trying to defend cultures as internally homogeneous, it is better to give due acknowledgment to the tensions, struggles, conflicting interpretations and antagonistic interests, which can be more proximate to the protagonists of life than the invisible pattern which gives structure to their life amid the familiar material artefacts. However, postmodern thought, unable to rest content with any transpersonal explanations, has questioned the whole intelligibility of the concept of culture (Abu-Lughod 1991; Hockey, Dawson and Allison 1997; Wikan 1999).

Yet even if the term 'culture' did not exist it would have to be invented in Europe or Africa, where the term is widely used. Empirical studies of, say, the buildings which people prefer show clear cultural patterns, despite widely differing personal preferences:

> The root of the confusion is the distribution of learned routines across individuals: while these routines are never perfectly shared, they are not randomly distributed. Therefore, 'culture' should be retained as a convenient term for designating the clusters of common concepts, emotions, and practices that arise when people 'interact regularly'. (Brumann 1999:51)

There are implications for identity and ethnicity, but there is no necessary correlation with what people actually think and do in culture, for the former categories mainly involve people's conscious and reflexive realization of who they are and to whom they belong. Confused or lost identities and ethnicities do not demonstrate the absence of culture, for all human life is as cultural just as much as it is historical. Culture is not just an optional diversion for the curious who do not subscribe to personalism, but an indispensable concept for explaining human perception and behaviour.

Culture is no abstraction, even if no thorough-going agreement can be expected, since definitions vary according to philosophical predilection, whether mentalist or behaviourist, idealist or materialist. Some accounts of culture focus on linguistic concepts, others on physical objects, but this opposition must be resolved. Culture here is taken to be a society's whole, accumulated response to its environment, where environment is the aggregate of the given external conditions affecting life with its physical features and primary resources. However, when the so-called 'virgin forests' of the world owe much to their symbiotic relationship with people who have managed them for millennia, considerable interdependence between environment and culture needs to be acknowledged in both directions (Seeland 1997). Indeed colonial suspicion that Karamojong herding was causing soil erosion justified cultural intervention, fixing the minds of colonial officers to this day (Anderson 1984; Beinart 2000:273; Wilson and Rowland 2001:2).

Indeed culture is not determined by any completely independent variable, whether genetic, geological or climatic. As 'all cultural behaviour is patterned', belief and behaviour are directed towards broad channels whose courses are implicitly known to all (Herskovits 1950:212f). Humanity is not only subject to culture, but the active subject in it, for 'a culture is a way of life of a people; while a society is the organized aggregate of individuals who follow a given way of life' (Herskovits 1950:29). It resolves the dichotomy between social and personal, enculturating personalities into the social structure while always enabling some cultural expression. Through collective choice processes, explicit and implicit, innovations are enculturated and the way of life changed, affecting the territorial, military, political, social, economic, legal, moral, personal, philosophical, technological, aesthetic, medical and ritual aspects of the culture. Traditions and institutions in all these are accumulated, maintained and developed. Complexity is inherent in culture, which fosters morphological growth.

Living in a mud hut and working alongside Karamojong culture concerning their interests in agriculture, water and health was a thorough way of becoming acquainted with it. Some rituals could be closely observed, but as severe insecurity, drought and famine were endemic from 1984 to 1986 and on my return visits, rain-making rituals were more common than the more celebratory ones that require auspicious occasions of peace and plenty. The most significant rites only occur twice a century. Insight into matters religious is not only earned by careful investigation, but is also given by disclosure. Some were disclosed to me, but others to various external observers of the Karamojong.

Communication

Communication is both intracultural and cross-cultural, as well as intimately connected to history by memory and the communication of tradition. Language is not merely an aspect of culture, but a carrier and presentation of it too. However structuralists and symbolic anthropologists have overemphasized it as the 'primary modelling system' through which we apprehend the world (Lotman 1990:x), with myth, religion, culture seen as secondary, text-based, modelling systems. Traditional Karamojong religion has no written and few oral texts, the *akigat* liturgy coming closest.

Language is not just an historical source as above, but semantics also generates meaning. Being familiar with the cognate lexemes not only lets the outsider into the resonance of meaning available to the speaker of Ngakaramojong, but also opens the way to etymologies they have forgotten. The basic morpheme of any Karamojong word is a consonant followed by a vowel. A consonant is added after the vowel to fill out particular, often related, meanings. Much of the rest of the morphology is comprised by the addition of prefixes, infixes and suffixes. For instance *nga-ki-le*[13] (milk); *eki-le* (male, husband); *aki-lek* (to vomit, give birth); *a-lel* (to flow); *aki-leleb* (to fill up); *e-lelya* (spring); *a-lely-an* (to be joyful); *aki-lem* (to harvest, reap); *aki-lep* (to milk); *e-lep-an-it* (grass *Dicanthium papillosum*); *e-lep-it* (wooden milking pot, mortar); *nga-lep-ito* (small termites which fly during the evening); *nga-lep-on* (dairy herd); *e-lep-un-oit* (boil, abscess); *aki-le-er* (to be clear (visible); *e-let-ot* (offspring, child, descendant); and so on. To see the connections seems even to expose the original process of assigning words to things and activities of building abstract terminology.

Morphology gives a clue, especially with grammatical, historical and cultural awareness, to what is basic and what derived or borrowed. For instance, Dyson-Hudson (1966:180), 'after three years of repeated questioning', was 'unable to discover the verbal source' of the word for elders (*ngikasikou*). Yet analysis of the language soon resolves his quest: *ngi-ka-si-kou* analyses to a number and gender marker, a demonstrative prefix, a causative infix and the stem, which is a Nilo-Saharan root. Its long-forgotten etymology is simply 'those made head', a valuable concept for understanding Karamojong politics. Inevitably this process begins to draw a word map of the culture, including the more abstract meanings. Yet it is important not to fall for idealist and nominalist temptations, and think that language, apart from culture and history, yields all knowledge.

Turning to cross-cultural communication, the Karamojong have only encountered non-Africans in the last 130 years. Most were seeking material advantage, ending in alien governments, colonial and independent (Knighton 1990). It is beyond the remit of this book to trace these encounters. Also significant for the religion is the contact with Christian mission. Ranger (2001) claims that 'Missionary archives offer the richest sources for pre-colonial African societies', but not here, as foreign mission did not begin until 20 years after colonial administration. Again he claims (1988:871), that it is 'impossible to write about any of the religions of Africa', whether traditional, Muslim, mission denominational or independent, 'in isolation from each other'. The story of Christian mission in Karamoja is a fascinating one with sources in archives, missionary memories or African responses, but neither space nor actuality permits it to be the governing narrative here. Enough of the story will be told to show that so far it has not diverted the course of traditional Karamojong religion. In this volume priority will be allowed to matters Karamojong so that the enduring traditional religion may be heard with as few Western presuppositions as possible. Instead of sceptically refusing to seek explanation rather than description, the exceptional case of the Karamojong will be examined.

5   Introduction to the Karamojong

Karamoja (a Swahilized term) is located in the northeast corner of Uganda bordering

---

[13] The hyphen is not part of orthography, but shows the reader the presence of prefixes, infixes and suffixes. *Ngakile* has a clear Proto-Eastern Nilotic (PEN) root, *le, and none of its Ngakaramojong derivatives here is a loanword.

Sudan and Kenya, where the boundaries are relatively natural both in terms of terrain (mountain or swamp) and ethnic homelands. The habitat of Karamoja is of peculiar importance for understanding the inhabitants' accumulated response to their environment. About 350 000 people of nine tribes inhabit about 27 321 km^2 (10 550 miles^2) in Karamoja, a larger area than either Israel (20 330 km^2), Wales (20 761 km^2), Rwanda (24 950 km^2) or Burundi (25 650 km^2). Of all regions in Uganda it has the lowest population density and its environment generally is more akin to that of neighbouring regions of Sudan and Kenya. Karamoja is part of the African peneplain, forming a plateau tilting downwards from the top of the Turkana escarpment of the East African Rift Valley to the Nile. At its eastern edge the plateau is about 1380 m (4530 feet) above sea level, falling to 1140 m (3740 feet) on the western side of Karamoja (Smith, P. 1987:1). The plains are interrupted by isolated mountains, 2–3000 m high, of ancient crystalline rocks and volcanic origin, while in the hillier country of the north and east inselbergs become a prominent feature. Around Mount Kadam, Tertiary lavas and volcanic tuffs are conspicuous. The herdsmen grow up to know large tracts of the land intimately.

Annual rainfall is lowest in the east central area, at about 600 mm per annum, rising to 900 mm in the south and west, more on Mounts Kadam and Moroto, but in all places precipitation is irregular, even in the wettest months of March to August (Dyson-Hudson, N. 1966:30–32; Dyson-Hudson, V.R. and N. 1970:95–7). Daytime temperatures usually fluctuate between 25 and 40°C, with the prevailing easterlies blowing cold in the morning and hot in the evening from the semi-desert of Turkana. It used to be thought that Karamoja was becoming steadily drier (Wayland 1931:190). There is no evidence in the data since 1923 to suggest that this is continuing. In Moroto the mean annual rainfall increased from 879 mm in the period 1923–40 to 890 mm in the period 1940–57.

In the pluvial periods much of Karimojong was under a vast, shallow lake formed by the reversal of the present Kafu-Kyoga river system (Tothill 1940:68–71). Since then, the rivers mostly drain into Lake Kyoga, whose level fell markedly in the northeast at the beginning of the twentieth century. Numerous water-sculpted, rock gorges in the hills of Karamoja tell of a much better-watered past (ibid.:84). Mount Toror, with its limestone caves, has completely dried out, preventing continued habitation since the eighteenth century. Agriculture was more possible in the Koten-Mogos area in the eighteenth century and at the end of the nineteenth than it is now. A county chief in the 1950s, when a stream had to be dammed to retain the water, recalled Lotome as a swamp full of hippopotami (Langdale-Brown, Osmaston and Wilson 1964:90).

Even the lowest rainfall area has 640 mm of mean annual rainfall, but the problem is the lack of continual rain in any one place to enable a plant to reach maturity, despite the desiccating effects of sun and wind. The standard deviation can often be a quarter of the mean annual rainfall, so often it is a case of too much rain or too little (see Table 1.1 and Map 1.1). Cattle can be moved to pasture not suffering from either, but crops cannot.

The bedrock is the Basement Complex, common to East Africa, and the plains of Karamoja are swamp deposits on it which form black cotton soil (*aro*) that is hopelessly sticky when wet and cracks when dry. It drains badly and is unsuitable for cotton. Its fringes have a 2–4 feet deep beach of pure sand. The higher ground

Table 1.1 Average annual rainfall at various centres in Karamoja

Location	Mean annual rainfall (mm)	Standard deviation (mm)	No. of years for which records are available	Standard error of mean (mm)	Source of information
Kaabong	693	–	10	–	2
Kotido	698	219	12	63	2,3,4
Alerek	1032	194	11	58	3
Moroto	896	227	43	35	1,2,3
Kangole	635	105	9	35	3
Matany	664	179	4	89	5
Lotome	660	140	16	35	3
Atumatak	750	201	38	33	1
Ngiminito	816	170	8	60	1
Nabilatuk	801	193	18	46	1,3
Iriri	979	178	9	59	3
Amudat	640	165	20	37	1,2
Moruita	951	87	3	50	1
Napiananya	1130	248	13	69	1,3
Namalu	1271	271	24	55	1,2
Karita	1054	260	16	65	1
Chepsikunya	692	–	2	–	1
*Kapraton	1225	276	14	74	1
*Kapwata	1588	305	15	79	1
*Bukwa	1073	124	10	39	1

Note: Centres marked with an asterisk * are not in Karamoja but they helped to decide the position of the isohyets in the average rainfall contours map below.

Source: Reproduced with kind permission from Paul Smith (1986a) who used the following sources of information: (1) computerized data at East Africa Meteorological Centre, Nairobi; (2) Lawes, EF 1969: 'Some Confidence Limits of Expected Rainfall' *East African Meteorological Department Technical Bulletin* 15; (3) Dyson-Hudson, N (1965) *Karimojong Politics*. Clarendon Press, Oxford; (4) Uganda Meteorological Department, Kotido; (5) Matany Catholic Mission.

(*ngitela*) has red loams, sand and gravels known as 'hot' soil, which shift after prolonged heavy rains, but for most of the year bake hard and scarcely absorb 20 per cent of precipitation. Though fertile, neither kind of soil lends itself easily to agriculture or heavy buildings.

Soil erosion has been seen, even to the present, as a most threatening feature of Karamojan ecology, whether gully, sheet or wind (Wilson and Rowland 2001:48f). The heavy storms and the large run-off wash away colloidal particles of clay and

The Challenges of Circumscribing the Other 21

Map 1.1   Average annual rainfall map of Karamoja (mm)

humus over wide areas, sometimes taking seeds or young crops with them, and pouring like soup into the river-beds to form raging torrents that sweep away banks and bridges. Before the rains, unrelenting winds and little whirlwinds stir up the sand and make red dust-storms. Even in the 1930s, before the human and livestock populations mushroomed, the area was thought to be in a process of reduction to desert (Wayland, Brasnett and Bisset 1937). Thus whether soil deterioration has been caused by continental climatic changes[14] or by local human culture is difficult to determine.

The removal of vegetation allows the sun's heat to be reflected back into the atmosphere, deterring the formation of rain-clouds, so overgrazing, overbrowsing by goats, and the destruction of trees for agriculture, bark and homesteads were perceived to denude the vegetation cover. By 1935, government assessments of Karamoja's cattle-carrying capacity had already been exceeded with 250 000 head each of cattle, sheep and goats (Eggeling 1938b:3). That soil degradation is not a one-way process is partly due to the recolonization by plants of areas eroded down to rotted rock which assists the percolation of water. Thus a cycle is created between savanna, steppe, bushland and dry thicket, and rotted rock (Langdale-Brown, Osmaston and Wilson 1964:89f). However the perceived dangers of overgrazing were to an extent more a matter of the colonial mind in this period (Anderson 1984; Beinart 2000:273).

Though the area has increased substantially since, to about 115 000 hectares, only 37 250 hectares were under grain crops in the whole of Karamoja in 1959, that is 1.4 per cent of the land area (Langdale-Brown, Osmaston, and Wilson 1964:78). The rest, apart from inaccessible mountain areas, is grazed for part of the year, though overgrown grasses in the wetter areas are not very nutritious and East Coast Fever in the southeast and the tsetse fly in the north limit grazing. However more recent calculations that the upper grazing limit is 750 000 mature cattle (Novelli 1999:XXXVIII) have already been surpassed, by estimates of more than 1 000 000 cattle with 750 000 sheep and goats. An accurate head count is hardly possible now, but with the unusually successful outward raiding of the last 15 years these figures might not be too large if it be recognized that more cattle are being grazed outside the borders of Karamoja, which had been moved in by the Protectorate government.

Karamoja is home to nearly half a million people who identify with one of nine ethnic groups.[15] The prescription that tribe and ethnicity are inventions of colonialism does not apply here,[16] for each regarded all the others as at least

---

[14] Mount Kenya lost 11 glaciers in the course of the twentieth century, which has been the empirical extent of global warming in the region (Climatic Research Unit 2001).

[15] It will be a long time before accurate demographic data can be marshalled. Questioning a participant in the 2002 census revealed an ambitious programme of officials visiting every residence. This was done in Kotido town, but not much beyond it. The results are simply not credible with annual growth rates of 9.7 per cent (see www.ubos.org).

[16] Of researchers into the Karamojong only Lamphear makes an effort to avoid the term 'tribe' and he has come back to it. 'In East Africa, where pastoral and semi-pastoral groups often lack strong kinship structures or centralizing authority, they frequently cut across territory and lineage, widening social contacts and instilling a sense of corporate, even

potential enemies, and some as possible trading partners, before British administration was effected belatedly in 1910. Indeed concepts of identity and enmity remain very strong within the Karamojong cluster (Gulliver 1952a), which dominates the plains. Their cradle is in the centre, the territory of the Jie people, the Dodosô are to the north and the Karimojong to the south, themselves divided into 11 territorial sections which are capable of both alliance and war. My mud-hut was in Kotido at the centre of Najie.[17] It was also the focus for research of the London anthropologists, Philip Gulliver and John Lamphear, both of whom found ritual to be most important for the functioning of society, but did not themselves address religion as a cultural aspect in itself.

The Karamojong are actually an invented people and Karamoja was a completely foreign word to them. There is no tribe or political unity of Karamojong, but a cluster of tribes (see Map 1.2);[18] not all can be called political unities in their own sense, thereby at once demonstrating how myriad forms of political and social organization are regularly reduced to tribes (Harvey 2000:9).[19] Tribalism was a favourite invention of colonial authorities (Ranger 1985), if only to explain resistance to their rule. Yet it is necessary to be careful not to deny to Karamojong, as to other Africans (Lonsdale 2000b), the politico-religious communities that they themselves imagine and identify with: Karimojong, Jie and Dodosô.[20] Apart from these proper nouns, they refer to their community simply as *ngitungakosi* (our people), where people can refer to human beings in general, but usually to Eastern

---

"tribal" unity' (Lamphear 1998:79). 'Indeed, tribe was the imagined community against which the morality of new inequality was bound to be tested' (Lonsdale 1992b:316). It is one thing to find a colonial construction of ethnicity among the peoples of Kirinyaga (Mount Kenya), quite another to deny the incorporated imagination of community to those that have it. The name one gives to that community is a secondary issue, except that any nomenclature can become tainted by pejorative use.

[17] It is still standing. The author lived in Kotido from 1984 to 1986 and revisited Karamoja in March–April 1998; January–February 2000 and March–April 2002.

[18] Gulliver (1952a;1956) coined the term, 'Karamojong cluster', which is still more precise, explicit and theoretically justifiable than the Central Paranilotes (Lamphear 1976b:1; Tucker and Bryan 1966). Those outside Karamoja, at least most of the time, are the Toposa, Dongiro and Jiye nearby in southeast Sudan and southwest Ethiopia, and the Turkana of Kenya who share the long north–south international boundary, which runs along the foot of the westernmost 600 m escarpment of the eastern Rift Valley.

[19] Pamela and Philip Gulliver (1953:40) find that the 'Jie tribe' are best seen as a unit, when the people assemble for ceremonies (Pazzaglia 1982:29). The term still has meaning in Uganda: 'Ethnic groups in Uganda are synonymous with tribes or nationalities' (Salih and Markakis 1998:190) indicating that nationality here does not refer to the state. Michael Little and Rada Dyson-Hudson (1999:16) still retain Gulliver's social stratification of 'tribal cluster', 'tribe' and 'tribal section'. Spencer (1998:18) defends 'tribes' in East Africa.

[20] Phonetically Kar*i*mojong is the better representation of what is pronounced by Karimojong, but J7 emphasized in speech 'Kar*a*mojong', which meant that he had come to the same terminological distinction between tribe and tribal cluster. The ring marker on Dodosô denotes a voiceless, breathed vowel.

Nilotes in particular. Lamphear's *ateker* does not lend precision for it means territorial subsection, clan and even distant relative rather than people, and is not in any case a political entity,[21] for clans are merely about kinship and hardly ever congregate. More important are the politico-religious communities, for which there are no more precise terms than 'tribe' and 'territorial section'. So straightaway multiple identities are found, and expected, for each person, for example, Karimojong (tribe), Pian (section) and Lip (clan) without considering age-classes, so it is necessary to typify the contrasting meaning of those identities.

In Karamoja it is the obvious observation that there are three related, but rival, tribes whose appellations and identities were not substantially invented by anyone but themselves, who collectively are called, and will be called for lack of any better indigenous term, 'Karamojong'. The Jie, like the Dodosô, function quite effectively in most circumstances as politically united. It is only possible to infer any unity for the Karimojong, the largest tribe, because they do still have some ritual and symbolic sense of collectivism and mutual relationship. They have 11 sub-tribes or territorial sections: the five original sections of Bokora, Pian, Maseniko, Tome, Osowa; two mixed sections, Mosingo and Pei; and four sections descended from Eastern Cushites, now quite dispersed: Mogos, Muno, Leeso and Kaala, who are partly absorbed by the Pian.[22] When they raid each other's cattle, they define other Karimojong as enemies, which is confessedly problematic for identity. Cattle-raiding is not sanctioned within the tighter political communities: the Dodosô, the Jie and each of the 11 Karimojong territorial sections. Those brought up in these communities will identify with its name, and members of the 11 territorial sections acknowledge themselves as being Karimojong. Identity can only be changed by a

---

[21] P12 supplied it as a word for tribe, but he explicitly excluded Jie, Turkana and Dongiro, while including Toposa and Dodosô. This separation is along the lines of current enemies and allies, having little to do with either origin or political community, even if it does lend support for a disputed concept of *ateker* peoples. As with *ngitungakosi*, *ateker* is a function of identity, or 'our people'. For P5 one's *ateker* is identified by one's cattle-brand (*emacar*) which is also used for clan, as one's cattle are branded according to clan, not herd.

[22] Every commentator after Neville Dyson-Hudson (1966:126ff,145) has observed there to be ten Karimojong sections (Pazzaglia 1982:39,77–82; Novelli 1988:12,33). P5 insists there are ten Karimojong sections plus the Mogos who are not really Karimojong by ethnic origin, but Maliri (Dasanec). Since they are now scattered between four sections they are not a political threat, being absorbed. The difference in the accounts lies in the Kaala, whom Dyson-Hudson (1966:126) counts as a sub-section of the Mogos, but two of the other three are also named as sections in their own right. What has happened is that the 'Maliri' already living north of Moroto before the Eastern Nilotes arrived fragmented into the small sections called Mogos, Muno, Leeso and Kaala. Now geographically dispersed, they retain their identity by having their own ceremonial grounds and a distinctive interest in animals uncharacteristic of the Karamojong (P3). The Kaala identity with camels is consistent with their Eastern Cushitic origin, not a 'Jie/Turkana' one (Dyson-Hudson 1966:138). The Nyakwai are sometimes said to be a Karamojong section (Wayland 1931:203;M1) and they are normally allies though, like the Abwor, they are known as a hybrid tribe ('half-brothers' instead of 'brothers' according to Dyson-Hudson 1966:150,229).

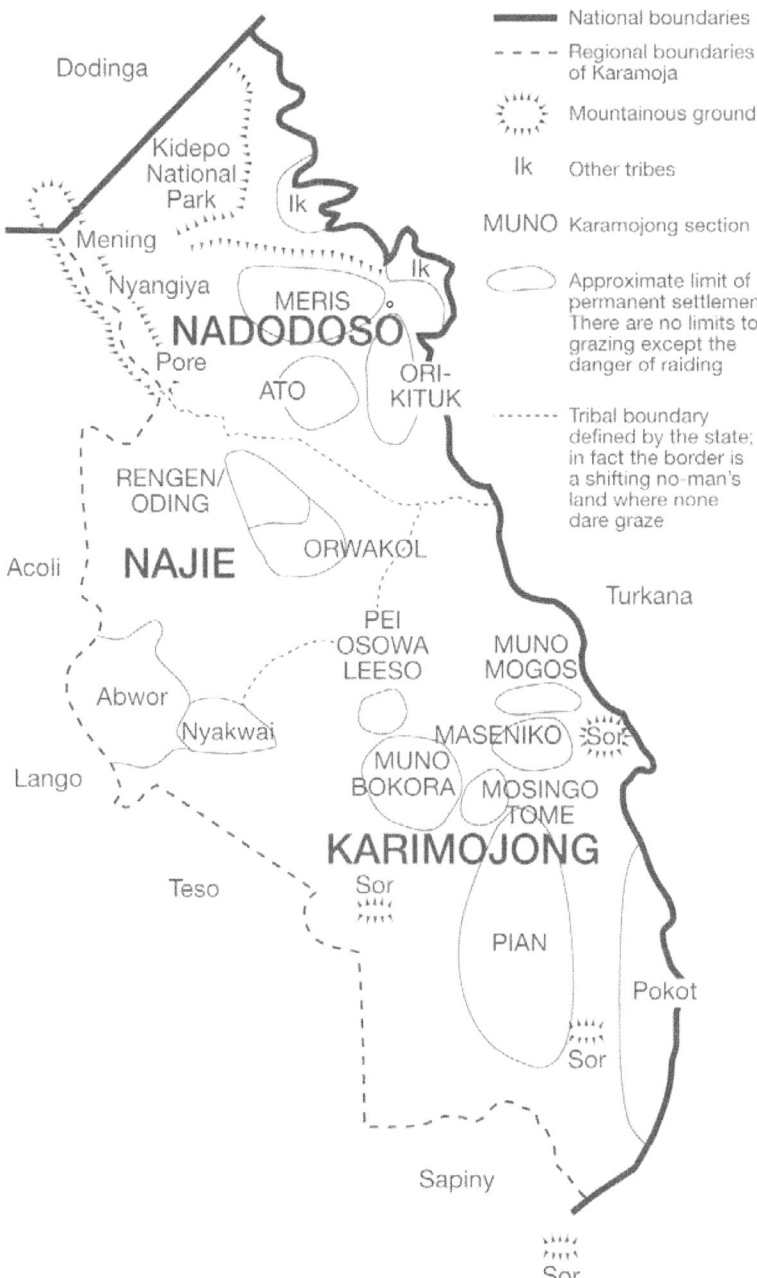

Map 1.2   The present political units of Karamoja

minority moving or marrying outside the community in which they were born. They all speak the same language and to the outsider are culturally very similar. They all appear as distinct from the several non-Karamojong tribes resident, often for longer than the Karamojong, in Karamoja. So the Karamojong, as a people, are an invention of outsiders, just as Africa or Asia is, but there are strong traditional identities and cultures. The Eastern Nilotic ones are designated, with popular usage, as Karamojong.

A 'Disappearing Tribe'?

For over 30 years the recurrent thesis in Ugandan academic circles, which tend to be detached from Karamoja,[23] is that the Karamojong are changing and will inevitably have to change in recognition of the need for modern agrarian and commercial development and in response to globalization. In particular 1979 is identified as a turning-point, when Amin's soldiers fleeing the Tanzanian Liberation Army left the munitions in the large barracks of Moroto available for distribution. Donkeys provided the mode of transportation for thousands of AK-47s that were eventually exchanged across Karamoja. Thinking driven by development agents and national politicians insists that, by using modern weapons, the Karamojong have forfeited their right to be a traditional people, and that the gun is itself undermining the culture, multiplying the casualties of raiding, and overthrowing the political rule of elders (excellently analysed just before independence by Neville Dyson-Hudson 1966[24]). The real power-players, it is argued, for the whole of the arid regions from Karamoja to the Indian Ocean, are big men, who are resourced by participation in national or international affairs, so can amass armies to pursue their own political and economic interests (Errington 1996:6; Galaty 1998; Belshaw and Malinga 1999). Such views are yet another expression of the assumption that European intervention must of necessity, for good or for bad, make traditional Africa evaporate before it (Orde Browne 1925; Root 1971; Ricciardi and Wan 1974). However, before capturing the wide-angle focus, it is advisable not to proceed without a ground-level shot.

Territoriality

A Karamojong child is not born just into a nuclear family but into a long series of

---

[23] See papers from the Workshop on 'Pastoralism, Crisis, and Transformation in Karamoja', Makerere University, Kampala 14–15.8.92 chaired by Mahmood Mamdani; for example, Mamdani, Kasoma and Katende (1992), Ocan (1992a, 1992b); and Okudi (1992). Hussein, Sumberg and Seddon (1999:413) criticize the 'conventional wisdom', which posits that 'the capacity of "traditional" institutions to manage and regulate competition is surpassed or diminished, and increasing violent conflict is the "inevitable" result'.

[24] Some 20 years after the Dyson-Hudsons' fieldwork, Paul Trappe (1978:57) commented 'at present, only a few people are ready to start something like a money economy'. Since Dyson-Hudson, there had been 'no important change in the social structure of the Karamojong'.

communities occupying progressively wider territory, which he soon learns from the activities of the rest of his family. Though this is by no means the only means of social aggregation, this introductory scheme needs to be given to allow some sense of domestic spatiality.

Yard The smallest unit of human geography is the yard (*ekal*), being a fenced area of about a square decametre, whose name could derive from a sheepfold (cf. *ikale*: lamb, kid) or the thorny brushwood (*ekalale*) which is split to make the fence (*alar*). It is the home of one married woman who has complete lifelong responsibility for it. It is her main working, living and sleeping area, and has a low door (*epiding*) to the outside world, which is blocked off at night by pulling in a branch (*egolit*), thorns pointing outwards. She has a private wattle and daub thatched hut (*akai*) for herself and her infants, and may have others for her older siblings, for whom *ekal* is home until they marry. It has basketwork granaries (*ngidulae*) on short wooden stilts and may have an *etem*, a meeting place covered by a flat roof (*eripipi*), where either women or men, but not both together, can sit informally for beer or just company. The husband has no private place of his own in the yard, only the right of access to his wife's hut.

Side Yards abut one another, with low doorways requiring the entrant to expose the back of his neck, to form a side (*ewae*) or wing, containing the mother, perhaps widowed, and all the wives and children of a married man, who as head of the house is the 'big man' (*ekapolon*), and the families of his younger, maternal brothers. It is the *ekal* a generation later. It includes small pens (*nganokin*) for milking the domestic cows, for calves, with whom the herdboys may sleep, and for sheep and goats. *Ewae* is the family unit. Sides and homesteads are named after the family heads.

Homestead The sides encircle one common cattle corral to form one complete homestead (*ere*). Ideally this contains all the wives and progeny of one grandfather, just as it is the home for his collective herd, but the permutations are endless. Also included may be poor clients, more distant relatives, inherited wives, or barren women, and in dangerous times *ngirerya* are built together for greater security, forming an endless maze of partially interconnected yards, pens and corrals. As a child learns his way round, so he learns about his agnatic kin.

Continual rebuilding goes on as people die and others, usually wives, come in to live. An *ere* is an *ewae* a generation on. Unity generally remains after the grandfather and even the fathers have died leaving only cousins, because it is focussed on the herd-owner, who is the head of the extended family (*elope ka ere*). He is responsible for homestead discipline and the general control of the herd, yet even he is always the guest of his wives.

Men can either congregate by the cattle corral in the nook (*aperit*) where the guards spend the night, or outside the *ere* in an open place (*ekokwa*) often on a hillock and under a shade tree (*ekitoi*) where inactive elders spend the day. There, homestead and herd problems can be discussed with relatives and neighbouring friends. Around, or slightly away from, the homesteads, the married women own small fields which they clear and fence round with thorns at the beginning of the wet season. There may be a problem with thefts of grain from the stalk in times of hunger, but the social exclusion of trespassers from unharvested fields, and the fear of divine punishment, mean more time is spent protecting the crops from wildlife than from humans. Men, as individuals, own no real estate at all, aspiring only to social status and rights in livestock, whereby they can harness the activities of the womenfolk and other men. Even a homestead head is only a steward for his sub-clan of the settled land in his care.

Neighbourhood Most *ngirerya* are clustered together irregularly, forming a neighbourhood (*edunyet*[25]) of not more than 13 or so, linked by well trodden footpaths. The population might be as high as 1000 men, women and children. Many may be agnatically related, thus composing a sub-clan, or even a small clan in its own right. Yet it is not geography or lineage alone that defines the community. 'Each [*edunyet*] is different: they sacrifice their own ox' (Dyson-Hudson, N. 1966:109). What unites the homesteads is a common allegiance to one sacred grove which serves as a place for sacrifice, for councils and for dancing. Between them the elders of a neighbourhood are the quorum necessary for an *akiriket* (church) with its own local variations on the common traditions of the tribe. It may also have its own fire-maker. The primary neighbourhood bond is therefore religious.

Territorial division At least one neighbourhood, or at most nine in densely populated areas, make up an *atyakatyaket a ngalup* (division of soils) that has its own place name, of which each neighbourhood is a part, or corner (*agule*). Its symbol of unity is again its sacred grove where large scale ritual activities are performed, especially rain-making (Gulliver 1952b:182). They still take place regularly at Nakwapua, the sacred grove of Panyangara, for instance. In the larger, wider spread Karimojong sections, however, this ritual unity has been transferred to territorial sub-sections, leaving a mainly geographical association of neighbourhoods beneath this level.

Subsection The five largest Karimojong sections, the Bokora (turtles), Pian (spirits), Maseniko (bulls), Tome (elephants) and Mosingo (rhinoceroses) have subsections, also with creaturely names, and each of these has sacred groves at which *akiriket* meets. The exception is the Pian who expanded so far south that they founded three subsections, Meri-emong, Taaruk and Nyanga, which were stretched into three north–south bands, while a more adequate expression of community was found by assembling the neighbourhoods that depended on one or other of the five major river-beds for water into river-units, named after the centre on the river; that is, Rengidwat, Bilatuk, Locat, Kakamongole, Pianyanya, for major ceremonies (Emoru 1998:24; Pazzaglia 1982:140f; Dyson-Hudson, N. 1966:265f). That subsections are also secondary territorial groupings is suggested by the Ngakaramojong *aperit* and *auryanet*, which are coterminous for the resting place for the herds outside the homestead, resonant with the gathering of the herds for *akiriket*.

---

[25] Cf. *akiduny* (to be near).

Section Apart from the promotion ceremony once in a generation, the section (*ekitela*) is the territorial community which forms the most effective religious, political and social grouping. The section, rather than the tribe, declares war and stages the major annual sacraments of Beseeching, Freeing the Cattle and Declaring War, with their huge sacrifices and multitudinous dances. Each is free to follow its own customs within the given ecclesial system (Dyson-Hudson, N. 1966:133f).

Tribe It is no accident that the unity of all territorially conditioned communities above the level of homestead or clan is constituted by the meetings of a religious congregation, the *akiriket* of elders and initiates. It is these that make frequent grandiose statements of tribal unity superfluous, for each assembly affirms the common values, the shared faith and the one people. For example, the opening prayer, 'The Jie, the Jie are here', gives an unforced, undisputed tribal identity to each member. This repeated affirmation is crowned for the Karimojong by the promotion ceremony when the pilgrim camps take up the position that their sections hold in the land.

Cluster The Karamojong tribal cluster includes the Toposa, Dongiro and Jiye nearby in southeast Sudan and southwest Ethiopia, and the Turkana in Kenya, as well as the Jie, Karimojong and Dodosô in Karamoja. Enmity between the Jie and the Karimojong or the Dodosô can be so bitter precisely because they recognize each other as rival bearers of a common culture, religious tradition and language. That common inheritance refuses exclusivity. Strangers are welcome in the land if they will adopt the religious and political tradition. The geography of Karamoja reinforces the sense of a common destiny because its plains within have more similarity than any terrain without. *Akwap* refers not just to a tribe's country but to land as it is known. At the margin it includes the whole earth, but the more agricultural terrains, with their soft, pot-bellied drunkards who do not consider it wise to lay down their lives in defence of the cattle, are not for the Karamojong, who adhere to the unalterable traditions of the elders. They see Karamoja, the cradleland, as a good place for decent values.

Nomadic Pastoralists

Herdsmen own no grazing lands, for it is not worthwhile defending plots that they can only use for short periods. Even enemies will not be ejected, if there is surplus grazing or if their ejection would incur too many losses to enforce, although small bands of unauthorized aliens are much deterred from casual entry by the likely loss of cattle and life. When grazing or water is in short supply, members of an *awi* or *alomar* ensconced near a water-hole will fight others if necessary, their own tribesmen with sticks to prevent overcrowding, but normally refusal of permission is accepted. Yet there is no defence of territorial boundaries in order to preserve exclusive use of land resources, contradicting the predictions of socio-biology.

> The case of the Karimojong indicates that energy costs for resource defense can be extremely low when common values and beliefs make ritual sanctions rather than overt defense effective in preventing trespass. The low energy costs only hold true if outsiders not enculturated into the beliefs are excluded. (Dyson-Hudson, V.R. and Smith 1978:37)

Karamoja's borders remain fluid. The Turkana, unable to satisfy all their herds on their semi-desert, were able to bring them up to Najie for months at a time, almost colonizing Loyoro, when the Dodosǒ inhabitants, dispossessed of cattle, had to flee to an Oxfam resettlement programme in the Kapeta Valley. As predicted (Knighton 1990:I,359), the Dodosǒ acquired more arms, and with them more cattle, and so reclaimed their traditional territory. The Jie and the Karimojong have effectively pushed their borders west, spending much of the dry season in Labwor, eastern Acoli, Lango and Teso, grazing their cattle in increasingly uninhabited areas. It is precisely this expansionism that the Uganda People's Defence Force, partly composed as it is of Acoli, Lango and Teso, is attempting to reverse, not least in the forcible disarmament campaign begun in 2002.

6. The Sacred

The sacred is not in opposition to a profane world. The sacred dominates and infuses the life-world. What is especially sacred or godly is the people and animals, places and events, which are the occasion for dense moments in the life of the people. Here the spiritual is maximally present. Such power must be regulated by custom, both to bring it out and to channel it for the common good.

Salvation History

The Karamojong have their own sense of salvation history, having been led to the good country of their own land, despite the threat of ogres and rivers in spate. Here they take the long view. Drought, famine, disease and defeat may be necessary to correct society by restoring it to the customs, but these are only temporary exigencies. When the culture is in harmony, peace and prosperity will break out as the great blessings of life, so that even enemies will come as clients to share in it and be welcomed into the community. Thus prayers may begin, 'The Jie, be there!' or whichever section or sub-section has assembled to reaffirm their divine mandate over the land. There is no need to deliberately determine the fate of interlopers who come with a different agenda, as their presence will not be permanent. The Dodosǒ adopted a relaxed stance towards the advent of British military administration in 1910–11, as they were sure they would be here for a short time. They themselves now think they were wrong, but eventually they were proved correct; British rule lasted only half a century, less than the normal span of a single generation-set.

History is evaluated religiously, not economically. The criterion is not an overwhelming crowd of ancestors who must be obeyed as a collective spiritual force. Ancestors are neither invoked nor beseeched in communal prayers. The forefathers are a differentiated part of history, not an eternal judge over it, for each can be assigned to age-classes identifiable with those of the living. It is the generation-set system which brings all together in time and space in the performance of the assembly, especially through overcoming generational tensions by demarcating them. It is in the material interests of young men to contest the command over resources, especially cattle, rigorously exercised by their fathers, but the junior generation-set also contains old men. The threat of the young men is represented symbolically at the assembly and its power thereby contained in it. Cultural health at any time is exhibited by the willingness of people to obey the elders. Continual refusal by any age-class spoils the country and besmirches the name of the age-class involved.

The archetypal fear is that the young men will go to dry-season cattle-camps and not return, but set up a rival society to the old men, women and children whom they leave behind. Since they have the cattle, they can acquire wives through bridewealth and so children, while the old men face starvation. Hence the popular etymology of 'Karimojong', 'the withered old men', has a multitude of derivations in story, with the community seeking legitimation preferring the part of the old men left behind by disobedient herders. That the fear of salvation history being rent by schism is based on actual historical events is exemplified by the secession of the Turkana from the Jie. That this has not happened more often is testament to religious means for resolving socio-political tensions.

Anointed People

Religious specialists are not the most important people in society, nor do they form a guild. Just as all males can participate in war and politics at a certain stage in life, so they can also participate in the religion. Having been anointed with the chyme of the ox that they spear, they become initiates in an age-class at the religio-political assembly. As mature men (*ngisorok*) they eat and pray in the supreme decision-taking body, being responsible for the butchery, cooking and serving of the sacrificial meat. They may exhort the elders to pray for pressing problems. When their whole generation-set is promoted, they become elders (*ngikasikou*) and, as their age-section graduates to seniority, senior elders. This is the most important religio-political office of the Karamojong, but it is not monarchical. The elders are a college or chapter of priests representing the interests and presence of the territorial sections and clans. Their rule is reactive and consensual rather than proactive and individual. Their first duty is to pray for the well-being of society. No initiation or concerted explicit plan of action can be taken without their permission and authorization.

Fire-makers (*ngikeworok*) have the potential to be monarchical leaders, as happens in more agrarian cultures, so the elders are cautious about anointing any. They find their rôle in agrarian ceremonies. The *emuron* (fem. *amuron*) is a more significant figure, although a number of sub-clans produce them to practise concurrently. Among more pastoralist peoples, such as the Turkana, they provide rare candidates for individual rule, and among the Karamojong as war-leader or adviser to a war-leader, they have a key rôle in military affairs. Others may categorize them as witchdoctors and medicine-men, and certainly they are the experts who counter witchcraft and provide medicine for magical and healing purposes. They may use incantations, sacrifices or herbs (*ekitoi*) to meet their client's needs. Though they do not cease to be herdsmen or mothers, nor face being set apart like the fire-maker, they come the next closest to being religious specialists. *Shaman* would be a misleading term as they do not normally go into ecstasy. They may exercise the charismatic gifts of the dreamer (*ekerujan*), the diviner (*ekesiemon*) or prophet (*ekadwaran*), but not necessarily all.

Ngimurok may specialize in, say, healing clients from a limited range of complaints, or may attempt many solutions. They are more than diviners, but common to all functions is the ability, using various techniques, to divine the efficient cause of the situations to which they address themselves. They must know who has made someone sick or caused them to die, they must discover the future, interpret dreams, signs or portents, figure out the presence and movements of enemies and diseases, identify the propitious domestic beast for sacrifice, or reveal the divine will or word, divining the hidden causes of many events. Since they not only practise divination, but have a wider presentiment of the implicit realities so as to offer remedies as well, the embracing term, 'divine' will be used to translate *e/amuron*.[26]

Anointed people have maximal effect when assembled in *akiriket*, the occasion for anointing people with chyme (*ngikujit*). This may happen at the level of the homestead or of the Karamojong as a whole at their promotion ceremony. At each level these ceremonies provide the dense moments in people's lives. Women have no place in assemblies called for livestock issues, politics and rain-making, but are present for all rites of passage even if they have to watch the men in the cattle corral from their side (*ewae*). They may issue their complaints or ululations from there. They do have their own age-set names which mirror the men's system. Though not allowed to pray in the assembly they have their own rites, which they perform to the exclusion of men. A large minority of traditional birth attendants are *ngamurok*.

Spiritual Places

There are many places associated with local gods or spirits, frequently mountains and hills (*ngimoru*), great rocks (*ngitaaba*), large fig-trees (*Ficus* spp.) and water where it is accumulated in any form. This is not to say that other places are profane or mere matter, for the whole land (*akwap*) is directly susceptible to social transgression. Digging deep into it has spiritual consequences and spirits in it are the cause of people stumbling. Local traditions may have tabus against the collection of firewood or cultivation, but a general one applies to the ceremonial ground or sacred grove, which is the meeting place for *akiriket*. Between sacrifices it is left untouched, but remains crying for another sacrifice to be carried out there (J20).

Sacramental Ceremonies

Ceremonies employ the will-to-life inherent in all existence. The medium is selected which confers sacrality on all associated with it. Cattle are both the medium of all social values, the means of livelihood and the stock of wealth. The sacrifice of cattle (*amurunot*) confers maximal efficacy in ceremonies therefore, and demonstrates that religion is not an escape or retreat from life, but a full-blooded engagement with

---

[26] It is one of the few terms that English-speaking Karamojong find largely untranslatable. Wizard or witch is used only in association with an interest to deprecate traditional religion, but these translate into Ngakaramojong as *ngikapilak*, malicious users of magic, whom it is the task of *ngimurok* to counter on behalf of society.

the rest of human culture in its different aspects. Social ceremonies include rites of passage: birth, initiation, marriage and death. There is the jural ceremony of the curse. The infrequent political ceremony of the promotion of a generation-set is augmented by annual and *ad hoc* ceremonies for a whole section to discuss current affairs. There are very explicit military ceremonies to open raiding, the night sacrifice before a raid and a special sacrifice for making peace. The economic life is marked by ceremonies to free the cattle and bring them back to the settled areas annually, while agrarian rites mark and sacralize seedtime, weeding and harvest. Ecological ceremonies beseech the elders to bless the country, and they meet to make rain. The healing of spiritual danger or ruptured social relationships is effected by ceremonies to deal with the killing of an enemy, to solve a fractious relationship, to cool down a heated social situation and to grant absolution to the accursed. The breaking of a tabu normally needs sacrifice to put it right. Without these, real sickness and misfortune are only to be expected.

Transcendent Beliefs

There is no dichotomy between the natural and the preternatural, though wonders are possible and are attributed to divine agency. Thus so-called 'nature spirits', gods (*ngakujŏ*) of the mountain or rock, and spirits (*ngipian*) associated with lightning, rain, rivers and ponds are firmly connected to the transcendent and do not constitute a problem for their belief in one God (Akujŭ) who made everything. Troubled and troubling deceased members of the family appear as ancestral spirits (*ngipara*), but do not attract much attention, much less worship. What transcends this world is still continuous with it. The sky is shaped like the inside of the roof of a mud hut, and represents the place of Akujŭ, and the great homestead (*ere apolon*) where the dead live (Emoru 1.4.02 Letter). Religion is associated with a cosmology, but that does not remove it from the other aspects of culture. In order to understand the whole, each aspect must be seen in its relation to the other, including religion. To suppose that faith is separate from knowledge is to interpose modernity into the one universe the Karamojong inhabit. That universe, and its interaction with other versions, is the subject of this book.

Chapter 2

The Series of Human Settlements in Karamoja

To assess to what extent anything is traditional it is necessary to explore as fully as possible the history of the traditions. Without this lengthy and extremely useful exercise the tendency is to make unwarranted assumptions about their history, for example, that traits and institutions have been present for millennia or alternatively were only diffused in the last few decades. When nothing is written, issues of temporal continuity are more likely to be ignored, for in talking of Karamoja the past is frequently claimed in support of one view or another. These considerations apply doubly to religion, which can be seen as an accumulation of memories and institutions regarded as culturally significant. Where memory is found to differ from history, yet more may be learned from ways in which people perceive their past and its reconstruction for their identity.

It is difficult not to depend on a wider knowledge of East African history than can be set out here, but the opposite error, and that usually made, is to present peoples like the Karamojong as isolated and without history. In fact it will be shown that their broad origins can be traced back further than the British, though inevitably this lacks simple precision. Yet the argument of the first three chapters of this volume is that this is much less misleading than skipping over the piecemeal evidence that there is. Indeed it is already overdue for Africanists to stop apologizing to other historians.[1]

1 The Prehistory of Karamoja

Little is written about culture or religion without at least implicit historical assumptions being made. Both are accumulations of traits and institutions over time. Merely to identify which cultural or religious traits are privileged now is to make claims on the past. However, without research, this discourse can often be the extrapolation of prejudice into the past, finding what was wished or expected. Yet *Historie*, as the past given beyond the interpretation of partial minds themselves the children of other histories, is full of surprises. Paul Ricoeur (1974:40f) thinks structuralism only fits the unconscious order of 'savage thought, which orders, but does not think itself'. Although it produces a system, stilted by its derivation from

---

[1] So John Sutton (personal communication). Lonsdale (2000a:10) tells the reminiscence of the Cambridge historian who refused to condemn oral history on the grounds that almost all his medieval primary sources, though documentary, were forgeries.

linguistic laws, its synchronic point of view reaches only the prevailing social function of a myth. Diachrony is a problem and, again, history is jilted. Ricoeur himself needs correction when he assumes that, compared with the Old Testament, 'savage' society is ahistorical and undifferentiated in consciousness.

The difficulty in researching East African history is, of course, the lack of written documents, before outsiders started making them, which, for Karamoja, has been for little more than a century. This alone has caused people to write tribal history off as unknowable and, therefore, irrelevant. The absurdity of Hugh Trevor-Roper's infamous remark that Africa has no history remains in Oxford's living memory. Such dogma has been used to denigrate all materials for a non-colonial history of Africa, which is then conveniently presupposed to have no effect on the present day. The result is that Karamoja is thought to be in a strange, unreal time-warp: its people have always been there, having been fossilized in an Early Iron Age culture for millennia. It is a museum of quaint freaks, dropped into the middle of unknown Africa from nowhere. Its display has nothing to tell of world history, because it is quite unrelated to real events. The fossils should bestir themselves, if they want to participate. Such a view is the intellectual blindfold of cultural imperialism.

Happily attempts are being made to fill a few of the gaping holes in our knowledge by using the laborious techniques of archaeology, linguistics and cultural anthropology; if documentary history appears easier it is not necessarily more accurate. It must be admitted that how their findings are to be triangulated is perpetually problematic, but their results will be brought together for Karamoja and a crude summary presented here on the grounds that identifying a few stars in the sky is better than presenting a universe where only the blue ionosphere exists. The etics of material culture, which the archaeologist has dug up, though not often enough in the pertinent areas, must be combined with the emics of the social and linguistic life of people poorly understood in academia. What is written now must, perforce, be highly tentative simplification of complex happenings over a long period, but to write nothing is to give the impression that nothing happened, which would certainly be farther from the truth. On the other hand there is an advantage over conventional history in the strength of an historical approach uncontaminated by the written word whose preserved prejudices have distorted and problematized European historiography.

East African Man

This sketch gives evidence for the idea that there is a prehistory of human presence in Karamoja, no doubt older than Europe's. The archaeological record is obviously piecemeal, not capable of accurate simplification, and not comprehensive, but this applies to most history. Perhaps the first *Homo sapiens sapiens* (who can at least be dated in East Africa from a skull 130 000 years old in the River Omo valley north of Lake Turkana) to wander over Karamoja were the hunting and gathering groups of the indigenous African stock of Bushmen, leaving their Stillbay[2] stone points and their lance-heads behind them, notably in a rock cistern on the eastern

---

[2] Stillbay is a site in South Africa, which has lent its name to an archaeological term for a pottery style associated with early Bushmen.

escarpment of central Karamoja. The well at Mogos was first chipped out of the rotting granite beneath an overhanging rock as long as 40 000 years ago in East Africa's Middle Stone Age by the first community to leave interpreted remains. Magosi (the Kiswahili name) once gave its name to an intermediate culture, thought to extend as far south as Zimbabwe. There was no hiatus between succeeding cultures, rather a continual process of transition into the Late Stone Age. The cistern was redug as the water level dropped in time of drought and stone tools of different millennia rubbed shoulders at the bottom (Cole 1963:54; Clark, J.D. 1982:283f).

The finely knapped microliths of the later community were used on the plains of Karamoja and Turkana. A little agriculture may also have been practised using digging sticks weighted by bored stones to break the hard earth. As rock paintings in South Africa show them being used thus, a Bushmanoid community is hinted at. Rock paintings are to be found in Karamoja of animals in dark red or white, and of geometric designs, such as concentric circles (Lamphear 1976b:62f). Such figures are visualized in the physical extremes produced by some dances and drugs. One site lends a dramatic focus, and a deep religious significance is altogether likely, since rock paintings generally are increasingly associated with religious drama, where the actors represent themselves as animals (James 2003:32).

Cushites

Some stone-flaking techniques in Karamoja resembled those used by the industries of the Saharan Neolithic (10 800–6700 years ago) and the Doian people of southern Somalia, also around granite inselbergs. Over 17 000 years ago a people entered East Africa from Northeast Africa, bringing an advanced technology in making fine stone tools. Microliths permitted the use of barbs, and so poison. Bows were also used to drill holes in seeds and ostrich eggshell for beads. If there were no sudden cultural change, it is likely that the Afroasiatic speakers gradually absorbed the local Bushmen.[3]

Man's habitat was not static. The uniformly high rainfall in East, North and Central Africa was reduced by global warming, leading to a dry period between 12 000 and 10 000 years ago, after which Lakes Turkana and Victoria began to rise again. This wet period, when rainfall was 165 per cent of modern levels, southwest Karamoja was under water (Tothill 1940:60ff) and Lake Turkana overflowed seasonally through the Lotakipi swamp into the Sobat River, lasted until 7000 years ago, when another dry period ensued for a millennium (David 1983:43). A final wet period prevailed 6000–3000 years ago, during which more Afroasiatics changed their location.

Cushitic[4] speakers of a distinct physique spread rapidly into East Africa from the

---

[3] There are four phyla (large groups) of African languages: Khoisan, associated with Bushmen, Afroasiatic, which includes Semitic and Cushitic, Nilo-Saharan, including Ngakaramojong (see Figure 2.1), and Niger-Congo, which includes Bantu (Heine and Nurse 2000).

[4] 'Hamitic' used to be the term for such Afroasiatic languages. Meinhof's (1912) 'Nilo-

north 3000–5000 years ago, with their domestic animals and new agriculture. The earliest, sure date for domestic animals in East Africa is 4000 years ago east of Lake Turkana (Robertshaw and Collett 1983:295). Deep-basin grinding stones for milling millet, deep-grooved pottery and Cushitic burial cairns have been found at sites across Karamoja. The Southern Cushites (SC) were absorbed by Eastern Cushites (EC), ancestors of the Dasanec, spreading to Karamoja from north of Lake Turkana 3000–2000 years ago (Ambrose 1982:111–13).

2 Black Populations on the Nile

Nilo-Saharan (N-S)

Apart from Afroasiatics, the first non-indigenous Africans to live in East Africa came from Khartoum. About 10 000 years ago pottery and bone harpoons were invented on the Upper Nile and spread to the Sahara and the Mediterranean. Yet the peoples on the Nile maintained languages distinct from the Afroasiatic ones that spread across North Africa and to the Horn. The Nilo-Saharan (N-S) phylum of languages (Figure 2.1) has an organic relationship with a common, ancient, mother tongue, which the linguists term a proto-language, 'P'.[5] Even if the Nilo-Saharan root for cow, *de/*te, did not go back to PN-S, it is quite different from the Afroasiatic *lo or *sa. Native, wild, long-horned, *Bos primigenius* cattle were domesticated independently in the eastern Sahara and known to the Nilo-Saharans 10 000–6500 years ago, spreading south in Africa from the west or northwest, so were not a later diffusion from expert pastoralists in the Ethiopian Highlands (Clark, J.D. 1982:497; Ehret 1983;1998:6–9; MacDonald 2000).

However, there is evidence to suggest that the Nilo-Saharans were only just coming to terms with cattle products for food. In order to stomach cow's milk, the human race must build up a genetic tolerance to lactose. The Bushmen of Angola have not begun to do this, while the pastoralists of the Horn have up to 100 per cent

---

Hamitic' hypothesis has long since been rejected with its inference of mixed languages and races, because of its unwarranted and unworthy association with the diffusion of any valued trait being from Indo-European influence. Conversely it can hardly be denied that the influence of Cushitic languages and cultural traits abound in parts of East Africa, to wit some current use of the term 'Paranilotic', attributed by Lamphear (1976b:1) to Tucker (Tucker and Bryan 1966), who had been using 'Nilo-Hamitic' (Tucker and Bryan 1956:106). Bender (2000:53) also condemns 'Paranilotic' as 'another step backwards' to 'extreme conservatism'.

[5] Greenberg's (1970) overall classification of African languages is basic to this discussion, its method of mass comparisons being 'universally accepted' (Nurse 1997:363), though the caveat must be borne in mind that the history of languages is not identical to the history of ethnic groups who, like the Lango, may adopt a 'foreign' language. For a counter-classification see Bender (1976) or Thelwall (1982:42) and Ehret (1983). Ehret (1998) is hotly disputed in Nilo-Saharan research (Blench 2002) as he is in Bantu studies, but Bernd Heine finds no convincing alternative to his model (Oliver *et al*. 2001:70–73).

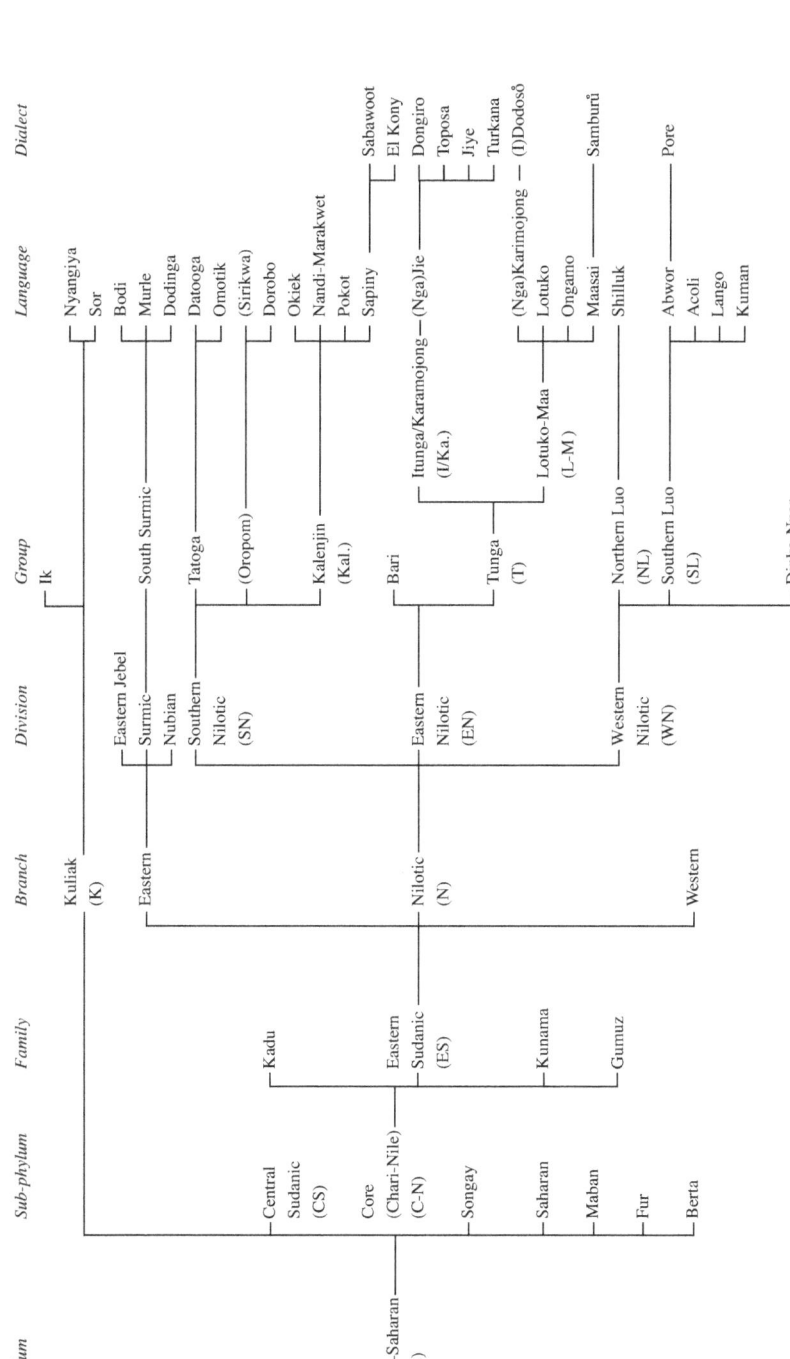

Figure 2.1   The linguistic classification of Ngakaramojong

tolerance. One of the most cattle dependent members of the Nilo-Saharan phylum, the Maasai, still have as low as 40 per cent tolerance (Vossen and Bechhaus-Gerst 1983b:562). Nilo-Saharan speakers' success in the agripastoral life, which also involved experimentation with wild grains, was encouraged by the progressive desiccation of the Sahara in the sixth millennium BC, even to the extent that they spread as far apart as the Niger River and Lake Turkana. In the process languages and customs diversified.

Chari-Nile (C-N)

The Chari-Nile (C-N) sub-phylum is being dropped from linguistic classifications (Ehret 1998; Blench 2002: 300), but its constituents Central (CS) and Eastern (ES) Sudanic speakers brought cattle into Central Sudan over 7000 years ago, being the first people there to produce their own food rather than garner it. As peoples pass from a hunter–gatherer to a food-producing way of life, the robustness of the skull reduces (David 1983:72).[6] They also took with them the common Nilo-Saharan discovery of the cultivation of sorghum (*Sorghum bicolor*) and bulrush millet (*Pennisetum americanum*), to the Khartoum area some 6000 years ago (David 1982:79), although cultivation probably did not spread much until the availability of iron tools.

Eastern Sudanic (ES)

The Eastern Sudanic family, which was begotten 7000 years ago near the Blue Nile, south of its confluence with the White Nile, slowly started spreading in different directions over the next millennium with its mobile stock of sustenance. The drier environment of 4000–3000 years ago opened up the Sudd grasslands for expansion, and during the following millennium the desiccation of vast areas of the Sahara and Nubia created a pressure to move on (Vossen and Bechhaus-Gerst 1983b:559). How people responded is unclear. Some went south up the west of the Nile to the Nuba Hills and along the margin of the Ethiopian Highlands on the east, where large areas were occupied by Nilo-Saharans over 3000 years ago, and millet and sorghum were being grown. Others went north to the Egyptian borderlands, despite the strong New Kingdom in Egypt. In 1400BC, there were two main groups involved: the Nilo-Saharan Eastern Sudanic, as evidenced by Egyptian loanwords in Nubian, and the Afroasiatic Northern Cushites. It may have been this contact which resulted in the Northern Cushitic Beja sharing the root for goat (*na) with Eastern Sudanic (Ehret 1983:392). Apart from language Nilotes and Nubians are also linked by the use of lip-plugs, and 'Nubi' is even named by a Jie elder as the origin of the Itunga (Lamphear 1976b:74; Wainwright 1954:119).

About 5000 years ago, a small, marginal branch of Nilo-Saharan[7] pioneered their

---

[6] The Teso even recalled their primal generation as tadpoles, men who were of short stature with large heads dwelling among swamps and on lakesides (Lawrance 1955:12).

[7] Roger Blench (27.11.01 E-mail) is reclassifying Kuliak as Central Sudanic, Bender (2000:55) as Nilo-Saharan, and Ehret (1998:81–6) as Eastern Sahelian, the problem being

way into Karamoja, assimilating and being influenced by any Late Stone Age inhabitants. This branch shares 3 per cent of its vocabulary with the largely Khoisan (Bushmanoid) language of the Sandawe of Tanzania. The number is insignificant but their meanings are not, for they indicate that the new settlers passed on new techniques of making knives, throwing spears, hoe cultivation, grinding grains and milking stock to wandering Bushmen.[8]

The Eastern Sudanic speakers are called the Kuliak,[9] who are now represented by the hill tribes, the Ik, the Nyangiya and the Sor, or Tepes, who still go hunting and gathering as well as tilling gardens, but whose present poverty, apart from modern agriculture in Nyangiya, does not reflect their previous dominance of the country. Probable memorials to the Tepes, the first Kuliak offshoot, range from the Tepes Hills in Dongiro (Tornay 1979a:310f), through the Dopes River in Najie, over Mount Kadam, called by the Kalenjin, Tabasiat or Debasien (Weatherby 1962:201) to Endebess, east of Mount Elgon, which again became their home for a while in the nineteenth century. Before stronger peoples came, then, it would appear that the Kuliak spread from the Ethiopian escarpment to southeastern Kenya. The Ik even have an oral tradition that, 'long ago', they were one people with the Nyangiya at Lomej (Gulliver, P. and P.H. 1953:98), which is midway between their separate destinations in the Nyangiya and Morungole hills.

The Jie remember former residents of their new land as Ngikuliak and, in 1916, the Turkana called the Teuso (the Itunga name for the Ik), Giluak (cf. Gulliver, P. and P.H. 1953: 98; Lamphear 1976b:69n; EA 4325: 29.2.16 Turpin's Report). They had cattle at some stage, but it may have been their very loss that drove them south so early. Whatever the reason, they use the Afroasiatic cattle terms, *lo, *sa, not N-S/ES *te, though they do employ the latter's root for 'many' or 'riches' (*bol) to describe their cattle corral (*bor*) but this might have been borrowed later from Ngakaramojong (Fleming 1983a:435).

The use of cattle and other terms poses the question of Cushitic links (Tucker 1967b:678). To this day travellers along the pass up the northeast escarpment to Kamion add to the little cairns on the path to quieten the spirits of the rocks. Even so it is a notorious place for travellers to go missing. Up here passed an old Eastern Cushitic people who also surged west into southeast Sudan, introducing loanwords there to Eastern Sudanic Dodinga and to Kuliak, ensuring the latter's continual bilingual position. According to Wilson's oral tradition (1970b:130f), which is substantiated by Turpin's 1916 report that many Eastern Cushitic Marille (Dasanec)

---

that their long contact with Eastern Sudanic languages, even adopting Ngakaramojong now, has masked their true origin. They entered at roughly the same time that domestic animals appeared in East Africa: humpless, long and short-horned cattle (*Bos taurus*) from Europe by way of Egypt, sheep, goats and donkeys (Marshall 2000). Yet their original word for cow, PK *lo, is much closer to SC *le than N-S *te, suggesting that they adopted a pastoralist practice from Southern Cushites.

[8] The alternative hypothesis is that Southern Cushites diffuse these practices to both Bushmen and Kuliak (Ehret 1967;1971:22–4; Elderkin 1983; Fleming 1983a; EA 4325:29.2.16 Turpin's Report; Lamphear 1976b:64–6; Weatherby 1988:210f).

[9] Ehret (1998) calls them the Rub.

climbed the escarpment even from Lake Turkana to visit the Ik, the 'Maliri' were settled in northern Karamoja until forced out by the Itunga. Because of the common use of the word '*kut*' for the hide of large animals, it has been surmised that a trade in skins existed between Maji in modern Ethiopia and the Nyangiya (Fleming 1983a:463; 1983b:551).

Nilotes (N)

The only sure trace we have of the original Nilotes is some of the vocabulary[10] which they passed down to their modern descendants, who have tended to preserve those derivative words which were closer to their continued identity and way of life. Fire (*imak) and rain (*ru) were important elements. Hunting was still important, for animals, such as the crocodile (*nyang), were trapped (*lok), speared (*rem), skinned (*yeng), and their meat (*ring) roasted (*cuny). Cows (*itang) and their udders (*nyaw) were vital, for milk could be stored in the form of oil (*myet) as ghee, a technique learnt, perhaps, from Afroasiatics (cf. Hausa *may*). Smoke (*pur) would rid their huts of flies and gnats.

Exploration (*rot) helped in finding pasture, when oxen, castrated by crushing (*dong) the testicles, could be exploited by drawing blood to be whisked or shaken (*pir) for eating clotted. Their urine (*ulak) could then be used to wash out the gourds. Dogs (*ngok) were kept for hunting in packs. Eggs were used, for beads as well as food. The Nilotes had a quinary numeral system, based on the fingers (*angwan, four) and hand (*kan, five). Aesthetic interest was given to feathers (*oper) and colours (*kweng, *ere) for decorating the body. The heart (*tau) of Nilotic man had a more emotional, psychological and spiritual meaning than belly. Social problems were caused by theft (*koko) and drunkardness (*mere) from consuming a surfeit of bulrush millet beer (Dimmendaal 1983:289ff; Hieda 1983:17ff).

Descended from the Eastern Sudanic language family 5000–6000 years ago, the likely cradleland of the Nilotes was immediately south of Gezira between the White and Blue Niles (Ehret 1983:392). Over 5000 years ago, Neolithic Sudan paralleled predynastic Egypt in pottery. Sandstone ochre grinders were used to make red pigment. Within the next 2000 years, the Gezira economy was built upon humpless cattle, using transhumance with dry-season cattle-camps near the rivers, and the cultivation of sorghum and bulrush millet near the more permanent dwellings. Just north of Khartoum, finger millet (*Eleusine* spp.) is also an African domesticate. Then Gezira came within Meroë's sphere of influence, so was subjected to perpetual acculturation from the north.

Between 4000 and 3700 years ago Egypt had occupied lower Nubia, which adopted Egyptian culture, building a temple to Amun, cemeteries with graves facing east and pyramids. Having already been known to the Greek geographer, the Kingdom of Kush came into its own 3000 years ago, adopting more African traits into its culture. After 850BC it was ruled by black ES Nubians, originally from west

---

[10] In linguistic reconstruction it is vocabulary that gives direct access to cultural terms and concepts (Nurse 1997:380).

of the White Nile, with the state's government and institutions closely modelled on those of Pharaonic Egypt. They used the Egyptian language exclusively for monumental proclamations and religious dedications, though Nubians, or Noba, continued to live in grass huts in the rural areas. Kush formed the 25th Dynasty, ruling Egypt from 751 to 664 BC and rashly fighting Sennacherib's Assyrians.

One of Kush's southern outposts was Jebel Moya. Here were tall, heavily-built people with 'extremely massive skulls and jaws' (David 1983:64f; Shinnie 1971a; Wainwright 1954:119). The two central, lower incisors had been extracted from 13 per cent of the males and 18 per cent of females. Quartz lip-plugs and iron bracelets with razor-sharp outer edges encircling the wrist were worn. The continuity of these cultural traits to the present Karamojong and other Nilotes does not alone establish this tall people as the ancestral Nilotes, who already extended over a broader area probably to the east, but Surmic and Nilotic people are the tallest people in Africa, indeed the world (Bender 2000:49).

Very different was the Roman influence that reached Meroë, but by 350AD Meroitic power was over. Around this time Jebel Moya served as an entrepôt between the Afroasiatics to the north and east and the Nilo-Saharans to the south and west mediating, above all, the use of iron. Around 550AD, Christian missionaries came up the Nile in the wake of literate Copts to Nubia and Meroë where their faith was established for 800 years in the new kingdoms of Nobatia, Makouria and Alwa, having a profound effect in the Nile Valley and beyond, until the Arabs invaded (Adams 1982:17).

3 The Spread of the Nilotes

Migration South

The Nilotes had begun to shift south over a millennium before any Christian influence, though at different rates, and changing in the process, but there is very little archaeological knowledge available of this time when the Nilotes began to split up into their Southern (SN), Eastern (EN) and Western (WN) divisions. Each inherited the Nilotic initiatory rite of dental evulsion and pastoral values. The Southern Nilotes have usually been to the east of their 'Eastern' Nilotic brethren, so it was they who had earlier contact with the Cushites of the Ethiopian Highlands, who gave them firstly the military organization, especially the warrior age-sets, to overcome rivals in drier environments, and secondly drought-resistant varieties of finger millet to cope with semi-arid climes (David 1983:93f). Thus they were the first Nilotic division to invade East Africa (Ehret 1971:6).

Southeastern Sudan was drying out 3000–2000 years ago, possibly leading to conflict with the fishermen cultures. Rearing the humpless (*Bos taurus*) cow had obliged a more farm-based economy and so more social ties with other locals (Vossen and Bechhaus-Gerst 1983b:566) but gradually a more nomadic exploitation of grazing became necessary as cattle became more populous in central Sudan. The initial expansion of the Nilotes was a function of their adoption of pastoralism and the potential for it in the southern Sudan lowlands (David 1983:94). They had also lacked a ready supply of iron spears to enable an easy expansion to the south, where the

Kuliak were the main casualties. Thus it was that the Southern Nilotes invaded East Africa first, while the other two divisions of Nilotes only entered in the last 500 years.

The First Nilotes in Karamoja

Less than 3000 years ago the first bands of Southern Nilotes began filtering south from their cradleland, north of Lake Turkana, along the Rift Valley, but no mention has been made of them traversing Karamoja also. That they might have done is indicated by the number of Southern Nilotic loanwords in the Sorat language. Although twentieth-century travellers have accordingly linked the Sor with the modern SN Kalenjin tribes neighbouring Karamoja, the Pokot and the Sapiny, these Kuliak people, now confined exclusively to the mountains of south Karamoja, have no common descent. The most likely solution is that a group of Southern Nilotes took over the plains of south Karamoja, leaving the mountains to the Sor, so that they continued to influence one another.

The Karimojong certainly knew of a cattle-keeping people, who lived north of Mount Elgon and west of the Turkwel, 'which was similar to us in habits, customs and language. The Oropom had nothing in common with the Suk [Pokot] group; they did not circumcise and the language of the latter was not understood by them' (Turpin 1948:162). The Oropom are remembered to this day to have lived west of Mount Kadam (P3), until dispersed or absorbed by the Pian after 1923 (Pazzaglia 1982:71f), and east of Kadam in 1927 before being scattered by the Pokot (Wilson 1970b:126f). Descendants absorbed into the Karimojong claimed to John Wilson that, in the distant past, the Oropom had spread over all of the southeast tip of Sudan, Karamoja (P5), Teso and Turkana, as far east as Lake Baringo and as far south as Mount Elgon and the Nandi Hills. Some substantiation is given by the place-names of Moru a Ropian in Nadodosô, Ongoropon in Najie, Oropoi in northwest Turkana and Najie and Rupa in Maseniko. The similarity with the marginal SN Dorobo (or Torrobo) people of Kenya and Tanzania is also noteworthy.

Oropom customs were largely Nilotic. They planted crops and kept humpless cattle, longer in the horn than Karamojong breeds, which they would milk and bleed for food. Bridewealth consisted of cows, goats and sheep, all of which had their horns reprofiled. The lower, central incisors were removed, and a stone, or perhaps, wooden lip-plug was worn. Men and women daubed themselves all over with red ochre and, like all Southern Nilotes around Mount Elgon, associated God with the sun (Ehret 1998:167f), but neither sex practised circumcision, unlike those Southern Nilotes who had been much influenced by Cushites. They had an age-set cycle, but no knowledge of iron-smelting, depending on small iron-working peoples.

Wilson (1970b: 144) has listed an Oropom vocabulary of 98 lexemes with basic meanings, which tends to omit Nilotic words, but still contains at least 18 per cent resemblances to SN words, notably the following:

Oropom	*Southern Nilotic*	*Kuliak*
emaa = fire	*ma* (Pokot, Nandi, ES)	
iyoo = mother	*iyo* (Pokot)	*iyo* (Sor)
meri = leopard	*meril*	*merihl* (Nyangiya)
muto = child	*mondo* (Pokot *muno* = son)	

More could be found by a full search of SN vocabulary which, when done for Ngakarimojong, yields 21 per cent resemblances.[11] Although clearly a member of the Nilo-Saharan phylum, 10 per cent of this Oropom list possibly resembles the largely Khoisan language of Hadza, ignoring the latter's clicks on the presupposition that these would be dropped as the words were adopted by the Oropom. This contact could be explained by the pioneer Oropom finding wandering Bushmen in Karamoja, some of whom migrated south, others being integrated into the newcomers to give the physiognomic features described by Wilson (1970b:133f, 144) and Elderkin (1983:506f).

Linguists have already established a contact relationship between Proto-Kuliak (PK) and borrowing in both directions (Fleming 1983a:426). When the Proto-Southern Nilotes (PSN), who dominated the plains from the Kidepo River in the north to the River Mara near the modern Tanzanian border in the south until 1000 years ago, began to split up, the strongest group, the Proto-Kalenjin (PKal), lost contact with the Ik to the north. Perhaps the place-name for the Ik territory, Timu Forest, was given by Southern Nilotes since they, unlike the Karamojong, used the Nilotic root *tim, meaning bush. It would appear, then, that the Oropom were the previous identifiable descendants from the Southern Nilotes who dwelt west of the Rift Valley. Thus their language would be cognate with, but not readily intelligible to, the modern Kalenjin who superseded them and inherited their Kuliak loanwords besides adopting Eastern Cushitic words and customs like circumcision and clitoridectome.

That the Oropom were connected to the Kalenjin is indicated by the Kalenjin stem, *rop, which, as in Eastern Cushitic Somali, means 'rain'. Furthermore the word the Pokot gave to Harry Johnston (1902:II,907) was Karobon, while the Nandi gave Macdonald (1899b:245) Torot, cognate with the Pokot High God, Tororut. The word for 'rain' in Africa is often cognate with the word for God and, sometimes, His people's name. It could be that the Oropom, like the later Dorobo, were named after their rain-god whose own name was supplied by the prolonged contact that the Southern Nilotes had from their early arrival in East Africa with Cushites (Ehret 1971:xi).

That the Oropom were not Eastern Nilotic is indicated by their long-horned cattle and their device of hiding them in great hollows in the ground, concealed by the lie of the land, which share their origin with the numerous Sirikwa 'holes' found on the lower slopes of Mount Elgon already known to be SN stock-pens (Sutton 1993:46). The Sirikwa, as they are called by some of their supplanters, the Kalenjin Sapiny or Sabawot, are an extension of the same submerged people who did not circumcise.[12] Also like the Oropom they had more than one room to their houses of stone foundations.[13] Lieutenant-Colonel Macdonald (1899a:147), who collected oral

---

[11] Using Greenberg's (1970) standard lists.

[12] This is evidence that the Kalenjin only adopted circumcision when they took over their SN forebears. Both the new initiation and the improved military organization necessary were probably borrowed from Eastern Cushites (Sutton 1990:50).

[13] Wilson (1970b:143) and Ambrose (1982:142) correlate Sirikwa hollows with Eastern Nilotes instead of Southern. David (1982: 82), like Posnansky (1967:637f), Oliver (1983:365) and Sutton (1990:41), think this 'probably wrong'.

traditions, believed the Kalenjin 'to be broken fragments of a powerful and wide spreading people' prior to the advent of the Eastern Nilotes and the Bantu. According to another tradition of the Kalenjin Nandi, they used to live on Mount Napak (Gulliver, P. and P.H. 1953:96). The Kalenjin were chipped off a block which modern scholarship knows as the Southern Nilotes. It is suggested, therefore, that the latter were well represented in Karamoja by the Oropom and in Kenya by the Sirikwa.

4 Eastern Nilotes (EN)

Cradleland

The Proto-Eastern Nilotes had trailed the Proto-Southern Nilotes south over a millennium behind, along the west side of the Ethiopian Highlands to the no-man's land where Sudan, Ethiopia, Uganda and Kenya now meet. Bari, Lotuko, Maasai, Teso, Jie (J8,12), Karimojong (P5), Dodosô (D5,9,13) and Lango traditions recalled their peoples coming from north of Lake Turkana, remembering coming 'together from a place called "Dongiro" which is far to the north' (Herring 1979a:56–8;1979b:286f; Mirzeler 1999:267). Today the Dongiro, or Nyangatom, live immediately north of Lake Turkana and the Lotakipi swamp. It is not known when the Proto-Eastern Nilotes emerged as a distinct body from the Nilotes for, while the Proto-Southern Nilotes went south again, the Proto-Eastern Nilotes remained in contact with Central Sudanic (CS) speakers for over 1000 years.[14] Archaeological finds yield evidence for hunter–gatherers surviving to 3830 years ago, followed by the presence of a pastoral people north of the Dodinga Hills 3000–1000 years ago (David 1982:83f), while Proto-Southern Nilotes remained dominant around the East African Rift Valley for most of the period. After they spread out they were succeeded by Proto-Eastern Nilotes, who had remained on the verge of East Africa until a millennium ago.

The 'topogenetic method' uses the criterion of the greatest linguistic differentiation within the relatively smallest geographical area to locate the point of dispersion (Ehret *et al*. 1974). In the Itunga group this happens in central Karamoja where the different dialects of Ngadodosô, Ngayen, Ngaturkana, Ngajie and Ngakarimojong converge with the bilingual Nyakwai and Abwor, while Ateso is spoken just 40 miles away. Oral tradition is available to pinpoint the home of the Tunga, but to find the home of the Proto-Eastern Nilotes the Bari and Lotuko groups, which account for 11 languages either side of the Nile as far north as Bor, pull the centre of gravity north and west to near where Sudan, Uganda and Kenya now meet, perhaps in the Dodinga Hills or, more likely, in the plains to the north round modern Kapoeta (Huntingford 1953a:10), itself named after the Proto-Tunga (PT) Poet, which settled in central Karamoja.

Kapoeta is now in the land of the Toposa, which again is remembered as a cradleland (Herring 1979b:286; Lamphear 1976b:81,97). This may have been the

---

[14] *Abatot* resembles CS *saba* (yam).

point of dispersal after pressure by a succession of eastward movements of various groups from what is now Ethiopia towards the Nile. Between the thirteenth and the sixteenth centuries waves of Hima, Huma, Hinda, Bako, Ober (whose descendants claimed Abac, that is Abyssinian, ancestry) and EC Oyima and Oromo migrated to Orom mountain in Karamoja, the Agoro Mountains in Acoli, and Bunyoro-Kitara to the Great Lakes.[15] Their incursion might have occasioned the Proto-Eastern Nilotes' moving right away from Lake Turkana to concentrate around Kapoeta, where the population grew after 1370 in a climate that could make only a pastoral people prosper. In particular Oromo moved west to the Agoro Mountains in 1517–44 at the same time as Proto-Eastern Nilotes were splitting and moving into East Africa. It was not until the fourteenth or fifteenth centuries that humpless cattle were replaced in the far south of Sudan by the Sanga breed which was a cross of the *Bos taurus* with the Asian Zebu (*Bos indicus*) from Egypt. Its better storage of nutrients and water in its hump, regulation of body heat, greater resistance to ectoparasites and diseases, harder hooves and lighter bones, and its capacity to digest inferior plants led to transhumance outdating concentrated mound villages, in favour of a freer existence on savanna and steppe (David 1982:85). It was the new breed of humped Sanga cattle that gave rise to the expansion of both Western and Eastern Nilotes (David 1983:94).

Language

The Proto-Eastern Nilotes (PEN) developed their Nilotic traditions, holding a clear distinction between the rocks and mountains (*meor) which they had encountered, and the open grasslands (*waka) which they preferred, but flooded rivers (*kare), rain (*kudyu), drizzle (*lilim) and thunderbolts (*kipiat) may have stimulated them to seek drier lands. Well-drained land suited their humped (*rruk), shorter-horned Sanga cattle, which lent a new emphasis half a millennium ago on cattle-herding (*yok; cf. Indo-European yoga, yoke). Here we find the modern roots for heifer-calf (*tago), milk (*le) and cow-dung (*woro), which found, with sheep dung (*kileleng), usefulness in plastering floors and walls of houses, which they built (*duk) with doorways (*kat) for a place to sleep (*dyot). The nanny-goat (*kined) found a new name.

PEN society was not purely nomadic. They had footpaths (*koty), fences (*maring) and boundaries (*kor) giving a concept of territoriality. They dug (*bok) gardens and planted a new finger millet (*kimaty) as well as the old bulrush millet (*marua) and sesame (*kinyom) which they reaped (*nger). The roots and fruits of the bush were also grubbed up (*rut), harvested (*deng), picked (*de) and plucked (*dot). Porridge (*tapa) was cooked on charcoal (*kuk) and meat on a spit (*dyepit). Shoes (*kamuk) were stitched.

---

[15] This is not merely the Hamitic hypothesis that has plagued Rwanda, but the oral history researched in Uganda by Herring (1979a:52;1979b:287). Bahima and Bahuma are used interchangeably in western Uganda oral history and are very probably Bantu versions linguistically related to the WN Oyima and Oromo from an original EC *yima and *oromo. Could Bahinda refer to *hindu? The Ober are a clan of the present-day Bako who speak an Afroasiatic Omotic language.

Servants from a subject people, probably Southern Nilotic Proto-Oropom or Proto-Dorobo, were rewarded (*rop) for their help (*ngar). From them they learned to cicatrize (*ger) their skin, for they had their own ritual body mutilations (*murun) linked with sacrifice. Life was directed by dreams (*rudy) or devilry (*dem) while the dead (*tuan) were buried (*nuk). Covetousness, or a grudge, could lead to someone being speared to death (*ar, Vossen 1981;1982).

Division and Expansion

The first schism was caused by the Bari moving west to the Kidepo Valley 500 years ago, according to oral tradition which Ehret (10.7.90 Letter) suspects of telescoping chronology. Their migration may have been precipitated by the wars of the Funj, often identified with the WN Shilluk, in the north in 1490–1530, and the Oromo pressing from the east. The Bari missed the cultural transitions which gave the PT their distinctive characteristics and linguistic morphemes, the most important of which divided all verbs into two classes, strong and weak, and introduced three different gender prefixes for all nouns. The former reflected, but overrode, the archaic PN-S distinction between intransitive and increasingly common transitive verbs, but the latter made the more manageable world personal by categorizing it according to sex or maturity (Heine and Vossen 1983; Dimmendaal 1983). Only the Bari of the Eastern Nilotes have not used the PN-S *tomon for ten, which is shared with the Ik *tomin*, the PSN *tommon and the EC *toban/tammam*.[16]

Why did the PT move on, many going south to still drier climes, to found the present Itunga tribes? Drought and disease on their own do not necessarily impel permanent migration. The Jie version of the 'parting of the waters' story, also told among the Tunga Maasai, Samburů and Turkana, may provide a clue.

> The reason why the Jie and the other people came to Koten was because an old woman called Napeikisina [she of one breast] came from a long way off, crossing many rivers, to the land, where they lived. She had a long knife with which she slew many people. The Jie and the others fled till they came to a large body of water, which was too wide to cross. One of the women begged God to make a path in the water, and the waters opened and the people crossed. Napeikisina followed them, but the waters closed and Napeikisina was swept away. (Sampson Looru, quoted in Lamphear 1976b:75[17])

In a place where rivers are dry one day, a raging torrent the next, and placid the day after, the story, given the axiomatic belief in a prayer-answering, saviour God, is

---

[16] The Karamojong worked out their word for hundred by logic (*ngatomonitomon*), while those, like the Southern Nilotic Pokot (*pokol*) or the Turkana (*pokol*), who had direct contact with EC traders around the Rift Valley, borrowed the EC Somali *bogol*.

[17] Huntingford (1953a:12) records the myth. Dyson-Hudson, N. (1962:786) gives the Karimojong version; EA 4325:1.1.20 Chidlaw-Roberts 'Compendium of Intelligence Reports', 26 lists it as a legend (Vansina 1965:73). Mirzeler's story (1999:179–87) recasts the woman as a manslaughtering Jiot aunt associated with a few common legendary motifs, but it is clear he is not passing on a fixed version of the tradition. Various versions of Napeikisina the ogre who will eat children abound (D5,12).

quite credible. The form of this *Wandersage*[18] has been diffused to many parts of Africa. The living Jiot, Lodoc, demonstrates that it is still in the minds of Karamojong by retelling the saga (Mirzeler 1999:181). Occurring also in the Old Testament, it is redolent of a Jungian archetypal myth that accords deeply with the human psyche (Jung 1977:657–9). It is thus more than a colourful, story-telling device but impresses a society's consciousness with the disagreeable past event which threatened its culture.

The appearance of God in the narrative is also an overdue reminder that history for many Africans is not merely a succession of deterministic events, such as the drought and population pressures, which have been detailed here, but a continuum, in which God is mysteriously at work. Disasters were attributed to an inadequate moral response by a society and frequently to the technically superior entreaties of the Almighty by rival societies, yet Akujů is still present to save that society. Though the divinity may be tribally defined, he, or she, can never be tribally confined, because a God who shapes and intervenes in natural forces cannot help but bless one society and judge another.

Being a primal event for the Karamojong, a few ancient memories have been attached to this memory of entry into the land: they had no iron, only sticks to fight with; the women had no clothes but grew ashamed 'on the way', so the women slaughtered goats to provide them with skins; they discovered gourds and their cultivation 'on the way'. Since the pastoralists had begun to use iron in East Africa by 700AD, since the Karamojong have a traditional tabu against female nudity so strong that it is applied to toddlers or women washing, and since gourds have been grown with cereals for millennia, 'on the way' appears to be an eternal pilgrimage. However it is possible that they did not have access to blacksmiths until after the Bari absorbed their *dupi*; they shared female nudity with Western Nilotes; and they learned about wide-necked (*abolokoki*) and narrow-mouthed gourds (*eboolo*) and stoppers (*abole*) from the Ik who decorate their gourds (*polo*).[19]

The factual nugget in this salvation history, which should be seen as an historical interpretation rather than as pure legend, may be the 'long knife' which could represent the scimitar of the Arabs who had conquered the kingdom of Alwa by 1500, with its spacious Christian cathedral at the capital Soba, but had lost power to the cattle-herding, nomadic Funj. These now ruled over a large proportion of Nilotic Sudan but, although they adopted and fostered Islam, Christian churches carried on, boasting 'crucifixes and effigies of Our Lady'. Since she was represented fully dressed, could she have given rise to Napeikisina among the enemies of Alwa? Contacts are indicated by the Western Nilotic Northern Lwo clan, Alwa, which passed through Karamoja, providing a constituent of the Kumam, who were in Soroti by 1580, and the Lango (Herring 1979b; Ogot 1967:50; Kropacek 1984:406–8). A Bokora tradition may refer back to this time, when their forebears lived northeast of Karamoja. 'But there they fought over grazing and cattle with

---

[18] This is not only a travel legend, but a 'travelling legend' according to Vansina (1965:73; 1985:90). The stereotypical form may still carry kernels of truth, which cannot *a priori* be rejected as ahistorical.

[19] It might be a common Eastern Sudanic cognate; cf. Murle *buru*.

unnamed neighbours who, over a period of time, inflicted many defeats on them. So they decided to move away in search of peaceful grazing areas' (Dyson-Hudson, N. 1966:262).

Another possible clue to the identity of these aggressors is that the 'long knife' could be equated with the 90 centimetre sword of the EC Oromo from southern Abyssinia, who raided the Lwo settlements in the Agoro Mountains in 1517–44. Though the Lwo repulsed them, their presence was unsettling and led to bands moving south. The EC name, Oromo, crops up at the River Oromo near Mount Lonyili, Mount (O)Rom, and in the Jie and Lango Orom(o) clans. The Ober clan of Lira claim descent from the Abac, and the Bako people of the North Omo River, whose namesakes lived west of Mount Toror in Najie until the eighteenth century, do indeed have an Ober clan. Moreover the Kareu, or Karewok, clan, though taking their name from the Lotuko Oghoriuk (Bari: Kuriak) clan, which absorbed CS speakers on formation, was also associated with the Oromo.[20] Not only does this demonstrate the intermixing and complexity of racial and ethnic groups in northeast Uganda, it also helps explain the presence of Cushitic, Semitic and CS lexemes in the language spoken by their integrated descendants (Herring 1979b:287,313; Buxton, D.R. 1970:51).

Vocabulary attributable to PT testifies to further concern with livestock. A new method of castrating (*gelem) oxen (*emongo) was introduced. Even the verb 'to milk' (*lep) is not traceable beyond this time though *le is very ancient. Names for the he-goat (*kor) and the ram (*merekeky) make an entrance here (Vossen 1981:54f). Attempts have been made to show that, through the mediation of EC by Southern Nilotes, the Proto-Ongamo-Maa (POM) were more sophisticated stock-herders, but nearly all the words adduced have Ngakaramojong equivalents: arrow for bleeding cattle (*emal*), bullock (*edonge*), bull-calf (*emanangit*), calf-pen (*anok*), lamb (*imesek/ikale*), branding-iron (*emacar*) and donkey (*esigiria*), of which at least one is derived from PEN, and two from PSN. If Proto-Karamojong did not have these technical terms initially, and it is difficult to imagine any Iron Age agripastoral society that would not have most, then they were supplied directly by Eastern Cushites or from Proto-Southern Nilotes before or after entry into Karamoja.

The bow (*kauw cf. Khoisan, *k"o) is used for the first time, and a new kind of pot (*moti). A new colour was identified with PSN assistance: blue-grey (*pus). This was a time of diffusion from neighbours, particularly the Proto-Southern Nilotes who mediated a breed of goat (*qoroi) which they may have shared with the Ik (*kol). They may have discovered Lake Turkana and its soda ashes (*makat) though since this is unknown to Ngakaramojong, it may be restricted to the POM and the Turkana. This was a time of trouble and disputes preceding the widespread expansion to come. They fought each other (*ara) and raided (*jore) cattle. Spearshafts (*morok) and shields became important. Sacrificial experts (*muro-ni) were needed to divine propitious moments for attack and defence. The conflicting interests produced new ideas of what it was to be a person or a people (*tungan).

---

[20] That this is an early absorbed Kuliak clan is more likely, though EC influences can never be discarded.

Soon, from the 1530s, the Lotuko split off, replacing the Bari in the Kidepo Valley, as they migrated further west. It was a time of drought so, in the opposite direction, the POM made for the west bank of Lake Turkana. The only people left were the ancestors of the Itunga, who coined gender prefixes, 'a', 'e' and 'i' for all common nouns. However the Proto-Itunga (PI) were already dividing on lines of occupation (see Figure 2.2 for a diagram of ethnic relationships).

Eastern Nilotes Invade Karamoja

Adverse conditions necessitated a choice between old cow-dung (*ngasike*) and beer dregs (*ngasinge*), between pastoralists and agriculturalists (Lamphear 1976b:87). The period 1587–1623 which, because of gaps in the data of the Nile levels, may have started earlier for all we know, had consistently below-average rainfall, with as many as two major droughts and famines. The first, in the 1580s, evoked these words from an oral historian: 'The stark spectre of starvation leaps from the traditions of this period as never before or since'.[21] Communities were shattered, instanced by an uncharacteristic outbreak of cannibalism. The splinters went south.

The agriculturalists, at least in the making, who would become known as (Ngika)Tap, 'the bread people', moved west after 1500AD to plant sorghum. In the wetter Kidepo Valley, they renewed contact with the Lotuko, and the Bari, with whom clan names were shared, before entering Karamoja by way of Mount Rom. Their southward migration coincided with that of Western Nilotes, from whom they began to learn Lwo language and customs.

For instance, the NL Jimos were in Najie, with their fire-making traditions, by 1570. The Bari/Lotuko Ngiminito merged with some of the Western Nilotic (Ngik)Omolo, who had probably come south from the Agoro Mountains in the sixteenth century, and mediated the Lwo 'drum complex' and bushbuck totem to the Sor on Mounts Moroto and Kadam. The (Ngiki)Lip(a)[22] or (Nge)Repo of Bari origin went to the east side of Karamoja, fusing with the Tepes and the Oropom to form the Lip clan on absorption by the Karimojong. The Riama crossed to southeast Karamoja; the Miro[23] carried on south, followed by the Pur, the Sera went west

---

[21] Webster, J.B., quoted in Herring (1979a:57); Lamphear (1976b:87). This fundamental, though not final, parting of the ways must have happened before entry into Karamoja to permit the different traditions of entry and settlement. For this period covered by oral history, Lamphear (1976b:chs III–V), Herring and Weatherby are the best sources, but such traditions need careful interpretation, and must be checked against other available information, primarily linguistic, but dating by glottochronology is suspect.

[22] People names are not given their full Karamojong form here. For a start these names were or are not always Karamojong, so their inflections make it unnecessarily difficult for the reader in English. The attempt is made here to give a consistent uninflected form. With neither prefix nor suffix, this normally leaves the simple root. Thus Ngikilipa (lit. the beggars) reduces to Lip.

[23] The Miro were known as the Lango Miro, that is the Proto-Langi. They were also known pejoratively as *lango tiang*, the people of the wild beasts (P3). Oral history remembers them as the first (Eastern or Western Nilotes) to reach Karamoja (P12) and associates them

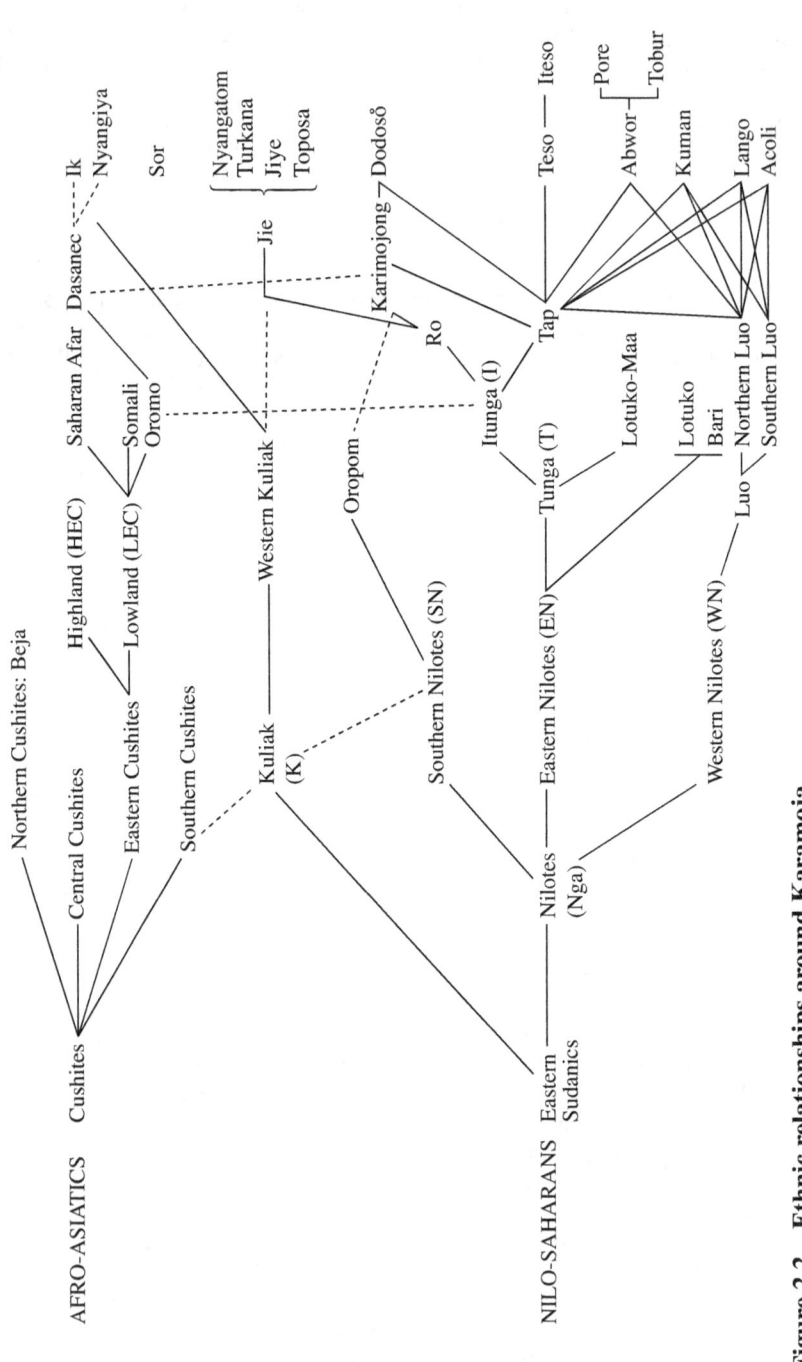

Figure 2.2 Ethnic relationships around Karamoja

Note: Dashed lines indicate subordinate influence/relationship.

followed by the Poet, while the Yen returned to stay on Mount Rom. These, with others, such as the Bako, would be the foundational clans for the Itesyo, Teso, Nyakwai, Pore and three tribes, whose language has become dominated by the Lwo with whom they mixed: the Abwor, Kumam and Lango (Cohen 1974:142; Herring 1979b; Weatherby 1979). Acoli also remain in the memory, though they could hardly have been more than an advance-guard: 'We all came together with the Acoli, but the Acoli left before we started the generation-sets. They went first. That is why we have the word "*akicolicol*" which means to leave first' (P3).

The ethnic mix was given a thorough stir by the disastrous famine in the 1580s and again in 1617–21. Under such pressure, adherence to the land and social identities was broken, both necessitating and permitting most societies in northern Uganda to enter a crucible wherein each would be fused with its neighbours. Out of it crystallized the tribes known today.

The impoverished pastoralists passed east of Mount Zulia and paused at a hill they named Koten.[24] They wandered further southeast along the escarpment of Karamoja, until they settled round a well at Lotisan, a location between the hills of another Koten to the north and Mogos to the south which afforded vistas of grazing lands to east and west. 'The Karamojong were at Koten' (P12). 'The Jie originated in the Sudan, came to Koten, and so to Daidai' (J12). All Karamojong and Turkana traditions agree that this was the first base of their forebears in Karamoja and the point from which they later diverged. They were there long enough to foster an ethnic identity but oral tradition, unlike the genealogical memories of their Lwo neighbours, does not penetrate into or before this time with any chronological sense whatsoever. Karamojong chronology, apart from a few catastrophic events, is dependent on their generation system (*asapanŭ*). That this was functioning before they dispersed is testified by their all taking an equally valid generation-set system when they went their separate ways.

The Beginning of Generations

There is no agreement between the sages of the tribes as to the name of the previous generation-set before the one named Palajamŭ,[25] which might only represent all the generations before their system started and so began their chronology according to Lamphear (1976b:163). The names, Ngisir and Ngikorio, were poorly remembered pre-existing groups, Ser(a) and Korio. Indeed the Ser were remembered, probably mistakenly when other Ser were Tap, as Mogos settled at Nakapelimoru (J12),[26] and the Korio as Tap. In other words, the Itunga concept of history which is mainly

---

with the (Nga)Riama who 'passed just north of' Namalu. It is an ethnic name that is also found in Kirinyaga District with Ngiriama in Coastal Province in Kenya and in southern Tanzania. Such a wide dispersion suggests rather a Southern Nilotic origin.

[24] Cf. *akiten* (to go ahead, lead).

[25] More unusually Palajamŭ is not named after a creature, but its etymology is 'wet hides' from *epalal* (it is wet) and *ngijamu* (ox-hides for sleeping), suggesting they had no shelter.

[26] Mogos were of Maliri (Dasanec) origin. This puts Herring's equation of them with the Bako into relief (1979b:307). They were both Ethiopian in geographical origin, however.

circular, grandfathers having already lived the generation of the grandsons, rolls back three revolutions and then promptly disappears into a misty blur in which the world or people began and heaven and earth were one. The Jie claimed that their leader in the Palajamŭ generation, Orwakol, invented the generation system (Lamphear 1989:243; 1976b:36). The obvious explanation is that the system only solidified in the uniquely named Palajamŭ generation-set in the mid-seventeenth century. This fits well with a date of migration to Koten-Mogos around 1600, give or take 20 years, forced by the 'widespread and devastating drought that continued for three decades (c.1587–1623)' culminating in the 1617–21 famine, that broke up many settlements over a very wide area (Herring 1959b:292).[27] No informant interviewed recently knew of a Palajamŭ generation-set, let alone its being the first, as memory of early generation-sets was extremely hazy. So this already indicates the need for a revision of Lamphear's chronology, particularly when he underestimates the span of a generation-set by about 32 per cent (see Chapter 6).

The corollary is that the full age-class system, not being a PEN trait, was constructed from people who had long had one, notably Eastern Cushites. The Upe (now called the Pokot) are mentioned as living in the vicinity, possibly becoming the Pei (wild dog) section (Lamphear 1976b:76; J18[28]), but it is more likely that this refers to their PSN forerunners, the Oropom, now living as part of the Karimojong 45 kilometres south at Rupa. Yet Koten-Mogos itself was inhabited by Eastern Cushitic Maliri (Marille, known now as the Dasanec), and 'generation-sets come from there' (P4). The Dasanec were only pushed back north of Lake Turkana by the Turkana in their nineteenth-century expansion. They are associated with an unusual aetiology of war, echoing the archetypal myth of enemies approaching through flooded rivers.[29] Dasanec obviously had the power to do so earlier:

> The [Proto-]Karamojong were using Lake Turkana, and their animals were drinking there. The Maliri were the other side of the Lake. Then they came fighting with sticks to water their animals first, then they threw stones. The Maliri entered the sea and started shooting with arrows. Then they were the first to get guns from Ethiopia. Then they entered the sea and shot with guns, so the Karamojong had to leave there. The Turkana joined them. (P4)

Clearly the Karamojong were militarily impressed with the Maliri, and an alliance allowed them into Karimojong polity at Koten-Mogos as whole sections, Muno (snakes or secret ones) and Mogos (unusually no intrinsic meaning in Ngakaramojong). Both claim Maliri descent (Wilson 1970b:132; Novelli 1988:33f).

---

[27] Herring (1959b) does not follow the logic of his own evidence: that his informants have telescoped the regional mass movements into a much later period does not mean they straggled over the whole period, but that they were more likely concentrated more at the turn of the sixteenth century during the 30-year famine than the three-year Nyamdere famine of 1725–8.

[28] 'Ngiupe were living here ... Long ago there was a famine, when Ngiupe separated themselves' (J18).

[29] 'Longiro, river Longiro ... May our enemies never cross your course. May our enemies be caught by your floods and swept away, or engulfed by *ngipian*' (Mirzeler 1999:244).

There is also a Mogos clan among the Jie, and *amagwoikin* means to be distorted, literally, to go to the Mogos. The Karimojong often ascribe greater religious power to the Mogos, so give them particular prominence in ceremonies including generation-set promotion (P5; Emoru 1988:24; Dyson-Hudson, N. 1966:139, 225).

The evidence, then, points to the Dasanec at Koten-Mogos, introducing the ritual organization of generation-sets, revolving every 36–60 years and dividing the men into the formal categories of fathers and sons. In contrast Lamphear (1989:241) believes the generation-set system to be foundational for the Eastern Nilotes, 'The Nilotic systems were originally based on generational principles, with biological age principles stressed by those societies, whose dynamic processes of migration carried them farther and farther from the ancestral homeland.' Yet WN societies which have travelled far less distance from the Nilotic cradleland do not show residual signs of a generation-set system as a unifying principle, and this is confirmed by Karamojong oral history that they were together with Western Nilotes who left Karamoja before they 'started generation-sets' (P4). On the other side, 'The structural affinity of Jie and Pokot systems with that of the Oromo is immediately obvious' (Gulliver 1953c:165–7). As the Pokot system was copied from the Karimojong, this leaves the Karamojong in a unique relationship with the Eastern Cushites.

There are considerable differences with Oromo systems (Baxter 1978) but the Karamojong do seem to have enculturated a single, basic principle of the Dasanec, that a person belongs to the opposite generation-set of his parents and children (Almagor 1989:145,148f). The most conservative tribe of the Karamojong, the Jie, have adhered to the genealogical principle with the strictest rigour, but it is not original. It should be seen, with simple monotheism, as the result of EC contact, impressed upon age-grading and initiation customs originating in hunting times many millennia before and associated with segmentary clan systems which were characterized by the belief in a range of gods or spirits, as found among the Southern and Western Nilotes.

5 Conclusion

Despite the lack of documentary evidence before the end of the nineteenth century, linguistic reconstruction and material culture allow many things to be said about previous human settlement in Karamoja and about Nilotic history. These are not entirely separate issues as the Eastern Nilotes mixed with and absorbed many ethnolinguistic groups on entering East Africa and since. The intermixing and complexity of racial and ethnic groups along the watershed between the Nile and Lake Turkana can hardly be overemphasized, except perhaps by over collapsing the large time spans involved. Cushitic, Southern Nilotic and Eastern Nilotic cultures have each been dominant in turn for several centuries, but such dominance has never totally excluded or expunged other cultural and linguistic features.

Already it can be confidently stated that Karamojong culture is neither timeless nor immutable. It has always been changing, often in far-reaching ways. Throughout there have been times of dispersal and times of absorption. If death has been an ever-present threat, life has continually revolved round the keeping of livestock for several millennia. This economic choice has affected life in all social structures, for neither the occupation of Karamoja nor the current system of generation-sets goes back beyond the seventeenth century, when the new pastoralism spread south into East Africa. In conjunction with this livelihood were certain characteristic approaches to divinity, from which the Karamojong were to adopt a unique combination.

Chapter 3

The Colonization of Karamoja and Christian Incursion

As with the whole pastoralist belt wrapping round the Horn of Africa from Sudan to the Indian Ocean, Europeans have never settled long or in groups of much more than a dozen. They frequently found these arid and semi-arid areas uncongenial, 'unhealthy' and isolated, not the best place in which to reproduce, so just as frequently doubted whether they had any mandate to 'civilize' them. For the last half-millennium, then, the dominant colonizers have been the expanding Eastern Nilotes from the north. Throughout this period the plains of Karamoja have been relentlessly occupied by their new pastoralism, leaving a basic choice for those who would continue to live in the region, between being absorbed by the Karamojong or taking refuge in the hills and on the mountains of its margins.

Government has congregated in a limited number of centres which it has selected and constructed largely from revenue raised elsewhere.[1] The only other modern institution to involve Karamojong collectively outside family herd and age-class is the Christian Church, which has eked out a fragile existence for 75 years, and that has seldom been self-supporting. Its story has been symbolic of many other attempts to assimilate the Karamojong to modernity, so the encounter of religions is instructive. Ranger (1988:871) has claimed that it is 'impossible to write about any of the religions of Africa ... in isolation from each other'. This is not a concerted attempt to prove him wrong, but conceptually in this case it would be misleading to talk of traditional Karamojong religion under the alien perspectives of the documentary shadow of Christian religion that has inserted itself in Karamoja without transforming its realities. While Karamojong identities were founded so much on their sense of territoriality in the plains of Karamoja and on their age-class systems, the relativization and desacralization of such identities in East Africa, or their new delineation, in the face of modernity could usually be found in profound religious changes. Did Christian mission have the catalytic capacity to enable this among the Karamojong? This is not the focus of a work on traditional religion, so it is necessary to analyse first the gradual crystallization of new Eastern Nilotic

---

[1] Ranger (1993:94f) finds that 'much of the continuing history of religion in southern Africa, whether of Christianity or of African religion, lies in the working out of "this dialectic between the local and the central"'. This would appear to contrast with the acephalous political systems of East Africa. Among the traditional Karamojong, religious assemblies and the abodes of traditional religious specialists are located normally outside of the townships: they certainly are not centralized even now and any original centres did not hold power over surrounding neighbourhoods.

identities in Karamoja that has shaped the cultural realties so much there that the Christian Church has been unable to shift them.

1 Colonies of the Ro

Famine Reunites and Divides

The pastoralist and agriculturalist branches of the Itunga, both having fused with other groups, renewed contact after a century. Again oral history shows that it is the Western scientific mind which sees famines dispersing settlements as the inexorable effects of macrocosmic laws of matter. To African minds they are often contingent, even upon human, microsocial activity, and have far more than a physical cause.[2] Thus a mortal quarrel between small bands of WN Lwo and EN Tap in Labwor was believed to upset the harmony of all life in northern Uganda, precipitating a great famine in 1587–1623 that dispersed many peoples over great distances and left others reduced to cannibalism (Herring 1979a:57).

The Tap who went east included some Lwo-speaking blacksmiths and, led by a certain Opio, contacted the settlement at Koten-Mogos,[3] bringing news of bountiful game east of Lokatap (place of *atap*, bread) Rock. The drought was also beginning to have its effect on the pastoral people on the escarpment: disputes were breaking out over water-holes, with the Proto-Jie concentrated to the north of Lotisan well around Koten Hill, and the Proto-Karimojong around Mogos to the south.

> They came to a rock (*etaaba*) between Koten and Mogos Hills called Karamojong.[4] Those who went ahead were unable to move because of famine. The Jie separated and came to Daidai [in central Najie] under one leader, Orwakol. (J12)

As the drought continued, more space was needed, so the Proto-Jie moved east, joining with the Tap to go hunting and trapping. According to the descendants of the pastoralist, 'Orwakol was the first to reach here, then Oding [the agriculturalist] came' (J3). They were the founding fathers of the two Jie sections, so are attributed comprehensive kinship.

> The eldest brother was Lopio, then Orwakol, then Oding Aparengen (father of the red Yen people). He was a cultivator. Orwakol refused animals for Oding to marry. ... there was a family dispute between Oding and Orwakol. Oding migrated to Mururwe. They were

---

[2] Science is just beginning to rehabilitate this ancient, theological idea (Barrow and Tipler 1986).

[3] There is no linguistic difference between Magos(i), the place-name on the published maps, and Mogos, the people of that place when the Itunga entered. The first vowel is neutral.

[4] Karamojong has a locative prefix, and is still used in its original meaning as a place name. J12's pronunciation of the second vowel was neutral, and his usage also lends weight to the use of Karamojong as a generic name now.

throwing fire at each other, and that led to separation.... Still Orwakol would have to use cows to buy grain from Oding to eat in the dry season.[5] (J12)

Traditions of Dodosô origins also fit the picture of dispersion of pastoralists from an eastern entry-point in Karamoja and of encounter with agriculturalists to the west. Three accounts are given below. The metonym of the grey bull is also associated with the central site for settlement and dispersal:

> All were called Karimojong after an *etaaba* (rock) near the River Apule. Beforehand they called themselves Itunga [people].... When they had all settled near the River Apule, then the fathers remained and others scattered. The fathers who remained were called the Itunga. Others when they returned found their father dead (*ekar*[6]). Itunga worked their ritual, and the father remained with the grey bull (*engiro*) there, and that was the origin of the Dongiro. 'Did the grey bull remain with the father there? Where is the father?' 'He has remained there.' 'You leave that old father and his cows there at Dongiro!' So Kangikaal [the place of the camels] is the place where both Dongiro and Turkana come for sacred clay. It is a holy place, so there can be no enemies at Nakadanya, only Itunga (*Ngitunga bon*). (D6)
>
> The Nadodosô came from the north by way of Karimojong at Apule River. They left the old people with some cows, while the young settled in Nadodosô with the girls. There was nobody here before, for the only Tap around were the Mening. (D9)

Reluctance to admit that a different identity had prior claim to the land through earlier settlement is common, and it is clear that for a while some Proto-Toposa coexisted on the eastern side having settled slightly earlier: 'The Nadodosô separated from the rock, passing through Narok ... The Toposa went north; they fought the Nadodosô at Loyoro' (J12).

So the cradleland of the Karamojong cluster lies between Koten Hill and the River Apule, but it was not merely a question of settling an empty land. The Tap peoples were already cultivating there, and many of them were to be absorbed, resulting in the agripastoral economy of the settled people, while some of their relatives moved on. For instance the Silang both were absorbed at Losilang and moved on to Toposa, or Adilang became Acoli (J12, 28). The Mogos of Nakapelimoru moved to Lango, but their kin to the east stayed behind and eventually became a section of the Karimojong. The Karimojong moved south in the Nyamdere famine[7] (1725–8) across the Apule River, which is still regarded by the Karimojong as their sacred, formative home. By the Laparanat famine

---

[5] This is interesting testimony that pastoralists were never continually self-sufficient in food production.

[6] This yields another etymology for Ngikarimojong: 'the dead old men', but it is a weird Karamojong myth that brings people back to life in this world.

[7] The names of the famines were given by the Acoli, as Lamphear (1976b:111,159) records, depending on his colleagues, but famines are so recurrent in Karamoja it is very difficult to distinguish one from another, and by my reckoning the Kok generation-set of the Jie finished their initiations by 1750, not 1800 (see Chapter 6). Nyamdere is Ngakaramojong for eating gourds, a bitter item for any menu.

(1780–1800) they had pushed the newly integrated Mogos, Muno and Pei sections before them to the Natoo River.

Traditional Ethnic Histories

Naturally these derivations of immediate ethnic identity are shrouded in myths. A pair in particular recurs, thus constituting what is called a 'central cliché', a simple statement of meaning, which refers to a more complex reality (Lamphear 1983; 1989:241). Since all myths do this, the term, 'archetypal myth', standing at the head and source of a society's consciousness and reflecting the psychological concerns of the elders, is preferred (Jung 1977:657–9).

The first myth is common among the Eastern Nilotes, having a Nilotic origin (Huntingford 1953b:12). The Itunga version focuses on a bull, 'the father of the herd', of particular blue-grey markings, denoted by the word *engiro*.[8] The place where it is providentially, if cunningly, appropriated becomes the tribal home of its new proprietors. Men do not own land; they own cattle, and the land is held in common for the cattle with whom the herders identify their lives. The cattle's wet-season grazing defines the area in which relatively permanent homes are built; the dry-season grazing defines the outer boundaries of the people's territory. The location of the bull sets up the ethnic land, livelihood and continuity. In the myth, *engiro* is the symbol of identity and security.

Attached to the central cliché are associated myths, all linked by the theme of a new cattle-herding community. Inevitably one recollection does not cover all the motifs. Rebellion against the elders is not part of the central cliché, but is a significant factor in founding a new pastoralist community and touches the elders' deepest anxiety. The perpetual fear of the elders that prevents them from often using their authority to have miscreant age-sets punished is that the junior generation-set will lose patience. The next generation-set must wait to inherit cattle from their niggly fathers who take all the major decisions and own most of the cattle with which they furnish themselves with yet more wives, while the herdsmen live a Spartan, dangerous life defending the families' cattle.

When personal relationships with fathers are strained, as is usually the case when fathers beget and employ many sons, the sons are tempted, when the cattle are freed for dry-season grazing, to take them and settle out of reach, where their wealth in cattle will fetch them wives and they will decide their own destiny. The elders are physically powerless to retrieve this dire situation, in which the present livelihood of the family is at once threatened and hopes of future prosperity shattered. The rebellious herdsmen in the myth symbolize the ever-present, fundamental tensions within society, with the concomitant anxiety and insecurity that spoil the feeling of well-being. Dislocating disharmony results from disobedience to Akujů's anointed elders. They can only make it religiously anathema but they cannot assert that it is without precedent. So the precedents are identified with enemies.

The Karimojong myth makes the Jie the disobedient, young men who ran off with the cattle from Koten-Mogos, leaving the withered, old men (*aki-kari-t*, to be

---

[8] Cf. *angiro* (dark) (Gourlay 1971b:C293); *emong ngolo ngiro* (Pazzaglia 1982:26–9).

thin; *e-mojong*, old man) behind. The myth also legitimizes any attempt to return the cattle to their rightful (by implication) owners and so too the subjugation of the Jie. 'Its value is clearly less as origin charter than as political myth that projects Jie and Turkana enmity into the past and so justifies action against them in the present' (Dyson-Hudson, N. 1966:263). However only the Karimojong accept the soundness of their own version and even they in the next breath insist that the Jie are not Karimojong and never have been (P12; Dyson-Hudson, N. 1963:401), while the other Itunga acknowledge the substance of the Jie story which does not see a schismatic rebellion of young men but the emigration of the whole Koten community.

Entry into the Land

The Proto-Jie took up the suggestion of the 'bread people', and explored what was to become Najie:

> So the people at Koten decided to go to the west with the Ekatapit [breadman/agriculturalist] to hunt those animals. They killed many of the wild animals, and then they captured the bull (*engiro*) which was also there, some grabbing its head and others its tail. The people saw that the place was good. (Peter Nakade, quoted by Lamphear 1976b:115)

They marked out family plots and, as there was no resolution of the Koten-Mogos disputes, moved there permanently to supplement their famine diet by hunting. Their centre was at Daidai, bounded by the current, tribal ritual grove of Looi on the west, with its hidden, long, rock sanctuary and slaughter-place and on the east by the River Longiro, from whose banks is dug the blue-grey kaolin used for ritual decoration, healing or exorcism. 'At first this river was not called Longiro – it had no name. It was named after the light grey bull (*engiro*) which the people found grazing there with the wild animals' (Joseph Lobalong, quoted by Lamphear 1976b:115).

The image is akin to the lion lying down with the lamb, for cattle need to be tended by humans, in this case the former residents of the place who had their own name for the river, but were driven off by raiders who renamed it as the Eastern Nilotes were wont to do with hills and rivers. Since *ngiro is an unlikely stem, it is probable that, in the light of the Nilo-Saharan use of a syntactic plural for a name, the people were called the Ngiro[9] whose sacred colour was blue-grey. 'At first our people were called "Ngiro" because we lived here in the land near the Longiro River' (quoted by Lamphear 1976b:129,211).[10] It is the people who are prior to the

---

[9] In order to emphasize the stem of collective names for people-groups, the plural prefix, Ngi-, will be omitted as well as locative prefixes which hide the derivation.

[10] Jie logic may see 'Ngiro' as prior. 'We don't know if the river got its meaning from the grey bull Engiro, or if the bull got is name from the river Longiro' (Mirzeler 1999:243). Mirzeler's sources retain the myth and associate Orwakol's spearing of Engiro with the secession of the Proto-Toposa and the Proto-Turkana and the curse of a prolonged drought that occasioned the Nayece saga. Nayece finds Engiro *redivivus*, who marks the spot and

place, inhabited places being named after people, so the colour for this river was not named according to the hue of its water, but after the people who lived by it, as was the Lo-ngiro River in the Eastern Nilotic cradleland of southeast Sudan. *Engiro* is a bovine personification of the Proto-Jie themselves, possibly the whole Karamojong cluster. The evidence points to (Ngi)Ro as an ethnic name, which has been lost in the closed circle of its derivatives, Longiro and *engiro*. If the name is indeed ancient it might be expected to occur in the other Itunga tribes yet it never appears as a clan name among the Karamojong.[11]

Najie proved to be overstated as a land of milk and honey and, with the social bonds established at Koten loosened by the move, groups of young men did make off with the cattle (1692–1750), probably during the Nyamdere famine.[12] The migration is remembered in the usual symbolic form by Turkana traditions:

> After the people settled in Najie, two bulls strayed away to the east. The grandfather of my grandfather, Angirokol [A-ngiro-kol, where '-kol' means patches on a white hide] whose generation-set was Ngipalajam, was the owner of one of those bulls, whose name was Engiro. My ancestors told me there is some connection between the name of that bull and the river called 'Longiro' in Najie. People tracked those lost bulls to the east and found them living with Nayece who was drying wild fruits at Moru Anayece[13] near the Tarash ...
>
> They saw the place was good, with fertile soil, good grass, and many wild fruit. They carried the news back to Najie and many young people decided to move to the east to the place of Nayece. All of this happened in the time of the Ngipalajam. (Lokimuk, quoted by Lamphear 1976b:119)[14]

---

occasion of the formation of the Turkana (Mirzeler 1999:253–77). However Mirzeler completely misses the metonymy of 'bull' for 'tribe'.

[11] Ngiro does appear in personal names: Ngiro (Karimojong, Pazzaglia 1982:144); Nyro (Jiot, Wayland 1931:226); Nangiro (Karimojong, Dodosô, Jie, M1, Gourlay 1971b:52; Gulliver 1955:116; Lamphear 1976b:176n). Above all *ro/ru figures in the Eastern Nilotic cradleland, Dongiro. Several places in East Africa have similar names: Nyero, near Ngora, in Teso; Mount Nyiru and the River Ngiro in Samburû; Naro Moru, near Mount Kenya; the River Ngiro feeding Lake Natron, and Ngorongoro, in Maasai country. Two Ugandan kingdoms, Bu-nyoro and To-ro, were subject to Western Nilotic domination (Cohen 1974:144). Ro/Ru might be an ancient name for Nilotic peoples, derived from N-S, C-N *ro/ru, name or self.

[12] Despite the different chronological base here, Lamphear also arrives at a date 'no later than about 1740' (1976b:119).

[13] Moru a Nayece is 'the mountain of Nayece'. The saga is confirmed by Mirzeler (1999:253–77) and by Huntingford (1953a:12) for the Turkana who also link it with the finding of a lost bull.

[14] No informant emerged at all who knew of Ngipalajamû, which might indicate a loss of memory over 30 years (Lamphear 1976b:108f), but Lamphear (1976b:93) forgets that Lokimuk specified that Nayece lived in the Palajamû generation-set. Lokimuk was a Turkana of the Moru generation-set (Lamphear 1972a:487) who was highly unusual in remembering the grandfather of his grandfather, a founding father of the Turkana who lived in the third generation-set of Lamphear's scheme (1976b:110). This is conclusive evidence that Palajamû

The other bull probably stands for another group from Koten-Mogos which went directly east in the wake of Nayece, the effeminate (because agricultural) Tap, who formed the Curo section of the Turkana. The *engiro* bull symbolized the dominant Ngiro, who formed the present nomadic and fiercely independent section, the Monia, whose elders nevertheless regard the Jie as their fathers in a spiritual and historical sense.

It might be this Jie association with the Turkana that gave rise to the Karimojong myth. Those who returned east were still identified with the band that had gone west to Najie. Having rebelled there, they appear to have taken men too from the Ro who remained at Mogos, the Proto-Karimojong, for there is a Turkana tradition of forebears who never went west (Lamphear 1976b:91). Hence the first schism could have promoted a second, leaving both the Jie and the Karimojong with indignant memories of recusant herdsmen.

The next group to diverge from the political centre at Daidai in the first generation was one which settled slightly to the north at Losilang (J3), where it mingled with the Tap Posa to form the two sections of the Proto-Toposa. After the Proto-Dodoso engaged them in battle at Loyoro (J12) and occupied their land, they drifted north in search of grazing. At Loyoro, a band splintered off, leaving a hill named after it, Nyangatom. The Nyangatom, or Dongiro, turned eastward towards the River Omo where a century ago there were two sections: the agricultural and fishing Purna and the pastoral Do-ngiro (Pazzaglia 1982:29–34; Tornay 1979a:311; 1989; Vossen 1982:64f). Continuing north, the Mosingo and the Kor sections of the Toposa turned westward, under pressure from the Turkana, to settle in Kapoeta by 1830. The Mosingo, a section originating from the Miro, allied with the Dodoså, while the Kor allied with the Jie and they still manage not to raid each other (J12). The Kor regularly return to Karabokol and the Longiro River for blue-grey kaolin and to be reminded of the traditions of the elders. 'In 1975 they invited the Kotiang clans, Nene and Korio to come and collect their sacred clay (*emunyen*) in Toposa' (J12).

In the same context of famine another schism occurred through an argument at an *akiriket* near Karabokol in Oding, when the Proto-Jiye went far to the north (J3). Hearing of a cattle disease at Daidai, they refused the elders' messages to return when the rains finally came. Tradition makes the original leader a woman, Nacere (she of the stars), who was either an extraordinary *amuron* or a mythical figure like Nayece. Afterwards in the eighteenth century their wealth in cattle proved an easy target for the Toposa and the Nyangatom, making the Jiye put up a fight (*ejie*) for their lives. Their two sections finally settled north of the Toposa. Their name does not derive from the Jie, which was a nineteenth-century appellation for the Ro on the Longiro River, but their language and customs do. They claim to have the closest possible intertribal relationship, sons of the same mother, and still return for sacred clay from Karabokol, though the Jie do not use that source (J3).

Although Lobbor (Labwor) and 'Aje' (Najie) are mentioned, the reports gleaned to the west in the 1870s–80s by Samuel Baker (1874:II,118f) and Emin Pasha

---

was the name for the first Turkana generation-set and for no other tribe. The Turkana split from the Jie, who cursed them, after the Jie had promoted its first generation-set.

(Casati 1891:263; Schweinfurth 1888:251f), who intended to visit the region, never refer to the Karimojong or names akin. Rather the inhabitants are called Lango, Lwo for 'people'. As they were related to the Tap who went west to modern Lango, this makes sense. All local traditions agree that the name 'Karimojong' does not date back before the Koten-Mogos days, yet the popular etymologies attached to the myth of origin are not only suspect but also deficient in explaining what is primarily a place-name. Unlike Jie, which needs the locative pronominal prefix, 'Na-', to define the place, Najie, Karimojong needs none, for it already has one in 'Ka-' or 'Ko-'.

The place name, Karamoja, was coined by outsiders, whether Abyssinian or Swahili (Persse 1934:110). Macdonald's expedition first mapped it as Karamojo, which was either a variant, or derived from the Sapiny name for their enemies, Karamoj (Weatherby 1962), as his base camp was in their territory. Despite this precedent three other early writers who had repeated contact with the people called them the Koromojo (Hobley 1897:183; Weinthal 1923:3,307; Purvis 1909:260-62; Leeke 1917:206); the first anthropologist called them the Karomojong (Wayland 1931:187); three called the place Koromoja (EA 1667:12.12.07 Cubitt to Dep. Commissioner; Lawrance 1955:29; Leeke 1917:204), while two called it Karomoja (EA 2957:31.11.13 Leeke's Report; Wayland 1931:191), but all six used the *ro stem. Further evidence is supplied by the Koromoic River near Moruita and by Abwor informants of Lamphear's (1976:90), who referred to a place called Koromoc, distinct from Karimojong, in the Koten-Mogos area.

The riddle is best solved by taking Koromojong as the original form with the emphasis on the third syllable, and the first two vowels neutral, which were heightened over time to 'Kara-', and then the modern 'Kari-'. The velar 'ng' is frequently voiced rather than sounded: hence, *emong* (steer) is shortened to *emo* and the (Ng)Atesot plural prefix is 'i-' rather than 'ngi-'. What then is the etymology? Either Ko-ro-mo-jong meant, 'where the Oromo stopped' (*a- jong*), which is unlikely though there is a hill named Rom eight kilometres east of Mogos and may refer to the Oromo connection, or 'where the (Ngi)Ro ox stopped', which would 'explain' why the herdsmen settled in Koten-Mogos and would be an apt name for the last branch of the Ro to leave the area.

'God himself gave Apule to the Karimojong' (Pazzaglia 1982:38). Captain Leeke (1917:206) met a senior elder around 1914, who had lived as a boy on the Apule River, from whose banks they did not begin to move until the Turkana, supplied by the Jie with spears from Labwor, pushed the Maseniko back up the escarpment. The Maseniko, who are still regarded as less than 'true Karimojong', share the name of their Monia section with the Turkana, so were possibly part of the herdsmen's secession east from the Ro. However these chose to settle, not in the plains like the Turkana, but on Moru a Siger with an ethnic mix of refugees from the plains, including Oropom, only to be overrun by the Monia Turkana in search of grazing and water. As usual some were absorbed by the Turkana as the Sigeere division while others fled 'up to Apule where they joined again with the Bokora' (Lamphear 1976b:198) to form the Siger clan.[15]

---

[15] This is the same name as the indigenous clan of the Pokot called Sekerr, which also

The Karimojong were so pressurized that they occupied the lands to the west, being vacated, as a result of the Laparanat famine (1780–1800), by the Ser(a) and other Tap, such as the Riama and Miro, who were to found leading communities in Teso and Lango (P4). 'The Ngikatap came along the Maniman River. We were fighting those people, so the Miro died and moved away via Matany. Three clans were captured, more than they were killed, by an encircling movement' (P4). The Pei and the Mogos, settled south of Najie, while the Bokora, the former Ro nucleus at Mogos, went west, as far as Nyakwai, building homes near Matany Hill. As 'the trunk of the Karimojong', with a coterminous history (P3; Dyson-Hudson, N. 1966:144), the Bokora should be of special interest, but no-one is sure of the meaning of their name. Their emblem is the swamp tortoise or turtle (*abokok*) but no attempt is made to relate this to their name, which might have been Bokoro, 'the Ro who dug' (*akibok*, to dig), reflecting their more sedentary tendency at Mogos. As such an agricultural meaning was not complimentary among herdsmen, it was conveniently forgotten.

The Mosingo section, themselves absorbed from the Miro cluster that was to found the Lango (Herring 1979b:296), captured large numbers of the previous inhabitants, Ruba, later known as Oropom, whose other settlements stretched south to Nabilatuk. The Pian, an offshoot of the Maseniko, went south to Lorengidwat, while the Maseniko occupied Moroto (P3). The dry years of 1825–40 saw them conquer the Oropom spared by the Turkana, crossing the Turkwel River, as far as Nasokol[16] and Kapenguria (P3). Oropom were absorbed even into clans regarded as constitutive of Karimojong ethnicity, since 'people were called in clans before we left Ethiopia' (P3). Their patrilineal descendants have full political rights, but remain conscious of their lack of breeding (P3).[17] The Karimojong also began to raid the Sapiny[18] on Mount Elgon at this time but they did not make permanent settlements any distance south of the Akinyo, or Omanimani, River until the next century. As a result of this continued expansion only 2.5 of the present 19 clans of the Karimojong were patrilineally descended from the Ro community. These were called the Ribor, Lobal and Lip *ngulu macarakejen* (those Lip who brand on the legs), 'the firestone clans', foundational to the Karimojong (P3; Dyson-Hudson, N. 1966:89; Pazzaglia 1982:84f), but not the first to dwell in the land, as they claim.

On the initial journey to Koten-Mogos, some pastoralists had broken off and

---

means cowrie shells used as decorations (Visser 1989b:9). Two items of early trade, donkeys (*ngisigirya*, PKal. *sikirio) and cowrie-shells (*ngisigira*), suggest that the original meaning of Moru a Siger was the 'Mount of traders', particularly as it offered a cool, wooded watering point in the middle of the intensely hot, dry plains of Turkana. At 35°E 3°06'N it is on the same latitude as Kotido and Koten.

[16] Na-sogol is the place of the long-horned ox.

[17] The women's ceremonial bundle of sticks (*ekeat*) distinguishes the more traditionally Karimojong clans from those who were absorbed later, by the number of sticks: five bound with strips of leather signify 'the real Karimojong. Those people (clans) with a single stick are the foreign Karimojong clans eg Oropom' (Emoru 1.4.02 Letter).

[18] Sapiny are known in Ugandan discourse today as the Sebei, their relatives in Kenya as Sabawoot.

crossed west to live by the Nyangiya. Around 1760, they crossed back to Loyoro as the Orikituk, seeing off the Toposa and separating them from their Proto-Jie brothers, while a party brought up some Proto-Karimojong from the Apule River who settled around Kaabong before 1800 as the Meris section. A third section, Ato, was formed at Kopus after the Dodosô captured large numbers of Tap Poet, known as Titi, around 1840. The Dodosô have the weakest sense of tradition and pride in warrior herdsmanship, but that is only relative. For their ritual system they look to the Karimojong to take the lead in announcing initiations, though their generation-sets have different names and are uncertain. This makes sense if only a minority underwent the formative social experiences at Koten-Mogos. The memory they still have is that, when they came into the land, the Proto-Dodosô found 'no holes for digging, so they used digging sticks (*ngakutae*). There were blacksmiths only in Nyangiya, so they were using sticks and stones' (D5).

The reason why Ro gave way to other names was not only the need to differentiate the newly emerging tribes, but also because at root, *ro may have meant, as it does in Nilo-Saharan languages, 'self' and only secondarily, 'to explore' as in *aki-ro* which, as a noun, means 'word' and as *ekiro* means 'name'. The archaic meaning may be reflected in the Ngakaramojong *elope* (oneself), if '-lo-' has derived from *ro and '-pe' from *epei*, one. The Ro are the people of the forgotten name, who have lost, and found, themselves in their new land.

2   The Ro Colonization Process

The formation of the present societies was never an absolute replacement of one clearly defined ethnic group by another, even when the demands of clarity and brevity inevitably leave a simplified account. It has been a story of one part of a group moving on and another part staying. Nor was this dynamic usually so pacific as it sounds, for the broad trends and even the oral traditions conceal the fact that the land was really occupied by others who had no wish to move out or be overrun. Conflicts were resolved by violence, though numbers normally killed in battle seldom ran to hundreds. Moreover captives were welcomed to bolster the incomers' strength in a reconfigured ethnic grouping.

There was not the slightest concern for racial purity, even among the endogamous Kuliak. What mattered was cultural domination, which the vanquished could only resist by emigration. However, if they stayed, they were soon given a full part in the religious and social life of the community. Marriage between the clans, which were the rumps of different ethnic groups, led to full integration, which was made smoother, because different customs could be retained by the clans, each of which perpetuated its own traditional history to this day. Indeed, with careful manoeuvring, a previously alien custom could be enculturated by the elders for the whole people. Such a process would be inconceivable for white colonists, especially with their tabu on intermarriage and their sense of absolute, 'civilized' superiority.

Thus the Sera-Miro peoples did not just happen to be migrating west, so creating a timely vacuum for the Ro to fill in the seventeenth century. In fact the population of central Karamoja was remembered as being larger than in the succeeding 300 years. Rather they were forcibly driven out or captured, an event made explicit in the traditions of those who fled and not in the memories of the victors or those who stayed to be absorbed. The lacuna served the need of tribal unity, perhaps, yet it does not make oral tradition worthless. That the Proto-Jie expanded west from Koten, 'would require massive evidence to challenge' (Herring 1979b:307f).

However it would be wrong to cast one group as active in the determination of history and the rest as passive. The Ro, though imposing their particular, pastoral way of life with its gerontocratic, political structure on the plains of Karamoja, were themselves moulded into a new culture by their move there. For instance, the Proto-Jie learned to build more permanent huts and to extend their agriculture, for the seeds of the west were also found to be suited to Karamoja. The honey-badger (*ekor*) was adopted as a tribal totem, while Lwo-derived clans retained the bushbuck (*akoloba*) as a clan totem. One of the two sections of the Jie, the Rengen,[19] was not Ro at all, but mainly Tap, grouped around the band of famine refugees who had gone to Koten.

The Rengen fire-maker, who did not fit into the generational leadership structure, took on the Lotuko office of rain-maker and the judicial function and ritual trappings, such as the symbolic axe or spear (*akwaara*) and the tribute of the first-fruits, which the Lwo associated with their hereditary king (*Rwot*). Only the Rengen fire-maker is accorded burial rites, which may imply an afterlife. He is buried with his clothing, sleeping hides, gourds of milk, ornaments and other possessions. People bring milk to pour on the grave and also leave food there. More than any other his spirit must be honoured to ensure well-being for the whole section. That such a 'royal' institution could have been integrated into the rule of elders shows a religious inclusivism born of a sense of need for unity.

The unity of disparate elements was tested and thereby proved in battle. If an alien (*emoit*) befriended the Ro to the extent of joining them on cattle-raids, he could build up his own herd and, with it, marry Jie wives. Though enemies were assumed to be a fact of life, no hard and fast, exclusive definitions were made as to their beliefs and behaviour. For instance, the Kuliak, acknowledged as autochthonous, were ridiculed for their circumcision and despised for their inability to defend, and so keep, cattle. Yet even these Kuliak, who were synonymous with a lack of cows, were thoroughly integrated into Jie society and granted the right to own stock.

Even declared enemies like the Poet were not beyond redemption, even if it were by way of enslavement. Poet was the generic name given to groups of unassimilated Tap who dwelt to the northwest of Daidai from Kaceri onwards. When they were forced west by the Laparanat famine, the Rengen spread out, occupying the inselberg called Poet at Kaceri. While some groups, like the Gule, stayed around Mount Rom after the famine, others like the Titi came back east. Kaceri was retaken, causing a major confrontation between the Poet and the Rengen, that threatened the existence of both. The war was decided by the Rengen's allies of the Orwakol section and the opportunistic intervention of the Dodosô.

As the Karimojong were used to do with the Oropom, the Dodosô and the Jie

---

[19] The Rengen were known formerly as the Rangyen, whose etymology is the red Ngiyen. The Yen are associated with Mount (O)rom and EC origin.

bound their captives with ropes and filed them home. Though enslaved, they were not drafted into an underclass of bondsmen, if only because pastoralists had no effective means of imprisonment. Anyway kindness could achieve more for the Ro than any amount of coercion, as the members of incorporated Poet clans are aware. Exogamy assured eventual integration through the exchange of cattle (Lamphear 1976b:190,164). Other movements, both within and into Karamoja meant that the culture was never static. Chickens, fat-tailed sheep, sesame, groundnuts, sweet potatoes and cow-peas were introduced to the Ro by Lwo speakers.

The ethnic response over a very long period to an unstable environment has been to move and to settle, to separate and to integrate, to fight and to unify, to mix and to merge, until the unique peoples who inhabit Karamoja emerged in the last 400 years. Yet this emulsification of diversity does not do justice to the Karamojong sense of their own salvation-history. Not only they, but all peoples, have been created in their place with their identity. Communities came to be and survived not merely by their own activity, vital though this may be, but also through the divine ordering and re-ordering of human affairs. Ecology and religion are not dichotomous, for divinity is to be associated with the water so necessary for livelihoods in semi-arid lands. The Creator not only brings the rain, but is so closely associated with it that He would be the rain were He not also transcending it. Certainly rain and water are spiritual. If the river in spate represents the tempestuousness of lesser spirits, divinity transcends them by bringing His people through the raging waters to protect them in their land against their enemies. The assumption is that the societies that settled the plains are internally constituted by divine order, and those members who forget it jeopardize everything.

3 The Advent of Christian Mission

Print-space alone precludes a fuller picture of the Karamojong encounter with 'red men': Arab, Swahili, Abyssinian, European and British, but this is available elsewhere (Knighton 1990:I,121–215). Since religion defines the focus of this book, this fascinating history gives way to a brief story of the most prolonged religious challenge brought by these outsiders without in the least meaning to diminish the explanatory power of other historical aspects. The Christian churches of Uganda were aware of a responsibility for mission to Karamoja ever since Bishop Tucker's indefatigable tours on foot had reached its margins on 28.2.09. 'Here to our great delight we found ourselves within sight of Karamoja country and within a two days march of Mani-Mani our original objective when turned from our course by absence of water on the caravan road' (Tucker 1911:342). But engagements at the centre of power in Mengo obliged him to postpone, like so many after him. This did not deter Archdeacon Buckley from his own territorially expansive dreams of mission: 'The land from the Nile to Abyssinia lies open before us. Surely the Church at home will not let the opportunity pass by' (Tucker 1911:342). She did let it pass for the Church Missionary Society (CMS). When administration began the next year, Karamoja was closed to missionaries.

In May 1923 CMS applied for, and was granted, permission to extend its activities to Karamoja following a letter from Revd H.G. Dillistone who was in charge of the mission in Teso District, offering his service for Karamoja. He had come to Uganda 22 years earlier as an independent missionary.[20] Only after the death of the appointed Pian county chief Aciya did government warm to any rôle for Christian mission to change the heart of the Karamojong. Even then it was couched in terms of countering 'the Mohammedan influence' guaranteed to excite the interest of missionary supporters in Britain.[21] Since CMS had not taken advantage of their permission, the Roman Catholic missions were informed 'that application for teachers to enter Karamoja will be favourably considered'.[22] In 1924, the new District Commissioner (DC), Tommy Preston, even urged CMS to send teachers. Exhausted of personnel, funds and zeal by the First World War, CMS, needing to make 25 per cent cuts in Uganda, was only able to establish, in 1924, two outschools in Labwor, neighbouring Lango and, in 1926, one in Moroto to be managed by the mission-station in distant Lira, funded by Teso Christians.

Eleazar Kyoko, a Lango from Lira, single-handedly founded the school at Moroto. Within a year he had his first adult Karamojong convert, Lokong, his houseboy and a former government headman from Kanawat in Najie (Paget Wilkes 1932a:40–43; J19, 24). Conversion required not only a spiritual metamorphosis and a decisive shift in social allegiances, but also a visible change in customs. Already being no longer a participating Jiot, because of his individualistic travels to Acoli, Lango, Moroto and Teso, the custom that had to go was a modern one, smoking. Eleazar insisted that to be Christian meant 'a real cut with the old life and all it contained': 'if I now started smoking again I should sooner or later go right back into the old heathen ways and lose the Gift of God' (Paget Wilkes 1932a:40–43). In 1928, a European missionary[23] came from 'Uganda proper' in order to conduct baptisms (ibid.:45), and Lokong took the name of Israel, seeing himself as the

---

[20] CMS G3/A7/0/100:7. Dillistone had visited Karamoja with the Archdeacon of East Uganda, Harry Mathers. By 4.10.23 the Mission Committee was minded to locate Revd T.L. Lawrence to Lira, while Dillistone's allocation to that place was to be reconsidered on the return of the Bishop of Uganda. He was reallocated to Bukedi and then Nabumali, where his wife took ill, dying of heart failure in England in 1927. He returned for 'special evangelistic work' at the age of 60 and died two years later without ever evangelizing Karamoja.

[21] CMS G3/A7/0/49:24. Boulton Ladbury, the CMS Secretary, wrote to the Chief Secretary (EA 1507/1908:23.5.23) asking whether the mission could start activity in Karamoja, but it had already decided, 'rather than open up work in Karamoja it would be advisable to build a station at Lira in Lango'. CMS did not wish to allow the Roman Catholics 'to take advantage of our opportunity for cultivating this fertile virgin soil in our portion of the Lord's Vinyard [sic]'. The Provincial Commissioner suggested a couple of mission teachers be allowed in the area between Soroti and Moroto, doubting the availability of a missionary (EA 1507/1908:31.5.23 PC, EP to Assistant Secretary for Native Affairs).

[22] EA 1507/1908:30.11.23 PC, EP to Chief Sec.: 'the time has now arrived at which, in my opinion, the entry of Missions into Karamoja should be permitted … the work of Missions would be advantageous in all respects'.

[23] This was no doubt T.L. Lawrence who reported on 16.12.28 that there were two adult baptisms. There were two communicants in Karamoja, 30 baptized and 11 readers, compared to nearly 50 000 baptized Christians in neighbouring districts (CMS G3/A10/P1/1929:5).

founding father of a new covenant people of Karamojong. He married Sarah, a Bokorait product of his first ministry in Kangole, and they were the first Karamojong adults to be baptized in the district. His life's course was to prove paradigmatic of Christian mission to the Karamojong, for the next year new missionaries would find him at his post and employ him.

Alfred Buxton, Home Secretary of the Sudan Interior Mission (SIM) in Britain, came up the Nile to reconcile with his famous, estranged father-in-law, C.T. Studd, and to resume a childhood friendship originating in their fathers' mission work in the Japan Evangelistic Band.[24] Hamilton Paget Wilkes bagged a couple of elephants in West Nile on a game licence in order to raise the first funds for Western mission in Karamoja. Together with Arthur Kitching, first bishop of the Diocese of the Upper Nile on whose map Karamoja was yet to be marked, they passed through the region in 1929 from Toposa in Sudan to the large CMS mission station at Ngora. Equipped to found a mission station at Kangole, the most significant junction of roads and the major river in Karamoja, they retraced their tyre-marks northeast. There they found Israel Lokong and, with him, climbed Moru Linga (the hill with a coloured patch of hair) 'to spy out the land and pray for it' (*MM* 10/117:120). However the elders refused to let them build at the foot of the hill as they herded their cattle there, and the people of Kalokengel to the east refused to have them. Government gave them permission for a base on unsettled land at Lotome (the place of elephants) by the River Omanimani on black cotton soil. Since the Karamojong choose to build their permanent settlements on the red soil ridges, this was uncontested, but the site was remarkably unsuited for either travel in the wet or for building.

The CMS missionaries would have accepted even the SIM presence, so 'appalling' was the lack of recruits, but SIM did not have funds for Buxton's project for mission to Rudolf District, that is the adjoining remote corners of Sudan, Abyssinia, Uganda and Kenya (CMS G3/A10/0). However, thanks to the largesse of two heiresses to the W.D. and H.O. Wills tobacco fortune, the Bible Churchmen's Missionary Society (BCMS) did. BCMS had seceded from CMS in 1922 in great acrimony as a stand against the growing preponderance of Liberal Evangelicals. Revd Fred Morris, who had gone out to East Africa on the 1913 Africa Inland Mission (AIM) expedition that C.T. Studd and Buxton left, arranged for his area of West Nile, ignored by the SIM, to be taken over by BCMS. However strong representations by CMS in London obliged BCMS to drop the plan. When CMS appeased the Conservative Evangelical interests in southwest Uganda by permitting the formation of the quasi-autonomous Rwandan Mission, it had twice frustrated BCMS' entry into Africa.

Now in the Diocese of the Upper Nile the old bitterness was overcome by the reluctance of CMS there to receive new missionaries of modernist views. Of Conservative Evangelicals at least BCMS was Anglican while SIM was not. Buxton's family and school connections helped arrangements between governors, administrators, bishops and societies. The Bishops of Mombasa and Upper Nile

---

[24] For the extensive family connections, starting with 'The Emancipator', Sir Thomas Fowell Buxton, see (Knighton 1990:I,389ff).

presented their CMS Africa Secretary with a virtual *fait accompli*. 'Buxton came to see us and we are willing to accept the offer provided the two Governments make no objection, as there is no prospect of the C.M.S. being able to undertake work in the area concerned' (KNA MSS/61/500 29.6.29; Heywood and Kitching to Hooper). 'We have all three interviewed the Acting Governor of Kenya today, commending the scheme' (29.6.29; Heywood and Kitching to Bartlett, BCMS).[25] Only afterwards did Buxton seek the approval of his own society (SIM: EB-1. 7.29; Buxton to Bingham). 'The Acting Governor gave permission so the B.C.M.S. is now definitely committed to the evangelization of this field, working in co-operation with the native Anglican Church in the Diocese of the Upper Nile' (CMS G3/A10/0).

With the financial turmoils of Western capitalism, the crash of markets and economic depression led some to despair of this world and hope for its end. BCMS was able to generate apocalyptic fervour to send out fresh men and women to convert the world in their lifetime. Their emphasis was on evangelism and preaching, and itinerated much on foot to that purpose. However they found little visible result beyond the naked bodies of responsive Karamojong to encourage the BCMS supporters in England, and soon found themselves slowed down by literacy and Bible translation. This obviously upheld their Reformation tradition, but they could not be oblivious of the normal mission practices in East Africa centred on mission-station and education. It was only houseboys and schoolboys who could be moulded into visible converts, adhering to a Western sense of hygiene and modesty, while Karamojong dances and ceremonies were to be strictly avoided as evil sorcery, witchcraft and wizardry. The healing power of the *ngimurok* divines was demonized as the devil's power to kill (Paget Wilkes 1932a:21–4, 31–5).

It took time for missionaries to begin to learn the ineluctability and value of Karamojong culture. When they did, they risked being misunderstood either by the Conservative Evangelicals at home or by their fellow missionaries on the field, who were very emotionally attached to the religious tradition that brought them there, and any departure from it could be interpreted as removing their *raison d'être*. A signal example of this was treatment of the Clarks, who were among the first young recruits to Karamoja. With the departure of the pioneers they soon became synonymous with the mission station at Lotome, and Bob became generally known as *Bwana* (boss) Clark. There is no doubt that he won the confidence of Karamojong elders and the Protectorate government, whose officers all beat a path to his door. By the 1940s, they regarded him as the authority on the Karamojong, holding influence with them. They lived between allegiance to government and attachment to the Karamojong, but with Doris working on Bible translation, hosting anthropologists and writing articles for the *Uganda Journal*, they gradually accommodated themselves comfortably to Karamoja, accumulating many livestock.

Since they worked in a period when centre–periphery relationships were at their most settled and relaxed, they were able to project an image of progress to London, which was always sufficient to convince Daniel Bartlett, the dictatorial General

---

[25] CMS G3/A10/P1/38–40, G3/A5 1929/101f; *MM* 17/216: 253; CMS G3/A10/P1/66. Six months later the Diocese of the Upper Nile was not in favour of handing over the Sapiny or any other tribe on Mount Elgon to BCMS.

Secretary of BCMS. It was his successor who would give ear to the jealousy of the Clarks' compatriots in the Society's Rudolf mission field. Soon afterwards the policy of the Uganda Protectorate was geared to the development of Karamoja in order to construct a more sustainable nation-state. Five-year plans were constructed to be funded out of the forced sale of cattle which was so hated by the Karamojong, and one of the chief beneficiaries was Lotome, for its educational and agricultural work. The BCMS missionaries felt obliged to accept government education grants as Italian RC missionaries, the Verona Fathers, would have benefited from all the grants for their schools. Such an expansion was beyond the capacity of the Clarks alone, certainly their financial and administrative acumen, so BCMS recruited many volunteers to assist, as the Clarks themselves had long urged. These young missionaries BCMS was soon to criticize as 'utterly impossible', 'of low intelligence' and 'most unpromising' (the latter of a future bishop), when before it had said there were too many old missionaries. The newcomers' threat to resign if something were not done with the Clarks convinced BCMS to 'sacrifice' them 'in the interests of the work' (BCMS:Uganda/Preparing Committee Karamoja 1952–8, 1.56 Sub-Committee). The bishop was not impressed, having appointed Bob as a canon in the diocese 'in recognition of his long, faithful, cheerful, and untiring work in Karamojo' and would have installed Doris also if he could (BCMS:Uganda/Bishop of Upper Nile, 5.9.50; Usher-Wilson to Houghton). Far afield *Bwana* Clark was thought to be 'very good, for he taught knowledge and agriculture' (D11). He was rude and used to beat people in school, but 'the Karamojong loved him' (J1). He could be 'wild' and quarrelsome, but he 'was a very good man, cultivating sunflower, which he introduced' (J28).

The DC backed the Clarks, 'right or wrong; they have been here for many years and have been very helpful to Government'. Yet BCMS quite relished dismissing episcopal and political pressure, even from the Minister for Local Government who regarded them and their work with the greatest esteem, but there were more searching questions to answer. Stanley Metters, who had preceded the Clarks to Lotome with Buxton, had opined that the reasons for the unhappy history of the field may be found primarily in the lack of leadership from the beginning (BCMS:Uganda/Preparing Committee Karamoja 1952–8, 5.11.55, Sub-Committee). The Clarks had expressed dissatisfaction with the church they had helped produce, so this was taken as evidence to condemn them. 'The Clarks themselves, especially Mrs., gave us very clearly to understand that as far as the church was concerned, they had failed miserably' (BCMS: Uganda/Preparing Committee Karamoja 1952-8, 1.1.57; Hacking to Houghton):

> You yourselves felt that that there had been a failure over the years in the building up of the Church on the right foundations and the evidence that has accumulated about the spiritual state of the church only serves to emphasize the truth of this. (4.1.57, Houghton to Clarks)

That building a church according to an English religious tradition was the seat of the problem never occurred to BCMS, so the Society made the Clarks pay the penalty for painfully discovering the bad news. Philip Gulliver (12.11.88 Letter) reflected that Bob was one of the truly best men I have ever met and a genuine practicing [*sic*], tolerant Christian .... He was there, as he expressed it to me, to bring God to them – not Western dress or shame about nakedness .... I was impressed by the affection and trust that the local people showed ... And amongst the best of missionaries I have met elsewhere in Africa, Bob Clark was, in my opinion, without superior ... I have seen a few who were genuinely good men able to transcend their own European culture. And Bob Clark was one such.

Instead of learning the lessons of mission failure, BCMS plunged headlong into fulfilling the Protectorate government's priority to educate the Karamojong before independence overtook them, in the hope that this would produce an educated leadership for the church. In this latter aim it was moderately successful, producing Karamojong clergy long before the Roman Catholics with their indiscriminate baptism policy. However whether either were able to lay the right foundations to mission remains open to question. Removing a few Karamojong children to boarding-schools did not mean that their culture could be eradicated in favour of one more acceptable to Western eyes, as Mary Morris Jones, a professional teacher, found in Lotome.

In February 1965, Mary only had one missionary couple owing to mass resignations after BCMS declined to pay school fees when government teaching salaries were more attractive. In the space of a fortnight a troublous spate hit Lotome. A boy died after the removal of eight feet of gangrenous intestine, so all his relatives at the school were taken away. A girl died of meningitis in their car when the missionaries were driving them to hospital. She was the daughter of Lobunei the local MP, who had already lost a son in the meningitis outbreak at Lotome, so he breathed murderous threats of reprisal against the school. It was rumoured that Lobunei had appointed men to kill two teachers, including Miss Jones, and four girls. Teachers refused to help Mary administer sulpha tablets to the girls. Teachers had to be taken to Moroto hospital with hysteria and hypochondria. The next month there were boy students in the girls' compound with a teacher and two girls. Teachers absented themselves without permission, and also started fighting. The outposts of church and state proved too fragile in Karamoja to allow such in-fighting. All the entrenched Karamojong suspicions of the immoral and misleading effects of boarding-school education for girls were abundantly confirmed to the point that teachers could be seen as *ngikapilak* (witches), and the whole place troubled by spirits. Ever since then the church has done little, apart from Sunday services and intermittent training, at its original centre of Lotome.

In common with other churches of the time, great hopes were placed in 'indigenous' clergy. The first one, Zephaniah Akamu from Ik, was said to be 'backslidden' for some years, though the Dodosŏ thought him 'a good religious leader who taught the word of God' (D4). He was speared to death by the Bokora as they reclaimed the bridewealth they had given him for his daughter's marriage in 1962. The second one to be ordained, Rufus Lorukude, followed his missionary masters into teaching, and was not employed by the church again. In 1987, after 11 years as a 'spiritually barren' missionary diocese (*MM* Spring 1976:1f), the Diocese of Karamoja appealed for external funding for transport, including a new Land Rover for the bishop and its mileage expenses, diocesan offices, a diocesan training centre, staff houses and churches, mills, vehicle workshops, tractors, lorry, cathedral, running costs for education and translation departments, a student bursary scheme, pastors' children's school fees, pastors' medical fees, the replacement of their looted property, archdeaconry offices and pastors' salaries (Lomongin 1987). Because of fighting and drought it was unable to fund this expansion internally. 'About Karamoja diocese, we are getting poorer and poorer every year, especially the pastoral ministry' (P3).

Many in Karamoja have been baptized and given a 'Christian' name, and 'a few have been truly converted', a transformation envied by the Roman Catholics; but, for the most part, allegiance to the church is superficial and secondary. Even Israel Lokong, the self-proclaimed father of the new covenant, married a second wife, Adia Loluk, in the 1930s and always participated in *akiriket* after returning to his Kanawat birthplace, becoming an outstanding authority on the oral tradition of his people (Lamphear 1972a:473) and bequeathing a homestead not visibly different from the next (J19,24). Thus even the relatively small number enticed into relinquishing the Karamojong world-view and its clear identities are quite capable of being absorbed back into their natal traditions most satisfactorily from the Karamojong perspective, but not the church's. Thus, while there has been considerable, sometimes amazing, interaction between churches and traditional religions in other more agriculturalist parts of Africa, in Karamoja the impact of Christian mission is unusually invisible. Traditional Karamojong religion can be considered as central to a continuing reality that has not been transformed by any missionary religion.

4 Historical Conclusions

Discontinuity

The present Karamojong communities were established from the 1830s, when different ethnic groups and customs were irrevocably amalgamated. The Jie did not receive their name until after the attempt to conquer them in the 1860s (Lamphear 1976b:211). The life of all societies in Karamoja was considerably interrupted by Erono, the disasters of the 1890s and, to a lesser extent, by the arrival of Abyssinian and Swahili adventurers, as well as the more insidious effects of the British Empire. Though the Karamojong have shown considerable hostility towards enemy cattle-herders, a large degree of tolerance has nearly always been shown to those who wished to settle with the herdsmen under their political system. It is certainly not the case that an eternally constant religion was holding the Karamojong as part of ahistorical Africa 'locked into an impoverished past' (Ranger 1988:864). Had the Karamojong, through their religion, not been subtle and adept at responding to the vicissitudes of historical change before, during and after the imperial episode, which could easily have been Abyssinian rather than British (Knighton 1990:I,122–81), their culture would have fractured in the face of state power. Rather it needs to be asked whether it was not the pragmatic flexibility of the decision-making process in the politico-religious assembly, constituted in age-classes, that enabled the Karamojong to manage change down the generations rather than be broken by it.

Continuity

The identity of the Karamojong has not been completely subject to the vicissitudes of famine and foreigners. The remarkable tenacity with which people have adhered to traditional values has enabled them to survive largely on their own terms in an uncertain environment. The economic aspect is neither an absolute determinant nor even an independent variable. Some Eastern Nilotes became Tap and grew less willing to die for the sake of their cattle and more willing to move to where there was rain, such as in Teso. The Ro and those whom they have absorbed have spurned this option, despite the ravages of cattle disease and raiders and in spite of the pressures of Protectorate and national governments to develop agriculture and restrict grazing as the economic means of sustaining a growing population.

Yet the Karamojong have achieved a military dominance over the agricultural peoples in, and even outside, Karamoja and have no intention of enculturating the priorities of modernity or of renouncing their traditional pastoral values. These are perpetuated, not merely by the economics of living in Karamoja, but by their *Weltanschauung* whereby their faith in Akujů led them through the river into the land. The arrival of the British was not the beginning of the subjugation of peoples or the introduction of different ideas and customs. These had been occurring from the prehistory of Karamoja. The effect of Europe was felt before a European was seen, for Karamoja has never been isolated from world history. Europe's technology, more than its ideology, affects Karamoja.

The more emphatic violence of the *pax britannica* did not lead to radical cultural transition. Colonial chiefs, who were deputed to suppress all killing and cattle-raiding, were not able to hold sway over acephalous communities. One, Aciya, who tried to exercise imperial authority over the movement of cattle and people, was simply killed by the elders for his folly, and the women celebrated in song and dance, beating the corpse of their compatriot with sticks (Knighton 1990:I,201–5). However the Protectorate's continual insistence on its exclusive right to determine the occasions of violent death did much, at great cost, to suppress the numbers of casualties from cattle-raids, if not the number of raids.

The enduring vitality of traditional Karamojong religion is shown precisely in the people's staunch intention to be independent of any state; they have no desire for it, and the mutual misunderstanding is great. The whole point is that these are nomadic pastoralists whose socio-political formation is markedly different from the state to which they were arbitrarily allocated and whose members despise and fear them for being different. The Karamojong seek their autonomy and prefer to be peripheral to Uganda, which they have never consented to join, not even at independence. Their religion is crucial to allowing them to do this, for it orally and spiritually validates, even empowers, a quite different value-set and their own convention of representative democracy. This happens because traditional Karamojong religion is not a spin-off from a religious tradition common to Uganda, nor is it submerged beneath one. Thus the Republic of Uganda is not the prime context for the Karamojong, and it would be a categorical error, caused by wearing state-coloured spectacles, to make it so. The history of the intervention of outsiders in Karamoja has proved surprisingly separable because the basic theme of that history has yet to change, still being expressed in current institutions and practices.

The Karamojong come to terms with external realities but do not sell their souls for them.

The Karamojong strategically chose to respond to the increasingly virulent presence of alien government and Church, not by the use of outright, certainly not vocal, opposition, but by deliberately ignoring their inappropriate demands, which could not be imposed without their tacit consent that was resolutely withheld. They have maintained, throughout their four centuries' occupation of the land in Karamoja, an independent communal life, sustaining a moral order that could not be bettered by alien law, except, perhaps, in intertribal cases.

So far the picture is that Karamojong culture was by no means static before the advent of the gun and the Republic of Uganda, and that acute challenges to traditions met an equal response. It is not so much that peripheral Karamoja has been ignored by an inattentive centre, but that the Karamojong have persistently resisted the various attempts of the centre to pull the region into its orbit. A basic and irreducible aspect of this resistance has not been violence, but their steady refusal to let their traditional religion atrophy in favour of a 'religion of children'. Christian faith has not been seen as harmful in itself, but as inappropriate in its social form to the pastoral life, because it is under the social control of largely uncomprehending aliens who do not share in a pastoralist livelihood with its concomitant priorities and values. Karamojong maintenance of a surprisingly autonomous culture and identity is not just due to geographical and economic factors; it has been greatly assisted by their not seeing any great need to appropriate a foreign faith, when they had long cultivated a much more satisfying means of appreciating the presence of a vital religion and a saving god in their pastoralist life. The bulk of this book will trace the ways in which that presence is sought and felt in Karamojong culture. Synchronic evidence will now be added to the diachronic to indicate that this religious life has been maintained through chance and change, and why.

Chapter 4

Spirit and Society

Religion cannot be understood apart from society in Karamoja, which is not to say that one can be reduced to the other. However, traditional Karamojong religion is to a great extent implicit in society. Persons are seldom any more mature in religious terms than they are in social status, though this can happen. There is no corpus of doctrine to be taught and no conversion required from unbelief to belief. Members of the community are enculturated very gradually and slowly into the full inheritance of their culture, and this may take the by-path of personal and circumstantial differences, just as they are socialized into the community. Thus rites of passage are extraordinarily important both socially and ritually (Cox 1998b), as their very continuance through historical change suggests. Thus it is necessary to delineate here some of the basic aspects of the culture in order to locate religion aright.

The danger of brevity is that diversity and marginality are not given due weight. Not all Karamojong in Karamoja can be described as nomadic pastoralists, which is one reason why the term 'traditional' is so inevitable, not only to distinguish what is different from alternative ways of living, but also to mark what is the mainstream, dominant form of life. There are indeed Karamojong teachers, clergy, government officials, labourers, prostitutes, development workers, brewers, retailers and traders. Yet, apart from the latter three, they are largely externally funded, and so a minority marginal to the life of the Karamojong whatever their income.[1] All may, in places, be outnumbered by people from other parts of Uganda, who find the Karamojong leave a relatively large number of vacancies in the bourgeois professions. Then exigency may have caused partial or temporary breakdown in the social structure. A culture subject to famine inevitably exports that part of its populace who would rather try to seek another way of life with greater security from poverty and death, yet that they are squeezed out is also evidence of the resilience of the structure that does not capitulate to their demands. A casual acquaintance with life in all its quirks may not yield much pattern to it, but it would be quite wrong to adopt the representation of society by some educated people that life is all disordered (Gray 2000; Mirzeler and Young 2001; Mkutu 2003). The common terms for living are still construed by traditional life so these need to be mastered.

---

[1] Some pastoralists may be councillors or seasonal labourers, but, so long as the acquisition of cattle for the family wealth remains a primary goal, they remain subject to traditional considerations and the interests of the community.

1 Kinship

Family

Ngakaramojong has no single equivalent for the word, 'family', which is defined according to the appropriate territorial unit. Of *ekal*, *ewae*, *ere*, the first two are used to emphasize closeness of relationship. All maternal brothers (*ngikaitotoi*) in a family (*ewae*) are called papa by their siblings, and the eldest becomes the 'big man' (*ekapolon*) in it. The larger concept of the family (*ere*) extends ostensibly to all the sons and grandsons of one herd-owner. The herd defines the family, so that, if a client or relative, not descended from the common grandfather, participates in the herd, it is 'as if' he were so descended. Thus, an agnatic nephew (*epapait*) may assert as in a previous generation:

> We say he is our grandfather. We are all 'cousins'. We live near together. We give each other cattle. Our herds are like one herd; our wives were all married from one herd. We are one Family (*eowe* [that is, *ewae* used in the sense that all are descended from maternal brothers]) and different from other people. (Gulliver 1955:109f)

Any *ere* family is named after its head, though he may be deceased, where it consists of coeval cousins (*ngikaiyeyai*). When the headship of the *ere* family is inherited, it passes to a maternal brother or by primogeniture through the first wife, so long as the heir is capable of carrying the responsibility of being herd-owner (*elope ka ere*). Family and herd go together and define one another. Control of one means control of the other, so that all stock allocations and disposals mirror *ere* family relationships. The men of the *ere* family have no right apart from poverty to deny another member a cow when he genuinely begs (*akilip*, to pray) for one. Having given it, its first heifer-calf should be returned to the giver, and its first heifer-calf, and so on, forging a bond, which may endure into the next generation. This cattle bond gives much of the distinction between 'our people' (*ngitungakosi*) and all others in the tribe to whom common hospitality is due.

Family and herd parallel one another. By analogy, a father is a bull, a mother a cow, unmarried men steers, girls heifers and boys bull-calves. No assignation is thought detrimental, rather natural. Indeed the cow (*aate*) is the essence of cattle (*ngaatuk*), its womb being acknowledged as vital. 'In Jie conceptions all significant inter-personal relationships rest upon connections through livestock' (Gulliver 1953a:155). Such a valuation continues.

Clan

Each *ere* family is a patrilineal lineage, and with neighbouring relatives forms a sub-clan. With other sub-clans in different places it composes an agnatic clan (*ateker*). In Najie, with its many small clans, one may consist of one to eight *ere* families. Each clan has a name which may describe its ethnic origin and may have a cattle brand which accords with its children's haircuts.

A wife must be brought from outside the clan and, indeed, from outside the husband's mother's, even grandmother's, natal clan, so that cattle bonds created by marriage are spread as widely as possible to ensure as many sources of help, when it is needed, as possible. Neither should a man marry a sister of his wife or of his brother's wife, in order that 'the cattle do not come mixed' (Gulliver 1955:225), which would happen if a fiancé were to beg cattle from his affines to give to his affines. Sexual relations within the prohibited degrees are tabu, punishable by Akujů, for every such girl is as a sister. There can be no future in such a liaison, for relatives from both sides would refuse to give or receive the bridewealth. The tabus presuppose that, by puberty, every girl or boy has been enculturated into the intricacies of kinship, though inevitably elders are more aware of the precise extent of kinship relationship, having lived longer.

School pupils might seek to elope, but to do so is to cut themselves off from their homes, and such unions are seldom successful. The girl returns to her home with any children, which legally belong to her family. Such restrictions go counter to the liberal conscience of the West, but they do display a very high valuation of the 'other' within society, leading to the different clans being fully integrated in the social order. Indeed marriage is the gateway for an alien to enculturate, and is recommended for the European man, so long as he pays the bridewealth and follows the customs, which none, as yet, has done to the full.

2 Sexuality

Sexual Orientation

It is a sacred duty for all healthy Karamojong, if they have the wherewithal, to marry. There is no other route to social fulfilment either for men or women. Those who fail to marry are object lessons of God's failure to bless, though, given this pervasive handicap, there are worthy functions they can perform in an *ere* family. Homosexuality is completely tabu. One informant (J22) had 'never heard of any homosexual activity at all', for it is the most difficult issue to raise when it appears to be so far outside their experience. If a male is identified as a homosexual, he will be known as *ekapilak* (witch, J18), who may in certain unfavourable circumstances face the death penalty. No healthy man is relieved of his social duty, not just to marry, but also to beget children. If he fails to do his best on any occasion, his wife will not be slow to tell her friends in the hearing of many others. Girls have the opportunity before they leave the parental home, that is marry, as they sleep together, but lesbianism is a punishable offence and is certainly abnormal.

Extramarital Relations

Gulliver (1953c:158) claimed a Jiot can marry and procreate children without initiation, which applies merely in the ritual sphere. This does happen, though usually in reverse order, for children are often born before marriage is completed. Gulliver has failed to distinguish between a norm and an exception which proves the rule. Locap states the rule, 'Initiation introduces young people to marry. No one is able to take full marriage without important initiation is done [*sic*]' (1989:1). Children are conceived, and marriage, which must be seen as a long process, not a single occasion, may be entered into, but not finalized, until initiation. This accords with the rule enunciated by the Karimojong, that a bride may not be taken to live in her man's home until he is initiated (Persse 1934:111; Dyson-Hudson 1966:198f; Pazzaglia 1982:103). Since marriages are not often completed before the man is approaching 40, there are relatively few discrepancies. To this day the Karimojong say that a man 'should be initiated before marriage, but there are exceptions' (P4).

That a strong sense of morality persists is demonstrated by the real fear which a lover has of entering his beloved's home at night because, if found by her parents, he will be beaten. Parents are most reluctant to send their daughters to school in case they learn promiscuity. There is no ideal of virginity before the completion of marriage, for sexual intercourse is a necessary part of the process, not a later consequence of it, but parents do seek stable, socially responsible liaisons for their children which will end in full marriage. Likewise there is no concept of illegitimate children. It is 'by good luck' that a girlfriend conceives even before any bridewealth has been paid (P3). Children are the blessing of Akujů and they need never lack for a legal father, even if it be the grandfather or uncle.

However, as always in traditional Karamojong life, a strong sense of what should be coexists with what is, involving minimal social disruption. There is always a grey area of concubinage, by which women live as clients of men without, at least for several years, undergoing the normal process. The change of the extent of this tendency, if it could be assessed, would be a measure of the secularization of the society.

Prostitution

Apart from the townships, where standards meet the temporary presence of civil servants and traders from other parts and prostitution (*akitiptowo*) is a paid multi-ethnic profession, there is the rôle of the traditional harlot (*amalaat²*), for which there no appropriate English term, as all are pejorative. 'She can go anywhere she is invited. She is a misfit in society whom no man can marry. She is effectively *ex communicado* and is not talked about' (J22).³ She is then that rare bird who can flout all custom and yet survive as an oddity in society by dint of her extraordinary talents, beauty or personality. The hegemony of men is never total.

This harlot is not a threat to a society which has a positive evaluation of sex, an even greater regard for marriage, and yet does not tie men into exclusive relationships. In this context, she functions for the stability of society, even if she is accorded no credit. Extraordinary beauty is not considered a desirable quality in a wife, for it tempts some men to contemplate what is strictly forbidden, adultery. Instead, if she seeks it, an irresistibly attractive girl in Karamojong eyes is given her

---

² Pl. *amalaae* cf. *akimal* (to greet, court) is not cognate to the loanword from the Kiswahili, which is derived from a Persian word for prostitute, *amalaya*, pl. *ngimalaya*.

³ I found this question and that of homosexuality the most difficult on which to obtain answers. While both are highly unusual, no-one could cite an instance of homosexuality. However it was not until I gave my own observation that my informant, with whom I had worked most closely, would admit such a rôle.

head. She is allowed a position in which she can choose any man she wants. This, as her dress indicates, distinguishes her from the prostitute (*atapitowo*) who puts herself at the disposal of anyone who will pay cash.

One evening, while I was tending my garden in Kotido, a woman who only spoke Ngajie went to the door of my sleeping hut. She had had no difficulty in securing unauthorized admission to the compound from the watchman, arriving, not in a textile dress favoured by town prostitutes, but in all the feminine finery that the local culture could produce, clean, black and well turned out. She was in her 30s, tall, dignified, assured, introducing herself as *aberu*, a (married) woman. Having said I did not want one, she made no attempt to plead or beg, as others like the brazen prostitutes of Kampala do, but turned on her heel and went as mysteriously as she had come. W.D.M. Bell (1923:57) came across one such over 80 years earlier, so even the woman who is a law unto herself is also a tradition.

Early Relationships

Parents may leave social life between the sexes, outside the forbidden degrees, to young people to arrange. They often pretend to take no interest, until sexual intercourse or conception has become an accomplished fact. Prior to that point, the siblings have scope outside the home to initiate relations with the opposite sex, beginning as young as ten for girls in lax families, and after puberty for the boys, before which they prefer the company of cattle. The main occasion for meeting is the dance, during which couples may go off into the darkness to explore one another. Also, when it is not too dangerous, older girls visit cattle-camps with sorghum and supplies for the herdsmen to churn and boil the excess milk into ghee. At night, they may lie with their boyfriends. Since there is more pleasure than responsibility at these occasions, women look back to them as constituting the best time of life.

However neither social nor sexual restraint is entirely lifted even here. Sexual relations are expected to fall short of copulation, most likely the girls use traditional techniques to prevent this, and both sexes have an interest in complying with this standard. While a man may have as many lovers as he can find, a girl risks a bad reputation if she cavorts, suggesting she will make a bad wife. This would be to let down her family, especially her brothers who depend, often directly for their own marriages, on a good asking price for bridewealth, which is a function of society's estimate of the girl as a future wife, worker and mother. Since marriage is virtually the only possible, let alone socially acceptable, route to her life's goals, and begins within a few years of puberty, she does not want to compromise her chances in life.

Men, on the other hand, are reluctant to embark on the laborious task of marriage, which presupposes a certain personal wealth in cattle, and involves much socializing in order to raise the rest of the bridewealth. His *ere* family may tell him straight that he cannot be married until his senior half-brothers, maternal brothers, and even his father again, are married first, or until his younger sisters have been exchanged for bridewealth. Of course if he can find a woman so weak and a family so marginal that they do not demand bridewealth then he might take her to his home as a concubine (P5). No marital system is ever so comprehensive as to rule out concubinage in practice. Normally, if he starts fathering children before he hands over the bridewealth, he must pay a fine of three oxen, or 30 sheep and goats, for each child, but still risks losing both lover and children to anyone who can come to agreement with the *ere* family and produce the bridewealth.

Thus it pays, in the long run, not to be distracted from the day-long task of herding, until such time as his personal herd is sufficiently large to open formal negotiations and, later, to support a family. Meanwhile he has the counter-attraction of the uncluttered purity of the nomadic life, free from most social and domestic pressures, having friends when he wants them, his beloved cattle all the time, and being able to use his own initiative to better his chances in life. He feels no pressing need to marry, until he finds his *asapan* brethren doing so. If he is wise, he will not force the pace.

3 Marriage

Courtship

The following valuation of marriage is from an account written by a Jiot:

> Marriage in Karamoja is the concern of the Community, hence, Choice of Partners [*sic*] is not only duty of boys even the Community is involved.
>
> It is a drama which involves every one as an actor, it is a duty, a requirement from the corporate society, a rythm [*sic*] of life in which every one must particepate [*sic*].
>
> Refusal to do so is to bring a curse to Karamojong Society and is to be considered a rebel law-breaker, abnormal and underhuman, thus the society will reject you in return. (Locap 1989:1)

Conservative families, who maintain tight control of their siblings, or have ones slow to approach courtship, still arrange marriages. Yet the Pian observe that education is bringing change for those few girls who spend much time in school, so that students agree to marry without parental advice (P5). With little participation in school after puberty, this remains a marginal threat, but one felt by elders always sensitive to any possible diminution of their power. Typically the girl is around 18 years of age, and the suitor 22 or older, often much older (P5). Some parents take the initiative. Having identified an eligible *ere* family, they visit the chosen girl's parents early in the morning, and broach the matter obliquely with a parable: 'They may say, one time they came across a certain donkey (girl) which they thought it [*sic*] would assist carry load for their boy ...' (ibid.). Yet it would be a mistake to suppose there is one trend from absolute parental control to the autonomy of youth. It used to be emphasized that the young people exercised their choice. 'Normally however no compulsion is brought to bear upon either party to a marriage' (Persse 1934:111), and if a pregnant girl had more than one suitor, she could prefer the one she loved most over the genitor of her child. 'The woman's consent is essential' (Wayland 1931:224). Thus there appears to be a shift over 20 years to the time when the suicide of girls denied the suit of their lover. Yet even this protest is a shrill witness to a girl's traditional rights in the matter, not to a downtrodden and compliant gender. However the temptation for a poor family, male and female, to marry their daughter to a richer and older man can be very great, and greed or necessity can overcome the dignity of one member of the family. The possibility of suicide, or elopement, is a check on such pressure, but these will not help the girl achieve her ambition of being fully-married to the man she loves.

Alternatively a suitor may make his own arrangements, as does an older man, but he must still consult his mother or his wives. A boy must start by wooing the girl (*akiting*) onto his side. When he is ready to be serious about a particular girl, he begs a trivial favour from her. This voluntary indebtedness is the sure basis for any reciprocal relationship (Novelli 1988:ch.VII). If she is interested in him, she will indulge his repeated 'begging' (*akilip*). Having established a relationship with her, he turns to begging from her friends in the 'girls' committee', her coevals in the *ere* family, as friendly relations are established through giving and receiving. For when her turn to marry comes, being old enough to decide, they determine who would be a suitable husband, and may even take the initiative in match-making without the parents' knowledge, but cannot force the girl to go through with the relationship.

Engagement

When the suitor has the approval of the girl and the girls' committee, they invite him to climb the fence into her *ekal* at night and they will not raise the alarm but, if her parents discover him, they may beat him, though, if they approve the match, this may be more token than injurious. If their anger at him does not abate, an ingenious and determined girl might take up residence in another home where her lover may visit her. Parents, however, do let daughters build their own sealed hut where a suitor can press his claim with sweet talk in privacy. Admission here is proof of engagement (*etinganŭ*, cf. *akiting*, to hold with the hands, to woo) for the girls, who will then discourage other suits. In the eyes of the young people, the girl is engaged (*atingat*).

Conception out of Wedlock

As soon as children are in the offing, any private affair becomes of public concern, not because anything shocking has been done, but because children are seen not as unwanted liabilities, but as valuable assets, who should never be removed illicitly from the *ere* family. However often children are begotten outside wedlock, that is before bridewealth is given, the practice remains less than exemplary, as indicated by the Karimojong requirement that an *emuron* (religious specialist) should have been conceived after his mother was 'married with cattle' (Dyson-Hudson 1966:120n). Conception outside wedlock is still an occurrence which requires the boy's parents to go to the girl's parents for *edyekir*, a time of apology and seeking unity (*akidyek*). There may be no great guilt displayed but, in the sense that regular social relationships have been disturbed, a sin has been committed. Whether such an engagement can grow into marriage depends on the quality of the lovers' relationship, and on whether the parents can come to terms.

Pregnancy Compensation

Whatever the future arrangements, the boy's parents are obliged to pay compensation[4] (*ecula*) of three oxen after the birth of a baby, not as a down-payment on either the child or the bridewealth, but as a provision for the welfare of the mother and child, whom the father may never see again. This is a stable expectation across the Karamojong (P5; J5,13),[5] which can be converted into the standard stock currency of 30 goats. The first compensatory payment (*ekicoli*) may be a cow in milk to provide for mother and child (P5). However the girl's father may delay asking for payment, until it suits him, a year or more later. He may be short of labour or feel his herd is under threat from cattle-raiders or disease. His rights are not time-barred.

There is a very real distinction between the genitor (*ekaurunan*) and the legal father (*papa*). Since the girl's parents are now very careful to see that mother and child do not leave home until after bridewealth has been paid, it is quite possible that the child will never bond with his genitor. It does not matter, for he has a father in whoever is his mother's guardian: her father, her brother or her future husband, and the child will be legally, ritually, and in every way apart from biologically, his (P3; Dyson-Hudson 1966:83f).

Betrothal

Marriage is only in sight after a series of deputations by the suitor's close agnates to the girl's parents and negotiations about bridewealth. One of these is called *eleto*, when the daughter's choice of her suitor is confirmed (J15). Having consulted important relatives who will receive shares in the bridewealth, the girl's parents will accept or reject the offer on the basis of the relative demeanour and standing in the community of the suitors, but most of all on the relative cattle holdings of the *ere* families. If her parents agree, the girl will be betrothed (*apudor*) as soon as he makes a part-payment of the bridewealth and should not be courted by other men. The eager suitor will make a part-payment quickly of any number above three to distinguish it from a pregnancy compensation.

If the *ere* family is keen, the girl is under strong pressure to accept the wisdom of their experience. Yet, if she is very determined, and counters all the arguments made about status and security, she can marry the man of her choice, even a poor one, so long as he is not kin. Her trump card is to threaten to hang herself, which is not an idle possibility (Clark 1953:75). Then her parents would be still worse off

---

[4] The courting couple have made a family relationship without obtaining the blessing of the family. The suitor must now make up for this deficit by feeding (*akicul*, to eat meat) the girl's family with livestock. This not an investment in future marriage but a restitution for liberties taken. It delivers the suitor of his obligation, but creates none for the girl's parents.

[5] A Dodosô informant cited ten cows, but said it depended on the customs of the clan (D1). What he meant was that it was subject to negotiation like bridewealth, so was referring to the down-payment on bridewealth, which can be any number above three cows, which the girl's family agree to accept, the excess being the first bridewealth payment.

(Dyson-Hudson, V.R. and N. 1962:48). The woman forced into marriage (*aberu ngina kitangikina*) is still known for, without the blessing of the girl's agnates and close maternal kin, she is assured of sterility, or 'the children will become ill and die' (Gulliver 1955:234). If they oppose a suit, but the suitor's clan forcibly carry the pseudo-reluctant girl off, they have to accept the fact and negotiate compensation for bride-capture.

Gathering Support

Both parties inform all their kinsmen, seeking their approval. If there is opposition, the match could fail at this stage, which opens the important business of drawing up the bridewealth demands of interested kin (Gulliver 1953a:150). If the girl's clan is large, many cattle will be required to satisfy all the relatives. The lead concept is again one of compensation for a life.[6] If the man's family is cattle-rich, then it can be a matter of honour[7] for both the parties that the bridewealth is high. The suitor shows that he has sufficient social and animal capital to pay, and the girl is, and feels, valued by the bridewealth. Once bridewealth begins to change hands, and part-payments (*ngaropar*) are common because of the difficulty of raising the full amount and the danger of enemies taking away what has been collected, the girl is pledged (*aroparitai*) as a fiancée, and her parents are morally obliged not to consider counter-offers.

Council of the Wand

The two parties meet again at the fiancée's home to approve the match. The Jie give him his wand (*ebela*). This one is special, in that it is very straight, with flat ends. This is the sign that he is officially ready to marry and is raising bridewealth to the amount which the fiancée's party demands. He fixes a white ostrich feather to the wand and/or in the head-dress or hair, and an oryx horn with a steer's white-haired tail (Dyson-Hudson, V.R. and N. 1962:48; P5; Locap 1989:2), which shows that he comes in peace when visiting bond-friends in other tribes. His intention is already clear, when he begins, 'I have come to beg.'

Food

A man will do well to have 40 per cent of the total cattle demanded available in his own herd. Another 40 per cent may come from the *ere* family herd, and the rest he must scratch around for from other kinsmen, maternal kin and bond-friends, though these are more likely to give him smallstock, which are also welcome as part of bridewealth. The fiancé may not meet the demands, and have to seek a downward

---

[6] To help someone raise bridewealth shares the same term (*akibut*) as compensating a family for the homicide of a member, and the standard number of cattle is the same. In marriage the girl's family give a productive life, a trained bearer of children and grower of crops, to an unrelated family. Congruent compensation is to be expected.

[7] The etymology of honour (*apolou*) is the 'the quality of bigness'.

revision, but so long as he has shown himself assiduous in his cattle-raising task, it may suffice for a father who calculated the formal demand to maintain his reputation. Or he may permit late payment of the shortfall. Adjustments are agreed, when the fiancé takes gifts of food (*akimuj*) to his fiancée's parents.

Cracking the Number

After many months of perambulating with his wand (Jie) or trumpet (*arupepe*, Karimojong), when the fiancé has enough cattle offered him to go through with the marriage, he goes with his close agnates to the home of his intended for what the Jie call *ebilanů* (Locap 1989:2; J15). They go with feathers, headdresses and giraffe- or ox-tail fly-whisks to ask for formal permission to wed. The fiancé announces the number of livestock each of the other party, cognatic and agnatic relatives, and also bond-friends will receive.

Announcing the Wedding

When all are satisfied about the composition and distribution of bridewealth, another meeting is held at the fiancée's home, where the two clan-parties gather together (*atukokin*), bring food and eat it sitting on an ox-hide (*ejamu*), to fix the wedding day. The wedding day is arranged. Usually it will come in a festive season after the harvest, not in a new moon, but counting from it. It is then announced (*alimor ekutan*, Locap 1989:2). There is no verbal distinction between the wedding day and the marriage process, both are *ekutan* (Ngadodosô and Ngajie) or *ekitanů* (Ngakarimojong), which suggests that the wedding only intensifies and symbolizes the process. From now until the wedding, claimants of bridewealth outside the bridal *ere* family may collect their share from the fiancé.

Driving the Cattle

Two days before the wedding, when as much bridewealth as possible has been assembled by the fiancé, he and his *ere* family show it off by wearing celebratory dress, including knee-bells and giraffe- or zebra-tail elbow whisks, and driving the cattle (*akiram ngaatuk*) round the fiancée's neighbourhood with the maximum of joyful noise. They are given beer, and steer-songs are sung by the fiancé and his friends with gusto. Well might he rejoice, for he has reached the position to fulfil all his obligations to his fiancée's clan, and can savour the sweet distillation of marital order, cattle.

Wedding

The wedding is the most important day of the marriage. The bridegroom's party gather in the morning, replete with freshly oiled beads and skin, and ilmenite and oil hairstyles for the women, ostrich feathers and knee-bells for the men. Each woman carries a straight stick to symbolize that the marriage will be straight and good, and dances and shouts on the way to the bride's home. On arrival in the cattle corral, the close agnates remove their sandals, and wait, while the bride's family feigns indifference. Eventually they are seated on the ground of the bride's mother's *ekal*, and the bride's father rises to open the men's business: 'I speak of cattle'. The oft-used arguments of the need for, and the lack of, cattle are rehearsed once more. Beer aids the tongues (P5; Dyson-Hudson, V.R. and N. 1962:50).

The bridegroom's party tells them the promised division (*akidwar*) of the remaining livestock and their hide-markings. The bridewealth settled, the bridegroom's group rejoins the rest of the party bringing the bride's father's share of the cows and two beloved oxen, one (*lokiriket*)[8] for the bride's elders, the other for her mother's mother. They pass to the right of the homestead, and then, when they are about 100 metres from the entrance, they charge into the cattle corral, singing the praises of the beloved-oxen. The bridegroom, who carries the oryx horn, and wears a leopard-skin on a cowhide cape, and one white ostrich feather in the midst of a mass of closely cropped black ones, tries to pass through the women of the bride's *ere* family. The woman who is able to snatch the white feather is entitled to claim, and receive, a number of cows (Persse 1934:111; Locap 1989:3).

All the young people begin dancing in the cattle corral, before moving to the neighbourhood dancing ground, where over a hundred people gather, and the bridegroom has the first dance. Weddings have a special dance (*ekamar*) where a male dancer can only jump in the air four times, and then give way to another. The male faces the group of unmarried girls also rhythmically jumping, with their leather skirts swaying from side to side. The consequent flash of thigh lends the erotic element for the men, but the dance is a disciplined and physically taxing rigmarole.[9] Meanwhile the bridegroom takes his close agnates aside to revise the bridewealth plans, and to sing his initiation songs, praising the emblem of his generation while miming its actions.

Hours later the bridegroom leads his sub-clan elders to the sleeping hides in front of the bride's mother's hut. Seated on a hide (*ejamu*) he promises the bride's sub-clan to hand over the remaining bridewealth. An old woman of the bride's clan fills a pipe with a clay bowl and a sorghum stem and gives it to the bride's father, who smokes it and rubs the ash into the sleeping hide. Then the bridegroom's father, then the bridegroom, then the bride's mother, and so all the elders 'smoke the tobacco pipe which signifies total unity and sharing of other things between the two families' (Locap 1989:3). They are feasted on sorghum *atap*, sometimes mixed with milk, and strong beer. The bridegroom's 'sisters', including half-sisters (*ngakaipapai*) and probably cousins (*ngakaiyeyai*) in the *ere*, are given a share of beer (*nakiruet*[10]) as a reward for watering the bridewealth beasts. The 'sisters' of the bride's clan are also given a share (*najaluntet*) to make it easier to part with (*akijal*) their sleeping companion.

The bridegroom's brothers come into the girls' area with a ram (*emesek*) and when they have cadged some of their beer, they push the ram into the bride's mother's hut, where she is supposed to stay for the whole day. If the bridegroom (*eteran*) and not his father or brother, wore the ceremonial dress, then he must go back home to spend the night.

---

[8] The one of the assembly (*akiriket*), which itself may have its origins in the kill of a hunt.
[9] The author was participant–observer in one such dance.
[10] Cf. *akiruet* (water trough).

Totting up

The next day, the two clans return to the bride's father's homestead where they agree the numbers of cattle handed over (*lomari*), and any outstanding balance. Marriage is the only occasion for which it is necessary to count (*akimar*) cattle. For the Jie, the wedding is a two-day feast, and the bridegroom's party come to collect the bride. The *lokiriket* (sacrificial) bullock is slaughtered by the bride's clan elders for everybody to eat (J30). For the Karimojong, it often coincides with the wedding day. Clan and *ere* family gather for a feast, to approve the bride's departure, despite her formal show of sadness.

The girl's parents anoint the visitors on the face and chest with sacred, blue-grey clay (*emunyen*). They tell them, 'Go, and multiply, and live peaceably!' (P5), to bless her in prayer for her fertility and happiness (P5; Gulliver 1953a:152). They tell the visitors to take the woman.[11] In deliberate exchange the visitors tell them when to come for the balance of the cattle. Her father may provide a few stock to ensure that she has access to milk. At this sorghum beer feast, the bridegroom and his *ere* family are still mere guests, but afterwards the ritual separation of him and the bride's mother is ended. Once bridewealth has been given to the bride's father, with the attendant celebrations, the marriage is sealed, the two clans have been bonded together, and both are committed to the marriage and individually to each other. 'You know a woman is married if stock have been given' (Gulliver 1955:228).

Leather Skirt

The bride remains a bride (*ateran*) while she continues to reside at her father's home. The biggest change in a woman's life is traditionally approached slowly, although a Karimojong bride usually leaves home on the wedding day and a Jiot bride the following day. From the *ere* family wedding, approval and blessing of the marriage is widened by the bride's father's age-set 'brethren' joining her clansfolk to perform a ritual (*lobwo*) to promote its success. She is allowed to wear a goat- or gazelle-skin skirt with gussets and flanges on the hem, whose number denotes her marital position. After this, she may visit the bridegroom's home for a few days.

Clan Ceremonies

Different clans have different rites, such as *loburia, lomalol, lobunat* or *lokidor*, to mark, and to assist, the transition of the bride from her father's clan to the bridegroom's (Gulliver 1953a:151–3; Lamphear 1976:82; Rowland 1983:9). They reveal the clan's origins, for the middle two involve the suffocation, with a woman's apron for *lobunat*, of a sacrificial animal reminiscent of the Western Nilotic Nuer and Dinka sacrifice to ensure fertility (Evans-Pritchard 1956:217), while *lokidor* (cf. *ekidor*, cattle-gate into the corral) is much more the orthodox Eastern Nilotic sacrifice of a bullock, with prayers to Akujů. Distinctive dresses for the bride are handed down from long ago.

---

[11] *Arikor* is also used of taking away a slave, and the hunting terminology of *rik suggests relics of bride-capture here. She may in fact be carried away.

Moving in

While the bride is in her father's home, her mother directs her household activities; in her new home, she will be accountable to her husband and his *ere* family, not to her mother at all. These separate lines of responsibility are not confused. Different clans have different ways of inducting a new wife, but all make clear her fresh duties and allegiances. She is escorted (*akiniamun*), led by the arms or carried to the bridegroom's home, while his party imitates their generation-set emblem. 'Before she enters the home, sacred grass (*emuria*, *Cynodon dactylon*) is dipped into the water in a gourd to sprinkle the girl to bless her. "You are welcome."' (P5) The first old woman to join that clan takes the lead in cleansing and washing away the custom (*etal*) of the bride's old home (P5; J15). She is taken through the cattle entrance (*ekidor*) and put into his mother's hut, where she might stay the first night. Grass is put in a gourd inside the hut. Sticks from sacred trees (*etirir* and *ekapelimen*, *Acacia spirocarpa* and *nilotica*) are buried in the floor of the hut. A small fire is lit in the middle, as is often done for warmth, and to repel insects, and the smoke envelops her. She is symbolically immersed in the domesticity of the social unit, to which she now belongs (Persse 1934:111; Clark 1952b:177). In many clans, she spends her first night with the bridegroom's mother who, no doubt, tells her about the clan customs and the idiosyncrasies of her son, if not the mother, her daughters, or the unmarried girls of the *ere* family, with whom she must work and take her place.

She lives alone, except for the bridegroom's mother or for small children, for the first two nights. Then her clan come for the balance of her bridewealth. If the livestock are less than stipulated in the contract, then they take their daughter back. She takes clothes and beer to her father's home. A week later she takes more beer there. Though she blackens her hair with ash from the bridegroom's home, she may go back to her father's home until such time as her husband calls her (J30).

If the bridewealth contract is fulfilled, then the bride can only come out of the hut in the morning, when, called by her mother-in-law (*akamuran*), she is taken inside the cattle corral. She removes her daughter-in-law's (*ateran*) decorations and dress, which are returned to her old home, to be given the clan status symbols of the married women in the *ere* family who have a peculiar solidarity, in that all were born outside it. After all her clothes and decorations have been removed, she is anointed with boiled ghee (butter oil) in a gourd. The daughters, who were born inside the *ere* family, also have a part in anointing her with ghee. She is taken inside a hut. The groom puts a necklet and belt of star-grass (*emuria*, *Cynodon dactylon*) as a sign of spiritual peace on the bride (P5), and anoints the top half of her body with ghee. Then she goes to the corral, where the men of the *ere* ceremonially beat her with *lokaliye* (*Grewia trichocarpa*) switches to prove her fealty. When she agrees to look after the livestock herded from home (*akitwar*), the bridegroom will give her one cow in milk (*anyarare*) for her children. When she drinks the milk straight from the teat, then she becomes a woman of the home. The women of the *ere* introduce her to the context of a woman's important tasks. She is allocated an *ekal*, with hut and granaries, some fields nearby, and a grindstone. The girls show her, in a manner which reminds her of her novice status, where to collect brushwood, and where to draw water, which she then does in obeisance to her mother-in-law (Persse 1934:112; Dyson-Hudson, V.R. 1962:52; Locap 1989:3f).

The bride grinds sorghum to prepare *atap* for the bridegroom. She goes in the hut to sweep it and smear it with cow-dung 'to prepare for her husband'. The night is spent in her new hut with the bridegroom, which will not be a comfortable time, especially on ox-hides. In the morning, they will be husband and wife, and not before, however many children she has borne or alternative rites they have undergone or been denied. 'After the husband sleeps with her, she is *aberu*, accepted by all' (P5). The couple will be recognized as fully man (*ekile*) and wife (*aberu*) and she as part of the *ere* family as few as three, or as many as 20, years after meeting (*Report of the Committee on the Revision of Marriage Laws* 1962:2).

Birth

The first birth from an approved union is blessed by the father sacrificing a bullock for his clan, and giving its hide to the bride to sleep on. The senior people of the new father's clan celebrate with *atap*, milk and beer. To become father or mother is to experience a significant rise in social status. The mother also is grateful for the additional security, that she is unlikely to be returned to her father for barrenness. So is her clan, who would have to return the bridewealth. If a woman for whom some of the bridewealth has been paid is near to giving birth at her father's home, she must be brought to her fiancé/groom's home to deliver. If it is too far then the grandmother or an elderly female relative from his home must go to attend the birth, so that she can name the baby when it first sucks (J30).

Traditional midwives are very efficient in their task, receiving the baby in front of the mother, while she pushes in a kneeling position. They wash it with cold water, tie the umbilical cord with fibre, cut it with a knife for a girl, or an arrow (*emal*) for bleeding cattle if it is a boy. Any Western programme of primary health care needs to work with the highly influential traditional birth attendants to achieve their aims for the health of the population (Graham 1999). They learn by watching their mother practise or for explicitly religious reasons, 'Akujů told me to', and some will be acknowledged as specially gifted, or also be an *amuron*. No special ceremonies are used, though traditional medicine may be, to assist mother and child in the process of labour (J30), which is seen as a primarily practical concern, but birth is not seen as a merely physical event. Children watching in the hut announce the birth outside. After childbirth the old women bless the eyes of the midwife, because otherwise she would be blinded by watching too much childbirth (Graham 6.4.01). Birth is an occasion, then, of dangerous power, an intense moment of life, followed by a time of vulnerability for the newborn baby, as careful precautions are made against possible witchcraft by some members of other clans. The cord and the afterbirth are buried in the cattle corral. A woman who has a gazelle-skin on her breast when she delivers will enjoy good fortune (Gourlay 1971b:84). Only in the early stages of breastfeeding will a woman wear a hide over her breasts to ward off the evil-eye.

The baby is given the names of a relative in its grandparents' generation and/or a name relating to the circumstances of the birth, if born in its father's home. The choice is made by the old ladies of the *ere* family sitting watching while they eat *atap*, take snuff (*etaba*) or smoke pipes. They recite possible names, until such time as the babe latches onto the breast, the coincident name sticking. Then the *ere* family sings, jumps and praises its oxen (J30). Feasting, music and dancing may follow. The moment of the baby suckling is of great moment, for it is at that point that the human being is attributed legal and social personality. Without sucking, it is no more than anonymous flesh that has succumbed to the action of spirits or witchcraft, which helps families to cope with high neo-natal mortality, if not preventing torturous grief.

For three days, mother and baby stay in the hut, and for many more the husband cannot even go inside (J30; Persse 1934:112; Rowland 1983:7). By that time the baby's umbilical cord has dried up. A tabu on sexual intercourse is common so long as the mother is breast-feeding, perhaps two years or more. Then they shave the baby's head, and the old women are given beer. A ritual is observed for twins (*etal a ngimuu*), whereby a ram or he-goat is sacrificed (Gourlay 1971b:142). The ram is a potent symbol of fertility as one may be sacrificed at four points in the marriage process.[12] Twins are welcomed except by clans reflecting Western Nilotic values, which see their birth as a misfortune, which may prompt infanticide. In any case the weaker twin is expected to die, but as a rule the more children the merrier for the Karamojong, for all are blessings, indeed answers to prayer, from Akujů. Yet, as for a breech delivery, still birth or miscarriage, a tiny shrine is constructed out of a bunch of dried grass under the eaves of the thatched hut in order to pacify any disturbed ancestral spirit that must have caused such an abnormality. Beer will be brewed from the first fruits of the harvest every year in order to pour a libation at the shrine.

Ram Sacrifice

To mark the birth, the father's mother sacrifices a ram (*emesek*), the head of the *ere* family receiving the tongue, a shoulder and some ribs, the women and children the rest. The ram's skin is used to make a sling for the baby, and the father will put its skull over the door of the mother's hut to protect her children (Persse 1934:113; Gulliver 1953c:152). The grandmother anoints the couple with ram's fat as they sit in front of the husband's old hut, blessing them, so that they may bear many children for society. With the meat as a sign, the father and mother 'save' or liberate each other, redeeming each other in marital bonds by which society has bound each to serve the other (Locap 1989:3).

Barrenness

Any marriage cannot be fulfilled until it has borne fruit in children. To be barren, which is not commonly a permanent condition among Karamojong women, is to be cursed by man or God, subject to the reproach of co-wives, and to be denied full adult status in society. Such a situation is not lightly entered into, so Karimojong like to see at least one baby born before the mother moves out of her father's home,

---

[12] Ram sacrifice in marriage is seen as an 'Old Semitic' development (Baldick 1998:133). Mirzeler (1999:136) notes the sacrifice of a black ram by women at the end of the weeding season to smear on the sorghum to protect it from insects and disease.

and the Jie two, preferably including a boy able to walk, which is encouraged very early instead of crawling. Should a bride prove to be barren, the bridegroom's *ere* family has the legal right to sue for the return of the bridewealth and the voiding of the marriage process. This right does not have to be exercised, but for the poor family, which cannot afford two marriages, it is a virtual necessity in order to have children for the continuation of the ere family as a viable unit. Marriage is to serve the *ere* family, so that the *ere* family can guarantee the marriage.

Under these circumstances, the bride should not move away from the support and protection of her *ere* family, until all the conditions of marriage in its fulness have been met. All is not lost, even if the bridewealth is returned, which is at least as difficult a procedure as paying it in the first place, and the bride returns to being a girl (*apese*). She may still be the object of attention for a man who accepts the position and the much reduced bridewealth involved, and, in time, she may well conceive. If a man's sterility is established, *ere* families on both sides will be less likely to contract a marriage whose future is hazardous. It is probable that an otherwise healthy and able man would be prepared to start his family with the help of an age-set companion, since the genitor is of less significance than the legal father. Or he can marry a girl who has produced children by another man who has failed to amass the bridewealth.

Polygyny

All of Gulliver's sample (1955:242) of 62 Jie men over 45 had at least one wife. The largest proportion, 37 per cent, had two, and 32 per cent had from three to six. With males marrying 10–40 years later than females in a population with a growing proportion of youth, polygyny still has a sound demographic future. In a growing population or one that has a significant adult mortality rate,[13] both of which apply to the Karamojong, older men, whose eligibility for marriage is defined by wealth in cattle, will always be considerably outnumbered by eligible girls. This is even so in absolute population terms as Karamoja has by far the lowest sex ratio in Uganda: 67–89.9 males to 100 females (Uganda Census 2001). Since marrying wives is a long-run route to wealth in stock, through rearing many cattle herdsmen and cattle-earning daughters, it remains attractive. A rich man has a social obligation to redistribute his cattle by marrying many wives, but which he can turn to personal advantage in terms of building *ere* family alliances. Rich *ere* families tend to intermarry with rich *ere* families, and it is difficult for a man from a poor *ere* family to satisfy a girl from a rich one.

The disadvantages of polygyny are the problems of success: competing interests between different *ngikalya* in the *ewae*, with wives championing the interests of their sons or themselves. Wife-beating is not the irrational response of frustrated men so much as an exercise in family discipline which is generally accepted. It does establish patriarchal primacy, but women are still vocal in standing up for themselves, individually and in groups.

---

[13] Cattle-raiding and polygyny are closely connected. The main motive for raiding is so that the raider can quickly marry several wives to establish his socio-economic position. If he loses his life in the process, then his behaviour lowers the sex ratio.

4 Instances of the Process of Marriage

To take a specific example of marriage, I have selected Apei Aleper, the daughter of Nacam, Lamphear's sole surviving informant, since I knew the family from 1984. The father was born in 1912 (J30), she about 56 years later, and a further sibling 86 years later. The active part of her marriage process so far was between 1987 and 1995. In 1987, she met Lokol, then about 30 years old, on the way to her locality (J5). He enquired about her, came to know her family, and attended the local dances. He used to go to her hut and talk with her privately. Then the family insisted they would not allow him in, as he would have to marry her according to custom. Without delay he gave Nacam eight head of cattle as down-payment of bridewealth, so that no-one else would take her. Aleper asked her female friends who knew him and her sisters, and they all approved, so they connived with her to allow him further visits.

When she became pregnant, his parents came to the homestead for the first round of negotiations, *edyekir* (apology, beseeching unity) and were told they could not take the girl, unless they bring cows. So they had to go home and organize another party to come for the second round, *eleto*, to check whether the girl is still for the match. Then in January 1988 they brought 90 head of cattle. At this point her family would have allowed her to be taken but, traditionally, she chose to wait for the process of *ebilanû* to be completed. The suitor puts a white feather in his hair, and goes round his relative and friends with an *ebela*, a wand, symbolizing that he is seeking contributions to his bridewealth. First they promised the exact contribution they intended to make, then they had to deliver. When the suitor had gathered, in this case the full number, both sides prepared beer for *atukokin*, a gathering of many people from both clans in December 1988 to fix the day of the wedding, which is the day of the official exchange of gifts.[14]

On the morning of *ekutan*, the bridegroom's party took more cattle to the bride's home. A ram was taken with a few sheep, so that the ram could be sacrificed for Aleper's step-mother to eat (her mother having died). The *lokiriket* (sacrificial) bull was slaughtered by the relatives of her father who all benefited from the bridewealth, and who in return had to pay a cow to the bridegroom's party. Aleper was taken to Lokol's home to shed the customs (*ngitalia*), clothes and decorations of her past life, to be inducted into those of her husband's family. There she acquired a mother-in-law (Naporit, J32) and three co-wives, though only one other (the first wife, Akut J4) had passed the stage of *ekutan*, because they had chosen to live with Lokol before he had brought sufficient cattle.

None of the wives had undergone the final stage of marriage, because Lokol has not been initiated. When he is, and *ekutan* has been performed, then the wives can share in their husband's initiation (*asapan*) by being anointed in her husband's homestead with ghee cooked in a clay pot (J20). Then, with her enrolment into the women's initiation group which shadows the man's, Aleper will have fully taken on the roles of wife and mother. She was still facing problems, particularly famine

---

[14] If the moon is 'dying', they do not fix the date until five days after the new moon has been sighted.

(*akoro*), because of the total harvest failure the previous August, but, with typical resourcefulness, she was still able to produce some groundnuts. However she did not look strong and fit and the shrine had been set up on the wall of the hut for libations to appease the angry spirit, which had taken away two of her four children.

There is nothing untraditional about the marriage of Lokol and Aleper. Moreover it fits her elderly father's separate account of marriage (J30), and others' through half a century (Clark 1952b; Gulliver 1953a;[15] Dyson-Hudson, V.R. and N. 1962:46–8; Locap 1989). Radcliffe-Brown's successors are disproving his dictum, 'We cannot have a history of African institutions' (1950:2). Other marriages adhere less closely to the norms, when the girl goes to live at the suitor's home without all the conditions for *ekutan* having been met, testifying to the fact that she came from a good home.

How protracted and irregular the process may be is instanced by the suit of Teko Apalomedica Lokwangiryang, who was initiated at 15, but is now white-haired, and Locia Lokero, about 33, who has six children and has lost two, and has been living in Teko's home for six years. Cattle had begun to pass, so she was rightfully engaged, but she had been willing to go to live in his home before there was any prospect of *ekitanŭ*. They had only reached the third payment of bridewealth, which consisted of two young oxen, two heifers, two beloved oxen, and two other oxen being taken round the corrals of the woman's Tiang clan at Cilapus in Oding. The suitor and his brother went from homestead to homestead in their ceremonial gear of headdresses with ostrich feathers, knee-bells and a modern whistle. An old lady carried the *ebilanŭ*.

At the woman's homestead they made a mock charge with their spears, and after waiting were invited into the cattle corral and seated around a large gourd of beer, where they were served with boiled sorghum and cow-peas. It was agreed that, in two days' time, Teko would spear a large beloved ox in an *akiriket* to discuss with the elders the day of *ekitanŭ*. It had already been agreed that the bride's uncle would have 13 cows, but the counting would not be completed until *ekitanŭ*. For an honourable marriage he knew the total would have to come to at least 60 cattle. So, though he had been having sexual relations with Locia for perhaps 16 years, Teko

---

[15] Gulliver claims many informants, but there are still grounds for confusion in his 15-stage account. He claims that *ekotan* [sic] is the whole process, but the Jie clearly associate it with the event of the exchange of bride for cattle. In ordering the 'stages', he overlooks the frequent occurrence, which he acknowledges even then, that children may be born before *ekutan* or, less commonly, that the girl has already become a concubine. Stages 9–15 are not stages in a common process, but ceremonies according to clan customs (*ngitalyo*). Gulliver (1953a:153) claims, 'Variations according to clan membership are not great and have no effect on the general pattern of the total process.' Indeed they do not, but that there are many different ways of initiating or confirming the bride into the customs of her new clan is attested by Lamphear (1976:82f), who associates particular customs with the origins of particular clans. The *ebele* is not 'an ordinary fighting stick', but a wand newly peeled of its bark and distinctively white. He overlooks the important ceremony of anointing. These inaccuracies disqualify the account from serving as a control, whereby all subsequent accounts may be judged as departures from a tradition.

had not quite reached the point of being able to announce the wedding. At *akiriket* elders preach about bridewealth not being paid, 'so many girls being taken by men, but the cows are not being brought'. Yet this is not evidence of a fatal crisis in marriage so much as a determination not to let sacred social institutions slip, despite the inevitable problems of life, all of which are topics for preaching and prayer. The family to whom pregnancy compensation is due may disturb the suitor 'every time, even daily'.

5 Challenges to Marriage

Adultery

Adultery is to have sexual relations with a married woman (*aberu*) usually by the risky method of entering the husband's home at night in his absence. It is as serious a crime as homicide, and is punishable in like manner, with much pragmatism. The punishment for adultery lies largely with the wronged family. If he is jealous and powerful, he and his clan may take the adulterer's life, and the adulteress's. It is permissible to punish the offender (*ekasecan*[16]) by death through driving a stick through the anus of an adulterer or the vagina of an adulteress, because the sinner has spoilt or polluted society by overturning the social order. The wife of a Dodosoit government chief was punished thus at Kopus in December 1997 (J33). Or the husband may require the adulterer to take her to wife on penalty of 60 cattle (P5). However the more tolerant or cattle-interested man can cut his losses by divorce and regain of all the bridewealth (P5). If a woman commits adultery after the final stage of marriage, anointing (*ekios*), it is believed that it will be shown with bloody diarrhoea which adversely affects the clans of both the man and his wife and their animals through many incidents (J20).

In order for forgiveness to clear up the social disaster, the adulterer must slaughter a ram, as a 'sacred animal for peace', in the wife's home for the land not to be polluted by the transgression (P5). The adulteress must provide sorghum beer, sacrifice a cow and a ram (her mother would have been given a ram as part of the marriage ritual), and the old women of the homestead must smear her with the sacred chyme (*ngikujit*) to cleanse her from her pollution (J20, P11). The real and extended value attached to marriage, as well as the institution of polygyny, mean only the rash aspire to adulterous acts, more likely with strangers than in a community where he will be soon known. Adultery, then, still brings more problems than it is worth, especially when sexual relations with the unmarried are not tabu.

---

[16] Literally, 'he who causes problems'. Punishing adultery with a person's life or the value in livestock of a life is confirmed by Gulliver (1953a:155 n1).

Source: Ben Knighton

Photograph 4.1 Teko and brother processing around the clan homesteads of his betrothed before making a bridewealth payment

Divorce

As divorce involves the repayment of bridewealth, it is an infrequent event, but for the Jie, whose marital process is even more protracted than the Karimojong's, it hardly ever happens. Since there are plenty of exit options before bridewealth is paid, most of the obstacles to a good marriage have already been encountered. If they cannot be overcome, the man is unlikely to be motivated to raise the bridewealth. When the wife does not go to a second man, she returns to her parental home with her children, who revert to the generation and family of the mother's brothers, unless the husband makes some special arrangement by granting stock to keep them. There is no evidence that divorce is increasing.

Rape

Rape is seriously tabu, since it pollutes the country by inviting the wrath of Akujů. It is punishable by a fine of 60 cattle, exactly the same as for murder and adultery, though the Pian may be more forbearing (J22, P5). The government itself has blessed the elders' sentencing policy of 60 cattle for adultery and rape which includes any sex in the open bush. There have been many allegations of rape by Karamojong warriors in districts to the southwest. This would appear to be a new development as raiding used to be more of a hit-and-run affair in the past, while recently massed cattle-camps (*ngalomarin*) have the military power to hang around agrarian settlements for weeks and be tempted to abuse it. However these atrocities have no bearing on domestic institutions, since they do not pollute the Karamojong land or society, and happen to foreigners who have no protection from Karamojong law. The main threat to Karamojong marriage would be in the importation of HIV which, despite, or because of, polygyny, has made very little advance in Karamoja. One elder (J30) was worried about HIV, because of its heavy publicity on Ugandan radio, but he had never seen anyone with AIDS. The Karamojong are most unlike other peoples in Uganda.

Illicit Unions

Cohabitation with no agreement between parents is more common in those areas most influenced by trade, education and Christian mission (Broussard 1989), that is, the vicinity of townships. It is here that young people have an opportunity to live away from parental discipline, especially in boarding schools. Those separated from the pastoral life are more influenced by the marital chaos prevailing in urban Uganda, and more likely to conceive children without any idea of how to be responsible for them. The children themselves become dependent on the streets, boarding schools and missions for food.

Youth Sub-culture

There is also a tendency for young people to take the initiative so far as to start cohabiting before the exchange of cattle,[17] instead of parents selecting a desirable

---

[17] Of Lokol's four wives (good going when uninitiated) only two had passed through

ere family for a marriage alliance. However the greater involvement of young people in marriage may well serve to perpetuate the traditional forms, where pastoralist values dominate, since the formal ceremonies have not been divested of meaning, rather, they may even take a notable place in a township. It is difficult for an outside observer to see anything but confusion when men, women and children are indeterminately related, and living in different places, but this is the inevitable expression of a marriage process which produces no final certainty and cohabitation, until it is completed, rather than a legal moment which suddenly defines the unmarried as married. Church weddings remain extremely rare and their symbols, such as the white wedding dress and bridesmaids, thoroughly European. All Karamojong women, and their children, desire the full status of customary marriage if possible.

Within the mêlée of sexual relations, there is still evident a high moral view of marriage, and the ambition of the young to inherit it is undimmed. Having entered the long process, appreciation of its wider import for society grows. 'Marriage in Jie–Karamoja is a very important activity as it creates families, conpensates [sic] parents for the bringing up of their daughters, bring [sic] unity or relationship to the society and putting couples in the respected position in the community' (Locap 1989:4).

Males appear to start begetting children at a younger age and at an earlier stage in the marriage process than in former times, but this impression needs statistical research. More serious for the long-term future of the culture is that, if the biological age between a father and his eldest son is reducing from 35–40 to nearer 20, the generation system will be besieged by more over aged men than it can handle, leading to the attenuation of the main institution, which prevents Karamojong society from splitting into blood-feuding segmentary lineages. If marriage can contain within its publicly acknowledged process the full expression of sexual intercourse, a structural social unity may be perpetuated. These criteria are themselves dependent on pastoralist values and the ritual performance of their faith in Akujů.

Paul Spencer's 'pastoral continuum' in East Africa, which recognizes a range of changing customs persisting through time, is typified by age-systems and marriage, especially polygyny (1998:2–4). For polygyny sustains a more viable family enterprise, favouring elders and delaying the marriages of younger men. To analyse the current state and trends of marriage is then to gain an insight not only into the strength of the social fabric, but also into the power of the gerontocracy.

Elders assert that in general marriage has not changed, and all ceremonies remain applicable (J10,30). A member of the junior generation confirms that the elders' power in this matter is being maintained (J23). There are certainly stiff sanctions available to support the institution. Waiving bridewealth, lowering the average amount exchanged or reducing it to monetary consideration would be a sure sign that marriage in a pastoral society is in disequilibrium or even crisis (Spencer 1998:87). The kinship

---

ekutan, though this seemed not to diminish their social seniority within the home. On the other hand the mother of a one-year-old baby, whose parents had only met the father's parents once, had not left her parental home (J15).

structure loses the binding power and trust created by the exchange of cattle between clans, and the introduction of cash into this highly symbolic social feature would signify the onset of cultural dependency on external capitalism and a calculative approach to the payment of bridewealth rather than trust in the promise of cattle. In many cases the promises take years to fulfil by the actual payment of livestock, but the system, built upon mutual trust, does not break down under the weight of frustration, whereas the medium of cash, being controlled by an alien government without regard to the effects of devaluation and inflation, has not evinced the confidence of the Karamojong for their future livelihoods, which depend on cattle.

Bridewealth continues to be paid. Only 4.5 per cent of girls on average achieve literacy (Uganda Census 2001) and they still want to be fully married if at all possible. In the terrible times of the 1890s bridewealth went down to only one or two oxen, but in the 1950s the mean was 63, ranging from 30 to 100, cattle or equivalent (Clark 1952b:177; Gulliver 1955:229). In the 1960s the figure could range from five to 200 (Dyson-Hudson, V.R. and N. 1962:46). It dropped in the great famine of 1979–82, but was raised to 100 in 1989 (Locap 1989) when raiding had multiplied cattle riches. The norm is 80 now, but can range from 75 to 120, the point in the range being defined by familial and personal differentials (J22). Thus the standard level of bridewealth is as high now as half a century ago, and rising. It is relatively very high for East Africa. The social valuation of marriage by the Karamojong is thus very strong, being independent of environmental determinism.

The payment is just that as a concept;[18] it is the releasing of a due, the fulfilment of a contractual obligation and the contract is not private, but social, between two clans as all marriage is exogamous. The bulk of its value must be in cattle, which remain the primordial sacrament of cultural well-being (Knighton 1990:I,343–5). When I last saw my friend Longoli (J23), he had five wives and 25 children. One of them had given birth to a baby daughter a couple of days beforehand, and the baby had been named, so could not now be classified as a neo-natal fatality. He was looking forward to claiming his three bulls in the course of the following year, now that the obligation of payment had arisen. 'The bridewealth for the first daughter is for the father to marry again,' he said. Thus it is explicitly for the benefit of patriarchy and polygyny. Sons, in order of age, can only expect to be helped with their bridewealth after the second daughter has married, if the father has no surplus, which in this instance was the case, since Longoli's cattle had recently been raided by the Dodosô and the livestock in his corral were on loan from a friend.

Yet the Karamojong system of marriage has always been able to absorb innumerable variations, especially involving the birth of children and the timing of bridewealth payments without the norms being overturned or forgotten (J7,J15). Women aspire to their full rôle in the culture, but when poverty and disaster intrude, as they frequently do in nomadic pastoralism, then arrangements are made pragmatically and provisionally according to circumstance or negotiation. Despite contingencies, Gulliver's assessment still applies (1953a:154): 'Carried out in the traditional order and manner, the whole process itself comes to have a mystical efficacy of its own in the minds of its participants.'

---

[18] Once the child has been named, 'he must pay even if she dies' (J23).

There is a warning for the future stability of marriage, in that the fathers have noted a tendency for both sexes to be marrying younger and having children younger (J10,20; P5). Marriage and cohabitation are begun at an earlier age, owing to changing expectations being mediated through the radio and other contacts from Ugandan society. If the mother is with child and has not moved from her father's home and famine strikes, difficulties may be caused when the suitor gives up that suit and starts another (J20). Irresponsible behaviour will bring its own retribution in the end, as less weight will be given in political affairs to the voice of the wayward, and no child is ever unwanted to the Karamojong, the legal father being more important than the biological.

However the effects of such a trend may be considerable in the long term. If young men gather several concubines or wives, it reduces the supply of girls available to others, including the elders, and means they have concerns, like the elders, in the home, at an age when their forebears were living the Spartan life of a warrior with the cattle. This luxury for younger men is probably connected to the current riches in cattle due to military superiority over their neighbours, so may pass with leaner times when greater dependency on their fathers for cattle returns. Alternatively the change can be seen as a continuation of the ebb and flow of the never-ending struggle between the generations for power in society and for control of the means of production, distribution and exchange of livestock. That is precisely what is symbolized by the generation-set moieties, whose ritual opposition and cyclical replacement in power have proved a most effective way of dealing with the tensions and taking the culture through to the future. There is also the muted resistance of women to the deliberate self-interest of patriarchs, who seem to have lost a battle, though not a sudden one, in allowing their daughters to choose whether they leave home before wedding, rather than extracting the maximum number of cattle.

6 A Contingent Conclusion

One father tries to balance the trends of continuity and change:

> Education is bringing change. Parents always used to advise, but now students agree on marriage themselves. But even educated girls want to go through the stages to *aberu*. The church is breaking the law not having a distinction between good and bad in society. Society does not recognize church marriage because it devalues society. There are no animals for a church wedding. One in a hundred marry in church to keep the law of the church, but before *ekitanû*. Church people may not have animals, not participating in raids. Holding *ekitanû* before a church wedding is advisable, but it has not happened, except once. That was the marriage of Timos[19] and Florence, but he later became a polygynist. Marriage in home is good for rural people. (P5)

---

[19] Timothy Talep Lokwakenya is famous for marrying Florence in the church only after *ekitanû* in 1969. The traditional institution of marriage took precedence in his life, since he married a second wife in 1973.

He is wary for the future, well aware of the potential implications of school and church for society. Indeed he is over-pessimistic of the impact that education is having on culture. Elders' control over choice of marriage-partners increased in mid-century, and is hardly less than what it was 70 years ago, despite current sensitivities. The challenge of the younger generation for the older is perennial, as is the capacity of the old to feel unsettled by the vigour of youthful waywardness. Though there is change, the vast majority of Karamojong girls remain Karamojong and greatly desire to become *aberu*. If men are to secure them, they are obliged to show their dependence on social relationships, not just on the well-tried method of raiding in order to raise the bridewealth. In fact the large size of the raiding-parties makes it unlikely that a warrior will bag many cattle for himself. Thus begins the slow and subtle enculturation of rebellious youth into a growing appreciation of its social and religious heritage.

There is no doubt that military, political and economic shifts could have a pronounced effect on all this. If the Maseniko were really to trade their guns for the siren offer of 'development', radical change would result, as in so many other parts of Africa. Sharon Hutchinson (1990; 1996) charts a link between chronic civil war and rising divorce for the Nuer. She even has to depict the growing reality of Christian perspectives and literacy, despite their secularizing tendency there (1996:345; 2001:325). Yet obviously the Karamojong situation is very different.[20] Their divorces have never gone to court, and are not a common feature of Karamojong society. They know in advance what research has identified, that an increase in divorce accompanies an increased vulnerability to male demands, so that more opportunities for divorce go counter to women's general interests (Hutchinson 1990:408f). Karamojong women tend to be more conservative than the men, and often take a very vociferous, collective lead in countering the perceived cause of some unfortunate development.

Karamojong do value women and their rôles. The bridegroom takes a special cow in milk with her firstborn calf, a gourd from his home and the old women of the *ere*, when they go for *ekutan*. For one male elder (J31) the most sacred moment of the whole protracted process is when the two mothers enter the hut of the bride's mother to share a drink of milk from the gourd. Karamojong marriage (it is not necessary here to use the 'traditional' qualifier as the process is eventually so all-encompassing that there is no viable alternative) is not so much about the male exploitation of women, which happens with the separation of gender rôles in a capricious environment, as the wholesome ordering of society. It is about 'good animals, eating and drinking, no trouble' (J31). This is the good life desired for the whole community. These are the blessings of the God of peace, '*Akujů ngina akisil*' (J31). Thus it is that Karamojong marriage gently, gradually and unobtrusively enfolds the spiritual and the social.

---

[20] It is interesting to note that traditional features persist as in Karamoja. Bloodwealth rates are also closely linked to bridewealth (Hutchinson 1996:123), indicating an ancient Nilotic system of values. A Nuer return to a more traditional valuation of marriage should not be ruled out if they can regain some autonomy.

Chapter 5

Religion and Social Control

It is not possible to distinguish here between tradition or law as fixed impositions and custom as flexible and owned by the people. Customs (*ngitalyo*) are frequently rigid, and are often subject, though not in Karamoja, to colonial codification as 'customary law' (Gluckman 1969). Karamojong law is not written; it is not *lex*, but a body of oral tradition founded on moral consensus. Custom itself does not predetermine the solution to every case, but customary procedure entails a jury of elders to decide difficult cases where the dictates of custom fall short. If a man acts, even violently, to assert his moral rights, he is acting properly, and will not be condemned by society, although the same acts in an immoral cause will be censured. Traditional law is therefore internal and plastic to the culture, seldom an objective 'given' to be obeyed. Such law and its application, like morality, are frequently open to negotiation.

> Legality stems essentially from morality, and is in practice that part of rightful behaviour sanctioned by physical force. Not all moral standards have a legal coefficient nor even necessarily those which are given the highest regard in society. Moral standards, which have legal effect are such as to give a certain minimum of security and stability in that society. (Gulliver 1955:263)

A shared sense of morality starts from a collective or social memory, so 'control of a society's memory largely conditions the hierarchy of power' (Connerton 1989:1).

Discipline starts in the home, where the family heads may correct family misbehaviour with the sanction of beating wives or children. A young man will have cause to boast if he can escape censure for behaviour generally regarded as unacceptable, and it is regarded as foolish to obey obstructive commands when there is a way round them. The individualism of the Karamojong is a noted feature, and the most precious freedom for any man is to be able to accumulate and maintain his herds according to his own judgment. Family loyalty and alliances with other cattle-herders are a means to this end, so if they restrict ambition too long, family relations are strained and alliances shelved. Each herd-owner can pursue his strategy, but not to the detriment of the political community, which reacts after the event, if it must, rather than predetermining action. Punishment 'comes as a result of something' (P3). Government is keen to see a traditional solution to crime, but is powerless to mobilize the elders unless they themselves have seen a real cause to act.

Each Karamojongait is enculturated into morality negotiated thus, not only by his upbringing in the homestead, but also by the sermons delivered at *akiriket*, when the ideals and values of society are verbalized and reinforced. Appeals to conscience as an internalized ideal law fail to appreciate the moral economy (Lonsdale 1992b) of the Karamojong pastoralist, whose first duty is to protect and provide for his family. The only restraints on this are the pressure of the community and the correction of Akujů. The solution to the latter involves recruiting the community, not by personal, spiritual repentance or belief in ideal commandments.

1 Jurality

'Legality' is not the best term for a system of enforceable moral economy, since it implies the letter of the law. What is jural concerns the practice of justice in society, not by the codification or accumulation of precedent in law, but rather by custom and consensus. If a person wants a quiet life, he must live according to custom. If he frets against this and transgresses, which he is free to do, he may get away with it or the culture may catch up with him as he finds that it is his beloved oxen that are selected for the sacrifice, testing his obedience to convention when it matters. There is no-one to police a fixed, externally imposed law, apart from the administration *askaris* who are ineffective unless cooperating with the communal will to bring a miscreant to justice. There is no legal profession, and consequent established distinctions based on a literary culture do not exist. There are no judges, but a jury who, representing society, wants to see justice done and the genuine criminal brought to heel. A criminal is defined of course by Karamojong jurality, not by the law of any state.

There is no great distinction between civil and criminal law, for adultery has the same procedure and remedies as rape and murder. The legal owner (*elope*) has unassailable rights over his livestock, except that he has an inescapable obligation to the elders, when they select one of his animals for sacrifice (Gulliver 1955:233). A man cannot sue for the recovery of debts, but, if a party is sufficiently strong, it may settle a grievance by force. If the other party is at all to blame, there will be no chance of redress, for there is no code of law to which it can appeal, only innocence, and the sense of justice of the elders, who are reluctant to embroil themselves in disputes unless they perceive a threat to the social order. Thus fights with sticks are allowed to settle arguments, and precedence, between boys or men within and outside *ere* families. A wronged party may exact retribution, in livestock or even a life, unilaterally and forcibly from a miscreant, who, unless he has a well-supported cause, is powerless to respond legally (Dyson-Hudson 1966:220). Justice may be fairly rough, but it should not disturb the community.

Forensic issues are formally aired when a consensus emerges that a significant wrong has been done that needs to be redressed. Disputes are brought before a session of elders, male or female, yet not both sitting together. A recalcitrant offender may have to be forcibly brought by his age-set companions or, if a group, by the age-set senior to them. The recalcitrants are caught, severely beaten with switches before the elders, and driven (*akime*) to their herds to collect sacrificial animals to declare their allegiance to the elders (Lamphear 1976:151,158). This is the pastoral discipline of *ameto*,[1] which stands for the enforcement of justice by

---

[1] Cf. *amet* (to possess livestock); *ekameton* (herdsman, drover, shepherd). Prior to

punishment. If the accused successfully resists arrest, the elders have recourse to the curse, like, '*Totwan'kaina*' 'Die on the spot!' (Pazzaglia 1982:101n), appealing to Akujů's judgment, as the matter is out of their hands.

Crimes against the Person and his Property

The two parties must stand in court (*akiwo*)[2] before the elders. The defendant is accused, and pleads, 'Oh my father!', stating his case. The elders question them and the witnesses as to matters of fact, until they jointly are satisfied of the guilt of one or the other. Then they summarily pronounce sentence. If a murderer is put in the hands of the relatives of his victim, he may be killed on leaving the assembly, and the case is ended. The tardiness and prevarication of state justice has long been a frustrating mystery to the Karamojong. In 1998, three different instances of mob justice occurred in Kotido and Moroto, where the mob forcibly took charge of capital punishment from under the nose of the state, even removing one suspect from police cells and killing him in the administrative offices (Kidong-Onyang 1998:23). Quite apart from the tardiness of impartial systems of justice, criminals can bribe their way out.

In contrast, Karamojong jurality may summarily order a thief, '*Totac elope. Tarama emong. Kicum emong*' (Pazzaglia 1982:101n), 'Compensate the owner! Bring a steer! Spear the steer!' Sacrifice must be made for the elders at an *akiriket*. An adulterer must pay compensation to the husband, and sacrifice an ox. A young man who has illicit sexual intercourse with a girl may be beaten or killed if caught in the act, but this is primarily a matter for the *ere* family, not a public hearing. A wife can bring her husband to a male court, if he has wronged her, or beaten her too severely, in which case he will be reprimanded. A legal father, or mother, who has been beaten by a sibling may take him to court for disciplining. Murder may find retribution by clan vengeance (P5). If the murderer has fled out of reach, the brothers of the deceased may still exact the death sentence on a half-brother of the murderer (J33). The elders will do nothing unless there is an outcry, neither is it likely that anyone will report either killing to the local administration.

Crimes against Society

Some crimes are felt to be so heinous as to constitute a sin against the land, in which case no effort should be spared to restore justice to the country. Raiding cattle from, or warring against, fellow members of a territorial unit, and murder, or a threat to murder, are 'believed by the Jie directly to affect rainfall and fertility adversely' (Gulliver 1963:134). A brutal rape in broad daylight or flagrant disobedience of the elders are also very serious matters. In such cases, the senior elders of the area affected by the crime form a tribunal, or council, *atuk(ot)*, where they act as a self-directing jury (*ngikatubok ngakiro*[3]).

Novelli (1999:338f) nothing had been published on Karamojong *ameto* as such, and he had read Knighton (1990:I) beforehand, which makes ten references to it.
  [2] Cf. *akiwo* (to stand, stop).
  [3] Those who cut (*akitub*) words, or divide affairs.

Towards the end of the colonial period, the neighbouring district of Lango had 37 times as many court cases per thousand of the population as Karamoja in 1955. Traditional law and morality was being eroded by economic development in the former, upheld in the latter (Knighton 1990:I,214f; II,118). Traditional law, as any other, does not operate by accident, but by assiduous application to fresh cases (Kakooza 1967). The neighbouring districts demonstrated how quickly it can atrophy. Law has effect according to publicly acceptable sanction, so jurality is the prior concept.

In Karamoja the obfuscating myth has been perpetuated throughout the twentieth century that the elders are losing power, that they can no longer control rebellious youth, and that this is especially so now that youth carry semi-automatic weapons. It is reminiscent of the rhetoric used by both parties in negotiating bridewealth: bewailing a dearth is in fact a claim for more, while to boast an abundance is to invite its loss. Elders have been to the fore in propagating this perception of perpetually declining power,[4] which to an extent is the timeless complaint of the aged in any society.

Thus anthropologists have tended to overlook the functional role of age-sets. Studies in East Africa used to find that they were non-political and non-military (Simonse and Kurimoto 1998:2). Gulliver's work on the Jie declared that the essentially ritual role of elderhood had no political consequences (1953c:165–7). Even when this old orthodoxy is being deliberately overturned,[5] Lamphear (1998:81) finds the whole age-system conferring power on the elders for the control of potential excesses of younger men in only two aspects: religious and economic.

Here it is the jural system of punishment, *ameto* that is selected for examination.[6] Abrahams, surveying the literature on the term, which is surprisingly widespread in the region, calls for further research into this significant institution (1978:49f, 60).

> The paradoxical result is that we have descriptions of an institution around the borders of a central area among peoples speaking very diverse languages (Lwo, Merle, and Kalenjin), and yet next to nothing is known about it for the otherwise rather well-documented central people from whom it seems certain to have spread.

---

[4] The further back they go in the oral traditions, the more they magnify the power of the elders (Lamphear 1976:156–8). Correspondingly, the closer to the present, the more they play down that power. An example is given in an Oxfam report (2001:25), but the particular circumstances of Lorocom are not revealed, when he blames poverty and the youth. He is not listed as an interviewee, and it is unlikely he is from Kotido District. Only five of the 103 listed have Karamojong names: all are government employees and four were in Labwor (Oxfam 2001:49–51).

[5] N. Dyson-Hudson had already done this for the Karimojong, stating the case for 'the fundamental importance of the age organization in Karimojong political life' (1963:397).

[6] Abrahams (1978:44) first refers to *ameto* among the Abwor as 'annual age-group gatherings', though their function is primarily to adjudicate, and only later is the most common description that they serve 'to punish wrongdoers' (ibid.:50) 'The people themselves tend to stress the disciplinary functions of the institution.' According to J22, '*ameto* is punishment'. The Ngakarimojong dictionary (Nadiket Seminary 1986) does not know the term.

Lamphear (1976:157f) speaks of *ameto* purely in the past tense, though it is clear it has never ceased to function. It has done so in competition with the formal jurisdiction of the institutions of the Ugandan state, and the Karamojong are careful to avoid ostensible rivalry, while retaining their own sanctions. Such a lacuna in the research is more typical than accidental. Karamojong do not like to talk freely with strangers about the key, powerful institutions that guarantee the cohesion of their society. These are infused with the awe of the numinous, and are profaned at the cost of that power to society, with the possible, if spiritual, consequences coming down to the individual (Knighton 1990:I,31–3).

It is still the case that the elder, the patriarchal head of extended patrilineal, patrilocal families, can correct family misbehaviour. In 1997, a youth was disturbing his family and selling his father's cattle. His parents arrested him and brought him to the police, with the result that he spent two years in the prison, seen as one of more merciful punishments. On release, the story was repeated. At last, when he reoffended, he was arrested by his father, uncle and other clan relatives, and was put before their firing squad (J22). There was no consequence for them. If a youth refuses correction by his father or elder, he can also be taken to his father's age-set (*ngikasapanak*[7]) who can decide to warn or give sentence. If the latter, then he must show signs fit for repentance (*akiki*) by sacrificing a bull for the elders to eat and by giving them beer to drink. If he has abused anyone from his own age-set upwards, he can be beaten at any time with a special whip cut from the *ekaliye* tree, which is only used for ritual purposes (J22). He can be beaten anywhere on his body, but it does not break his bones. Dangerous characters can be tied to prevent use of guns. If an offender picks up any weapon such as a gun, spear or knife, he may be termed an *emoit* (stranger, enemy). This is a terrible sanction and can easily be imposed on an individual. Such excommunication means his cattle can be stolen by his own people and he can be killed with impunity. He may no longer identify with the tribe, but is a foreigner, an outlaw.

If he has also 'spoilt' or polluted his age-set by his transgression, bringing any shame on them, the age-set leader convenes the group and then the transgressor may have to sacrifice a bull or a ram, and provide beer for his age-set. The Jie are 'very serious about discipline here' (J22), yet there is no Karamojong tribe or section that is reputed to have dropped *ameto*. The Bokora, notorious for their warriors, who have even raided Matany Hospital, exercise it, so do the Pian (P3,5). If the offender avoids authority, 'the elders' council can still send age-mates to fetch someone who has gone against our law' (J22). They will want to hear the whole case history. Having reached a consensus, they can require the criminal to render compensation to any victim. Anyway, he is obliged to make a sacrifice of one of his oxen and submit to a beating before or after this highly symbolic profession of fealty to the elders. To sacrifice an ox for the benefit of an individual is a confession of his kingship in African society (Simonse and Kurimoto 1998:19,28n8). For the Karamojong it is the elders to whom sovereignty belongs.

---

[7] The term means 'those of the initiation (*asapanû*)'. When a Karamojongait is initiated defines his age-set and generation-set (Knighton 1990:I,304–13; Tornay 1998:104–15; Dyson-Hudson 1963:366f).

A customary punishment for adultery, rape and murder used to be 80 head of cattle. President Amin, in his drive to outlaw Karamojong customs, reduced it to eight, but the rise in crime made the elders increase it again to 60, and this has the tacit backing of local government (J22). Since these trespasses are crimes against a life, one would expect the fine to return eventually to 80 and an equivalence to the standard level of bridewealth.[8] The main alternative, after all, is the death sentence, though, at least since colonial times, an elders' council has been discouraged from pronouncing it. There could hardly be a clearer demonstration of the way in which Karamojong culture, though shifted out of its cultural groove by external forces, gravitates back to the traditional, continuing external forces notwithstanding.

Again there is surprising conformity across autonomous communities, from Kasile to Namalu.

> Elders say 'Don't kill a person! Don't steal! Don't commit adultery!' If you are caught, you must kill your own bull for the elders. You have to pay a fine of 60 cows for adultery because they have wanted to stop adultery. The punishment system is there (*Ameto eyai*). The government's civil law is eight cows. The government would say, 'Why are you using age-sets to police these matters?' Only those who resist traditional discipline will be left to the government. (D4)

> *Ameto* is still working. There has to be a problem (*asecit*), something wrong, bad, for example, a youth insulting an elder, adultery, rape, murder, stealing including cattle-theft, incest. The wrongdoer's own age-set must take responsibility because their name is damaged. They gather to look for the culprit. When they get him, he must kill (*akingol*) a bull for forgiveness and mercy (*akidyek*, *akisyon*). They beat him with a whip (*ekaliyet*, or of *topojo*, *Lannea humilis*, or of *apongai*, a bush). He eats the bull with the elders, who pray beforehand for Akujŭ to forgive ... If the age-set declines to act, then an aggrieved clan will collect the culprit's animals. The elder age-sets only advise. If the age-set fails to act, all are sinners. Then many members of the age-set will be called, 'Why has this come?' When the elders find the reason, they deal with it. If some individuals were misleading others, they will be punished. People do not stand out for long; a solution needs to be sought. The authority, the strength of the elders is all there. (P5)

The compensation among the Pian for the life of a woman is 100 cattle, for a man it is 60. On the other hand it may be only seven to ten for rape. Rape is no bar to marriage, if the girl's parents are willing (P5), which is quite possible if the bridewealth would be lowered for another man because of the rape.

If the criminal refuses any stipulated punishment, he can be excommunicated or even cursed. It is the outlaws, or at least those who are clients of the relatively few with major interests in the capitalist economy, who resort to banditry on the roads. 'Bandits are individuals; a few are outlaws. Businessmen incite their brothers to

---

[8] Marriage adds a life to a family; adultery, divorce or death takes it away. As, according to Gulliver (1953a:155), 'In Jie conceptions all significant inter-personal relationships rest upon connections through livestock', cattle must be transferred to acknowledge and compensate the shift in the relationship. Otherwise, human life and social relationships are not valued. 'Adultery was traditionally regarded as grave a crime as homicide, involving the death of a man concerned or a compensation payment equal to that for murder.'

waylay vehicles. The elders are against banditry, but they may not be knowing. They can only curse the bandits, which is an excommunication. They may come back for forgiveness.' (P5) Since elders owe no duty to the *ngimoe* who travel through their country, it is easy for them to take no notice.

Of course Karamojong law is not statutory and nowhere is it written, even by colonial authorities who did not therefore invent it. While there are customary jural procedures and convictions, there are cases which are cleared up in rough and ready ways which, if they themselves are not unjust, do not attract the active attention of the elders. In 1996, at a dance in Lokitela-ebu, warriors let their guns off. A bullet accidentally went through a boy, killing him, and on into a girl. The brothers of the boy called the killer, who expected forgiveness. They made him lie down next to the corpse of the boy, and shot him dead. There was no further action, either from the elders or from the government. In 1995, Arupan at Lopie was refused support from his father to marry the girl whom he loved. He shot the father in his hut with six of his friends and three more friends outside. He hid, but was eventually tricked by someone he knew, captured and stoned to death, capital punishment being the automatic consequence of such a socially polluting crime (J33). The action of the boy in shooting ten men before anything could be done is precisely what causes observers from the towns to doubt the power of the elders, and certainly it will make them think twice before treating their sons harshly. However the status quo was efficiently restored, and sons too will not see shooting their kin as a means to get their own way. The main complaint of the Karamojong about British administration was that it had become 'a woman' in its dispensing of justice (Bataringaya 1961; Knighton 1990:I, 210–13).

The elders are quite capable of giving justice subtly. My old friends, Longok and Butong, were visited by their drunken brothers-in-law who started to beat them with sticks over a bridewealth dispute. In defence, they picked up *pangas* to cut the sticks. Since the in-laws regarded themselves as giving the defaulters their due punishment, they called them '*ngimoe*' for grabbing the steel weapons, and a large group was organized to arrest them. The elders heard their statements, and found for Longok (J22) and Butong, but they had to sacrifice a ram and make beer for the elders, who smeared them with the ram's chyme (*ngikujit*) to remove the stain of the accusation. The brothers-in-law had to sacrifice two bulls and be beaten, for they had arrogated to themselves the power of elders to determine punishment (*ameto*).

Vengeance belongs to the elders, for they are closer to the God who ensures that age rules, and not segmentary clans. This is not merely the rhetoric of ritual, for the age-set clearly functions as the traditional police force as well as a unit of moral economy for mutual encouragement and discipline. Abrahams is mistaken to underestimate this use of controlled violence for the internal regulation of society and to continue to assume that the Jie age-system 'is in any case of little secular significance' (1978:47). This is not minimal government enforcing a minimal social contract, but a highly effective jural means of social correction which, unlike the bureaucratic system, can distinguish in practice between cultural offence and insignificant transgression. Though age-sets infer the ineluctability of human mortality, the generation-set principle ensconces the religio-politico-jural power of elders across clan lines.

> The writer had the good fortune to attend an '*Atuk*' immediately after arriving in the district and while still a stranger to the tribe. The case was the murder of a girl by a young man and the procedure was simplicity itself. In a grass hut were seated the judges, twenty or more of them; the prisoner, led in at the end of a hide rope fastened round his neck, was placed before the court. The father of the murdered girl acted as prosecutor and produced himself and others to prove the case against the defendant, who was allowed to testify in his own defence. The court conferred for a perfunctory minute or two, for the case was to all appearances a clear one, and found the prisoner guilty, whereupon the bereaved father led him out to his doom. There was a slight scuffle, a gurgle, and the sound of a falling body just a few feet away. Justice had been done! (Shearwood 1921:202)

Under civil administration British justice was deemed to prevail over homicide, but the Karamojong have now reappropriated capital punishment in a country where life has been very cheap, though they never completely ceded that right. Tanner (1970a:20) noted that there were 86 reported murders in Karamoja in 1963, but that one 'inter-tribal incident', a cattle-raid, accounted for 68. He therefore deduced considerable underreporting. It is unlikely that anyone would report a justifiable revenge killing or a jural punishment, and the aggressors in any raid would like it not to reach government ears. The possession of firearms makes *ameto* more dangerous to police, but criminals who raise their guns at a search party, if they escape, are cursed and outlawed, and can only live a life of banditry or espionage. Unlike in the army barracks, discipline has prevailed within the Karamojong sections.

The older women have their *ameto a ngaberu*, and act as judges in their tribunal, held in a field, or near an anthill or tree. They can try anyone, male or female, who infringes rules in women's affairs, chiefly agriculture and water. Planting or hoeing in another woman's field commits the social crime of mixing (*akinyal*) the seed. This, or sorcery, or other things, even a nesting hawk (Dyson-Hudson 1966:111), may hold back (*akilal*) the rain. Women may also be punished in the same way by elder women's age-sets. There would not normally be a sacrifice of an ox.

When the rains are delayed, the women approach the person they hold responsible with sticks, and threaten to kill him, unless he reveals the location of his handiwork. If he confesses, they command him, '*Taar akine. Kinyaku akiru*' (Pazzaglia 1982:101n), 'Kill a goat! Bring back the rain!' This done, the women are anointed with chyme, and the initiated men eat the goat, which has been roasted whole and unskinned, while the head, neck and lights are sent to the wife of the guilty man, who may not himself partake of them. '*Ebuni akiru, arumor*' (ibid.), 'The rain is coming, it is finished.'

Such law still runs in the townships as well as the countryside. Thus it can be seen that the age-system has considerable power to control miscreant individuals and even groups. The threat of excommunication and the risk of shaming one's age-set are not only active deterrents for the most selfishly materialistic, but are also continual reinforcers of identity: what it means to belong and the terror of not being allowed to belong. Even armed groups cannot stand out against their own political community for long, in considerable continuity with the past. The only exception is when an age-class is powerful enough to found its own autonomous tribe, but this has not happened for two centuries. Rather than permanent schism, there has been the integration of other ethnic groups, who had no solution to the depredations, which Karamojong morality and jurality encouraged. As Tanner (1970a:36) found, 'the Karamojong are far less aggressive within their own tribal communities than most of the other tribes in Uganda'.

2 Gauging the Effects of Military Change

The postmodern perspective of scholars looking at Karamoja intermittently over the last decade has sought to emphasize discontinuity between the past and present uncertainty. Mirzeler and Young (2000), in an article entitled 'Pastoral Politics in the Northeast Periphery in Uganda: AK-47 as change agent', arising out of Mirzeler's research for a PhD dissertation (1999), 'Veiled Histories', claim to lift the veil with this central assertion to their argument: 'The large-scale infusion of AK-47s after 1979 introduced a new dynamic, again favouring the emergence of warlords and the decline of the elders. The guns, and the power that came out of their barrels, were in the hands of younger men, grouped and led by warlords' (Mirzeler and Young 2000:419). The argument is retrospective, making the Jie military saviour at the beginning of the last century, Loriang, a 'warlord'. It is the first time he has been called thus, being styled by Lamphear as 'war-leader'. The Karamojong, of whom the Jie are but one strong ethnic identity, know no lords.[9]

Military Leaders Old and New

Loriang and his successors possess the functional appellation of *ekapolon ka ajore*, the big man of the fight, raid or battle. Loriang earned a unique place in Jie history, unprecedented by any leader of his people, and imitated by no-one who came after him. This was not because he created a new office for himself, but because he provided the answer to the most serious crisis in Jie history; indeed out of it they became known as *Ngijie*, the fighters. They were squeezed by simultaneous, aggressive campaigns by the Dodosŏ from the north and the Karimojong from the south, 'like the testicles of a donkey' (Lamphear 1976:214). Loriang developed the traditional system of mobilization and battle tactics in order to prevent his people from being overwhelmed.

However even Loriang was directed by the strategic planning of the congregation of elders, and dependent on fire-makers, divines and diviners for religious expertise. He still had to gain permission from the very old men in order to lead the Jie in one army (Lamphear 1994:75,79). Thus, when the campaigns were

---

[9] The attempt of County Chiefs to appropriate '*Ekapolon*' as a title and bedeck themselves with all the finery they could acquire was for display to their colonial masters primarily, but even the latter had to remove the chiefs, when the populace, sooner or later, resisted their attempts at accumulation of resources. A year after the most active chief, Yakobo Lowok, was awarded a medallion in person by the Queen for limiting raiding, he was unseated by popular demonstrations, so large police reinforcements were required all the way from Gulu (Field 8.5.90 Letter; Cleave 1996:34). The Pokot killed County Chief Lorike. 'Chiefs didn't work in Karamoja' (Powell-Cotton 22.2.89, Interview).

frustrated, the crucial leadership of Loriang merged back into long-term norms of Jie culture.

> While brilliant and far-ranging, Loriang's military changes emanated essentially from traditional structures. ... Because of cosmological constraints derived in part from their perception of themselves as 'the centre' of their universe, the emerging Jie community was consistently resistant to radical changes, and tended to cling to venerable political and religious forms. Thus fundamental perceptions concerning the status and role of the army remained basically constant despite Loriang's innovations. (Lamphear 1994:86)

There was no problem of succession, for there was no successor to a monarchical office. The normal leadership was the acephalous, decentralized, consensual rule of elders, which Loriang never tried to replace. If he displaced it for a season, it was only because there was a consensus that his innovations and leadership were necessary for the exigency (Lamphear 1976:202–62[10]).

Owners of the Gun

It is true that the state's claim to a monopoly of violence, having been used by Amin to great excess in the cause of clothing the naked, encouraged the Karamojong to take advantage of Uganda's fleeing second battalion. As soon as it fled before the Tanzanian liberating army in 1979, the Sor, Maseniko, Bokora, Pian and Jie were quick to empty the barracks at Moroto of all its munitions, even if it meant using donkeys for transport. This greatly added to the stock of firearms held by Karamojong, especially of Kalashnikov semi-automatic rifles. However it would be as foolish to suppose that this event changed nothing as it would be fatuous to argue that this changed everything *ipso facto*. It could be expected that there would be a ripple-effect through the culture due to this shift in the availability of the products of Western technology. Apart from this, it soon became evident that the balance of power had been seriously upset.

The Turkana from Kenya, the Maseniko, Bokora and Jie were the main winners, while the Dodosô, Ik and the Abwor, in the north and west of Karamoja, were the main losers, especially the former, many of whom were made destitute, when the 1979–81 drought meant they lost their crops at the same time as their cattle were raided. However even events as calamitous as these are swings and roundabouts in the long history of the region, where even in the days before firearms arrived, in the 1870s, the technology and trade of ironware nevertheless was a factor in military matters.[11] All the Karamojong peoples relied on trading relationships with outsiders

---

[10] Even Lamphear falls into the trap of periodization by entitling chapter seven, 'The Era of Warfare, Disasters, and Strangers', but quite clearly all these recur throughout oral and documentary history. The distinction given by Lamphear's informants emphasizes massed battles with thousands on each side. Though thousands may be mobilized today on one side, it is the usual aim of warfare to acquire cattle for individuals, not to eliminate the opposition. Bokora raided Jie 'as young men do' (Lamphear 1976: 202f). The Karimojong rationale for failing to overrun, disperse and absorb the Jie was that they needed a reservoir of cattle close at hand, which they could raid (Novelli 1999).

[11] The capabilities of the tools of war are seldom likely to be ignored, but the current

for their spears and hoes. None had blacksmiths, and it was the Abwor who were. Since 1998, the Dodosô have redressed the balance and are again raiding the Jie (J20, 23).

Government only becomes a real proposition for the tribes when it has the will and capacity to enforce a policy. Museveni's new administration tried to disarm Karamoja by torturing people with the method called *kandooya*, tying the arm up behind the back, sometimes breaking or paralysing it (Amnesty International 1988:82), in order to extract information on the whereabouts of arms. As clumsy reprisals, different armies previously burned whole neighbourhoods near Namalu, Iriri, Lopei and Panyangara. This insecurity leads to denser neighbourhoods, as before Empire, but out of sight of the roads, since soldiers dare not stray far from vehicles. After a company of soldiers was eliminated near Kotido in 1987, it was clear that the government had not the capacity to impose its will, so it preferred to see the Karamojong raid the neighbouring tribes, who were resisting a government dominated by southerners. A young, 'saved' Karimojong, David Pulkol, was appointed as Minister for Water Resources, and an unusual effort was made to send famine relief. The main military problem facing Karamoja remains the raiding of the Turkana and the Pokot, threats to peace dealt with more effectively in *atukot* and *akiriket* than by modern armies of the state.

Yet Mirzeler and Young (2000:419) go beyond finding mere change, asserting 'a new dynamic'. Tracing the continuities with the old is not their agenda, when it is apparent to them that an African people must be the victims of Western technology. They even hypostatize this 'power that came out of their barrels', at the same time trying to socialize it in the young men. This supposedly autonomous power, without further explanation, becomes the power of young men, and then, with another mysterious shift, it becomes the power of warlords. All are taking away power from the elders. 'Locally, the balance of power has clearly shifted away from the elders who were once the lynchpin of authority' (ibid.: 426). Here lies the core of their argument and of many in the peace industry (Walker 2001:18f;[12] Frank 2002:74; Leggett 2001:47; Mkutu 2003:6,11).

Firstly, Mirzeler and Young assume, without discussion, that elders have no guns. Yet guns, like spears, can be traded, and elders generally command more resources than their juniors. The elder is the owner (*elope*) of the family herd. His sons cannot marry without his cattle and his blessings. Any girl or children a son may have can be suddenly forfeit to another who can pay the bridewealth. That raided cattle have not shifted privilege to young warriors is evidenced by the continued practice of polygyny. The bridewealth received by a Jie father for the first marriage of a daughter of his is his privilege to use as bridewealth for a further marriage of his own, even if he should already have five wives (J23). Through their own diligence as herd-owners, as raiders in the past, and as fathers, they are likely to have accumulated more cattle than the youth, who only have raiding and what their fathers and friends

---

history of war is tending to subordinate them to the ideas and institutions of warfare. Modern military history is really playing down the role of weaponry (Lamphear 15.8.01, E-mail).

[12] In fact Walker (2001:19f) begins to question the received view: 'the assumed situation of "declining power of elders" may in fact be more complex than often portrayed'.

give them. If elders want guns, no-one can stop them, but they have no need when they instruct junior age-sets as their armed police. Across Karamoja those visibly moving with guns are the younger, more athletic men, while elders more commonly move with spears, or even just sticks. There is no great change here. An elder entrusts his herd to sons, agnatic nephews or affines to tend. It is their duty to look after the cattle, to find grazing and water, often far from the home, and to live in a cattle-camp (*nawi*). The primary responsibility is to protect them from wild animals and enemies, so they must be armed in order to accomplish this.

Perceptions of Chaos

Mirzeler and Young (2000:426) see 'endemic disorder', but, if there were, elders would no longer be entrusting their wealth to their sons, and separate communities would emerge as in formative historical shifts, when warriors make off with the herds, leaving their cursing fathers behind, later to be identified, for example, as Turkana and Jie, respectively (Lamphear 1992). If attention is not paid to ritual, then the order imagined by a community is missed by the scholar, for 'an ordered social world is enacted emphatically in ritual' (Bollig 2000:361). The violation of social norms that happened among the Turkana did not occur among the Jie, because of their distinct cosmology (Lamphear 1994:90). Established ethnic identities are as strong as ever among the Karamojong,[13] even if political unity among the ten Karimojong sections is more an exception than a rule. They have never raided in permanent alliances. 'What appears to emerge is a stable form of disorder' (Mirzeler and Young 2000:426). Put simply, there is no catalepsis, for Karamojong culture is continuing.

Who are the 'young men'? Despite the literature, Mirzeler and Young enter into no discussion on generation-sets, which define seniority more according to the order of begetting than to age. If they had really read their Dyson-Hudson (1966:188,198f), they would be aware that, when the senior generation-set becomes few in number and incapacitated, owing to the natural death of their peers, the culture regularly enters a period of crisis. Older uninitiated men drift into raiding, as the only means whereby they can increase their standing in the community. The junior generation of initiated men, which itself contains men older than the most junior age-set of the senior generation, is itching for power. They will show, short of revolution, various displays indicating that power should now be handed over to them, while some rituals fall into abeyance for lack of elders, and men move their herds totally independently. Yet Dyson-Hudson (1966:199) observed for himself that, when the junior generation was promoted and a new generation was opened into which their sons could be initiated, the former rebels now conformed. Men again deferred weddings until after initiation. There was a quick, visible return to the pattern of allocated rôles and the corporate emphasis on the age system.

---

[13] What was the picture a quarter of a century ago remains so now: tradition and ethnicity coincide to a great degree, and political struggle is not sought in the national arena (Kasfir 1976:143). However 'passivity' was and is a total misreading of the autonomy of Karamojong politics, then and now (Dyson-Hudson 1966).

However, even given the increasing internal disequilibrium in the cycle of generations, fieldwork after Mirzeler's[14] suggests the power of elders has not disappeared; rather it never has been very visible to the outside observer. If the researcher approaches elders with questions about raiding, the answer is predictable, but if one enquires about jurality and religion, they respond with marked affirmations. Every generation of elders has lamented that they do not have the power their forebears exercised. Back in 1951, Jie elders complained of their lack of control of their young men.

> Yet I think that the old men would always have liked more authority than they actually had and in ideal they should have had. I remember that I picked up a few stories about the pre-colonial days when the young men were raiding under 'war leaders' and, allegedly, disregarding the elders of that era. After all, the authority of elders must always have been rather fragile (control of livestock, of marriageable girls, of ritual and access to Akuj, etc.) and probably the elders themselves remembered how, as young men, they too had not altogether heeded their elders ... older men had a sneaking respect and admiration for the headstrong, wilful young men who were acting as they themselves had once done and would still like to do. In any case, don't older men everywhere complain that youth are going to the dogs and do not heed sufficiently the superior wisdom of older people? So I would be very cautious concerning complaints of contemporary Jie elders, that their authority has been weakened in recent times. (Gulliver, P.H. 19.6.90, Letter)

Many factors need to be taken into consideration here. It is the universal experience of leaders to find that, after decades of yearning for real power, when having climbed to the top of the greasy pole, they find nothing there. Moreover power is concentrated in no individual, but in the congregation or assembly, which is in the gift of no one elder. The voice of a strong, wealthy herd-owner may carry the day on one occasion, but not on another. If his peers suspect that he is just furthering outside interests, their consensus will swing against him, so that he is reminded of his corporate loyalty. Thus there is no one representative of a political unit to which an outsider can go to receive an answer, or on whom he can apply leverage, and the congregation will not meet at the behest of a stranger or of one or two elders. The inability to find a political insight into the Karamojong so perplexed British administration used to indirect rule through chiefs that it sponsored an Oxford anthropologist to research Karimojong politics. Neville Dyson-Hudson (1966) found there was indeed no handle that they could grasp in that way, for the only unitary being who held power in Karimojong society was a deity who responded to sacrificial prayer. On deity, as on the most unifying political institution, the generation-set, Mirzeler, Young and the ever-revolving NGO circus are silent.

Alomar Leaders

Probably for the first time in African studies, there has been a study of warlords, where none are named or characterized. They are entirely anonymous and shadowy

---

[14] There is no indication that Crawford Young has done any fieldwork in Karamoja, only a little in neighbouring Sebei, while resident in Makerere in the early 1960s.

warlords, who move wraith-like on the borders of Sudan and Kenya, where 'large informal markets for weapons and ammunition flourish' (Mirzeler and Young 2000:422).[15] A market for semi-automatic rifles, pistols and ammunition is reported and these are allegedly 'controlled by *kraal* leaders or warlords from Sudan and Kenya as well as Karamojans'. In no case are they even identified ethnically, which is generally regarded as an important feature of warlords. Perhaps there is a brief attempt to identify them with state politics. In fact there is no evidence apart from the dispersed involvement in arms-trading, which features on the flier on William Reno's book on warlord politics, that these are warlords at all, but he depicts them thus: 'enterprising strongmen are joining in with marginalized groups to exploit regime weaknesses, opposing groups are trafficking in illegal drugs, weapons, and natural resources, and are even forging foreign commercial partnerships' (Reno 1998:257).

In fact there are identifiable military leaders in Karamoja, especially when warfare demands it. Dr Arthur Banks undertook a medical mission to the Jie cattle-camps in 1980, and has probably spent more time there than any other person not a member of the Jie political community. At a time of the most serious drought and famine in the twentieth century, he followed and worked among one cattle-camp of 10 000 men, women and children herding 10 000 cattle. Only in the extremest times of hunger do mothers leave the permanent settlements, so cattle-camps usually have a much lower population. To concentrate so many cattle reflects an intense military threat, so fearful that it overcomes the normally prevalent desire to realize herders' freedom by exercising grazing decisions according to their own pastoral judgment. Massing cattle in the bush can only be an attempt to counter large numbers of an adjacent enemy. In the mid-1980s, when heavily armed Turkana were grazing in Najie, there were three Jie *ngalomarin*. The cattle-camp during dry season grazing is known as *awi*, and is based on family herds sometimes joined with the herds of friends and age-mates. When large numbers coalesce, it becomes known as *alomar*, meaning coming in and going out. Every herder has the freedom to join the camp or leave it. It is not a conscripted army, unless the elders require it for tribal defence in the direst crisis, so it would not be true to say that any one man can put 10 000 in the field. However, if a number of warriors do come together, then they are bound by a very strict communal discipline. Those not attached to herds must go home, even if it means starvation, for 'any diminishing of the spiritual authority of the priest–general, any unlawful contacts with the enemy would not be tolerated' (Banks 3.4.90:2, Letter). 'You either kept your cattle there and submitted to the camp's authority, or you were back to the village' (Banks 3.4.90:4, Letter).

Leadership, as in any military organization, is very well defined. The general of the warrior host, *ekapolon ka ajore*, may frequently be a divine, *emuron*,[16] because

---

[15] A market for semi-automatic rifles, pistols and ammunition at predictable prices is reported at Karenga (Oxfam 2001:12), but this is likely to be a traders' enterprise. Guns can be exchanged for sorghum in Kotido or for cattle anywhere. There is no evidence of any monopoly.

[16] Exemplifying what became a strong feature of Turkana politics (Lamphear 1992), the Turkana-born *alomar* leader in Maseniko, Apaloris (father of the leopard), was an *emuron*,

of the need to use medicine to confuse the enemy, or at least an *ekesiemon*, because of the need to be a haruspex to read the entrails of the sacrificial ox. If his leadership is based on military strategy alone, he will need to work in tandem with an *emuron*. He may also need a younger man to lead the troops into battle. He will be the most skilful and courageous warrior, *ekadedengan* (*dedeng*, fierce), primed with the testicles of the ox sacrificed for the raid. This leadership commands 'a tight security conscious military unit – entirely united in the twin aims of defending their own cattle and acquiring the cattle of other tribes' (Banks 3.4.90:2, Letter).

The military aim is not related much to national politics; in fact it has little to do with politics as academics now know it, for cattle-camps 'were primarily a religious organization on the move', very useful for unity and morale, but useless for warlords seeking to exploit weakness in a national régime, unless it has cattle to raid. 'Many pastoralists in the area are unclear about the country of their citizenship' (Frank 2002:72). In short, Karamojong have nothing in common with others named as warlords around the world seeking commercial gain and state power through the barrel of a gun. Indeed Mirzeler and Young (2000:426) come close to admitting this in finding that the Karamojong are 'not interested in a separatist movement or a national project', that they do not threaten the state even though they only give Ugandan sovereignty minimal acknowledgment.

The context for Reno (1998) is the state, but the Karamojong only have as much time for the state as the external coercion it can bring to bear. Even the colonial state, whose superior military power in full-frontal showdown was never contested, came to be derided by the Karamojong as a 'woman' in the latter days of colonial office sensitivity and Parliamentary papers (Powell-Cotton 22.2.89, Interview). However the restraints on traditional Karamojong freedom for a growing Karamojong population became exceedingly irksome. 'Since the arrival of European rule, our land has been spoiled. If there were no poll-tax, it would be rich. European rule has squeezed our cattle and our people, so we pray, "Divert! Go!"'.[17] Nevertheless the Karamojong did not want to join independent Uganda, preferring the continuation of British rule, the Munster Commission found (Munster 1961:156). Baganda bureaucrats, who feared the Karamojong even more than they despised them, were not to be trusted. Karamojong 'ignore as far as possible the criminal law of the Central Government and carry out their traditional raids' (Tanner 1970a:24). It can be argued that the Karamojong have never been closely governed in many aspects of their culture by any state, mainly because of their collective will to self-determination that cannot abide any overrule, whatever the peace and prosperity it may bring.

If the defining function of the Weberian state is to control its borders and the use of violence within them, then the Republic of Uganda should draw a line at the borders of Bugisu, Teso and Lango. However it cannot even defend these against armed Karamojong incursion. When it suits them, or in order to mollify an outraged government, tacit compliance can be adopted, but only as long as necessary.

---

who made decisions on moving camp and finding grazing based on his reading of the intestines of sacrificial oxen (Banks 3.4.90:1f, Letter).

[17] A retranslation of G. Pellerino's (1973) Karimojong text in Novelli (1999:342 n46).

Source: Ben Knighton

Photograph 5.1 Herders in the cattle-camp: most are out grazing the livestock

'Governments change and the weather changes ... but we continue herding our animals' (Lorocom, quoted by Leggett 2001:78). The Karamojong rely far more on traditional politics and military than on the unfavourable mercy of an alien power. Régime weaknesses can certainly be exploited, but not because the Karamojong have any interest in the state, or in appropriating its powers of taxation or standing army. The Karamojong are for the Karamojong, so the rule of elders and the policing of warriors are quite enough for them.

3 A State of Revenge

To advance the hypothesis that the AK-47 has brought unprecedented, radical change by fuelling violence and disorder, it is necessary to deal with the history of Karamoja. The nomadic pastoralists of Northern Uganda and Kenya have traditionally raided each other's livestock, an activity that flows naturally from their cultural frameworks for life. During the raiding season, raid is typically followed by counter-raid with considerable loss of life possible. Ever since they became neighbours, raiding has gone on intermittently, not only between Karimojong and Pokot, but also between them and Jie, Dodosô, Turkana, Samburû, Marakwet, Sapiny or Sabawot, and Bukusu. In the nineteenth century, Turkana and Karimojong were attacking neighbouring peoples, assimilating them or driving them on (Knighton 1990:I,96–100). In the first half of the nineteenth century, 'Large scale raids in which hundreds of warriors were engaged became the most successful strategy to "harvest" other peoples' livestock' (Bollig 2000:360). 'Mount Elgon was the scene of intensive inter-tribal warfare during the whole of the nineteenth and early decades of the twentieth century, when the Sapiny-speaking semi-pastoral tribes living on the mountain were involved in conflict with cattle-raiders from the surrounding tribes' (Weatherby 1962:200)

In 1902, the British were impressed by the 'ever recurring petty quarrels and blood feuds'.[18] Abyssinian and Swahili were happily joining in the local raiding (Garretson 1986; Knighton 1990:I,122–48). A Jiot (J25) carries the memory from this time that 'So many people were killed because of guns.' In 1910, the first year of administration, there was 'constant' tribal fighting with the Pokot (Barber 1965:34) and raiding of the Turkana (Lamphear 1976c:233). Even if the police report that 90 per cent of Jie warriors had guns in 1911 was propagated by the enemies who feared firepower (EA 19/1911:Lt E.G.M. Thorneycroft to OC, Troops 11.2.11), Lt Williams did find 16 Gras rifles, 6 muzzle-loaders and 113 rounds of Gras ammunition in one *ere* the next year. After rounding up cattle and burning deserted homesteads, it was believed that the disarmament of 60 Gras rifles was completed in September 1912 (EA 2957:Diary by Capt W. d'E. Williams 20.10.12; Tufnell, DC Rudolph Province, Report 6.10.12). Of course the guns had just been 'dug into the ground and hidden in caves' (J25).

In 1920, the British pushed the Pokot, Sapiny, Karamojong and Turkana into conducting a peace ceremony, but hostilities only subsided for six months, as the

---

[18] Harry Johnston, quoted by Barber (1968:57).

Pokot, growing in numbers, sought to expand into Karamoja, which they did for the next 70 years (Weatherby 1962:210; Brasnett 1958:118f; Knighton 1990:I,348 n12). 'Peace with the Upe is always like that, it never lasts long' (women in Alwyn 1998). Incomplete district records show that six different ethnic groups between 1929 and 1983 killed some 3000 Turkana, the hardest and fiercest of all nomadic pastoralists in the region, and took some 100 000 cattle (Oba 1992:9). Between various tribes and sections involving Karimojong, 15 000 cattle changed hands at a cost of 50 lives, including at least two women, in the first seven months of 1958. Government cattle stockades were raided 16 times, that is, more than fortnightly (Dyson-Hudson 1966:246f).

The end of empire and the beginning of independence was a time of great military activity by the state to stop cattle-raiding once and for all. Yet, in the 1950s and 1960s, large, well-organized traditional armies were revived by the Jie with as many firearms as they could muster for huge raids on the Karimojong (Lamphear 1994:80). The skeleton in Uganda's nation-building cupboard was to be exorcized by building roads across the remote passes, by manning police posts and by laying down airstrips for spotter-planes to report every assembly and movement of men and cattle, in order to make their control more complete. Spears and guns were subject to strict regulations, and even the ritual culture felt under pressure from suspicious eyes in the sky (Marshall Thomas 1965:61f). However the colonial administration had failed to meet even its top priority throughout its occupation of Karamoja: law and order, while there was a preponderance of spears.[19] Without the energetic actions of a super-tribal umpire, mortality would have been worse, even if the long-run effects of colonial rule in raising population, while limiting dry season grazing, were not sustainable.[20] Only a jural reform would have changed effective sanctions on homicide.

In 1982, the Acoli, equipped with military vehicles and munitions, invaded from the west and shot many Jie. In the eventful years of 1984 to 1986, the author lived in a mud hut among the fighting people, the Jie. In 1986, Museveni took Kampala by force from the government of General Tito Okello, an Acoli with a Jie grandmother.

---

[19] In 1964, the spear was the most common weapon in homicide in Karamoja, with the gun only accounting for 10 per cent, as in most other districts. There was no correlation between availability of weapons and homicide (Tanner 1970a:13,39). Thus it was not the gun that caused the Karamojong to have the highest reported homicide rate in Uganda over five years, and most of this was due to seasonal, interethnic cattle-raiding (Tanner 1970a:20,30,58). The figures do not include those killed by Karamojong in neighbouring districts.

[20] The census figure of 171 945 in 1959 had grown by 200 000 in 32 years according to the unreliable census of 1991, but it probably demonstrates that the ecological limits were greater than those feared by officialdom. Casualty totals can be expected to be seven times greater than those seen before 1919 in order that proportions remain constant; 0.4 raiding casualties per thousand of the population is small compared with infant mortality and less than what happened either side of the colonial period, but the important point is that British rule only suppressed this violence towards the enemy without lessening the motivation sufficiently.

What was deservedly called 'the worst army in the world' fled fresh from its genocide of the Baganda in the Luwero Triangle towards its Acoli homeland in stolen vehicles. The Jie shot them all the way, leaving far too many corpses for the devouring hyenas and vultures to cope with the next day. Yet this was neither a bid for state power, nor an alliance with the Baganda, but the Jie taking advantage of a passing opportunity for revenge, and to collect more arms and ammunition for their future raiding exploits. There was no warlord in control, for there were no warlords, just captains of companies formed for military purposes only.

In July 1999, Jie warriors reacted to an army and vigilante operation at Panyangara to recover 40 cattle raided from the Maseniko by destroying two Buffalo armoured vehicles, which had previously been effective in recovering Bokora cattle (J9). Two days later the Jie performed the sacrifice of a dog at the very spot where the vehicles were burned, followed by a communal cursing of the officers to foil the operation. In five days a Buffalo was struck by lightning and another crashed into a house in Kotido. By October two commanding officers and the Residential DC were all away recovering from unexplained illness. However hundreds of Jie cattle and many other livestock were forcibly taken by the 5000 troops posted to Kotido in reprisal (*Sunday Monitor* 24.10 and 1.11.99). With helicopters providing aerial cover, there was little more the Jie could do, even though the cattle started to die without new pasture, and soldiers ate or sold them. Some Jie said they had been taught a lesson (P3), but since then army commanders have defected to Kampala rather than be operational in Karamoja.

In June 2000, Dodosô raided Jie, and then 10 000 cattle from Turkana grazing Kidepo Valley National Park, right on the deadline the Uganda government gave them to leave (*New Vision* 22.6.00). Men who raid successfully gain not only wealth in cattle, but also standing in the community, the capacity to father repeatedly, through the adulation of maidens who seek a secure and well-provided home, and a saga of courageous exploits to sing in the dance. The incentives to acquire more cattle by raiding cannot be suppressed by prosperous elders for long, and the urge to counter-raid to restore lost cattle is intense. When the author stayed with his Jie friend Longoli in 1998, all his cattle had just been raided by the Dodosô, and when he was staying with a Pian friend, Revd Andrew Emoru, two years later, the Pokot had just tried to raid his brother's cattle and the Pian had counter-raided. In Kenya, a Nairobi newspaper, *The East African* carried a long and well-informed story:

> The Night of Monday, January 24, is one the Pokot will want to forget. It was a night of slaughter as some 700 Karimojong tribesmen from Uganda, armed with 47 assault rifles, opened fire on unarmed Pokot herdsmen in Mor[u]ita Hills, some 400 kilometres northeast of Kampala.
>
> Estimates of casualties vary from 14 to 100 dead, including women and children. The lower figure was given by the commander of the Ugandan Army's eastern division, Col. Geoffrey Tapan. A Baptist bishop who visited the site, Rev John Ladinyo, gave a figure of 100 dead. The injured were admitted at Am[u]dat dispensary at the Kenya–Uganda border.
>
> The Karimojong made off with 1,800 head of cattle, 5,000 sheep and goats and camels. About 2,000 Pokot survivors escaped with their livestock and were reported to be organizing a major revenge attack....

The counter-raiding continued while the author stayed with the Pian, who were selling the cattle in Namalu market in case state authorities should come, perhaps with their former owners, looking for oxen sporting Pokot brands. The greatest incentive for the Karamojong to sell their wealth and livelihood in cattle is not price, but the prospect that they are going to lose them anyway.

On 30.3.00 *The Monitor*, a journal published in Kampala, reported:

> Kumi and Katakwi districts have recruited 1,400 army veterans and former militia to fight the Karimojong cattle rustlers. The recruits who form the local defence units, are to be armed with guns recently given to the districts by President Yoweri Museveni.
> ...Over the weekend, the Karimojong raided 26 head of cattle from ... [Teso] and uprooted four acres of cassava ...
> They camped in the MP's home where they ate the raw cassava.

On 5.4.00 *The Monitor* reported the Uganda People's Defence Force in a full-scale battle:

> Heavy gunfire yesterday rocked Apeilolim [*sic*], Moroto [the largest town and barracks in Karamoja], during a UPDF counter-offensive to dislodge about 1,000 armed Karimojong warriors.
> 'We've captured Apeitolim which was the base of the (Karimojong) warriors and our men are completely in control of Apeilolim [*sic*] and the general security situation,' a military source told The Monitor in Soroti town April 04 after the fighting.
> Karimojong warriors had April 03 attacked Kapelyebong, and Katakwi, and killed 11 UPDF soldiers and a deputy commander, according to military sources.

The government's disarmament campaign of 2001–2 led to potentially new balances of military power, which all armed parties, including the UPDF, then sought to test by raiding those thought to be less well-armed (Knighton 2003e). Seldom has there been raiding in so many directions at once at the same time. In early 2003, the Bokora raided the Pian and the Pian raided the Pokot, who struck back (M1). The Maseniko allied with the Jie to raid the Pian. To avoid having enemies on all fronts the Pian elders held a sacrifice for peace (*akisil*) with the Tome and Bokora in May 2003. So the cycles of revenge interleave with times of peace, with the state as just another player, both in terms of raiding cattle and in being a vehicle for revenge by Teso or Lango soldiers, officials or militias.

Government has not been so powerless for 80 years as it is now to prevent or solve cattle-raiding, despite promoting ingenious peace meetings and sending battalions of the Uganda Peoples' Defence Force to Moroto or Kotido. Yet the army and officials of the state are also complicit in revenge and banditry, being quite capable of raiding and killing on their own account (Knighton 2003e; Frank 2002:72,75,81). Mirzeler and Young (2000:426) are correct in asserting that 'the state has no possibility of matching the performance of the colonial state in disarming the populace', but they fail to follow the logical conclusion that the Karamojong have little to do with state politics,[21] and would have less if they could.

---

[21] Karamoja had the lowest registration rate, the lowest turnout and the highest percentage of spoilt ballot papers in Uganda's Constituent Assembly Elections on 18.3.94

The traditional politics of the Karamojong keep state government at bay by clever tactics of dissembling and obfuscation, knowing that the government, or its policy, will change. Being an acephalous society, there are no individuals which the state can use for leverage on the society. As Mirzeler and Young (2000: 425) rightly note, Karamojong born and bred MPs are guilty of cultural defection purely because of their incorporation into the state. 'Those who cast their lot with the national system to some degree sever their full membership in local society.'

It has been asserted (Mamdani 1981:19; 1986:*passim*) that 'the Karamoja problem' is merely a projection of colonial violence,[22] or the side-effects of the breakdown of the African state in the neo-colonial age with big men, that is, national political players raising private armies, or that the firearm has upset and overturned the essentially chivalrous harmony of traditional culture (Okudi 1992; Belshaw and Malinga 1999; Galaty 1999; Leggett 2001:47). In this, Mirzeler and Young are faithful representatives of the assured results of modern scholarship in the University of Makerere and of government opinion. The discouragements on the routes to Karamoja abound so much that many touring scholars never reach there. If they do, their minds are already more than half-formed. Yet nowhere has it been demonstrated that national political players, even Karamojong ones, have any military clout in Karamoja. Museveni's government has fostered local committees to take local decisions, with considerable success, and has appointed a chairman in each county to chair the Karamoja Initiative for Sustainable Peace (P4). They tried to call the Karimojong for a peace meeting at their united ritual grove at Nakadanya, but they refused to go, not wanting to be directed either by traders or by government desires for peace. The elders will not be coerced by unitary power if they can avoid it.

Church leaders based in Moroto tend to identify with the interests of their national church, and therefore with state action. 'The bishop of Karamoja diocese blamed Karamojans for their reckless use of guns, expressing the fear that the Karamojong would not survive in the next ten years.'[23] The Christian Church, as the

---

(Geist 1995:98f), which meant that only 37 per cent of an unreliable 1991 Census voted, and nearly half of those were likely to be non-Karamojong.

[22] 'Colonial rule produced a new type of drought, new in its intensity and frequency' (Mamdani 1986:88). Gartrell (1985) trenchantly criticizes Mamdani and his colleagues for their evolutionary model, which like so many developmental plans sees progress primarily in terms of sedentary agriculture. Despite his emphasis on popular democracy, Mamdani does not canvass the opinions of the Karamojong and ignored social and religious views on cattle (Gartrell 1985:109), an approach which he fostered in the subsequent study of Karamoja in the Centre for Basic Research, Kampala.

[23] Mirzeler and Young (2000:408) quote *The Monitor* 23.9.99. Taking Christian conversion as one index of incorporation into the state, they cite the spectacular increase in the number of Catholic converts, to 150 000 by the 1980s (ibid.: 426). This reveals a poor understanding of the realities of Karamoja and a willingness to believe anyone's story. Even if as large a proportion of the population of Karamoja as 43 per cent had been baptized, this was due to an aggressive, indiscriminate baptismal policy. In the 1979–82 and other famines, joining the Roman Catholic Church was for many Karamojong akin to signing on for famine

major expression of 'civil society', has no purchase on the life of the Karamojong, for it associates cattle with guns, and guns with killing, so expects good Christians to live without cattle in a nomadic pastoralist culture. 'Church people may not have animals, not participating in raids' (P5). Thus the church, apart from kinship patterns, is practically disengaged from the culture, providing mainly chaplaincies for townspeople, who also may not belong to the Karamojong political community.

On the other hand, Karamojong beneficiaries of raiding will admit no fault. If challenged, men or women will admit nothing, for fear the government will want to return the livestock to their former owners. They will sell the branded cattle as quickly as they can at the new cattle markets for slaughter in Kampala to avoid detection.[24] Yet, if they are raided, the complaining will be great, the losses may be exaggerated, and why the enemies raided will be a mysterious calamity quite undeserved by the 'victims', the warriors (*ngikajok*). 'We are innocent I tell you and yet we are constantly attacked. They keep taking our cows yet we have not killed anyone' (Maseniko woman, in Alwyn 1998). Thus it was that Gray's Bokora and Pian women informants leave her with a picture of the Bokora and the Pian having their cattle raided, lacking arms to defend them, and their culture being disrupted. Gray (2000:410) seems unaware of Bokora raids on the Tome, Jie and Maseniko from the early 1980s, not to mention the 1950s, while the Pian have in recent years being forcing the Pokot back, despite a desperate lack of grazing due to drought in the Cheringany hills. 'Conflict is not the strange, dangerous new phenomenon that some current analysts seem to want policy-makers to believe ... many researchers agree that violence has long been one form of interaction among these groups...' (Hussein, Sumberg and Seddon 1999:413).

4   A Warrior Culture

There are three main enemies to the good life as a cattle herder: drought, disease and raiders. The most intensely fearsome are the latter. A bullet may come out of the blue; your hopes of accumulation in cattle who are Akujŭ's blessing of all that is most desirable in social relationships, and the very mediation of the Sacred may disappear in a trice, and you are left suddenly as a marginal pauper. 'A man is a man in cattle.' For, without any, women will be ashamed of you (Frank 2002:81), and women enculturate men from birth into this susceptibility to shame as a spur for them to show virility and bravery in battle: 'Male infants are named after successful raiders, and grow up being told they must fulfil their legacy by being an even fiercer, more powerful raider. All ages and genders go about in fear of the *ngimoe* (enemies), who will strike when you least expect'.

---

relief. Only a small fraction attends church, and the drop-out rate is high, like the 88 per cent drop-out rate from school (Oxfam 2001:36). The Verona Fathers admit that their Church has made little fundamental change to lives, and now their resources are dwindling with 'indigenous' Ugandan leadership, the church's appeal is reducing (Knighton 1990:I, 480–85).

[24] The raiders would prefer to be able to keep the cattle, and would do so without government interference. It is not the same business as much cattle-raiding in the southern half of Kenya. 'The Kuria have been in it for the money for 80 years' (Fleisher 1999:241).

It is commonly said, and vouched for by the testimony of elders, that there was a golden age of Karamojong spear-headed chivalry, when women and children were unharmed (Leggett 2001:47f).[25] Greater chivalry in the past is a romantic notion, even if espoused by both present-day Karamojong and observer, which coincides with the internationalist dogma that all disruption can be blamed on the insertion of the Westerner and his, primarily military, technology.[26] Later idealized accounts of traditional war were the norms of colonial chivalry imperfectly imposed by the British. The restraint on killing women was, in fact, the colonial imposition of Victorian morality by the only super-tribal umpire, for pastoralists see women as part of the war effort, blessing their men when they go out to fight and giving military strength by procreation. The cicatrice on the shoulder has for innumerable generations denoted the killer of an enemy (Wayland 1931:222–7); 70 years ago three in 20 men were decorated on the right shoulder, having killed a man, and one in 20 men were decorated on the left, having killed a woman despite the colonial proscription of homicide.[27] The ratio of three men slaughtered to one woman is easily explained by men and boys being exclusively responsible for herding the cattle and guarding the cattle-camps. They are the ones usually in the way of any military action,[28] so the killing of women is, and was, much more the expression of total war or the escalation of revenge, but it is certainly not a novel phenomenon. Aleper Apothia's memory of 1902 (Paget Wilkes 1932a:8–10) makes it quite clear that there were no tabus on raiding of homesteads and killing of women and children.

The killer may also be honoured by the assumption of an enemy-name. He sacrifices an ox in the presence of elders and may then cut notches in the ears of his beloved ox,[29] that is the ox whose name he has already taken and whose praises he

---

[25] Disembowelling pregnant women seems no more likely in the past than now. It happens rarely, being motivated by a rage to reduce the production of more enemies to raid one's own herds. At this point, violence is decidedly ethnic.

[26] The Sabawoot prophet, Arap Koburrkoin, was famous for prophesying the coming of the white man and the widespread peace he would bring. Even the hated sub-imperialism of the Baganda was seen as a fulfilment. With the reduced need to prophesy raids and raiding opportunities, the Sabawoot declared, 'they did not need' prophets any more (Weatherby 1962:208,212).

[27] 'Only warriors who have raided cows and killed enemies can decorate their bodies with scars and show them off at the dances. Women only choose men with good scars. So a real man's body must be decorated with scars' (Alwyn 1988). This demonstrates complete continuity with customs (Novelli 1999:279) as far back as records and memory go. I have seen newly cut *ngageran*. The Karamojong's neighbours to the south, the Southern Nilotic Sabawoot, cut a 2.5–3 inch scar on one side of the chest or other. *ger is a Nilotic root indicating a venerable history to scarification as one decoration or another.

[28] Karamojong women are hardly shy and can express themselves forcibly, even in a raid by the Sabawoot in 1909: 'Four Karamojong were called and then the women came after them crying, and two of them were killed' (Weatherby 1962:211). Sabawoot women had to defend themselves when raiders came to their homes with bow and arrows.

[29] Novelli (1999:279) gives details of Karimojong cuts. *Ngageran* on humans and *ngamunyen* on oxen are there to be seen today.

will sing in the dance. If satisfied as to the details of the event, the elders permit him to use a name which relates to the enemy whom he killed, such as Lokwarasmoi (he of the enemy who bore spears). The cicatrices (*ngaloka* or *ngageran*) are a link to a life of hunting and trapping (*akilok*).[30] Indeed, the Karamojong's fellow Eastern Nilotes, the Teso, call them Ngilok, people you cannot trust (P3). The Langi similarly call them Ngikalokak, which is not how anyone would want to describe themselves (P4). In this naming rite, we may see an initiation rite that predates *asapanů*. Killing an enemy or carnivore had been a precondition for initiation and marriage.[31] Hence the culturally required killing of enemies dates back before the 'new pastoralism' adopted by the Karamojong on their entry to East Africa to many centuries ago when hunting and trapping were a more important feature of their economy (Knighton 1990:I,334f).

The accumulation of tradition does issue in empirical behaviour. 'Karimojong are so committed to their policies as to push them frequently to the point at which they take both the lives and the herds of others, and risk the loss of their own' (Dyson-Hudson 1966:247). Proving manhood has long not been a factor in homicide among the agricultural peoples of Uganda, but there were Karamojong raids 'in which the offender could have gained his end of stealing cattle without homicide but that he chose to wait in a situation, either before or after the raid, in which homicide was almost inevitable' (Tanner 1970a:36). It has been estimated that a third of those who go on a raid inside Karamoja will be wounded and only one in 40 will die in hospital (Oxfam 2001:16,30), but such claims merely seek to exaggerate the violence by dehistoricizing it. Current expressions of Karamojong violence are not an aberration, but just the modern outcome of old practices, ideas and institutions of Karamojong warfare. Raiding is so popular now that even educated people go (J7). In other words, mortal violence against the other in Karamojong history has very little to do with the gun, Western technology and globalization. Though Uganda nationalists quite understandably attempted to put warrior traditions behind them, the military aspect of any culture tends to be persistent, so that it is difficult to disagree with Borgerhoff Mulder's comment (in Gray, Sundal *et al.* 2003:23): 'For pastoralists raiding and militarism are practically synonymous.'

A picture should not be formed of the Karamojong's continual enmity with all neighbours of a distinct political community. Trans-ethnic alliances may be made at personal, clan and, temporarily, tribal level. There may be intermarriage, and friendships are valued as insurance against disaster. Barter and trade may be useful, even necessary. There are clans, self-sufficient in cattle, who want peace and are said never to have gone raiding (P3). The elders, largely being those who are rich in cattle as opposed to younger men who have yet to establish their own herds and marry wives, may refuse to open the raiding season, or curse those who go raiding

---

[30] The old Nilotic practice of dental evulsion, knocking out the bottom, middle two incisors, is associated with this past (P3).

[31] The drive for a *moran* to be the one bravest in the band hunting a lion, in killing a lion by stabbing him in the throat, is undiminished in the pastoral Maasai today. The reward is the lion's mane.

without their blessing (Gourlay 1971b:144; Knighton 1990:I,330–42). There is de-escalation of raiding, not just escalation. There are ritual peace meetings, for there is a time for war and a time for peace. Karamojong frequently pray for peace, and political and economic circumstances will repeatedly combine to make it good sense.

5 Gun Metamorphosis

History is simple when it all turns on a single event. Before 1979, Karamoja was peaceful, pastoral and traditional, but that year ushered in the 'new era' of guns (Mirzeler and Young 2000:409). 'There is one single and identifiable cause of the change – the proliferation of automatic guns' (Leggett 2001:47). Since then the culture has been unequivocally infected by the ills of modernity. 'AK-47 raids currently represent the single greatest risk to the persistence of the pastoralist system and to the continued survival of the pastoralists themselves' (Gray, Sundal *et al.* 2003:23). It is just a matter of time before death will be pronounced. However the symptoms have not yet been adequately identified and measured.[32] Mirzeler and Young (2000:407f) write that there are 30–40 000 AK-47s in Karamoja, while Gray (2000:407) goes by a rumour that there are 100 000 automatic rifles there. A conference accepted the figure of 150–200 000 (Mkutu 2001:20). In fact, no-one knows at all, for there will be no counting.[33] Many warriors, and some herd-boys,

---

[32] Gray, Sundal *et al.* (2003:23) argue that cattle-raiding with automatic weapons is the 'single greatest threat to their biobehavioral resilience', with 'profound evolutionary costs', while stating that cattle-raiding used to be an adaptive component of a successful subsistence strategy with remarkable staying power. The AK-47, whose availability is linked inextricably to cattle acquisition that still shaped every aspect of Karimojong culture in 1998, just as it had done in the 1950s, now ensures cultural survival (ibid.:3–6). Their data however do not support the maladaptive threat: Bokora infant mortality dropped from a high of 37 per cent in the 1970s to 24 per cent in the 1980s, and 11 per cent in the 1990s (ibid.:19); the probability of Bokora and Maseniko children, both under fives and under tens, dying, halved in the 1980s and 1990s as compared with the 1960s (ibid.:8f); adult male mortality due to raiding increased from 22 per cent in the 1950s to 37 per cent in the 1970s, but fell to 33 per cent in the 1980s and 1990s, when the government peace initiative clearly changed no paradigms (ibid.:15). Even if the data gathered from women's memories in 1998 of relatives dying are reliable, causation by cattle-raiding or pastoralist ownership of guns cannot be established. Perhaps the major agent of violent death is predation by the state, which would certainly explain the large increase in the 1970s under Amin's regime, and the army killed many Karamojong in the 1980s and afterwards for no clear reasons (on my first day in Karamoja we stopped on the road to inspect the remains of two shot by the army; see Knighton 2003e for early 2002). 'We were running, running from the soldiers' (ibid.:18), not from the cattle raiders. In any event there have never been more Karamojong people or cattle than at the start of this millennium.

[33] If 700 of the most aggressive section of the Karimojong carried 47 assault rifles to a raid on the Pokot (*New Vision* 16.2.00), then the deduction can be made that less than 7 per

carry firearms. Some arms are buried under rocks. There is nothing very new about the gun, for it has been present since the 1870s. The colonial government licensed some, and there have always been at least a few illicit guns, however secretly traded in. The northern Turkana were never thoroughly disarmed, so they provided a constant potential supply of guns from Ethiopia. Failing that, Karamojong would manufacture some out of pipes. These are known as *ngamatidai*, closely connected in name to iron hoes with v-shaped handles *ngimatidoi* (Wilson 1973b:91). Illicit weapons increased after independence, and the Ugandan soldier has had continued difficulty in not looking upon his rifle and ammunition as a way of augmenting his income through sale.

Firearms are not novelties for the Karamojong; indeed they have enculturated them with very little fuss, just like other iron implements, all of which have to be bought from foreign blacksmiths like the Abwor and the Mening. The home-made gun and the iron shield (until the high-velocity rifle rendered them obsolete) may be fashioned by Karamojong, but guns are still made from imported metal, indubitably stolen or recycled from government or NGO pipes. Yet Mirzeler and Young (2000:409) try to argue that the 'new era' after 1979 can be seen in the desacralization of society. Their unnamed source opines that the power of spears emanates from the 'the soul, *etau*' of iron ore in sacred Mount Toror, and this has led to a change of ethics. Again comes the anonymous authority to say, 'As the hoes made from the ore of Mount Toror ruptured the earth which gave life to the sorghum grain, the spears made from the same ore pierced the bodies of the warriors and released their spirits' (Mirzeler and Young 2000:423).

Furthermore, with their observation that the 'people of North-East Uganda'[34] buried the hoe at the beginning of harvest and buried the spear to initiate war', they assert that 'the soul of iron ore' is the 'dominant metaphor for death and life'. Yet there is no recorded Karamojong custom of burying hoes,[35] which are just discarded when worn out with use, and spears are only buried to make peace, not war. Abwor

---

cent have access to AK-47s. Suppose the population of Karamoja has been growing by about 2 per cent a year since the 1991 census, giving a total figure of 443 400. Assume 83.8 per cent of Karamojans are Karamojong (371 660) and that 20 per cent of them are warriors (74 332), then, extrapolating from the one raid, those with AK-47s are 4991. To this may be added other firearms. The UPDF claimed in 2002 to have collected 10 000 guns and, having lost the trust of the Karamojong through the use of force, and by sparking an escalation of raiding, will recover few more.

[34] The 'people of North-East Uganda' most likely are not Karamojong at all, but rather Abwor, who are the Lwo-speaking blacksmiths of Karamoja, especially as they claim that 'spears blessed by the ancient spirits of the iron-makers in Alerek [Labwor] brought victory and justice to those who used them'. The source here is probably Lodoc, who is the Jie storyteller around whom Mirzeler's dissertation revolved. He spent a 'long time' in Labwor living near the government hospital at Abim, while his father was dying (Mirzeler 1999:313). He seems to have picked up some Abwor traditions there, which Mirzeler is trying to smuggle into a common Karamojong view.

[35] Novelli (1999:287) describes a Karimojong ceremony blessing the hoes before they are used for the first planting.

hoes have been replaced by those manufactured by Chillington in Britain from the 1930s,[36] and then by Chinese hoes, without in the least desacralizing agriculture and the rôle of women. Undaunted, they go on to build their argument.

> In the 1980s a new strain of sorghum was introduced, accepted as more productive, but believed to lack the spiritual properties which made customary sorghum beer effective. In the words of an elderly woman informant, 'we still offer sorghum beer during peace ceremonies, but like the guns of *wazungu* [whites] their grains lack souls'. (Mirzeler and Young 2000:423)

Having been involved in the multiplication of Seredo sorghum, which was introduced in the 1970s from Hubert Doggett's plant-breeding work at Serere in Teso, it is true to say that there was some consumer resistance to our distinctive seed. So taste trials were undertaken. It is quite possible that Seredo beer was not considered 'real ale',[37] yet plenty of the hybrid grain was grown, because of its superior yield, especially in drought. The Karamojong have never been utter traditionalists.

> Suppose a man comes to Najie from the west with seeds he has borrowed there. Suppose he digs his garden and plants those seeds while the person in the neighbouring garden plants his usual seeds, those of Najie. And lo! The person who has borrowed the new seeds finds that his garden has yielded well. Is he not well-pleased? Will he not say, 'These seeds have suited me well!' Will he not continue to use the seeds he has borrowed? (Amuk, quoted by Lamphear 1976:126)

Private opinions on matters of taste should not be projected onto a whole culture, but Mirzeler and Young (2000:423) carry on to claim that AK-47s have made many Karamojong elders question the spirituality and social implications of semi-automatic weapons.

> Many Karamojong elders agree that a spear made from the soil of Mt. Toror releases the spirit of the dead person which goes to the bush to join the rest of the ancestral spirits and seeks justice. The spirits in the bush are said to threaten to curse the people who do not accept full responsibility for deaths and losses. However, death and destruction caused by AK-47 bullets made from unknown soil are said to send the spirit of the dead person to unknown places instead of the bush where the ancestral spirits live. Because of this ancestral spirits could not seek justice and threaten to curse the person who might be responsible for death and destruction. (ibid.)

---

[36] One of the first Christian converts, Yakobo Lowok, was trading hoes for hides to sell in Soroti in order to augment his catechist's salary (Lorec 1981:12).

[37] Yet if 'Karamojong will buy sorghum beer before health care' (Mirzeler and Young 2000:424), it is preposterous to suggest that Karamojong would refuse it, just because it was made from Seredo sorghum. According to Mirzeler (1999:410) Serena-type sorghum is distributed as part of the agrarian rites in Kaceri instead of a traditional variety. The special concern is only for the succession of the Jimos fire-maker, who is required not to eat any alien food.

It is still difficult to know just how common such a view is, but it is certainly an interesting one. The main distinction is not from magic or lack of it in the soil, but in the issue of the ceremonies to deal with the vitality of the vengeful spirit (*ecenit*) as given above. A spear is blooded, so there is an object that has to be, or at least can be, consecrated, and a victim whose features are known at once. With a shooting, the enemy may die at a distance, and since warriors of either side are always left where they fall, the enemy may be more likely to remain *incognito*.[38] Without the blooded spear, the ceremony is robbed of its most potent symbol. What the above view does is to give a rationale for not having to follow the old customs used in the event of killing an enemy. The avenging spirit (*ecenit*) is seen as sent to the unknown places where the bullet came from, and not the bush where it can cause problems (*ngican*) for the killer. Thus there is no need in this case to be so closely associated with the victim, or to disengage from him, or to cease to use the gun, as had been the case with the spear. However the disruption to custom should not be exaggerated as it was not uniform anyway, for Pazzaglia noted two different ceremonies (Novelli 1999:278–80), and some note an ox being sacrificed, others a goat. Rowland (1983:9) considered that the spear-blooding and sacrificial animal-spearing are separate rituals, but all versions appear to include the latter, probably as the elders' recognition of the warrior's deed without which there is no entitlement to the public signs of enemy-name, cicatrice and ear-notches.

Mirzeler and Young (2000:423) conclude that 'the escalated armament has intensified local conflict within Karamoja':

> The culture of the gun, and the cultural changes triggered by the omnipresence of the AK-47 pretend far-reaching changes in social relationships, which are only beginning to work themselves out. The equilibria, which have sustained Karamojong survival in a taxing environment, and their normative embodiment, seem at risk. The soulless AK-47 is eating away at the soul of Karamojong culture.

However the Karamojong do not believe in souls, certainly not in Greek philosophical terms as immortal substances, nor even as the disembodied part of a person, regarded as a separate entity, and as invested with some amount of form and personality. *Etau* should not be translated as soul or spirit, if either refer to existence after death. For it is precisely death which marks humanity's loss of life-force (*etau*). The heart (*etau*) stops beating in the dead. That which causes a human being to be is no more. All that is left is vestigial spirit, whether *eparait* or *ecenit*. What this critical reflection does find in Mirzeler's shadowy material is that the Karamojong world is all connected by shady spirit, whether man, beast, seed, soil or metal. In this sense, the gun is not soulless. It is made by outsiders (*ngimoe*) as are spears, and all other metal. It may be acquired by exchange with outsiders, just like spears. The only difference is that the origin is unknown, situated in a far continent, and that very difference is used by a few Karamojong at least to rationalize their use without the spear-cleansing rituals.

Even when peace was at a premium in the mid-1990s, a variety of views were

---

[38] There will no doubt still be sufficient noteworthy circumstances for the killer or his age-mates to devise an enemy-name should he be lacking one.

expressed to the camera, but only the bereaved voiced what government wanted to hear.

> A prayer of the *emuron* at the sacrifice, 'May our enemies leave us in peace! May our weapons keep them away and may their cattle come to us.'
> Longora, a vigilante, 'Women only choose men with good scars ... My sons look after the calves; when they grow up, I'll buy them guns ... Guns are good ... And with a gun you can kill people. This will please your girlfriend. Then you are a real man and the girl will want to marry you.'
> His wife said, 'The one thing we objected to in him is his obsession with peace meetings. We preferred him when he used to raid ... Anyway without guns in Karamoja, people would die and we would be like dogs again. We thank the gun for what we have. You see a man without a gun is not a man at all.
> Maseniko woman, 'This is our land; the Upe took it from us by force. Now we've reclaimed it, thanks to the gun.' (Alwyn 1998)

The gun is 'not like the spear which was our own' (P5). Yet that is no reason to ban it, for '*Atom* (gun) has brought improvements, but it is also killing many' (P5). One improvement is that the enemy cannot easily steal cattle. A disadvantage is that men can even kill their wives when drunk, whereas before a spear would be sheathed for civil activities. Still this is a merely incidental, not a structural side-effect of guns. 'Nobody is using guns to get their own way in the family. The age-sets can still disarm rebels if they do not go far' (D4). The possession of guns is no defence against the pursuit of justice by clan vengeance upon a murderer or his herd.

Far from desacralizing Karamojong culture, the gun is being determinedly used by them to preserve their autonomy, their traditional politics and religion. Lamphear (1994:87) observes that, a century ago, alien technology, where it was borrowed at all, tended to be merely grafted loosely on to traditional structures. In their enculturation of innovations, little has changed. Whether you point a gun or a spear at Lokapel Hill, the spiritual effects are the same (J31).

Lurking still in the occidental mind, perhaps, is the assumption that traditional African peoples must succumb to the power of the Western technology. If it is now considered immoral for colonialists to use arms against African peoples and for neo-colonialists to supply or trade arms with them, it is assumed that Africans must remain passive to their power. It is the Ugandan or Western observer who retains a greater fascination with the modern icon of the gun than do the Karamojong themselves, who pragmatically rely on them to function merely as big spears. The word for gun (*atom*) has long been in use.[39] Cattle as a mediation of the Sacred remain the supreme good, and guns find their economic value and spiritual legitimation in their usefulness in defending and obtaining cattle.

Guns being let off in marriage celebrations just produce another impressive noise to add to the occasion, not a degeneration to the gun-law of Western films.[40] They

---

[39] *Atom* was the name of the Jie war-leader, grandson of the tribal military saviour, Loriang, who organized huge raids on the Karimojong using some firearms (Lamphear 1994:80).

[40] Though Tanner (1970a:21,24,36) kept likening Karamojong and North American disdain for central law.

were part of the dance in 1909, being used competitively to produce the most noise, smoke and fire (Bell 1949:137).[41] That guns are used in the bridewealth should not be seen as the profanation of marriage, which continues past traditions and its important cultural rôle. A senior Jiot showed horror and disgust at the thought of the Acoli considering grain, tobacco, beer and even agricultural implements as valid tender for bridewealth in 1955 (Brasnett 1996:26), but a gun is one thing, apart from human life, that has a price in cattle (three to four), precisely because it is closely associated with both. It may be concluded that the gun has been so enculturated that it is a suitably valuable means to acquire the cattle to perpetuate the beloved age-class and conjugal rites of the Karamojong.

However the value of a gun is a small fraction of that of the life of a member of the political community. The gun has not spoiled its coherence. What it has done is to allow inner tensions increasingly to be resolved by projecting them onto neighbouring peoples. If any young man lacks cattle, he has the age-old remedy of raiding them. Yet, since Museveni, there is a great imbalance of force with the Karamojong's Ugandan neighbours. Cattle ownership in Kotido District is 271 times greater per person than in Kitgum district, where a population of nearly half a million owns a paltry 3276 cattle. The ownership rate of sheep and goats is 20 times as great (Oxfam 2001:35). Since the demise of a northern-based government in Uganda, the Karamojong have raided its neighbours clean of cattle, but may bring them back for dry-season grazing. In their success they are in expansionist mode, yet even this is not a new departure; as was noted before the advent of the AK-47, 'revenge raids are a means of asserting dominance over an area permitting an expansion for grazing and watering' (Tanner 1970b:63).

The evils of success attend, for young men sell raided cattle and become drunk on beer and locally distilled spirits with the proceeds. It is the Acoli who used to be despised as pot-bellied drunkards. There are more shops and stores, markets, cattle sales and cash (J20), which take some of the edge off recent droughts. 'The culture is not changing,' avowed one patriarch (J10), 'there are only improvements.' Even the most senior elders, though dismayed by people being attracted to drink more than their Spartan pastoral duties can afford, sometimes approve the new self-sponsored developments (J30). To the Karamojong therefore the culture, far from rotting away, is thriving. The abundance of cattle assured by the instrumentality of the gun provides the means and the confidence to celebrate the traditional values at the assembly. Akujů is answering the old men's prayers at the sacrifice, which must then be seen as efficacious. The warriors are able to carry out their duty of feeding the elders, to whom Akujů is present. While other traditional religions have waged an underground war or appropriated modern disguises, the Karamojong have maintained the religious high ground, which is itself a vital factor in maintaining internal social control as well as allowing political unity to expand. However the morality of valuing *ngimoe* as expendable to Karamojong ambitions is not one calculated to be acceptable to others.

---

[41] Guns already had a long history of being used in dances, as Tosh (1978:85,91) records for the neighbouring Lango, who certainly encountered hostile guns in 1872.

Chapter 6

The Constitution of the Assembly, the Paradigm for Time

Traditional Karamojong religion, in its dominant form, is implicit in the way leading males assemble to decide military, jural, political, social and economic affairs to the extent that none of these can be adequately understood without attending to their deeply religious nature. East African pastoral societies are ordered primarily by age-systems (Baxter and Almagor 1978; Beaton 1952; Bernardi 1952;1985; Clark 1950; Gullliver 1953c; LeVine and Sangree 1962; Kurimoto and Simonse 1998; Peristiany 1951; Tornay 1980b; Wolf 1980). Though these may lack clear military and other functions, they do offer the vision of constituting an identifiable culture by instituting a social means to unity (Fleming 1965; Prins 1970; Stewart 1972;1977). Thus the assemblies of nomadic pastoralists are so likely to be crucial to understanding how they cohere that they must be researched in detail. Enough is already known of age-systems to see them not only conferring social status, but also defining time. The Karamojong understanding of time is not chronological, but event-oriented. The memorable political events are the promotions and initiations of age-classes. What the literature may not appreciate fully enough is the political import of what can be easily overlooked as quaint, vestigious ritual in a changing world.

1 Assemblies

The American anthropologist, Elizabeth Marshall Thomas (1965:139,141), likened the sacred places of the Dodosŏ to 'ancient churches', and a ceremonial sacrifice to 'an important church service'. No other writer has used the word, 'church', of the Karamojong, probably because assemblies have been analysed as functions of society rather than religion and, in any case, nothing would seem more foreign to Karamojong practice than either the Western or the Eastern traditions of the Christian Church. Yet that is to stand at the end of two millennia of continuous Church history which separates the current referent from what was originally a borrowed concept for assembly. At least there is no danger of Western Christian religion being cast as the prototype of Karamojong religion. Karamojong have three words for their assemblies.

Atukot

Both people and their cattle (*ngaatuk*) gather (*atuko*) primarily for political purposes, that is, to make a corporate decision about community policy or action. All political meetings involving the elders, and therefore concerning the community as a whole, are manifestly religious events. As the objective is for elders to agree a decision, it is better called a council.

Akero

Communal threshing floors are used as dancing grounds, which makes them especially sacred sites.[1] Thus the largest ceremonies are for the *ekimomwor* dance, which is a community celebration. *Akero* refers to a place, not the people, and may be the site for an assembly.

Akiriket

Akiriket[2] means both the sacred grove in which ceremonies are performed, and whose trees must never be cut, and the assembly which meets there. An example of a sacred grove is the little-known 'shrine' of the Orwakol section of the Jie, Nayen, which belongs to no sub-section. Long ago it was surrounded by homesteads, but the people,[3] under military pressure, moved to Kotido, leaving the bush to grow. Yet it can only be used for firewood after the sacrifice of an ox to open the wood-cutting season. The site of assembly itself is marked merely by a small mound to which the passer-by must add stick, stone or bone 'to keep the place happy'. Jie do not like to go there when it is dark, nor to take strangers there.

The assembly of initiated men, having stacked their weapons against a tree, sit in the shape of a horseshoe, opening in the direction of the commonly accepted tribal cradleland. The Karimojong open out to the north or northeast towards Nakadanya by the Apule river and the Jie and Dodosỏ east towards Koten and Loyoro. The senior elder sits facing out of the opening with the largest tree, often an old fig, or tamarind, behind him, flanked by the other elders. Members of the junior generation-set compose an outer ring, and behind them uninitiated men are sometimes permitted to sit, watch and learn. This formation is adopted at every level of community above the family, for all religious ceremonies, and for political and legal decision-making by the elders, who conduct the discussions and have the last word (Pazzaglia 1982:98f). Quarrellers may be reconciled at the assembly which is the hub of all public action. The act without which a gathering would not be *akiriket* is sacrifice (understood provisionally as making a sacred drama) for Akujů, to whom prayers are made, that the community might be blessed. *Akiriket* is the sacred assembly of the Karamojong, and constitutes their politico-socio-religious

---

[1] Cf. *akerit/akiker* (to be afraid, revere, honour)

[2] Cf. *akirik* (to guide, surround, hunt) suggests that, in the unutterably dim and distant past, the main point in men assembling was to combine for a hunt, whereby game was driven into a place where it could be surrounded and overcome. Such an occasion was, and is, among hunting peoples appropriate for religious activity.

[3] Most likely a Tap people, the Yen, who were absorbed as the Rengen (*ereng* Yen, red Yen) by the Ro. Other Yen settled below Mount Rom to the northwest.

organization. '*Akiriket* is continuing as normal with the elders praying and cursing evil. Only a few old men take a little meat back home ... There has been no change in the last 30 years, because they follow exactly what the elders have done'(D4).

A section may have a combined annual assembly with representatives from each sub-section, who bring an ox for the sacrifice. For instance the Jie section, Oding, held one in their sacred grove at Namoja in January 1998, while the other section, Orwakol, held one around October 2001 at Daidai (J10), the place of their very first sacrifice in Najie even of the grey bull, Engiro, and in March 2002 at Kotiang. The senior elders decide on place and time, according to moon, well in advance in order to declaim and pray over current affairs. *Akiriket* is also necessary before the sub-section may go ahead with the pivotal operations in both pastoral and agricultural management. Each homestead must kill a black goat before starting to clear their fields for the new planting season. No-one may do this until the elders have agreed at the sub-section *akiriket*. 'If they go ahead without the *akiriket*, their fields will be affected by stem-borers and other problems. It does not matter how many chemicals or machines[4] that are used, the crop will be bad' (J10). There is similar ritual for weeding time. They reveal a clear preference for a traditional world-view over a rational–scientific one.

Akiriket provides a living record. First its full members are men. They are not there merely to exclude women from power in society, nor even as representatives of their families or clans. They are there as a summation of society before Akujŭ and, under His guidance, to take responsibility for that society and act on its behalf for its common welfare. Secondly, the men are strictly ranked in order of seniority. Uninitiated men have no proper voice in the assembly and have a status relative to it similar to that of women, as *ngikaracuna* (they of the apron) or boys (*ngidyain*). The initiates are divided twice, into generation-sets and into age-sets contained within the generation-sets, but all initiates have an equal right to speak in the assembly, even if different voices carry different weight. The whole system, or part of it, is called *asapanŭ* (initiation) from *asapan* (to initiate) derived from '-si- apa-' (to make a father).[5] Initiation is not just a matter of man being father to an ox, for normally he will still not have the married status of fatherhood, for it enfranchises him in society. Herd and family go together.

Initiations are only held in good years, and any planned for years that turn out to be bad are stopped. For instance, there were no initiations in 1962 (P4), even though Namalu, like most district centres, had its highest annual rainfall for 20 years in 1961 (Baker 1977:153). There was sorghum in the granaries, but because the 1962 harvest failed, it was not a propitious year for initiation ceremonies, with hunger and

---

[4] The informant was a former Jie County Chief and a leading contract farmer with the Karamoja Seeds Scheme. His mention of chemicals and machines refers to the arguments and resources he received from its agronomists. There are empirical grounds for not planting first, as the early crops may be decimated by pests, or birds at harvest.

[5] 'Apa-' is not the normal word for father (*papa*) as in Nilotic, but that used for the ox-name, which a young man acquires. It is thus a formal appellation, and may well have been borrowed, with the generation system, from EC who use *abba*. On the other hand, it could be a throwback to PN-S/C-N times, when *aba was used for man.

war with the Turkana. The poverty, impotence and infertility of the year would have been passed on to the age-set being initiated, which boded ill for the country when they would be senior elders. Ritual must maximize its associations with blessing (Emoru 1998:24). The uninitiated are always keen for their turn, but 'the elders say, "No!" because problems would be inherited, not blessings'(P4). Initiations are continuing now, but, because there is no peace, no new age-set will be initiated, for the problems must remain with the old names. Thus Karamojong ritualism holds together the real and the nominal, the political and the symbolic, power and convention, causation and time.

2   Asapanŭ

'Elders decide for children or grandchildren which animal they will be initiated under when they are 18 years old'(J30). Yet the elders consider that the late 40s is a good age for initiation. Uninitiated men have to wait, not only for their fathers to be initiated, but also for their mothers to receive the anointing (*ekios*) of ghee, which is the final rite of marriage (J8,22). Moreover brothers must be done in the order stipulated by the elder, which means waiting for a certain age-set to open (Gulliver 1953c:155); in fact they like to be distinguished from their brothers by identifying with a distinct age-set or age-section. One 46-year-old father is still waiting for the Boko age-set to open to be initiated, even though his generation-set, Tome, has been open for 46 years and his age-section, Kwei, for four (J8). There is no maximum age, which at once demonstrates the primacy of the age-system over arithmetical age, for it is not a rite of passage marking the shift between adolescence and the age of majority. Thus the system is never merely the repetition of the past, but elders respond to contingencies, while at the same time showing that they have the prerogative to direct the system.

The animal names for age-classes may have been determined by the *atapapaa* long ago (P3),[6] but these have been largely forgotten as a chronological series by all but the old men who have time to talk over them and maintain their memory. The old names have then to be consciously memorialized by being reinstituted by the senior elders (J13). One may be guided by Akujŭ in a dream (Gulliver 1953c:152). There is also room for divergences between different parts of the social structure. Nacam (J30), in the Kaceri extension which he pioneered of the Caicaon sub-section of the Oding *ekitela*, ridge or territorial section of the Jie, had only one other age-mate in the whole of Kaceri. He wanted to remain true to his long record as an innovator, so opened a new age-section called Kwei. This depends on the elders in any sub-section or even clan, and Nacam was happy to watch others catch up with him. 'I just wanted to push them.'[7]

---

[6] Nilotes absorbed or developed ritual, age-sets and cattle-herding together possibly around two millennia ago (Ehret 1998:155).

[7] As families have joined his Caicaon extension from other subsections, it might be the case that Nacam is trying to promote Kaceri into a new sub-section, though he himself retains the set of seven. It could be that he is making political moves within Caicaon to take the lead.

Over in Orwakol, the other Jie territorial section, the elders of Losilang territorial sub-section had not begun initiations into the same age-set, due to be opened in October 1997, for their own reasons, but recognized that in Nakapelimoru they were doing something different. These differences are usually due to seeking a propitious occasion in every sense, and various localities may have bad harvests, deferring initiations until a good one comes. Again in Kalokorwakol, at Kanawat, on the road to Kaceri, the Kwei age-set was opened in 1986, at least two years after Kaceri. Moreover 'the elders were to decide the name of the new age-set' (J13); they were not going to be bounced into other people's decisions.

The normal designation of an age-class is an animal, but other natural features, such as rocks, mountains and trees, may be included. The Tome generation-sets are exclusively entitled to wear ivory armlets, and to make elephant noises and dramatic representations at the dances. What confuses the decoding of what does not appear at all systematic is that various other names are introduced to it with little differentiation by the informants. Every generation-set has its *ngikangarak*, openers. In other words a new generation-set, which only happens every half-century or more, is opened by the first round of initiations, without a separate new age-section or age-set being opened; they take the name of the generation-set only. It is a great honour to stand at the head of the new generation, and it is one for which they will have had to wait many frustrating years, while as many initiations as possible were being completed in the previous generation-set.

For half a century the Karimojong have been very clear about the nomenclature of their age-system. Moru and Gete generation-sets alternate.[8] Precisely because grandsons have the same name as their grandfathers, it is necessary to distinguish between them with another name not in current double use, and an old name, Mirio, has already been chosen long in advance to distinguish the next Moru generation-set. Karimojong are clear that in each generation-set there are four age-sections (P3,4). The Verona Fathers are equally convinced, following Neville Dyson-Hudson (1966:256), that there are five (Pazzaglia 1982:95; Novelli 1988:45,49). If the generation-set name is also counted as an age-section, as effectively done by the Jie, then this would be so, but the Karamojong do not consider *ngikangarak* (openers) to be a self-standing age-class. The Karimojong see the system belonging to the order of creation,[9] so laid out in fours.[10] There are four age-sections, each with four

---

[8] Each generation-set and age-section distinguishes itself by its chosen style or colour of decoration: head-dress, feathers, ear-rings, lip-plugs, armlets and even stool. For instance, the Gete-Tukoi generation-set adopted aluminium, the Moru senior generation-set favour copper, the Gete brass, and the Mirio generation-set yet to be opened will have copper as they are already defiantly wearing it, despite overlapping with their grandfathers (P3).

[9] Karamojong very much subscribe to what we call in English the four points of the compass, which are also linked to the apparent movement of the prevailing wind and of the sun from east to west, and the third (or perhaps in their world-view, fourth) dimension of up and down, sky and earth. An informant justified the significance of four with an example of the liver in a sacrifice always being cut into four (P4).

[10] This pattern in the informants' minds easily leads to seeing the generation-sets in a cycle of four, but generation-set names are only repeated alternately, Gete and Moru. If the

age-sets, lasting theoretically four years, each of which could have an initiation if auspicious (P4,P9). However each age-class begins with one round of initiations which take the name of the whole age-class: thus they may be known as Tome without any age-section name. They are designated as *ngikangarak*, which is not a name, but simply means 'openers': Pazzaglia and Novelli have picked up names to distinguish Moru *ngikangarak* as white, but this is more likely to refer to their decorations than to a fifth age-section. *Ngikangarak* may be succeeded by the first age-section in the same year or else not until up to two years later. Karimojong emphasize the names of generation-sets and age-sections and remember them well, so that the same eight names of the last two generation-sets have been consistently collected since Doris Clark's time (1950:215). Clark notes six names, but repeats Owa and includes *ngikangarak*, yet the confusion is more in the minds of the observers than in those of the people, as Table 6.1 tries to portray.

Because of circumstances and their auspices, age-sections and age-sets depart far from the mentally conceived pattern of 16 and four years, respectively, so that an age-section may turn out to be very short or to last more than 30 years. However in aggregate it somehow comes right, without any calendrical calculation being made. The implicit pattern of the mind gives a generation-set 64 years, but three age-sets being opened after one is promoted would reduce the span notionally by 12 years, and *ngikangarak* initiations would expand it by five years in practice, giving a typical result of 57 years, though always highly contingent on the relative strengths of a senior and junior generation-set towards the end of the former's reign and of rival political communities.

Individual honours go to the hereditary leader of the particular age-class, known as its spokesman (*ekeseran*), who is clearly demarcated by being the very first to spear his ox. Here age gives no seniority, for the rules of heredity may require that the youngest boy in the age-class be first to be initiated. The ideal is that the grandson will open the same age-set of the same age-section of the same generation-set as his grandfather did. 'The one who opened the age-set is leader, but he must operate in tandem with the age-set' (J22). Power is never vested in an individual, but in an age-class. Any members of the most senior age-section, after the promotion of their generation-set, at once become the most senior elders in the whole society. Among them the order of precedence still runs according to initiation ranking.

Typically there is no system that automatically comes into play at its own appointed time to regulate the transfer of age and generation-sets. No individual leader gives hegemonic direction. Among the Jie a group of the junior generation-set, interested in being promoted as the senior generation-set for the political leadership and ritual privileges conferred, will go to a senior elder to present him with gourds of milk, *atap* and beer. Having convinced him of this proper expression of loyalty and fealty to their seniors, they may say, 'The generation has grown big' (J30). The request means that the initiations for that generation-set have been largely completed and that there is now pressure from their sons to be initiated,

---

next generation is initiated as Moru-Mirio, it will be six generation-sets since those names were first used in combination.

Table 6.1   Karimojong age-classes

1.	**Kwangai** (white ones)	
2. c.1633	**Gete** I (Grant's gazelles, *Gazella granti brightii*)	
3. c.1690	**Moru** I (mountains) **Mirio** (field-mice, *Rodentia muridae apodemus*)	
4. c.1747	**Gete** II (Grant's gazelles, *Gazella granti brightii*)	
5. c.1804	**Moru** II (mountains) **Ngatunyo** (lions, *Panthera leo*) *ngikangarak*	
a.	Taaba (rocks)	
b.	Putiro (wart-hogs, *Phacocoerus aethiopicus*)	
c.	Dokoi (grey monkeys, grivets, *Cercopithecus aethiops*)	(Rengelem red ostrich feathers)
d.	Baanga (ducks, *Anas sparsa*)	
6. c1861	**Gete** III (Grant's gazelles) **Tukoi** (zebras, *Equus burchelli granti*) *ngikangarak*	aluminium
a.	Meguro (bat-eared foxes, *Otocyon megalotis*)	
b.	Owa (bees, *Apis mellifera*)	
c.	Wapeto (eland, *Taurotragus oryx pattersonianus*)	
d. 189?	Ru (small plant with green leaves and yellow fruit)	
7. 1897	**Moru** III (mountains) **Dokoi** (grey monkeys, grivets) *ngikangarak*	copper
a. 1898	Taaba (rocks)	
b.	Putiro (wart-hogs)	
c. 1913	Cubae (blue monkeys, *Cercopithecus mitis stuhlmanni*) Rengelem (red ostrich feathers)	
d.1942–3	Baanga (ducks)	
8. 1956	**Gete** IV (Grant's gazelles) *ngikangarak*	brass
a. 1956	Meguro (bat-eared foxes) there were initiations in 1957, 1959, 1964, 1966 at least	
b. 1975	Owa (bees) now closed – many initiates	
c. 1999	Wapeto (eland)	
Forthcoming		
d.	Ru (small plant with green leaves and yellow fruit)	
9.	**Moru** (mountains) **Mirio** (field-mice) *ngikangarak*	copper

Note: **1. Generation-set**, a. age-section.

which cannot happen until their father's generation-set has been ceremonially promoted. There are arguments, when elders have become few and feeble, that the effective political and legal leadership of society becomes atrophied, in which case the good of the whole community would be served by a transfer of power. Ceremonies marking the seasons and raiding may lapse for lack of elders. However the last to be initiated in the senior generation-sets have waited a long time for their age-set to reach seniority in their generation-set, and for them to agree to the request means they will be eclipsed for ever in politico-religious affairs. Their generation-set rolls at once into history. That only two generation-sets, one senior and one junior, may be active at once is the norm.

If the senior elder agrees, he can send them to another senior elder, and so on until the reform group has gone round all the remaining members of the senior generation-set. Thus, even where there is an emerging consensus, determined individuals have plenty of opportunity to delay proceedings, and issues of chronology do not enter. Though the elders come to recognize the political need for a transfer of power, they will not judge the time right until an auspicious year is reached, one of peace and plenty, for to do otherwise would blight the whole of the next generation-set, as everyone recognizes.[11] There are then considerable incentives for the reformers to be praying for such a year, and it is the prayers of the most senior elders that weigh most, so they must still be paid even higher honour.

> There are four age-sections. When all are finished initiating, the Karamojong sit together, 'All the ranks have finished initiating, and we want to start initiating into a new generation-set.' If the elders of the Mugeto [the senior generation-set] refuse, all of them will die without a generation-set opening. It is not done just anyhow; they must have permission from the elders. They don't know the year the promotion will be, for it is finally fixed only when the elders all agree. People go round the elders (*ngikasikou*) to ask them to decide. When they have sat and decided, the information as to the ceremony will be passed out. The same thing is done in other tribes [of the Karamojong cluster]. They gather together in subcounties [sections], 'You go and tell the same message!' So senior Tome go to equivalent generation-sets in other tribes. (J21)

This is a statement of what should happen, not what actually did, when Orwakol elders refused, and the Tome generation-set was opened without their permission while they yet lived (J20). In contrast the Oding section opened the Tome generation-set in line with the Karimojong, even though the previous promotion had been some 20 years out of synchronization with their enemies. Not to promote when your enemy does and to retain a weak leadership is a dangerous strategy. If constitutional standards were slipping before, they are not now when the Tome generation-set has been initiating for at least half-a-century. Though delays due to prolonged disaster can be seen as partly the responsibility of the senior Karamojong generation-set for their lack of ritual efficacy in bringing down solutions, religious authorities may easily point to the transgressions of the youth, particularly in

---

[11] Such a system of political succession stands in stark contrast to modern ones, where the incentives for the opposition lie in causing trouble, so that political opinion swings against the rulers.

raiding, for being the efficient cause of spoiling the country. Even if general dissatisfaction prompts a decision to change, the ceremony still cannot be held until the propitious time occurs, which could be a few years later.[12]

When the ceremony does happen, it involves all men over 18 years of age (J30). Gulliver (1953c:149[13]) and Lamphear (1976:39) were told that the transmission of power occurred at Nayen, the sacred grove in Orwakol, while Pazzaglia (1982:29) was informed during his journey that it happened at Kotiang rock, though united ceremonies happened at Daidai, the long rock in the River Longiro that is the focus of origin of the Jie people. Already, then, there is evidence that *akitopolor* is not necessarily a ceremony for the united tribe. 'Ngitome did not open with a combined ceremony, because the grandfathers refused, so initiations went ahead illicitly and locally' (J20). Moreover Nacam testified that ceremonies are held at different times by the Oding[14] at the section's ritual grove, Namoja, and the Orwakol at Nayen.

> Grandchildren will be of the same generation-set and age-set of the grandfather. There are two generation-sets, Ngitome and Ngimugeto. When one section meets, they must invite two or three of the other section. Everything should be done together, including opening age-sets, but obviously there is a difference between the idea and the actuality. (J22)

Separate promotion and initiation ceremonies were considered no threat to unity derived from there being observers at each, and each was kept informed of the plans of the other, while not feeling bound by them. This would appear to support Gulliver's thesis that ritual defined nothing political,[15] but rather it is to misunderstand, as Europeans so often do, the radically dispersed nature of power. There is no central authority to govern the uniting institutions of even a single Karamojong tribe. No section of the communion of elders can be ordered to do things, only entreated. This remains true even with a growing proportion of youth in the population, for the very survival of old people makes them more special.

That the ceremonies are separate is also testified by their dates, both sources being quite specific about their dates in general and quite able to trust their interviewer. Others present could have questioned their dating. Nacam was quite clear that the Oding *akitopolor* took place in 1956, the same year as the Karimojong ceremony. Lodio (J13), despite having read Lamphear, was equally certain the Orwakol started their Tome initiations in 1961, and neither referred to the other in

---

[12] The last Karimojong promotion ceremony in 1956 had to wait five bad years.

[13] Gulliver is mistaken on two counts: Nayen is not 'the tribal ritual grove', but only that of Orwakol; neither is it used only for promotion ceremonies, for seven bulls were slaughtered there in 2000 and 2001.

[14] Rengen is more the term used of the Oding by the Orwakol, but though they do not refuse the appellation, Rengen, the Oding like to bring attention to their own founder, Oding. Gulliver (1953c:149n) rightly noted a separate Rengen ceremony, but the age-system he observed still enabled him to 'write as if the whole tribe were a single unit'.

[15] Gulliver (1953c:163f) found the Jie to be politically atomistic, 'Sociologically, the limits of the Jie tribe can be best described in ritual terms. People of a district and of the whole tribe are kept together by indispensable ritual needs.' The age system existed chiefly to serve the ritual system, so neither could be political factors!

line with the general reluctance to make authoritative statements on someone else's territorial section (J17). Lamphear (1976:46), whose closest sources were Orwakol, was sure that the date was 1963, and he started interviewing only six years after that. Nevertheless there is no good reason to doubt the former sources, for it is clear that Lamphear has assumed that there was one ceremony for the whole of Najie. Oral traditions still do not relate well to the Gregorian calendar. Even where memories are accurate and not conflated to more immediate experiences, there is scope for much confusion concerning names (Lamphear 1976:41).

Since Tome is the name for each alternate generation-set in the cycle, many informants refer to it, especially when elderly, recently disenrolled Tome are still alive, as Osowa after the first, large age-set in the new Tome generation-set. If it is asked when the Osowa started their initiation, a later date will be given, for the openers (*ngikangarak*) were initiated in the first round of Tome initiations, then the Osowa age-section was opened for the next round. For Oding this happened a year later, in 1957; it is quite likely that for the Orwakol the Osowa began to spear their oxen in 1963, but two years after *akitopolor* as the harvest failed in 1962 (P4). The choice of 1961 was obvious, as it saw the best rainfall for two decades, following poor years since 1957 (Baker 1977:153). Furthermore J22 was himself initiated as Ngatunyo in 1986, a good year following three poor ones, after the age-set had been opened by an *akiriket* at Namoja in 1981. This agrees with the Orwakol date for opening Ngatunyo of 1986 (J13). It is likely that they had, or decided at, a ceremony at Namoja to synchronize with the Ngatunyo age-section out of sympathy with the Orwakol after a gap in initiations of four years. Thus both sections were then able to open the Kwei age-section in 1996.

Comparing names is further complicated by unsystematic preferences. An age-set or age-section can also be known either by the description of the ox speared by its first initiand or by the decorations with which initiates adorn themselves to mark out their identity. The same word, *asapan*, is used for generation-set, age-section, age-set and any initiation, so there is plenty of room for confusion.[16] Thus Rionomong is the black ox killed by the first initiand of the age-section led by the Osowa or of the Ngatunyo age-set within it.[17] Similarly the first age-section of the Mugeto is known as Rengelem after the red ostrich pom-poms that distinguish them (J30). It is to be expected that confusion arises, even in Lamphear's list (1976:36f) of age-classes, which includes as generation-sets and age-sets the names of their associated oxen and decorations. He himself describes (1976:41f) how he unmasks the age-section name, Osowa, as a means of distinguishing the particular Tome generation-set, but names the other as Koria instead of Mugeto, even though none of his Jie informants own the name. He may have been misled here by some research 'noise' from the Abwor, whose alternating generation-sets were known as

---

[16] Dyson-Hudson's specification (1963:358) of *asapanet* for age-set and *anyamet* for generation-set is scientifically helpful, but common usage is not so precise, being characterized by interchangeability.

[17] Lodio claimed to be the first initiand of the age-set charged with the responsibility of spearing the black ox, which as a grandson of the last Jie firemaker was entirely likely but it is still difficult to tie this to age-set rather than age-section.

Osowa and Koria (Abrahams 1978:39). As there was intense Jie influence on the Abwor at the turn of the nineteenth century, it is possible that this nomenclature was used among the Oding, but an Orwakol research assistant and reader of Lamphear completely refuted Koria instead of Mugeto as the name of the alternate generation-set to Tome (J20,22). This shows that patterns are elusive, being hidden in a hundred inconsistencies and exceptions, but most adults know the pattern sufficiently well for their purpose of finding their own way in it; the rules are seldom imposed in any systematic fashion, so that irregularities are easily absorbed and contradictions not highlighted.[18] This is in itself a picture of how life in general proceeds. Somewhere in it all is meaningful coherence, but there is no need to worry about the apparent confusions, for they will all be resolved as the cycle of life turns.

Both the Orwakol and the Oding have to bring gifts to their outgoing generation-set in multiples of seven to represent the number of territorial subsections in each of the two sections.[19] Each sub-section must bring an ox, a ram, tobacco, and seven gourds of milk for *akitopolor* at the sacred grove. In return the most senior member of the retiring generation-set ritually hands over to one ideal representative of the generation-set being promoted, who has already demonstrated his capacity to keep tabus (*ngitalia*[20]) concerning his gender role: he must not look in a pot on the fire, he must not look in a granary, and he must not drink from a broken gourd. All these three symbolize the integrity of the womb, which a man should have the wisdom not to look into, for these are women's matters that should be entrusted to women. Then a ram is slaughtered and its chyme used to smear the representative to cancel the effect of any tabus he may have broken. Fibres are tied to the back of his head as ritual confirmation of his fitness for promotion. The new generation-set all make the noise of their emblem, topi in the last ceremony. Then it is for the sacrifices and prayers to be made, and for the elders to feast as usual.

The issue of the length of generation-sets is not yet completed. While Gulliver (1953c:148) and Dyson-Hudson (1963:359, 389) thought that the span was between 25 and 30 years, Lamphear (1976:45–8) considered it to be around 40 years after trying as hard as he could to establish the date of the previous *akitopolor* in 1920–23. Yet Gulliver was absolutely convinced it was in 1935. The precise question put to informants is crucial, since *asapan* is used for generation-set, age-section, and age-set. To ask when the Osowa or the Tome speared their oxen is not the same, even when they are used interchangeably to denote the same generation-set. No-one hitherto has spotted the time gap between the initiations of the new generation-set and the first age-section. The first round of initiations in a generation-set comprises the older men and elder brothers, who have long been waiting for the

---

[18] This picture of 'illumination and obfuscation' is extraordinarily similar to Baxter's (1978:157): 'Boran do not find gada puzzling because they do not seek to explain it all together; as if it were something simple like cricket. They find their way through its maze of rules and of rituals as they need to, without any trouble at all. It is only foreigners who use other, and more naïve, cognitive categories who need a guide or notice dissonance.'

[19] Lamphear (1976:21) lacks three Oding subsections and the order of precedence, which are as follows: Pelok, Duman, Atap, Caicaon, Bwolin, Riwo and Doket.

[20] Ngajie has *ngitalia* compared to Ngakarimojong *ngitalyo*.

generation-set to be opened.[21] They are known as the *ngikangarak* and take the name of the generation-set and no other animal-name, though they may be known by the features of the ox that is first speared or the exclusive decorations allowed to that age-class. The same goes for the openers of each age-section. The names that any informant gives may be due to a host of factors, all rational, such as the prominence of an age-class, the current popularity of a name and personal preference.

No informant has yet been found who can set out the whole pattern comprehensively and systematically, yet memory has an implicit way of cyclically reviving the old names, so that few are dropped, except if they are associated with a disobedient and disastrous age-class, whose very name spells dislocation. Gulliver (1953c:148n) writes of 'vague recollections', yet 'nevertheless the theoretical principle remains in men's minds'. Though Lamphear has been able to open up a generational history of profound significance, inaccuracies would suggest that he has not sufficiently established names and dates. Analysing the average ages of his Jie informants (1972:466–82) shows an order of age-sets rather different to that compiled from his informants' testimony. For instance, Lamphear (1976:37) puts Korio two age-sets above Tukoi, when his Korio informants were actually 6.7 years younger on average.[22] Then, despite trying to avoid this in other respects, he appears to have conflated his understanding of age-classes before his living informants with those of the Abwor, through collaboration with contemporary researchers to the west (Lamphear and Webster 1971:39; Abrahams 1978).[23] Though the Abwor age-system was derived from the Jie, it would be odd if the names were all identical.

The Karimojong ceremony of *akitopolor* has been described by Dyson-Hudson (1966:186–95) since his fieldwork occurred shortly after the last one. At a time when it was alleged that the authority of the elders had broken down, it was fascinating to hear the oral tradition of an informant who had not been aware of the previous ceremony, but was being made conscious of the one to come. The three core clans of the Karimojong, Ribor, Lip and Danya, meet,

> when the latter hosts a custom (*etal*) seeking blessing from God, and the three sit together in consulting each other. 'What can we do this year or next if society goes wild, how can we bring it back to peace, obedience, respect? There are ferocious people (*ngitunga adedengata*). There is failing custom, because there are not people keen to keep the traditions and there seem to be few living beyond 80, compared with when they had responsibility.' They realize the trends and consult one another and decide to say, 'We

---

[21] The oldest mean age for an age-class interviewed by Lamphear (1972:466–82) in 1970 was 68.1 years, which means that in 1961 they were 59 at initiation, perhaps more according to the age and number of those who had died in between. They identified themselves as Rengelem, which clearly indicates the decoration for the openers (*ngikangarak*) of the generation-set.

[22] Lamphear rightly follows Gulliver against his informants. On the other hand Gulliver (1953c:151) omits Tukoi altogether from his exhaustive analysis of Kotido territorial subsection, yet Lamphear finds a 65-year-old one there. Most likely he had been called Rengelem, when Gulliver was there.

[23] The source of conflation could alternatively or also, come from three of his young Jie research assistants all being very well-acquainted with the Abwor (Lamphear 1976:263f).

need to go back to where they began to name them: Bokora is called the hind legs (*amuro*), the first wife, Pian the second wife, Maseniko the third.' There are three major sections, but a total of 11.[24] (P3)

The metaphor of 'wife' has nothing to do with gender, but shows how each section is conjoined to the Karimojong and ranked in order of precedence. Each section is given its identity, not like the Jie in battle, but at the cradleland of the Karimojong on the margins of Karamoja. It is there whither Karimojong must return in order to rediscover their original unity.

There is a distinction between clan and section. Clans have an unusually significant rôle here compared to the Jie and the Dodosŏ. Though pastoralists in general, and the Karimojong in particular are frequently dubbed a pragmatic people,[25] a clear sense of the ideal is reflected here. Clans, unlike sections, are seen as ethnically pure, at least in patrilineal terms, for the strict rule of exogamy ensures a continual genetic mix. Yet it is the three lineage-based clans, Ribor, Lipa and Danya, though spread across Karimojong, that are seen as the bearers of Karimojong culture in its most ideal form, conferring on them the right to lead in this rare convocation. Again these appear as inventions of the imagination, for some Oropom have been incorporated into the Ribor clan (P3), but then Karimojong are quite aware of these complexities and discount them before enunciating their beliefs. If every qualification were allowed to predominate, then nothing could be said.

It could be argued that mere ritual precedent, occurring only once in a lifetime and flying in the face of social reality, has no political validity, but that is to miss the peculiarly ritual foundation of Karimojong politics. The ceremony is not forgotten; it lurks in memory and expectation, and when it eventually happens, as it is in the interest of many to happen, it has profound political consequences. One of the hoped-for consequences is the restoration to full visible working order of cultural institutions that may have atrophied because of practical circumstances. Of prime importance among these is the rule of elders, which necessarily goes through a crisis before the ceremony can be staged. So long as there is any strength left in the ruling generation-set, it will delay the promotion that disempowers them from taking place. Societies as a whole, even those absorbed from different ethnic origins, such as the Southern Nilotic Oropom-derived clans, look to the ethnically pure segments to resurrect the culture. This is not mere ideology, for it is given as the reason why the attempts to bring together all the Karimojong sections[26] by the

---

[24] The Nyakwai are sometimes said to be a section represented at Nakadanya (Wayland 1931:203; M1) though, like the Abwor, they are known as a hybrid tribe ('half-brothers' Dyson-Hudson 1966:150,229) associated with blacksmith work rather than pastoralism, so contribute the special spear for the Nakadanya promotion.

[25] 'The Karimojong are a people pre-eminently pragmatic, as we said' (Novelli 1999:lxiii); Dyson-Hudson (1963:382,385) writes of 'practical wisdom derived from long experience in worldly matters' ... 'as in many aspects of their social life, the Karimojong are pragmatic'. Novelli's view has been much influenced by the writings of Dyson-Hudson, though that is not to deny the Karimojong their worldly wisdom.

[26] All published lists enumerate ten Karimojong sections (Dyson-Hudson 1966:136–47; Pazzaglia 1982:77–84).

Karamoja Initiative for Sustainable Peace failed. Focusing on politics to the exclusion of other aspects of culture in Karamoja is not in fact practical.

The three main territorial sections are also idealized as the 'wives' or firestones (*ngikenoi*) of the Karimojong. Despite being usurped in the ritual leadership of the 1956 promotion ceremony, the Bokora have always been, and still are regarded as, the most important section, 'the trunk', 'the true Karimojong' (Dyson-Hudson 1966:144–7), the first 'wife', the hind-legs, that is the seniority and the strength of the Karimojong. Behaviour for the ceremony is also surrounded by tabu, representing an ideal, which may often be far from normal in everyday society, especially among young men, but is nevertheless normative. That this is not mere rhetoric is demonstrated by elders needing to approximate to such behaviour, if they are individually to earn the dignity of their social status formally conferred by membership of their generation-set and age-set. Among their peers, exemplary behaviour gives a voice weight in the assembly, while an ox-thief, though an old man, can be beaten by the owner in public, whether it was he or his sons who were the actual culprits. Though occasional ritual can be the only reason for a tabu on sex for elders, whose duty it is to satisfy all their wives, the exigencies of the cattle-camp often impose a Spartan life for the warriors.

In 1950, there were only two elders surviving in Lotome, the place of the Tome section (Clark 1950:215). Promotion did take place 'not many years hence', and the Gete, Grant's gazelles, as they were known in advance, speared their first oxen in 1956. It is said that the next Moru generation-set will be opened between 2010 and 2020 (P3). In 2000, the nearest elder to Namalu, Lokol Apalomongole, was 30 kilometres away at Kobeyon, and he died a few months later. '*Akitopolor* occurs in Nakadanya after about 50 years, so it is growing near now, but there are many Pian still to be initiated' (P4). For a senior Gete, who has an interest in promotion, '*Ngimoru* are near' (P10). Similarly Lamphear (e-mail) found in April 2001 that Jie 'preparations for the inauguration of the new *Ngimugeto asapanu* are well underway', but it is clear that the Orwakol must open at least four age-sets first.

The new Karimojong generation-set will be known, as was said immediately after their fathers' generation-set was opened, as Mirio (mice)[27] after their great-great-great-great-grandfathers of the first distinct generation-set of the Karimojong. Even though they are not initiated, they are already beginning to wear the copper ornaments associated with Moru generation-sets, as a deliberate, ritual provocation to stimulate the grandfathers to consider retirement. If the elders do not have the heart or the power to enforce rigid discipline on ornamental matters, then it is time for them to go. This is the dilemma the uninitiated want to manufacture, but of course the elders in their wisdom will not be drawn by such a ruse. The enforcement

---

[27] This contrasts with Dyson-Hudson's expectation (1963:360,400n13) that they would be called Ngatunyo, which is now not on the agenda, thus disproving his theory of a rotating cycle of four names. The cycle is restricted to two, Moru and Gete, while they may both be distinguished by additional names. It is quite possible that Ngatunyo proved, even at the beginning of the antecedent generation-set, an unwelcome name, when the previous Ngatunyo cursed their juniors, resulting in the worst dislocation of people and land in memory.

of discipline is reserved for what really matters to them, whether the disobedience is symbolic or behavioural.

So what is, in general, the average span of the generation-set? In 1950, Doris Clark (1950:215) noted that it was a 'great many years' since a promotion ceremony had been performed. Dyson-Hudson (1963:396) estimated it to be at the turn of the century, giving a span of '50 or 60 years', yet he still chose the biological one at half the length, despite finding the 1956 succession to be the only one remembered (1966:205). Lamphear (1976:46–8) arrived at 40 years for Jie generation-sets, based on his dating of two promotion ceremonies in the twentieth century, the Mugeto in 1920–23 and the Tome in 1963. The latter date has been shown to be inaccurate by as many years as his fieldwork was distant from the supposed event. He has testimony for both 1920 and 1923, yet much depends on the age of Lokepon and his being the first initiate for the whole generation-set, even as a boy, and not for an age-set or age-section within it.[28]

Even if 1920 is being testified to, all the informants cited belong to the Orwakol section and not Oding, which could well have been earlier, as they were in 1956. Opening the same age-set could be 20 years apart in different Abwor sections (Abrahams 1978:65). Only four of Lamphear's 'grandfather' informants were born after 1905, and they still could have been initiated after the 'father' generation-set had been opened (1976:47). Indeed Lamphear's own observations (1976:45n) ten years after the 'grandsons' generation-set was opened in Orwakol was that initiations of the under aged 'fathers' could go on for about 20 years after their generation-set has been theoretically closed. The most decisive evidence could be given by the average estimated ages of the survivors of the first age-section of the fathers' generation-set, who were born around 1902. However it is not possible to adjust for older initiated men who later died, or for those who categorized themselves as wearing the distinguishing decoration for the generation-set, while being initiated in a lower age-set. There was clear testimony by an outstanding informant, Lobilatum (Lamphear 1972:471; 1976:240) that Loriang's army was officered by the 'great-grandfathers' and the 'grandfathers', presumably as senior and junior generation-sets at the time. Thus it is unlikely that *akitopolor* could have taken place before 1911, and that a date of around 1915 or anything in the second

---

[28] Gulliver (1953c:149) identified the hereditary 'senior leader' of the Mugeto generation as being born in about 1917 and too small to even lift a spear for an ox-spearing in 1920, while Lamphear (1972:470) estimates 1910. Since Lamphear's leader was from Kotiang while Gulliver was concentrating on Kotido men and believed that the Mugeto generation-set opened in 1935, it is not clear that they were talking about the same men. (Though it seems unusual for there to be two young 'senior leaders', when they are selected for being the eldest son of the eldest son of the senior leader in their grandfathers' generation-set. Most likely Gulliver is referring to an age-section, not a generation-set.) Not only is there a hereditary spokesman ('leader' is too strong a word, referring only to going first in the spearing of his ox, which will be of the emblematic colours of his age-section) for the whole generation in a section, who is also the spokesman of the first, opening age-section, but there are spokesmen of all the other age-sections and age-sets. Michael Lodio, as he was pleased to tell me, was first to spear the black ox of his age-set in 1974.

decade is possible (see Table 6.2 for a reconstruction of Jie age-classes). Given that there are still possibly seven age-sets to be opened before the next *akitopolor*, it is unlikely to happen before 2020, but then three of them could still be opened after promotion.

The Karimojong expect to open their last age-section in this generation-set between 2010 and 2020, having only opened their last one in 1999. In the previous generation-set, the last age-section was open 13 years before *akitopolor* (promotion), but this time political pressures may intervene. One informant elder, remarkably comfortable and accurate with dates and ages, was sure that not only the Moru/Dokoi generation-set was opened in the nineteenth century, but also the first full age-section, Taaba (P4). His father he reckoned to be born in about 1887, and considered him, like himself, to be initiated after his generation-set had been promoted, in 1907 among the last age-sets initiated. Similarly his grandfather was born around 1840 and initiated in the last age-section of the Gete/Tukoi generation-set. An age-section mate, less comfortable with dates, was sure that 'The Ngitaaba opened when the British came; Locukut was camping in the slope in the river' (P13).[29] Locukut has never occurred in the literature, but it most likely refers to the Honourable Algernon Hanbury Tracy of the Royal Horse Guards. He was the first European to enter Karamoja, rather than skirting the perimeter, in order to establish an advance depot at Manimani among the Pian on the banks of the Omanimani River.

Lt Hanbury Tracy was in Karamoja for three weeks in September 1898, buying pack-animals, and in December was sufficiently '*persona grata* with the Karamojo [*sic*] natives, amongst whom he had spent considerable time in the past year', to prevail on them to organize a dance for 100 men and women (Austin 1903:70,80, 222f,239). This was the very first time that the Pian could have seen the British, or rather a Briton, in their territory, and they associated him with an *acukut* (bank or valley). Major Macdonald's main force went through in September, but he was known as Bilic, the bull with the broken leg (Pazzaglia 1982:55). So this gives the clearest possible date of 1898 for the opening of the Taaba age-section, with the *ngikangarak* (openers) of the Moru generation-set probably being initiated the previous year in 1897, which satisfies the oral tradition that it happened before the British came (P11). The same source carried the memory that the Cubae age-section fought the British, when they first saw them. This clearly refers to 20.8.1913, when angry Pian attacked a patrol of the Northern Garrison under Captain R.H. Leeke of the Rifle Brigade touring from Acoli. The warriors from Locoworyan lost two casualties before a more politic deputation went into his camp at Manimani to 'acknowledge their errors' (Barber 1968:127). All of this is most consistent with the rough Karimojong estimation that a generation-set lasts about 50 years (P3,P4; Novelli 1988:49). It is consistent with Neville Dyson-Hudson being unable to unearth memories of the previous promotion ceremony (1966:205; 1963:396).

The conclusion emerges, then, that there can only be two ceremonies a century at most, but that, judging just from the last completed one, the Jie generation-set lasts only 40 years and the Karimojong 60. The Karimojong by 1897 had suffered

---

[29] P3 could only put it at 'before 1910'.

a great mortality and emigration of elders, possibly so that they became too few to rule and had to hand over to the Moru generation-set. Many of those who sought refuge among the Kumam and Pokot were killed. Others went to the River Turkwel and beyond, settling in Trans-Nzoia, and staying with the Bikusu south of Mount Elgon, only to die of smallpox (Turpin 1948:163f).[30] Though the Jie were similarly hit by the same disasters of the 1890s, the Karimojong response was more drastic for the home society, after the elders cursed the junior generation-set (Dyson-Hudson 1966:217). It is most likely that a promotion ceremony was called to bring a closure to the time of Erono, and there was awareness through prophecy that a new era was dawning. However there is evidence that generation-set spans are now reconverging as the Oding section of the Jie had their last ceremony in the same year as the Karimojong and both will have the next some 60 years later.

The Jie are rather different, for they tend to emphasize more the names of their age-sets and their decorations or sacrificial oxen attached to them or to age-sections or even to generation-sets. They are not very clear about age-sections, yet it is apparent that some names are more inclusive than others. Though the Jie hold to a fourfold pattern, it only works if *ngikangarak* are counted as one of the four. Gulliver (1953c:150) was correct to find 'about three' age-sets in three age-sections if he was trying to identify numbers of distinctive animal names in an age-class. He deduced that the age-section takes its name from its first age-set (ibid.:152), when rather it is the case that the members of the first age-set are initiated into the name of the age-section, being its openers. Though there is greater articulation of detail of age-sets by the Jie, they can omit age-set names in any age-section to give the same irregular outcome in practice.

The Dodosŏ age-system may be sketched similarly (Table 6.3). Initiations must be into the generation-set following the father's. The span of a generation-set is reckoned at 50 years, but of course the informant could not possibly have attended two promotion ceremonies (D6). As with the Karimojong and the Jie, no Dodosoit informant recognized the Palajamŭ generation-set at all, as the first to be explicitly associated with Nakadanya was Murya (D9). Unprecedentedly they share the same name for a generation-set before that: Kwangai (white people[31]) with the Karimojong (D9). This gives a pattern: when a tribe crystallizes by leaving the ancestral stock in enmity, it does not remember the previous, shared names of the generation-sets. The Jie have no clear memory before Tome of the Kwangai initiating and the Turkana have no clear memory before Palajamŭ of the Jie Tome initiating, or before that of the Kwangai initiating.

---

[30] Lamphear 1976:223–5; Jackson 1930:237; Turpin 1948:162–4. There is no record of their being 'in a very impoverished state' (Macdonald 1899a:136). 'The Karamojo are a magnificent people of great stature ... possessing immense herds of cattle, donkeys, sheep, and goats'. Austin (1903:70f) simultaneously observed that 'some men were the most magnificent specimens of humanity I had ever seen with grand powerful limbs, chest, and shoulders'. They seemed more successful hunters than hunting and gathering tribes but preferred to trade some game with the Kitosh for flour. However it is footloose warriors who may be expected to have the strongest physiques in society thanks to better nutrition.

[31] If the colour derives from the white clay there, this would suggest the previous generation-set was associated with Nakadanya.

Table 6.2 Jie age-classes

1.
2. c.1633 **Tome** I (elephants, *Loxodonta Africana*)

3. c.1692 **Mugeto** I (topis, *Damiliscus korigum*) **Kok** (army ants, *Dorylus* spp.)
a. *ngikangarak*
b. Risai (leopards, *Panthera pardus*)
i. *ngikangarak*
c. Korio (giraffes, *Giraffe camelpardalis rothschildi*) Lukumong (ox's horns curving down/in)
i. *ngikangarak*   Eleki (earrings)

4. c.1750 **Tome** II (elephants, *Loxodonta Africana*) **Siroi** (dikdik, *Rhynchotragus kirki*)
a. *ngikangarak*
b. Osowa (buffaloes, *Syncerus caffer*)   Rionomong (black ox)
i. *ngikangarak*
ii. Ngatunyo (lions, *Panthera leo*)
c. Kwei (jackals)

5. c.1808 **Mugeto** II
a. *ngikangarak*
b. Risai (leopards)   Rengelem (red ostrich feathers)
i. *ngikangarak*
ii. Tukoi (zebras, *Equus burchelli granti*)
c. Korio (giraffes)   Lukumong (ox's horns curving down/in)
i. *ngikangarak*   Eleki (earrings)

d. Murya (duikers, *Sylvicapra grimmi*)   Kokol (black-spotted ox)
i. *ngikangarak*
iii. Tiira (trees, *Acacia tortilis*)

6. c.1866 **Tome III**   Black and white ostrich feathers
a. *ngikangarak*
b. c.1870 Osowa (buffaloes)   Rionomong (black ox)
i. *ngikangarak*
ii. c.1874 Ngatunyo (lions)
c. c.1885 Kwei (jackals, *Canis adustus*)
i. *ngikangarak*
ii. Lobai (hartebeests, *Alcelaphus buselaphus jacksoni*)
iii. Boko (tortoises, *Geochelone pardalis babcocki*)
iv. Beri, (grasshoppers, *Zonocerus variegates*)
d. 1895 Dewa (grass-snakes yellow and white stripes, *Natrix* sp.) Nyangamong (yellow ox)
i. *ngikangarak*

ii.	Suguru (wait-a-bit thorns, *Acacia brevispica*)	
iii. 1905	Moru mountains	
iv.	Kolimoru (rock doves, *Columba livia*)	

7. c.1915–20   Mugeto III

a.	*ngikangarak*	Rengelem (red ostrich feathers)
b.	Risai (leopards)	
i	*ngikangarak*	
ii.	Tukoi (zebras)	
c. 1923	Korio (giraffes)	Lukumong (ox's horns curving down/in)
i.	*ngikangarak*	Eleki (earrings)
ii.	Gete (Grant's gazelles, *Gazella granti brightii*)	
d. 1935	Murya (duikers)	Kokol (black-spotted ox)
i.	*ngikangarak*	
ii.	Tiira (trees, *Acacia tortilis*)	
iii.	Wapeto, (elands, *Taurotragus oryx pattersonianus*)	(red and white striped ox)
iv.	Kerekerei (woodpeckers, *Dendropicus fuscescens*)/Baanga ducks (*Anas sparsa*)	

8. 1956/61 Tome IV   Pokoi (ivory armlets)

a. 1956	*ngikangarak* of Oding only	
b. 1957	Osowa (buffaloes)	Rionomong (black ox)
i.	*ngikangarak* of Oding; Orwakol in 1963 (Lamphear 1976: 41, 46)	
ii.		
iii. 1974		
iv. 1981	Ngatunyo (lions) (Orwakol section in 1986)	
c. 1996	Kwei (jackals, *Canis adustus*)	
i.	*ngikangarak*	

Forthcoming

ii.	Lobai (hartebeests)	
iii.	Boko (tortoises)	
iv.	Beri (grasshoppers)	
d.	Dewa (grass-snakes yellow and white stripes)	Nyangamong (yellow ox)
i.	*ngikangarak*	
ii.	Putiro (warthogs, *Phacocoerus aethiopicus*)	
iii.	Moru (mountains)	
iv.	Kolimoru (rock plovers)	

9.   Mugeto IV

Note: **1. Generation-set**, a. age-section, i. age-set.

Table 6.3 Dodosŏ age-classes

1.		**Kwangai** (white ones)
2.	**c.1633**	**Baanga** I (ducks, *Anas sparsa*) **Murya** (duikers, *Sylvicapra grimmi*) Inaugurated at Nakadanya
3.	**c.1690**	**Tome** I (elephants, *Loxodonta africana*) **Buin** (hyenas, *Crocuta crocuta*)
4.	**c.1747**	**Baanga** II **Owa** (bees, *Apis mellifera*)
5.	**c.1804**	**Tome** II **Putiro** (warthogs, *Phacocoerus aethiopicus*)/**Ngoletiang** (bald wild animal?)
6.	**c.1861**	**Baanga** III **Korio** (giraffes, *Giraffe camelpardalis rothschildi*) *ngikangarak*
a.		Kerumo (hornbills, *Tockus* spp.)
i.		*ngikangarak* (the openers)
ii.		Ngoroko (ox spotted like a cheetah)
iii		Tukoi (zebras, *Equus burchelli granti*)
b.		Osowa (buffaloes, *Syncerus caffer*)
c.		Wapeto (eland, *Taurotragus oryx pattersonianus*)
d.	c.1930	Rionomong (black ox)
7.	**c.1899**	**Tome** III **Kamar** (wedding-dancers) *ngikangarak*
a.	1900–	Ngatunyo (lions, *Panthera leo*)
i.		*ngikangarak*
ii.	1915–	Gete (Bright's gazelles, *Gazella granti brightii*)
iii.	1920–	Moru (mountains)
iv.	1920–	Rengemong (red ox)
b.	1928	Meriemong (spotted ox)
i.		*ngikangarak*
ii.		Risai (leopards, *Panthera pardus*)
c.	c.1949	Rianamong (light brown ox)
d.	1952	Nyamong (yellow ox)
8.	**1959**	**Baanga** IV **Aleeso** (ostriches, *Struthio camelus*) *ngikangarak*
a.	1960	Kerumo
b.	1965	Osowa
c.		Wapeto
d.	1977	Rionomong (not yet opened in Kaabong)
Forthcoming		
9.		Tome I Dooi (field-mice, *Rodentia muridae* sp.) denotes the generation-set that has not been allowed to open.

Note: **1. Generation-set**, a. age-section, i. age-set.

The Dodosô identify very closely with the Karimojong, from whom they claim to take the lead for opening new age-classes and being present at all ceremonies at Nakadanya. Dodosô senior elders went in 1999 to Nakadanya with their Karimojong counterparts to fetch the sacred white clay and to sacrifice. There were many problems of killings, diseases, drought and snakebites, so they wanted to consult. 'Then the senior elders decided' (D6). Collaboration demonstrates political unity was the message. 'For us we are Karimojong' (D6). Yet the Dodosô have their own system of names and their own times for opening new age-classes, not dependent on the Karimojong;[32] in fact timings are closer to the Jie, both opening a Rionomong age-section within three years of each other. However it is unity with the Karimojong that must be emphasized, when it is the Jie who are the perpetual raiding enemies. Every year in Kopus the senior elders process in single file to a goat sacrifice, and then announce an annual general assembly for Dodosô, which will give dos and don'ts for the whole tribe. A tribal *akiriket* can be held at Nakwakwa and Lokumro, when there is peace for Akujû to appreciate their activity. '*Akiriket* sorts out problems' (D6). Despite interruptions, and the Dodosô suffering the worst calamity of all in the great famine of 1979–84 when all their herds were lost to drought or enemies and the senior elders died so that no ceremonies were held, 'their culture has returned to normal. Initiations are going on in good years' (D6).

These results shows that Paul Spencer's mathematical model, based on Samburû demographics, gives more accurate results than the estimation of social anthropologists and oral historians, for his model came out at an optimum span of a Karamojong generation-set in a stable system of 55 years, or 57 years given certain preferences (Spencer 1978:108f). These are the rules of the Jie system inferred by Gulliver and amended by Lamphear, on which Spencer depended:[33]

1 Only two generation-sets, senior and junior, are formally constituted at any one time.
2 Preceding and succeeding generation-sets are so predictable that the generation-set, past or future, of any male can be told by that of his father or son.
3 The remnant of the grandfathers of the junior generation-set will inevitably be small, and even this will expire quickly.
4 Full membership of a constituted generation-set is only received through personal initiation. Generation and not age gives entitlement to membership of a generation-set.
5 A new generation-set is opened once all their fathers have been initiated, but there is no formal closing of the group.
6 There are strong links between grandfathers' and grandsons' generation-sets.

---

[32] Dodosô elders are aware of certain differences in customs (*ngitalyo*) with the Karimojong, as in the burning of sacrificial animals in funerary rites (D5), though they do bury the sub-anal, iliac gland (*angarwe*) (D6).

[33] Though the four principles isolated by Spencer (1998:99) reflect Gulliver (1953c), the corollaries do not. In particular Spencer's emphasis in his first principle is quite different from Gulliver's fifth. Gulliver virtually contradicts himself, for if the generation-set is not closed, then the possibility remains that it is open to more initiations.

These rules of the system hold just as true today, though some qualification is required of his interpretation then. In (3) Gulliver did not realize he was looking at fathers whose generation-set had been promoted at least 30 years before, and in (5) that some of those fathers had been initiated after their generation-set had been promoted (Lamphear 1976:45,47). This means that the grandfathers had 30–40 years before Gulliver arrived to die out after the promotion of the fathers.

Frank Stewart (1977:28–44) formulated rules for the Jie system of generation-sets:

1   Sets are ordered.
2   There is no overlapping.
3   There are two sets.
4   Sets dissolve in order.
5   There is a minimum enrolment age.
6   There is single membership only.
7   There is no resigning, except by leaving the society for ever.
8   There is no rejoining.
9   There is no shrinkage, for every son of a member of a set himself joins another set.
10 This is an ideal generation-set model, because a man joins the first set to begin recruiting after the one his father joined.

Again Stewart's assessment is purely theoretical, but he was quite correct to note that the generational principle would result demographically in a widening age-span shown in 'underaging', when boys beneath the minimum enrolment age would be initiated into a set being closed to recruitment, and 'overaging', when the minimum enrolment age was passed by the uninitiated waiting for their set to start recruiting (ibid.:48f). Indeed he believed that the model was a false representation of the actual, with genealogies being rewritten, and rules not being strictly observed. Only structural amnesia allowed the fiction of a system to be perpetuated, while at the same time Stewart (ibid.:221) speculates that in Jie consciousness both generation-sets overlapping in recruitment was a sign of social and ritual degeneration causing drought, illness and impotent initiations.

Dyson-Hudson (1966:196–204) and Stewart (1977:66,222) were informed of two additional rules concerning the Karimojong: the uninitiated could not go raiding, and the uninitiated could not marry. The first rule is scarcely credible as anything more than a notional ideal, since all men and boys who are herding cattle are exhorted to fight to the death for them, and *ngikajok* (warriors) have always been conceptually distinct from *ngisorok* (initiates of the junior generation-set). '*Ekajon* has no connection with *asapan*, age, marriage, or fatherhood. He is just a defender or attacker' (P3). *Ngikacaruna* (uninitiated) currently provide many warriors. It is possible that the nineteenth century battalions were composed of initiates for large, set-piece battles, but there were still opportunities for the uninitiated in scouting and the baggage train.[34] The second rule has more credibility as traditional norm, but

---

[34] That nineteenth-century Jie battle formations were divided exclusively into age-sets

Dyson-Hudson does not clarify what he means by marriage, which is a long-drawn-out process. Now there is no sense that initiation is a requirement of Karimojong marriage at any stage (P5). Dyson-Hudson (1966:202f) concentrated on rules that allowed self-righting mechanisms:

Demotion   When all members of a retired generation-set have died, recruitment to the senior generation-set is closed. Remaining candidates are directed into the junior one.

Promotion   A son born to an unmarried mother will be initiated into the generation-set of his uncles, reflecting a legal paternity: effectively the mother's father occupies this rôle, not the immediate genitor.

Simultaneous recruitment   The senior generation-set is kept open as long as possible to ensure a supply of vigorous men to maintain the authority of the elders.

Of the self-righting mechanisms, promotion and simultaneous recruitment are standard features among Jie and Karimojong, though the latter is, just as Dyson-Hudson and Spencer (1998:110–13) depict, offset by the desire of the junior generation-set to assume power from a dwindling number of elders and of the overaged uninitiated to be initiated as members of the assembly at last. The first could not have been observed by Dyson-Hudson coming at the turn of generation-sets as the grandfathers were long dead, so he could not have witnessed their underaged candidates being initiated, against the generational rule, into the fathers' generation-set.

In fact the ethnographies are good so far as they go, but Stewart's and Spencer's use of them to demonstrate two contrasting systems needs to be questioned, as do their predictions of degeneration. Though the maintenance of the systems is undoubtedly decentralized, both within and between tribes, there are harmonizing mechanisms at work taking the form of a 'local, aggregated process' (Dyson-Hudson 1966:197). As in business location, competition as well as cooperation may lead to ceremonies of the promotion of a generation-set being brought as close as possible. For one tribe to be governed by a few aged and senile elders is a security risk, when the enemy has promoted a large and vigorous generation to power. Then why did the Jie hold their promotion ceremony between 1915 and 1920, when the Karimojong had held theirs in the late 1890s? The answer lies in the terrible times of the 1890s, known simply as *Erono* (bad). It is quite likely that the Karimojong suffered more than the Jie, as many were obliged to take refuge west of Elgon and around Kitale, or to perish in Teso (Austin 1903:70f; Turpin 1948:163). The same environmental disasters afflicted the Jie, but they seemed to escape with a lower mortality, by living off hunting and gathering, sheep and goats, or bond-friends and

---

(Lamphear 1976:230) is denied by his own evidence (ibid.:213) that the battle-leader Acuka was killed trying to rally the remnant of his territorial subsection. The territorial structure may have been ranked according to generation-set, but the decisive military innovation used by Loriang is the institution of his central and hierarchical direction and of his bodyguard.

relatives in nearby Labwor or Eastern Acoli (Lamphear 1976:223–5). Thus Karimojong recongregating in Karamoja would have found themselves bereft of their old men, because of famine, disease and emigration. Unstoppable pressures would then have arisen from the junior generation to be promoted in order to fill the power vacuum. Why did the Jie not follow suit? Despite their being numerically smaller, the next decade found the Jie snatching the ascendancy from their neighbouring rivals to fight on Karimojong territory. As there were men of the senior generation-set fighting effectively in the victorious Jie army, it clearly had plenty of vigour left. It would certainly have been strange to have had a promotion while Loriang and his age-set were still alive in the fathers' generation-set (Lamphear 1976:229,260). He would have been around 60 had he lived up to 1915.

Hence it is not difficult to see why promotion ceremonies should diverge, but why should they come back together? In the next round the Oding section of the Jie hold theirs in the same year as the Karimojong, and the Orwakol only five years later. Of Lamphear's informants nine years after the Orwakol promotion, 38 per cent of those identified as initiated men were of the grandfather generation-set aged mid-70s on average, while Gulliver (1953c:148) thought that no-one of the grandfather generation-set might survive at all to promotion. Clearly Spencer's demographic model based on biological age does not explain the Jie promotion after about 40 years, while satisfactorily accounting for the Karimojong span of 58 years. Promotion is not merely an internal dynamic of competing peer groups, but can also be affected by strategic military considerations. The 1950s were a time of raiding, and the Jie considered that they needed to have a new generation-set to mobilize the people, not because they might run out of members of the senior generation. The possibility remains that a merely ritual unity is still sought among the Karamojong. This might account for the observation that the Jie did not retire or dishonour their elders as they observed amongst the Karimojong (Lamphear 1976:153f). The Jie grandfathers' generation-set allowed promotion on the understanding that they were not retired, while encouraging a greater mobilization of mature men. However, all other things being equal, it can be predicted that both Jie and Karimojong generation-sets will last about 55–60 years, so that most men will only experience one promotion in their lifetime, while more will see none rather than two. This helps explain why no-one can give an overview of the whole age-system. Is it then stable?

There are demographic features which must tend to destabilize any model based on a generational principle. For instance an aged elder like Nacam (J30) sired his eldest surviving son, Nakwaki, when he was around 36 and sired a son from another wife when he was 86. Suppose he leaves a widow of 20. She will be inherited by a younger brother or son of Nacam, but any child born will be counted in the generation-set of Nacam's sons. A text from Pian is in complete accord.

> My mother was inherited by her husband's eldest son, who became my father, whose *asapan* is decided by the legal father. Legally I was a brother to the biological father who has not rights in inheritance: he is raising up, begetting, children in his father's name. Therefore a man can be producing children in his name for 70 to 80 years. In the old times a lady would lie on a man of property in order to conceive to distribute to the poor ... [on being challenged whether this was merely an old custom]. You are right ... it still happens. (P3)

His legal father and biological grandfather was of the Gete generation-set. Even though his biological father was of the Moru generation-set, he was initiated into the same one despite being too young, 12 at the most, to spear his ox before the Moru were promoted. Clearly there was little pressure to end further initiations, as he was initiated when he was 22. It is perfectly possible for the progeny of one man to have a span of 70 years. In the next generation-set it is conceivable that the span lengthens, if the youngest son is equally prolific, to 140 years, then to 210 years and so on. How can a system hold when a generation-set lasts less than 60 years?

The system does in fact do much to accommodate the underaged by allowing overlapping. That is, when a generation-set has been promoted as senior, it may continue recruiting new initiates for another 40 years, thus encompassing a range of nearly 100 years. Jie testified that Mugeto could still be initiated 37 years after their generation-set had been promoted, provided they were sons of the previous Tome generation-set (J13), very few of whom could still be alive.[35] The few who are too underaged for this and so undoubtedly born posthumously to a widow who gave birth at a relatively advanced age, would be able to take advantage of the slip mechanism that allows a man to drop down two generation-sets (P3). He still would not be much overaged, being little more than 30, and his initiation would not violate the strict generational principle, since he would become a member of the grandson's generation-set, who are considered as identical substitutes for their grandfathers. In their terms, 'Grandchildren recur' (P3). Thus there is no reason for underaging to be progressive, destabilizing the system. What it does do is to protract the tension between retiring elders and ambitious *ngisorok* by ensuring that some of the former are younger than some of the latter, yet this is considered to be of social value, no doubt by elders due to be retired, in order to give their generation-set more vigour and time in power. Here the bulk of a generation-set must eventually find precedence over the stragglers of the previous generation-set.

Two informants aged about 55 were initiated into the Moru generation-set exactly ten years after it was promoted and the Gete generation-set started initiating. They still had not reached the phase of senior elder as members of the last age-section, Baanga (ducks), even though it started initiating 58 years before (P4,11). The final age-sections and age-sets in a generation-set are frequently named after birds, who otherwise do not figure. The Kucila (*Ploceidae* spp., weaver-birds) are an age-set of Baanga. It is as if those initiated out of the proper time for a generation-set's recruitment have been able to fly into the system rather than walk. The Jie have rock-plovers, woodpeckers and ducks.

Overaged sons, that is sons born near the beginning of their fathers' generation-set, may die before their generation-set is opened for them to be initiated (Dyson-Hudson 1966:198; P3; J11). This is not a rare occurrence. If there are still two age-sections to initiate in the fathers' generation-set, it is pointless for the sons to agitate for a promotion. One informant (J6) died aged 40 years with the possibility of initiation unlikely for another ten years or more; another (J29) is over 45. The first wife of four for Lokol was wed (*ekutan*) 20 years ago, meaning that he is likely to

---

[35] At the end of the century there were no grandfather Tome found alive in Najie and no grandfather Gete Pian, thus indicating that the system was not out of kilter due to underaging.

be 50 or more, but he is not initiated (J4,6). His father was initiated not long after the previous promotion ceremony (J32), indicating that Lokol will have to wait until after the next promotion ceremony.

However, if a man dies uninitiated, his sons may take their father's place in his generation-set, which may account for the relatively young leaders of an age-section (J20). This would satisfy Karamojong notions of fairness, but it is the only definite exception to the predictable generational principle: 'Grandchildren will be of the same generation-set and age-set of the grandfather' (J22), and it has not been picked up by researchers before. These are initiated into a generation-set succeeding that of their grandfathers and they do not follow in the generation-set after that in which their father would have been initiated. Yet the whole point is that their father was not initiated, so he does not count in the system, however illustrious he was. Thus the sons may be initiated in the generation-set in which the father took no possession. Even if the father was as old as 60 when he died before initiation, his son will be around 30, a normal age for initiation, so this is an obvious and fast-acting, self-righting factor of the overaging problem. Thus the generational principle remains inviolate in the form in which Karamojong express it, if not in the way that Spencer (1998:99) does, and in their social context: 'you cannot be initiated in the same generation-set as your father or your son' (P3).

It would be strange in Africa for rules to be always hard and fast.

> Timos Loram Lemukol, an Ekegetait born in 1918, had a girlfriend, Iriama, and by good luck she bore Lomongin, but another man brought bridewealth, Loduk Aporkomoli, an Emorait, an Ecubait. When the time came for initiation, Lomongin remained with his uncles who considered him as a brother, so he was initiated as Emorait, because the father of his mother was an Etukoit [Gete]. Legally he should have been the son of Loduk. (P3)

What it is at issue is not the generational principle, but the legal definition of father, for there are three candidates. The biological father, Loram, who was son of the successor to Aciya as county chief of the Pian, is ruled out, for he never paid the bridewealth. Loduk did, but his legal rights appear to have gone by default, through his son living with his mother's brothers. Had there been a divorce and the bridewealth repaid, then it would be clear that his mother's father would be his legal father.[36] Logically this was not the case, and Lomongin was only *de facto* in the homestead of his mother's father. For the purposes of initiation, then, he was considered quite naturally to be the son of his maternal grandfather.

The other complication brought here gives some semblance of support to Stewart's assertion that widow inheritance rules were not strictly observed and to his unfounded conclusion that the age-system depends on 'structural amnesia' in

---

[36] When Neville Dyson-Hudson (1966:199) finds that in divorce siblings count as children of the divorcee's brother, this only makes sense in the absence of her father. His report of second initiations makes little sense and has to be put down to either misreporting or the temporary crisis before the promotion ceremony. There is a clear, if unintentional, error in his sentence: 'Inherited widows transmit to their children, irrespective of the genitor the right to join the generation of [sic; should read after] her deceased former husband' (ibid.:205).

order to work in practice (Stewart 1977:221). 'Men can have wives, so that children can be initiated into different generation-sets' (P4). Now he may have meant age-sets and that sons of different wives should be initiated into variously named age-sets is indisputable[37] (Gulliver 1953c:154; Dyson-Hudson 1966:205; J11), but when I raised the generational principle he admitted 'there were exceptions we allowed'. The accepted norm is that 'Children of the youngest wife are considered to be in the same generation-set as children of the first wife' (P3). However it is difficult to imagine why a young man, or his family, would want him to be initiated into a junior generation-set even if his peers did, when a senior one was still recruiting. If it had closed at last, he could drop down two generation-sets. Dyson-Hudson may not have realized this (1966:202), 'but it is possible to put the very young back two generation-sets' (P3). 'The youngest normal age for initiation is 10–15' (P3; 12 years old for D6), for the initiand has to be able to 'hold a spear and make to spear the ox' (J20), even if another kills it. Daniel Lopul of Lotome and Loduk Aporkomoli are cited as being initiated in the generation-set below that predicted for them (P3). There may be peculiar reasons for these cases, and the latter suggests a reason why his wife's son, Lomongin, found a way round the rules, but in neither case is the generational principle flouted; it is just that a generation-set has, exceptionally, been slipped. It is then possible to arrive at that rare conclusion in African Studies, a law: 'you cannot be initiated in the same generation-set as your father or your son' (P3).

There are other norms, which are appreciated despite the reality. One is that a man 'should be initiated before marriage, but there are exceptions' (P4). This would be normal enough with initiation typically between 18 and 30 and marriage between 30 and 40, or at least that phase of marriage (*ekutan*) where the bridewealth is satisfactorily paid. Since a man always has to wait his turn behind his father or brothers to gain wives, this phase of marriage is not going to be hurried however low the age of sexual intercourse is brought (J10,20). The problem comes with overaging. Where this became acute before a promotion ceremony, it was ignored (Dyson-Hudson 1966:198f), as it often is today, when many young warriors have become cattle-rich through raiding. Exigency has led to a variant custom being enculturated by the Jie. They have no norm of initiation before bridewealth, which mutually reinforces household ranking among sons of one father, but they are very strict on initiation before the final ceremony of marriage and the status that it confers, especially on the woman. A woman is not fully a wife, and may not be initiated into the women's age-sets that shadow her husband's, until she has been anointed with oil in the ceremony called *ekios*. Without it Jie marriage is not complete even though it may come decades after *ekutan* (J4).

> You can complete marriage without initiation except the last stage of smearing cooked oil in a clay pot on the bride in the husband's home. If she commits adultery after sharing the *asapanů* of her husband, it will be shown with bloody diarrhoea, which affects the clans of both man and wife and their animals in the situation of many incidents … there is a relatively small proportion reaching this far. (J20)

---

[37] Brothers positively want to be divided, for it gives them a fresh identity for their different ages (P3).

If the husband dies without initiation, then marriage never happens. So the pressure for every man to be initiated remains, but compared with the Karimojong, this allowed the Jie when outnumbered on all sides in the latter half of the nineteenth century to concentrate on the serious business of increasing the tribe's lesser population unhindered by formal constraints. The Karimojong carry out an anointing (*akinyonyo*) as an initiation into the bride's new clan after she has come to live as a member of it (J22). Her husband's initiation does not affect her status as fully married woman (*aberu*).

The rule is that women should be initiated into the age-class parallel to their husbands. Entrance into this important status for any woman is at *ekios*, when all the other marriage rituals have taken place and the husband has been initiated. Women's age-classes though derivative of the men's system certainly have their social and jural importance. They meet to discuss women's affairs and have the mandate to deal with crime committed by women that is not already solved by the family or clan or by vengeance from another clan. Since a wife always changes clans and her father's clan will not welcome her back for fear of having to repay her bridewealth, it may well be that age-sets are needed to decide and enforce discipline through specific punishments (J22).

3 Dualism

Their generation-set system has classed the Karamojong among the societies that believe the cosmos is structured by the interaction of opposing ultimate principles (Maybury-Lewis and Almagor 1989:2). Their cosmologies embrace the age-old oppositions between agriculture and livestock, light and dark, male and female, life and death. The two generation-sets or moieties are indeed an opposition, a duality, for they divide all initiates into fathers and sons.

Father and Son

The fathers hold wives and cattle while restricting the ambitions of their sons in the same direction. The sons must spend Spartan lives caring for the herds of their fathers and defending the nation. When, at ceremonies, the junior generation-set makes a mock charge at the senior generation-set, their spears stabbing the air within centimetres of the elders' faces, it is not merely a display of their ability to defend their people but also contains the latent threat of the younger wishing to displace the older. Unflinching, the elders look them in the eye with the moral courage that comes from acting for the *summum bonum* and not for personal aggrandisement.

The opposition is more marked among the Karimojong, for the generation-sets vie to initiate the underaged, each seeking to bolster and prolong its power against the other in the knowledge that, once retired, they will be dumped into ignominy (Dyson-Hudson 1966:203f). Every *akiwodokin* ceremony is a potential crisis, for the juniors have every opportunity to go off with the cattle to form a new society with themselves as elders. That this is a rare event is a testimony to the unifying factor of *asapanů*.

Maybury-Lewis (and Almagor 1989:13) claims that dualistic theories offer equilibrium by the harmonious interaction of contradictory principles because they are in a cosmic scheme. Almagor's (ibid.:144) fifth component of dual organization states: 'the commitment to social and symbolic dualism includes the sense, that the whole is more important than any of its parts'. Yet this indicates an ultimate monism, not utter dualism.

Moreover the generation-set system is not connected with any of the usual oppositions; neither generation-set is characterized as evil. Nor is the Karamojong cosmic scheme fundamentally dualist, while acknowledging evil. It is in the generation-set system itself that the interpenetration of the divine and the mundane is seen, though it might be fair to add that the fathers represent the more spiritual side of a scale, and the sons the more worldly. There is no fundamental dichotomy if *asapanû* meant to make a young man a father. Rather, there is a progression from the passions of youth to the wisdoms of age in which the growing seniority of age-sets and generation-sets provides perceptible steps. In due time the sons are destined to become the fathers, likewise to guard the traditions, if they will only be patient.

If dualistic theories offer harmonious equilibrium, it must be questioned whether they are really dualist. Static, binary oppositions are not fundamental here, for they are ever in a process which produces a dialectical third. Though two generation-sets only are formally recognized in the cycle, they are never alone. Elders of the retired generation-set hang on and sons to be initiated in an unopened one are continually being born. The very old, the young, and women, who have their vocal say in the home, are constant reminders that *asapanû* functions to serve the whole community, of which the two generation-sets are but a representative part. A synchronic study of *asapanû* may give a dualist father–son appearance, but a diachronic one will yield a triadic movement: grandfather–father–grandson in a rounded whole. Reality is dynamic and its 'deep structure' is trinitarian, not dualistic, neither dangerously idealistic nor degenerately pragmatic.

Generation versus Age

The main tension in the system is between the ideal of the genealogical principle and the remorseless fact of biological age. The Jie and the Karimojong strike different balances. While the former revere age at the end of the system by not stripping elders in the retired generation-set of their authority, the latter acknowledge age at the beginning of the system by initiating the underaged into the generation-set following their proper one. Both imply a relaxation of the alternation of generation-sets, the Jie valuing old age more, the Karimojong maturity. In Labwor and Turkana 'the rôle of the generations is very much attenuated and young men are initiated into age-groups much more clearly according to their age' (Abrahams 1978:56f). Thus the Jie are accurately reflected as the conservative idealists of the group, the Karimojong as the expansionist pragmatists, the unruly Turkana and the divided Abwor as more individualistic (Gulliver 1955:252ff).

Unity

A comparative analysis of the Itunga points to the generation-set system as one of the chief unifying factors of a people. Naturally politico-socio-economic considerations enter in here but the mainspring, in proportion to the intensity and persistence of unity, seems to be religious and preternatural, though not removed from the natural. It is the system's task to employ and perpetuate 'the fundamental political and ritual assumptions' of Karamojong life (Dyson-Hudson 1963:367). It is no accident that initiated men, when they act in accordance with *asapanů*, are not merely concerned with the apparently trivial, personal decorations that specify their status within it, but are acting, whether territorially, politically or otherwise, for the unity of the whole community. 'The form, object of devotion, aims and occasions of ritual are identical for all territorial groups, which can therefore act independently or in varying combinations as the purpose requires' (Dyson-Hudson, N. 1960:286). The 'church' of the Karamojong comprehends most territorial and social divisions, because its faith unites all those holding pastoralist values.

Since women are only represented by men at the *akiriket*, this unity might be less than voluntary, if they do not share the same faith, the same theological and cosmological presuppositions (see Chapter 9, 'Women's Affairs'). From a society-wide view, Abrahams suggests (1978:62) 'that, notwithstanding the many difficulties involved in actual operation, the model of a system of generation groups succeeding one another has certain formal and substantive properties which make it well-nigh ideal as a conception of the well-ordered progression of a society through time'. This is also endorsed by Lamphear (1989:253), as implying the 'transcendence of mortality'. As women, Rada Dyson-Hudson and Elizabeth Marshall Thomas are not derogatory about the communities with which they lived, the latter (1965:59) perceiving in *asapanů*, 'the order and the immortality of the nation'.

4 Male Initiation

The closest translation of *amuronot asapan* is a sacrificial rite to initiate. It is not merely the slaughter of an animal for a feast, but a sacred, religious occasion, where the death of the victim is the instrument of consecrating the initiands. This is clear from the cognate terms, *amuro*, to sacrifice, and *emuron* or *amuron*. That these are all religiously significant terms is given unintended support by traditional Christian approaches that emphatically associate them with witchcraft and sorcery. The sense of threatened rivalry for religious allegiance is only compounded by the fact that nearly all baptized informants are also initiated at some later date, and come to value that initiation. It seems that the attempted ban by the use of such highly pejorative language is only upheld by those who are excluded by being given only a distant prospect of being initiated according to the age-system. In other words the spiritual condemnation of such sacrificial practices has rebounded because the mass of Karamojong have accepted the rite of nominal Christian initiation without it affecting their cultural rights. Any attempt by the church to presume baptism means the end of animal sacrifice will be rejected as yet another instance of Europeans not being able to understand the goodness, irreducibility and sheer inevitability, whatever their personal preferences or ideals, of their African tradition. Yet the enquiry needs to be made here whether it is merely an issue of traditionalism.

Conditions

It is the elders of the clan who suggest initiation of candidates for their son's generation-set (P1). A good year is required, in order to hold initiations (*ngasapan*) so that there are sufficient surplus oxen and grain for the ceremonies, which are held after the sorghum has ripened from July to November, to be real feasts. The elders will fix the time and the place. It is best to initiate in the first quarter of the moon, and worst when there is an eclipse of the moon (Pazzaglia 1982:104). A candidate must have permission from his father or whoever is head of his house, and the local elders, to participate in a ceremony which will include as many young men whose ranking allows them to be initiated. It depends on the extent of territory covered by the participating elders as to where the ceremony will be located. It may be at the territorial sacred grove (*akero*), or in a secret place in the bush, which the elders have chosen beneath a fig-tree (*ebobore*, *Ficus sycomorus*), which the elders have selected to sit under. If there are only one or two initiands, it can be held in the cattle corral at home (*lore*) (P1).

Given that a man is of the eligible generation-set, he must wait for his siblings who are older, or born of a more senior wife, to be initiated first. It is not the custom to be initiated in the same age-set as a full brother (Gulliver 1953c:154). Thus at every level the seniority of primogeniture and age within a family is reinforced. The would-be initiate (*esapat*) must find a fat bullock to spear from a friend or his father's herd, but usually this is considered to be the candidate's expense. So he must beg a bullock from a bond-friend or exchange livestock with a friend to acquire one (P1). Initiation is not just of ritual importance, for it has social and political ramifications. Normally it is the rite of passage for adulthood, and candidates must be at least 18 (J30), except when a generation-set is about to be closed, or for the hereditary opener of an age-class. Yet it certainly is a great ritual moment that cannot be confined to the spiritual, but responds to and infuses physical life, because the distinction simply is not made. There are no Ngakaramojong terms for 'spiritual' and 'physical'. Thus no diseased person may be initiated, for disease in itself effectually symbolizes in advance the absence of the very blessing that the ritual is supposed to effect and to celebrate, thus emptying it of meaning. He must be healed first, just as initiation must not be held in a time of famine. It would be to bless disaster and so court it for the future.[38] Though sexual relations are not forbidden to the uninitiated, who can start the marriage process, it used to be the case in living memory of the Karimojong that he may not pass the stage when he takes his betrothed from her father's home to his own until he is initiated and has

---

[38] It is at points such as these that the Christian faith, with its message of the cross and spiritual blessing in the midst of disaster, finds a natural *entrée* into such religious systems. The appeal to the marginalized is great, but the mainstream will only be diverted to consider these issues when the culture is seen to be failing their long-term interests after very many years of suffering. The Dodosô suffered most after 1979 and did not recover many cattle until the mid-1990s, but still they refused to accept the message given them by Christians, witnessed by the author in 1984, that their tribulations were due to their refusal to repent of their old ways. Charity they would accept, but no obligation to change their minds.

paid the bridewealth. Since his father, or head of house, controls the latter, he has an effective veto in the matter, so that the uninitiated never has the right to found a family of his own without the connivance of his affines. If he has managed to take a girl to his own home, he faces possible divine judgment before initiation, in that, 'if the wife should die, the man would die as well' (*ani etwani aberu, totwan ekile dang*; Pazzaglia 1982:104; cf. Persse 1934:110). While initiation will usually take place in a man's 20s, he will not be a married man until nearer 40. The procedures will be followed of an initiation that was enacted on 1.4.02 in Lokitela-ebu in Orwakol, Najie, but in continual comparison with other such ceremonies in order to isolate local peculiarities.

Preliminaries

The initiand (*ekasapanan*) may shave his head or pluck out his pubic hair. He has his obedience to his ritual seniors tested by their begging from him his more precious personal possessions, such as his sandals, or sheet (*asuka*). He must comply, as he relies on them for the gift of the symbols of his initiation. Personal finery is meticulously prepared by all who attend. The men prepare their leopard skins, head-dresses and ostrich feathers; the women soften with ghee their goat or gazelle-skin skirts, which nowadays are reserved for festivals such as this. They may also use ghee as ointment for their own skin. They polish their bead, iron, copper or brass necklaces, bracelets and anklets. On the eve of the sacrificial opening of the ceremonies proper, the initiand's kin, friends and co-initiands gather to sing and dance the night away (ibid.:105).

Contrary to Gulliver's dictum (1953c:153) that there was no 'school of instruction in matters of tribal lore', Lamphear (1972:512) was tutored by his jural father in the observances he would have to keep after he was initiated, such as 'not to look directly into a cooking pot, not to sit on the stool of a member of a senior asapanu [*sic*], and ... which parts of the sacrificial ox it was proper to eat'. A Karimojong initiand is told on the morning of the sacrifice by his father or maternal uncle, with all solemnity, the history of the generation-sets and age-sets and the symbols of that he is about to enter (Pazzaglia 1982:106), but it rather depends on the father. A senior member of the same generation-set, here an Etomait opener, will lead the proceedings under the supervision of his *asapan* fathers.

Spearing the Ox

The victim must be a bullock (*emongin, edonge*) except that a younger maternal brother is covered by the ox of his older brother if he spears a he-goat at the same event. The object is to spear the victim in the corral, using the right hand, behind the first ribs of its right flank, so that the spear penetrates the heart (P1), killing the ox as quickly as possible. If it is an adult who misses, he may try to spear again in the right place (P1). If the initiand fails, his sponsoring seniors will take over to ensure that it falls on its left side. It is a bad omen if it does not, but a very good one if its head points towards the tribal cradleland. The ox, Logarapus (that of the blue stripes), was speared at 9:00am and fell in the ideal position.

Source: Ben Knighton

Photograph 6.1 Lotuko (he of the zebra): the ox to be speared at initiation tethered in the cattle corral on the morning of the ceremony

Dismembering the Sacrificial Victim

First the tender meat below the rectum (*elamacar*[39]) is cut out with a spearhead and reserved for the elders to start the banquet (P1). However, for the first time at an ox sacrifice, the initiand may be allowed to kneel down at the carcass and, with his face in the stomach cavity, to drink deeply from the pool of blood collecting there. '*Italeo akimat ngaokot ngitunga ngulu eroko nyesapana*' (Pazzaglia 1982:109n; 'It is tabu for people to drink blood, who are not yet initiated'). It is in entering into what was formerly tabu without danger that signifies the initiate is 'elevated into manhood' (P1), and a one- or two-legged stool-cum-headrest (*ekicolong*) which he will always carry, may be awarded to denote that elevation. Consuming the blood is imbibing the life-force released by the sacrifice of the victim. All parts are cut into pieces by the junior generation-set. The 12 main pieces of each carcass are heaped on leaves. After fetching firewood and delivering the empty stomach sacs to their mothers they must braise cuts of meat for the elders, who are not slow to tell them the intricacies of their new duties, while they themselves begin to eat. The butchery is done by up to six Tome, while a kite (*eculi*) flies overhead. First the *elamacar* (sub-anal flap) is removed for the initiates. Then the flanks and the hind legs are removed, which anyone can eat, and, after 45 minutes, the entrails.

An *ekesiemon* (haruspex) may come at any time to divine the entrails or not. An *ekerujan* (dreamer) will come if he has a message to impart from Akujů. Unless a haruspication of the entrails reveals an urgent problem, the stomach sac is slit ten minutes later, to reveal the most sacred element of chyme (*ngikujit*). The Oding would do the anointing at this point. At 10:10am the first butcher drinks of the blood, followed by his colleagues. Blood spilt on the ground by the spear 'is for Akujů', but it is thought bad to spill much. 'This is our church: the Karamojong church,' it is explained. The joint of the hind legs is cut with an axe at 11:00am, and the head and neck are taken out of the corral to the yard, where the women cut it up for soup. At noon fire is brought from the home and the *elamacar* is roasted. The flank is roasted on a spit. The ruling age-section (Korio) roast the hind legs, the strongest part, but the initiand must help by holding up the tail, so that its hairs are not burned. The senior elder takes a foreleg and holds it for an initiand to bite off small pieces of hoof to spit on his own chest.

The Anointing

At 12:30pm the senior generation-set, Mugeto, remove any clothes of the initiand, who will never wear them again. Then a senior in the initiand's own generation-set anoints (*akijuk*, *akitujuk*) him with the steaming chyme taken from it, chiefly on the initiand's forehead, temples, chest, shoulders, and the outsides of the hands and feet. He holds his *lokaliye* wand. Everyone there who is willing is anointed with chyme as a blessing (P1). 'Smear' is the word used by English observers, but this is to focus on the material being used, rather than on the profound significance of a sacred act. To be anointed with chyme (*ngikujit*) is to be given God's blessing for your life and

---

[39] *Akila*, to be clean; *emacar*, brand, mark.

any evil spirit is driven away. The anointer may add his own by spitting in the anointed's face. '*Tobar, togogonyar! Toruko ka ngikonei ngula [sic] alalak: Toruka ka ngaberu ngulu alalak. Tomojong*' (Pazzaglia 1982:110; cf. Dyson-Hudson 1966:165; Be rich! Be strong! Be together with many friends! Be together with many wives! Become old!). The implications of the change are immediately brought home by a ritual beating by the initiand's seniors with a switch (*lokaliye* from the *ekaliye* tree) which sends him running from the place. His age-mates haze him out of the gate, trying to avenge any former slight.

Cutting the Sacrifice

Separating the hind legs (*akidung amuro*) with an axe effectually symbolizes the release of the ox's greatest strength for the empowering of the community through the elders. 'There is nothing else apart from praying ... After cutting *amuro*, they should pray.' The owner of the corral leads prayers, and then the paternal uncle of the initiand prays, carrying the right hind leg of the sacrifice on his right shoulder to add weight to the prayers, 'May cows be in abundance in this homestead!' Three times he must use his right hand to wipe some juice off the rear right thigh as it cooks to rub on his own lower back, signifying the transfer of the ox's greatest strength through the sacrifice.

Preaching and Prayers

By 12:50pm there are 139 initiated men in the corral. Different sections and clans have different *ngitalia* (tabus or sacred customs). Initiation ties the clan into the age-system. The local clan starts the ceremony, with elders of other clans arriving later, and sitting in their clans or territorial sections, if represented, under the leadership of the host, that is, the initiating, clan (Lamphear 1972:512, 520). Seniors sit in the front row and more towards the apex of the horseshoe formation. The senior elder present from the host sub-section sits at the fulcrum of the assembly shaped like ox-horns. The leader of the ceremony, who may himself be a senior member of the same generation-set, rises with his wand to speak and then pray. As the first prayer-leader (*ekagatan*), he declares the presence of the gathered political community.

> We the people were gathered here to see how to give pleasure to he who has gathered us here together. That's why I say, 'Let the Losilang people be together. So even the Panyangara people be together. The Kotido people be together. The Nakapelimoru people be together. The Rengen people be together. All those ones who are even here with their *atap* (bread[40]): they are our visitors. So let's see our fathers who are here. I have to show you that this is an example that there is Akujů, who has really brought us here together, that today is a big day. Even those who are jealous of us sitting here, pray to let them be removed from us. So let them go away from us ... So today this bull is for the Kotido people. Now he is urging these people that the Nakapelimoru people come and pray, even Rengen, Panyangara, and Losilang peoples. So let them pray for all of us. So let us enjoy

---

[40] This is a reference to Tap non-cattle people, such as the Acoli visitor who was present.

this bull here, so as to give us life. So here it is now time for you to pray for this animal before it is cut [its intestines]. So hear all of you the Jie gathered here before Akujů, 'Let Akujů in our prayers! So all the bad things that are within us, which are bad, let them be calm, and also let them go away!' (at Lokitela-ebu 1.4.02)

So each sub-section occupies a short length of the horseshoe, and the whole assembly replies in unison to give hearty voice to a regular, antiphonal liturgy, which is yet spontaneous and dramatic, when well led. Then the goodness, the spiritual harmony, of the land is affirmed, dismissing anything that threatens it. Each section provides an *ekagatan* to continue the prayers.

The style of the *agat* may vary according to the inimitable style of each *ekagatan*, but the chief items that are begged (*akilip*) of Akujů alter little, as comparison with a version recorded over 40 years earlier among the Tome Karimojong shows. The difference between imperative and indicative mood may be ascribed to a sense of whether the times are good or bad. On this occasion they were felt to be dire, so there was decided urgency in the prayers.

Leader	*Assembled*
The Jie people in their country, be there!	Be there! ...
Evil that is against the Jie, disappear!	Disappear! ...
So for the evils, let them go away!	Go away! ...
Well-being, be there!	Be there!
Well-being in this home, be there!	Be there! ...
Akujů has heard.	He has heard.

I: [Invocation]	There is well-being in our country, is there not?
R: [Response]	There is!
I:	It is here.
R:	It is!
I:	Yes. Evil is going away.
R:	It has gone!
I:	It is leaving.
R:	It has gone!
I:	Well-being is with us.
R:	It is!
I:	It will always be with us, will it not?
R:	It will!
I:	It will.
R:	It will!
I:	Will it not?
R:	It will!
I:	God has heard.
R:	He has heard!
I:	He has heard.

R:	He has heard!
I:	The sky, the cloud-spotted sky here, it has heard.
R:	It has heard! (Dyson-Hudson 1966:167)

He prays for peace to come down on animals, people, food, grass and rain for the future, after cursing all evils. 'Anything bad, let it go set with the sun, everything is carried by the wind or Akujů' (P1). This is effectually dramatized with the westward motion of his spear-laden right arm. If all evils are transferred to the Acoli and the Kumam, so much the better. Wealth in cattle, in sorghum and in descendants is beseeched for both the owner of the corral and the son being initiated.

Leader	Assembled
Our son who has been initiated, grow rich!	Grow rich!
Samuel [the jural father] from this home here, grow rich!	Grow rich!
Cows in this corral, grow rich!	Grow rich!
Granddaughters in this home, be there!	Be there!
Small children in this home, be there!	Be there!
be there!	Be there!
be there!	Be there!
This corral, be enlarged!	Be enlarged!
Sorghum in these granaries, fill!	Fill!

Eating happens intermittently during the prayers and at 2:00pm the men alone number 200, spilling outside the corral, while women watch through the fence from their yard. In half an hour this host soon consumes the rest of the ox the elders will distribute and then begin to disperse.

Tongue, Stomach and Cold Dripping

Beer is passed round the invited groups of the initiated. After visiting elders and friends have finished the fellowship meal and left the cattle corral, the initiand is consecrated as an adult member of his grandfather's homestead.[41] A father has no place of his own in the *ere*, so it is his mother, or surrogate, who kneels before his son. Some ribs, the lungs, bronchia, heart and tongue had been given to the initiate's mother to boil in a pot for the evening meal. In the initiand's home the stomach is boiled, pulped and mixed with sorghum flour, pumpkin, beans, roasted cucumber

---

[41] The conceptual bond is with the grandfather over against the father, which is a useful way of containing within society the filial frustrations that arise. A Semitic father is not permitted to watch his son sacrifice his bull, only the grandfather (Baldick 1998:133).

seeds and ghee into a consistent mash. The women put the broth in a gourd and mix it with flour. The hostess passes pieces of the meat and a gourd of the broth between the men of the senior generation-set and the initiand. 'It is very rich and drunk by the elders alone' (P1), starting with the most senior who is the last to leave. As in the sacred grove, they all sit on their stools facing their Karamojong cradleland. More prayers may be said. The bare bones are flung into the cattle corral with the wish that they will multiply into oxen for the grandsons to use at their initiation.

In the evening (or the following morning) the initiand is called to sit on a cowhide outside the father's hut between his two wives with their children, his sons and their families. The old lady then brings cold portions boiled from the neck and makes the initiand bite at a lump in her hand three times. This is repeated with the rest of the family. Then she brings a rib, for the initiand to bite at the cold fat (*akuring*) on the end, also thrice. When he has eaten, all eat. Finally the old lady brings a gourd of beer, forcing the initiand to drink deeply thrice and to spit some on his chest. It is 'a blessing of the family'. Thus belonging, both to kin and to age-set, is stressed in initiation.

The Naming

Then the initiand joins a group of his generation-set to drink beer and sing a few times the anthem extolling (the spearing of) the animal, from which their generation-set takes its name. The Tome Jie anthem to the elephant has persisted through most of the generation-set's initiations:

Iyaa, ooo, o imiliakial. Iyaa, oh!	The tusks glitter
Imilia elosia	It glitters when it is going
Kiremo inyakapolon	We speared the big one
Kiremo nyetome tigor imilia ngikial	We speared the big elephant with glittering tusks (Lamphear 1972:515)

It is not that the ox represents the elephant, though in the distant hunting past it could well have been a requirement of initiation to kill a dangerous animal instead of an ox. Rather, the elephant and the ox stand for the initiand. He is now Etomait (he of the elephant). The ox, part and parcel of his life hitherto, he has speared. He has sacrificed part of himself to God, but he does not die. Instead, he is born into a new and better life in the order of creation, as an elephant, and has taken a leap along the road which leads to the time when he must give all of himself to Akujů at death.

Elal nyikore kicaki ne, ii	That which trod here was big, eee
Papakothi kicaki ne, iii	Our father trod here, eee
Lokolimoe, nyetome kicaki ne	Lokolimoe, the elephant trod here
Lomeako, nyetome kicaki ne.	Loomakol, the elephant trod here. (ibid.)

Names of 'fathers' are applied to elephants but, taken literally, the fathers' generation-set is Mugeto (gazelles). The grandfathers were Tome and this is explicit in singing *papaakosi* (our grandfather). The grandfather, indeed each alternate forefather, comes alive again in the new generation-set of grandsons, in that their names are revived, and their memory hallowed. As members of the junior generation-set they must be subordinate to their seniors in it, symbolized by their control over personal decorations and the ritual beating. Each age-class helps to regulate its own decorations, whose fashions, especially in headdresses, may change over the years. Now one of them plaits a small ring into the hair at the back of the initiand's head with the injunction that it should not be removed for 14 days.

The initiand may take an ox-name from the ox that he spears, which can stick for life. For example an ox marked with stripes on it hide yields the ox-name, Apalotuko (father of that of the zebra). The initiand is now made a father in the formal constitution of male politico-social ranking. It has nothing to do with kin and little with age, but is a religious change. He may be addressed by the uninitiated, whatever their age or other status, as *papa*. However the only naming that is explicitly done in the ceremony is incorporation into age-class names, and the elders invite the initiand to appear before them to receive them. Every member of the Tome generation-set is named by the elders, Etomait. This is obvious and predictable from conception. The rest is at the discretion of the elders, and may not be determined by anyone else before this point. If the initiand is among the openers (*ngikangarak*) of the generation-set, there is no other name to give. Otherwise they must decide on the age-section name, for they may have decided to open a new one. If the initiand is among the openers (*ngikangarak*) of the age-section, there is no further name to give. A Jiot would now be Etomait Ekwoit. Otherwise he will also have an age-set name as well, though which he will use depends on the context. Precisely because the elders like to preserve their discretion, discouraging expectations, it is most abnormal for anyone to articulate the whole system.

Clearly naming the initiand is the point of transition from disenfranchisement to ritual maturity; from relative anonymity to incorporation into generation-set and age-set names, which will be etched on his people's oral history for ever, from the generality of people to the sacred ranks of Akujŭ. The initiands are now fully entitled to a place at the sacrifice, and to eat sitting behind the elders. Visiting relatives return finally to their own homes, for the feast is over. The young man (*esapat*) is an initiate (*esapanit*).

Anointing with Clay

Initiation confers the right to begin to wear adult head-dresses. A tuft of hair, left to grow at the back of the head, used to be worked up with blue clay into a bun to fashion the *emedot* head-dress. Plaits of ox tendons tied there after the sacrifice are replaced by two small chains, and the clay allowed to dry hard. This becomes the basis for the aloket (the wire frame which supports a ring of ostrich feathers). The tendon strings and chains may both be echoes of the hunting past when they were useful for trapping (*akilok*) and snares (*ngaloketa*). To the sedentary Teso, the Karamojong tribesman is *eloket*. Now it is the permanent anointing with the sacred blue clay (*ajukot ke emunyen*) which carries meaning. The wearer shows to all that he bears the holy traditions of his tribe, but these ones change in shifts. The *emedot* head-dress is more associated with the senior generation-set, and what is in vogue now is the removable head-dress (*etimat ngolo bubura*), which is only worn for rituals. However, with the ostrich and its egg being hunted out, it is difficult to obtain ostrich feathers to adorn head-dresses now, so initiates go without the *emedot* and the senior generation-set satisfy themselves with a wide-brimmed hat with one side pinned up.

Signifiers

The initiate's new place in the ritual strata is apparent at all times to those who can read the signs. Apart from the obvious head-dress he is now entitled to a particular design of one- or two-legged stool-cum-headrest, which is carried at all times, if not in use. Uninitiated men are not allowed a stool, or to eat *atap* with the long wooden spoon (*abolokoc*). Now he is granted one to use instead of his fingers or a piece of gourd. It is as if on spearing his ox a man grows up to dissociate himself from agricultural produce. He may help produce it and will certainly eat it, when at home, for the rest of his life, but he is still distanced from it. Anointing with chyme has changed his orientation. As a youth he would sit with the women at home during a rain-making sacrifice and eat worms (*ngikukur*), an unwelcome manifestation of spirit, in that they eat the crops. '*Nyepedori tokona akimuj ekukurit, nyisub nabo amok*' (Pazzaglia 1982:122). (Now you are not authorized to eat the worm, nor perform the rite any more.) Responsibility for the crops, and the spirituality involved in safeguarding them, belongs to women. Good Karamojong derive their spiritual sustenance from cattle.

Initiation is not merely, or mainly, a personal event. It is a familial, communal, creational focus, under Akujů, of the values held by the whole society and embodied in the ritual and political structure of *asapanů*. Thus the initiate's new status and its symbols are not just of psychological importance to him. His incorporation into the customary way of organizing and preserving unity, because it is ultimately dependent on the one Akujů, is an effectual sign of hope for the future. He too will bring his sons to initiation. Another generation-set is being willingly enlisted to uphold the traditions for another cycle.

Sacrifice of a Ram

To ensure that there are no disturbing consequences of a highly transformative drama, further sacrifice is made the next morning. The initiand must provide a ram (*emesek*), which is taken to a tree 200 yards outside the homestead. He should hold the ram by its back right leg and spear it through the heart, just behind the right shoulder. As with the ox, lung and heart have been pierced, so that air bubbles out of the slit. The head, tail and all the legs except the right front are cut off, for the latter to be handed by the initiand clockwise round his knees thrice. Then he taps his knees with them, and throws them behind him, through his legs to the west. The sacrifice is 'to get rid of any bad thing', 'to throw every bad thing from me'. 'The ram is a good animal for sacrifice, as it dies quietly', so that this quality is transferred to the initiand in order that he might not overreach himself, but be a quiet member of society. The rest of the ram is cut up, and the intestines and rib cage removed 'to throw every bad thing' from the initiand. A few Tome must be gathered to drink the blood, and only initiates may eat the roasted meat. Everything must be finished on site, for none can be taken home.

5 Promotion

As the senior generation-set nears its end, the junior generation-set becomes perturbed at being continually put down by an ever decreasing number of increasingly senile seniors who find it more difficult in practice to have their decisions implemented, as they must be enforced by age-sets in the disgruntled junior generation-set. The juniors seek the advice of the prophets and the senior elders in order to win the authority of age to their side. At last the breakdown in the normal order of things reaches a crisis, perhaps in the unpermitted and unpunished usurping by a junior age-set of some insignia of their seniors, when the only option left is for the junior generation-set to be promoted so that order can be restored. This non-violent power contest is sharper in Karimojong because the solution involves the retirement of the senior generation-set from power, sometimes to the extent that they are verbally abused.

In Najie there is more continuity between old and new senior generation-sets, with the oldest men continuing to lead prayers and participate in decision-making until they die, but the Mugeto generation-set was opened some years after the British came in 1910 by the oldest outgoing Etomait, Apainyangainyang Aring, demonstrating that the new senior generation-set had been promoted (J25).

> The ceremony to promote [*akitopolor*, literally to make big] the Ngimugeto [our, that is, Ngikosowa/Ngitome's, sons] was held at about the same time that our grandsons, the Ngitome, began their initiations. The Ngikosowa and Ngimugeto went to Nayan [*sic*;[42] section sacred grove] where many oxen were sacrificed. The Ngikosowa were on one side and the Ngimugeto on the other. Then the Ngikosowa blessed their sons and raised [promoted] them up and told them, 'Come! Sit here on this side with us. Be elders.' But those Ngimugeto were not really able to do anything after this ceremony that they could not do before. The Ngikosowa still have the power [*apedor*], and we shall have it until we are all dead. The Ngimugeto must still ask our permission before they can do things. (Dodoi and Longoli, quoted by Lamphear 1976:154)

The Karimojong regard the three clans (*ngamacarin*), Ribor, Lip and Danya, as ancestral. They are the three stones (the central props for any cooking-pot) of the Karimojong, traditional bearers of the dominant Eastern Nilotic culture.[43]

> Information is circulated to meet there at Nakadanya, for all the clans (*ngatekerin*) who are represented. This is appointed a year in advance. The clans (*ngatekerin*) gather together according to section in the traditional places to sleep there for a certain number of days, reassuring people they do not need to steal, fight, insult, be drunk, to refuse tobacco (*etaba*), no lying with women. It is a holy movement. I am gone (*alosit*) to Apule and Nakadanya. A number of animals are identified for sacrifice there. Ngipian meet first with Ngitome, Ngimosingo, and Ngibokora, and later Ngimaseniko join at a certain place, and Ngipei, Ngikaleeso, and the others. The three clans give the lead through being true Karimojong, not having been absorbed. The three clans were the first to sacrifice because they are a blessing to the rest. (P3)

---

[42] Mugeto were first initiated at Nayen (J21).

[43] 'People were called in clans before we left Ethiopia' (P3). Neville Dyson-Hudson (1966:89) and, later, Novelli (1999:182) make Lobal one of the three 'original clans'.

The three clans can appoint the time a year in advance according to their lunar calendar. The Ribor are custodians of 'the boat for the sacred clay (*emunyen*), and the sacred water to be transported' (P3). The Lipa are keepers of the ceremonial axe, while the Danya carry the wooden drill for making fire. The three clans diagnose the problem, and will lead others to Nakadanya for any serious common problems (P4). They are the first to sacrifice their oxen. Attempts by the politicians of the Karamoja Initiative for Sustainable Peace to convene a meeting at Nakadanya failed, because they were not led by the three clans (P3). Information is circulated to all the clans, as they will be represented at the promotion ceremony. However the territorial sections have their place in reinvesting the age-system with authority. 'Generation-sets come from' Nakadanya (P3).

Place of Installation

Promotion is the only tribal-wide ceremony that the Karimojong normally perform. They have always used Nakadanya near the Apule River, which involves a mass pilgrimage for all those who have the resources to attend. '*Alosit Apule na Nakadanya*' (P3) ('I am gone to Apule and Nakadanya'). 'The succession journey is part of the most specific and important affirmation of tribal values that any of its participants will see in their lifetime ... in intent and symbol it is the tribe which is gathering' (Dyson-Hudson 1966:189).

> The clans gather together according to section in the traditional places to sleep there for a certain number of days, reassuring people they do not need to steal, fight, insult one another, be drunk, or to refuse the elders *etaba*, snuff. There is no lying with women, for it is a holy movement.[44] (P3)

A number of oxen are identified in advance by haruspication for sacrifice there. From their perspective the Pian first meet with the Tome, Mosingo and Bokora, and later the Maseniko join at a certain place. 'The Bokora are always first for they are the mothers of the system' (P4). Yet, in 1956, the Bokora lost their traditional leadership to the Maseniko and the Mosingo (Dyson-Hudson 1966:147). The remaining sections come in. Men carry 'the things of celebration': musical horns (*ngaluto*) of ox, gazelle, eland, kudu or oryx, wooden trumpets (*ngarupepe*), knee-bells (*ngitworoi*), leopard- or baboon-skin, and cow-hide capes, and feather head-dresses. The boys herd sacrificial oxen and milking cows, followed by young women. The religious nature of the activity forbids any stealing or quarrelling, which usually breaks out when men who have been avoiding their stock obligations for years are finally confronted by their claimants. Different sections, according to their historical seniority, undertake sundry tasks in building the camp of sacrifice (*awi a amuros*) and preparing for the ceremonies. On the eve of the ceremony, they sleep in the river. The next day they kill the oxen as a sacrifice for the elders to give them rain (P4).

---

[44] It is fair to collate these two sources though 40 years apart since they both report the same event in 1956. The value of oral tradition is shown in that there is no fundamental contradiction, for P3 has never been to Nakadanya.

Severing the Hind Legs

A specified ox is sacrificed but on this occasion alone the senior elder distributes the sacred perineal flesh (*elamacar*), to the junior generation-set instead of the elders as in every other ox-sacrifice. He leads in prayer to God, for him to bless it in its responsibility for the tribal country. All the meat is eaten, save the very sacred hindlegs (*amuro*) wherein lies the strength of the ox. The tradition is still recorded that the special long spear has been brought from the blacksmiths in the west of Karamoja through all the Karamojong sections by the Pei (Pazzaglia 1982:81n), but it appears that this spear was rejected in 1956 as a 'foreign thing' that caused the disasters around the turn of the century (Dyson-Hudson 1966:147).[45] Thus the Pei custody of the sacred spear passed to the Mogos.[46] The presiding Mogos elder grasped his own spear near the blade and, with as many juniors as can gain hold of the shaft of the spear behind him, he severs the flesh of the hips. He cuts the sacrifice (*akidung amuro*). So holy is this act that, if the blade needs sharpening on a rock, another ox must be sacrificed in order to atone for the imperfection.

Unlocking the Age-set

After the sacrifice is consumed the pilgrims return home, now able to do what before was never done: to begin the initiations of those mostly overaged men in the next generation-set, so that in unlocking the age-set (*akurwor asapanet*) which had waited many years to be opened, as many as 100 men may be initiated in a single session.

Rock of the Country

Next, some of the retiring generation-set and that being promoted journey again to Nakadanya, driving older calves into a large ritual enclosure, centred on the rock of the country (*emoru a akwap*). Oxen are sacrificed and both cattle and people are anointed with their chyme. The participants assemble round a heap of white pebbles, symbolizing calves as in boys' games. The senior elder stands and 'announces the custom' (Dyson-Hudson 1966:192), exhorting the elders designate to live up to their responsibilities. When the sacrificial meat has been eaten the newly initiated scramble for the pebbles and the ashes of the fire that roasted the meat. Precisely four calves are selected from particular clans and marked with the clan's brand (*emacar*).[47] Just as a new generation of people is brought into being by

---

[45] This is further evidence that the promotion ceremony was in the 1890s and was not regarded as the harbinger of peace, because of the smallpox, the disruption occasioned by those in search of ivory and slaves, and the Jie victories.

[46] The Nyakwai, sometimes said to be a section represented at Nakadanya (Wayland 1931:203,229; M1) associated with blacksmithing rather than pastoralism, so contribute the great spear for the Nakadanya promotion. Yet they are not credited with being the owner of the spear, an honour which devolves on an elder of religious renown, who is a member of a true territorial section of the Karamojong.

[47] Again the sacred number, four, appears. There are four horizontal slits cut in the ox's

the grandsons replacing their grandfathers in the constitution, so another generation of cattle is given to them on which to live.

New Generation

On their return home the newly married women dip grass brushes into water in their milking vessels and spray the pilgrims and their cattle. Both grass and water are symbols of peace and blessing which accord with their spiritual principle. Each man puts the pebbles (*ngakookes*) from Nakadanya in the milking vessel, from where they are redistributed to every family to be kept in the large churning gourds to clean them. All unbranded stock are branded according to clan.

These renewals are paralleled by New Fire, which is kindled with newly cut firesticks being drilled in old wood by the new initiates before the assembly. The fastest runners then take embers to the permanent settlements (Pazzaglia 1982:98). The opening of a new generation-set is the opening of a new age, literally, for Karamojong time is divided up into generation-sets. The incipient and decrepit disorder previous to the promotion ceremony provides a vivid contrast to the hopes for the next generation of peace, order and plenty. Mature, vigorous men now occupy senior positions in the assembly to intercede to Akujů for the people, yet still in the alternating current of tradition perpetuated over the last four centuries.

---

stomach at *asapan* and *akiwodokin*; the women dance four times at *ngasuban*; after birth the mother carries four sticks when first emerging from the hut to ward off the evil-eye (Pazzaglia 1982: 120).

Chapter 7

Sacral Leaders and Sacramental Representation

Traditional authority is ritually constructed (Deeley 2004). Therefore religious legitimation is vital to traditional leadership. Its formalization promotes a powerful, but constrained, voice of authority, which can in turn delegate authority to lesser voices, thus establishing the foundation of social organization. The terminologies of ritual, ceremonial, customary and religious leaders all have a misleading connotation in English, suggesting that these are not the real leaders. They are part of the superstructure of a false consciousness, when attention should be given to those with 'real' politico-socio-economic power. Forsaking any dichotomous or functional concept of ritual, this chapter will investigate the use and means of power in the religious terms of the Karamojong. Even the Weberian concept of the charismatic personality must be adapted, for charisma inheres in, and is attributed to, corporate groups, not just individuals. Certain people are selected by various criteria to ensure the blessings of Akujů on the community for the good of all. Vulnerability to overt political challenge may be assessed according to the restriction on access to the necessary qualifications and the existence of a broad social consensus that authority represents a sense of the order of creation and liberation (Bell 1992:121).

1 Leadership

Corporate Office

Priests Asapanů is administered by the elders (*ngikasikou*) who are defined as the senior generation. The most senior elders are the age-section still in power, which requires an unquantifiable quorum of surviving old men. When they become too few or too weak to give an effective lead to others, the burden of leadership will be taken up by the next age-set. The definition of elder is therefore completely formal. Only within an age-set does age count as seniority and, even there, a younger man selected on hereditary grounds to spear the first ox will be senior to older age-mates, and may be the spokesman (*ekeseran*) for the whole age-set. As age-sets advance in the cycle they gain in seniority by approximating, through their nearness to death and to Akujů, the preternatural source of all authority and power.

> The age-sets of the oldest men have the most power. That is because they have grown close to God over many years. They can truly bless the people. Even if they become foolish and speak like children, still they are wise, because they are the oldest age-sets. Until they die, they are the most powerful. (Mabuc, quoted in Lamphear 1976:153)

Even the Karimojong called the sole surviving age-set of Ngitukoi in 1957, *ngikasikou*, after they had been officially retired (Dyson-Hudson 1966:181). The quintessential elder is a member of the most senior age-set.

Thus the insignia proper to the senior generation, whether red, white or black feathers, red or yellow 'iron' (copper or brass), may be necessary but not sufficient for recognition as an elder, whose badges of office traditionally include a baboon-skin cape, an ivory bracelet, a rectangular belt of chain-metal, a finger-hook and a certain design of stool-cum-headrest, or anything else an age-class decides upon to declare their exclusive identity. They have power to control the wearing of all personal decoration.

Neville Dyson-Hudson (1966:180n) was never able to elicit the etymology of *ekasikout* by questioning, but linguistic analysis makes the answer plain (cf. Pazzaglia 1982:96); '- si-*akou*-' applies a causative prefix to *akou* (cf. N-S and Afroasiatic, head). An elder is not just old, but one who has been made head. There are no particular chiefs in Karamojong religion and society, for chieftainship, or oversight, including judicial authority, is exercised by a corporate office, 'a praesidium of elders', as Wilson (1988:4) puts it, 'in fact, those with priestly function and power'.[1]

> As the most junior men are thus playing their menial role during rituals, the most senior men demonstrate their supernaturally derived powers and their proximity to God, by leading the prayers and in general supervising the ceremonies upon which the Jie community relies for its well-being. (Lamphear 1976:155)

The elders' 'most important characteristic in Karamojong eyes is an ability to intercede with the deity for assistance ... to control the environment for the benefit of the community as a whole, or for any recognized segment of it gathered together' (Dyson-Hudson 1966:212).

In the assembly, the eldest sit nearest to God, lead the liturgy and exhort the people: 'Akujů wants for an elder to have more spiritual power than others in the family to lead them. *Asapanů* is the divine ordering of society' (J31). 'Akujů is with the elders. He is invisible, but they know. There is no separation; He is existing. Akujů is above in power, but has not left them. Akujů answers prayers; it depends on when and how they consult Him. If there be no response, they kill another animal' (P5). This informant also claimed that the heart of a dead elder goes to Akujů, but, on being challenged, that this was a new religious concept, as a Roman Catholic, he agreed. This does represent one of the few points where Christian thought was coming in. In any case elders were never thought simply to cease to exist, but death brought them closer to Akujů than any living person could afford to be. That is exceedingly close, when 'Akujů is the brother of old men' (J13).

---

[1] The elders (*presbuteroi*) of ancient Greece had a similarly important social status. 'In the order of society the elders receive respect and authority on the ground of their experience and wisdom.' (Brown 1980:I,192ff). Likewise the elders of Israel, translated by *presbuteroi*, the Greek origin of 'priest', are seen as 'the representatives of all Israel'.

Deacons The primary meaning of the Greek root *diakonos* is one who serves at meals, centuries before it declined to a brief, transitional stage in a sacerdotal hierarchy (Brown 1980:III,546). In Karamoja, the most recent initiates perform the menial tasks in ritual sacrifices, collecting firewood, sorghum stalks and grass, on which to roast cuts of the sacrificial meat, and then laying it before the elders. The latter repeatedly test the obedience of their juniors by imposing petty tabus and demands, such as giving 'the junior age-set minute shreds of meat to roast, the loss of which can cause a punishment to be meted out to the entire age-set' (Lamphear 1976:154).

Older age-sets are employed by the elders to enforce the requisition of the sacrificial ox, proper decorum as regards personal ornaments, which are the tokens of ecclesial office, and the disciplining of offenders. They serve the elders by imposing the *ameto* punishments, like beatings or the confiscation of cattle, to maintain order, because they recognize the spiritual power of the elders, demonstrated by their sovereign survival in an inclement and modern world. Their proven wisdom in treating with God will therefore be the deacons' surest hope for the future, when their turn to be priested comes (Novelli 1988:48).

The usual word for members of the junior generation (*ngisorok*) is translated as 'adults', but this is not satisfactory, failing to bring out its specific role in the generation system, yet its derivation is not obvious. Since the cognate *akiroga* (to be about to die, cf. *agaa*, chameleon, ES *ga, to change) and *erokit* (sacred medicine) suggest a link with the cluster of meanings around the root, *ro, there is a case for seeing the causative particle, '-si-', undergoing vowel harmonization, as in *esokod*, giving the original meaning of *esorokit* as one made sacred or divine. Initiation then becomes a consecration to an attributed maturity. The promise of the ox-name beginning Apa- is now fulfilled in that his proper form of address is now *papa* (father) irrespective of age or procreation. Even those older than him might address him thus. It is a conferred convention, not an earned reward. It shows reverence to an institution more than to informal authority. In the end every member of the political community wants to be initiated, including churchmen. Those who are denied initiation until after the next promotion decades away are tempted to seek higher status by some non-traditional means as traditional routes are effectively closed.[2] Even a highly successful cattle-raider cannot earn a seat in the assembly.

Hereditary Office

Ngimurok Known variously in English as wizard, witch, witchdoctor, medicine-man, *laibon* (Maasai), physician or diviner, no accurate translation has yet emerged for *emuron*, or the female, *amuron*. Certainly his ordinary function, except in Turkana where his leadership rôle has been developed, is in the realm of healing. In Africa this is not a confined area. Since the well-being of creation depends upon the Creator, the overlap of the sacred with the created order is considerable. The root

---

[2] J14 is a good example, who used his capability to be a contract-farmer and in the church's development work. Though aged about 50 his understanding of Jie traditions is surprisingly limited.

meaning is unmistakable: *amuro* (the sacred, hind legs of a sacrifice, to make a sacrifice), *amuronot* (a sacrificial ceremony), and *amuros* (sacrifice). To be consistent with these current meanings, *emuron* is a sacrificer, which tallies with his tasks as a healer and his prominent part in divination. This basic meaning is made explicit by the saying, 'He inherits the sacrifice' (Dyson-Hudson 1966:120n).

His rôle in the public sacrifice of cattle is subordinate to that of the elders, who must call an assembly for the purpose. He can advise the elders when to assemble or advise a client to ask them to assemble but he may not sacrifice cattle on his own. Even in *akiriket* he does not necessarily play a fixed, formal role, except in supervising ritual procedures, particularly haruspication when present. He has no exclusive tasks but, because he is a technical specialist, especially if he is known to be a proficient one, his dreams, divination, choice of sacrificial animals, sermons and prayers will carry greater weight in proportion to his closeness to Akujů. For private healings he can order and perform the sacrifice of smallstock, so becomes well-versed in haruspication.

The *emuron* is not rootless, but is attached to a community. If he is unavailable and his heir is not ready, a *locum tenens* must be sought from elsewhere. The rules of inheritance are revealing: the Karimojong seek the first son begotten of the *emuron* by his first wife, provided she was 'married with cattle' and not inherited and he was conceived after marriage. If these rare conditions are not met, then the first son of the next wife will succeed, if he and his mother qualify (Dyson-Hudson 1966:120n). The Dodosô gave Marshall Thomas (1965:167–81) a more functional description of the selection of *ngimurok*, though theirs had wives and mothers as *ngamurok*. Akujů is known to have granted the power to a particular boy or girl, when he or she begins to receive Akujů's messages at night and divines in dreams. All *ngimurok* are persons thought by the Jie to inherit the shade or shadow (*etorobe*; cf. *atorobe*, chest, bosom) of a previous *emuron* (Israel Lokong, quoted by Lamphear 1972:339). The charisma of the *emuron* becomes known in childhood. He will be seen to shake with ecstasy, or be possessed and run away, or else he will be very quiet. An associated wonder may help, for example, if he stands on the roof of a house, falls, but is not hurt (P5). As with the insane it is assumed that those most liminal to mundane life are closest to Akujů.

Qualified and practising *ngimurok* in the clan will assess the aptitude of the candidate. When satisfied they will mark the appointment to the office by sacrificing an animal with a beard, normally a black goat. The skin from its back and hind right-hand side legs will be decorated with cowrie shells for the boy to wear around his chest and back. The tail of the goat will come over his forehead. The skins he will wear for a time as a protection against the headache and tremulations of the heart in this spiritually dangerous profession. He will put on copper, brass or aluminium bracelets.

What emerges is a man apart, imbued with special knowledge that can only be imparted through intimate relationships with parents and spouse. Some clans or sub-sections become noted for producing skilful *ngimurok*. Marshall Thomas's privileged association with the renowned Lomotin presents a deeply spiritual man, almost fanatical in his work, carrying his medicine-bag containing curative roots to visit those of whom he dreamed, to warn and heal them. Though apparently careless of his own worldly interests he is benevolently concerned for all aspects of the welfare of his parish, including its defence.

Ngimurok charge 'doctor's fees' for counsel which frequently involves anointing with clay or chyme, small tabus, charms, the sacrifice of dogs instead of the usual goat, and the wearing of specific parts of an animal. This may give him a more than adequate revenue in livestock. As a haruspex he generally reads the intestines at the sacrifice, and divines the signs concerning rain, sun, enemies coming, and so on (P5). At the sacrifice the *emuron* 'is spoken to by Akujŭ who reveals how people can be protected against disease and attack' (P11). Yet the *emuron* is the nearest the Karamojong come to a holy man and to the sacerdotal concept of priest, since his office is not dependent on *asapanŭ*. Because *ngimurok* are generally the wisest in things sacred, they are best suited by the term 'divines'.[3]

Ngimurok vary in quality. Those only peddling medicine are considered lesser. One such is the only *emuron* in Kotido town, as those with a wider ministry shun close contact with strangers and their different lifestyles. This one specifically declares he uses neither ritual, sacrifice, incantation nor knife, and can only assist specific complaints such as diarrhoea, cough and those spirits of madness (*ngikerep*) that beat people, and even then only a recent attack. His only method is medicine (*ekitoi*) from the bush (*namoni*), and he has two other occupations, besides of course his herd, as a farmer and as a trader of fish, goats and cattle. Those whom he cannot manage he sends to the church dispensary, which was once amazed to find that he had healed an AIDS patient who had come coughing to him with a swollen stomach. This earned him a visit from Entebbe, but he has never claimed to be able to cure *eslim*. He was keen for his work as a healer (*etic ka emuron*) to be recognized, so asked for a paper certificate from the government. On 20.7.97 he attended a workshop for 'Traditional Healers and Herbalists' in Kotido and was registered, the least traditional *emuron* in Karamoja.

The greater the *emuron*, the more he encompasses skills in all the preternatural functions and it seems that no *emuron* could be famous without the abilities of a prophet. Such was the case with the Jiot, Loingolem (he who practises divinity), who prophesied in the mid-nineteenth century that one day pale-skinned people would appear in Najie. Also *ngimurok*'s travelling makes them better informed.

> Loingolem, the great *emuron* of Panyangara, was known by all the Jie because he always saw the future clearly. If he said enemies would come, they would really come. If he said the rain would fall, it would really fall. Most other *ngimurok* were just big liars. The things they said would happen never happened. (Cope, quoted by Lamphear 1972:341; cf. Lamphear 1976:248)

The hereditary office of the divine is not only an opportunity for young men to take religious responsibility, but for women also, who often function as invokers of spirits (*ngakalemak*), sucking out diseases through the skin using a soft sisal ball or an ear of bulrush millet, but the profession is as meritocratic for women as for men. As a medium she will keep two small gourds (*ngakaae*) at a shrine in her hut and carry them round with her. They contain stones normally used to clean the milk gourds, which talk as husband and wife in a low buzzing noise. These she audibly

---

[3] A distinction is needed between a divine and a diviner who here is taken to practise the two main methods of divination, but the rôle of *ngimurok* is much deeper and wider.

consults for guidance, and feeds with libations of beer (Graham 6.4.01 Interview). She may be able to identify the voice of the dead (P5). At this point in an interview the local Anglican pastor interjected to say it was a fraudulent business with the voices being supplied by men behind the house speaking through holes. Yet his RC friend gently asserted that he found mediums true, for they help the living, and certainly conduct a healing ministry with specific roots and tablets. An *amuron*, Lodul, was pre-eminent in early nineteenth-century Najie, foretelling enemy raids and the rain (Lamphear 1972:340f) and she was not the only effective woman: 'Before the Dodos attacked the place called Tiira in Nakapelimoru, my own grandmother, Awapawothit, an *amuron*, had already predicted they would come' (Nakade, quoted in Lamphear 1976:228).

Ngimurok are consulted before embarking on a raid, and brave men are they who ignore the augury given. The activity of certain birds provides omens here. Since highly dependable *ngimurok* are a rare and extremely valuable resource for risky operations, they are sought beyond the borders of the tribe, even amongst enemies in a war, not that an *emuron* would betray his own people, but the work of a great one transcends partial interests even while he deals in them. He tells what he sees but takes measures to protect against consequent hostile action. In this way an *emuron* enters into widespread influence, though his reputation will always depend on performance. A few are so impressive that they are promoted to the realms of legend and immortality, the only trans-tribal focus.

Fire-makers *Ngikeworok* are religious leaders whose Nilotic religion, controlling the annual agricultural cycle, atrophied with the concentration on pastoralism and the rise of *asapanŭ* at Koten-Mogos, so it is difficult to judge the weight that should be put upon them. Their influence varies in Karamoja roughly in accordance with the renewed impact of WN Lwo and EN Tap. Neville Dyson-Hudson (1966:109) seemed to be aware of the rite of fire-making but not the office. Each section might have one, assisted by others based in subsections or neighbourhoods. Fire-makers extract little obedience but the elders turn to them in times of hardship or seasonal shifts like *angola* and *akiwodokin* for the fresh start which new fire brings, following the extinction of all domestic fires. Then the fire-maker kindles new fire, using sticks from the *adome* (*Cordia sensensis*) tree for the promotion of a generation-set (Novelli 1999:215) or to recover from a common disaster (Gulliver, P. and P.H. 1953:40). It is taken to every hearth to resume a blessed life after the crisis.

The Jimos clan give the impression that fire-making has always been their preserve, but there are oral traditions that it was inherited through women by default at one point. 'The firestick (*epit*) and fire-making came originally from Kanawat. The Lep clan made fire for the *akiriket*. There were no heirs in the clan, for one girl went to Losilang and one to Kotiang' (J14). Lamphear (1976:121) found Orwakol to be the primordial Jie fire-maker from the Toroi clan, so this would deny the Jimos clan the honour, even if it does not quite fit with Kanawat, unless Orwakol was the one who married the girl of the Ngalep clan already settled as cultivators.

> Fire-making originated from Kanawat. The fire-maker was left with two daughters and no sons. The eldest daughter went to Losilang, and one to Kotiang where she married into the

Toroi clan. The Toroi clan count fire-making back to Kanawat ... When the fire-maker died he appointed one of his daughters, who was married at Kotiang, and carried fire-making there ... There was fire-making in the sacrifice for the whole of Orwakol around October 2001. The Jimos tried to make fire and failed, so it was given to Kotiang. (J10)

Clearly the current rôle is very much under the authority of the elders.

Even a 'saved', counter-cultural Christian finds the prospect of a fire-maker exercising monarchical power attractive. 'The fire-maker makes fire, opens the planting season, reconciles people as a man of peace. For his royal qualities, elders may go to him for advice; he will tell people to be self-disciplined and they can take heed' (J29). 'The fire-maker is closer to Akujů in that he can prevent war, disease, and so on, by giving orders' (J2). Fire-makers were responsible for ceremonial rites, settling disputes, preparing warriors for battle, and rain-making using the yard-long, wedge-shaped stones left by the Tap around the homesteads of the Jimos clan in Najie. They were responsible for bringing rain. They would also bless the people and the sorghum seeds, determining when sowing should begin and being entitled to the first fruits of both grain and beer. The elders selected a new one from the sons of the old on the criterion of quiet, kind, gentle humility, to the point where they no longer appoint one for the Orwakol section (Lamphear 1976:27,121–7,156,169–81).

There has long been a dispute over who is the true heir in the Jimos fire-maker's family. The last fire-maker to be installed was Lotum, who died in the early 1950s,[4] and is buried alongside his famous father, Dengel, in the sacred grove looking north outside the *ere*. Uniquely they are not buried in the cattle corral, and have stone cairns for a memorial. There is a method of trying the candidate. In 1996, one put out sandals with oil on top, but he was proved to be a fraud by their being eaten by a hyena (J13). There were two candidates, Dengel Kamare[5] of Losilang and Lomuleu Epuriapua. However Kamare had broken the rules: keeping fire burning and drinking pure sorghum beer is not unusual, but eating tepary beans and defecating in the corral is most odd. 'A fire-maker could only eat meat from the sacrifice' (J10). A fire-maker should be old, so as not to move up and down, and should eat no alien food. He should have no wounds from wild animals or enemies (J13). He should be chosen by the remainder of the Tome generation-set in a good year according to the behaviour of the candidates, but clearly the Tome elders do not want to appoint a quasi-monarchical figure for their generation.

---

[4] The Gullivers (1953:40,50) were told that the last time fire had been made centrally at Moru Ewur, Lotum's homestead, was in 1938, so the custom of new fire was already falling into desuetude under colonialism. However new fire for all Orwakol is only needed for a crisis.

[5] Dengel was the name of his grandfather, the penultimate and renowned fire-maker, while Kamare means 'he of the tepary beans' (*Phaseolus acutifolis*). Where this leaves Nakapor, Mirzeler's active Losilang fire-maker, is not at all clear: 'Nakapor, the current *ekaworan* [sic] (political–religious leader who demonstrates his traditional power by making fire from wet branches of *essegese* tree)' (Mirzeler and Young 2000:420; Mirzeler 1999:91,369,374). As his fieldwork was done before these interviews, it would appear that his account is confused with Nakapor making new fire in Kaceri. Even there Nacam had already done it for his new community, though there is no installed fire-maker for the Oding section (ibid.:411).

The fate of the Jimos clan's cattle lies according to how the fire-maker lies. He has a tree for shade with long low branches, which is called Lokatum, 'the parliament' of the Orwakol section, when new fire is made. In the morning he lies in the direction in which the livestock should be driven for their grazing, and then he turns round for their return. People come to him from around the section for his blessing before they plant their first seeds of the year. He gives back the seeds he received from them when they brought the first fruits of the previous harvest (Mirzeler 1999:134–6). 'Taking grains to his granary was for emergency; he would take the seeds when needed' (J10). Planting may then begin together, the most effective way of minimizing loss of grain to birds.

White clay is collected by youths from the sacred site at Karabokol and brought to him to bless. He grinds it to dust in the hole in the rock outside his *ere*, mixes it with water and anoints the messengers. Then it is distributed by his age-set to the seven Orwakol sub-sections, who may use it for initiation or promotion ceremonies, firstly at the sacred grove of the section at Nayen, then at the sacred groves for each subsection, such as Lokitoipeta (the place of planting), Lomos (the place of people), Lodukanit (the place of rain) and Looi (the place of war). One sacred grove is chosen each year to sacrifice one bullock. It is divided up for distribution to the seven sub-sections, who can pray for the long rains and the grass rains. The portion for the Jimos clan is the scapula (*eseket*, J13).

2 Sacraments

Sacraments are ceremonies sacred to life. They are pointers to human culture being more than craftsmanship of a few individuals, but a shared reality which both incorporates and transcends the individual possessing identity. If the ceremonial is at the heart of the way collective structures are mediated in culture, it is also crucial for understanding cultural difference (James 2003:6f,17,299). The imagined community is possible through ceremonial, so that the ceremony becomes sacred to the initiated, however quaint or obsolete it may appear to the outsider. The sense of the sacred does not separate religious thought and action from the rest of life, but draws all the aspects of culture into an intricate harmony, too complex usually to articulate in the round, but, being implicit in the words and ritual of ceremony, it does promise a consciousness of unity, order and purpose in a world whose contingency is saved from caprice and confusion.

Karamojong ceremonies represent the best of life, as greetings between senior men indicate (Novelli 1985:194): '*Maata nakero* (Let us frequently be going to our ceremonial grounds!); *Maata lotal*! (Let us frequently be celebrating custom!); *Maata ngasuban*! (Let us frequently be holding ceremonies!)'. The prayers also show that ceremonies are integral to the good life: indeed are, as this one was, the prime public means to achieve it.

Leader	*Assembled*
Yes! Good ceremonies in this home be there!	Be there!

In this family,	
let there be no cough!	Let there be no cough!
All good ceremonies,	
be there!	Be there!
Even in the night,	
be there!	Be there!
Be there!	Be there!
Be there!	Be there!
Be there!	Be there!
Be there!	Be there!
Be there!	Be there!

Good ceremonies and sorghum and cows together with the people here, even my fathers, mothers, and the children,

be there,	Be there!
Be there!	Be there!
Be there!	Be there!
Be there!	Be there!

It is very rare to repeat a response as many as six times. So long as Karamojong life has ceremonies, cows, people and sorghum, probably in that order, it is abundantly rich, for the spiritual and the mundane will then be mysteriously fused.

The problem is that English words have a history intertwined with the religious understandings of English people down the ages, but 'sacrament' is a term that still has possibilities that are not predetermined by a particular Christian doctrine. In Ancient Greece *mysteria* were mystery celebrations, in which the initiated attained salvation and deification through their participation in ceremonial and dramatic acts rather than through being instructed by plain words (Brown 1980:III,505). Mystery defied being reduced to words, and sacrament, a sacred engagement, is from *mysterion*'s Latin translation. Sacrament then is a symbol conveying a numinous element spiritually perceived and made efficacious (James 1962:15). Faith, that is trust in the sacred, unfolds in various actions which are individually perceptible. Despite the inevitable Western associations which all English words must have, its meaning may be more appropriate than the problematic 'ritual'. There is no one concept provided by Ngakaramojong. There are *ngitalyo* again, *ngipeyos* (the roast offerings of a guest), or *ngasuban*.

Ngasuban are feasts and rites. *Losuban* is the festival month. It is the harvest moon, when the stirring stick remains dirty with food. It is the time for the celebration of marriages and for initiation, the time to dance the *ekimomwar* and eat of the *ngimomwa* being harvested to serve the sorghum stodge (*atap*) and to drink the new season sorghum beer (*ngagwe*). The married women dance publicly four times, a number associated with the created order,[6] though if they have eaten really well they dance eight times to rejoice in a double blessing or second helping

---

[6] Four is a sacred number often employed by the Karimojong, denoting the order of creation. There are points on the horizon; north, south, east and west. There are four horizontal slits cut in the ox's stomach in *asapan* and *akiwodokin*; the women dance four times at *ngasuban*; after birth, the mother carries four sticks, when first emerging from the hut to ward off the evil-eye (Pazzaglia 1982:120).

(Pazzaglia 1982:12). Since the cattle are based at home for the wet-season grazing, milk is relatively plentiful, and ghee, the real sign of the fat of the land, is made. Appetites can be satisfied and skin anointed to look its lustrous best. The body itself declares which moon it is. The cattle herders are at home, the raiding season is still at least two months away, and there is peace. Turkana bond-friends and relatives come to participate in the harvest and renew old relationships. All these show that blessings from on high have come down on the land (*akwap*) which also means down, beneath, below or under. This happy state of affairs cannot happen by accident, nor can it be stage-managed. It is the fruit of cosmic harmony, and all that man can do is not to spoil it by transgression.

It is not always so. Rainfall being extremely patchy in terms of both time and space, not more than one harvest in four is a bumper; just as many are failures, and twice as many are less than adequate, so usually the *Losuban* celebrations are funded with the knowledge that, if one is not careful, the grains at least will all be consumed before the next harvest, by when some will be trying to eat aid seed with its chemical treatment. Then the cosmic harmony is lacking, shattered by some significant transgression or at least limited by the people's ritual or customary disobedience, so that it is the prayers and sacrifices of enemies that are heard and savoured, and their actions favoured. Thus it is that the good times are dependent on how people live throughout the year in all their activities. The individual cannot do as he pleases without consequence for the ecological health of the community. It is precisely the incipient capitalist, or those who use unrecognized cultural ways to better themselves, especially if they break any tabus, who may be accused by the women at the next planting season of tying up the rains.

However, the absence of blessing does not mean the desinence of ritual, for it is precisely through ritual that the world can be put the right way up again. Even though the rite (*asuban*) specifically means the dance at the beginning of the festive season, *ngasuban* is the most suitable word to employ for ritual in general. *Akisub* is to create, prepare, repair, put right in this cosmic religious sense. It is certainly associated with the work of the religious specialist, the *emuron*, and with the cosmic Creator above, Akujů. There are therefore seasonal rites to ensure the people are in line with the cosmic order, and moveable feasts to request the restoration of the world or demand the repentance of the errant members of the politico-religious community. There is then a clear difference between *ngasuban* and *ngitalyo*, which is well translated as 'custom', and is a far more general term, including *ngasuban* with its note of celebration but also tabus and sacred traditions (Pazzaglia 1982:107n). '*Erai etal kozi akitiya ngakiro konaga.*' (It is our custom to do things like this.) (Novelli 1999:lxxix)

Both customs and rituals are things that are done. Being etic, they provide definite standards by which all behaviour can be assessed. As might be expected of a traditional culture, these are the primary test of communal acceptance and recognition, which requires orthopraxis before orthodoxy. However, when a miscreant is before the elders, his approach to them and emic indications of his motivation, morality and values will be of crucial importance. They will determine how the punishment fits the crime. That ideals are implicit does not connote their absence, merely that they are fleshed out by visible behaviour. Thus the various notions that some members pick up from schools or outsiders provide no immediate threat to the community. So long as they keep to the customs and participate in the rituals as required then they are good members. That power is perceived in Nilotic ritual by other peoples is evidenced by the Kuria designating their ritual elders, who alone can make ritual use of chyme, as *umu-sub-i* (Ruel 1997:29). For Karamojong, ritual is associated with power in a number of ways, not just political and social (Bell 1992:198f).

Rituality is a concept that comes easily to them in a holistic sense uncomplicated by Western myth–ritual dichotomies. It is not merely the sum of customs (*ngitalyo*), which is the shorthand for the way a Karamojongait is exhorted to live (Novelli 1999:303–14), but it also encompasses rites or ceremonies, which themselves are the embodiment of implicit beliefs. However rituality has been so used and abused that the concept of sacramentality will be explored, bracketing out its special Christian usage that yields relatively esoteric meaning. The primordial sacraments of initiation and promotion have already been treated in Chapter six.

Beseeching

Each section has a ground dedicated to this ceremony, when the section beseeches the elders to intercede to God for the good health of the people and livestock, a bumper harvest and a wide berth for hunger, disease and pestilence. It is as close as the Karamojong come to a New Year ritual, for it occurs at the beginning of the wet season (Pazzaglia 1982:80f) in or after the lunar month called *Lodunge* (that which cuts, or divides, the wet from the dry season). It comes when dust winds have been blowing, granaries are emptying and stomachs are rumbling, but the start of a new agricultural year offers the possibility of an end to hunger as well as its intensification. Like most feasts in Karamoja it is moveable and will be called when the section faces great stress, perhaps widespread enough to warrant use of the tribal sacred grove.

The Karimojong call the ceremony *akitocol* (to cause to compensate with cattle). It is an *epeyos*. The junior generation-set offers livestock for a sacrifice in honour of their seniors, for such an act of subordination to age is good for the land. The Jie and the Turkana call the same ceremony *angola*.[7] Each territorial division or Karimojong sub-section sacrifices its oxen and rams or he-goats, and the stomach of each is slit as many times as there are subsections. The elders, having prayed for their economy, feast on the meat which is supplemented by gifts of milk and tobacco. They bless the livestock and the fields. All the people file through a makeshift gate constructed out of branches cut from a tree with a ritual axe, for the senior elder to spatter them with a blend of sacred clay and water, also blessing each by calling down Akujů's favour upon him. Another may sweep the way clean for them. They go through in the acknowledged order in which the territorial sections were formed (Lamphear 1976:133; Dyson-Hudson 1966:89). Thus, at a time when divisiveness and accusations of witchcraft may abound in the face of hardship, the critical unity of the generations as well as neighbourhoods and clans is maintained by faith in a God-given hope for the future.

---

[7] Cf. *akingol* (to slaughter).

If drought or famine have a cumulative effect after two or more bad years and the normal ritual solutions have had no effect, it must be because the people themselves have sinned (*akisec*) against their country, spoiling the world (*akwap*). The ultimate sacrifice to restore peace with Akujů after this catastrophic disobedience is a human one. So a child may be carried to the highest mountain, Moroto, for sacrifice, to approach nearer to Akujů in order to propitiate His anger (cf. Alan Root's 1971 film, 'The Karamojong'). Novelli (1999:163–6) tells of the sacrifice of a donkey which is scapegoated with all the diseases afflicting people, and the mountains are beseeched by an *amuron* as the homes of malevolent spirits. The donkey is cut in half and the participants pass through the middle without looking at it. The format is the same for human sacrifice as happened on the order of an *emuron* to a Roman Catholic priest from Madi.[8]

In 1985, after three poor or bad harvests, a Pore *emuron* in Karenga discovered by dream or divination that five Jie youths should die to save their people from an army operation. As with sacrificial oxen, descriptions were put out of the required victims who were ceremonially despatched to their maker. Though folk in Kotido saw this as a terrible thing, it was no more than a reflection of the dire straits of the time. There were no protests from any quarter, yet the killings were apparently not implemented on an order from the elders. If such a thing could effect an improvement, then there was something good about it, and no-one wished to meddle in rites so potent as these, though the elders put a stop to similar human sacrifices in the Moroto area (Rowland 1.8.90 Letter). The inference is that the response of human sacrifice to severe crises is not historically an EN custom, but is ingrained in some *ngimurok*-producing clans with WN or Kuliak origins.

Rain-making

The prime condition for healthy herds and a good harvest is rain. The only members of society who can make rain are the elders who have the holy ability to intercede with God successfully. In Najie, if the fire-maker's ceremony of washing a black goat at a Losilang rock cistern fails to work, the elders can organize an ox-sacrifice at Lodukanit water-hole, the place to sacrifice for rain, Looi sacred grove, or any sub-section's sacred grove (Gulliver, P. and P.H. 1953:48; Lamphear 1976:174). Rainfall can be extremely localized. Their prayers, begun by the senior elder with a freshly cut stick or wand, claim that the rain will come. The prayers of senior men, who have kept the traditions, avail to change the habitat.

Even when rain has begun to soften the hard ground, work cannot be done in the fields until the rites have been performed. After the fields have been cleared of thorns the seed, having been stored by each woman and tied to the ceiling of her hut, in a bag (*egogol*) made out of a bull's scrotum to ensure germination, is strewn, and small gangs of women hoe the seed into the soil, away from depredations of ant and bird. It may germinate but, if the rains have reached no consistency, the tiny plants

---

[8] Poorly attested reports of human sacrifice west of Karamoja lack this feature, so should not be attributed to Karamojong religion (Oxfam 2001:19).

soon wither and die. The labour is in vain and must begin again. Good timing, the responsibility of *akiriket*, overcomes this curse on agriculture.

Gourlay (1971b:142) and Novelli (1999:287) write of blessing hoes and seeds, '*ajulot ngina iwosere ngakutai ka ngaetin*', which, when spelt out, translates thus: an animal sacrifice to anoint with oil the long-handled ace of spades hoes and the seeds. They would be smeared with animal fat to aid the penetration of the sacred soil and the fertility of the crop. *Ajulot*[9] is not related to the normal vocabulary for sacrifice, but only that concerning crops. It is therefore likely that those sacrifices were brought to Karamoja by Tap and have been integrated as lesser rites in the Karamojong church. The Jie call it *asulany* (Mirzeler 1999:135).

The persistence of traditions through time and cultural change is indicated by the fact that the seed-growers of Kotido, more capitalists than tribespeople, being involved in trade and local government, arrived at the Karamoja Seeds Scheme office all on the same day asking for tractor cultivation, despite being requested every year to cultivate earlier, as ploughing and sowing, agronomically, need not be simultaneous. It is now the *emuron* who declares the official opening of seed-time at *akiriket* (Rowland 1.8.90 Letter). With no installed Orwakol fire-makers, the sub-sections meet at the sacred groves of the sections and each sacrifices an ox in order to open the planting season (J13). A Tap clan, Dioki, make fire for all of Oding. There is a central fire-making ceremony at the sacred grove in Lokatap Rock, followed by ceremonies at each sub-section. The new settlement at Kaceri now has its own *akero* at Atapar ka Amurkwang (the dam of the white sacrificial gatherings). In the absence of anyone else there in 1953, the pioneer Nacam made fire by himself. Then, at neighbourhood level, a ceremony for planting (*apoka*) is held in the month of cultivation, Lomaruk, that is the third moon of the solar year. The fire-maker at that level goes from homestead to homestead to tell the women to brew sorghum beer. The following morning the elders drink the beer in each cattle corral, and then pray ritually for success, for the well-being of the homestead, and for disease to leave the cattle (J8).

If rain does not come in sufficient continuity then the people must please the elders again by feeding them in rain-making ceremonies for the affected locality so that their curses may be eliminated and their strongest blessings effected. The warriors' vigour, yet their obedience to the elders, is dramatized in mock spear charges. A bullock, or sometimes a full-grown bull, or a fat cow, may be speared and its chyme spattered on the worshippers and on their fields. In April 2002, elders in Oding were looking for a black ox 'to sacrifice very soon' for rain (J8). Prayers are led by respected elders (Rowland 1983:2) and the *emuron*, sticking his unsheathed spear upright in the ground. The prayer-leader or the congregation may dramatize the source of rain, the east, or the destination of disease, the west, by pointing arms, stick or spear in the appropriate direction.

Leader	*Assembled*
Kiera, E, e, akirru [sic] adwere paadoa ?	Ado.
Adoba ?	Ado.

---

[9] Cf. *akijul* (to turn upside down, alter).

190   The Vitality of Karamojong Religion

Adoba ?	*Ado.*
E, e, Ngatuk [sic] paa emwoko ?	*Emwoko.*
Emwoko ?	*Emwoko.*
Emwoko ?	*Emwoko.*
E, e, Ngimomwa arupon paaruputwa ?	*Aruput.*
E, e, Arukum kalotunga aporori papora ?	*Aporo.*
E, e, neni karononi aporori papora ?	*Aporo.* (Persse 1934:115)

(Listen! Yes, yes,[10] the rain I have prophesied, has it not fallen?	It has fallen.
Has it fallen?	It has fallen.
Has it fallen?	It has fallen.
Yes, yes, the cows have they not been satisfied?	They have been satisfied.
They have been satisfied?	They have been satisfied.
They have been satisfied?	They have been satisfied.
Amen, amen, the sorghum has germinated. Has it not germinated?	It has germinated.
Yes, yes, the cough of the people, it has flown away, has it not flown away?	It has flown away.
Yes, yes, the evil there has flown away, has it not flown away?	It has flown away.)

If this is an accurate retranslation of what Persse heard then the verbs are in the perfective aspect, as indicated by the prefixes and the negative particle (*pa*), while local translations of prayers into English usually adopt the future tense, in order to make the prayers intelligible to empirical Englishmen. In actual fact the rain has not yet fallen and the cattle are far from satiated, which is why the ceremony is being held in the first place but something has already happened that starts a process, which will end ineluctably in rain or welfare, and which the prayers reinforce by verbalizing, in faith. The event which starts the process in such an unpromising environment is the death of the sacrificial victim.

Almost 70 years on, there are still prayers for rain whenever the sacrifice of an ox allows a pressing need to be asked of Akujů. There are repeated prayers for rain seen as part of the natural, yet sacral, order

Leader	*Assembled*
Now pray for rain,	
be there	Be there!
Rain with our own animals, be there	Be there!
Rain with our own animals, be there	Be there!
Rain come	Rain come!

Hey Akujů, you want to return back these cows again and all these animals got finished some time back. So rain for our animals.

Come!	Come! ...

---

[10] The interjection, *e/ee*, usually meaning 'yes' is here not answering a question, but is related to what the prayer-leader is about to say. If this is the case, he is using the word with a similar declaration of prophetic power to Jesus' use of 'amen' in his sayings (Jeremias 1967:112–15).

We pray for rain now. We are asking you to pray for rain. You can see that the cows are now in problem, for the cows really have no water. They are now in problems. They are now in problems because there is no water, no grass. So let's pray for rain. Today you should know that there is no rain. Now it is time to pray.
Ei. Akiru, akiru, ngaatuk (Yes. Rain, rain, cows)
Ei. Akiru ka ngaatuk (Yes. Rain of cows)
Ei. Akiru, (Yes. Rain,)

today come!	Come!
Come heavily!	Come heavily!
Has it stopped?	It has not stopped!
So the rivers, have they become full?	They have become full!
Have the cows become satisfied?	They have become satisfied!
So when it rains, will the seeds germinate?	They will germinate! ...

Rain, rain to cows,	
come back!	Come back!
Our grandmothers,	
be happy!	Be happy!
Now River Naokot,	
be full!	Be full!
River Kopus,	
be full!	Be full!
So Kopus, our cows,	
let it keep!	Let it keep! ...

During that time when there was no rain, they killed a certain bull at Lolukwangit, the rain came down.

Rain,	
pour down!	Pour down!
Pour down!	Pour down!
Cows,	
rejoice!	Rejoice!
Rejoice!	Rejoice!
The children who got lost some time back, with rain	
let them meet!	Meet!
Rain in Jie,	
be there!	Be there!
Rain in Jie,	
be there!	Be there!
Peace in Jie,	
be there!	Be there!

Despite the attempts of the Uganda People's Defence Force to keep Karamojong herds inside the district boundaries at the hottest point of the dry season, when the bare earth bakes, and the rivers lie empty, the prayer of faith still goes up. 'Today' it is commanded to come, and without a rain-cloud in the clear blue sky, it is asserted that it has not stopped! In the perfective aspect the cows under threat of a fatal epidemic have become satisfied in the time of the prayer. The answer is in the prayer. The world changes immediately when the old men ask, whatever the lack of environmental evidence, because Akujů has heard and it is only a matter of time before creation catches up with the divine fiat. The sorghum will germinate, not if the rain falls, but when.

Forensically, if it be found that the elders are not speaking the words of Akujŭ, there must be a reason. Sorcery or antisocial practice can wrong the country and 'tie up' (*akikujukuj*) the rain.

> Such an instance occurred in the summer of 1951 when a man boasted publicly that he had buried 'medicine' in a pot to prevent rain. The women of the neighbourhood, who always act in cases where rainfall is threatened, marched to the man's homestead, dug up the offending pot with the medicines inside and broke it into pieces. (Gulliver, P. and P.H. 1953:49)

Since women are totally responsible for providing water for the home and for managing the fields, they take it upon themselves to root out the cause of the crop rains failing. They may visit places where there is water, to pour it as rain, or they address rivers by special, probably spirit names, and sing how they have flooded the land or, if they suspect someone, they take a stick in either hand and proceed, singing and swaying, as they walk to his home (Gourlay 1971b:139).

A leading trader in Kotido had consulted an *emuron* in order to prevent the government prosecuting him for *magendo* (making supernormal profits). The *emuron* advised the sacrifice and burial of a dog near Mount Toror. Years later, in 1985, the same *emuron* pinpointed the dog's grave as tying up the rains, presumably because they upset the rain-bearing spirits of Toror. So the women of the town stampeded to his shop and looted it. A ceremony, no doubt involving a sacrifice of an animal and a fee for the *emuron*, was performed to cancel the effect of the previous one. The rich and influential cannot gainsay the power of this world-view, and ignore the local customs that ensure social responsibility at their peril.

There is a sacrament (*ajulot ngina ka akiru*, sacrifice for rain) when a dry spell threatens the young crops, which counters selfish or evil practices for the benefit of the whole community (Gourlay 1971b:138). David Burnett, a scientist by training (1988:13f), chronicled a visit in Najie in June 1983, a month usually given to drought in the middle of crop growth, receiving as little as 15.9 mm and having at most a 1:6 chance that any rain would fall at all in 24 hours (cf. Dyson-Hudson 1966:32; Dyson-Hudson, V.R. and N. 1970:97). Najie is generally drier than the centres of the south. Rain normally comes from an easterly direction, so much so that it is tempting to say that 'west' was wrong.

> ... I could sense the excitement and the anticipation. It was going to be a great day. Then I looked up to the sky. It was now about 9am, and the sun was climbing into a clear blue sky. There were only a few wisps of a cloud visible, and it had all the indications of being another hot, dry day in Karamoja.... Did they honestly think that by offering a sacrifice they would cause rain to fall?
>
> The little group of men began to lead the black bull into the open area just on the outside of the village. The bull had to be black, I was informed, because that was symbolic of the clouds which would come from the west.
>
> ... Eventually one of the old men stood near the remains of the carcass and began to shout his prayers to God, 'Akuj, send rain on your people.' The people in the circle echoed

the refrain. All the old men took their place and in turn led the people in the prayers while the meat was being cooked on the fire.

Suddenly the cooked meat was being offered around, and the people began to jump up and dance. I scarcely noticed that the thin clouds had thickened, and from the west the sky slowly began to darken. The dance continued into the afternoon, and the air of anticipation grew. Finally, at about 3 pm, a few spots of rain fell, and then the rain began to fall so heavily that everyone had to run for shelter. (Burnett 1988:13f)

The Karamojong believe their sacraments have power to change the course of nature and to redeem the spoliation of creation.

Freeing the Cattle

When the grass around the settled areas begins to dry up in October or November, the cattle herdsmen become restless, wanting to move away to the dry-season grazing lands with their herds. Embarking on the nomadic life each year is seen by the herdsmen as liberation for both them and their cattle. They will often be scores of miles away from their paternal herd-owners and the cattle will be able to roam as far afield as they need in order to satisfy their appetites. Together they represent the future well-being of society; the herdsmen are the rising generation and the herds are the social and economic capital. The elders know that, if the herders resolutely refuse to return to their families, there is little they can do to stop the dissolution of their tribe or section. The most fatal of curses will not undo the damage done, if the threat of it is ignored. Thus it is of the utmost importance that the herdsmen leave in a sanctioned and amicable way.

The public ceremony of *akiwodokin* provides for this departure for the cattle-camps (*ngawiyoi*). As with *akitocol*, the original meaning has changed, at least for the young unenculturated people, to what they see as the function of the ceremony, namely here, freeing the cattle, driving them, or assembling. *A-dokin* means to emigrate, run away, go away in anger (Lamphear 1976:29). That is precisely what the schismatic groups did who founded the Turkana, Toposa, Nyangatom and Jiye as independent tribes. The entire intention of *akiwodokin* is to stop another repetition of these socio-political tragedies. *Akiwo* means to stand or stop. *Akiwodokin* is designed to stop the warrior herdsmen going away in anger by turning the event from self-won independence to a happy blessing by the elders, incorporating a reminder of their duty to return.

As the herdsmen grow restless, one of them, an *esorokit*, asks for a council (*atukot*) to decide a date for *akiwodokin* and the move away. Until this happens it is an act of wilful disobedience, punishable by a beating and the sacrifice of an ox, to take cattle off to the dry-season pastures. Oxen are sacrificed to please the elders, who divine the propitious occasion. A facilitator (*ekeseran*) is appointed to announce and organize the assembly with the aid of a kudu horn, so that all the males may attend the sacred grove of the section with as many herds as possible – no mean operation. The elders feast on the sacrificial oxen and gourds of milk. The herdsmen and the stock in their care are blessed with the chyme and the elders' prayers. Then the herdsmen leave, in the accepted order of clan or locality, through the brushwood gate and are given a clay spray blessing and a token beating with a switch to remind them of their duty to the elders (ibid.:155).

The herds are led, by the *ekeseran* blowing his horn, to a prearranged dry-season water-hole, whence family herdsmen can exercise their precious right within the guidelines set by the family heads who are the herd-owners, to herd where and with whom they will. It is apparent that it is only the shared cattle loyalties, united in the sure belief that Akujů can in fact bless men and herds through the elders' prayers and execute their curses on the recalcitrant, which prevents the disintegration of society.

The Pian hold their opening *akiwodokin* at the sacred grove of the Kaala. This day of blessing is fixed according to the moon months in advance. Visitors are welcome and Pian subsections will send observers, before each holding their own ceremonies. The wooden trumpet (*arupepe*) is blown and there is much meat and beer for this celebration. The bullocks are driven round the crowd four times and through the door (*ekidor*) at pace. The blessing is given by one of the most senior Kaala elders. Then the *ekimomwor* is danced four times, and the herds are free to go to dry-season grazing (Emoru 1998:24).

Angola and *akiwodokin* are a pair of sacraments. One is usually held at the beginning of the wet season, the other at the beginning of the dry. They signify a renewal of life (J21). Both involve the sectional assembly and blessing of cattle and the orderly dismissal through the symbolic gate (*ekidor*) made with *edodoi* (*Kigalia aethopica* fruit) fibres, with the anointing of clay and the ritual beating. Broken pots, ashes and small sticks are put out, and the fire-maker kindles new fire with his firestick (*epit*; J21). The gate perhaps signifies entry into or exit from settled society with all its regulations on behaviour which stipulate Akujů's justice.

In both case there is no looking back and no sacrifices as the cattle herders march off. They go to the east for *angola* and to the west for *akiwodokin* in order to found the dry season cattle-camps. *Akiwodokin* is a celebration of herders' freedom, as the young men leave their fathers at home. Yet the subtlety of sacralizing these moments in economic livelihood is that, moving through the gate, the herders are further enculturated into the cosmology of the religion, and are stopped from emigrating (*akiwodokin*). Woe to the one, like chief Aciya, who tries to prevent the ceremony of the door that frees the cattle! Movement is symbolized here, not the blessing or sanctifying of territory. Diseases are not waved on, but left behind and closed off, as it is the change of environment which will be as good as rest for the cattle. Out in the bush a man can be alone with Akujů in His spiritual creation. The cattle which society has blessed continually mediate Akujů's providence to him. In such a gracious environment, however hostile and threatening to others, he can work out his own salvation.

There are two more sacraments, whose timing is conditioned by the seasons.

Harvest Festival

On average no more than one year in three will yield a fairly good harvest or better (Dyson-Hudson, V.R. and N. 1970:116). Since rainfall is highly localized, some neighbourhoods may have little grain on the crop, even though the section as a whole is doing quite well, in which case, or if *akitocol/angola* has not worked, all the adult men of the neighbourhood will visit each suffering homestead for one last supplication to God for the welfare of its fields, crops and livestock in a sacrifice for sorghum (*ajulot a ngimomwa*; Gourlay 1971b:142; Gulliver 1955:81). Sorghum, unlike maize, has an amazing capacity, given late rain, to produce a crop despite having been bleached white by the sun. In this hope the women of the homestead provide blood, milk and sorghum *atap* for those who pray.

In the one good year in three, each homestead blessed by God takes turns to sacrifice an ox in its cattle corral for all the adult males in the neighbourhood. God's beneficent handiwork is publicly acknowledged and prayers made for next year's rains to be just as timely and abundant. Here there is opportunity for the clan traditions of each family, in whose name thanks and petitions are made to Akujů in prayer (ibid.:82). These feasts are *ngasuban*, and are genuinely a festival of creation (*asubet*) with dances by the women to celebrate the fruit of their toil (Pazzaglia 1982:120). They are held around July (*Losuban*) when the first ears of sorghum can be reaped. A good crop is the prime condition for holding weddings and initiations over harvest (*aet*). All these ceremonies are performed (*akisub*) out of the bounty of the Creator (*Ekasuban*).

War Sacrifices

There is a season for going to war, usually starting after *akiwodokin*. It may continue until the wet season makes travel difficult, brings the herds back home, preoccupies the men with other tasks or gives sufficient food to damp any *Wanderlust*. Since raiding, even by an enterprising, small group of friends can bring severe repercussions on others, the elders feel a need to control the eagerness of the young men to acquire a herd of their own the quick way, as the elders may lose theirs in a counter-raid. In 1965, the elders were in no mood for war and not only refused the young men this sacrament but also cursed them if they went raiding (Gourlay 1971b:144). All the political ingredients, including the spy intelligence of the *erotot*, for a decision go into haruspication. An *emuron* will examine an ox's entrails in search of propitious signs for the section's elders to decide whether to grant permission to raid. A Pian informant (P5) claims that the elders do not give a ceremony to open raiding and did not use to, though this could again be a feature of the lack of elders at the end of a generation-set (Dyson-Hudson 1966:215). Raiding is the concern of youth; the ceremony is conducted by the *emuron*, but he only advises the spy or war-leader. Yet this sounds too much like an apology for older members of society, distancing their responsibility for raiding. Raiding against the Pokot and the selling of their cattle was going on in Namalu while the interview was being conducted (P7), and there was no indication that this did not have the blessing of the herd-owners. It is possible that a ceremony to open the raiding season has been dispensed with for 30 years in some sections, but it was always the case that, within the raiding season, the cattle-camps were free, on the advice of an *emuron*, to determine their own raids and tactics.

The sacrifice that opens fighting (*amuronot ngina angaar ajore*) produces extremely shrewd results. The choice of the weakest enemy is anything but arbitrary. Radio news is not disdained, especially as it tends to cover parts of Uganda other than Karamoja, giving an advantage over its neighbours. Internal news travels very fast along the strata of the age-system, with many people on the move between the centres and the outlying areas. Certainly the Jie were waiting for

General Okello's troops to retreat home from Jinja through Kotido in January 1986.[11]

The timing and place of a particular attack is settled at a raiding feast (*epeyos ngolo jie*). This is held on the eve of the planned raid and so often at night for the warriors 'to make their hearts fierce' by drinking ox's blood (Paget Wilkes 1932a:8; Docherty 1957:33; cf. Dyson-Hudson 1958a:177). If it is held at night the ox cannot be speared running with the herd as usual but is held by men with a thong round its hind leg, and another tries to thrust his spear through the heart at the first attempt to ensure good fortune. The blood is drunk from the chest cavity, elders first. Adult warriors are given chyme with which to anoint themselves, while the elders anoint the uninitiated, uttering a personal blessing, like, '*Topolor! Tomojong! Tobaru!*' (Be great! Become old! Be rich!). An *emuron* uses it to daub on small stones, making patterns that glisten in the dark, while muttering incantations over them.

Medicine (*ekitoi*, tree) has always been significant in the hunt and the raid to 'confuse' the victims, but currently the Jie have combined their cattle into three great *ngalomarin*,[12] which each have an *emuron* attached to advise the war-leader (*ekapolon ka ajore*) if he is not 'a high priest' himself (Banks 3.4.90 Letter). His advice on who to take, the route there and back, or the tactics will weigh as much as his reputation in these matters allows. However a younger man is chosen to lead the raiding party into action, the bravest and most skilful warrior. As leader (*ekadedengan*[13]) he may be offered the bull's testicles to eat so that its power may be transferred to him.

The young women sing and clap in the background, while the initiated men eat and young men join them for the dance (*ekimomwor*) 'to put heart into a man' (Gourlay 1971b:144), whipping themselves up into a drunken frenzy. The songs extol oxen and courage, the very attributes most attractive to girls, not least because they offer the greatest mortal security. Warriors will seldom go to raid unless their mothers bless them in the home, where they may anoint themselves with ritual clay to prevent harm from bullets, spears and arrows. Women are very much part of the war effort, castigating the cowardly and praising the brave, also being acknowledged as the producers of warriors to protect the country, so enemy women are also treated as combatants.

A community under threat from a small, impending raid holds an ordinary sacrifice at its sacred grove (Marshall Thomas 1965:ch.5). However, in times of full-scale war, the leaders and the warriors gather into an *alomar*, which becomes a fighting unit on full alert for the defence of their cattle and people. In 1980, Arthur Banks (3.4.90) was present, in the bush, when the Jie were under very real threat of attack, and watched the whole group of several hundred warriors at a 'prayer-meeting', called

---

[11] Tito Okello himself had twice gone to the elders of east Acholi for the equivalent ritual there to decide whether he should launch a *coup d'état*. The second time, he successfully marched on Kampala.

[12] Cf. *alomar* (to go in).

[13] Cf. *dedeng* (fierce).

to put a curse on the enemy, and it was terrifying in the power of evil or at least pagan vitriol being poured out in the amazing unison of the curses – the rolled 'R's' and exhaled hisses – no, more deep and sonorous than hisses, more like the power of the bottom note on a cathedral organ, or a vicious rumble of thunder close by.

Any sacrifice may be the occasion for a curse, which, in the absence of the accursed can be dramatized thus: the senior elders leave the place of sacrifice, but still stand facing east. They pick up stones or gravel, and hurl them backwards between their legs towards the west. This will be the fate of anyone who would intervene in their affairs. Victory in battle and the restriction of the growth in enemies' human and cattle populations which is essential, ultimately, for the survival of the tribe is in the hands of Akujů who will favour those who have done things wisely and well.

Receiving an Enemy-Name

Though the culture provides incentives to kill the enemy, as does every culture in its military aspect, the spiritual harmony of the killer's world is radically jeopardized by the seizing of life (Tornay 1989:866ff).

> Someone kills a person; Akujů is therefore not happy and the spirit of the victim might disturb his mind or give chronic disease leading eventually to death. His wife may be barren, or his children die, and other problems (*ngican*). To appease Akujů or the spirit of the victim, it is necessary to kill a white he-goat, for all men, even enemies, have a connection with Akujů. The skin is cut in the form of a rope. A long piece is tied round his neck and shorter ones on the joints of the limbs and the waist. He may be given an enemy-name, summarizing how the enemy was killed, for example, Lokwarale (he who was run through with a large spear). (P3)

During a battle, if a man has blooded his spear, which is much rarer with the increased use of firearms, he licks the blood 'to prevent him feeling faint' (Rowland 1983:9),[14] as an internalization of the enemy's life-force or heart (*etau*[15]). It must be dealt with. He may never use it as before, lest its taint will surely cause him to die, so it is broken up and used as a knife or given away. Otherwise, he may stick the spear into the ground to return it to the creation, or burn the blood off the spear (*akicun*) before it can be reused (P5). Not only may the dead person's family seek vengeance but his spirit (*ecenit*[16]) may too. Since most enemies die by bullets now,

---

[14] President Amin, an EN Kakwa, is believed to have performed a blood-tasting rite on his dead enemies of state (Kyemba 1977:108f).

[15] e- is the masculine gender marker, -ta- is a strong causative infix in the Karamojong verb, while –u denotes an abstract noun. Thus e-ta-u is the quality that causes a person to be, so is that which is lost at death. As with animals, this life-force is not annihilated at death, but released with cosmic potential.

[16] When a person dies, his personal, human existence is no more and can be no more. There is no resurrection among the Karamojong, but neither is there a complete and utter end to life, for its origin is spiritual, in life-force. Thus the human fades into the sub-human, a mere trace or vestige of his former being. He becomes either an ancestral spirit insubstantial

this custom must be rare, unless a knife is applied to the corpse, as nothing similar is done with guns.

A killer must purify himself before Akujů to 'free himself from the stain of death through the sacrifice of a goat. He eats the goat and cuts the goatskin into strips, which he wears to show that '"the enemy blood has been washed away"' (Marshall Thomas 1965:119). Should he not undergo the ritual cleansing symbolized by the white goat-skin thongs (*ngarukanes*) above his elbows and below his knees, it is believed he will fall sick (Rowland 1983:9), overcome by the life-force of the other.[17] He may also don a necklace of white (traditionally, ostrich shell) beads, also as a charm against avenging spirits whose symbolic colour, being of the world of shades, is black (Knighton 1990:I,133f).

In order for his act to meet with public approval, he must submit himself to the elders by sacrificing an ox, white probably being the propitious colour. If satisfied as to the details of the event, they will authorize him to take an 'enemy-name' which picks up some distinguishing item. So the name 'Lotongomoi' means 'he of the angry enemy'. It may become the name by which he is known for the rest of his life.

He will have a pattern of cicatrice (*ngaloka* or *ngageran*) made by plucking the skin with a thorn and cutting it to leave scars on the right shoulder denoting a man, on the left a woman. Spearing an elephant, lion, the now extinct (in Karamoja) rhinoceros or buffalo also used to merit a decoration and slits in the ear of the beloved ox. Although not now a necessity for initiation or marriage, killing has been significant for partaking of tribal identity. The Teso call a Karimojongait, *eloket*. *Aloket* is an animal trap, or the wire appendage which doubles back over the headdress of a previous generation-set to suspend a rabbit-tail or monkey fur bob (*etuleru*) over the forehead. The Karimojong have been viewed, not so much as cowherds but as Ngilok (trappers, hunters, killers; Clark and Totty 1953:3). In these rites, then, may be the last vestiges of an initiation ceremony that predated *asapanů*,

---

image (*eparait*), if the person dies as an established member of the community, or a revengeful spirit (*ecenit*), if the person dies as an embittered member of the community or an enemy. Neither sub-creature is personally recognizable, or generally visible; their presence is known by contrary circumstance or by divination. Enemies who have been killed in battle can naturally be expected to bequeath *ngicen*, so it is vital that a ceremony is performed to nullify this loose and invisible cannon of a life-force. Otherwise, the killer can be sure to be dogged by *ngican* (problems, Kiswahili *matata*). '*Ngicen* bring *ngican*' (P5). This provides a sure insight into the Karamojong view of causation: visible events have invisible causes, however mysterious. Theories of Karamojong pragmatism or functional religion are thereby limited. Ugandans fear Karamojong not just for their military prowess, but because of their proficiency in dealing with the invisible or spiritual, which gives them confidence in killing the enemy with neither bad conscience nor fear of impunity.

[17] The Sabawoot had a similar ceremony, 'On arrival home he received a white goat (white for purification) which he took into the bush and killed. The man had to remain there alone for fourteen days, during which time he was allowed no sexual intercourse. ... If any man broke this rule it was said that the woman would not be able to bear afterwards; and that the man would lose his strength and become ill' (Weatherby 1962:204).

dependent on an economy based more on hunting, and was a precondition for initiation and marriage.

Of 59 Dodoso males examined by Wayland (1931:222-7), 20 per cent had cicatrices, and, of 62 Jie, 16 per cent. Of all these, 16 were on the right shoulder and six on the left. The impression is that their frequency has not reduced today. So telltale a sign, as with the strips of goat-skin, may be delayed until after the raiding season, so as not to present too tempting a target. The scarification is performed after a month, when a white ox is also sacrificed for the elders, with the head and neck going to the women of the family. This is one occasion when Karimojong elders eat the perineal gland (*angarue*). The killer wears strips of its hide around waist, wrist and ankles (Novelli 1999:279).

No doubt this occasions some psychological security for the killer, and it is interesting that he still needs to undergo this means the culture has for sanctifying the brutality exercised upon enemies. Yet, unlike the Ugandan caricatures of the Karamojong, they are human and have normal sensibilities, despite their low valuation of the life of the outsider. Those Karamojong with maturer religious sensitivity are aware that the sacraments dealing with the spiritual dangers of homicide do not work *ex opere operato*. 'People can sacrifice for sin, but Akujů's curse will run its course. Killers may not be forgiven on earth or in heaven, as the man may be the continual enemy of Akujů for shedding blood. Akujů is not happy: He may listen to the enemies' sacrifice' (P5).

Peace-making

There is a time for war and a time for peace. The tribes of Karamoja are not fighting with all of their neighbours all of the time. Throughout hostilities, a Karamojong tries to uphold his relationship with an alien stock associate, despite the public opprobrium, for he knows that there will be a time in his life when he will need him. Ties of marriage also exist. Repeatedly, political and economic circumstances will arise which make peace good sense. This is fine, especially for the elders, for society as a whole regards peace with prosperity as the most desirable state, one for which they often pray. It is mainly those who want to make their mark on the *status quo*, who take the benefits of peace for granted.

Peace (*ekisil*) may break out at any time, even after a crushing defeat, for wars are never fought to build an empire, only to secure space in which to live and eat. In 1983, a durable peace broke out between the Karimojong, Jie and Dodosô who had been fighting intermittently for three decades, but it was no accident, being arranged by the elders. The warriors went on raids together in Uganda, Sudan and Kenya. Internal disruptions, such as there have been between sections in Karimojong, were settled in the late 1980s. Jie and Turkana held a peace-making ceremony in the mid-1990s, which Akujů answered with rain.

Respected leaders visit the enemy under a truce and sue for peace. If there is sufficient will on both sides a meeting of the two generation-sets from both sides is fixed, either at a neutral site or at one another's sacred groves in succession (Rowland 1983:10). The nature of the ceremony appears to have changed little in 200 years. At the end of the eighteenth century the Toposa and the Dodoso broke their spears and buried them in a river bed (Pazzaglia 1982:35). One was held in

Rengen in 1901/2 to end the Jie–Acoli war, with elders from all parts of Najie attending and the local ones officiating (Lamphear and Webster 1971:30). The thigh-bone of a sacrificial ox was broken, presumably with its foreleg, between the two parties to give a peace which largely held, with much mutual contact and intermarriage, until 1982. To share in a sacrifice to Akujů, even when very different conceptions of Him are held, is a highly effectual sign.

In 1920, when the British pushed the Pokot, Sapiny, Karamojong and Turkana into making peace (*akisil*), the ceremony also consisted of the elders of each side exchanging white and red ostrich feathers tied to long sticks, the former symbolizing peace and life, the latter anger and bloodshed. One accepts the other, past atrocities, present vengeance and all. Then they walk over crossed spears, crossed arrows and crossed shields. The central act is still the breaking of the right thigh bone, seen as the essence of the ox's strength.[18] Representatives of the parties hold the ends and presumably keep them as tokens of the formally ratified peace. They also hold up razors, take a peace oath and bury the razors.[19] An *ekimomwor* dance follows for the young people to celebrate the new political relationship, and provides an opportunity for sexual relations and courtship between the sexes and the tribes. The treaty between the Pian and the Pokot was remarkable for its long run inefficacy but this was due to the imposition of the ceremony by the British. Karamojong sacraments are commonly rooted in reality; if not, they promote disembodied ideals which have little to do with life as they see or experience it. When they, as tribes or sections, are ready for peace, and not before, they will still conduct the *akisil* ceremony to usher in a time of peace.

There are occasional personal bonds, which may bind the participant's kin or age-set. A sign of peace at any time is to rip up a handful of grass and bear it to the other party. A practice which used to be widespread over East Africa when the interior was first encountering strangers from the coast was the mixing of individuals' blood to forge a blood brotherhood for life (Bell 1923:63).

Funerary and Memorial Services

Those who die in the homesteads are taken out into the bush (*namoni*) and laid in a thicket (*amoni*). The function of this must be to prevent the vultures from disfiguring the corpse by day but to allow the hyenas to dispose of it all in the night. The dead, though lost to the land of the living, are thus taken closer to the sacred sphere. Rowland (1983:10) witnessed the corpse of an old lady being taken out by

---

[18] WN Nuer blood feuds are permanently defused by sacrifice involving 'breaking of the bone' (Hutchinson 1996:123).

[19] EA 5857: 15.12.19 J. Barton, DC, Kacheliba to OC Troops, Turkana; 25.10.20. Report by Chidlaw-Roberts and K. Hunter, DC, Kacheliba. The razors were probably traditional ones, which were used at least until 1970. A stone blade (*aketunetunet*) was chipped off chert, felspar or quartz and used for shaving (Wilson 1973b:84). Obsidian was used in the past for its very sharp edge. The symbolic use of stones gives a manifest continuity with ancient times. Raiding soon resumed (EA 4325: 10.7.20, Capt. E.V. Otter to KAR, Nairobi; Weatherby 1962:210; Brasnett 1958:118f).

her son, who broke in his hands a small gourd of ashes, throwing them against the deceased. The war dead are left where they lie, unless they are near the settlements, but only local men will be covered with branches. People who die without issue are cut off from the land of the living, for it is the duty of sons to arrange rites, and of siblings to remember their parents.

Only the herd-owner must be buried, and his first wife in his grave. This is dug in the moist earth in the middle of his calf or sheep pen and he is buried on his side, with his head pointing toward his tribe's known cradleland. The corpse is covered with dung and earth, stamped down hard to foil body-snatchers. He may be buried in the hide of his beloved ox: 'the ox will be killed to accompany its master on his last long journey' (Clark 1952a:69). Two beloved oxen were killed when Nacam was buried in his cattle corral on 14.12.01 (J8). An upright gravestone is a reminder that the spirit of the deceased still watches over life of the *ere*. The Dodosô cut the legs of the ox sacrificed for the whole clan, smear them with the chyme, and then burn all the meat, having done the same for the family with a ram, which is also burned (D5).

Respects are paid by the weeping and wailing which goes on for several days. Men have the front of their heads shaved, women all of their heads. All neck ornaments are removed and the widow's ear-rings too. Women and children put on tatty clothes until hair recovers the head, when the mourners rub themselves down with dust (*apua*) and shake it off, to cleanse themselves of the stain of death (Clark 1953:76). Then personal ornaments can be restored.

All the deceased's beloved oxen must eventually be sacrificed, as nobody is allowed to inherit one. This is a funerary rite (*apun*),[20] which is for the sake of the living (P5). The deceased's age-set companions will eat them in a meal called *akurwor*, which unlocks his spirit from his earthly home but, uniquely, no prayers are said and no rite is performed with the *amuros*. Rich wives bring an ox for sacrifice, poor or young ones a ram, the same beast that they receive when their daughters marry.

A year after the death of a mature man or woman the family will sacrifice an ox for a funeral banquet (*amon*). Its hide is pegged out, upside down, in the homestead to dry in the sun. The next day the friends and relatives come in and sit round the sides of the *ekal* to drink the beer that is offered them, married women at one end and the men at the other. It is a quiet, low-key affair, but of good humour. The proper thing has been done for the deceased, and his spirit may rest in peace. Nacam's son, though he is educated, a sub-county chief[21] and a Roman Catholic, is planning the final memorial for his father, which he calls *lokinyom* (that of the seeds), if there is a good harvest (J8).

Memorial services are not held only for people. *Atwa*[22] is held every five to ten years, when the owner of a beloved ox, which has become too old or ill to keep up

---

[20] Cf. *apunor* (to cut open an ox).

[21] In fact Butong is nicknamed Bwanalam, referring to G.H. Lamb, whose reputation as an active administrator still continues after 80 years (D3,4), meaning he takes his employment very seriously.

[22] Cf. *atwanare* (to die).

with the herd, is able to find friends or relatives in the same position. Then they fix a venue by a river between harvest and *akiwodokin* at a time of peace and invite bond-friends, affines, relatives and neighbours. For days there will be much milk and beer to go with the meat from the sacrifice of the outgoing beloved oxen, and there is the celebration of the blessings of Akujů that crosses most social barriers with prolonged dancing (Emoru 1998:24; Novelli 1999:xlvi,275f). The owners will replace their beloved oxen with young ones of identical hide markings and horn profiles, though these need to be hammered into position. As usual this ceremony is a continuous tradition (Dyson-Hudson 1966:216; Pazzaglia 1982:86).

Cooling Down

When a community, below the level of a territorial division, suffers great stress because of an outbreak of diseases or deaths among people or cattle confined to it, spirits of one sort or another are blamed. If it is cholera or dysentery, *ngipian* are angry. Trouble might be caused by spiritual machinations of sorcerers or by disturbed ancestral spirits. Accusations begin to fly, about either how someone has wronged the spirits or how someone is a sorcerer, and tempers grow steadily more heated until life for all becomes miserable (Gulliver 1955:95f,113; Rowland 1983:6f).

The solution is to have a 'cooling down' ceremony (*akitolim*[23]). Now a human's shadow (*etorobe*) represents his vital being and the stem, *lim, is associated with a range of spiritual things: rain, water, cold, advice and stain (*akilimet*) as in death. *Akitolim*, by cooling down a situation, placates hot, angry spirits. It serves to restore the spiritual world, and therefore of necessity the human and material worlds, to a more harmonious order. This is done by sacrificing a steer, or in smaller family affairs a goat, and praying that Akujů will soothe an inflamed, putrescent, social situation. That He does is testified by the high degree of solidarity in neighbourhood and extended family, despite endemic hardships.

An *amuronot a lore* (sacrifice of the home) may be held to reduce the family tensions exhibited by problems like madness or barrenness. The elders are called and an ox, provided by the head of the family, is sacrificed in his cattle corral. The elders exhort the community and pray over a situation where barrenness has prevented the payment of bridewealth.

Leader	*Assembled*

Now take care of these problems, so that when we are given these animals, something does not again come to disturb the womb of our daughter. So now I can say this,
For the child who brought this case, cattle,

multiply!	
Multiply!	Multiply!
	Multiply!

All those problems that were about to entangle him,

will pass away!	Will pass away!

Even the blood that is in her womb will, and

---

[23] Cf. *etolim* (cool shade, shadow of inanimate object).

the child in the womb will become!	Will become!
the child in the womb will become!	Will become!
the child in the womb will become!	Will become!
the child in the womb will become!	Will become!
And Longaren	
will become happy!	Will become happy!
will become happy!	Will become happy!
And Loutan	
will become happy!	Will become happy!
And all the Pore people [clan]	
will become happy!	Will become happy!
When they are eating the ox,	
they will become happy!	They will become happy!
Akujů now hears the problems!	He hears!
He hears!	He hears!

It is in this context that bold accusations can be made without the risk of the breakdown of relationships.

Why should one person become tough?	Why should one person defeat you?
Why should one person become tough?	Why should one person defeat you?
Why should one person become tough?	Why should one person defeat you?

Whoever is against Modo, whoever hates him, let that person meet with the cobra.

They dramatize the killing of a cobra, and then curse whoever is the cause of the problems. The accused, or anyone with a grudge against Modo, must perforce keep very quiet after this ceremony. As a result of the sacrifice and prayers, Akujů now hears so as to act to bring fertility, cattle and happiness, and the hot feelings against 'that person who has charmed my daughter' are cooled. It is in this context that bold accusations can be made without the risk of the breakdown of relationships.

Absolution

When youths or men disobey the elders or the social norms which the latter uphold, they lay themselves open to the legal, physical punishment of *ameto* or to the preternatural curse (*akilamakinet*) of the elder(s). The distinction is a fine one, for *ameto* often results in a religious sacrifice, and the curse in physical suffering, and the elders instigate both. However the punishment with potentially greater effect is the curse. It is not used if the elders can avoid it, for they would prefer that theft, for instance, were sorted out between the parties rather than bring contempt on their preternatural powers by overuse in the mundane. Yet the curse is used to salutary effect.

Just as the elders pray for something good, and it is at once asserted by the response to be the case, so it is in reverse. As soon as they curse (*aki-lam/pyed/cen*), the world has been changed and it is an urgent priority for the accursed to do everything he can to revoke the curse before it is too late. There is no question of waiting to see what happens. Even if we take the most sceptical view of actual effect on the accursed's health, wealth or life, specified by the curse, it is undeniable that

Source: Ben Knighton

Photograph 7.1 The *Agat* litany: praying for a baby to be implanted in the womb of a daughter during a sacrifice in the homestead (*amurunot a lore*) of Moding

an unrevoked curse will lead to his being cut off from his people. As an outlaw he must either live as a desperate bandit, move to a town or go into exile among enemies who would use him to assist their raids. Elders do not relish any of these alternatives, and would rather he submitted to their authority, but there are no negotiations on an equal footing.

In 1965, when the elders cursed those who went raiding, they retaliated in kind by holding their own ceremony to free themselves from the elders' power. Each transferred the curse heaped upon him to his beloved ox, which was driven into the bush (Gourlay 1971b:84,144). It was a means of sacrificing cattle directly to God, without going through the elders, and the clearest possible example of an ox substituting for a man. This rebellion against the authority of the elders was not caused by the influence of modernity except inasmuch as it fostered population pressures since the curse was taken seriously, but by social and economic pressures to acquire cattle, when cattle holdings were more than the environment could sustain. The elders would not have recognized the warriors' repudiation of their curse but have seen its effects in the bad famines over the next two decades.

There is a sacrament to enable the accursed to come into line and to recognize the elders' God-given authority. In proportion to the gravity of his offence he, or they, must offer tobacco, beer or sacrificial stock to the elder, or an ox for the assembly. The elders make clear what is required. The ceremony (*akidyek*) takes it name from the central dialogue.

Offender: 'Father, father, let me be. Help me. Leave me alone. I will not do these things again, truly. I will not repeat them.'
Elder: 'Very well. Have you believed?'
Offender: 'I have.'
Elder: 'Or do you still argue?'
Offender: 'No, I have believed.' (Dyson-Hudson 1966:182)

The offender may be cleansed by crawling through (and being momentarily gripped by) the elder's straddled legs or he may be anointed with chyme at the sacred grove. The former cleansing seems a microcosm of the gate that the juniors have to pass through at *akitocol* and *akiwodokin*, all emphasizing submission to the elders as the divine authority in society.

Yet Dyson-Hudson's translation of *akidyek* as 'let me be' gives the offender's view of what he is doing rather than what he must do, in the elders' eyes, for them to revoke the curse. This is borne out by his connotation of 'someone struggling with a force greater than himself that may only be removed at its behest rather than his own' (ibid.:182n). Of course, the accursed is in the act of imploring and beseeching the elders, but he is doing something far deeper than asking them to get off his back: he must be, or they would not cleanse him.

When the accursed says, *adyek aiyong*, he does not command 'let me be', but confesses he is sick, guilty, evil.[24] From the admission that he has done wrong he is in a position to repent, to promise never to do wrong again. Having confessed and

---

[24] *Akidyak* means 'to miss the target', an old English meaning of sin, and *adyak*, probably the primitive verb behind both 'to be ill' (cf. *adyak*, sickness).

repented, he can properly say that he has believed, that the authorities are constituted by God and he will not argue with them. Whether every offender fully understands it this way or simply as a means of getting out of trouble is a secondary issue, common to all sacraments. Dyson-Hudson's other examples (ibid.) can be retranslated: a man with a dying child, 'Akujů, I am sick; Earth, I am sick!'; a thief apprehended in the act, 'Father, I am guilty. I shall not do these things again. I shall not repeat them. Please forgive me'; a would-be adulterer, caught by her menfolk because of the woman's alarm, 'Father, I am a sinner; Mother, I am in the wrong!' Assumed fault is common to them all.

Killing the Sacred

The Oding hold an annual sacrifice after harvest in Losuban for the ratel or honey-badger (*ekor*), which it is tabu for that section to kill or hurt.[25] It may be considered as a rare totem, for it is a very serious matter even to wound a honey-badger by accident, let alone kill or eat it. An ox would have to be sacrificed before elders as soon as possible in order to prevent ecological consequences overtaking either the perpetrator or the community. At this ceremony only is it killed for the 'community', specifically 'for the oldest men'. Beer is brewed and the number of oxen sacrificed depends on the number of subsections present. Though they eat the flesh, the oxen are not an offering to the elders. The ritual question is asked, 'Who told you to kill the grandfather?' (J8). The oxen die as a sacrifice to Akujů to remedy the slaughter of the animal with which the section has connections of origin. The sub-text is that the danger posed by latent desires to kill the grandfathers are purged by this sacrifice which alludes to them.

3 Sacramentality

All the sacramentals of the Karamojong have not been set out here. Indeed that would be an endless task, for minor rites abound for healing and cleansing.[26] Yet most of these could hardly be called sacraments, as they avail just for individuals and families in isolation. They do not bring society together before God; they do not involve a meeting of the assembly (*akiriket*). On these grounds marriage might arguably be excluded, since each marriage only involves two families and clans and

---

[25] Lamphear (1976:129) also finds the honey-badger (*ekor*) to be an Orwakol emblem. Ngikorwakol could be translated as 'those of the black and white honey-badger', which would make the leader Orwakol merely a construction of the section's name rather than the converse.

[26] Novelli (1999) gives a longer ethnography of customs, though he had read Knighton (1990) before publication, while this book was contracted before the present author discovered Novelli's work. 'Yes, I read your thesis. An enormous work, an invaluable reference point for any further research in this field. My sincere congratulations, and thanks, once again for your kindness to allow me to read it' (Novelli 4.9.01 Letter). Now deceased, he assisted the author with his books and correspondence.

sundry friends, though the collective import of marriage for society is undoubted. Also it is a process which takes years to complete, not a single sacramental act.

In general the above sacraments are intrinsically salvific for the individuals and communities who are represented in them. They are all performed in the presence of Akujů and prayers are addressed to Him at some point to bless the people in all the main aspects of their culture – social, political, economic – and to remove the threats from which they need to be saved. They are the points at which it is acknowledged that Akujů comes to man in creation, particularly through the mediation of sacrificial cattle, and in redemption, wrought either by Akujů's responsive intervention in the world or by the obedience of the people to His authorized ministers. In Karamojong sacramentality creatures, whether human, animal, vegetable or mineral, symbolize and proclaim Akujů Himself.

Chapter 8

Mediation and Revelation

To take seriously the voices of Karamojong, it is necessary to bracket the secular Western perspective. The West has often exported its problems in a vain attempt to solve them, not least by intervening in nomadic pastoralism in the name of development (Dyson-Hudson 1985:158). 'For of the last stage of this cultural development, it might be truly said: "Specialists without spirit, sensualists without heart; this nullity imagines it has attained a level of civilization never before achieved"' (Weber 1930:182). The study of Africa, despite the position the world assigns it, teaches that the inclusion of religion is irreducibly necessary in order to understand cultural patterns and change, in short the meaning of earthly existence. To remove it out of the equation does the researcher no service.

> the decline of the sacred is intimately connected with the changes in society and human psychology. It cannot be considered as merely a contingent fact: it is associated with the collapse, whether temporally or finally of traditions, cultures, and values.
>
> From the religious point of view, humanity has entered a long night that will become darker and darker with the passing of the generations, and of which no end can yet be seen. (Acquaviva 1979:201)

How naïve the optimism was in the 1950s and 1960s of both colonialists and Ugandans, that a new nation could be built on the back of social science.[1] To solve their problems, disciplines need to cooperate rather than cling to their fetishes. This approach is not designed to exclude the findings of behavioural studies or the force of social and economic realities. Rather it seeks to coordinate these on the matrix of the cultural cohesion afforded by extant tribal religion. Cultures, like disciplines, need integrating factors. Oddly, when religion was depicted as a social function, it was Malinowski (1948:53) who observed that religion 'bestows on man the gift of mental integrity'. The sacred, understood not as an opposition to the profane, but as an intensity of the spiritual dimension of existence that is already there, is an irreducible and universal occurrence in human life. Religiosity in some shape or form touches on every other aspect of culture. Paul Ricoeur objects to Geertz's 'thick' description of language or culture, when the essential dimension of language begins beyond the closure of signs. Immersing oneself in the thickness, in the direction of sublexical units or, in Geertz's terms (1975:10), 'transient examples of shaped behaviour', makes us realize the closure of language. 'The greatest opening out belongs to language in celebration' in praise of the sacred (Ricoeur 1974:96f).

---

[1] 'The assumption in a scientific age is that it must be possible to find a solution to all social problems' (*Uganda Argus* 24.9.58 Editorial). Its leading question, 'Is this so in Karamoja?' now hangs over all Uganda.

1 Mediation

The sacred is mediated continually to the entire community. This mediation has prescribed ritual channels in order to condense the sacred who makes Himself felt in the particular, but the same mediation extends to all aspects of the culture which draw together and build up the whole life of the community. Thus the sacred is mediated in, not to, Karamojong territoriality, sociality, economy, polity, jurality, morality, personality, mentality and musicality, as well as its religion and language.

Territoriality

Long before the Nilotes emerged as a distinct ethnic group, their forefathers kept cattle which constituted the main reason why Ngiro were able to colonize, and abide in, Karamoja when Tap were being forced out by drought. Territory is elastic to allow for the grazing needs of the herds.

Sociality

Without cattle, no new Karamojong family can come into being, for until bridewealth has been handed over in cattle, neither the bride nor her children leave her extant family. When a man raises the bridewealth from his kin (*ngiyeneta*) and his bond-friends to give it to his affines, a whole network of stock associates (*ngiyeneta a ngaatuk*) is created and two clans are linked by common interest. The closeness of each relationship is precisely expressed by the relative number of cattle given. So the man likes to express his love and his willingness to provide for his bride by raising the highest practicable bridewealth and she is suitably impressed. A person without cattle, who is not a client dependent on a herd-owner, is not a member of Karamojong society. 'A Man is a Man in Cattle' (Marshall Thomas 1965:146); 'People with cattle are Turkana, Karimojong, or Jie, whereas people without are not' (Gray, Sundal *et al.* 2003:22).

Economy

Cattle are not just bridewealth, but wealth in its fullest possible sense. A Karamojongait cannot be poor with cattle, or rich without them. The milk, blood, meat, fat and marrow of cattle are vital to Karamojong subsistence. Hides are used as sleeping mats, working surfaces, capes, skirts, bell collars, sandals, armlets and anklets. Horns and hooves are carved into snuff boxes (*ngigilita*), feather boxes, food containers and musical horns. Urine is the washing-up liquid for all food and water utensils, and it also curdles milk. Faeces make fertilizer, parget and floor surfaces. The scrotum is used to store seeds for the next growing season.

Cattle are in great demand by neighbouring peoples to the extent that no one item of other goods is equivalent, with the notable exception of the gun, so that smallstock, or ghee, make a more flexible means of exchange. If a Karamojongait wishes, he can trade cattle for guns, ammunition, spears, wrist- and finger-knives, ox- and knee-bells, metal waist- and neck-bands, anklets and armlets, decorative chains, removable head-dresses (*ngitim ngulu buburak*), leopard- or baboon-skin cloaks, giraffe- or zebra-tail elbow whisks, grain, tobacco or even money, but that is only necessary for town beer, lengths of cloth (*ngasukai*), poll-tax receipts and school fees.

Polity

The most self-sufficient member of society is the herd-owner (*elope*) who is the head, or big man (*ekapolon*), of his extended family, whose membership is defined by shares in the collective herd in his gift. Such men are those most entrusted with political influence, since their policies are most likely to promote the common good, precisely because of their interest in cattle as a fund for social relations and welfare. If a man wishes to increase his influence, he must add to his herds in order to build exchange relations with as many other herders as possible, or to marry more wives and gain in affinal support. Thus political affairs often revolve around the protection of cattle belonging to members of the community or the planning of raids to acquire more from enemies. The primary object of all military activity is the acquisition and protection of cattle. The attacking battle formation is in the shape of an ox's head.

The Karamojong political community is led by a group of elders, supported by other herd-owners, who direct the achievement of the common good according to pastoralist values. Members have particular territorial rights and the assurance of security for themselves and their livestock, but that membership can be forfeited by any standing refusal to obey the elders and to adhere to the polity. An outlaw and his cattle are fair game for anyone. Seniority in the political constitution is ranked according to when a man speared his ox and was initiated. Herds may be present at ceremonies and every assembly of the political leadership revolves around the sacrifice of cattle.

Morality

In the Karamojong scale of values cattle are the 'greatest' (Dyson-Hudson 1966:94). They are the highest good. Given a mutually exclusive choice between the worst possible of evils, the loss of one's cattle or one's wives, many men would opt for the loss of wives, since the possession of cattle soon brings wives, while the converse is not so true. This ranking is displayed by the behaviour of herdsmen in living far away from the *ere* over long periods for the sake of cattle, which they will be most reluctant to slaughter for their families in the harshest of famines. Even the cattle-rich will trade an ox for grain, rather than kill it, for the demands of the *akiriket* for sacrifice are hard enough to bear. The loss is real, even when compensated. As before, 'A Karimojong loves his cattle above all other things, and for these cattle he will give his life' (a Karimojong statement in Dyson-Hudson 1966:102).

Jurality

To steal cattle is tantamount to a declaration of war, unless the thief is a member of the same tribe, in which case it is a heinous crime. Compensation in all crimes and civil actions is in terms of cattle, as are any additional penalties.

Source: Ben Knighton
Photograph 8.1 Drinking the blood and sucking out the marrow at an ox-sacrifice

Masculine Personality

Differences in physique and character are a source of fascination and amusement, but all have their place. Karamojong society is not repressive, except perhaps to those who seek to live a lifestyle separate from the culture. Rather it encourages each child to have its head in what comes naturally in such a context: the girls to seek the approval of their peers and, before long, of men; boys to acquire a deep interest in cattle. As soon as they can understand, boys join in the games with pebbles as cattle, either in miniature stick corrals or in a series of pockets in the ground, where one 'eats' another's cattle. In adolescence boys may have no high regard for their fathers, the elders or their traditions, but want to make their own way in the world, by building up a personal herd in order to be master of their own future.

Identity may be expressed in the beloved ox and in novel, personal decorations, but, in this last, a young man comes up against the rulings of the age-sets and generations. He may treat absolution (*akidyek*) just as a way out of trouble, and sacrifice as a means of feeding the elders to keep them happy, but soon he wants to be initiated, and then to marry. He learns the meaning and import of ritual, and sees the need for society to observe certain rules. Next, he looks forward to being an elder, for the responsibility, power, status and privileges which that brings, and he finds himself fully enculturated, jealously guarding the traditions that he learned, except that, now, it seems, young people no longer have the fear and respect for senile authority that he had as a lad.

School education seeks to mould personalities differently, as small windows on the Western world, but even after half a century of British administration, only 3 per cent of the population received primary education. 'To have resisted western civilization so persistently and maintained tribal institutions intact suggests considerable force of character and staying power' (Munster 1961:155). In 1940, a group of elders near Lotome ritually buried a pen in their sacred grove to curse education as a symbol of oppression. As a result of young men appealing for the curse to be removed, a ceremony to unearth it was performed in November 1995, but this did not quell the reservations about education's notoriously dissocializing impact. 'My boys have never gone to school. The cattle-camp is their school ... Why does the education that is given in schools make the children run away from our homes? Why does it make our children disrespectful to their parents and elders?' (Leggett 2001:50f).

Even now the secondary schools and teacher training colleges are largely filled with Abwor and youths from outside Karamoja, looking for a school place, who do not entirely escape the spiritual background. Though more bush schools were founded, and filled in the famines of the 1980s and 1990s with the attraction of food, they are no more popular now than before, and with very low morale among teachers, who may be threatened by warriors and absent themselves because of insecurity (Oxfam 2001:37). In the whole of Karamoja, which is about 83 per cent Karamojong, only 24 per cent of the school age population are enrolled in primary school, while 1 per cent is in secondary school. Enrolment does not mean that they are there when there are livestock to herd or crops to cultivate and harvest, or when there are adequate supplies of food from either source. As a well-educated Jiot (J20) and sometime government employee dispassionately observes, 'the government's free education mean resources for famine'. The illiteracy rate of all people, lumping together pastoralist, agriculturalist and employee, over 15 years old in Karamoja is 78 per cent.

Even for the educated, very few are incapable of eventually being re-enculturated into a traditional world-view and allegiance. As one educated, former County Chief asserts, 'You have to initiate even if you have education. If the big does not, the small will not. Education will not work properly and will bring other things to your life' (D6). Initiation is more important for life in Karamoja than education. This man took great pleasure in noting that a Baptist missionary, no less, had been initiated. One Dodosoit claimed service with the 1st KAR in Yemen, Germany, Italy, Tanganyika and Turkana, then with the Agricultural Department. He was baptized and educated by *Bwana* Clark in Lotome. Now as an old man in his 80s he claims both to go to church, which was a rare event according to his pastor, and to teach others in *akiriket*. He 'can pray for rain and it comes' (D11). He initiates new men.

> The system is working well and is very necessary. It is like a school, just as good. There is similarity in the two religions. They are one. They are all good. For example the church teaches children to respect parents; *akiriket* teaches the same: to be loyal to parents. When educated boys and girls do not listen to parents, or defy elders, they are cursed. (D11)

Education is equated with the Christian religion, as was common for his generation when both were *dini*. What is important about it for the old man is what the traditional religion already emphasizes. Quite contrary to the objective of the missionaries, it is firmly established in his mind that there is no need to leave the traditional when it is complementary to the modern.

A boy grows up with a 'four-legged brother' (Wilson 1988:1), a bull-calf, of the hide markings of the beloved ox of his grandfather or great uncle after whom he was named. It is given to him when he is three or four to herd with the other calves and sleep with. He may beg other oxen of the same hide markings from family or friends, so that most men have about five (Gulliver 1952b:72–4). As it grows older, he will witness the reprofiling of its horns into a shape of his choice and its branding with the clan brand which parallels his own haircut. He composes songs for it. It is his beloved ox (*emong ngulu aminat*) and he weaves for it a succession of bell collars, making first a bell of a tortoise shell with a wooden clanger, until he can beg an iron one. School terms, if they come round at all, are usually mere interludes in this most intimate of a boy's relationships. He will see it castrated when its testicles are crushed with a stone, or wooden, hammer (*aramet*). Then the beast is a bullock or steer (*edonge/eutut*). By the time of his initiation his peers will call him by a name (*ekiro emong*) describing his beloved ox, of which he is said to be father by his own ox-name. For instance if the ox is decorated with stripes, it will be called Lotuko (the one like a zebra), while its master is named Apalotuko (father of the one like a zebra).

He will lay down his life to defend his beloved ox, and if he needs preternatural strength to do so will cry out its name (*akiwonga*) for inspiration. If he kills an enemy or a fierce, wild animal he will make slits (*ngamunyen*[2]) in its ears and his

---

[2] Cf. *emunyen* (sacred clay).

beloved ox 'becomes happy' (Dyson-Hudson 1966:100), contrasting with the ox who 'despises' the man unable to kill. If it dies, he goes into mourning, occasionally to the point of suicide. Most pragmatically look for another ox of the same markings to carry on the name by which his stock associates know him. If he dies and is buried, they will usually wrap him in the hide of his beloved ox, which must be sacrificed. Such an enculturation cannot but leave all men with the profoundest emotional attachment to cattle. A man's responsibility to herd constitutes his personal freedom. He will even swear by the ox of his naming: *abere ngolotimong atuman* (My goodness! My fat ox). Beloved oxen 'are more highly esteemed than parents, wife, children, or any other possession, and the relationship becomes a religious one, as of a man to his guardian angel' (Clark 1952a:69). Beloved oxen die, with their master and father at the funeral. Bovine valuation has not changed, crucially for the culture, when 'Cows are the home. Cows are a woman (anointed wife).' The homestead may be burned, wives may be captured or killed with their children, but if a man has cattle he can regain all these, while a man without cattle for his corral is poor indeed, so had better go and live as the client of one who has.

Mentality

Karamojong language and categorization both corroborate the primacy of cattle. Whereas there is a disappointingly undifferentiated vocabulary for birds, that for different descriptions of cattle has infinite permutations. Each beast is named according to its colour, markings, shape, size, horn profile or size, decorations, sounds, similitude to other things in the created order, or any detail characteristic of it (Gulliver 1952b:73f). The number of different names so far counted is 327 (Gourlay 1972b:247). A man neither numbers nor counts the herd in his charge, but catalogues each beast in the mind. As the herd returns to the corral, he leafs through his mental file, ticking each, as the animal it represents presents itself to him. Whereas the Karamojong have not developed mathematics as a science, the West has not developed mental catalogy.

Descriptions of cattle are the source of many personal and social names. Every man is distinguished from his beloved ox by prefixing his *ekiro emong* with 'Apa-' (father) but mutuality is not lost, for as he fathers the ox, causing it to be what it is by naming it and exalting it above its fellows, so does the beloved ox help create the man by conferring upon him a new name. Age-sections acquire names after the cattle they sacrifice. Ngirionomong (they of the black ox), Ngiyangamong (they of the light brown ox) and Ngimeriemong (they of the spotted ox). One section, Ngimaseniko, is supposed by them to be derived from bulls (*ngimaniko*).

Musicality

Songs No-one is unmusical in Karamoja, for singing and dancing give common pleasure and an escape from cares and fears, yet music is not idle. 'A man sings and dances because all men sing and dance; so strong are the pressures of socialization that without music he would cease to be Ekarimojongait' (Gourlay 1971b:122). Songs may concern individuals or groups, both displaying their identity, by means of singing about their ox or emblem, or singing about past events, personal and political. 'Every man has his own song', and he spends his herding hours composing or rehearsing it to his livestock. The beloved ox is immortalized in song, which gives social status to the owner (*elope*), who thereby finds his self. The common topics for the ox-song (*eete emong*) include the praise of the beloved ox, his character, his horn-profile, begging and giving oxen, the dangers of herding, cattle-raiding and the difficulty of fighting (Gourlay 1999:92f). Beer parties are not for becoming blind drunk, but for loosening the tongue together. All songs, as opposed to mere hums, are sung by a cantor and chorus method. Rôle models are eulogized, and the folly of departing from known ways is chronicled, so that socially acceptable behaviour is unconsciously inculcated. Because the lyrics affirm what they already sense to be true, even sad stories reassure.

Dances In the young people's evening or night-time dance (*edonga*), the men successively sing their ox-songs, shout their ox's name to rhythmic clapping, and jump vertically in the air and descend flat-footedly (*akidong*[3]), dancing sandals hitting the ground with a resounding thwack, while the girls, in the other half of the circle, bob up and down on the balls of the feet opposite the solo dancer, their weighted leather skirts swinging audibly through the air. A girl may declare her fancy by the flick of an elbow whisk. A variant for weddings (*ekamar*) allows only four jumps to each leader (*ekamaran*).

There is a modern dance more Lwo than Karamojong in the pioneer community in Kaceri, similar to those in Labwor. This is a night-time dance, depending on a band of instrumentalists playing melodies, to which the young people sing. The instruments appear to be descendants of the *opook* and the *nanga*, sketched by Wayland (1931:197) in Labwor. Metal has replaced the tortoise carapace for the sound-box in the six-stringed harp (*lodunga*; apart from the prefix, an onomatopoeia), and the strings have given way to iron strips of varying length, which are fixed to the sound-box at one end and plucked at the other. Both instruments are popular in Kotido, and with schoolboys, throughout Karamoja. Ox-songs are not necessary for this music. The dance, too, is different, with a circle of men surrounding girls bunched in the centre, fanning out for each to dance opposite the man of her choice. Both dance individualistically in a modern African style.

However there are two important continuities with tradition. Girls may approach particular men with erotic mimes, which the men may disdain. Later in the night, this may lead to sexual play, away from the dance, or in the girl's courting hut, if the man can gain entrance. A few precocious 10–11-year-old girls may indulge in this, which could be a novelty, but the men are between 17 and 35, boys taking their herding duties more seriously. The musical form may be imported, but the content of the songs is certainly not, relating notable events in the tribe, such as the heroic defence of the Jie against the Acoli invasion in 1981.

Apart from music, Karamojong aesthetics is confined to the regalia displayed at dances and ceremonies. Men don a leopard skin, and an ostrich feather head-dress, encircling the head (*agyat*) or right down to the feet. Bunches of white ostrich

---

[3] Cf. *edonge* (bullock, or any castrated animal).

feathers, (*ngikawaleta*) are held by sockets (*ngikujwaleta*) in the head-dress, and the ostrich's black feather (*etimu*) is used for a more fearful aspect, or one dyed blood-red, the colour denoting a particular age-class as permitted by the elders. An oval-shaped, shiny metal plate (*akaparaparat*) may be suspended from the septum of the nose, and the rectangular metal belt (*erikot*) is worn. The left elbow is adorned with a giraffe- or zebra-tail fly whisk, the knees with bells (*ngitworoi*) and the feet with square-toed elephant-hide sandals, all of which add greatly to the sound of the dance. Since the impoverishment caused by the 1979–81 famine and the consequent relief aid, this impressive finery is less common, and contrasts with the shabbiness of dirty, tattered clothing worn by many for its prestige in Uganda, but also disdained by many. Though younger women have *en masse* gone over to light Ugandan dresses for work, regarding glimpses of the thigh as unfashionable (J20,14), they all wear their leather skirts for the dance, paying attention to their hair, skin and ornaments (J10).

Ekimomwor is the most formal and communal of all music and dancing, and requires a good harvest of sorghum (*ngimomwa*) to warrant the festivity it crowns. Crowds converge, singing their group songs, to the rhythmic accompaniment of wooden trumpets (*ngarupepe, ngaburucu*) and horns (*ngamomwar*). It forms part of the harvest festival, and the ceremony to declare war, or may be occasioned by a wedding. The dust rises high into the air and the sound can be heard from afar. Being so public, with the warriors distracted and disarmed, makes it a security risk, which lays the people open to a raid. It would have been the height of irony if the *ekimomwor* dance, at which Loriang surprised the Pei and the Bokora (Lamphear 1976:242), had been one to declare war on the Jie.

Ekimomwor is a circle dance, whether all male, or women alternating with men, who twirl them. The leader is led by a stamper (*ekapeton*) in the middle, who begins to stamp (*akipet*) with his right foot, turning on the spot. He sings the first phrase of an *ekimomwor* song, and the whole circle, joining hands for the chorus, starts stamping, each finding his own expression of the blaring rhythm, aggregating into a wave movement (Gourlay 1971b:185–92). They kneel on one knee for the solos, but the stamping of 2000 feet, or more, raises a cloud of dust into the afternoon sun to be seen for miles around. Outside the circle, isolated old women, or groups of girls, mimic the emblematic animal of their husbands' generation, or their sub-section or section. When the older people retire, the energetic may call the changes for *edonga*.

Significance of ox-songs 'A soloist not only sings about the ox; in so far as human limitations permit, he becomes it' (Gourlay 1971b:162). His arms mimic the horn-profile of his beloved steer, and his torso represents its head. The cow, which is praised in group songs, is an expression of sociality, while the bull is the symbol of authority and virility, precisely those attributes which he is not allowed to have outside the association of young people, until society is willing to give him them. Until initiation and marriage have formally established his ecclesial status, and his legal fatherhood in society, he can only be 'father' to a beast of lesser attributes, an ox, which is castrated, that is, a steer or bullock (*edonge*), which also means a eunuch or any castrated animal.

As a 'lesser' creature it enables a man to becomes its father and to show the affection which an 'ideal' father would bestow on his child but which, in his own case, is lacking. As a 'greater' creature, the ox enables a man to admire and praise its size or the shape of its horns without the danger of venturing into the forbidden territory of sexual potency and authority. The ox is specifically warned in songs to 'keep away from bulls', for it is not one of them. Identified with the ox, a young man is able to achieve self-respect (for its admirable qualities), assured that he is in a 'safe' position from which he cannot be accused of venturing into 'bull-territory'. The ox's emasculation is its own, and its owner's salvation (Gourlay 1972b:252). Young men are enculturated through their single sex peer group of wandering herdsmen, emphasizing rôles of membership and leadership, not predetermined, as in the *ere* family, where sexuality is restricted to preserve social stability. Now the Dodosô proverb is plain, 'A bull is father of the herd, but an ox encourages a man' (Marshall Thomas 1965:163).

Gourlay (1972b:247) recorded over 200 song-texts among the Karamojong. The names of cattle occurred 673 times and in 84 per cent of songs, while the majority of the remainder either referred to an ox without naming it or were too short to permit inclusion. This empirical finding substantiates the local assertion that 'all Karimojong songs are about cattle' (Dyson-Hudson 1966:99) and some are still sung to cattle. In one song the singer calls to his ox, 'Answer to your name!'; in another people are described as 'feasting off the ox'; a whole series relates to either tying or knocking the ox's horns into the prescribed shape; in recounting the events of a cattle raid, the singer names his friends, adding, 'We protected the ox, Losiangole'; a further group relate to the begging and giving of oxen: 'Some friends talked Kakuro into giving me Lopusimedo', 'I admired Apalogolokongu's herd; he gave me Locuba'; 'I begged a man to give me an ox; he gave me Lokorilima'. The generic term for these is ox-songs (*ngieosyo ngimongin*) and they are still sung (*akiruk*[4]) at beer parties and dances.

Communal dancing started with 'traditional songs' which praise the cow (*aate*) as the epitome of cattle and the common interest of the group whose traditions are being rehearsed. 'The cow mooed and we were excited' (Dyson-Hudson 1966:100). The Maseniko, when they sang the traditional songs about their own section, also performed the cattle dance 'leaping and frisking like young cattle, shaking heads like bulls or staring' (Clark 1952a:70).

Individual men compose a short ox-song (*eete emong*) to which he has exclusive copyright as his own solo (*eete elope*, Gourlay 1972a:242) to which the rest of the men and girls will sing a chorus.

Solo: 'When I kept company with Loyaale,
people said that the Father of Loluk [Apaloluk]
was becoming bad.'

Chorus: 'O the curses given me for my bad ways!
O Loluk, now that Lomagol has been slaughtered,
you are free from blame.' (Gourlay 1972b:248)

---

[4] Cf. *aruk* (ox's hump).

The song relates how the soloist, Apaloluk, fell into bad company and so into transgression, as a consequence of which he had to sacrifice an ox, Lomagol, in order to atone for his disobedience to the elders but it is his beloved ox, Loluk, who is said to be free from blame. Though they are distinct, Apaloluk is the man and Loluk is the ox, they clearly have the same experience and stand in the same social position. The ox stands for the man, as all the singers know. The two are inseparable and identical in song, and the same applies to his other beloved oxen, which are the subject for further solos. Thus a man parades his self-identification in public. In, and after, a beer party he sings (*aporojan*) the praises of his beloved ox, however discordantly.

Rituality

At all ceremonies involving the elders as the representative leaders of the community an ox, at least, is sacrificed and herds of the participants are massed. Unless the family is too poor to afford more than a goat, which is still ineligible for initiation, an ox is sacrificed at all rites of passage: initiation, after a wedding, after the birth of the first-born, homicide and divorce. When a man dies his beloved ox is sacrificed, after the period of mourning for any parent an 'ox of mourning' is speared in the usual way.

At the sub-section (as distinct from the clan) rituals the colour and markings of the ox are critical. A black ox may be unusually efficacious. Thus someone's beloved ox may be required by the elders as fitting the specification but refusal to part with it will result in its forcible seizure by herdsmen executing the elders' order. The owner does not lose wealth, for he is compensated with a heifer by the slaughterer, as it is a great privilege to be chosen to spear the ox, but bad omens will be suspected if it is not speared in the heart through the first ribs.

After the intestines (*ngamoliteny*) have been read, the iliac gland is carefully removed to be buried. Then the surrounding perineal flesh (*elamacar*, the sacred brand) is carefully cut out to be eaten by the elders. The junior initiated men slice up the carcass to braze on an open fire but the joined hind legs (*amuro*) representing the sacrifice of the strength of the ox are left in the horse-shoe shaped assembly of elders, while they invoke Akujů with an antiphonal litany concerning cattle, people and Akujů. The *amuro* is the most sacred joint of the ox and can only be eaten by elders.

The stomach sac is also highly symbolic. It is cooked for the final stage of the initiation ceremony. The number of the slits is symbolic, for instance, of the sections in the tribe. The chyme is squeezed out. This too is sacred. After all, it is Akujů who sent the rain, and His spirit, who made the grass grow and constituted the water, which the life-sustaining cattle eat and drink. The stomach is the source of the ox's strength that turns what it eats into an offering fit for Akujů and man. Thus it is smeared (*akijuk*) on fellow elders, on their juniors, on initiands and on their herds as an effectual sign of Akujů's blessing. 'It is the outward symbol of men, who are in a state of grace because the deity has heard their prayers and taken note of their need' (Dyson-Hudson 1966:94). Akujů is mediated spiritually to men by the chyme (*ngikujit*) of cattle. The locus of the spiritual medium in the mundane, day-to-day life of the Karamojong is unavoidable. It is cattle. Karamojong culture is not alone in having cattle mediate 'between man and the spiritual world' (Gourlay 1972b:245), so long as it is firmly understood that the spiritual world is this one seen by those who have eyes to see.

2 Revelation

The Karamojong have no scripture, though the remembrance of Akujů's past works is held in the salvation histories attached to generations and to clans, which may be retold by elders reminiscing in their daily gathering outside the homestead or, where pertinent, in ceremonial speeches; in song by herdsmen in the cattle-camp, or by girls at the dances. These will recount the deeds of brave men and the overthrow of enemies. Mythology recounts Akujů's guidance in the unchronicled past, but is limited, because relatively few have a common history. The Tesyo and Ser clans of the Jie even subscribe to the Teso name for God, Edeke (Lamphear 1976:84), which in Ngakaramojong means disease or pestilence, though in public, ritual prayers are made to Akujů and unity maintained. This shows the connection between suffering and the diverse revelation of the divine to enemy tribes, whose capacity to intercede is grudgingly recognized.

Certain individuals become the mortal instruments of Akujů for the function of making known his specific instructions (Gulliver 1953c:161). Akujů gives words (*ngakiro*) directly and in his own timing to those with charismatic gifts, which are the preserve of no office. Each charismatic is as good as his last revelation and only remarkably accurate ones will gain standing outside his neighbourhood.

Dreamers

Any vivid message in a dream might be from Akujů, but they are only important when they bear on the welfare of a whole community or its ritual procedures. Thus a dream might reveal the propitious day for a raid, or a ceremony, pointing out the appropriate sacred grove and the colour and markings of the sacrificial ox for it. Such understanding usually requires the dreamer (*ekerujan*) to be an *emuron* or an elder. He is able to warn of misfortune but is himself unable to do anything about it. That is the corporate responsibility of the leaders of the community who may consider a particular dream as only one factor in their decision-making, overruling it to avoid a greater evil (Dyson-Hudson 1966:226).

Prophets

The conscious contact of a prophet (*ekadwaran*) with the divine enables him not only to predict (*akidwar*) some future events but also to avoid or precipitate them for the people's protection. Akujů speaks to him in the bush (*namoni*), a place on the borders of the world of men and so close to Akujů. Such a one will usually have long experience of life, and will have outlived mundane family responsibilities to grow closer to Akujů by reason of his proximity to death. His age and his powers make him a greatly revered man in society, whom nobody would choose to cross, but his greatness depends on his prophecies. The great prophets are about the only figures who can live a transethnic existence without government support.

Alternatively, those males or females marginal to society, usually the physically or mentally handicapped, who forgo sexual relations and are freed from normal social responsibilities, are candidates for the prophetic vocation. As rare unmarrieds (*ngikadwarunak*) they have the time and the incentive to acquaint themselves with history, mystery or religion, otherwise the province of old people. Even the mad who have a superfluity of spirits (*ngikerep*) may have a word from Akujů, if it comes to pass.

A Lotuko prophet, Ikwaibong, whose home was diversely reported to be a mountain in Sudan, Nadodosô or Acoli, which argues for the vicinity of Mount Lonyili where the borders of all three intersect, was much sought. He travelled all over Karamoja throughout the 1950s, for his ability to make rain with his rain-stones and to bring prosperity wherever he dwelt lent great value to this prophet. He was said never to grow old, could not be injured by a spear or a bullet, and could make sticks go into rocks (Dyson-Hudson 1966:225; Marshall Thomas 1965:162). He even had a group of disciples, each of whom 'could make rain simply by pulling up a tuft of grass'. A popular Jie story relates that his last visit to Najie ended with his being locked up in a windowless room by a government chief. During the night he vanished from the room, never to be seen there again, although in the morning the lock on the door was found to be intact (Lamphear 1972:342f n).

A District Officer (Allen 1.10.00 Interview) remembers a prophet of the same Lotuko school, Lomiluk, whom Acoli, among others, went to consult.

> Special Branch brought him into Kitgum in January 1958, because his son was reputed to have caused resistance to the Sudanese government. The police offered him a good room. He said, 'It hasn't rained for a long while has it? I must do something about it.' Then he disappeared. There was a tremendous, monstrous thunderstorm that night. Around May or June Lomiluk returned to Kitgum saying he wanted to die in a bed, as he had not been in one.

He was taken to hospital and examined, but the doctor found nothing wrong. 'Could he have a bed for the night? Yes, there was an empty ward. Next morning he was dead and the doctor could find nothing wrong or the cause of death. He left behind his stick, which was known everywhere, since with it he had often made rain.'

Yet the function of a prophet is not to arouse wonderment but to serve as Akujů's oracle in order that rain may be brought or stopped, and otherwise unpredictable threats to a people's well-being, such as raiders, diseases, locusts, stem-borers and army-worm, averted by the people responding in accordance with the prophet's prescription. When North Karamoja was catastrophically hit by cholera in the 1979–81 famine, a prophecy was given that the epidemic would not spread to Kotido if two giraffes, never normally seen in that centre of population, were seen to come from the west and to go away to the north. Such an event was observed and no Kotido inhabitant died of cholera, despite drought, malnutrition and starvation. The story was recounted by a Musukufu (J29) strongly predisposed to reject the 'superstitions' of traditional religion. The prophet can only speak from Akujů, as He chooses, so cannot direct day-to-day affairs, for there will be times when he has nothing to reveal. Instead leaders and even senior government officials will not neglect to consult him as an oracle.

Diviners

Most elders and all *ngimurok* are likely to have tried their hand at divination, though only some will emerge as skilled.

Haruspication   The will of Akujů is particularly manifest in the bowels of a sacrificed animal and a handful of the more senior or skilled men present will crouch round to interpret them. The rumen is put on the ground and the intestines in their integument are laid on top, providing an uneven surface representing the countryside. Various irregular features, like tumours, ulcers and capillaries, are taken to be fires, raiders, live or dead people, the colour of the ox for the next sacrifice, and so on. Black spots, for instance, may be read as threatening raiders. The bowels are read like a book by those able to decipher it, who will discuss together what they have learned before coming to a conclusion (Marshall Thomas 1965:143f). The best place in which to graze cattle can be ascertained. Warnings are usually seen as conditional, so if the community employs the correct ritual or other prescribed response, the danger may be averted. He who performs this function accurately is a haruspex (*ekesiemon*[5]), who can see beyond the distinction between human and divine affairs.

Erisa Longok, who was still alive at Losilang in 1998, was famed for his haruspication of goat intestines. From reading the entrails in 1969 he divined that, if a goat were not killed, a mother in labour would develop complications. It was not, she did, and she died. Early in 1978 he divined that there would be no cattle in Najie; the Dodosô raided and the cattle were taken (J17).

Sandals   A pair of elephant, buffalo or giraffe-hide ceremonial sandals (*ngakaloro*) may be cast down (*akilamilam*[6]) on the ground several times in succession and their position on landing interpreted in order to infer the shape of things to come. So the future of a young married couple may be foretold, or the best means to prosecute a raid. More often assistance will be sought by men making their intricate and manifold decisions regarding herds, families and journeys. Youths may spend their time in this fashion trying to master the art.

Akujů also occasionally manifests his action in the world by miracle (*akujwanut*[7]) and by works of power (*ngatyoniso*). This is when Akujů Himself intervenes in the created order, but human functionaries are not necessarily ruled out

---

[5] *Ekesiemon*, *amoni*, pl. *ngamon* (forest, thicket) and *amon* (funeral feast) all point to liminality and the divine and, as the only forms of the root, *mon, invite a connection with the divine name of the Ancient Egyptians, Amon/Amun. *Eke-si-emon*, with the causative infix, -si- (Dimmendaal 1983:296), means, etymologically, 'he who makes divine' and, in common usage, diviner.

[6] Cf. *akilam* (to curse); in Nuer *lam* is to invoke (Hutchinson 1996:329).

[7] Cf. *akiwan* (to spoil, break).

where there is no clear boundary between the spiritual and the natural. What, to me, was a good case of a miraculous cure of a dying lad, when neither local ritual nor Western medicine had the answer, evoked no wonderment among his people. To them a miracle is more immediate to Akujů than normal preternatural events.

The Spiritual

It would be importing religious concepts to assert that the Karamojong assume two different worlds, one visible, the other invisible. Certainly they recognize invisible beings, but their importance lies in that they make themselves felt one way or another in this world. Rather the ingrained assumption is that the spiritual infuses and suffuses this world. Indeed the very concept that there are things spiritual separate from materiality is a pure abstraction not present in traditional thought, though it may be encountered in Christian teaching. There is considerable resistance to any dualistic notions, though, because the invisible is closely related to earth whether in it, above it, or below it. Concepts of spirit are closely connected to the Karamojong idea of will. Everything that is has a will-to-life, a strength of the heart (*agogong ke etau*), which is by no means unique to humans. It is shared by all things that have not been utterly destroyed: spirits, animals, trees, plants, rocks and materials. The will-to-life is the stuff of being. To will is to be able (*apedor*) to some extent, and to prove one's manhood or womanhood is to test the extent of one's ability in a world full of contrary wills, without provoking them to be ranged against one. At this abstract level, which is suggested to be an explicit description of what lies beneath consciousness and behaviour, the Karamojong are closely related to wider African consciousness, which itself is not exclusive.

In life a person pursues their interest, but when they perceive they are rousing wills-to-life against them, either they need considerable spiritual fortification to continue, or they drop the matter so that the spiritual can cool down. Thus it is possible to interfere in someone else's interest, but to bring that person to naught is to invite spiritual retaliation of the most dangerous kind. So if a certain course of action becomes hard and difficult (*agogong*), there is a reason. It is because one is encountering the will to life of other creatures, however unknown. To continue on that line is to invite their anger. In this sense all things are personal. Animals are beings in the neighbourhood whose most inconvenient characteristics Karamojong chuckle about, as though they would a difficult relative. In neither case is there any spiritual freedom to eliminate one kind of being, and considerable consequences are to be expected from any systematic attempt to dominate any particular feature of either the order or the confusion of creation. Everything is spiritual, though the intensity of that spirituality differs, so that fatalism can be overcome by acts of will, or rather a determined life, a force to be reckoned with in the world. In the end religion is necessary because, above all other aspects of culture, it sheds light on the competition of personal wills, including unknown spirits, which life comprises. Religion brings a person to the blessings of life by providing the means towards a spiritual harmony with the plethora of divergent wills.

Though deeply feared at times, evil is not felt to be dominant in society, except by aliens. The greatest expression of evil (*karononi*, lit. bad things) is not an overbearing, simple, spiritual force (*akapil*) so much as hard times, for there is no distinction between spiritual and material oppression; both are bad, evil (*erono*), both the evidence of malicious will, whether within or without. Thus to sin (*akisec*) is not just to commit a moral offence but to spoil the order of things; its meaning is as much ecological as ethical. The PEN root *dem (to bewitch) becomes *akidem* (to rob). The problems and deficiencies (*ngican*[8]) of everyday life, though causally untraceable, are not due to blind chance but, somewhere along the line, may have a connection with the spirits (*ngicen*[9]) of those who died with vengeance in their hearts. Thus evil is a privation of good, but its cause is by no means impersonal. Each difficulty in life is caused by the contrary will of someone or something.

This explains why people consult the *amuron*, because her *ngililae*, though themselves potentially malevolent spirits, represented in the bestiary as small, dark snakes, give access to the personal wills hidden from the eye. There are two ways a person grows quiet: either they become resentful or covetous (*alilat*), or they become conciliatory or peaceful (*akisil*). One way leads to evil, the other to good, the accidental choice of created beings in society, not a cosmic dualism, for goodness is prior. Rather evil can be ascertained in the activities of rival societies, such as a Kuliak dance (*elilya*) or the Teso God (Edeke) whose name was given by Karamojong to Johnston (1902:II,905) when he sought a name for the devil. For Karamojong it means a disease, tuberculosis of the spine, just like Jok Lubanga of the Lwo (Wright 1940). Every disease is willed, which is why the sick fall into fear so much, for they worry that they are falling under the power of another.

The only word the Karamojong have for devil is the Afroasiatic Sitan. As might be expected with a loanword, this is used by peoples adjacent to Karamoja and not uniformly within. The use of bored stones by the ancestral Sapiny, or the Oropom, for divination or sun rites, is called *setanik* (Dyson-Hudson, V.R. 1962b; Wilson 1970b:138–42). The use of the root is not new, for it has established Ngakaramojong form in *akisitakin* (to accuse somebody) and *isitana* (he is an habitual accuser). There is no evidence for a preoccupation with, or worship of, the devil.

It appears that most terms for evil are secondary, being cognate with mundane words, though the materialist and positivist would argue that all abstract and religious words are derived from concrete referents. There is only one pair which commonly arouses fear and hatred: *akapil* (to practise sorcery) and *ekapilan* (sorcerer). The sorcerer is typically embittered and malevolent, a social dissident who has secret, evil designs on his enemies and those who arouse his jealousy. A few families may have a tradition for producing *ngikapilak*, and will intermarry, but they may be enemies within. They are the opposite of the *ngimurok*, for whom they generate much business. They prowl around at night like the hyenas[10] on which they are reputed to ride, seeking whom they may devour by disinterring the recently buried or using fingernails or hair[11] from their intended victim to gain power over the essence of his life. Disease and death are often attributed to his spells and, if found around another's home at night, a sorcerer can be lawfully killed (Marshall

---

[8] Cf. Nilotic, *can, lack.

[9] Cf. WN, *cien* (ghostly vengeance).

[10] Cf. *kapel(i)* (spotted, as the hyena).

[11] Cf. *akicud* (to remove hair, bewitch).

Thomas 1965:176–8). A successful, public accusation leads to the *ekapilan* being stoned, or bound and beaten, to death.

In the day-time malicious people with sinister powers can cause sickness by staring at an individual. Someone caught casting an evil-eye (*akibem*) with unwelcome results will be accused of being a witch (*ekabeman*).[12] Especially vulnerable are infants and anyone while they are ingesting, which may be a factor in the sexes normally eating apart. A serious offence may attract ostracism or death, since death is often attributed to it.

Spirit is an involution of Akujů in the form of wind (*ekuwam*), rain (*akiru*), thunder (*agiro*), lightning (*ekipye*[13]), rainbow (*alokakinet*, a 'trap' of vapours encircling the sun, moon or earth), a certain tree (*epye*), grass (*nga-nya*), the crocodile (*aki-nyang*[14]), flood (*akalele*) and spring (*elelya*[15]), as the active agents of His will in the world (Dyson-Hudson 1966:212; Clark 1952a:70; Pazzaglia 1982:82n). These are 'the angels of Akujů', but they do not displace Him, for 'Akujů is there' (J31). There is a multitude of ungraded, unnamed self-willed beings or spirits (*ngipian*) directly responsible for each. Thus 'The rain is *ekile apolon*' (Marshall Thomas 1965:187): it has autonomous personality. The common element associated with all these created features and beings is water (*ngakipi*) whose source is Akujů. To pray to them as witnesses in and of the divine panorama is to pray to Akujů.

Leader	*Assembled*
Akujů hear us! Star hear us! Moon hear us! Sun hear us!	
The lost cows taken by the Dodosô and the Bokora, come back!	Come back!
The cows that went to the Karimojong, come back!	Come back!
Yes, Akujů hear us!	Akujů hear us!

Akujů's presence is denser in high places, especially on a dominant mountain (*emoru*) which reaches into the heavens above the clouds and so therefore is closer to His abode. Mountain people, particularly the Ik and Sor, inevitably have a spiritual potency denied to the plains people, at least so long as the former are in their mountain homeland. Because of the presence of other tribes and clans who were absorbed by the Karamojong, mountains may be associated with gods distinct from Akujů, and are frequently named after them. For instance, Mount Toror is

---

[12] Novelli (1999:129,197,264).

[13] Cf. *akipyed* (to call down death or misfortune). Storm and lightning are manifestations of *ngipian* (J31). Lightning is of the foremost spiritual significance for the WN Nuer (Beidelman 1971:395; Hutchinson 1996:107f).

[14] Cf. *akinyan* (to avenge). The crocodile was an expression of divinity in Ancient Egypt (Moret 1972:398) and among WN (cf. N *nyang: Evans-Pritchard 1956:66f,126–8; Lienhardt 1961:1.III). The Nyanga sub-section of the Pian refuse to eat it, as they identify with it, when portraying it in their sectional dances.

[15] Cf. *alel* (to flow; *alelyakin* (to love greatly).

named after the Pokot high god, Tororut. Yet this is not to the exclusion of Akujů's Spirits (*ngipian*), who dwell in the mountains and the hills. These are believed to be responsible for bringing rain, being sent by Akujů for that purpose, so in prayers for rain, generally addressed to Akujů, the Spirits may be entreated: 'You, Toror, come! You, Moroto, come! You, Maru, come!' and so on (Lamphear 1972:340n). 'Bad rains mean a bad *ekipye*. Whether an *ekipye* is good or bad is judged by their actions' (J31). To an extent *ngipian* are a device that maintains the irrefragable goodness of Akujů. 'There is no separation between Akujů and *ekipye* ... A higher or stronger *akuj* is there in a high mountain, which means one is free to climb or take a stick or stone' (J31).[16]

Akujů in spirit is 'in the rocks' and stones (*ngamoru*) of many places, though some clans descended from other traditions may speak of the 'god of that rock'. The word used here may be Akujů or *ngakujo*, which some Karamojong translate into English as 'charms', or 'magic'. In either case, Akujů is felt to be present, indirectly, in the world, through divine Spirit or spirits and can have a deleterious effect on those who trangress upon the divine locus, whether a fall, an illness or an absence of blessing. Whenever a bit of the physical world 'hits back' at a person when, for instance, they stub their toe on a stump, the phenomenon is always explicable by divine judgment for some minor violation of the world order of Akujů for which and to whom atonement must be made to ensure good health (Paget Wilkes 1932a:22).

Rowland (1983:11) observed a Jiot boy fall on the rocks so badly that his injuries endangered his life. After he had been to hospital and recovered he was ritually beaten for his misdemeanour in disturbing the deity. Some small accidents may even be beyond redemption. Wayland (1931:222) came across a casualty (a porter) who literally gave up the ghost and died of no natural cause: 'They [Dodosŏ] told me that when a man is "called" [by an ancestor] he first loses power over his legs, then his belly swells, and in three days from the moment of being called he expires.' Three days, almost to the minute, the scientific Wayland asks us to believe, from his initial fall into a ditch, he 'vomited a large quantity of clear liquid, turned over and expired'. For that period his companions thought him, 'for all practical purposes, dead already'. This concept of a spiritual creation with everything in its place, and humans in theirs, also helps account for Karamojong lack of interest in major building and engineering works. Apart from grass, bushes, and the wild animals they hunt, they are innate conservationists.

Akujů is not as 'otiose' as most observers tend to conclude when their enquiries meet with evasive answers about a shadowy, impersonal, remote figure (ibid.:221,225). These are governed by the need to preserve the transcendence of Akujů who has never descended to inhomination and so cannot be ascribed human personality or actions in any direct way. Since the normal response of a European to the thought that God should sit in the tops of trees is an inward chuckle, the African cannot be blamed for keeping his counsel. Though it is simple for him to

---

[16] This is contrary to the duality emphasized by van der Jagt's (1990) interpretation of Turkana religion, which begs the question of whether this derived more from structuralist theory than from Turkana understanding; for them *ngipian* are not mere symbols but real causative forces in their world.

state the transcendence of Akujů, it is too complicated to explain how He is present in the manifold, without undermining the prior assertion of transcendence. Thus Akujů is not an identity with the god (*akuj*) of a rock, for there is a necessary distinction between the Creator and the created world. Yet there is no separation, for the created order is imbued throughout with Akujů as Spirit.

Is this concept of Spirit a mere theological construct? The sin of omission committed by Wayland's unfortunate porter was, though chasing a hare, knowingly failing to contribute to a stone cairn (*asenorit*). Thus he disobeyed the spirit world, provoking it into retaliatory action in order to restore the continued harmony, briefly threatened, of Spirit and the created order. It was at this point that Wayland (ibid.:222) discovered the deeper meaning of the extremely common word of greeting or approval: *Ejoka*? (How are you? Literally, Is it good?); *Ejok*, (Fine! It is good!); 'but the deeper significance attached to it in less profane affairs is that of "The Dead" as a community of spirits'. The incident provided a happy disclosure for Wayland (ibid.:188), which no amount of rigorous research or interviewing would have thrown up of necessity. Educated Karamojong can be questioned minutely but not a shred of an insight will they impart concerning traditional religious views. If the spiritual does not wish to be disturbed, neither does it wish to be disclosed,[17] to be distilled from what patently exists, for consciousness to be differentiated from the unconscious, so that the given world order may be rent asunder.

Wayland's discovery establishes what is already strongly suggested by the obvious derivation of *ejok* from the central concept of the sacred, *jok*, present in all Western Nilotic languages, used for Spirit, spirits and so forth (Evans-Pritchard 1956:160; Lienhardt 1961; Burton 1991), while the word does not feature so generally among EN and SN. For the WN Lango *jok* is an omnipresent, creative presence, but invisible 'like moving air' or a potential energy dwelling in rocks and hills, springs and pools (Driberg 1923; Gresford Jones 1926:133; Hayley 1940, 1947; Butt 1952:179; Ogot 1961; p'Bitek 1963:27f[18]). Thus it is not that *ejok* has a

---

[17] Goldschmidt (1969:8f) thought the cultures of NE Uganda 'peculiarly difficult to penetrate' owing to the 'scarcity of verbal and symbolic elaboration. The Sapiny and their neighbours are laconic. Their world is peopled by spirits but they speak very little of them. They have tales, but among the Sapiny at least these are told only by the young and the very old; ordinary adults literally do not know them ... The portals by which we usually enter alien culture are thus narrow to the point of being closed'.

[18] This three-cornered debate between British observers, p'Bitek and Ogot is fascinating. The British are trying hard to assimilate the WN phenomena to religious concepts known to them, while the presuppositions of Ogot's theist idealism and p'Bitek's agnostic empiricism, resonant more of postwar Oxford than Uganda, are diametrically opposed. However both acknowledge the conceptual plurality of *jok*, even if Ogot's application of vital force has more to say to Karamojong religion than p'Bitek's political segmentation of *jok*, which is a common British misreading of Evans-Pritchard (1956) and Durkheim (1915). Yet Ogot's analysis would be better summed up by refracted monotheism than the 'cultural monism' that justifies having no opposition parties, though he is right to point to the dualism inherent in so much Indo-European thought that has not been inherent to Africa.

common, profane meaning overwhelming a rarefied, sacred one so much as the spiritual infusing the ordinary and commonplace. To say, '*Ejok*', as is done many times a day, is to say that the world is in its cosmic order as normal. There is no great polarity, or opposition between the divine and the mundane, for the transcendent Akujů cannot be confined, even to the above: 'Akujů is everywhere ... because He can be in the wind, the sky, here; He is not confined to one particular thing' (P11). 'I don't know where Akujů is; Akujů is everywhere' (J31).

The Karamojong only make stone cairns, as a funeral rite, for hereditary firemakers (Wayland 1931:208; Lamphear 1976:187). However, when travelling along a steep and rocky path beyond their territory, each still makes his contribution to cairns on the way, picking up a stone, a twig or two, or a handful of grass, imparting a blessing by spitting on it, exclaiming, '*Ejok*!', and adding it to the pile. This minor rite functions as travel insurance against mishap on the journey, not to ensure compensation but to prevent death by the hand of strangers, mysterious disappearance, theft, bad health and hunger, lending weight to the hope of hospitality at the end of the road. The spirits of the place are appeased, and afford their protection to those who have acknowledged them. Some cairns may be dedicated to particular men of renown. It is then the spirits (*ngipara* or *ngawiyenito*) of the departed who give mind to matter, but in themselves they carry no weight, for Karamojong do not believe in ghouls or ghosts, unlike the Sor on Moroto or the Nuer (P11; Laughlin and Allgeier 1972a; Beidelman 1971:401; Hutchinson 2001:312).

The cairn is but one example of the way ancestral spirits are seen to affect later generations. Should an unwelcome, uncontrollable event, or above all a series of events, occur to a person, family or clan, the cause will be sought in a malevolent will, whether alive or 'dead', or in ancestral spirits, male or female, singular or plural, who have been annoyed by a wrong attitude, a breach of tradition or an omission in ritual. The ancestors try to have the wrong put right by penalizing their errant descendants. The appropriate response of the living is to ensure that everything they do is done precisely according to the traditions of their forefathers, especially all the prescriptions and proscriptions involved in custom, for 'ancestors participate, like Akujů, at the sacrifice. Ancestors (*atapapaa*) receive milk, beer, libations at the grave in the corral (*atamanawi*) and the home. The Karamojong seek blessings from the living dead, as power is available from the clan and the society' (P11).

> In times of trouble, sickness or perplexity, it is not unusual for some clans to gather at the old man's grave, with his children and grandchildren, and there milk the cows, bring out the tobacco, kill the ox, smearing the stomach contents over themselves and over the burial stone, and crying out, 'Oh father, help us. What shall we do? Are our cattle to die? Are our children to die? We never disobeyed you. O father hear us. Give us life.' By thus honouring the memory of the elder, they trust that God will hear their prayers and remove their trouble. (Clark 1953:76)

If this fails to turn the tide of misfortune, its cause will be assumed to be a malevolent will. Though ancestral spirits are not moving in the air, they are thought to be present and sensible at their grave. The Christian son of the church-teacher's wife, Sarah Lokong, said by her grave, 'She is hearing us talk now', and prayer was made (J19). This was before the memorial service, which might be expected to release the spirit from earth to sky.

East African pastoralists are taken to be free of spirit veneration (for example, Goldschmidt 1979:24–7) and anthropologists in Karamoja have assumed this to be so for the Karamojong. Relative to mountain and agricultural tribes, there is indeed very little recognition of spirits in public worship but it would be wrong to go on to excise them from Karamojong cosmology. In certain seemingly unthreatening situations, self-confident, educated, nominally Christian young men become petrified. They still live in a world surrounded by terrible, unseen forces, which man can only cross at dire peril.

Nevertheless these ever-present powers have their master, for the spiritual world is not chaos. It is as orderly as the visible world which it infuses. The spirits of the dead are different from the spirits, or hearts (*ngitain*[19]), of the living. The proper abode of ancestral spirits is *kakujů*, the place of Akujů distinct from the earth (*akwap*) but there is no separation, for 'God is One', the guarantor of ultimate unity in the spiritual universe. To Akujů must prayers be addressed, for He is the one who has decisive power to stay death's onslaught and to give life: 'Akujů! Help this girl to be pregnant!'

Cosmology

Death is the irreversible event, when Akujů calls a person to be with Himself. Someone far removed from death has been 'refused' by Akujů (Lamphear 1972:523). This refusal is a blessing of this life, but implies its transience. All men die, irrevocably. Close relatives will be disconsolate for a time, with a brother immediately seeking blind revenge in cases of homicide, and a wife, or a mother, going into hysterics, self-abuse and uncontrollable wailing. Women used to keep a cord in their granary for hanging themselves in just such an eventuality (Clark 1953:75). Yet death is not quite so tragic for the dead, especially when they die at a ripe old age, having spent a lifetime gradually drawing closer to Akujů and withdrawing from the passions of the human struggle for existence.

When a Karimojongait dies,

> he finds a ladder which leads him to a great village in heaven (*ere apolon*) where all the other Karimojong who died before him are living.
>
> He announces himself to the others who will tell him to enter. He will receive food, shelter and he will stay with the others talking and, from time to time, looking down at the other Karimojong who are still on earth. (Novelli 8.2.89, Letter)

Above the sky is situated a vast homestead (*ere apolon*) with enormous herds (Gulliver 1965:187). Without this corroboration by Gulliver from an earlier time and for a different tribe, it might have been suspected that the *ere apolon* was a depiction of a Christian heaven, but Novelli's evidence is substantial (1999:20–24) and supported by Emoru (1.4.02, Letter) who insists that *nakujů* is the new way of

---

[19] Cf. WN Nuer *tie* (soul), if that be an accurate translation.

referring to a heaven traditionally called *ere apolon*. The stars might be represented as the little fires of the inhabitants. However there is no expectation of seeing Akujů face to face, or in glory, nor of a personal judgment. Divine judgment happens on earth through the curses, penalties and retributions of his own people or through 'natural' calamities. The notion of a ladder is another indication that heaven and earth are not cut off, as in many Eastern Sudanic myths. The good life and timely death are not so far away as may be supposed. 'Bless (*emwamwakis*[20]) all our lives and take them away Akujů!'

Those elders who on earth were known to be in especially good communication with heaven may return posthumously to their sacred sites in the guise of a black Egyptian cobra with a white feather rising from its hood. Such snakes must not be killed and snakes in general are not eaten.[21] Death is not the end. Akujů is responsible for the death even of children and babies, more than starvation, disease, wild animals, enemies or witches. Their mortal bodies may be fit for the agent of death, the hyena, but no-one can deny them continued, if marginal, life as spirits (*ngipara*).

Ethereal, as opposed to ancestral, spirits (*ngipian*) are dependent on water, whether as a liquid (*ngakipi*) or as a vapour, characteristic of the rainy season (*akiporo*). Where there is a spirit (*ekipye*), there is water. So related are the spiritual and the physical, the ethereal and the real, that the converse might also be true, so that the spirits are the masculine form which constitutes the empirical feminine substance, water. Thus the spirits can fly (*akipor*), being seen in lightning and in the mist below the clouds.[22] 'Sometimes they roam the earth, following the rivers, and appear above wet places early in the morning like wraiths' (Marshall Thomas 1965:180f). They are not devoid of form, and the angrier ones are predominantly russet in colour, as is water after a storm in Karamoja, more like soup than aqua-vitae. 'And as Lopore described the spirits, they seemed like water, for they are transparent, iridescent creatures, human in form, with billowing, many-coloured hair. "They have hair like Europeans," Lopore once told me' (ibid.). The house-girl of a missionary doctor, and so well-used to Europeans, was once confronted by a Briton, remarkably round in shape and red in hair and beard. She shrieked and fled in terror for safety. With my sun-reddened skin and my beard comprising black, brown and ginger hairs, my appearance has often sent children screaming from my fearful appearance. No doubt we seemed to be veritable incarnations of *ngipian*.

Ngipian are radically ambivalent, good and bad as human creatures. They can be mischievous, destructive and unpredictable, but are not socially bonded, so it is for the human community to come together to sacrifice to Akujů to solve any serious

---

[20] To spit at someone is to bless them; to spit away from them is to curse them. For God to spit is to send rain. The sacramental value of water pervades.

[21] A cobra, killed by a missionary in Nuer, required compensation, 'so that the god in it would not be angry with them for letting it be killed' (Evans-Pritchard 1956:69). The Dinka believe in an underworld, 'a land of the cobras, a land like Dinkaland but inhabited by cobras'. Some Dinka are 'really' cobras and could change their form into that of cobras (Lienhardt 1961:117).

[22] Cf. ES *pur (smoke).

problem they might bring. They cannot be taken lightly and often deflect behaviour. One family recently moved its whole *ere* (homestead) uphill 'because the old one was small and snakes from the trees were infesting it because of *ngipian*: Egyptian cobras (*ataloupal*) and green snakes (*ngikoliterak*). We do not cut the trees because of *ngipian*, which used to throw stones into the house by the whirlwind (*epiripirit*)' (D5). It is people who need the power of the sacrifice to protect them against any malevolent spirit, not the spirit, which derives its own from water. Other than that it is important not to provoke *ngipian* by trespassing on their preserves.

Spirits normally dwell below the surface of the earth for, as any Karamojong boy or girl knows, water does not only exist above the earth in a river or a pool (*ekipwor*) but extends down into it.

> They keep their cattle under the rivers, letting their cattle come to the surface at night to walk in the grass. When you hear the spirit cowbells ringing in the darkness, you know, say the Dodoth, that the little magic cattle are grazing near.
>
> In their homes below the rivers, the ngipian have spirit wives, who grow up, grow old and die as people do. When an *ekipi* [sic] dies, the *ngipian* family abandons its pool and moves elsewhere and the pool goes dry. The *ngipian* control the rain, the rainbows, the mist, the clouds, the water level in the pools, and must be treated with respect. If you displease them, they can make your cows stick in the mud or catch you in the whirlwind, *ekuwam ngolo ipiripiri*, which will drive you mad. If you throw your stones in the water, the *ngipian* will think you are stoning them and will want you to die.
>
> To please the *ngipian*, you can throw the chyme of a goat in the water. It also pleases the *ngipian* to see the lips of cattle drinking far above them at the surface of the pool or to see calabashes dipping as people fill their jars with water. (Marshall Thomas 1965:180f)

Despite being subterranean creatures, *ngipian*, in their spiritual and watery nature, are close to Akujů. Humans similarly close to Akujů, such as one with the gift of making rain, are related and are welcome in their deep homes underwater to talk, rest and drink milk from the little spirit cows. Yet they can be dangerous.

> An *ekipye* can arrest someone at the dam (*atapar*),[23] and sacrifice will be necessary in order to be released. ... If you take one of the smooth stones (*ngabulangataruk*) for grinding tobacco (*etaba*), the *akuj* or *ekipye* can follow. The rain will come or the *akuj* or *ekipye* will take the stone back. ... You should salute the *ekipye* at Lodipoc water pond in Kamimuget River, or the oxen will be stuck there until a goat is sacrificed. (J31)

'War originated from water' (P4). The only solution for such difficulties is a religious invocation of the most sacred.

Akujů is anything but a local god amongst others. 'God created the Tepes on their mountain, Moroto' (Lamphear 1976:65). The Tepes, or Sor, have a very different religion, being attributed magical powers that can bring famine on those who attack them, and they call God Belgen. 'Akujů gives even enemies a chance to raid when

---

[23] It is interesting that the artificial ponds made in colonial times to provide water are just as associated with spirits as any other water. Innovations enculturated by the Karamojong do not secularize.

they bother Him' (J31). 'He may listen to the enemies' sacrifice' (P5). 'All men, even enemies, have a connection with Akujů' (P3). Yet this does not disturb the Karamojong belief in a High God who divided the whole world into territories for the peoples He had made.

Cosmogony

The Karamojong world has a beginning: it is not timeless. It began in the above (*kidyama*; cf. PEN *kudyo, rain), when heaven (*kakujů*) and earth (*akwap*; cf. *kwap*, beneath, south) were one. 'Akujů is supreme; He is above (*kidyama*)' (P11). 'Akujů is up, because rain, also sun, moon, starlight, clouds, come down from above. From the north (*kuju*) comes rivers, waters' (J31). The common substance was water.[24] The parallels with the Afroasiatic rain-God associated with the storm-cloud and the sacrifice of black animals are marked (Baldick 1998). Thus creation occurred by dividing the waters into the rain-bearing sky (*adis*) and the earth which brings forth water when a well (*akuja, akare*) is sunk into its heart. Time was divided as well as space. Year and season (*ekaru*) are divided by rain (*akiru*). Day (*akwar*) and night (*akwaare*) are differentiations of the same thing.

No Karamojong creation myth has been recorded, but the Toposa have a version of the common WN myth that heaven and earth used to be joined by a rope which, as a result of sin, folly or the malice of wild animals, was cut, leaving a permanent, wider separation. The Toposa believe that 'men originally lived with Nakwuge [*sic*] in the sky' but many came down to earth by sliding down a rope which then broke (Gulliver, P. and P.H. 1953: 92). Karamojong, on the other hand, at least where faith is vital, take the presence of Akujů as normative; neither He nor heaven are ontologically cut off. 'There is no separation; He is existing. Akujů is above in power, but has not left them. ... Akujů can make a separation, if sin is there. He is near, but He may turn deaf ears and can curse His peoples' (P5). Anyway humankind was created on earth: 'Karamojong believe they are made of soil and will return to it' (P4).

The Karamojong have their own ways of categorizing the visible world. The vault of heaven is perceived as the inside of the thatched roof of a large hut. Every feature of the landscape is named, usually by describing it, or associating it with animals, people or events. Living under the stars, they have named several constellations, which have yet to be accurately identified. *Lomeritom* and *Ngiremotom* (Great Bear, Orion) were used to signal the start of the hunting season, which parallels the SN Nandi *Koremerik*, which, if the roots are common, means, 'that of hunting with spears', but is identified with Pleiades. *Ngakuliak, Akanyerit, nganareny* (Pleiades) are used to determine the start of the rains and, therefore, of seed-time. Since the lunar months, and the change in the length of the day, are inadequate for the Karamojong to fix a solar year, they look to the astral sign of Pleiades, setting probably, to start the year, with its ancient, universal promise of rain (Frazer 1963:Spirits I,317f). A shooting star (*etop ngolo eremonor*), is a

---

[24] *kwai is a universal root for water; for example *kwe*, Sorat for rain, cf. *aki-kwa-ar* (to stop raining), *aki-kwang* (to swim).

message spearing down from Akujů, to declare the source of an imminent raid or disease (Marshall Thomas 1965:254).

The Karamojong colour scheme seems to have no distinction between blue and grey, and much in common with Victor Turner's primordial classification of reality.

> The colour triad white–red–black represents the archetypal man as a pleasure–pain process. The perception of these colours and of triadic and dyadic relations in the cosmos and in society, either directly or metaphorically, is a derivative of primordial psychobiological experience – experience which can be fully attained only in human mutuality. (Turner 1966:82)

For instance, the predominant colours of head-dress feathers and decorative pigments are white (*ekwang*[25]), red[26] (*ereng*) and black (*iryono*) or dark blue. I was unable to dissuade a Christian Karamojan in Kotido from the home-bred conviction that the black man was bad (*erono*) and the white man good. Black, unusually, symbolizes sexual passion, as well as death, so that the girls' use of ilmenite (*kupoi*) to blacken and spiral their hair (*ayerit*[27]) for social events is supposed to be successful in winning men, and women are praised for it.

The Creator

Everything known to humankind has a simple, unitary, ultimate source, Akujů, who is acknowledged in all the significant occasions of Karamojong life. That 'God is One' is the surest assertion that can be made about the divinity, even though there is a plural term (*ngakujo*), which applies to the god or spirit of a mountain, rock, tree or stream. There is unresolved confusion here with Akujů, who can quite properly be called a High God, even a sky-god (James 1963; Setiloane 1976:77), but there is connection and continuity, despite distinction. In either case Akujů is felt to be present in the world indirectly through divine Spirit or spirits and can have a deleterious effect on those who transgress upon the divine locus. 'There are gods (*ngakujo*) like people, cruel or mischievous' (J31). 'The Karamojong did not know any other way of worshipping Akujů and so they keep two ways. They acknowledge Akujů and *ngakujo*; there are not distinct gods. Where they gather, the supreme Akujů is being consulted there' (P11).

Akujů is the Creator (*Ekasuban*) of everything that is, however manifold and distant from the divine. He makes the sky change its appearance, the wind blow, the rain fall and the earth quake. He determines a person's lifespan. Everything comes from Akujů in the end. The notion of a refracted monotheism is helpful here, where the oneness of God is more emphatic than among WN such as Nuer and Dinka (King 1970:28–30) and quite different from the lack of a unifying principle among Acoli, Lango and Uduk (p'Bitek 1963; James 1988). This suggests that the Cushitic

---

[25] Cf.*kwai (water); *akikwang* (to swim).

[26] Cf. Indo-European *roudhos; *akired* (to redden, stain with blood).

[27] So symbolic is it of sexual passion that a girl seduced by a man she dislikes laments that she left her *ayerit* by a tree (Gourlay 1971b:78, 81,83)!

contacts (Baldick 1998) of the Eastern Nilotes[28] or the crucible of their own sense of salvation history as they entered East Africa across the dry plains have moved them to a greater sense of personal divine presence and coherent activity. Though there have been changes in past millennia, the Karamojong are good bearers of 'a single level of the preternatural, a single spiritual Force or Presence' associated symbolically with the sky and rain that featured in the postulated Sudanic religion encompassing both Cushitic and Nilo-Saharan peoples from around 6000–5000BC (Ehret 1998:145).

Though addressed as 'Papa', grammatically Akujů is a feminine form, but since verbs, pronouns and adjectives do not distinguish gender, it is reinforced little. Nevertheless that the only name for God should be feminine in a strongly patriarchal society might surprise structuralists. There is a measure of gender ambivalence; the father of a bride, as a part of the process of marriage, dresses in the clothes of his wife. A widow in mourning wears her husband's sandals, even at night, and carries his stick and his gourd (Clark 1953:76). Women play a prominent part in mythology (Lamphear 1976:75; Mirzeler 1999). People of both sexes may be given names of the opposite gender.[29]

It is possible that the word, Akujů, takes its gender from the root meaning of PEN *kudyu (rain) as liquids are generally given feminine form, but they are also generally plural. Akujů is not diminutive or neuter in gender, rather He transcends gender. He may fit the masculine typology of sky-gods (James 1963), for the concept of Akujů has nothing in common with the Earth Mother type. Men are the sons of Akujů, who is called father, though in the sense of an impersonal Creator and so in a figurative way that does not locate Akujů in the male type which pronouns never reiterate. Given the monopoly of the Akujů tradition, and its linguistic affinity to the WN *kot/ kwoth[30] association of rain, Spirit and God, it can be said that belief in this divinity predated the attribution of a gender marker less than 500 years ago by at least two millennia. Until such time as a collective gender pronoun is coined for English, 'He, Him, His' will be used to refer to Akujů on the understanding that

---

[28] If van der Jagt (1990:16f) is right that Turkana never use *ngakujo*, it might be claimed that they have developed a less refracted monotheism, though their usage of Akujů expresses immanence. The Southern Nilotes, being the first to enter East Africa, tend to hold to a High God, but there they first adopted from the Southern Cushites a divinity associated with the sun, Asis, which also influenced Bantu in the area from 300BC (Visser 1989b:91–5; Ehret 1998:164,167).

[29] Of Lamphear's 262 male Karamojong informants (1972:466–83), 23.3 per cent bore names of feminine form, 52.7 per cent masculine, 4.2 per cent diminutive, 3.8 per cent collective and 16 per cent were unmarked as to gender. Of 20 Jie women named by Wayland (1931:228), 50 per cent had names with a masculine gender marker, 40 per cent with a feminine, and five per cent each with a collective and a diminutive. Names of males and females are interchangeable. This ambiguity is reflected in that both the collective and feminine forms of the locative prefix ('ka-' and 'na-') are used for 'the place of God' (ibid.:221), while the adjective, godly (*ekujwana*) is set with a masculine gender marker.

[30] cf. Indo-European *ghut (Onions 1966:I,866). The common testimony that Akujů and Kwoth are everywhere and so here now is remarkable (James 1963:3).

this does not have an exclusively male connotation, but reflecting the fact that, if pressed on the gender of Akujů, the Karamojong opt for male. It certainly means that the Karamojong have not gone the whole way in adopting Afroasiatic gender markers, which distinguish the masculine as 'big, strong, and important' (Baldick 1998:149).

For Westerners there is the immediate problem of theodicy with a Creator who provides a harsh and capricious environment in which famine, disease and death are a common hazard, but there is no basic problem for the Karamojong. Firstly, they do not see their environment as menacing, for they love their land, only moving their homestead after the gravest social crisis, and often returning to the same locality. Disaster has a remarkably high degree of acceptance and it is a fundamental, undisputed tenet of faith that Akujů is good. Yet ultimately it is Akujů who ties up (*akikujukuj*) the rain. The blame for drought is not laid at His door, but at the feet of the efficient cause: the enemy, or sorcerer who is successful in his malicious magic; or else intercessions for rain have been nullified by ritual incompetence or sins which have 'wronged the country' (*akwap*). The created world, as distinct from the Creator, is a perpetual conflict of wills, and Akujů cannot be faulted for asserting His in order to bless some of them.

The serious question for life on earth is whether Akujů will bless the Karamojong, or some section of them. He is free to do what He will, but they make their demands clear to Him in prayer, just as people will make open demands to their elders to do their duty to them as their God.

> Hey Akujů, you want to return back these cows again and yet all these animals got finished some time back.
> So rain for our animals,
> come! Come!
> *Hoita-hoita-hoita-koi*! [prolonged expletive expressing shock] O Akujů, you don't even forgive us? O Akujů, O Akujů, even you Akujů, are throwing us away. O Akujů, O Akujů, even you are throwing us away. O Akujů, who is even our Akujů, you don't want to throw us away? O Akujů who is even our Akujů, you don't want to remove the sickness that is killing our animals? You remove it away! Take it away to the west!

Though the *ekagatan* on this occasion was a convinced Roman Catholic (J3), and there are echoes of the God of Moses here, such an approach to God is not recognizable in the generality of European or African Christians. It is not a matter of grace that the Lord of all should deign to show favour on his reprobate subjects, but a matter of obligation that a munificent father should respond to the justified demands of his deprived children. Another preaches, 'Let's pray to Akujů today as He is our Father, because our cows are in problems.' Put another way, the approach is not one of reverence so much as familiarity, though it is only in the context of the sacrifice, where the people are 'gathered here before Akujů' that such a conversation is conceivable.

Akujů is not like a man that He should behave like a man. The person who is most like Akujů is not passionate, angry, noisy, violent, troublesome, proud, ambitious, greedy or lustful, but is gentle, kind, humble, wise, impassive and, supremely, quiet, just like the traits of benevolent old age. Caprice is not in Akujů's nature but He may show, just as old people may show, apparent indifference and lack of interest to the point of apathy. Akujů is not apathetic, however, for He regularly, if not automatically, responds in the interest of those who pray aright, and reveals His justifiable unhappiness against those who shed blood (P5). He is the source of every blessing, even on those of another country:

> Father, when going back to their country, nothing bad, no stumbling on the road,
> will he meet! Let him not meet!

Akujů is also inscrutable. Akujů can be entreated, His will can be divined, but Akujů may neither be questioned nor cursed. This unaccountable power makes something like bereavement in cases of untimely death a lonely and inconsolable experience, in which the world of the bereaved temporarily collapses around him to the brink of suicide. Life is complex (*emaditana*) and the judgment of Akujů is to allow it to be reduced to confusion: for the order (*akiciket*) to become chaos (*akinyalinyalakinet*). In Himself, he is peace, 'Akujů *ngina akisil*' (J31).

The otherness of Akujů is a basic premise of the Karamojong. Akujů is radically transcendent, being above all in every sense. 'God is above the sky' ('*Eyau Akujů kidyama nadis*') (Rowland 1.8.90 Letter, cf.P11; Gulliver, P. and P.H. 1953:47). Although the name of God is Akujů, it is wrong to suppose an identity with the Biblical firmanent (*nakujů*) as with any other visible feature of the creation. Akujů is invisible and abides above the blue firmament, riding on the back of the clouds. The distinction with the material world is brought out by referring to the heavens (*kakujů*) as the dwelling-place of Akujů. Speculative or experimental theology is unknown, for Akujů needs neither introduction, explanation nor justification. Akujů is simply there, not just as part of the universe of the Karamojong, but also over and beyond, forming it. 'Akujů is with them. He is invisible, but they know Him' (P5). His intimate presence among the whole people is demanded at the sacrifice.

> O Akujů, before these children,
> draw nearer! Draw nearer!

He is immanent and transcendent.

3 The Great and Powerful God

Thus the Karamojong have a religion, the symbolic integration of belief and behaviour, rather than a theology. All that needs to be said is communicated in the words and drama of sacrament as it draws together all the threads of life, and lifts them towards the ideal which is neither removed from, nor abandoned within, the real. The ideal is in the real and changes it. There is no call for theology, at least in the public domain, outside of the prayers and exhortations which indicate the different ways Akujů is likely to act, or the kind of people He is apt to approve. The paucity of self-critical reflection tends to seek the integration of society by the alienation of most outside it, but theology is not absent.

The greatest act of faith is the presumption of Akujů. No arguments are needed for or against the existence of Akujů; the only choice is to accept His presence or to ignore it. To do the latter is to ignore the Karamojong and the heartbeat of their culture. Commentators on Karamoja have noted the obeisance paid to Akujů but they have not done justice to the way He has shaped its environment and culture. Yet even a study of Karimojong politics leads ineluctably to Akujů 'as the source of all values' (Dyson-Hudson 1966:94) or, more euphemistically, 'A careful examination of Jie myths and historical traditions ... shows that the Jie system is deeply rooted in fundamental cosmological concerns' (Lamphear 1989:8). 'Sociologically, the limits of the Jie tribe can best be described in ritual terms. People of a district and of the whole tribe are kept together by indispensable ritual needs' (Gulliver 1953c:165).

All gods and religions are of course culture-specific, even Allah. Yet there is little significant difference between the way the term 'God' is commonly used in Europe and the way 'Akujů' is used in Karamoja, with the exception that the name is taken in vain much more in the former, as also in Anglophone Africa. The first Christian missionaries at once alighted upon this name and there has been no question ever since that Akujů would always be used in their Ngakaramojong translations. Once Akujů is there in Scripture and worship, Christian Karamojong have been encouraged to feel that, whatever the missionaries and their devotees teach, their traditional religion is validated. The Christian influence on their beliefs in Akujů has been remarkably small. That Novelli (1999:16), a Verona Father since 1957, from Verona, spending a lifetime among Eastern Nilotes, cavils against the commonality suggested between Christian and Karamojong notions of God is one indicator that Christian mission has not tried to appropriate traditional religion and that it has not been reworked to the approval of the Church.

There is no evidence to suggest that traditional beliefs have been invented by either missionary or colonial rule. Macdonald (1899a:137) noted in 1898 that the Karamojong had 'the same belief in one Supreme Being and in various omens' as the Maasai. Since neither had experienced missionary or imperial rule or even white men, it cannot be claimed that Karamojong religion had already been distorted by others before then. The Karamojong had not witnessed any white men before that expedition, and no missionary would come for over 30 years. There is no question that the term and the associated concepts are traditional, though not immutable, for issues such as the goodness of God can never be closed.

The time-spread of twentieth-century sources indicates little change in religious beliefs, and the implicit nature of belief has proved an effective defence against the incursions of state, mission, NGOs and global communication. The outsiders motivated to be agents of change have very seldom seen any need to initiate a religious discourse on Karamojong terms, when they themselves do not propagate belief verbally. The transmission of the faith is by sacramental osmosis, and it is those who have long been in the process who can articulate it when asked. Nevertheless it is that faith on which the cultural world-view stands and thrives.

Chapter 9

Enduring Vitality and its Challengers

The book so far, whether starting from history or from culture, has pointed towards Karamojong cognizance of Akujů as the transcendent figure, implicitly and explicitly, who is immanent in their normal lives by his presence and activity. Though he may be responsible for amazing signs, it is the regular, natural rôle that he plays in their cosmology which integrates their communal life in the face of global, environmental and governmental adversity. It is 'Akujů, who has really brought us here together', and when they assemble of their own accord, it is invariably for the purpose of sacrifice and prayer, in their terms. Thus the meaning of these activities, so central to the enduring vitality of their culture and the religion that suffuses its every aspect, warrants further elucidation. They will be weighed against those factors of change which are likely to displace the currently beating heart of Karamojong culture.

1 Sacrifice

To sacrifice (*amuro*) cattle is a much more sacred affair in manifold ways than slaughter, for 'the sacred meal is at once a sacramental communion and a sacrificial oblation' (James 1962:17). In a deconstructionist world notions of ritual cuisine are more palatable, but even the French Hellenists gave place to the belief of the invited gods being present (Heusch 1985:18). Luc de Heusch (ibid.:3,14) finds the Durkheimian separation of the sacred and profane inapplicable to African sacrifice, but then arrives at a theory of sacrifice that puts the world back in its dichotomous, structuralist order where gods, spirits and ancestors belong in the sky, while men are bound by their prohibitions to the earth. In adhering to Lévi-Strauss, the disciple of Marcel Mauss who shared Durkheim's sociological school of thought, de Heusch has not escaped the trap of Indo-European dualism. All have missed, however narrowly, the more likely African presupposition for which the Karamojong are a particularly clear example.

Though certain people, animals, places and things may be marked out, even spatially separated on occasion, as especially sacred and supported by various prohibitions, this does not mean the rest are profane. On the contrary all existing things are sacred, and even the scapegoat, the outcast and the enemy are not totally cut off from sacred power. The sacrifice of the enemy may attract divine blessing. Here God cannot be sufficiently explained as a metonym for society as He can set himself over against society. Hence the need for atonement (Heusch 1985:18). Yet, if there be atonement, the divine is united with the human community. God is present, not absent and opposed. The rightly ordered world has the divine infused in it. Thus the sacred is not defined by the exceptional, the tabu, the separated and the transcendent so much as by presence in and to humanity, animals, plants, rain, rivers and rocks. The sacred is not conceived of in terms of polarity, but according to intensity. The created order is generally spiritual, not profane, and ceremonial events, above all sacrifice, provide an especially dense moment not merely in some esoteric, mystical religion, but in the whole life and ecology of the sacrificing people. It remains to be seen how this is worked out in the interpretation of Karamojong ritual.

Feast

Killing the cattle branded by the clan is not done unless they are about to die anyway, for they are the family treasure. An equivalence of people and cattle is expressed in bridewealth and compensation for the loss of a person. Thus killing their herds was not an option for the people of Nakapelimoru, for example, in 1984–5, even though their crops failed totally. Either they lived off milk and blood, hunting and gathering, even famine relief, or they went hungry. With cattle, or livestock that could be exchanged for cattle, there was a future, because bridewealth assured progeny. Yet progeny assured nothing if there were no livestock. Therefore the feast (*peyos*[1]) is generally a sacrifice of one sort or another (*amuronot*,[2] *ajulot*), when death is a precondition for a carnivorous meal. 'An animal is food for man. *Epuot* is killing a fat beast for slaughter as respect for a relation' (P11). Thus sacrifice is unavoidably a meal by which social relationships are expressed (Smith 1901). The culinary features of sacrifice cannot be denied, and it is these that the young men and the sceptical will emphasize, for no human society is homogeneous in its religious appreciation and beliefs.

Giving up the Victim

The sacrifier[3] gives up part of his livelihood for each sacrifice. The herds may be assembled at the sacred grove, an act which itself consecrates the occasion by its display of unity (Rowland 1983:11). When the elders see an ox of the markings prescribed by divination at the last sacrifice, an absolute requirement is laid on the

---

[1] Cf. *akipe* (to roast).

[2] The common root for things sacrificial, *mur, even agnates (*ngikamurak*) who are related through sacrifice, probably has its origins in pre-pastoral times, perhaps with the sacrifice of hunted animals, such as the duiker (*amur*). The ES root for ox (*mor) suggests a linguistic connection. The only parallel with the Semitic use of stones for marking sacrificial places is the 'the rock of the land', Karimojong, at Nakadanya (Dyson-Hudson 1966:192) and the rain-stones possessed by the Jie, but an association is suggested by the PT root for rock (*moru), and Gulliver (1953c:151) even misspells stones as *ngimuru*. However it is the spirit or god of the rock, for example of Moru Apolon, to whom sacrifice may nominally be made.

[3] The sacrifier is one who funds the offering, who owns the sacrificial victim, while the sacrificer is the one who executes the sacrifice (Hubert and Mauss 1964).

owner to hand it over. Unless it is a beloved ox, his bovine son who shares his name, he can do quite well, for the spearer must compensate him with a heifer, and so becomes the sacrifier.[4] In fact the beloved ox is too close to its owner to be sacrificed. 'You cannot spear your own ox; it is like killing yourself' (P1). The perfection of identity means that it is too threatening a substitute, for the perfect sacrifice must separate from the divine curse, while uniting sacrifier to the sacred.

Finding someone willing to take up the rôle of sacrifier may require some time, for parting with cattle, even for a public ceremony, is no light thing; it represents human livelihood, not just having, but being as well. 'A man is man in cattle', so it is intrinsically a sacrifice in the Christian sense of self-denial. Resentment is expressed at those who always come to eat, but never spear an ox. The victim is always costly, because cattle are related to human beings, denoting their social and economic transactions and constituting their social capital, but at least one of their number must die.

Spearing the Victim

A man never spears his own ox but an exchanged one, except at initiation, and even then he is given it by his *ere* family or a bond-friend. The sacrifice creates relationships in its cattle transactions. There is a special, large spear (*atum*), which is not normally carried, for central sacrifices. The ox should be speared behind the third rib through the heart, and it is a great honour to accomplish this at the first attempt. The spearer's mother will be given the head, tongue, neck and lungs to boil, even when the spearer is compelled to sacrifice for tying up the rain.

Any mishap in the spearing is bad form, even an omen, and may be attributed to the reluctance of its owner to part with it, to the bad hearts of participants or to any breach in the formal procedure. The event is not merely social, but filled with spiritual import. The ox may run a mile with the spear between its ribs, but it can do no other, it is believed, than return to the sacred grove where it has been ordained to die, ideally on its left side with its head towards the sacred place of tribal origin. The victim cannot desert the communion feast any more than a man can opt out of his social or religious obligations, when all are spiritually bound.

Cuts of Meat

In Karimojong sacrifice the meat of the two sides of the carcass is then shared between the two sides, or horns, of the assembly. Starting from the base of one 'horn' and going along it, a front thigh is given to the most senior elder, one side of the chest to the second, a knee-joint, (*asukongiro*) to the third, a shoulder (scapula)

---

[4] Thus a man is never required to sacrifice his own beloved ox, either as sacrifier or as sacrificer. That would be like spearing himself, so close is the identity (P1). It is only reasonable to find a substitute. Nevertheless an owner cannot withhold his beloved ox from being sacrificed by another, if an ox of his particular markings or horn profiling has been divined or decreed for sacrifice. The having of the individual must give way to the well-being of the community.

(*eseket*) to the fourth, a hip-bone to the fifth, and one side of the lower back to the sixth, and the pair of each is distributed at the same time to the other side. The ribs of each flank (*apol*) are distributed to the elders. An elder cuts part of the tongue into strips; together with the head, neck, lungs and heart, it is carried away by the women. The rest of the meat is given to the initiates. The elders extract the marrow from the bones by cracking them between two stones and slurping it.

Then attention is turned to what they consider to be the strongest part of the ox and the source of most beef, the rear thighs (*amuro*), again a word resonating of sacrifice. The *amuro* is brought to the elders (P1). One of them cuts the flesh with a spearhead, and the Karimojong and Dodoso extract a small gland from between the legs (*angarwe*), which is put under chyme and reserved for Akujů. If the elder cuts it by mistake, he must at once sacrifice a goat or a sheep to rescue him from the danger of transgressing such a sacred tabu (P1). Then they break the hind legs apart. The elders separating the hind legs (*akidung amuro*) is regarded as so significant a moment that Clark (1950:217), followed by Neville Dyson-Hudson (1966:187) and Novelli (1988:43;1999:211) use the term as the name for the promotion ceremony. Though this moment may be used as a surrogate for the whole ox sacrifice, it is a feature of every ox sacrifice, not just those for marking the succession of generation-sets. The flesh of each hind leg is cut into six portions for the elders only to eat.

An Offering

With the death of the ox, the ceremony begins in earnest and the previous business can be forgotten. The passing of its life is a solemn event that releases, they say, power and peace on earth. Those present are morally bound to put aside personal, familial, clan and generational quarrels, and turn their minds towards the blessing of the whole community. The victim is cut open (*apunor*) and the perineal flesh is carved out first for the senior age-section to eat. The Karimojong, but not the Jie, carefully put side the iliac gland (*angarwe*) as the portion for Akujů, buried at the foot of the sacred tree. He communes with them, savouring the gift of the sacrifice through the smoke of it cooking and through eating the blood absorbed in the ground (P11). The participants do not indulge in theophagy and eat divinity, for the victim stands between them and the danger of the dense presence of the sacred. All the cuts of meat made by the deacons are allocated to specific categories, as in initiation, and eaten the same day by the assembly. It is a precious offering of a part of what the Creator has provided for His people, the part representing the whole (Durkheim 1915:229). It is a piacular offering, a sacrifice for sin not just in cases of wrong-doing, since it is the only adequate answer the community has when it is faced with privation of the blessings of Akujů, and it always costs an ox. If an ox does not die, the problems will eventually kill people instead. When the country has been spoiled by transgression,[5] and the persistence of problems proves they have

---

[5] There is a clear sense of the socially and ecologically polluting contagion of transgression, and of the dangers of not taking preventative or remedial action, but little apprehension of either individual purity or inherent sinfulness. Persons are assessed

been caused by transgression including the omission of sacrifice, there is no alternative but to put it right by the restorative effects of sacrifice (Beattie 1980:42).

The Communal Presence of Akujů

The entrails reveal the will of Akujů by divination. As the cattle eat the grass, which is itself the product of the divine spirit in rain on the sacred earth, so the organs that contain this heavenly gift are themselves a particularly sharp revelation. When the stomach sac is slit, the chyme (*ngikujit*) is used for anointing cattle and men. 'The intestines are read by the *emuron*, who divines the signs: rain, sun, enemies, or whatever is coming. He tells then the remedy' (P5). It is at the sacrifice that '*ngimurok* are spoken to by Akujů, Who reveals how people can be protected against disease, attack, and such things. It may be other dreamers, diviners, prophets, who reveal' (P11).

> The Karamojong see a tree as sacred, where they worship. Chyme marks it out as sacred, where they consult Akujů to pray. Akujů is Supreme: He is above (*kidyama*). The prayer-leader intercedes to Akujů. They choose a tree for shade, which encourages people to meet, so they make it sacred. It is for people to consecrate, where Akujů hears their prayers. It is a place where they talk to Akujů. Akujů is everywhere, so He will be there. It can be Akujů rustling the top of the tree, because He can be in wind, sky, the here and now. He is not confined to one particular thing. (P11)

Akujů is also blessed by smearing (*akijuk*[6]), when chyme is put on the trunk of the sacred tree, in the top of which Akujů moves, rustling the leaves. 'A whirlwind (*epiripirit*) comes to see where they have gathered and greets them' (J16). He not only observes proceedings, but evidently plays a quasi-human rôle in them. 'Stomach chyme is thrown to the sacred tree for Akujů, who also tastes the smoke through smell and eats blood spilt on the ground' (J8). 'Akujů participates in the sacrifice through the blood, chyme, and smoke' (J16). These make him happy. Chyme is the most effectual symbol of transmitting the blessings of Akujů.

---

according to their attitudes and behaviour, finally by whether they meet with prosperity or calamity, and not how altruistic their motives are. There is overlap between sin and spoiling, but the word to translate these, *akisec*, is linguistically very close to that used by Roman Catholics to be pure (*akiseg, asegar*), applied by Karamojong to the antisocial who avoid people. To be pure, then in Karamojong thought, is to transgress social norms, and to be purified is to undergo an expiatory rite (*amok*) to stop one being hunchbacked! Dichotomies of clean and unclean seen in the Old Testament do not go far here (Douglas 1975).

[6] *Akijuk* is a strong verb and so more primitive than the weak verb (Dimmendaal 1983). *Akijuk* (to push) may be an example of the reversal of root consonants ('k' and 'j'). It may be cognate to *ejok*, which would connect with its use in the cairn custom and the frequent use of *akijuk* (the weak verb) for to travel, for example 'to push to Moroto' as though one went distances only by pushing up a cosmological blanket or through a heavy atmosphere irradiated by the prayers and charms of strangers, in order to move forward. Thus *akitujuk* could mean not only to smear, but also to make good or divine. In either case we have a spiritual dimension to a material activity and the indication that *jok/juk might have been derived from *kudy (rain).

Source: Ben Knighton

Photograph 9.1 *Akidung Amuro*: cutting the joint of the hind legs of the sacrifice. The blood waits in a gourd and the chyme is speared to the ground

A sacrifice is a communal repast 'to feed the elders' as the representatives of the community. In order of seniority they drink the life-giving blood (*ngaokot*) from the chest cavity. 'The smallest drop of blood contains the same active principle as the whole thing' (Durkheim 1915:343; James 1962:25f).

> An animal dies in the place of people as the prevention of problems. When life goes out of an animal, it releases power; through the animal Akujů acts there. Akujů will have power on earth to tell enemies to return. That is why it is the best time to pray ... only initiates drink blood and Akujů is near at this point. It is a sacred moment, so the eldest in the age-set drinks first. The closest to Akujů drink first.[7] (P11)

Those who drink it are united in a fellowship, bonded by the ingestion of a common, life-giving substance. Having drunk, they wipe their gory lips on the right hind leg of the victim, which symbolizes the strength of the ox.

The Nature of Sacrifice

As might be expected, Karamojong sacrifice is accessible by many theories. It is a gift to a deity, since Akujů partakes of the smoke, blood or perineal gland of the victim, whose sacrifice is certainly intended to make Him happy. Akujů is honoured by a gift in homage and gratitude. In the blood-covenant the initiates share in the being of the victim by drinking its blood. It is obviously a fellowship meal that unites the political community in communion with Akujů. It is clearly a piacular sacrifice since it is the primary way of dealing with either an actual or a potential transgression, and can do so with great assurance. Expiatory sacrifice is an easy concept, when sacrifice is the only known solution for the country which has been wronged or spoiled by man's inhumanity to man.

It is patently a substitutionary sacrifice, when 'An animal dies in the place of people as the prevention of problems' (P11). This is supported by Gourlay's analysis (1972b:248) of the identification of man and ox that finds in sacrifice absolution from a curse for ox and man. Contrary to the urban and urbane scruples of bourgeois liberals who prefer to denounce anything that might lead to transgression occurring, substitution is a fundamental principle of sacrifice here (Heusch 1985:23f). For the Jie the foundational sacrifice is that of Orwakol and his people as they take possession of the land (Mirzeler 1999: 243–8). Yet the ox that they kill is Engiro, the metonym of the tribe. By all spearing him or letting the uninitiated eat the meat, their lack of customary control lets loose the cosmic power of sacrifice, so they are killing themselves; indeed terrible schism, drought and famine follow.

Substitutionary scapegoats would appear to grant validity to Girard's notion (1977) of the displacement of violence onto a sacrificial victim, which would have more mileage were it not that Girard started from Freud rather than Africa. Even the killing of a divine king in order to restore the future of his people has an echo in the

---

[7] It is difficult to maintain with Novelli (1999:lxxix) that Karimojong have no explanation for their rites other than that it is custom. It is not surprising that he cannot find evidence for propitiatory sacrifice, despite its general association with identity (James 1962:34).

scapegoating of the 'asapan-man', the senior elder of the closely-related Nyangatom or Dongiro who sacrifices an ox, loses his mind and wanders off into the bush to die as a symbol of the retirement of the senior generation-set (Tornay 1998:106–8). Such a practice has not been discovered in Karamoja, but human sacrifice is there as testimony to the implicit belief that a few men should die for the nation threatened by severe famine or disease. Yet the community is believed to be ordered by peace, not conflict, and there are effective social sanctions for limiting violence. The virtues of old age, the sacred of society, do not include as much as a violent temper. Sacrifice is not needed to deal with Girard's omnipresent violence before Christ does away with sacrifice,

Barrett (1998) emphasizes that Turkana sacrifice is all about an exchange relationship whereby Akujů is given a sacrifice in return for Him answering prayer. This suits Karamojong sacrifice, but he misses in Turkana thought[8] what has also been demonstrated in Karamojong belief. 'When life goes out of an animal, it releases power; through the animal Akujů acts there. Akujů will have power on earth to tell enemies to return. That is why it is the best time to pray' (P11). Karamojong come back to sacrifice so often because they trust it has real power to solve their problems in the world, especially the ecological ones. Yet this power is unquantifiable, immeasurable.

Hubert and Mauss (1964) still hit more right notes than any other, especially if the Durkheimian bifurcation between sacred and profane is removed. The 'expulsion of sacred spirit' is the primordial concept of sacrifice (ibid.:6), as the event is more cosmos-shaking than a comforting communion. Sacrifice 'always implies a consecration'. The thing consecrated serves as an intermediary between those who receive the benefit of the sacrifice and the divinity to whom the sacrifice is addressed. Sacrifice is always the destruction of a victim, and through its consecration it modifies the condition of the moral person who accomplishes it (ibid.:9, 11–13). There is a perfect constancy of rites and a similar constancy in the mental state of the sacrifier, who is obliged to undertake the expenses of the sacrifice in person, and of the sacrificer concerning the gods, victim and petition. There is unshakeable confidence in the automatic result of sacrifice. The religious act must be accomplished by the religious frame of mind, for the act carries faith. There is in the victim a spirit, which it is the aim of the sacrifice to liberate, conferring the perfect religious nature on the victim. Death releases the divine principle making consecration definitive and irrevocable. It is a solemn moment, for the intensity of the forces of life cannot be concentrated in an earthly object without destroying it. The purpose of consumption is the complete elimination of the animal from its temporal surroundings. The most perfect way of effecting communication with this necessary intermediary is to hand over to the sacrifier a portion of the victim which he consumes. Portions are distributed to priests, each of whom represents a god. There is an alternating rhythm between expiation and communion (ibid.:28–33, 38–40, 43, 94f). Man and God are not in direct contact, which would

---

[8] On participating in the sacrifice of a goat at Oropoi in 1985, Turkana elder told me in answer to my questions that, when the animal died, power was released which would lead to an outbreak of peace on earth.

immediately cause the death of the man. Thus drinking the blood is not a direct fusion of human and divine life, it is only food (*akimuj*, P11). The value of the victim is that it separates God and man, while uniting them. Through death God can be one with the victim and so vicariously with man (ibid.:9,43).

Yet power and spirit remain names for the unanalysed invisible. What happens in sacrifice for Batailles (1989) is that the sacrifier is destroying his own animality to become truly human. The sacrificial victim is at once identified with and distinct from the sacrifier, who relates through the victim to his own spirit, so is able to come to a higher self-consciousness. If he were not able to recognize his own spirituality in the animal's otherness, he would only be retreating into the isolation of self by destroying the other, but because he identifies, even loves, the other, he finds in death's release of the spirit his own liberation from mere consciousness. Sacrifice reconstitutes his humanity, rather than being an evolutionary anachronism of bestial violence. Whatever the reasoning, sacrifice is the dense moment not only of traditional Karamojong religion, but of the whole culture, while the sacred grove is crying for someone to perform a sacrifice there (J8).

Social scientific explanations of sacrifice are likely to make human practice the centre of attention, but this does not reflect Karamojong cosmology. Humanity is not alone in the world, a subject over against freedom-threatening objects. In the performative scheme of sacrifice there are three actors. There is no freedom without cattle, even if the life of one ox is only a sixtieth of a human one. Similarly there is nothing without Akujů. There is a delicious metonymy here. The ox is man's 'four-legged brother', while 'Akujů is the brother of old men' (J8). Identity and distinction do not have to be forced at all, when Akujů mediates Himself through the chyme (*ngikujit*) of cattle and the elders are gods (*ngakujo*). Of course it is tempting to jump to the conclusion that Akujů and cattle are just transferred names for humans. Yet, if these other beings are mere projections of false consciousness, where is the spirit and the power?

Superstructure cannot change socio-economic structures, but the Karamojong look to sacrifice to mend broken and spoiled communities, to make the dry land bloom, and to exile the sickness of their cattle. Spoiling the world removes Akujů from it; sacrifice ensures that He is still here to bless His people. There is a dialectical relationship with Akujů, for to be close to him is to receive His blessings, but to be closer is to die, as no flesh can survive intense spirit. Thus the Karamojong find their self-consciousness taken up through sacrifice, which allows them to die only to their old selves. The warrior cannot remain perpetually trying to prove his manhood over against the other. Just as he finds consolation for his impotence to control the family herd in a castrated ox, so he finds his place in the age-system by spearing an ox. When he starts his own herd and family, he looks to the prayers of the elders to bring down rain from heaven, so his own selfish autonomy must be resolved. When the community finds its own being through the momentous sacrifice of its bovine brother, the encapsulation of all social values, it becomes itself the history of the sacred spirit. That is the dynamic power at work in the world.

2 Prayer

In the sacrifice the junior age-section lightly roast the meat on an open fire. They 'slice and cook the meat, which is heaped in one place. The elders eat the *elamacar* from below the tail. Then they pray because Akujů is there. Whenever they kill the sacrifice they have first to pray' (P5). 'The animal belongs to Akujů, so it is believed they should not eat before getting blessings from Akujů, who is in life and death' (P11). 'Akujů listens to prayers and blesses. Three requests are made: for the health of the people, the multiplication of animals, and good crops' (J8). Of course those who expect a 'Hush, please! Eyes shut and hands together!' approach to prayer will be disappointed, but the exhortations make it plain that the most powerful men, not little children, should take prayer very seriously. 'So we don't make this day as a joke, but we make it a day of prayer; prayer is our seal, and it is good to pray... So here is now time for you to pray for this animal before it[s intestines are] cut... So now prayers stay' (J3).

The elders are enjoined to be godly in their praying, as they of all people are close to Akujů. Hot and angry spirits should be cooled, and the badness within human beings should be cast out, if the requests of Akujů are to be effective. They are reminded of the need to pray. They do not merely supplicate for themselves, but also intercede for others. 'So now I am telling you that you pray for this boy [a man of 47 being initiated] ... And also we pray for the owner of this homestead.' Whoever is to be the recipient of the answer to the prayer is introduced to Akujů, not that, as all-seeing Father of his people, he does not know them, but they are to receive the blessing that all depends on him favouring the right people.

Leader	Assembled
Akujů, these are the children of Moding. Do you accept them?	Accept them!

Litany

At a large event the most senior elder (*ekapolon*), still holding a wand standing up from his exhortations, opens the prayers, pacing up and down, and gesticulating with the wand especially to denote direction.

Leader	Assembled
Kirak! Kirak! Kirak!	
Neni karonan a lotunga kang a ngaatuk kang,	
Neni karonan a lomomwa,	
Neni karonan a ngakipi,	
Neni karonan a lonyo,	
Neni karonan a lorotin,	
Neni karonan a ngakimuj,	
Neni karonan a daadang,	
Nyawosit awot arokosi ka kolong!	*Ee, arokosi!*
Nyacei emam.	

Ngitunga eya a?	*Eya!*
Ngaatuk eya a?	*Eya!*
Daadang eya a?	*Eya!*
Ngimoru eya a?	*Ka ngikingidwe?*
Ngigete eya a?	*Eya!*
Ngidokoror eya a?	*Eya!*
Ngaatuk eya a?	*Eya!*
Ngibaren eya a?	*Eya!*
Ngimomwa eya a?	*Eya!*
Nyakiru nyatiaun?	*Atiaun!*
Ngaatuk daadang ka ngikeyokok nyarukun?	*Arukut!*
Akujů ekirar erar a?	*Irar!* (P5)

(Listen! Listen! Listen!	
Anything bad connected with my people and my cattle,	
Anything bad connected with sorghum,	
Anything bad connected with water,	
Anything bad connected with whatever,	
Anything bad connected with paths,	
Anything bad connected with food,	
Anything bad connected with everything,	
Have they not gone on a journey, emigrated, set together with the sun?	They have set!
It is not alert!	
The people are staying, are they?	They should stay!
The cattle are staying, are they?	They should stay!
All are staying, are they?	They should stay!
The senior generation-set, the Rocks, are staying, are they?	And not the children?
The junior generation-set, the Gazelles, are staying, are they?	They should stay!
The uninitiated, the Rats, are staying, are they?	They should stay!
The cattle are staying, are they?	They should stay!
The riches in cattle are staying, are they?	They should stay!
The sorghum are staying, are they?	They should stay!
Did not the rain come?	It did come!
All the cattle and the herdsmen, did they not come together?	They did come together!
God, is He not hearing what we hear?	He is hearing!)

The prayer-leader uses the *lokaliye* wand to walk, to motion from left to right, and to caste all evils to the west. The same style of litany for supplication is used for all occasions of sacrifice (P5).

Although it is termed as asking or begging (*akilip*), what is actually done is to command Akujů. This is the style of the antiphonal *agat* invocation. It begins with the imperative mood being used to Akujů himself: 'Akujů listen!', 'Akujů hear us!', 'Draw nearer!', 'Accept!' He is charged to set his priorities aright, for instance to remove sickness: 'You remove it away! Take it away to the west!' Akujů's attention having been engaged, it is now His creatures who are commanded: the elements, such as rain, clouds and rivers; other animate beings, such as sorghum, cows and people; artifices, such as cattle corrals; activities, such as ululations and good speech; the good, such as goodness, peace and riches; and the bad, such as sickness, enemies, evils and evil spirits. When Akujů is present with them in the sacrifice, the elders have His authority and power to command every feature immanent in the world, even in places on the other side of the world.[9]

The assembly assumes that even the greatest efforts of people may avail them nothing against the adversity of enemies and environment, so they appeal regularly to a higher authority by praying (*akigat*). Whichever elder should lead the antiphonal prayers is known as *ekagatan*. He pronounces extempore versicles in a stylized way, to which the congregation responds in unison. Having asserted who the people and cattle are, who have assembled, he prays for blessings like rain to come (*akigatun*) and for evil like disease or enemies to depart (*ekagator*). 'He prays for peace for the animals and people, for food, grass, and rain for the future, after cursing all evils. Anything bad, let it go set with the sun. Everything is carried by the wind/Akujů' (P1). Prayer is assumed to change reality, even within the course of the prayers. Often the past tense is used, for whenever the third person prefix is a- , it marks a past tense. Thus they pray for rain as though it has already rained. This is the prayer of faith, not of function. Frequently a concluding prayer is, 'Akujů has heard, has He not?', to which the sure response is, 'He has!', and another prayer-leader begins. 'Prayers continue while initiated men are roasting and eating and Akujů is happy' (J8). This may even go up to five hours or more, that is whenever the congregation arrives at a consensus that 'prayers have been enough' (Rowland 1983:4).

Changing the World

Prayer, though it is accompanied by the cutting and eating of meat, is a serious business for the Karamojong. It is an act, indeed a series of repeated acts, of faith, on which the life of the community depends. This is how elders see their ceremonies, and this is how women and youth see their rôle. It is the responsibility of elders to pray for rain, because they have the greatest access to and fellowship with Akujů. 'Akujů is the brother of old men' (J8). Prayer is assumed to change reality by begging (*akilip*), petitioning Akujů. Even within the course of the prayers their belief is that 'Akujů answers prayers'. Forensically it depends on when and how they consult. 'If He gives no response, they kill another animal' (P5). This is the point at which religion does not remain in comfortable harmony with the way things are. It is believed that they can be different, and that, through religious practices, they will be different. To believe (*akinup*), as the Karamojong do, that their prayers will make the rain fall, disease disappear and enemies stay where they are, in an environment where drought, chronic ill-health and insecurity are endemic, appears to be absurdly optimistic, even inhumanely unrealistic. They pray for individuals, families, clans, subsections, sections and for the tribe, as represented in the assembly, but there is no recorded case of praying for another tribe. Their faith in the efficacy of *akiriket* cannot be gainsaid. 'You Apalotinga! You Acuk! All the

---

[9] One informant wanted to know about my children and, as often, to keep photographs of them. His memory was not dulled by the passage of 16 years, 'Your children were Akujů's gift, as the elders prayed for you to have children' (J21).

problems[10] there that are mentioned, even if they are defeating you, they cannot defeat us, can they?' Individuals or families cannot speak for Akujů in disputes wider than the family. It is only in the *akiriket* that the elders as a corporation can give His word that will solve the problem.

It is axiomatic that Akujů does intervene, or refuse to intervene, in what would otherwise be a continually inclement ecology. Faith works and the proof is the survival of the community. Individuals may not survive in the real Karamoja, but the community, the culture, can and does. Only if its very existence is disintegrating is there room to consider other beliefs; only if it has been overwhelmed may they be adopted. Yet I have seen their life on the rack. The Dodosô in the early 1980s had no cattle and no crops, and the survivors were dependent on famine relief. Some fell prey to the social engineering attempted by Oxfam to resettle them on black cotton soil in order for them to become tillers of the ground. Then they had to endure the message of repentance brought them by Christian clergy drawn from the Karimojong. Since they were suffering privation of blessing, they must have earned the curses of Akujů predicted in Deuteronomy for a disobedient people. Such a hard message is congruent with the way Karamojong see Akujů. If grass, livestock, health, even life itself, disappear, it is the correction of Akujů, and no-one can fight against Him. However He cannot lose his quality of intervening on behalf of his people.

With religious observance sufficient to turn the hearts of the people back to the tried and tested customs, Akujů will surely bless his people sooner or later, whereas the foreign religions could not be trusted. Had they not brought confusion to marriage and young people? They could not understand the nomadic pastoralist way of life and brought no sustainable alternative that could be associated with freedom. It was the lot of the loser. There were no responses to the Protestant preaching, no change of heart won by the Roman enticements among people who appeared to have nowhere to turn. They silently, somewhat sullenly, held their peace and waited for the year when they would rediscover their dignity in cattle. About a decade later they were able to acquire guns, which allowed them to raid and retain cattle, and so did not depart from Karamojong culture, though apparently victims of it for so long. It is imperative for a blessed future, the Karamojong believe, that they enculturate new generations into the old faith (*anupit*). 'Sacrifice is finding redirection and home through prayer' (J8).

3 Women's Affairs

It is easy to suppose that women are dominated by a self-interested patriarchal gerontocracy. Even a brief acquaintance with the relative stature of men and women shows that, while the women are left to suffer the consequences of recurrent crop failure, men can benefit from a highly nutritious diet so long as they can graze their cattle in distant camps. Women are by strict custom the hewers of wood and the drawers of water for the homestead. It is tempting to think that it would be in the

---

[10] Problems (*ngican*) are implicitly assumed to have a spiritual cause (*ngicen*).

interests of women to overcome the traditional gender dichotomy of cattle and sorghum, especially as this was never absolute, and opt for all the innovations offered by NGOs and Ugandan life.

While women are excluded from sacrifice and assembly, and so the ultimate politico-religious court of the Karamojong, it would a great mistake to assume that they are voiceless, passive or subordinate in society. There is great affection between mother and son, and women can have rights in land and even livestock, when gender roles are clearly demarcated between crops and cattle. Sorghum or 'beer is the cattle of women' (Dyson-Hudson 1966:96) and each is fundamentally equivalent when 'Akujů created cattle and sorghum on the same day.' Women's ceremonies are seen as parallel and complementary to men's, so instead of an animal sacrifice, the women offer beer before the elders. The old men bless the women by anointing them with the brewer's grains, so that the goodness of Akujů is mediated to them too.

Women's Initiation

Whenever a new, male age-class is opened, it must be formally named (*akiwor*). This word is also used for times when women gather to name an age-set, into which they are initiated, and they 'identify themselves' (Gourlay 1971b:89,111; Emoru 1998:25). Women follow the paradigm of male age-classes and theirs mirror them, while retaining distinctive names. While the men spear their oxen, the qualifying moment of women for initiation is marriage, since their generation-set and age-section must mirror the husband's, making it doubly clear which generation-set their son should join. She will wear the same metal as her husband, and take the name of his generation-set, though she will apply no personal name of his to herself. The women's age-section name, which revolves in track with the male one, identifies her with a category of coevals. Those in the senior generation-set are honoured and listened to as *ngakimak*; they are venerable old ladies, so hold privileged status relative to both women and girls.

The initiands bear gifts to an elder and ask him permission to hold their initiation underneath his tree. Then, with the help of a group of young men, they sacrifice an ox and smear themselves with the chyme (Novelli 1999:221–6). An *ekimomwor* dance is held. This may last five to ten days for the same ceremony to be repeated daily. The sacrament culminates with a blessing (*awatun*) used for a person returning after being lost, now that the girl has completed her term on the margins of society to come back as a fully fledged member of the association which unites women from different clans. The initiands, followed by their escorts, crawl through the corral gate and an elderly couple sprinkle (*akiwat*) black cotton soil (*aro*) over them with the following commands of blessing: *Toyara, tobara, torwyuta ngidwe ngulu alalak, topolo, talalata, tomojong kinwaka Akuj* (Pazzaglia 1982:127; 'Live! Be rich! Give birth to a great many children! Become great! Multiply! Become old! Give light to God!').

Charismatic Women

Even more neglected is women's more explicit religious activity. Naturally the focus has been on the men's *akiriket* as a public, daytime ceremony. A woman may have her shrine to a disturbed spirit under the eaves of her hut, but that is a family affair only insofar as it affects fertility. Yet women do gather for their own intensely religious meeting. Women in a clan gather in the personal space of one woman (*ekal*) in an *ere*, while the older boys and men are away in a cattle-camp. After dark, when supper has been cleared away, all kneel, haunches on ankles, in a circle. Children are unavoidably present. They chant and clap with the object of attracting a spirit into one of the women. They believe that this occurrence could be seen as a woman manifestly went into an ecstatic trance. Her face would change and she would stand up and shake or dance. If privileged, she would receive a word of knowledge about some domestic matter that could help somebody unknown to them. There was nothing grotesque, fearful or erotic in the occasion, just a welcome sense of the numinous, and all went to their huts quiet and satisfied about midnight.

This domestic smoothing of the uncertain was a contrast to the formal, public sacrifices of the men. This undercover spiritual freedom is perhaps an antistructural response to the comprehensive hegemony of the male-dominated sacrifice, though it hardly threatens male governance. It is a women's affair, and fits well into theory of ecstatic religion that confers a sense of spiritual power on the marginal (Lewis 1971). Karamojong women are not generally marginal to the culture, though they clearly are to the *akiriket*, being forbidden either to be present or to eat the roast meat of the sacrifice. Furthermore their nutrition depends to a larger extent on the crops they can harvest, while herders in the cattle-camp can still grow to a disproportionate height on a diet of blood and milk. Certainly, despite Gray (2000), women in an *ere* family do not consider themselves the losers, and, compared with women in neighbouring districts, they are not. Agents of development have found women to be more conservative than the men (Smith, P. 1987:9). Concerning relations with outsiders or with those suspect members of the community whom they may accuse of tying up the rain through actions not according to custom, they can be extremely vocal and impossible to handle. A man or his power can be ruined by women united on the warpath.

Women's Healing

Women on the directions of an *amuron* can gather to engage the spirits anywhere for healing purposes. In the backyard of a Kaabong town house women and girls, totally independent of men, were rhythmically drumming on plastic jerry-cans and tins with sticks, or shaking plastic bottles, or drumming on a gourd in a basin of water. They were singing repetitively to chase the spirits (*ngipian*) and spirits of the madness (*ngikerep*). The songs recalled the names of place and objects associated with a spirit (*ekipye*). A black goat was tethered nearby. Though participants asserted it had nothing to do with the performance, it was there for a reason, and it is possible that the spirits could be induced into it or the water. Spirits have to be chased, so the more noise the better. A woman of 30–37 years, obviously suffering psychologically, was said to be sick, and her friends, on their initiative, were trying to find out the particular sickness. This would happen when the spirit manifested itself in a girl who would dance and jump, or in a drummer who would go into a trance. If the spirit did not manifest itself, they could do nothing.

Source: Ben Knighton

Photograph 9.2 Women's healing session, Kaabong

There was little sign of spirit possession, and the participants were trying to cure a long illness. An old lady wanted an informant to resume drumming, and was angry that the patient was distracted. No great conflict was felt with church adherence. A male *emuron* was sceptical of the efficacy of this treatment for mental illness and felt it could do more harm than good: it 'can make a person worse in the brain' (J21). Yet the women take no heed of men's opinions, whether Christian or traditional, of their affairs. The participants would engage in this lengthy ritual once a week on average.

Some women (*ngakalemak*) can heal by using the technique of rubbing the skin with an ear of bulrush millet or a soft sisal ball, sucking out the disease, and then picking foreign bodies out of the skin. There are many other methods used by women, especially *ngamuron* for healing, yet only research on traditional birth attendants has been done (Graham 1999). Some women are able to charge a fee and are known as witches by the educated, despite their wholesome intentions. Healing is not a closed system, when no system provides most of the solutions, and women have been very open to the Church's primary health care programme, including vaccinations and eye operations, continuing a pragmatic response rather than adopting a scientific world-view. With fewer facilities, Ngakaramojong health statistics are considerably better than in neighbouring Kitgum (Oxfam 2001:36). HIV/AIDS and orphans are rare.

Such spirit-religion may only be an isolated innovation from Lwo sources, but since women are trans-clan after marriage, it is unlikely to be confined. It fills a religious gap and fits women being more concerned with spirits and men with the structured worship of a sky-god, disdaining spirits. While it is the rôle of old men to pray for rain from the Creator, it is the rôle of women to draw water for the family, and spirits (*ngipian*) are present there, enjoying the dipping of gourds. The stories of *ngipian* belong to women and children, but are of no consequence to men until something serious happens. Though women recognize that their spirit-religion may be a problem for Christian Europeans and their own men, it is very much part of their life and can be happily practised in tandem with church attendance. It is the religious practice into which their children are first enculturated. It is at the men's sacrifice, marriage and the combined dances that their ululations are to be heard at their loudest.

While their more distinctive religion has more in common with their Uganda neighbours than the austere customs of their men, there is very little sign that there is a movement to displace the dominance, with it concomitant obligations for the whole culture, of the male *akiriket*. They invoke specific blessings for women of all ages.

Leader	*Assembled*
Granddaughters in this home, be there!	Be there! ...
O Jie, be happy!	Be happy! ...
Our grandmothers, be happy!	Be happy! ...

The Jie,	
be there!	Be there! ...
Brides,	
be there!	Be there! ...
A beautiful head, my daughter's head,	
be there!	It is there!
Be there!	It is there!
Be there!	It is there!
Be there!	It is there!
Be there!	It is there!
Be there!	It is there!
You say like that, it is there!	
Even if[11] it is a girl in the womb of the girl,	
let it be there!	Be there!
Be there!	Be there!
Be there!	Be there!
(Singing while women are ululating with happiness.)	

Every girl or woman wants to be a bride and a mother. Women's happiness is necessary for the good life, and often they appear to have that condition rather than the *Angst* haunting so many cultures of the postmodern world. They have discretion over many affairs and a loud voice in the homestead. Women can be the more conservative sex, and it is they who create a hullabaloo against any who bring unwelcome or suspect change and innovation.

Of course the culture yields casualties. A few are able to improve themselves and find roles as Ugandan citizens, while thousands lose their patronage or their wealth in cattle, so escape to other cultures or non-agripastoral livelihoods. Yet even those who succeed do not strike envy in those who stay true to their forebears. Most recusants have to deny their Karamojong ethnicity in order to survive elsewhere. On the other hand there is always the possibility of being welcomed back as a participant in perpetuating the pastoral values and customs at home, so long as a family-head agrees.

4 Religious Innovation

In most of Africa the study of traditional religion, indeed the whole culture and modern history of a people, needs to be understood much more than it has been as interpenetrated with Christian mission and church. Among the Karamojong and their nomadic pastoralist neighbours it is different. Christian mission has been there for three-quarters of a century and has been studied elsewhere (Knighton 1990:I,389–525), but lasting effects of interaction in fusion or reaction are remarkably insignificant. As with other strangers who have had an interventionist agenda motivating enough for those determined enough to brave the insecurity, the

---

[11] The 'even if' concession also applies in the opposite direction to the cursing of a woman. A male is first choice for both the blessing of progeny and the curse of evil-doing, yet women too are valued, responsible human beings, who are also subjects of life and death.

Karamojong have watched the Christians and appropriated little more than what they needed to continue their traditions. Whatever conflicted they soon rejected. If being baptized in a denomination or enrolled in a school gave access to food in time of famine, or any other benefit, then it could support the interests of the community. Since the church did not demand cattle, it could be long tolerated. Yet, without the wealth of the people, the church can only remain poor and marginal. Agricultural and water resources development was economically valuable and could make its agents friends, but they did not warrant the abandonment or reform of any traditional ceremony. Even with no official fire-maker, the demands of the agronomist could not prevail over an unspoken ceremony for the section to start planting.

The Karamojong response is typified by the life-story of one man, Israel Lokong. Having lost his mother, he left home as a young man without responsibility and, through contacts with Christian missions and other lifestyles in and from neighbouring districts, he was converted in 1926. He was recruited by the new Evangelical mission in 1929 and was soon employed as teacher, interpreter and 'headman' over all the routine of the station. Back at home near Kotido he seceded from his *ere* family in the early 1940s, which was seriously affected by what was believed to be prolonged witchcraft from outside and by the fears and accusations involved (Gulliver 1955:113; 19.6.90 Letter). Lokong was one of few Christians in Najie then, and he had been taught to see his countryside bound with 'the fearsome chains' of the devil (Paget Wilkes 1932a:24). That his wife was Karimojong and Christian deepened others' suspicion, so they built a new house 100 yards away. Despite the clash of cultural views, they were still considered as part of the *ere* family, maintaining reciprocal stock rights in the family herd. By the 1940s, they had ceased to be active in the church, and in the 1970s, though living in Lokong's old age at Kanawat, never attended worship (Rowland 1.8.90 Letter). Instead Lokong became 'an outstanding informant' on the traditional history of the Jie, even if he had come to interpret religion in terms of 'souls' (Lamphear 1972:339,473). The capacity of the Karamojong to reabsorb its rebels should never be underestimated.

The philosophy graduate from Makerere can return to be a warrior. Two daughters of the Jie élite have graduated from university (J11), but only one in a hundred in the whole of Kotido District are ever enrolled in secondary school. One quarter may be enrolled in primary school, but the drop-out rate at both levels is 88 per cent (Oxfam 2001:36). If the future of the Church is still considered to lie in education, she is going nowhere. The culture remains predominantly oral, speaking Ngakaramojong. It is true that many Karamojong have been baptized, but few contribute much to the church. All my Karimojong informants had 'Christian' names, 60 per cent of the Dodosô and 68 per cent of the Jie. Over 23 per cent were confirmed in the church, including three pastors. That Christians, nominal or not, as with Lamphear's research, should provide such a fertile source on Karamojong traditions, past and present, and validated longitudinally, is itself a telling datum. Despite many attempts of Christian mission to replace or displace Karamojong culture, failure has been almost constant. In the very long run, Christian Karamojong tend to grow in their appreciation of their people's traditions, while mission agencies despair at the capacity of the churches to be self-supporting. If the keeping of cattle is not ethical for Christians, how can the church be built on the local economy? She remains an alternative lifestyle at its purest, not even a counter-culture, for her adherents do not have the means to marry and reproduce among themselves alone. Mirzeler and Young (2000:426) are profoundly mistaken to take Christian adherence as evidence of Karamojong incorporation into the state.[12]

5 Vanishing Tribes?

European observers were lamenting that traditional African culture was evaporating around Mount Kenya, even in the first decade of the last century (Orde Browne 1925). Yet these are crocodile tears, for it is necessary for the self-belief of the West that Africa be associated with savage backwardness, and also that Western contact cannot help but dispel it. These insidious presuppositions are perpetuated in television series such as Anglia's *Vanishing Tribes of Africa* (Root 1971) and Channel 4's *Disappearing World*, as well as global ethno-tourism (Turton 2002: 2004). It is possible for a religion to lose its shape and authenticity.

> There was a hum, and a tiny airplane flew over, the police plane looking for raiders. But Uri thought the police were looking for sacrifices. People attending sacrifices have been spotted from the air and then arrested, for the government believed sacrifices were preludes to raids ... Uri watched it go. 'Our religion is dying,' he said again, 'and the government wants it to.' (Marshall Thomas 1965:61f)

Indeed both officials and missionaries were working for the introduction of a more modern world-view. Uri need not have worried, for his religion shows signs of outlasting both imperial and national governance. The Karamojong are continually presented with innovations as the globalizing world grows in its incapacity to restrain itself, but to suppose that determines all responses to irreversible change is to jump to conclusions.

> Nevertheless there remains the problem of discerning between novel features that are historically unique and recurrent aspects that are characteristic rather than unique. Expressing this as a 'problem of generations' is to suggest that earlier transitions may also have involved independent striving among younger men at the expense of their obligations to their seniors and a recurrent aspect of career pattern ... The problem facing the interpreter of ethnography is to strike a balance between novelty and persistence, and

---

[12] They cite a spectacular increase in the number of Catholic converts to 150 000 by the 1980s, but this reveals a poor understanding of the realities of Karamoja and a willingness to believe anyone's story. Even if as large a proportion of the population of Karamoja as 43 per cent had been baptized, this was due to an aggressive, indiscriminate baptismal policy. In the 1979–82 and other famines, joining the Roman Catholic Church was for many Karamojong akin to signing on for famine relief (J11). Only a small fraction attends church, and the drop-out rate is high. The Verona Fathers admit that their church has made few fundamental changes to lives (Knighton 1990:I,480–85). Now that their resources are dwindling with 'indigenous' Ugandan leadership, the church's appeal is reducing.

to ascertain how far 'change' is no more than traditional society in modern dress. (Spencer 1998:232f)

Tradition was not invented for the Karamojong by colonial rule, which was minimalist in its governance for all but the last decade of its half-century reign, so there was little 'transforming flexible custom into hard prescription' (Ranger 1983:212). As soon as any ethnography is done, there is the danger of that happening, but Karamojong society is not literally led, and my distribution of 20 copies of Lamphear (1976) seems to have ossified nothing, for the purchasers have lost their copies to the few educated lads still thirsty to understand. One of them categorically refutes his schema for Jie generation-sets (J11), so Karamojong understand their culture better than some researchers who receive non-committal answers suppose. They are nobody's fools, being justifiably suspicious of the motives, attitudes and agendas of interlopers, which is not to say that they cannot be generous and tolerant in their friendship with those who live amongst them.

Africans have their own ability to invent tradition. My students in Kenya were very quick to identify anything that happened twice in the college as a tradition. Neither they nor the Karamojong should be denied this essential feature of human living. As Vansina (1990:257) says, 'Traditions are historical phenomena which occur everywhere.' Yet the Karamojong do not need to invent tradition to bolster new and artificial social institutions, for much of their tradition is given, and so long as they can decide collectively through many small incidents how that givenness is to be interpreted and applied, they will adhere to it. Rather traditions enculturate their identities, because Karamojong want continuity with them, and since their traditional politics continue through colonialism and independence, sustaining a relatively large measure of autonomy, they have the power to reinterpret them. They are their traditions and the ideas, images and symbols which they embody give them a sure identity. As a former Jie County Chief (J7) put it, 'Our culture is not changing: only improving.'

Ranger's observation (1983:247) of pre-colonial Africa remains equally true for the Karamojong before, during and after the colonial period: 'These societies had certainly valued custom and continuity but custom was loosely defined and infinitely flexible. Custom helped to maintain a sense of identity but it also allowed for an adaptation so spontaneous and natural that it was often unperceived.' The authority of elders has always been challenged, which itself is the source of current and traditional identity for the Turkana and Karimojong as descended from youths who rebelled against their fathers in Najie and absconded with their cattle, and for the Jie and Karimojong as the withered old men who have stayed behind. Any attempt to infer the death of tradition from elders' laments at their loss of power are scotched by the same story being told over 90 years ago, when Tufnell observed that they 'have no authority over the younger men who, to any remonstrance, simply reply "You did the same thing in your day and now it is our turn"' (Barber 1968:148). In any case, 'age systems are bound up with problems of succession' (Spencer 1998:5). It is true here that the 'full expression of collective identities ... depends on their articulation by elites' (Ranger 1998:148), but that élite comprises the elders who represent every homestead in the political unit, giving a representative democracy the style of which England has not known since before the Norman conquest. Youth and women are relatively marginalized, but the latter are observed to be a more conservative force in society.[13] Even though elders may pursue their own interest, they may also learn to transcend it. 'Elders are gods' (J8).

Developmentalists reject tradition as an independent variable, or cause of behaviour, replacing it with economic considerations (Baker 1974:11). Development is primarily an economic aim and it is difficult for its practitioners to envisage any other *telos* (end) than the developed economies of the West. Randall Baker published a number of studies with a view to planning the economic future of Karamoja. He asserted, on the basis of his study of *ad hoc* imperial measures, that there is 'no middle road' between the traditional pastoral system and a planned alteration of 'the whole basic strategy', executed on the back of detailed research (Baker 1977:155). 'What we are witnessing now are the painful death throes of a traditional order, and it is no longer of any value to continue treating symptoms. It is necessary now to build a whole new system: nothing less will do' (Baker 1974:17). Yet traditional Karamojong culture in all of its aspects has not died, is not vanishing, and will not disappear with the present government disarmament programme, despite the torture. The stubborn fact of religion may yet prove that it was not so alien to real human freedom.

To ignore the visible changes coming even to the more remote settled locations would be folly. There were, it is acknowledged (J11) 'more shops and stores, markets, cash, and cattle sales' because of the peculiar conjunction of peaceful transport encouraged by Museveni, abundant cattle raided from neighbouring peoples and hunger due to crop failure for four years up to the good harvest in 2001.[14] Unusually men are prepared to sell cattle to buy beer, maize, radios and clothes. Will this trend towards commoditization at last bring Karamoja into Uganda? Are the Karamojong about to come post-traditional?

Jürgen Habermas's view of post-traditional society is one that develops as Europe has done, leaving traditional society on the bottom rung of an unavoidable ladder, for he writes of the 'irresistible irony of the world-historical process of enlightenment' (1987:155). He assumes a complete dichotomy between postmodernity and monotheism: 'growing autonomy can come to pass only to the extent that the constraints of material reproduction no longer hide behind the mask of a rationally impenetrable, basic normative consensus, that is to say, behind the authority of the sacred' (ibid.:145). Yet he finds his integral and normative concept for social theory empirically strongest in 'archaic societies, where structures of linguistically mediated, normatively guided interaction immediately constitute the supporting social structures' (ibid.:156). However nostalgia does not fit Karamojong culture; it is not archaic, but contemporary and vital, preserving autonomy for families at least through the generations, without resort or capitulation to such an evolutionary post-traditionalism.

---

[13] For example, the wives in Alwyn (1998) complaining about their husbands giving up raiding, even though it is because he has achieved his objective of obtaining them with the booty of his raids.

[14] However, transport and trade depend on security, which is still being contested as the army tortures local Karamojong leaders (*UN IRIN* 8.3.02).

David Simon (1997:3) sees 'post-traditionalism, emerging as a result of development failures and a reassertion of the durability of indigenous cultures and identities. These new forms have much in common with postmodernity and post-colonialism'. This is because 'we have a rich tapestry of crosscutting continuity and change, of old, new, and hybrid identities, of reason and reaction, of gender and power relations, of the preservation versus the transcendence of categories, and of how and by whom they are negotiated, defined, and safeguarded' (ibid.:35). Yet the historical lesson is that this rich tapestry has always been there, and the Karamojong make unlikely glocalists. Are the Karamojong at heart traditionalists who are bound to present a reactionary front against any social or communicative action? *Ngitalyo* (customs) are the fall-back position and the tested option. Decorations distinguish each age-class change in order to express particular belonging across the political community (J15), but they are only functional.

The community is greater than an individual, or family, clan, age-set or even generation-set. Karamojong do not believe in the passing decorations and fashion associated with any. Women always have to change clan; in ordinarily wearing modern dress, they have suppressed the most frequently seen *ngitalyo*. Thus Karamojong do not believe in *etal* (custom) as more than a cultural standard, and are not traditionalists in the sense of trusting exclusively to past customs. They rely on *asapanů*, the age-system, which rolls the whole society into the future and 'is the divine ordering of society' (J16).

That the Karamojong nevertheless see their institutions as having continuity and stability is, I suggest, due largely to their age-system and to the time dimension which it provides. However, the new generations which displace the old also recreate them: individually by the practice of naming children after members of the grandparental generation and collectively by the symbolic association of alternate generation-sets. Successive phases of Karamojong society, as its personnel are replaced, can, moreover, always be accommodated within the span of a single age cycle and thus blended into each other. The result is a sense of social continuity, of time and traditions continually recreated and relived (Dyson-Hudson 1963:399).

Ultimately Karamojong uphold the *telos* of the age-system to which gathering age continually approximates, Akujů, the God to Whom they pray at the sacrifice and Who answers their prayers to deliver them from whatever disequilibrium or crisis they might find themselves in (Knighton 1999). Thus the vitality of traditional Karamojong religion continues, not so much the legitimation of a certain social structure as the heart of a culture, living by the faith of its people. In this the Karamojong are not of a strange order: it is just that they repeatedly invent their communities in unusual continuity with their past in order to preserve their autonomy for the future. They are not in a world of their own, but steadfastly refuse to be homogenized by someone else's. However the one who would be close to Akujů might take His discontent with bloodshed and His universal accessibility more seriously.

Bibliography

A Abbreviations of sources

BCMS	Bible Churchmen's Missionary Society, archives then in 251 Lewisham Way, London
CMS	Church Missionary Society, archives in University of Birmingham
EA	Entebbe Archives, Uganda
edn	edition
ed.(s)	editor(s)
FAM	Friends of Africa Mission
FAO	Food and Agriculture Organization, United Nations
FO(CP)	Foreign Office (Confidential Prints), now in the Public Records Office, Kew
HMSO	Her Majesty's Stationery Office
IAI	International African Institute
KNA	Kenya National Archives, Nairobi
MM	Missionary Messenger/Mission Magazine (Bible Churchmen's Missionary Society)
nd	no date
PP	Parliamentary Papers, now in the Public Records Office, Kew
RHO	Rhodes House, Oxford
SCM	Student Christian Movement Press
SIM	Sudan Interior Mission, archives in Scarborough, Ontario, Canada
SOAS	School of Oriental and African Studies, University of London
SPCK	Society for the Propagation of Christian Knowledge
vol.	volume

B Primary sources

Key to Indices

D0–14	Dodosô
J1–33	Jie
L1	Lugbara (a Central Sudanic people based in West Nile)
M1	Mosingo Karimojong
N1–2	Nyakwai
P1–13	Pian Karimojong
Po1	Pore

S1   Somali
T1–2   Teso
This is total of 69 local informants.

C   Secondary sources

A full bibliography for Karamoja is attempted here, as well as giving some other intellectual material for this book and neighbouring peoples. In fact 908 items have been collated here that refer to Karamoja in any way, its peoples, animals or places. This total is about 850 more than in any existing bibliography on Karamoja. This section serves as a simple index to references in the text, and backgound material, as well as a full bibliography for Karamoja, since all writing on Karamoja reflects the interaction of African and occidental cultures. Those writings known to refer directly to any matter in Karamoja are asterisked *. A modified Harvard system provides the form for references and notation. The nature of each work, whether collected work, monograph, periodical article, contribution to collected work, unpublished thesis, mimeograph or typescript, is distinguished in the notation with only substantial published titles being italicized. Collected works to which noted articles contribute are normally included separately under the editor's name with a short reference being given with the author and title of the article.

Abrahams, RG
* 1971: 'Reaching an Agreement over Bridewealth in Labwor' in Richards and Kuper 1971:202–15
* 1972: 'Spirits, Twins and Ashes in Labwor' in La Fontaine 1972
* 1978: 'Aspects of Labwor Age and Generation Grouping and Related Systems' in Baxter and Almagor 1978:37–67
* 1986: 'Dual Organization in Labwor?' *Ethnos* 51/1–2:88–194
Abu-Lughod, L
1991: 'Writing against Culture' in Fox 1991
Acquaviva, SS
   1979: *The Decline of the Sacred in Industrial Society* Oxford: Blackwell
Adam, S
   1981: 'The Importance of Nubia: A link between Central Africa and the Mediterranean' in UNESCO 1981:II,226–43
Adams, WY
   1982: 'The Coming of Nubian Speakers to the Nile Valley' in Ehret and Posnansky 1982
Adoko, Judy
* 1997: Did the constitution mean to legalise customary tenure or to lay the foundation for the demise of customary tenure? Oxford: Oxfam
ADOL
* 2001: 'Arms Trafficking in the Border Regions of Sudan, Uganda and Kenya' Kampala: Action for Development of Local Communities

* 2002: 'Karamoja Response to Disarmament: 60 months later' Kampala: Action for Development of Local Communities

Adong, Florence
* 1993: 'The East African Missions of the Bible Churchmen's Missionary Society 1929–1962' MA dissertation, Trinity College, Bristol

Aerni, MJ
* 1969: 'An Anthropological Report for the Karamoja Children's Relief Service' Moroto

Africa Research Bulletin
* 27.2.2000, quoting *New Vision* 17, 14004 B, Political, Social, and Cultural Series

Aherne, Mollie
* 1987: 'Adult Education for Women in Karamoja' *The Outlook* Winter pp. 200–205

Ahmed, Abdel Ghaffar M, Abdel Ati, Hassan A, *et al*.
* 1996: *Managing Scarcity:Human adaptation in East African drylands* Proceedings of a regional workshop held on 24–26 August 1995, Addis Ababa, Ethiopia: OSSREA

Akol, Joshua WL
* 1959: 'Ngakarimojong Grammar Lotome' mimeograph
* 1965: 'Orthography of Akarimojong' mimeograph
* 1966: *Ngiemuto a Ngikarimojong* Nairobi: East African Literature Bureau
* 1983: 'Socio-Cultural Roots of the Disaster' paper at Uganda Red Cross Conference, Kampala 19–21.3.85

Almagor, Uri
   1971: 'The Social Organization of the Dassanetch' PhD thesis, University of Manchester
   1989: 'The Dialectic of Generation Moeties in an East African Society' in Maybury-Lewis and Almagor 1978:143–69

Almond, DC
* 1962: 'Explanation of the Geology of sheet 15 (Kitgum)' Entebbe: Government Printer

Alnwick, DJ
* 1981: 'Towards a Food Aid Policy for Karamoja' Kampala: UNICEF, mimeograph
* 1985: 'The 1980 Famine in Karamoja' in Dodge and Wiebe 1985

Aloka, Aloysius L
* 1992: 'Narratives and Songs in Karimojong Oral Literature' MA thesis, Makerere University, Kampala; also London: SOAS
* 2000: *Iteo Alive* Kampala: Fountain Publishers

Amaza, Godfrey Ondoga ori
* 1998: *Museveni's Long March: From guerrilla to statesman* Kampala: Fountain

Ambrose, Stanley H
   1982: 'Archaeology and Linguistic Reconstructions of History in East Africa' in Ehret and Posnansky 1982:104–57

Amnesty International
   1985: *Uganda Six Years after Amin* London: Amnesty International
   1988: *Annual Report* London: Amnesty International

Amselle, JL
* 1974: 'Les ethnologues, le ciel at l'enfer' *Cahiers d'Etudes Africaines* 14/2:54
* 1979: 'Le sauvage méchant' *Le Sauvage à la Mode* pp. 243–58

Anderson, David M
    1984: 'Depression, Dustbowl, Demography and Drought: The colonial state and soil conservation in East Africa during the 1930s' *African Affairs* 82:321–43

Anderson, David M and DH Johnson (eds)
    1995: *Revealing Prophets: Prophecy in East Africa today* London: James Currey

Anon.
* 1933: *Ekitabu ŋolo akilip ŋa nituŋa dadaaŋ* London: SPCK
* 1938: *Abuku lina arukitor: Liowsio ka akilip ka lakiro ja Akuju (Hymns, prayers, and scripture texts for use in Karamoja, Taposa, Turkana)* London: SPCK
* 1951a: *Acts: Ɖiticisyo a ŋikiyakya* London: British and Foreign Bible Society
* 1951b: *John: Eemut ikwaŋ inapei kigiria Yokona ŋolokwaŋan* London: British and Foreign Bible Society
* 1957: *Ngakilipeta ka Ngieothiyo* London: SPCK
* 1964: *Review of Recent Progress in the Work of Bible Churchmen's Missionary Society* London: Bible Churchmen's Missionary Society
* 1974: *The New Testament in Karimojong: Akitutuketŋina kitete* Kampala: United Bible Societies
* 1981: *Akarimojong: Prayer and Hymnbook* Kampala: Centenary Publishing House
* 1982: 'Karamoja Update' *Disasters* 6/1:70f

Archer, GF
* 1963: *Personal and Historical Memoirs of an East African Administrator* Edinburgh: Oliver and Boyd

Associated Christian Churches of Kenya
* 1982: 'Karapokot Water Supply Project: Application to NORAD for financial support' Nairobi: ACCK

Austin, HH
* 1899: 'Journeys to the North of Uganda II: Lake Rudolf' *Geographical Journal* 14/2:148–55 Aug
* 1903: *With Macdonald to Uganda* London: Edward Arnold

Avirgan, T and Honey, M
    1982: *War in Uganda* London: Zed

Ayo, S
* 1963: 'Why are the Karimojong still Backward?' *Kangole TTC Call* 2

Ayoo, SJ
* 1995: 'The Ik Research' Kampala: Oxfam

Azarya, V
    1996: *Nomads and the State in Africa* Aldershot: Ashgate

Baker, P Randall
    nd: 'Sociological factors in the Commercialization of Cattle in Africa' pamphlet
* 1967a: 'Environmental Influences on Cattle Marketing in Karamoja' Department of Geography, Makerere University, Occasional Paper 5
* 1967b: 'A Geographical Appraisal of Karamoja as a beef production area' Faculty of Agriculture, Makerere University, African Studies Program RDR 43

* 1968a: 'Problems of Cattle Raiding in Karamoja, Uganda' in Berger 1968
* 1968b: 'Problems of the Cattle Trade in Karamoja, Uganda' in Berger 1968: 211–26
* 1968c: 'The Distribution of Cattle in Uganda' *East African Geographical Review* 6:63–72
* 1972: '"Development" and the pastoral peoples of Karamoja: An example of the treatment of symptoms' study for XIIIth International African Seminar, on 'Pastoralism in Tropical Africa' Niamey, Niger, in Monod 1975:187–205
* 1974: 'Perceptions of Pastoralism' University of East Anglia: Development Studies Discussion Paper 3; also in Smith, AJ 1976
* 1975a: 'The Administrative Trap: The conflict between administration and ecology' University of East Anglia, Development Studies Discussion Paper 5
* 1975b: 'Pastoralism and Progress: Readings on the development of traditional cattle herding areas in Africa' University of East Anglia, Development Studies Reprint 6
* 1976: 'Cattle Marketing in Karamoja' University of East Anglia Occasional Paper
* 1977: 'Polarisation: Stages in the environmental impact of alien ideas on a semi-pastoral society' in O'Keefe and Wisner 1977:151–71
* 1979: 'Perception de l'état pastoral, interprétation du rôle sociale du bétail en Afrique' *Environnement Africain* 46: Supplement 3–17

Baker, Samuel W
* 1874: *Ismaila: A narrative of the expedition to central Africa for the suppression of the slave trade* 2 vols London: Macmillan

Baldick, Julian
   1998: *Black God* London: IB Tauris

Banton, M (ed.)
   1966: *Anthropological Approaches to the Study of Religion* London: Tavistock

Barber, James P
* 1962: 'The Karamoja District of Uganda' *Journal of African History* 3/1:111–24
* 1964a: 'The Macdonald Expedition to the Nile' *Uganda Journal* 28/1:1–14
* 1964b: 'Karamoja in 1910' *Uganda Journal* 28/1:15–23
   1964c: 'The Black Man's Burden: Problems Facing East African States' University of New South Wales, typescript
* 1965: 'The Moving Frontier of British Imperialism in Northern Uganda' *Uganda Journal* 29/1:27–43
* 1968: *Imperial Frontier* Nairobi: East African Publishing House

Barrett, Anthony
   1977: *Incarnating the Church in Turkana* Eldoret: Gaba, Spearhead 52
   1987: *Dying and Death among the Turkana* Eldoret: Gaba, Spearhead 97–8
   1998: *Sacrifice and Prophecy in Turkana Cosmology* Nairobi: Paulines

Barrow, JD and Tipler, FJ
   1986: *The Anthropic Cosmological Principle* Oxford: Clarendon

Barth, Fredrik
* 1974: 'On Responsibility and Humanity: Calling a Colleague to Account' *Current Anthropology* 15/1:99–102 Mar

Barton, Juxon
   1921: 'Notes on the Suk Tribe of Kenya Colony' *Journal of the Royal Anthropological Institute* 51:82–99

Bascom, N and Herskovits, MJ (eds)
   1959: *Continuity and Change in African Cultures* Chicago: University Press
Batailles, Georges
   1989: *Theory of Religion* New York: Zone
Bataringaya, BK (chairman)
* 1961: *Report of the Karamoja Security Committee* Kampala: Government of Uganda
Battle, Vincent M
* 1970: 'Selective Conservation in Culture Contact: A Study of Educational Adaptation in the Karamoja District of Uganda' MA dissertation in Faculty of Teachers College, Columbia University
* 1975: 'An Historical Analysis of Educational Development in Karamoja District' *Makerere Historical Journal* 1/1:65–83
Battle, VM and Lyons, CN (eds)
* 1970: *Essays in the History of African Education* New York: Teachers' College Press
Baxter, Paul TW
   1972: 'Absence Makes the Heart Grow Fonder. Some Suggestions Why Witchcraft Accusations are Rare among East African Pastoralists' in Gluckman 1972: 163–91
   1975: 'Some consequences of sedentarization for social relationships' in Monod 1975
   1978: 'Boran Age-sets and Generation-Sets' in Baxter and Almagor 1978: 151–82
Baxter, PTW and Almagor, Uri
* 1978: *Age, Generation, and Time* London: Hurst
Baxter, PTW with Richard Hogg (eds)
   1987: 'Property, Poverty and People' Manchester: University of Manchester
Beaton, AC
   1952: 'The Bari: Clan and age-class systems' *Sudan Notes and Records* 19: 109–46
Beattie, John HM
   1973: 'Understanding Traditional African Religion: A Comment on Horton' *Second Order* 2/2:2–11
   1980: 'On Understanding Sacrifice' in Bourdillon and Fortes 1980:29–44
Beattie, John HM and Lienhardt, RG (eds)
   1975: *Studies in Social Anthropology* Oxford: Oxford University Press
Beattie, John HM and Middleton, John
   1969: *Spirit Mediumship and Society in Africa* London: Routledge, Kegan Paul
Becker, G
* 1984: 'The Social Regulation of Sexuality' *Current Perspectives in Social Theory* 5:45–69
Beckwith, Carol and Fisher, Angela
   1999: *African Ceremonies* 2 vols New York: Harry N Abrams
Beidelman, TO
   1966: 'The Ox and Nuer Sacrifice: Some Freudian Hypotheses about Nuer Symbolism' *Man* 1/4:553–67

1971: 'Nuer Priests and Prophets: Charisma, authority, and power among the Nuer' in Beidelman 1971:375–416
1971: (ed.) *The Translation of Culture: Essays to EE Evans-Prtichard* London: Tavistock
* 1973: 'Review of Colin M Turnbull, The Mountain People' *Africa* 43/2:170f
1981: 'The Nuer concept of *thek* and the meaning of sin' *History of Religions* 21: 126–55 Nov
1982: *Colonial Evangelism: A socio-historical study of an East African mission at the grassroots* Bloomington: Indiana University Press

Beinart, William
2000: 'African History and Environmental History' *African Affairs* 99/395: 269–302

Bell, Catherine
1992: *Ritual Theory, Ritual Practice* Oxford: Oxford University Press

Bell, WDM
* 1923: *The Wanderings of an Elephant Hunter* London: Country Life republished by Neville Spearman 1958
* 1949: *Karamojo Safari* London: Victor Gollancz republished by New York: Harcourt Brace 1964
* 1960: *Bell of Africa* London: Neville Spearman

Belshaw, D, Averr, S, Hogg, R and Obin, R
* 1996: 'Report of the Evaluation Mission: Integrated development in Karamoja' Norwich: Overseas Development Group/New York: UNCDF

Belshaw, D and Malinga M.
* 1999: 'The Kalashnikov Economies of the Eastern Sahel: Cumulative or Cyclical Differentiation Between Nomadic Pastoralists?' Paper presented at the First Workshop of the Study Group on Conflict and Security of the Development Studies Association, South Bank University, March

Bender, M Lionel
1971: 'The Languages of Ethiopia' *Anthropological Linguistics* 13/5:165–288
1976: (ed.) *The Non-Semitic Languages of Ethiopia* East Lansing: Michigan State University
1981: (ed.) *Peoples and Cultures of the Ethio-Sudan Borderland* East Lansing: Michigan State University
* 1996: *The Nilo-Saharan Languages: An essay in classification* Munich: LINCOM
* 1997: *The Nilo-Saharan Languages: A comparative essay* Munich: LINCOM
* 2000: 'Nilo-Saharan' in Heine and Nurse 2000:43–73

Bennett, Clinton
1996: *In Search of the Sacred: Anthropology and the study of religions* London: Cassell

Bennett, G
1952: 'The Eastern Boundary of Uganda in 1902' *Uganda Journal* 23/1:69–72 Mar

Berger, H (ed.)
1968: *Ostafrikanische Studien* Nürnberg: Alexander University

Berleant-Schiller, R and Shanklin, E (eds)
* 1970: *The Keeping of Animals* Totowa: Allanheld Osmun
Berman, Bruce and Lonsdale, John
   1992: *Unhappy Valley: Clan, Class and State in Colonial Kenya* 2 vols London: James Currey
Bernardi, Bernardo
   1952: 'The Age-System of the Nilo-Hamitic Peoples: A Critical Evaluation' *Africa* 22:316–22
   1959: *Mugwe: A failing prophet* Oxford: Oxford University Press
   1970: 'Dieu et l'absolu chez les primitifs' in Catholic Church Secretariatus pro Non-Christianis 1970: *Religions: Thèmes fondamentaux pour une connaissance dialogique* Rome: Àncora pp. 237–65
   1977: (ed.) *The Concept and Dynamics of Culture* The Hague: Mouton
   1985: *Age-Class Systems* Cambridge: Cambridge University Press
Bertinazzo, G
* 1981: 'History of Missionary Involvement in Education in Uganda and Particularly in Karamoja' Moroto, mimeograph
* 1982: 'Notes on the Karimojong Grammar/Introduction to Karimojong Grammar' Moroto
Best, Günter
   1978: *Von Rindernomadismus zum Fischfang: Der soziokulturelle Wandel bei den Turkana am Rudolf-See Kenya* Wiesbaden: Studien zur Kulturkunde
   1983: *Culture and Language of the Turkana, NW Kenya* Heidelberg: Carl Winter, Universitätsverlag
Biellik, RJ and Henderson, PL
* 1985: 'Mortality, Nutritional Status and Diet during Famine in Karamoja, Uganda 1980' *The Lancet* 2:1330–33 121281; also in Dodge and Wiebe 1985
Bishop, Mrs and Ruffel, D
   nd: 'History of Upper Nile Diocese' Department of Religious Studies, Makerere University, manuscript
Bishop, WW
* 1958: 'Miocene Mammalia from the Napak Volcanoes, Karamoja, Uganda' *Nature* 182:1480–82
* 1962: 'The Mammalian Fauna and Geomorphological Relations of the Napak Volcanoes, Karamoja' *Geological Survey of Uganda Records* 57–8, Entebbe
Bishop, WW and Clark, JD (eds)
* 1967: *Background to Evolution in Africa* Chicago: University Press
Bishop, WW and Posnansky, M
* 1960: 'Pleistocene Environments and Early Man in Uganda' *Uganda Journal* 24: 44–61
Blake, Gerald H
* 1997: *Imperial Boundary Making: The diary of Captain Kelly and the Sudan–Uganda Boundary Commission of 1913* Oxford: Oxford University Press
Blench, Roger M
   2002 : 'The Classification of Nilo-Saharan' *Afrika und Übersee* 83:293–307
Blench, RM and MacDonald, KC (eds)
   2000 : *Origins and Development of African Livestock: Archaeology, genetics, linguistics, and ethnography* London: UCL Press

Blumenthal, JV
* 1976: 'Le Groupe Karimojong (Ouganda)' in *Encyclopédie Alpha des Peuples du Monde* entier II, 17:82–9

Boccassino, Renato
1939: 'The Nature and Characteristics of the Supreme Being Worshipped among the Acholi of Uganda' *Uganda Journal* 6/4:195–201

Bollig, Michael
* 1990a: 'Ethnic Conflict in North-West Kenya: Polot–Turkana Raiding' *Zeitschrift für Ethnologie* 115:73–90
* 1990b: 'An Outline of Precolonial Pokot History' *Afrikanistische Arbeitspapiere* 23:73–92
* 1993: 'Intra- and Interethnic Conflict in Northwest Kenya: A multicausal analysis of conflict behaviour' *Anthropos* 87:176–84
2000: 'Staging Social Structures: Ritual and social organization in an egalitarian society. The pastoral Pokot of northern Kenya' *Ethnos* 65/3:341–65

Bonté, Pierre
1975: 'Cattle for God: an Attempt at a Marxist Analysis of East African Herdsmen' *Social Compass* 22:381–96
1977: 'Non-stratified Social Formations among Pastoral Nomads' in Friedman, Rowland, J and M (eds) *Evolution of Social Systems* London: Duckworth
* 1979: 'Les sociétés des pasteurs nomades' in *Être nomade aujourd'hui* Neuchatel 29–46
* 1981: 'Les éleveurs d'Afrique de l'Est, sont-ils égalitaires?' *Production Pastorale et Société* 9:23–37

Bourdillon, MEC and Fortes, N
1980: *Sacrifice* London: Academic Press

Bozas, Robert du Bourg de
* 1906: *De la Mer Rouge à L'Atlantique* Paris: Rudeval

Brasnett, J
* 1958: 'The Karasuk Problem' *Uganda Journal* 22/2:113–22 Sept
* 1996: 'Basic Administration' in Brown 1996:25–30

Bredon, RM and Thornton, DD
* 1965: 'Grazing Proposals for South Pian' Ministry of Agriculture, Entebbe, mimeograph

Bredon, RM and Wilson, JG
* 1963: 'The Chemical Composition and Nutritive Value of Grasses from Semi-arid Areas of Karamoja as Related to Ecology and Types of Soil' *East Africa Agriculture and Forestry Journal* 28:134–42

Broch-Due, Vigdis
* 1990: 'The Bodies within the Body: Journeys in Turkana thought and practice' PhD thesis, University of Bergen
1999: 'Creation and the Multiple Female Body: Turkana perpectives on gender and cosmos' in Moore 1999:153–84
* 2000: 'The Fertility of Houses and Herds: Producing kinship and gender among Turkana pastoralists' in Hodgson 2000:165–85

Brown, Colin (ed.)
1980: *The New International Dictionary of NT Theology* 3 vols Exeter: Paternoster

Brown, Douglas and Marcelle, V (eds)
* 1996: *Looking Back at the Uganda Protectorate: Recollections of District Officers* Dalkeith, W Australia: Brown

Brown, LH
1971: 'The Biology of Pastoral Man as a Factor in Conservation' *Biological Conservation* 3/2:93–100

Brown, Monty
* 1989: *Where Giants Trod* London: Quiller

Brumann, Christoph
1999: 'Writing for Culture: Why a successful concept should not be discarded' *Current Anthropology* 40: S1–28

Bryan, Margaret A
* 1945: 'A linguistic no-man's land' *Africa* 15/4:188–205
1959: 'The T/K Languages: a new substratum' *Africa* 29/1:1–21
1968: 'The *N/*K Languages of Africa' *Journal of African Languages* 7/3: 169–217

Bryan, MA and Tucker, AN
* 1948: *The Distribution of the Nilotic and Nilo-Hamitic Languages of Africa* Oxford: Oxford University Press

Bryden, Jessie
* 1974: *Akitutuket ngina Kitete: Ngina a ekapoloniyok ka eketeyiaran Yesu Kristo* Kampala: Bible Society of Uganda

Bundt, C et al.
* 1979: 'Wo ist "vorn"? Sinn und Unsinn entwicklungs-politischen Eingreifens bei ostafrikanische Hirten-nomaden' *Sociologus* 29/1:21–59

Burke, FG
* 1964: *Local Government and Politics in Uganda* New York: Syracuse University Press

Burnett, David G
* 1983: 'Report on Visit to COU Development Project in Karamoja' mimeograph
* 1988: *Unearthly Powers* Eastbourne: Kingsway

Burton, JW
1974: 'Some Nuer Notions of Purity and Danger' *Anthropos* 69:517–36
1987: *A Nilotic World* New York: Greenwood
1991: 'Nilotic Cosmology and the Divination of Atuot Philosophy' in Peek 1991:41–52

Buss, Andreas
2000; 'The Evolution of Western Individualism' *Religion* 30/1:1–25

Butt, AJ
1952: *The Nilotes of the Anglo-Egyptian Sudan and Uganda* London: IAI

Buxton, David R
1970: *The Abyssinians* London: Thames and Hudson

Buxton, Edith
* 1968: *Reluctant Missionary* London: Lutterworth

Buxton, Jean
1973: *Religion and Healing in Mandari* Oxford: Clarendon

Byaruhanga-Akiiki, ABT (ed.)
* 1971: 'Occasional Papers in African Traditional Religion' 5 vols, Department of Religious Studies and Philosophy, Makerere University

Calhoun, JB
* 1975: 'Plight of the Ik and Kaiadilt: a Chilling Possible End for Man' in Bernard, HR (ed.) *The Human Way* New York: Macmillan pp. 383–91

Calvocoressi, Roy
* 2000: 'Blessed are the Peace-makers' *The Door* Oxford May

Cappelletti, R
* 1983: 'La musica dei Karimojong' (Uganda) Un'esperienza di ricerca', Tesi di Laurea, University of Bologna

Carrithers, Michael
  1992: *Why Humans have Cultures: Explaining anthropology and social diversity* Oxford: Oxford University Press

Cartwright, Peter G
* 1965: *Getting a Move On in Karamoja* London: Bible Churchmen's Missionary Society

Casati, Gaetano
* 1891: *Ten Years in Equatoria and the Return with Emin Pasha* London: Frederick Warne

Cefalo, R
* 1972: 'The Diocese of Moroto' *Leadership* Kampala, Aug pp. 49–52

Cernea, MM (ed.)
  1985 *Putting People First* Oxford: Oxford University Press

Chaillé-Long, Charles
  1876: *Central Africa* London: Sampson Low, Marston, Searle, and Rivington

Chidlaw-Roberts, JR
* 1920: *Report on Karamoja District* Entebbe: Government Printer

Christensen, Palle Rolf
* 1974: 'Generationsmods ae tringene sat: System, samfunds maessig organization paa basis av alder, etnografisk rapport fra Labwor', Moesgaard: Aarhus Universitet

Cisternino, Mario
* 1979: 'Karamoja: The Human Zoo' MSc. dissertation, Swansea: University of Wales
* 1984: 'Socio-economic Evaluation of the Crash Labour Employment Programme in Karamoja' Moroto, mimeograph
* 1985a: 'Crash Labour Intensive Employment Programme' International Labour Organization, Geneva, mimeograph
* 1985b: 'From Pastoralism to Agriculture in Karamoja' Moroto, mimeograph
* 1985c: 'Famine and Food Relief in Karamoja' in Dodge and Wiebe 1985

Cisternino, M and Rowland, JRJ
* 1980: 'Some Guidelines in the Development of Karamoja' Moroto, mimeograph

Clark, Doris
* 1950: 'Karamojong Age-Groups and Clans' *Uganda Journal* 14/2:215–18 Sep
* 1951: (tr.) *Gospel of John* London: British and Foreign Bible Society
* 1952a: 'Memorial Service for an Ox in Karamoja' *Uganda Journal* 16/1:69–71 Mar

* 1952b: 'A Karamojong Wedding' *Uganda Journal* 16/2:176f Sept
* 1953: 'Death and Burial Ceremonies among the Karamojong' *Uganda Journal* 17/1:75f Mar

Clark, D and Totty, A
* 1953: *Looking at East Africa* London: Bible Churchmen's Missionary Society

Clark, J Desmond
* 1957: 'A Re-examination of Industry from the Type Site of Magosi, Uganda' in 3rd Pan-African Congress on Prehistory 1957, London
* 1982: (ed.) 'From Earliest Times to 1500 BC' Vol. I in Fage, JD and Oliver, R 1982: *The Cambridge History of Africa* Cambridge University Press

Clark, Robert S
* 1945: *A Karimojong–Swahili–English Vocabulary* Kampala: Uganda Bookshop

Clarke, JI
* 1985: *Population and Development Projects in Africa* Cambridge: Cambridge University Press

Clarke, Peter B
    1988: 'Introduction: African Religions' in Sutherland, Houlden, Clarke, and Hardy 1988:821–4
    1998: (ed.) *New Trends and Developments in African Religions* Westport, Connecticut: Greenwood

Clarke, Peter B and Byrne, Peter (eds)
    1993: *Religion Defined and Explained* London: St Martin's Press

Clay, E and Everitt, E (eds)
* 1985 'Food Aid and Emergencies' Report on 3rd IDS Food Aid Seminars, University of Sussex, DP 206

Cleave, JC
* 1957: 'Matheniko Survey' Moroto, manuscript
* 1996: 'First Posting' in Brown 1996:30–37

Cleave, JH
* 1961: 'Bell in Karamoja' *Uganda Wildlife and Sport* 2/1:7–18

Climatic Research Unit
    2001: 'Global Air Temperature' Available at http://www.cru.uea.ac.uk/ Accessed 13.12.01

Coates, R
* 1970: 'The Carvers of Karamoja' *African Arts* 3/4:75f

Coates, R and Feldman, BJ
* 1973: 'New Cattle Sculpture in Uganda' *African Arts* 7/1:16–19,81

Cohen, DW
    1974: 'The River–Lake Nilotes from the fifteenth to the nineteenth centuries' in Ogot 1974: 135–49

Cohen, Yehudi, A (ed.)
* 1968: *Man in Adaptation: The cultural present* Chicago: Aldine

Cole, D
* 1967: 'A Reinvestigation of Magosi and Magosian' *Quarternaria* 9:153–68

Cole, Herbert M
* 1974: 'Vital Arts in Northern Kenya' *African Arts* 7/2:12-23,82

Cole, Sonya
* 1963: *The Prehistory of East Africa* London: Weidenfeld and Nicolson
Coleman, Simon J
* 1998: *East Africa in the Fifties: A view of late imperial life* London: Radcliffe
Collins, RO
* 1961: 'The Turkana Patrol' *Uganda Journal* 25/1:16–23
* 1962: 'Sudan–Uganda Boundary Rectification and the Sudanese Occupation of Madial' *Uganda Journal* 26/2
Collison, RL
* 1981: *Uganda: A bibliography* Oxford: Clio
Conant, FP
  1965: 'Korok: a Variable Unit of Space' *American Anthropologist* 67:429–35
  1966: 'The External Coherence of Pokot Ritual Behaviour' *Philosophical Transactions of the Royal Society of London* B, 251:505–19
  1982: 'Thorns Paired; Sharply Recurved' in Spooner, B and Mann, HS (eds) *Desertification and Development* London: Academic Press pp. 111–22
Connerton, P
  1989: *How Societies Remember* Cambridge: Cambridge University Press
Cordery, RD
* 1996: 'Idi Amin as Soldier: While acting in support of the civil power' in Brown 1996:249–52
Corrain, C and Capitanio, M
  1979: 'Quelques observations hémotypologiques sur les Pokot du Kenya' *Anthropologie* 83/2:253–9
Cox, James L
  1998a: *Rational Ancestors: Scientific rationality and African indigenous religions* Cardiff: Cardiff Academic Press
  1998b: (ed.) *Rites of Passage in Contemporary Africa* Cardiff: Cardiff Academic Press
Cox, Peter SV
* 1963: 'The Mountains of South Karamoja and the Karapokot' *Mountain Club of Uganda Bulletin* 8:15–22
* 1966: 'Brucellosis – a Survey in South Karamoja' *East African Medical Journal* 43/2:43–50 Feb
* 1967: *The Amudat Story* London: Bible Churchmen's Missionary Society
* 1968: 'A Comparison of the Rapid Slide and Standard Tube Agglutination Tests for Brucellosis' *Transactions of the Royal Society of Tropical Medicine and Hygiene* 62/4:517–21
  1969: 'The Value of Mobile Medicine' *East African Medical Journal* 46:1–5
* 1972: 'The Disease Pattern of the Karapokot and its Relationship to their Environment and Culture' MD thesis, University of London
  1974: 'Planning for the Future in a Nomadic Community' in Anderson, C and Kilama, WL (eds) 1974: *Parasitoses of Man and Animals in Africa* Nairobi: East African Literature Bureau
* 1979: 'My Bit of Africa' unpublished memoirs, typescript
* 1983: 'COU Health Survey of Karamoja' mimeograph
* 1985: 'The Karamoja Health Service: A Proposed Revolution' in Dodge and Wiebe 1985

* 2000: *Bring Your Medicine If You Like* Leeds: E Cox
Crazzolara, JP
* 1960: 'Notes on the Lango-Omiru and Labwor and Nyakwai' *Anthropos* 55: 174–214
* 1967: 'General Sketch Grammar and Vocabulary of the Language of the Ik' Kangole, typescript
  1969: 'The Hamites – Who Were They?' *Uganda Journal* 33/1:41–8
Curley, Richard T
  1973: *Elders, Shades, and Women: Ceremonial change in Lango*, Uganda Berkeley: University of California Press

Dak, O
* 1968: 'A Geographical Analysis of the Distribution of Migrants in Uganda' Department of Geography, Makerere University, Occasional Paper 11
Daniele, S
* 1973: 'Grammatica Karimojong' Moroto, mimeograph
Darley, Henry
* 1935 [1926]: *Slaves and Ivory* 2nd edn, London: Witherby
David, Nicholas
  1982: 'Prehistory and Historical Linguistics in Central Africa' in Ehret and Posnansky 1982:78–95
* 1983: 'The Archaelogical Context of Nilotic Expansion' in Vossen and Bechhaus-Gerst 1983b:35–107
Davire, KA
* 1935: 'Geological Observations on a Traverse through Karamoja' *Geological Survey of Uganda Bulletin* 2:37–9
Dawkins, HC
* 1954a: 'Northern Province Mountains: Speculations on Climate and Vegetation History' *Uganda Journal* 18:58–64
* 1954b: 'Timu and the vanishing forests of North-East Karamoja' *East Africa Agriculture and Forestry Journal* 19/3:164–7 June
Deeley, Peter Q
  2004: 'The Religious Brain' *Anthropology and Medicine* 11/3:245–67
Dellagiacoma, C
* 1969: 'The Catholic Church in Northern Uganda, 1910–69' Gulu, mimeograph
* 1972: *Karimojong Dictionary* Kisubi: Marianum Press
Delmé-Radcliffe, C
* 1905: 'Surveys and Studies in Uganda' *Geographical Journal* 26:481–97
Deshler, Walter W
* 1954: 'Factors Influencing the Present Population Distribution in Dodoso County in Karamoja District' paper for East Africa Institute of Social Research, Kampala
* 1957: 'The Dodos Country: A Study of Indigenous Settlement in a Semi-Arid Area of Uganda' PhD thesis, University of Maryland
* 1960: 'Livestock Trypanosomiasis and Human Settlement in NE Uganda' *Geographical Review* 50/4: 541–54; also in Mansell Protheroe, R (ed.) 1972: *People and Land in Africa south of the Sahara* Oxford: Oxford University Press

* 1964: 'The Dodos: A Cattle Keeping Tribe in East Africa' in Thowan, RS and Patton, DJ (eds) 1964 *Focus on Geographical Activity* New York: McGraw-Hill
* 1965: 'Native Cattle Keeping in Eastern Africa' *Man, Culture, and Animals* 78: 153–68
* 1975: 'Drought and Food Shortage in North Karamoja 1916-mid '50s' paper at eighteenth Annual Meeting of African Studies Association 1910-11175, San Francisco

Devlin, Heather M
* 1998: 'Patterns of Morbidity in Karamoja, Uganda, 1992–1996' MA dissertation, University of Kansas

Diener, Hans
* 1986: 'Final Report, Forestry Programme' International Labour Organization UGA/80/002

Dietz, Ton
* 1986: 'Migration to and from Dry Areas in Kenya' *Journal of Economic and Social Geography* 77/1:18–24
* 1987: 'Pastoralists in Dire Straits: survival Strategies and external interventions in a semi-arid region at the Kenya/Uganda border, Western Pokot, 1900–1986' PhD thesis, University of Amsterdam, Amsterdam: Instituut voor Sociale Geografie, Universiteitvanth
* 1993: 'The State, the Market, and the Decline of Pastoralism: Challenging some myths, with evidence from Western Pokot in Kenya/Uganda' in Markakis 1993: 83–99

Dimmendaal, Gerrit J
* 1983: 'The Two Morphological Verb Classes in Nilotic' in Vossen and Bechhaus-Gerst 1983b:271–309

Docherty, AJ
* 1957: 'The Karamojong and the Suk' *Uganda Journal* 21/1:30–40 Mar

Dodge, Cole P
* 1986: 'Uganda – Rehabilitation, or Redefinition of Health Services?' *Social Science and Medicine* 22:355–61.
* 1990: 'Health Implications of War in Uganda and Sudan' *Social Science and Medicine* 31:691–8.

Dodge, Cole P and Alnwick, DJ
* 1986: 'Karamoja: A Disaster Contained' *Disasters* 10/1:15f

Dodge, Cole P and Raundalen, M (eds)
1987: *War, Violence, and Children in Uganda* Oslo: Norwegian University Press

Dodge, Cole P and Wiebe, PD (eds)
* 1985: *Crisis in Uganda* Oxford: Pergamon

Donham, Donald L
* 2003: 'Concluding comments: Collective identities in a complex world' *Africa* 73/3:456–60

Donham, DL and James, Wendy (eds)
* 1986: *The Southern Marches of Imperial Ethiopia: Essays in history and social anthropology* Cambridge: Cambridge University Press

Douglas, Mary
1975: *Implicit Meanings: Essays in anthropology* London: Routledge, Kegan Paul

Driberg, JH
   1923: *The Lango: A Nilotic tribe of Uganda* London: Unwin
   1932a: 'The Status of Women among the Nilotics and Nilo-Hamites' *Africa* 5: 404–21
* 1932b: 'Lotuko Dialects' *American Anthropologist* 34/4:601–9
Durkheim, Emile
   1915: *The Elementary Forms of the Religious Life* London: Allen and Unwin
Durojaiye, Moa (ed.)
* 1970: 'Psychological Studies in Karamoja' Kampala: Makerere University Department of Educational Psychology
Dyson-Hudson, Neville
* 1955: 'Sanction and Political Structure among the Nilo-Hamitic Tribes of East Africa' BLitt. thesis, University of Oxford
* 1957: 'Dry-season Water Supplies in Pian' Kampala: East African Institute of Social Research
* 1958a: 'The Karamojong and the Suk' *Uganda Journal* 22/2:173–80
* 1958b: 'The Present Position of the Karimojong' monograph for the Government of Uganda
* 1960: 'The Karimojong: A study of political relations in a primitive pastoral society' DPhil. thesis, University of Oxford
* 1962: 'Factors Inhibiting Change in an African Pastoral Society: The Karimojong' *Transactions of the New York Academy of Sciences* 24/7:771–802; also in Middleton, J (ed.) 1970: *Black Africa* London: Macmillan 49–77
* 1963: 'The Karimojong Age System' *Ethnology* 2/3:353–401
* 1966: *Karimojong Politics* Oxford: Clarendon
   1972: 'The Study of Nomads' *Journal of Asian and African Studies* 7; also in Irons and Dyson-Hudson 1972:2–29
* 1980: 'Resources Strategies among the East African Pastoralists' in Harris, CR (ed.) 1980: *Human Ecology in Savannah Environments* London: Academic Press
   1985: 'Pastoral Production Systems and Livestock Development Projects' in Cernea 1985:157–86
Dyson-Hudson, N and VR
* 1982: 'The Structure of East African Herds and the Future of East African Herders' *Development and Change* 13/2:213–38 Apr
Dyson-Hudson, V Rada
* 1960a: 'Men, Women and Work in a Pastoral Society' *Natural History* 69/5:42–57
* 1960b: 'East Coast Fever in Karamoja' *Uganda Journal* 24/2:253–9 Sept
* 1961: 'An Ecological Study of a Pastoral Tribe' *Sudan Journal of Veterinary Science and Animal Husbandry* 2/2:176–9 Nov
* 1962a: 'A Nomad Ecology' in 'Proceedings of 10th Annual Conference of the Philosophcal Society of Sudan' pp. 10–21
* 1962b: 'An Akarimojong–English Check List of Trees of South Karamoja' *Uganda Journal* 26/2:166–70 Sept
* 1972: 'Pastoralism: Self Image and Behavioural Reality' *Journal of Asian and African Studies* 7/1-2:30–47 Jan–Apr; also in Irons and Dyson-Hudson 1972: 30–47
   1980: 'Towards a General Theory of Pastoralism and Social Stratification' *Nomadic Peoples* 7:1–7

* 1983: 'Understanding East African Pastoralism: An Ecosystems Approach' in Berleant-Schiller and Shanklin 1970:1–10
* 1999: 'Turkana in Time Perspective' in Little and Leslie 1999:24–40
* 2000: 'Processes of Discovery and Modes of Commentary through Time: Karamoja and Turkana as illustrative cases' *Abstracts of the Annual Meeting of the American Anthropological Association* 99:190ff

Dyson-Hudson, VR and N
* 1962: 'Marriage Economy: The Karamojong' *Natural History* 71/5:44–53
* 1969: 'Subsistence Herding in Uganda' *Scientific American* 220/2:76–89
* 1970: 'The Food Production System of the Karimojong' in McLoughlin 1970: 92–123
   1980: 'Nomadic Pastoralism' *Annual Review of Anthropology* 9:15–61

Dyson-Hudson, VR and Little, MA
   1983: *Rethinking Human Adaptation* Boulder: Westview Press

Dyson-Hudson, VR and McCabe, JT
   1983: 'Water Resources and Livestock Movements in South Turkana, Kenya' *Nomadic Peoples* 14:41–6

Dyson-Hudson, VR and Smith, EA
* 1978: 'Human Territoriality: An Ecological Reassessment' *American Anthropologist* 80/1:21–41 Mar

EAAFO
* 1962: 'Special Edition' *East Africa Agriculture and Forestry Journal* 27 Mar

Eck, Diana L
   2000: 'Religion and the Global Moment' *Macalester International* 8:3–26

Edwards, KA
* 1979: 'Summary of the Results of the Atumak Experiments' *East Africa Agriculture and Forestry Journal* 44:224ff Special Issue

Edwards, KA and Blackie, JR
* 1979a: 'The Atumak Research Project' *East Africa Agriculture and Forestry Journal* 44:192–5
* 1979b: 'Aspects of the Hydrological Regime of the Atumak Catchments' *East Africa Agriculture and Forestry Journal* 44:206–11 Special Issue

Eggeling, WJ
* 1938a: 'A Plant Collection from Karamoja' *Uganda Journal* 6/1:43–53 Jl
* 1938b: 'The Savannah and Mountain Forests of South Karamoja' Imperial Forestry Institute, University of Oxford: Paper 11
* 1948: 'A Review of Some Vegetation Studies in Uganda' *Uganda Journal* 12: 139–52

Eggeling, WJ and Dale, IR
* 1952: *The Indigenous Trees of the Uganda Protectorate* Glasgow: Glasgow University Press

Ehret, Christopher
* 1967: 'Cattle-keeping and Milking in East and South Africa: The Linguistic Evidence' *Journal of African History* 8/1:1–17
* 1971: *Southern Nilotic History* Evanston: Northwest University Press
   1972: *Ethiopians and East Africans* Nairobi: East African Publishing House

* 1974: 'Cushites and the Highland and Plains Nilotes to AD 1800' in Ogot 1974: 150–69
* 1981a: 'The Classification of Kuliak' in Schadeburg and Bender 1981
* 1981b: 'Revising Proto-Kuliak' *Afrika und Übersee* 64/1:81–100

1982: 'Population Movement and Culture Contact in the Southern Sudan c3000 BC to AD 1000' in Mack and Robertshaw 1982

1983: 'Nilotic and the Limits of Eastern Sudanic' in Vossen and Bechhaus-Gerst 1983b:375–421

1998: *African Classical Age: Eastern and Southern Africa in world history 1000 BC to AD 400* Oxford: James Currey

Ehret, C and Posnansky, M
1982: *The Archaeological and Linguistic Reconstruction of African history* Berkeley: University of California Press

Ehret, C et al.
1974: 'Some thoughts on the early history of the Nile–Congo watershed' *Ufahama* 5/2:85–112

Ekström, Bengt
* 1955: *Ädventyr i Karamoja* Stockholm: Foldet i bild

Elderkin, ED
* 1983: 'Tanzanian and Ugandan Isolates' in Vossen and Bechhaus-Gerst 1983b: 499–521

Eliade, Mircea
1958: *Patterns in Comparative Religion* London: Sheed and Ward
1959a: *The Sacred and the Profane – The Nature of Religion* San Diego: Harcourt Brace Jovanovich
1959b: 'Methodological Remarks on the Study of Religious Symbolism' in Eliade and Kitagawa 1959:86–107
1960: *Myths, Dreams, and Mysteries* London: Harvill
1985: *History of Religious Ideas* 3 vols Chicago: University Press

Eliade, Mircea and Kitagawa, Joseph M
1959: *The History of Religions: Essays in methodology* Chicago: University of Chicago

Ellen, Roy F
* 1982: *Environment, Subsistence and System* Cambridge: Cambridge University Press

Emoru, Andrew DE
* 1998: 'The Role of Music in Evangelism in the Rural Church with special reference to Namalu Parich, Anglican Church of Uganda in the Diocese of Karamoja' Research Paper for the Award of Diploma in Specialised Ministries, Mukono: Uganda Christian University

Equipe Ecologie et Anthropologie des Sociétés Pastorales
* 1979: *Pastoral Production and Society* Cambridge: Cambridge University Press

Errington, Sarah
* 1996: 'Taming the Gun' *BBC Focus on Africa* April–June

Evan-Jones, P
* 1960: 'The Karamoja Development Scheme: A report on the work during the years 1955/59' Kampala: Special Development Section, Uganda Protectorate

* 1963: 'Report on Karamoja Rehabilitation Scheme 1955–60' Kampala: Uganda Administrative Office

Evans-Pritchard, EE
  1954: 'The Meaning of Sacrifrice among the Nuer' *Journal of the Royal Anthopological Institute* 84/1
  1956: *Nuer Religion* Oxford: Clarendon
  1962: *Essays in Social Anthropology* London: Faber and Faber
  1965: *Theories of Primitive Religion* Oxford: Clarendon
  1976: *Witchcraft, Oracle, and Magic among the Azande* Oxford: Clarendon

Even, W
* 1986: 'Towards a Primary Health Care System in Southern Karamoja and Pokot' Amudat: Church of Uganda

Everton, RE
* 1964: 'Karamoja Paper' *Royal Engineer Journal* 78: 399–408

Fage, JD and Oliver, RA (eds)
* 1975–: *The Cambridge History of Africa* Cambridge: Cambridge University Press

FAO
* 1966: *East African Livestock Survey* FAO/SF21Reg

Fardon, Richard
  1990: *Between God, the Dead, and the Wild: Chamba interpretations of religion and ritual* Edinburgh: Edinburgh University Press

Fardon Richard, Binsbergen, Wim van and Dijk, Rijk van (eds)
  1999: *Modernity on a Shoestring: Dimensions of globalization, consumption, and development in Africa and beyond* Leiden and London: EIDOS

Farina, Felice
* 1965: *Nel paese dei bevitori di sangue: genti nuove alla ribalta: il popolo Karimojòng. Pagine vive di attualità* Bologna: Nigrizia
* 1972: 'Karimojong Grammar' Moroto, mimeograph
* 1973: 'Dizionario Karimojong–Italiano' Moroto, mimeograph
* 1986: *Ngakarimojong–English and English–Ngakarimojong Dictionary* Verona: Comboni Missionaries

Farrant Russell, S
* 1972: *Full Fifty Years* London: Patmos

Fasholé-Luke, EW et al. (eds)
  1978: *Christianity in Independent Africa* London: Rex Collings

Featherstone, M
  1995: *Undoing Culture: Globalization, Postmodernism, and Identity* London: Sage

Field, M
* 1967: 'A Visit to the Karimojong' *African World* 7

Fivaz, D and Scott, PE
* 1977: *African Languages* Boston: GK Hall

Fleay, Martin
* 1996: 'Karamoja's District Team and Development Scheme' in Brown 1996: 20–35

Fleisher, M
   1999: 'Cattle Raiding and Household Demography among the Kuria of Tanzania' *Africa* 99/2:238–55
   2002: '"War is Good for Thieving!" The symbiosis of crime and warfare among the Kuria of Tanzania' *Africa* 72/1:131–49

Fleming, Harold C
   1965: 'The Age-Grading Cultures of East Africa: An historical enquiry' PhD thesis, Pittsburg University
* 1983a: 'Kuliak External Relations: Step One' in Vossen and Bechhaus-Gerst 1983b: 423–78
* 1983b: 'Surma Etymologies' in Vossen and Bechhaus-Gerst 1983b:523-55

Fleuty, MJ
* 1968: 'Explanation of the geology of sheet 27' (Moroto) Entebbe: Geological Survey and Mines Dept

Forde, CD
* 1970: 'Ecology and Social Structure' *Proceedings of the Royal Anthropological Institute of Great Britain and Ireland* 15–29

Foster, P
* 1961: *White to Move? A Portrait of East Africa Today* London: Eyre and Spottiswoode

Fournier, A
* 1966: 'Chez les Karimojong' *Revue des Postes Belges* 25/6:206–8

Fox, RG (ed.)
   1991: *Recapturing Anthropology: Working the Present* Sante Fe, NM: School of America Research Press

Frank, Emily
* 2002: 'A Participatory Approach for Local Peace Initiatives: The Lodwar border harmonization meeting' *Africa Today* 49/4:69–87

Frazer, JG
   1963: *The Golden Bough* 3rd edn 9 vols London: Macmillan

Friedmann, Herbert
* 1964: *A New Swift from Mt. Moroto, Uganda* Los Angeles: Los Angeles County Museum

Fukui, Katsuyoshi and Markakis, John (eds)
   1994: *Ethnicity and Conflict in the Horn of Africa* Oxford: James Currey

Fukui, Katsuyoshi and Turton, D (eds)
   1979: *Warfare among East African Herders* Osaka: National Museum of Ethnology

Galaty, John G
   1998: 'Pastoralists and Forced Migration' paper presented in the Forced Migration series in Queen Elizabeth House, University of Oxford, 25.11.98

Gans, Gde
   1986: 'Taking Indigenous Knowledge Seriously: The Case of Pastoral Strategies among the Turkana' manuscript

Garretson, Peter P
* 1986: 'Vicious cycles: Ivory, slaves, and arms on the new Maji frontier' in Donham and James 1986:196–218

Gartrell, Beverley
* 1985: 'Searching for "The Roots of Famine": The case of Karamoja' *Review of African Political Economy* 33:102–10
* 1988: 'Prelude to disaster: The case of Karamoja' in Johnson and Anderson 1988:193–217

Geertz, Clifford
1966: 'Religion as a Cultural System' in Banton 1966:1–46
1971: *Myth, Symbol, and Culture* New York: Norton
1975: *The Interpretation of Cultures* London: Hutchinson

Geist, Judith
* 1995: 'Political Significance of the Constituent Assembly Elections' in Hansen and Twaddle 1995:90–113

Gibbs, JL (ed.)
* 1965: *Peoples of Africa* New York: Holt, Rinehart and Winston

Gidudu, Henry
* 1996–: 'The Impact of Inter-Ethnic conflicts, Cattle-Rustling, and Armed Violence on the Karimojong family: A case study of Moroto District' in Network of Uganda Researchers and Research Users 199?: NURRU Policy Briefs No. 2 Kampala NURRU

Gifford-Gonzalez, D
1998: 'Early Pastoralists in East Africa: Ecological and social dimensions' *Journal of Archaeological Anthropology* 17:166–200

Girard, René
1977: *Violence and the Sacred* Baltimore: Johns Hopkins University Press

Glenday, DK
1980: 'Acholi Birth Ceremonies and Infant Baptism' *Missiology* 8/2:167–76 Apr

Gluckman, Max
1965: *Politics, Law, and Ritual in Tribal Society* Oxford: Blackwell

Gluckman, Max (ed.)
* 1969: *Ideas and Procedures in African Customary Law* London: Oxford University Press
* 1972: *The Allocation of Responsibility* Manchester: Manchester University Press

Goldschmidt, Walter
1968: 'Game Theory, Cultural Values and the Brideprice in Africa' in Buchler, IM and Nutini, H (eds) 1968: *Formal Approaches to Social Behaviour* Pittsburgh: University Press pp. 65–74
* 1969: *Kambuya's Cattle: The legacy of an African herdsman* Berkeley: University of California Press
1971: 'Independence as an Element in Pastoral Social Systems' *Anthropological Quarterly* 44:132–42
* 1974: 'The Economics of Brideprice among the Sebei and in East Africa' *Ethnology* 13/4:311–31.
* 1976: *Culture and Behaviour of the Sebei* Berkeley: University of California Press
1979: 'A General Model for Pastoral Social Systems' *Equipe Ecologie* 1979: 15–27

Gomes, Nathalie
* 2002: 'Interregional Cattle Rustling in Northern Uganda: Triple Standards for Offence Management?' paper presented at BIEA/IFRA Conference 'Crime in Eastern Africa: Past and Present Perspectives', Naivasha, Kenya 9.7.02

Gomes, Nathalie and Mkutu, Kennedy
* 2003: 'Breaking the Spiral of Violence: Building local capacity for peace and development in Karamoja, Uganda' Utrecht: Pax Christi/Kampala: SNV

Gommery, D, Senut, B, Pickford, M and Musiime, E
* 2002: 'Les nouveaux restes du squelette d'Ugandapithecus major (Miocene inférieur de Napal, Ouganda' *Annales de Paleontologie* 88/1:167–86

Goody, Jack
1987: *The Interface between the Written and the Oral* Cambridge: Cambridge University Press

Gould, LN and Garrett, JL
1977: 'Amin's Uganda: Troubled Land of Religious Persecution' *Journal of Church and State* 19: 429–36 Aut

Gourlay, Kenneth A
* 1967: 'Review of Dyson-Hudson's Karimojong Politics' *Uganda Journal* 31/2:222f
* 1969: 'Cross-Cultural Reactions to Music as Indicators for Anthroplogical Research' Makerere University, Uganda Social Science Council Conference, Makerere Paper 67
* 1970: 'Trees and Anthills: Songs of Karimojong women's groups' *African Music* 114–21
* 1971a: 'The Making of Karimojong Cattle Songs' seminar paper for Institute of African Studies, Makerere University; also in Discussion Paper 18, Institute of African Studies, University of Nairobi
* 1971b: 'Studies in Karimojong Musical Culture' PhD thesis, Kampala: University of East Africa
* 1972a: 'The Practice of Cueing among the Karamojong of NE Uganda' *Ethnomusicology* 16/2:240–47
* 1972b: 'The Ox and Identification' *Man* 7/2:244–54
* 1999: 'The Making of Karimojong Cattle Songs' in Floyd, M (ed.) 1999: *Composing the Music of Africa: Composition, interpretation, and realisation* Aldershot: Ashgate pp. 92–105

Graham, Sally
* 1999: 'Traditional Birth Attendants in Karamoja, Uganda' PhD thesis, South Bank University

Gray, John M
1947: 'Ahmed bin Ibrahim the first Arab to visit Uganda' *Uganda Journal* 2: 80–97
1952: 'Acholi History 1860–1901 Part II' *Uganda Journal* 16

Gray, Sandra J
* 1998: 'Butterfat Feeding in Early Infancy in African Populations: New hypotheses' *American Journal of Human Biology* 10/2:163–78
* 2000: 'A Memory of Loss: Ecological politics, local history, and the evolution of Karimojong violence' *Human Organization* 59/4:401–18
* 2003: 'A Memory of Loss: Ecological politics, local history, and the evolution of Karimojong violence' *Peace Research Abstracts* 40/2:123–26

Gray, SJ and Akol, HA
* 2000: 'Reproductive Histories and Life History of Bokora and Matheniko Karaimojong Women of Northeast Uganda' *American Journal of Physical Anthropology* 30:191

Gray, SJ, Sundal, M *et al.*
* 2003: 'Cattle Raiding, Cultural Survival, and Adapatability of East African Pastoralists' *Current Anthropology* 44/S:3–30

Greenberg, Joseph H
  1950: 'Studies in African Linguistic Classification V. The Eastern Sudanic Family' *Southwestern Journal of Anthropology* 6:143–60
  1955: *Studies in African Linguistic Classification* New Haven: Compass
  1957: 'Nilotic, Nilo-Hamitic and Hamito-Semitic' *Africa* 27:364–78
* 1970: *The Languages of Africa* 3rd edn Bloomington: Indiana University Press

Greenwald, HP
* 1972: 'Patterns of Authority in Two Herding Societies' *Administrative Science Quarterly* 17/2:207–17 June

Gresford Jones, H
  1926: *Uganda in Transformation 1876–1926* London: CMS

Grinker, Roy Richard
* 2000: *In the Arms of Africa: The life of Colin M Turnbull* New York: St Martins' Press

Gros, Paule M and Rejmánek, Marcel
* 1999: 'Status and habitat preferences of Uganda cheetahs: an attempt to predict carnivore occurrence based on vegetation structure' *Biodiversity and Conservation* 8/11:1561–83

Groves, CP
* 1955: *The Planting of Christianity in Africa* 4 vols London: Lutterworth

Grubb, Norman P
* 1942: *Alfred Buxton of Abyssinia and Congo* London: Lutterworth

Gubert, R (ed.)
* 1987: 'Riflessi sociali dei piani di sviluppo in Karamoja, Uganda' Trento University degli Studi
* 1988: *La Sfida dello Sviluppo: In una società pastorale dell'Africa orientale, Karamoja–Uganda*' Milan: Jaca Books

Guerin, C and Pickford, M
* 2003: 'Ougandatherium napakense *nov.gen. nov.sp.*, le plus ancien Rhinocerotidae Iranotheriinae d'Afrique' *Annales de Paleontologie* 89/1:1–35

Gulliver, Pamela and Philip H
* 1953: *The Central Nilo-Hamites* London: IAI, Ethnographic Survey of Africa: East Central Africa Part VII

Gulliver, Philip H
* 1951: 'The Name "Lango" as a Title for the Nilo-Hamites' *Uganda Journal* 15: 111–14
* 1952a: 'The Karamojong Cluster' *Africa* 22/1:1–21 Jan
* 1952b: 'Bell-Oxen and Ox-Names among the Jie' *Uganda Journal* 16/1: 72–5 Mar
* 1952c: 'The Family Herds' PhD thesis, University of London

* 1953a: 'Jie Marriage' *African Affairs* 52/207:149–55
* 1953b: 'The Population of Karamoja' *Uganda Journal* 17/2:178–85
* 1953c: 'The Age-Set Organization of the Jie Tribe' *Journal of the Anthropological Institute* 83/2:147–68
* 1954a: 'Jie Agriculture' *Uganda Journal* 18/1:65–70 Mar
* 1954b: 'The Blood of the Karamojong' *Uganda Journal* 18/2: 195f Sept
* 1955: *The Family Herds* London: Routledge, Kegan Paul
* 1956: 'The Teso and the Karamojong Cluster' *Uganda Journal* 20/2:213–15
* 1958: 'The Turkana Age Organization' *American Anthropologist* 60:900–922
  1959: 'Counting with the fingers by two East African tribes' *Tanganyika Notes and Records* 51:259–62
* 1963: *Social Control in an African Society* London: Routledge
* 1965: 'The Jie of Uganda' in Gibbs 1965:157–96
* 1967: 'The Problems of Pastoral Peoples in Contemporary East Africa' African Studies at Makerere 1963–6
* 1968a: 'Age Differentiation' in Sills 1968:I,957–62
* 1968b: 'The Jie of Uganda; The Turkana' in Cohen 1968
* 1969: (ed.) *Tradition and Transition in East Africa* London: Routledge, Kegan Paul
* 1972a: 'Nomadic Movements: Causes and Implications' in Monod 1975:369–86
  1972b: 'The Turkana of North-Western Kenya' in Molnos 1973:II,316–24
  1973a: 'The Turkana of North-Western Kenya' in Molnos 1973:III,373–84
* 1973b: 'Review of "To Live with Herds" [Film]' *American Anthropologist* 75: 597f

Guyer, Jane
  1996: 'Traditions of Invention in Equatorial Africa' *African Studies Review* 39/3:1–28

Habermas, Jürgen
  1984 & 1987: *The Theory of Communicative Action* 2 vols Cambridge: Polity
Hacking, H
* 1955: *Tangled Thickets* London: Bible Churchmen's Missionary Society
Haddon, EB and Thomas, HB
  1968: 'Early Christian Activities in Northern Uganda' *Uganda Journal* 32/2: 200ff
Hailey, Lord
  1950: *Native Administration in the British African Territories* London: HMSO
Hall, SW and Langlands, BW (eds)
  1975: *Uganda Atlas of Disease Distribution* Nairobi: East Africa Publishing House
Hansen, HB and Twaddle, M (eds)
* 1988: *Uganda Now* London: James Currey
* 1995: *From Chaos to Order: The politics of constitution-making in Uganda* Kampala: Fountain
Harvey, Graham (ed.)
  2000: *Indigenous Religions: A comparison* London: Cassell
Hastings, Adrian
  1997: *The Construction of Nationhood: Ethnicity, Religion, and Nationalism* Cambridge: Cambridge University Press

Hayley, TT Steiger
  1940: 'The Power Concept in Lango Religion' *Uganda Journal* 7:98–122
  1947: *The Anatomy of Lango Religion and Groups* Cambridge: Cambridge University Press
Hazel, R
* 1979: 'Les formes traditionnelles de pastoralisme en Afrique Orientale, Pratiques économiques et normes idéoliques' *Anthropologie et Société* 3:22–54
* 1985: 'Livestock Camps and Male Exclusivism' discussion paper, Department of Anthropology, McGill University, Montreal: East African Pastoral Systems, project 3
Heaton, Tom
* 1989: *In Teleki's Footsteps* London: Macmillan
Hegel, GWF
  1895: *Lectures on the Philosophy of Religion* 3 vols (tr. Speirs, EB and Sanderson, JB) London: Routledge, Kegan Paul
  1931: *The Phenomenology of Mind* (tr. Baillie, JB) London: George Allen and Unwin
  1956: *Philosophy of History* New York: Dover
Heine, Bernd
* 1971: 'The Kulyak Languages of Eastern Uganda on Genetic Relationship and the Case of the "Nilo-Hamitic" Languages' *Journal of East African Research and Development* 1/1:19–28
* 1974: 'Tepes and Nyangi – zwei ostafrikanische Restsprachen' *Afrika und Übersee* 58:263–300
* 1975: 'Ik – eine ostafrikanische Restsprache' *Afrika und Übersee* 59:31–56
* 1976: *The Kuliak Languages of Eastern Uganda* Nairobi: East African Publishing House
  1980: *The Non-Bantu Langages of Kenya* Berlin: Dietrich Reimer
* 1985: 'The Mountain People: Some notes on the Ik of NE Uganda' *Africa* 55/1: 3–16
* 1999: *Ik Dictionary* Köln: Köppe
Heine, B and König, C
* 1988: *Plant Concepts and Plant Use II: Plants of the So of Uganda* Saarbrücken: Breitenbach
Heine, B and Nurse, Derek (eds)
* 2000: *African Languages: An introduction* Cambridge: Cambridge University Press
Heine, B and Vossen, R
* 1983: 'On the Origin of Gender in Eastern Nilotic' in Vossen and Bechhaus-Gerst 1983b:245–68
Heine, B, König, C and Brenzinger, M
* 1988: *Plant Concepts and Plant Use: An ethnobotanical survey of the semi-arid and arid lands of East Africa* Saarbrücken: Breitenbach
Heine, B, Rottland, F and Vossen, R
  1979: 'Proto-Baz: some aspects of early Nilotic-Cushitic contacts' *Sprache und Geschichte in Afrika* 1:75–91
Henderson, JP
* 1949: 'Some Aspects of Climate in Uganda' *Uganda Journal* 13/2:163

Henin, RA
    1969: 'Marriage Patterns and Trends in Nomadic and Settled Populations in Sudan' *Africa* 39 July
Herring, RS
* 1971a: 'Production and Exchange in Labwor, Uganda' Makerere Institute of Social Research
* 1971b: 'The Origin and Development of the Nyakwai' seminar paper, Makerere University
* 1973: 'Centralization, Stratification, and Incorporation: Case Studies from NE Uganda' *Canadian Journal for African Studies* 7/3:497–514
* 1974: 'A History of the Labwor Hills' PhD thesis, Santa Barbara: University of California
* 1976a: 'The "Origins" of the JoAbwor and JoAkwa' Department of Geography, Kenyatta University College Staff Paper 10:1–29
* 1976b: 'The Nyakwai: On the Borders of the Lwo World' in Odongo and Webster 1976
* 1976c: *The Nyakwai* Nairobi: East African Literature Bureau
* 1979a: 'Hydrology and Chronology' in Webster 1979:39–86
* 1979b: 'The View from Mount Otuke: Migrations of the Lango Miro' in Webster 1979:283–316
* 1979c: 'Iron Production and Trade in Labwor, NE Uganda' *Transafrican Journal of History* 8/1:75–93
Herskovits, MJ
    1926: 'The Cattle Complex in East Africa' *American Anthropologist* 28:230–72, 361–80,494–528,330–64
    1950: *Man and his Works: The Science of Cultural Anthropology* New York: Alfred Knopf
    1955: *Cultural Anthropology* New York: Alfred Knopf
Hetzron, Robert
    1980: 'The Limits of Cushitic' *Sprache und Geschichte in Afrika* 2:7–126
Heusch, Luc de (ed.)
    1985: *Sacrifice in Africa: A structuralist approach* Manchester: Manchester University Press
Hewitt, Gordon
* 1971: *The Problems of Success: The History of Church Missionary Society 1910–42* London: SCM
Hieda, O
    1983: 'Some Historical Changes in Nominal Stems in Nilotic Languages' in Vossen and Bechhaus-Gerst 1983b:311–35
Hoben, Susan Y
* 1979: 'A Select Annotated Bibliography of Social Science Materials for Uganda' Washington: USAID
Hobley, CW
* 1897: 'Notes on a Journey round Mount Masawa or Elgon' *Geographical Journal* 9/2:178–85 Feb
* 1902: 'Eastern Uganda: an Ethnological Survey' Anthropological Institute of GB and Ireland, Occasional Paper 1

1929: *Kenya from Chartered Company to Crown Colony* London: HF and G Witherby
Hobsbawm, Eric and Ranger, Terence (eds)
   1983: *The Invention of Tradition* Cambridge: Cambridge University Press
Hockey, Jennifer L, Dawson, AH and Allison, James (eds)
   1997: *After Writing Culture: Epistemology and practice in contemporary anthropology* London: Routledge
Hodgson, Dorothy L
   2000: 'Taking Stock: State Control, Ethnic Identity, and Pastoralist Development in Tanzania 1948–1958' *Journal of African History* 41/1:55–78
* 2000: (ed.) *Rethinking Pastoralism in Africa: Gender, culture, and the myth of the patriarchal pastoralist* Oxford: James Currey
Hogg, Richard
* 1983: 'Destitution and Development: The Turkana of north-west Kenya' *Disasters* 6/3:164–8
Hohenberger, J
   1958: 'Some notes on "Nilotic, Nilo-Hamitic, and Hamito-Semitic" by JH Greenberg' *Africa* 28:37–42
Höhnel, L von
   1895: *The Discovery of Lakes Rudolf and Stephanie* 2 vols London
   1919: 'The Lake Rudolf Region' *Journal of the Royal African Society* 18
Hooton, WS and Stafford Wright, J
* 1947: *The First Twenty-Five Years* London: Bible Churchmen's Missionary Society
Hopkins, TK
   1969: 'A Study Guide for Uganda' Boston University African Studies Center, USAID
Horton, Robin
   1984: 'Judaeo-Christian Spectacles: Boon or Bane to the Study of African Religions?' *Cahiers d'Etudes Africaines* 24/4:392–436
   1993: *Patterns of Thought in Africa and the West: Essays in Magic, Religion and Science* Cambridge: Cambridge University Press
Hubert, Henri and Mauss, Marcel
   1964: *Sacrifice: Its nature and function* London: Cohen and West
Hughes, Lotte
* 2003: *The No-Nonsense Guide to Indigenous Peoples* Oxford: New Internationalist/London: Verso
Hulley, DM
* 1923: *Vocabulary and Grammar for Use in Turkana, Karamoja and Toposa* Kampala
Huntingford, GWB
   1930: 'Further Notes on Some Names of God' *Man* 30/79
   1950: *East African Background* 2nd edn London
* 1953a: *The Northern Nilo-Hamites* London: IAI, Ethnographic Survey of Africa: East Central Africa
   1953b: *The Southern Nilo-Hamites* London: IAI, Ethnographic Survey of Africa: East Central Africa 8

* 1956: 'The Nilo-Hamitic Languages' *Southwestern Journal of Anthropology* 12: 200–222
* 1963: 'The Peopling of the Interior' in Oliver, R and Mathew, G (eds) 1963: *History of East Africa* Oxford: Clarendon pp. 58–93

Hursh, CR
    1952: 'Forest Management in East Africa in Relation to Local Climate, Water and Soil Resources' East Africa Agriculture and Forestry Organization Report

Hussein, Karim, Sumberg, James and Seddon, David
    1999: 'Increasing Violent Conflict between Herders and Farmers in Africa: Claims and Evidence' *Development Policy Review* 17:397–418

Hutchinson, Sharon Elaine
    1990: 'Rising Divorce among the Nuer 1936–83' *Journal of the Royal Anthropological Institute* 25/3:393–411
    1996: *Nuer Dilemmas: Coping with money, war, and the state* Berkeley: University of California Press
    2001: '"A Curse from God"? Religious and political dimensions of the post-1991 rise of ethnic violence in South Sudan' *Journal of Modern African Studies* 39/2: 302–31

Huxley, Elspeth
* 1951: *The Sorcerer's Apprentice* London: Chatto and Windus

Ilukol, Margaret
* 1990: *Child of the Karimojong* South Melbourne, Victoria: Macmillan

Imbeck, K
* 1987: 'Karamoja' *Geo* 12:76–96 Dec

Ingham, Kenneth
    1957: 'Uganda's Old Eastern Province' *Uganda Journal* 21/1:41ff Mar
* 1958: *The Making of Modern Uganda* London: Allen and Unwin

Ingrams, W Harold
* 1960: *Uganda: A crisis of nationhood* London: HMSO

Intelligence Branch, Army HQ, India
* 1911: *Frontier and Overseas Expeditions from India Vol. VI Expeditions Overseas* Calcutta: Superintendent Government Printing

Irons, W and Dyson-Hudson, N (eds)
* 1972: *Perspectives on Nomadism* Leiden: EJ Brill

Islington Conference Papers
* 1968: *Mission in the Modern World* London: Patmos

Jackson, Frederick J
* 1930: *Early Days in East Africa* London: Edward Arnold

Jagt, Krijn A van der
* 1983: 'De Religie van de Turkana van Kenia: Een anthropologische studie' PhD dissertation, University of Utrecht
* 1990: *Symbolic Structures in Turkana Religion* Assen: Van Gorcum
    1991: 'Equivalence of Religious Terms across Cultures' United Bible Societies Monograph Series No 4

James, EO
  1933: *Origins of Sacrifice: A study in comparative religion* London: John Murray
  1962: *Sacrifice and Sacrament* London: Thames and Hudson
  1963: *The Worship of the Sky-God* London: Athlone Press
James, Wendy
  1988: *The Listening Ebony* Oxford: Clarendon
  1997: 'The Names of Fear: Memory, History, and the Ethnography of Feeling among Uduk Refugees' *Journal of the Royal Anthropological Institute* 3/1: 115–31
  1998: 'Questions old and new in the anthropology of religion' lecture in the series Methodological Approaches to the Study of Religions, Christ Church, Oxford 1.12.98
  2000a: 'Kuria and the Passages of Life: Review of Ruel 1997' *Journal of Religion in Africa* 30/1:121–6
  2000b: 'Anthropologists, Missionaries, and the Study of Religion in Practice' open lecture, Oxford Centre for Mission Studies 5.12.00
  2002: 'Ritual and Religion' Lectures in the series 'Issues in Contemporary Social Anthropology', ISCA, University of Oxford 15.10.02 and 1.11.02
  2003: *The Ceremonial Animal: A new portrait of anthropology* Oxford: Oxford University Press
Jameson, F and Miyoshi, M (eds)
  1998: *The Cultures of Globalization* Durham: Duke University Press
Jeffery, Roger and Vira, Bhaskar (eds)
* 2001: *Conflict and Co-operation in Participatory Natural Resource Management* New York: Palgrave
Jeremias, Joachim
  1967: *New Testament Theology* London: SCM
Johnson, Douglas H and Anderson, David (eds)
* 1988: *The Ecology of Survival* London: Lester Crook Academic Publishing
Johnston, Harry H
* 1902: *The Uganda Protectorate* 2 vols London: Hutchinson
* 1903: *The Nile Quest* London: Lawrence and Bullen
Jones, PE *et al.*
* 1961: 'Report on the Dyson-Hudson Study on the Karamoja District plan, 1953–8' mimeograph
Jorgensen, Jan J
* 1981: *Uganda: A Modern History* London: Croom Helm
Jorgensen, JG
* 1972: 'Variations on Traditional Concerns: The Neofunctional Ecology of Hunters, Farmers, and Pastoralists' in Jorgensen, JG (ed.) 1972: *Biology and Culture in Modern Perspective* San Francisco: WH Freeman 328–31
Jost, C, Stem, C, Ramushwa, M *et al.*
* 1998: 'Comparative Ethnoveterinary and Serological Evaluation of the Karimojong Community Animal Health Worker Program in Uganda' *Annals of the New York Academy of Sciences* 849:327–48
Jung, Carl G
  1977: *The Symbolic Life* Vol.18 in Herd, H *et al.* (eds) 1977: *The Collected Works of CG Jung* London: Routledge, Kegan Paul

Kabera, JB
* 1985: 'Populating Uganda's Dry Lands' in Clarke, JI 1985:112–22
Kakooza, JMN
* 1967: 'The Evolution of Juridical Control in Uganda' BLitt. thesis, University of Oxford
Kant, Immanuel
　1929: *Critique of Pure Reason* (tr. Norman Snaith) London: Macmillan
Karamoja Diocesan Synod Pre-Lambeth Conference
* 1988: 'Draft Resolutions' Moroto, mimeograph
Kasfir, Nelson
* 1976: *The Shrinking Political Arena: Participation and ethnicity in African politics with a case study of Uganda* Berkeley: University of California Press
Keane, AH
* 1904: *Africa Vol. II South Africa* 2nd edn London: Stanford
Kerfoot, O
* 1959: 'Check List of Vascular Plants growing on the Atumak (Lodoketominit) catchment: Pian county, Karamoja, Uganda' manuscript, Nairobi; Kew: Royal Botanic Gardens
Kesby, John D
* 1977: *The cultural Regions of East Africa* London: Academic Press
Kidong-Onyang, Mike
* 1998: 'Uganda: Mob justice in Karamoja' *New African* 363:23
Kihangire, Cyprian B
　1957: *The Marriage Customs of the Lango Tribe (Uganda) in Relation to Canon Law* Friedburg bei Ausburg: Palloti
King, Basil Charles
* 1949: *The Napak area of southern Karamoja, Uganda: A study of a dissected late Tertiary volcano* Colchester: Benham
King, GR
　1937: 'The Topotha' and 'The Jiye' in Nalder 1937:2/1
King, Noel Q
　1970: *Religions of Africa: A pilgrimage into traditional religions* New York: Harper and Row
　1971: *Christian and Muslim in Africa* New York: Harper and Row
King, NQ (ed.)
　1965: 'Reflections on Baptism in parts of Tropical Africa' *Dini na Mila* 1/2: 1–4 Sept
Kinloch, BG
* 1955: 'Obituary: Karamoja Bell' *Uganda Journal* 19/1:106–9 Mar
Kirby, CP
* 1968: *East Africa* London: Ernest Benn
Kitching, AL
　1935: *From Darkness to Light* London: SPCK
Kmunke, R
　1913: *Quer durch Uganda: Eine forschungsreise in Zentralafrika 1911/1912* Berlin: Dietrich Reimer

Knighton, Benjamin P
* 1988a: 'The Gospel and Development Work' *Mission* /2:14fJun
* 1988b: 'Beyond the desert of criticism we wish to be called again' Bishop Robertson Divinity Prize, University of Durham
* 1989a: 'The Source of the Authority of the Church in Karamoja, Uganda' paper at Ecclesiology Seminar, Department of Theology, University of Durham, 2.2.89
* 1989b: 'Missionaries of Empire? A Reflection on Anglican Mission in Uganda and Karamoja' paper at Imperial History Seminar, University of Durham, 22.5.89
* 1990: 'Christian Enculturation in Karamoja, Uganda' PhD thesis, University of Durham
* 1999a: 'The Meaning of God and the Meaninglessness of Well-meaning Christian Mission: The experience of Christian enculturation in Karamoja, Uganda' *Transformation* 16/4:20–27
* 1999b: 'Traditions and "Traditionalism" among the Karamojong' paper presented to North-East Africa Seminar of the Institute of Social and Cultural Anthropology, University of Oxford 4.12.99
* 2000: 'Other Religions and the Meaning of God in an African Traditional Religion: The encounter in Karamoja, Uganda' *Asia Journal of Theology* 14/2: 399–430
* 2001a: 'Forgiveness and Disengagement in a Traditional African Cycle of Revenge' *Exchange* 30/1:18–32
  2001b: 'Globalization: Implications of violence, the global economy, and the role of the state for Africa and Christian mission' *Transformation* 18/4:204–19
* 2002a: 'School for Progress: The re-routing of BCMS missionaries into education for the end of empire in Karamoja, Uganda' *International Review of Mission* 91/361:256–77
* 2002b: 'The *Longue Durée* in Karamojong Ethnography: Variation and stability of traditions over time as a corrective to the perception of trends' paper presented to the Association of Social Anthopologists Conference, 'Perspectives on Time and Society: Experience, Memory, History' in Arusha, Tanzania 11.4.02
* 2002c: 'Historical Ethnography and the Collapse of Karamojong Culture: Premature Reports of Trends' paper presented to the African Studies Seminar, St Antony's College, University of Oxford 13.6.02
* 2002d: 'Karamojong: Criminals or Warriors?' paper presented at BIEA/IFRA Conference 'Crime in Eastern Africa: Past and Present Perspectives', Naivasha, Kenya 9.7.02
* 2002e: 'The Power of Sacrifice: An anthropology of traditional Karamojong religion' paper presented at the African Studies Association Conference, University of Birmingham 9.9.02
* 2003a: 'Anthropological Perspectives on Transformational Development' *Transformation* 20/2:91–9
* 2003b: 'Saving Space: Women's times in traditional Karamojong religion' paper presented at the International Gender Studies Centre, University of Oxford 5.6.03 and at 'Gender and Theology in Africa' Theological Society of South Africa Conference 20.6.03
* 2003c: 'Market Rationality and Karamojong Cattle' paper presented at the Pastoral Markets Panel, Pisa 9.7.03

* 2003d: 'Dichotomies and diffusions of orality and literacy' paper presented at the Workshop on Orality and Literacy, 'Language, Power, and Society', 18.7.03 SOAS
* 2003e: 'The State as Raider among the Karamojong: "Where there are no guns, they use the threat of guns"' *Africa* 73/3:427–55
* forthcoming: 'Belief in Guns and Warlords: Freeing the Karamojong from Africanist theory'

Knutsson, K-E
* 1985: 'Preparedness for Disaster Operations' in Dodge and Wiebe 1985

Köhler, Oswin
    1950: 'Die Ausbreitung der Niloten' *Beiträge zür Gesellungs- und Volkerwissenschaft* (Festchrift Richard Thumwald) Berlin 159–94
    1955: *Geschichte der Erforschung der nilotischen Sprachen* Beihafte zu Afrika und Übersee 28 Berlin: Dietrich Reimer
* 1970: 'Field Notes on the Karimojong Language' Cologne

Koryang, L
* 1980: 'The Christian Marriage and Karimojong Traditional Marriage' Department of Religious Studies, Makerere University

Kotido PRA Team
* 1999: 'Kotido District Report' Kampala: Uganda Participatory Poverty Assessment Project

Krätli, Saverio
* 2002a: 'Educating Nomadic Herders out of Poverty: Culture, education and pastoral livelihood in Turkana and Karamoja' Brighton: IDS, University of Sussex
* 2002b: 'Cultural Roots of Poverty? Education and pastoral livelihood in Turkana and Karamoja' Brighton: IDS, University of Sussex .pdf file

Kropacek, L
    1984: 'Nubia from the Late 12th Century to the Funj Conquest in the Early 15th Century' in UNESCO 1984:IV,398–422

Kuhn, T S
    1970: *The Structure of Scientific Revolutions* Chicago: University of Chicago Press

Kumm, Karl
    1907: *The Sudan* London: Paternoster

Kurimoto, Eisei
    1992: 'An Ethnography of Bitterness: Cucumber and sacrifice reconsidered' *Journal of Religion in Africa* 22/1:47–65
    1998: 'Resonance of Age-Systems in Southeastern Sudan' in Kurimoto and Simonse 1998: 29–50

Kurimoto, Eisei and Simon Simonse (eds)
* 1998: *Conflict, Age, and Power in North-East Africa: Age Systems in Transition* Oxford: James Currey

Kyemba, H
* 1977: *State of Blood* London: Corgi

La Braca, P Anthony
* 1980: 'Social development in Karamoja, promoted by the Catholic Church' Moroto: Diocese of Moroto
* 1982: *Ekoy a Yesu* Bologna: EMI
* 1984: *Ngikoyo Ngulu Ka Akuj Ngulu alo tooma Ngisabitui* Verona: VF

La Fontaine. J (ed.)
* 1972: *The Interpretation of Ritual* London: Tavistock

Lamphear, John E
* 1970: 'The Inter-Relationships which brought about the Jie Genesis' Kampala: Makerere University, Department of History
* 1971a: 'The Inter-relationship which Brought About the Jie Genesis' Seminar Paper 5, Department of History, Makerere University
* 1971b: 'The Jie Genesis' Department of History, University of Nairobi East Africa and Nile Valley Seminars, Paper 11
* 1972a: 'The Oral History of the Jie of Uganda' PhD thesis, University of London
* 1972b: 'The Jie of North-East Uganda' in Molnos 1973:II,308–15
* 1973: 'The Desire for Male and Female Children and Jie Naming Customs' in Molnos 1973:III,365–72
* 197?: 'The Development of Jie Nationalism' Evanston: Northwestern University
* 1976a: 'The Origin and Dispersal of the Central Paranilotes' in Odongo and Webster 1976
* 1976b: *The Traditional History of the Jie of Uganda* Oxford: Clarendon
* 1976c: 'Aspects of Turkana Leadership during the Era of Primary Resistance' *Journal of African History* 17/2:225–43
* 1979: 'When the Ngitome Speared their Oxen: Problems in Reconstructing the Chronology of the Jie' in Webster 1979:263–82
* 1983: 'Some Thoughts on the Interpretation of Oral Traditions among the Central Paranilotes' in Vossen and Bechhaus-Gerst 1983a:109–26
* 1986: 'The Persistence of Hunting and Gathering in a "Pastoral World"' *Sprache und Geschichte in Afrika* 7/2:227–65
* 1987: 'The People of the Grey Bull: the Origin and Expansion of the Turkana' *Journal of African History* 29/1:27ff
* 1989: 'Historical Dimensions of Dual Organization: The Generation Class System of the Jie and the Turkana' in Maybury-Lewis and Almagor 1989: 209–34
* 1992: *The Scattering Time: Turkana Resistance to the Imposition of Colonial Rule* Oxford: Clarendon
* 1993: 'Aspects of "Becoming Turkana": Interactions and assimilation between Maa and Ateker speakers' in Spear and Waller 1993:87–104
* 1994: 'The Evolution of Ateker "New Model" Armies' in Fukui and Markakis 1994:63–92.
* 1998: 'Brothers in Arms: Military aspects of East African Age systems' in Kurimoto and Simonse 1998:79–99

Lamphear, JE and Webster, JB
* 1971: 'The Jie-Acholi War' *Uganda Journal* 35/1:23–42

Langdale-Brown, I, Osmaston, HA and Wilson, JG
* 1964: *The Vegetation of Uganda* Entebbe: GovtPrinter

Langlands, BW
* 1962: 'Early Travellers in Uganda' *Uganda Journal* 26/1:55–71 Mar
* 1967: 'Burning in East Africa' *East Africa Geographical Review* 5:21–37
* 1971: 'The Population Geography of Karamoja District' Department of Geography, Makerere University Occasional Paper 38
* 1974: 'Atlas of Population Census 1969 for Uganda' Department of Geography, Makerere University, Occasional Paper 9

Langlands, BW and Namirembe, G
* 1967: *Studies on the Geography of Religion in Uganda* Kampala: Department of Geography, Makerere University College

Langness, LL
  1974: *The Study of Culture* San Francisco: Chandler and Sharp

Laughlin, Charles D
* 1972: 'Economics and Social Organization among the So of Northeastern Uganda' doctoral dissertation, University of Oregon
* 1974: 'Deprivation and Reciprocity' *Man* 9/3:380–96
* 1975: 'Lexicostatistics and the mystery of So ethno-linguistic relations' *Anthropological Linguistics* 17:325–41

Laughlin, CD and Allgeier, ER
* 1972a: 'Kenisan – economic and social ramifications of a ghost cult among the So' *Africa* 42/1:9–20
* 1972b: 'The So of Karamoja District, Eastern Uganda' in Molnos 1972:II,300–307
* 1973a: 'The So of Karamoja District, Eastern Uganda' in Molnos 1973:III, 352–64
* 1973b: 'Maximisation, Marriage, and Residence among the So' *Canadian Review of Sociology and Anthropology* 10/3:199–213 Aug; also in *American Ethnologist* 1:129–41 1974 Aug
* 1974: 'Age generations and political processes in So' *Africa* 44:266–79
* 1979: *Ethnography of the So of NE Uganda* 2 vols New Haven: Human Relations Area Files

Lawrance, JCD
* 1953: 'The Karamojong Cluster' *Africa* 23:244–9
* 1955: 'A History of Teso to 1937' *Uganda Journal* 19/1:7–40
* 1957: *The Iteso* Oxford: Oxford University Press

Leach, Edmund (ed.)
  1974: 'The Future of Traditional Primitive Societies' SSRC Symposium, Cambridge, Dec

Leach, Robert J
* 1960: 'Grazing Control: Karamoja District' typescript
* 1962: 'Pasture Development on the Intensive Reclamation Area' *East Africa Agriculture and Forestry Journal* 27 Supplement: 53f

Leakey, MD
  1943: 'Notes on Ground and Polished Stone Axes of East Africa' *Journal of East African Natural History Society* 17

Leeke, RH
* 1917: 'The Northern Territories of the Ugandan Protectorate' *Geographical Journal* 49/3:201–8 Mar

Leggett, Ian
* 2001: *Uganda* Oxford: Oxfam/Kampala: Fountain
Lévi-Strauss, Claude
  1963: *Structural Anthropology* New York: Basic Books
  1966: *The Savage Mind* London: Weidenfeld and Nicolson
LeVine, Robert Alan and Campbell, DT
  1972: *Ethnocentrism: Theories of conflict and group behaviour* Grand Rapids: Zondervan
LeVine, Robert Alan and Sangree, W
  1962: 'The Diffusion of Age-Group Organization in East Africa' *Africa* 33/2: 97–110
Lewis, IM
  1971: *Ecstatic Religion: an anthropological study of spirit possession and shamanism* Harmondsworth: Penguin
  1972: 'The Dynamics of nomadism' in Monod 1975:426–42
Lienhardt, R Godfrey
  1961: *Divinity and Experience* Oxford: Clarendon
  1997: '"High Gods" among some Nilotic Peoples' *JASO* 28/1:40–49
Little, Michael A and Leslie, Paul W (eds)
  1999: *Turkana Herders of the Dry Savanna: Ecology and biobehavioural response of nomads to an uncertain environment* Oxford: Oxford University Press
Little, Michael A, Dyson-Hudson, R *et al.*
  1999: 'Framework and Theory' in Little and Leslie 1999:2–23
Livingstone, I
  1977: 'Economic Irrationality among Pastoral Peoples: Myth or reality?' *Development and Change* 8:209–30
Locap, Rufus
* 1989: 'Marriage and Bride Price' typescript; also transcribed in Knighton 1990:II,76–84
Locheng, Zach, Logiro, Peter, *et al.*
* 1996: *Nakiro nunga Ajokak Ikotere Nitunga Daadang: Akamunet nina kitete* Kampala: Bible Society of Uganda
Lokut, J
* 1983: 'A Christian View on Cattle Raiding among the Karimojong of Uganda' paper for the Department of Religious Studies, Makerere University
Lomongin, Joseph
* 1999: 'Church Marriage among the Karamojong – Pian, Karamoja, Uganda, 1929–99' BD research paper, Mukono: Uganda Christian University
Lomongin, Peter
* 1987: 'Diocesan Financial Requirements 1987–91' Moroto: mimeograph
* 1988: 'Bishop's Report for Fourth General Synod Of Karamoja Diocese' Moroto, mimeograph
Lonsdale, John
  1992a: 'African Pasts in Africa's Future' in Berman and Lonsdale 1992:203–23
  1992b: 'The Moral Economy of Mau Mau: Wealth, Poverty, and Civic Virtue in Kikuyu Political Thought' in Berman and Lonsdale 1992:315–504

2000a: 'Agency in Tight Corners: Narratives and initiative in African history' *Journal of African Cultural Studies* 13/1:5–16
2000b: 'The State of African Studies, 2000' *ASAUK Newsletter* 5/19:1–4
Loor, J Logyel
* 1976: *Ngakarimojong–English Dictionary* Kampala: Mission Combianum
Lorec, John RA
* 1981: 'Christianity in Karamoja 1929–80' research paper for Diploma in Theology, Kampala: Makerere University
Lorukude, Rufus
* 1958: *Old Testament Stories* Kampala: Uganda Bookshop
Lotman, IUM
1990: *Universe of the Mind: A semiotic theory of culture* London: Tauris
Lovell, Nadia
1996: 'Religion and History: Review of Chrétien 1993' *Journal of African History* 36/1:120f
Lynch, BM and Robbins, LH
1977: 'Animal Brands and the Interprtation of Rock Art in East Africa' *Current Anthropology* 18/3:538f
1978: 'Namoratunga: the first archaeo-astronomical evidence in Sub-Saharan Africa' *Science* 200:766–78
1979: 'Cushitic and Nilotic Prehistory' *Journal of African History* 20:319–28

McCarthy, Nancy, Swallow, Brent *et al.* (eds)
2000: *Property Rights, Risk, and Livestock Development in Africa* Washington, DC: International Food Policy Research Institute
McClellan, Monique
* 1982: 'Without Magic, the Struggle Goes On' *One World* 74:11–13 March
Macdonald, JRL
1897: *Soldiering and Surveying in British East Africa 1891–4* London: Edward Arnold
* 1899a: 'Journeys to the North of Uganda I' *Geographical Journal* 14/2:130–48
* 1899b: 'Notes on the Ethnology of Tribes met with During Progress of the Juba Expedition of 1897–99' *Journal of the Anthropological Institute* 29:226–47
MacDonald, R
* 1962: 'Explanation of the Geology of Sheet 36, Nabilatuk' Geological Survey, Entebbe: Government Printer
McEwen, AC
* 1971: *International Boundaries of East Africa* Oxford: Oxford University Press
MacGaffey, Wyatt
1970: *Custom and Government in the Lower Congo* Berkeley: University of California Press
MacGregor, JP
* 1962: 'Explanation of the Geology of Sheet 10, Kaabong' Geological Survey, Entebbe: Government Printer
McKnight, Glenn H
2000: 'Land, Politics, and Buganda's "Indigenous" Colonial State' *Journal of Imperial and Colonial History* 28/1:65–89

Mack, J and Robertshaw, P (eds)
  1982: *Culture History in the Southern Sudan* Nairobi: British Institute in Eastern Africa, Memoir 8
McLoughlin, Peter FM (ed.)
* 1970: *African Food Production Systems: Case and theory* Baltimore: Johns Hopkins Press
Maconi, Vittorio
* 1959: 'Roti funebri e culto dei morti presso i Karimojong' *Anthropos* 63/4: 841–51
* 1963: 'Note su alcuni aspetti economico-sociali dei Karimojong' Ateneo di Scienze, Lettere ed Arti, Bergamo
* 1967: 'Alcuni problemi urgenti della ricerca etnologica presso i Karimojong, Uganda' *BIC* 9:23–6
* 1973: 'L'iniziazone ai gruppi d'età femminili presso i Karimojong' in *Festschrift zum 65 Geburtstag von Helmut Petri* Cologne and Vienna: Böhlau Verlag pp. 344–59
* 1976: 'Persistenza di una cultura tradizionale e dinamica culturale in Uganda' in Chiozzi, M (ed.) 1976: *Etnicità e Potere* Padova: Cleup pp. 111–21
* 1979: *L'uomo e il bue Una culturra resistente* Genova: Mondini and Siccardi
* 1985: 'Dualismo della vocazione magica presso i pastori dell'Africa Orientale (I Karimojong)' *De Magia* pp. 114–20
* 1986: 'Nascita per stimolo di una produzione plastica presso i pastori karimojong dell'Uganda' in Bassani, Ezio (ed.) *Arte in Africa* Modena: Panini pp. 38–40
* 1987: 'I razziatori di bestiame diventano eroi' *Geodes* 8f
Mahndevan, P and Parsons, DJ
* 1960: 'Pastoral Systems' Uganda Protectorate, Department of Agriculture Series 3: Systems of Agricultural Practice 5
Mair, LP
  1962: *Primitive Government* Baltimore: Penguin
Malinowski, Bronislaw
  1944: *A Scientific Theory of Culture and other Essays* Chapel Hill: University of North Carolina Press
  1945: *The Dynamic of Culture Change* New Haven: Yale University Press
  1948: *Magic, Science, and Religion* New York: Doubleday
Mamdani, Mahmood
* 1981: 'Colonial Roots of the Famine' paper delivered at the Conference on Rural Rehabilitation and Development, Faculty of Social Science, Makerere University 9.81
* 1982: 'Karamoja: Colonial roots of famine in north-east Uganda' *Review of African Political Economy* 25:66–73
* 1985: 'Disaster Prevention: Defining the problem' paper at Uganda Red Cross Conference, Kampala 19–21.3.85 *Review of African Political Economy* 33:92–6
* 1986: 'Colonial Roots of the Famine in Karamoja: A rejoinder' *Review of African Political Economy* 36:85–92
Mamdani, M and Oloka-Onyango, J (eds)
* 1994: 'Uganda: Studies in Living Conditions, Popular Movements and Constitutionalism' *Journal für Entwicklungspolitik*, Vienna

Mamdani, M, Kasoma, PMS and Katende, AB
* 1992: 'Karamoja: Ecology and History' Working Paper no. 22, Centre for Basic Research, Makerere University

Management Systems International
* 2002: 'Addressing Pastoralist Conflict in the Karamoja Cluster of Kenya, Uganda, and Sudan' March 2002 Report on Conflict Assessment Nov–Dec. 2001; available at www.usaid.gov/regions/afr/conflictweb/reports/karamoja.pdf accessed 13.3.03

Manfredini, C and Vigano, M
* 1985: 'Report to the Uganda Government on the Karamoja Italy–Uganda Borehole Project' Kampala: Ministry of Rehabilitation

Manning, HL
   1956: 'The Statistical Assessment of Rainfall Probability and its Application in Uganda Agriculture' *Proceedings of the Royal Society* B144: 460–80

Mantovani, MA
* 1963: *An Introduction to the Karimojong Language* Gulu: Catholic Press
* 1985: 'A New Karimojong Grammar' Moroto, Nadiket Seminary
* 1986: 'Value in English of the Karimojong Verbal Tense' Moroto

Mantovani, MA and Roncari, G
* 1973: *Appunti di Grammatica Karimojong* Gulu: Catholic Press

Markakis, John (ed.)
* 1993: *Conflict and the Decline of Pastoralism in the Horn of Africa* London: Macmillan Press

Marshall Thomas, Elizabeth
* 1965: *Warrior Herdsmen* London: Martin Secker and Warburg

Martin, WS
* 1938: 'Note on Soils and Soil Erosion in Karamoja' in Wayland and Brasnett 1938

Matheson, JK and Bovill, EA
* 1950: *East African Agriculture* Oxford: Oxford University Press

Matson, AT
   1958: 'Uganda's Old Eastern Province and East Africa's Federal Capital' *Uganda Journal* 22/1: 43–53
* 1965: 'Macdonald's Expedition to the Nile' *Uganda Journal* 29/1:98–103
   1968: 'Macdonald's Manuscript History of the Events of 1897–9' *Uganda Journal* 32: 217–19
   1970: 'Macdonald's Manuscript History' *Uganda Journal* 34/1:83f

Maxwell, David
   1999: *Christians and Chiefs in Zimbabwe: A social history of the Hwesa people c.1870s–1990s* Edinburgh: Edinburgh University Press

Maybury-Lewis, David and Almagor, Uri (eds)
* 1989: *The Attraction of Opposites: Thought and Society in the Dualistic Mode* Ann Arbor: University of Michigan Press

Mazrui, Ali Al'Amin (ed.)
   1977: *The Warrior Tradition in Modern Africa* Leiden: Brill

Mbiti, John S
   1968: 'Christianity and East African Culture and Religion' *Dini na Mila* 3/1:1–6 May

    1969: *African Religions and Philosophy* London: Heinemann
    1970: *Concepts of God in Africa* London: SPCK
    1971a: 'Notes for the collection of material on African traditional religion' in Byaruhanga-Akiiki 1971: I
    1971b: 'Sources for the Study of African Traditional Religion' in Byaruhanga-Akiiki 1971: I
Medeghini, A
    1973: *Storia d'Uganda* Bologna: Nigrizia
Meinhof, Carl
    1912: *Die Sprache den Hamiten* Hamburg: Friederichsen
Menghesteab, T
* 1978: 'A Study in Karimojong and Christian Initiation Rituals', Diploma in Theology Research Paper Gaba National Seminary, Makerere University
Meyer, Birgit
    1996: 'Modernity and Enchantment: The image of the devil in popular African Christianity' in Veer 1996:199–230
Meyer, Birgit and Geschiere, Peter (eds)
    1999: *Globalization and Identity: Dialectics of flow and closure* Oxford: Blackwell
Meyerhoff, EC
    1981: 'The Socio-Economic and Ritual Roles of Pokot Women' Lucy Cavendish College, Cambridge
Meyers, CH
    1979: 'Man, vrouw, ritueel; onderlinge verhoudingen binnen een lokale gemeenschap in West-Pokot, Kenya' Hendrik Kraemar Institut, Oegstgeest
Middleton, John
    1955: 'The Concept of Bewitching in Lugbara' *Africa* 15 July
    1960: *Lugbara Religion* London: Oxford University Press
    1968: 'Some Categories of Dual Classification among the Lugbara of Uganda' *History of Religion* 7/3
    1970: *The Study of the Lugbara: Expectation and Paradox in Anthropological Research* New York: Holt, Rinehart and Winston
    1997: 'Religion and Ritual' in Middleton 1997:III,562–9
Middleton, John (ed.)
    1997: *Encyclopedia of Africa South of the Sahara* New York: Charles Scribner's
Middleton, John and Winter, EH (eds)
    1963: *Witchcraft and Sorcery in East Africa* London: Routledge, Kegan Paul
Mills, C Wright, Gerth, Hans and Weber, Max
    1991: *From Max Weber: Essays in Sociology* London: Routledge
Mirzeler, Mustafa Kemal
* 1999: 'Veiled Histories and the Childhood Memories of a Storyteller' PhD dissertation, University of Wisconsin-Madison
* 2004: 'Oral Tradition as a Remembered Memory and a Repeated Event: Sorghum as a gift in Jie and Turkana historical consciousness' *Ethnohistory* 51/2:223–56
Mirzeler, Mustafa and Young, Crawford
* 2000: 'Pastoral Politics in the Northeast Periphery in Uganda: AK-47 as change agent' *Journal of Modern African Studies* 38/3:407–30

* 2004: 'Pastoralist Conflict, Governance, and Small Arms in North Rift, Northeast Africa (Karamoja-Uganda, West Pokot, Samburu, Laikipia in Kenya)' University of Bradford, PhD thesis
* 2005: 'Pastoralist Violent Conflict in Karamoja: Examining gender issues' Utrecht: SNV-Uganda

Mkutu, Kennedy
* 2001: 'Pastoralism and Conflict in the Horn of Africa' London: Africa Peace Forum/Saferworld/University of Bradford
* 2003: 'Pastoral Conflict and Small Arms: The Kenya–Uganda border region' London: Saferworld

Molnos, Angela (ed.)
* 1972–3: *Cultural Source Materials for Population Planning in East Africa* 4 vols Nairobi: East African Publishing House

Monod, Theodore (ed.)
  1975: *Pastoralism in Tropical Africa* Oxford: Oxford University Press Studies at 13th InternatAfrican Seminar, Niamey 1972

Moore, Henrietta L, Sanders, Todd and Kaare, B (eds)
  1999: *Those Who Play with Fire: Gender, fertility, and transformation in East and Southern Africa* London: Athlone

Moorehead, Alan
* 1962: *No Room in the Ark* Harmondsworth: Penguin

Moroto Diocesan Synod
* 1982: *Pastoral Plan* Kisubi: Marianum Press

Morton, WH
* 1967: 'Rock Engravings from Loteteleit, Karamoja' *Uganda Journal* 31/2:208f

Moyse-Bartlett, H
* 1956: *The King's African Rifles* Aldershot: Gale and Polden

Mudimbe, VY
  1990: *The Invention of Africa* Oxford: James Currey

Mugerwa, PJN
* 1969: 'Status, Responsibility and Liability: a Comparative Study of Two Types of Society in Uganda' *Ideas and Procedures* 279–91; also in Glurkman 1969: 279–92

Mugobera, Peace Nyiramahoro
* 1998: *And the Lord Took Him* Kampala: IFES-PAFES

Muhereza, Frank Emmanuel
* 1996: 'Agriculture and pastoralism in Karamoja: competing or complementary forms of resource use?' in Ahmad and Abdel Ati 1996
* 1997: 'Analysing the Nature of Agro-Pastoral Relationships in Karamoja: A Case Study from the Bokora of Moroto District' Kampala: Centre for Basic Research, Working Paper no. 50
* 1999a: 'Violence and the State in Karamoja' *Cultural Survival Quarterly* 43–6
* 1999b: 'Cross-border grazing, and the challenges for development in the dryland areas of eastern Africa: The case of Karamoja' Addis Ababa: Ethiopian International Institute for Peace and Development
* 2000: 'Question d'histoire: Guerre et paix au Karamoja (Ouganda)' in Compagnon, David and Constantu, François (eds) *Administrer l'environnement en Afrique* Nairobi: IFRA-KARTHALA
* 2001a: 'Ranchers and Pastoralists: The restructuring of government ranching,

Uganda' in Salih and Ahmad 2001:100–133
* 2001b: 'Conflict Prevention, Management and Resolution' Capacity Assessment Study for the IGAD Sub-Region, Phase 2: Implementation, Report by National Experts for Uganda IGAD and Centre for Development Studies, University of Leeds, July

Muhereza, FE and Bledsoe, D
* 2001: 'Land Sector Analysis: Common Property Resources Component' Kampala: DfID

Muhereza, Frank and Ocan, Charles Emunyu
* 1994: 'Report of the Second CBR Pastoralism Workshop on Pastoralism and Crisis in Karamoja' 28–9.1.94 Moroto, Kampala: Centre for Basic Research

Muhereza, Frank and Otim, Peter
* 2002: *Pastoral Resource Competition in Uganda: Case Studies into commercial livestock ranching and pastoral institutions* Kampala: Centre for Basic Research/Utrecht: International Books

Mukherjee, R *et al.*
1955: *The Ancient Inhabitants of Jebel Moya* Cambridge: Cambridge University Press

Munster, Earl of (Chairman)
* 1961: *Report of the Uganda Relationships Commission* Entebbe: Government Printer

Murmann, C
* 1974: *Change and Development in East Africa Cattle Husbandry: A study of four societies during the colonial period* Copenhagen: Akademisk Forlag

Nabofa, MY
1985: 'Blood Symbolism in African Religion' *Religious Studies* 21:289–405

Nagashima, Nobuhiro
* 1969: 'Historical Relations among the Central Nilo-Hamites' Makerere University, Uganda Social Science Council Conference, Makerere Paper 608:338–77
* 1998: 'Two Extinct Age Systems among the Iteso' in Kurimoto and Simonse 1998:227–48

Nalder, LF (ed.)
1937: *A Tribal Survey of the Mongalla Province* London: IAI

Nancholas, Renny A
* 1983: 'Misrepresenting the Famine in Karamoja' Development Studies Annual Conference, Institute of Development Studies, Sussex University
* 1984: 'The Erosion of Pastoralism and Limitations of Relief Intervention in Karamoja' MPhil. thesis, University of Bath

Narman, Anders
* 2003: 'Karamoja: Is peace possible?' *Review of African Political Economy* 95: 129–33

Nelson, CM
* 1970: 'Archaeological Survey of the Kotido Area' Uganda Monuments Section Monthly Report, Apr. Ministry of Culture

Newman, Las
2001: 'A West Indian Contribution to Christian Mission in Africa: The career of Joseph Jackson Fuller (1845–1888)' *Transformation* 18/4:220–31

Niamir-Fuller, Maryam
* 1999: 'Conflict Management and Mobility among Pastoralists in Karamoja, Uganda' in Niamir-Fuller 1999:149–83
* 1999: (ed.) *Managing Mobility in African Rangelands: The legitimation of transhumance* London: Intermediate Technology
  2000: 'Managing Mobility in African Rangelands' in McCarthy and Swallow 2000:102–31
* 2001: 'Conflict Management and Mobility among Pastoralists in Karamoja, Uganda' in Jeffery and Vira 2001:19–38

Nicol, B
* 1968: 'An Investigation into the Situation of "Wandering Children" in Moroto, Karamoja' Makerere Department of Social Work, mimeograph

Novelli, Bruno
* 1985: *A Grammar of the Karimojong Language* Berlin: Dietrich Reimer Verlag
* 1987: *Small Grammar of the Karimojong Language* Verona: Comboni Missionaries
* 1988: *Aspects of Karimojong Ethnosociology* Verona: Comboni Missionaries
* 1990: 'A man went out to sow his seed (Luke 8:5): Moroto Diocese silver jubilee, 1965–1990' Moroto: Diocese of Moroto
* 1999: Karimojong Traditional Religion: A contribution Kampala: Comboni Missionaries

Novelli, B and La Braca, PA
* 1980: *Pastorale Missionaria Nuova: Un'analisi critica dell 'attività missionaria dei Comboniani tra i Karimojong e una realizzazione pratica* Bologna: EMI

Nsibambi, A and Byarugaba, F
* 1980: 'Problems of Political and Administrative Participation in a Semi-Arid Area of Uganda: A Case Study of Karamoja' *African Review* 9/2:79–96

Nurse, Derek
  1997: 'The Contributions of Linguistics to the Study of History in Africa' *Journal of African History* 38/3:339–91

Nzita, R and Niwampa, M (eds)
* 1995: *Peoples and Cultures of Uganda* Kampala: Fountain

Oba, G
  1992: *Ecological Factors in Land Use Conflicts, Land Administration, and Food Insecurity in Turkana, Kenya* Pastoral Development Network Paper 33a London: ODI

Obbo, Christine
* 1988: 'What Went Wrong in Uganda?' in Hansen and Twaddle 1988:5–33

Obwoch, G
* 1976: 'Karimojong Image, a day through the eyes of Karimojong' BSc dissertation, Makerere University

Ocan, Charles Emunyu
* 1992a: 'Pastoralism and Crisis in North-eastern Uganda: Factors that Have Determined Social Change in Karamoja' paper presented in the workshop on Pastoralism, Crisis and Transformation in Karamoja, 14–15.8.92, Moroto, Kampala: Centre for Basic Research Working Paper no. 20
* 1992b: 'Pastoral Crisis in North-eastern Uganda: The Changing Significance of

Cattle Raids' paper presented in the workshop on Pastoralism, Crisis and Transformation in Karamoja, 14–15.8.92, Moroto, Kampala: Centre for Basic Research, Working Paper no. 21
* 1994a: 'Pastoral Crisis and Social Change in Karamoja' in Mamdani and Oloka-Onyango
* 1994b: 'Pastoral Resources and Conflicts in North-Eastern Uganda: The Karimojong case' *Nomadic Peoples* 34/35:123–35

Odhiambo, ES Atieno *et al.*
* 1977: *A History of East Africa* London: Longman

Odongo, JM, Onyango, KU and Webster, JB (eds)
1976: *The Central Lwo during the Aconya* Nairobi: East African Literature Bureau

Ofcansky, Thomas P
* 1996: *Uganda: Tarnished pearl of Africa* Boulder, CO: Westview

Ogot, Bethwell A
1961: 'The Concept of Jok among the Nilotes' *African Studies* 20:123–30
1967: 'The Impact of the Nilotes' in Oliver 1967:47–56
* 1974: (ed.) *Zamani: A Survey of East African History* Nairobi: East African Publishing House/Longman
1983: 'Language, Culture, and Ethnicity in the Precolonial History of Africa' in Vossen and Bechhaus-Gerst 1983a:23–33

O'Keefe, P and Wisner, B (eds)
* 1977: *Land Use and Development* London: International African Institute

Okech, A
* 2000: 'Needs Assessment Survey for Functional Adult Literacy in Karamoja, Uganda' Kampala: Ministry of Gender, Labour and Social Development/WFP

Okengo-Okuda, J
* 1972: 'Juok – Labwor, Karamoja, Uganda' in Byaruhanga-Akiiki (ed.) 1972: 5/44

Okudi, Ben
* 1992: 'Causes and Effects of the 1980 Famine in Karamoja, Uganda' paper presented in the workshop on Pastoralism, Crisis and Transformation in Karamoja, 14–15.8.92, Moroto, Kampala: Centre for Basic Research, Makerere University, Working Paper no. 23

Oliver, Roland
1952: *The Missionary Factor in East Africa* London: Longman
1957: *Sir Harry Johnston and the Scramble for Africa* London: Chatto and Windus
1967: (ed.) *The Middle Age of African History* Oxford: Oxford University Press
1977: (ed.) 'c1050–c1600' vol.3 in Fage and Oliver 1975–
1983: 'The Nilotic Contribution to Bantu Africa' in Vossen and Bechhaus-Gerst 1983b:357–74; also in *Journal of African History*

Oliver, Roland *et al.*
2001: 'Comments on Ehret, "Bantu Expansions"' *International Journal of African Historical Studies* 34/1:43–81

Oloka-Onyango, Joe
* 1993: 'Pastoral Crisis and Transformation in Karamoja' Dryland Networks Programme issues paper, International Institute for Environment and Development 43/XY

Oloka-Onyango, Joe, Zie, G and Muhereza, FE
* 1992: 'Pastoralism, Crisis, and Transformation in Karamoja' paper presented in the workshop on Pastoralism, Crisis and Transformation in Karamoja, 14–15.8.92, Moroto
* 1993: 'Pastoralism, Crisis and Transformation in Karamoja' *International Institute for Environment and Development* 43

Omara-Otunnu, Amii
* 1987: *Politics and the Military in Uganda 1890–1985* New York: St Martin's Press

Omolo, Leo Odero
* 1996: 'Foreign Prospectors Clash with Locals in Karamoja' *New African* 344:34f

Omondi, WA
  1983: 'The Lyre, "Thum", in Luo Society' in Vossen and Bechhaus-Gerst 1983a: 127–44

Omwony-Ojwok, R
* 1972: 'Kwer – Customary rites in Karamoja, Uganda' in Byaruhanga-Akiiki (ed.) 1972: 5/42

Onadipe, Abiodun (ed.)
  2002: 'Neither in War nor in Peace: Perspectives on the Karamoja problem and its effect on neighbouring communities' London: Consiliation Resources

Onions, CT (ed.)
  1966: *Oxford Dictionary of English Etymology* Oxford: Oxford University Press

Onwurah, E
  1987: 'Remaking of African traditional religions under the influence of modernity' *Journal of Dharma* 12:180–91 Apr–June

Opio-Odongo, Joe Martin Aldo
* 1971: 'Social Structure, Ideology and Rural Development: The Lele of Kasai-Congo, Kinshasa, and the Karimojong of Uganda compared' Kampala: Makerere University College, Faculty of Agriculture

Opuli-Watum, DR
* 1980: 'The Karamoja Problem is a Land Question' *Forward* 2:3f

Orde Browne, G St. J
  1925: *The Vanishing Tribes of Kenya* London: Seeley, Service

Otim, Peter
* 2002: 'Local Pastoral Institutions: The Case of Karamoja' in Muhereza and Otim 2002:111–71

Owen, William
* 1935: *Kitabu: Ekitabu ŋolo akisom ŋolo kisyaunet. Akaramojoŋ 1st primer for Karamoja, Taposa, Turkana* London: SPCK
* 1936: *Kitabu: Ekitabu ŋolo akisom ŋolo kisyaunet. Akaramojoŋ 2nd primer for Karamoja, Taposa, Turkana* London: SPCK
* 1989: 'Memoirs' manuscript

Owen, W and Buxton, AB (tr.)
* 1933: *Genesis: Ekitabu ŋolokisyaunet a Musa* London: British and Foreign Bible Society

Owen, W and Sogol, Caleb (tr.)
* 1933: *Prayer and Hymnbook* London: SPCK

* 1934a: *Luke: Eyemut ŋolo kolong egiritai a Luka ŋolakwaŋan* London: British and Foreign Bible Society
* 1934b: 'Gospel of John' manuscript
* 1934c: 'Grammar of Karimojong' manuscript

Oxfam
* 2001: 'Conflict's Children: The human cost of small arms in Kitgum and Kotido' Oxford: Oxfam

Paget Wilkes, A Hamilton (ed. tr.)
* 1930a: *Prayer and Hymnbook* Kaimosi: Friends Africa Mission
* 1930b: *A First Reader* Kaimosi: FAM; also in 'Suk'
* 1930c: *A First Catechism* Kaimosi: FAM
* 1931a: *St. Mark in Shamba Swahili*; also in 'Suk' Kaimosi: FAM
* 1931b: *St. Mark in Karamojong* Kaimosi: FAM
* 1932a: *Lokong – Tells His Story* London: Bible Churchmen's Missionary Society
* 1932b: *Mark: Eemut ngolo kolong kigirio la Marako lokareunan* London: British and Foreign Bible Society

Palmquist, Stephen
    1992: 'Does Kant Reduce Religion to Morality?' *Kant-Studien* 83:129–48

pa'Lukoba, O
    1971: 'Acholi Dance and Dance Songs' *Uganda Journal* 35/1:55–61

Parrinder, E Geoffrey
    1968: *African Traditional Religion* London: SPCK

PARTICIP
* 1992: 'Evaluation of Karamoja Development Project, Phase II' European Development Fund Project no. 5100.33.42.46 Wehingen: PARTICIP

Paterson, EPC
* 193?: *Trekking in Toposa* London: Bible Churchmen's Missionary Society

Patterson, KD
    1969: 'The Pokot of Western Kenya 1910–1963: The Response of a Conservative People to Colonial Rule' Syracuse Occasional Paper 53, New York

Pazzaglia, Augusto
* 1973: *I Karimojong* Bologna: Editrice Missionaria Italiana
* 1982: *The Karimojong* Bologna: Editrice Missionaria Italiana

p'Bitek, Okot
    1963: 'The Concept of Jok among the Acholi and Lango' *Uganda Journal* 27/1: 15–29 Mar
    1965: 'Acholi Concept of Fate – *Woko, Wilobo, Run-Piny*' *Uganda Journal* 29/1: 85–94
    1970: *African Religions in Western Scholarship* Nairobi: East African Literature Bureau
    1971: *Religion of the Central Luo* Nairobi: East African Literature Bureau

Pearce, RF
* 1941: *Light in the Darkness* London: Bible Churchmen's Missionary Society

Peek, PM (ed.)
    2001: *African Divination Systems: Ways of knowing* Bloomington: Indiana University Press

Peel, JDY
  2000: *Religious Encounter and the Making of the Yoruba* Bloomington: Indiana University Press
Peristiany, JG
* 1951: 'The Age-Set System of the Pastoral Pakot' *Africa* 21:188–206, 279–302
* 1954: 'Pakot Sanctions and Structure' *Africa* 24:17–25
  1964: *The Social Institutions of the Kipsigis* London: Routledge, Kegan Paul
* 1975: 'The Ideal and the Actual: the Rôle of the Prophets in the Pokot Political System' in Beattie and Lienhardt 1975:167–212
Persse, EM
* 1934: 'Ethnological Notes on the Karimojong' *Uganda Journal* 1/2:112–15
Philip, MS
* 1958: 'A Working Plan for the Labwor Hills and Otukei Central Forest Reseves, Karamoja District, 1958–67' Uganda Government: Department of State and Public Insititutions, Forest Dept.
Pirouet, Louise
* 1978: *Black Evangelists: The Spread of Christianity in Uganda 1891–1914* London: Collins
Platvoet, Jan G
  1993: 'African Traditional Religions in the Religious History of Mankind' *Journal for the Study of Religion* 6/2:29–48
  1999: 'Contexts, concepts, and contests: Towards a pragmatics of defining religion' in Platvoet and Molendijk 1999:463–516
Platvoet, Jan G and Molendijk, Arie L (eds)
  1999: *The Pragmatics of Defining Religion: Contexts, concepts, and contests* Leiden: Brill
Plinius Secundus, Caius
  1582: *Historia Mundi Naturalis* Frankfurt: Sigismund Feyerabend for Martin Lechler
Polanyi, M
  1967: *The Tacit Dimension* London: Routledge, Kegan Paul
Pomeroy, DE and Tushare, Herbert
* 1996: 'Biodiversity of Karamoja: Ground Survey Results and Analyses' Kampala: Ministry of Tourism, Wildlife, and Antiquities
Posnansky, Merrick
  1966: (ed.) *Early Stone Age – An Interpretative Approach in Prelude to East African History* Oxford: Oxford University Press
  1967: 'The Iron Age in East Africa' in Bishop and Clark 1967:637ff
* 1974: 'The Prehistory of East Africa' in Ogot 1974:52ff
Posnansky, M and Cole, G
* 1963: 'Recent Excavations at Magosi, Uganda' *Man* 63:104–6
Posnansky, M and Nelson, CM
  1968: 'Rock Paintings and Excavations at Nyero, Uganda' *Azania* 3:47–66
Posnansky, M and Sekibengo, W
* 1959: 'Ground Stone Axes and Bored Stones in Uganda' *Uganda Journal* 23:179–81

Posnansky, M and Wilson, JG
* 1961: 'The later stone age of Northern Uganda in the light of recent discoveries from Karamoja' *Uganda Journal* 25

Powell-Cotton, PHG
* 1904: *In Unknown Africa* London: Hurst and Blackett

Prins, AHJ
1970: *East African Age-Class Systems* Westport, Conn: Negro University Press

Prunier Gérard
1999: 'Uganda and Southern Sudan, 1986–1989: New regimes and peripheral politics' in Hanson and Twaddle 1999: 178–87

Puccioni, N
1948: 'Una nuova carta etnica dell'Africa Orientale e la diffusione delle tribö Nilo Camitiche' *Rivista Geografica Italiana* 55: 5

Pulkol, David
* 1994: 'Karimojong Inter-Country Raids and Roads Insecurity: the leadership crisis in the case of the Bokora and Matheniko counties: Moroto District between 1989–91' Kampala
* 1999: 'Knowledge, Practice, Institutions and Natural Resource Management: A Study of Rupa Sub County in Moroto District of Karamoja' ALARM Working Paper 11, Kampala: Centre for Basic Research

Purvis, JB
* 1909: *Through Uganda to Mount Elgon* London: Fisher Unwin

Quam, MD
* nd: 'Social Change in Karamoja' Kampala, MISR, Namugaba Conference Paper
* 1978: 'Cattle Marketing and Pastoral Conservatism: the Karimojong District 1948–70' *African Studies Review* 21/1:49–71
* 1979: 'Pastoral Economy and Cattle Marketing in Karamoja' PhD thesis, Indiana University
* 1997: 'Creating Peace in an Armed Society: Karamoja, Uganda 1996' *African Studies Quarterly* 1/1, available at http://www.clas.ufl.edu/africa/asq

Radcliffe-Brown, AR
1952: *Structure and Function in Primitive Society* London: Cohen and West

Ranger, Terence O
nd: 'The Early History of Independency in Southern Rhodesia' mimeograph
1965: 'African Attempts to Control Education in East and Central Africa 1900–1939' *Past and Present* 32:57–85
1983: 'The Invention of Tradition in Colonial Africa' in Hobsbawm and Ranger 1983:211–65
1985: *The Invention of Tribalism in Zimbabwe* Gweru, Zimbabwe: Mambo
1993a: 'The Invention of Tradition Revisited: The Case of Colonial Africa' in Ranger and Vaughan 1993:62–111
1993b: 'The Local and the Global in Southern Africa Religious History' in Hefner 1993:65–98
1995: 'Religious Pluralism in Zimbabwe' *Journal of Religion in Africa* 25/3: 226–51
1998: 'Concluding Comments' in Yeros 1998:133–44

1999a: 'Taking on the Missionary's Task: African spirituality and the mission churches of Manicaland in the 1930s' *Journal of Religion in Africa* 29/2: 175–205
1999b: *Voices from the Rocks: Nature, culture, and history in the Matopos Hills of Zimbabwe* Oxford: James Currey
2001: 'Review of Peel 2000' *African Affairs* 100/401:653–6
Ranger, TO and Kimambo, I (eds)
1972: *The Historical Study of African Religion* London: Heinemann
Ranger, TO and Vaughan, MO (eds)
1993: *Legitimacy and the State in Twentieth Century Africa* London: Macmillan
Ranger, TO and Weller, J
1975: *Themes in the Christian History of Central Africa* London: Heinemann
Rattray, JM and Byrne, O
* 1963: *Reconnaissance Survey of Karamoja District* Rome: FAO
Ravenstein, EG
* 1891: 'Messrs Jackson and Gedge's Journey to Uganda via Masailand' *Proceedings of the Royal Geographical Society* 13/4:193–208 Apr; also in *Uganda Journal* 12/2 1948
Rawicz, Slavomir
* 1986: *Kilun Moroto* Soul: Hangulu
Rayani, S
* nd: 'The Karimojong of Uganda' Makerere University
Rayne, Henry
* 1923: *The Ivory Raiders* London: Heinemann
Rees, Garth ap
1996: 'The Last Intake of Administrative Officers' in Brown 1996:59–62
Reynolds, GW
* 1956: 'Three New Species and one new variety of Aloe from Karamoja, Uganda' *Journal of South African Botany* 22:135–44
Ricciardi, Mirella and Wan, Barney
1974: *Vanishing Africa* London: Collins
Richards, Audrey and Kuper, A (eds)
* 1971: *Councils in Action* Cambridge: Cambridge University Press
Richards, Charles and Place, J
* 1960: *East African Explorers* Oxford: Oxford University Press
Ricoeur, Paul
1974: *The Conflict of Interpretations* Evanston: Northwestern University Press
Rigby, Peter
1969: *Cattle and Kinship among the Gogo* Ithaca: Cornell University Press
1981: 'Pastors and Pastoralists: the Differential Penetration of Christianity among East African Cattle Herders' *Comparative Studies in Society and History* 23/1:96–129
1985: *Persistent Pastoralists: Nomadic societies in transition* London: Zed Books
Robbins, Lionel H
* 1970: 'Rock Paintings at Napudeh Hill, Karamoja' *Uganda Journal* 34/1
Robbins, LH, McFarlin, S *et al.*
* 1977: 'Rangi, a Late Stone Age site in Karamoja district, Uganda' *Azania* 12: 209–33

Robertshaw, Peter (ed.)
   1990: *A History of African Archaeology* London: James Currey
Robertshaw, P and Collett, D
   1983: 'A New Framework for the Study of Early Pastoral Communities in East Africa' *Journal of African History* 24/3:289–301
Robinson, Susan
* 1980a: 'Background briefing document on Uganda/Karamoja: Prepared for the Church Missionary Society medical team' London: International Disaster Institute
* 1980b: 'Karamoja famine relief, July–September 1980: debriefing report' London: International Disaster Institute
Robinson, S et al.
* 1980: 'Famine Relief in Uganda' *Lancet* 849–51
Rodhain, F et al.
* 1989: 'Arbovirus infections and viral haemorrhagic fevers in Uganda: A serological survey in Karamoja district 1984' *Transactions of the Royal Society of Tropical Medicine and Hygiene* 83/6:831–54
Roncari, G
* 1981: 'Vento, sabbie e spine di Karamoja' *Geodes* 3/Jul.
Roncari, G and Mantovani, M
* 1973: *Appunti di grammatica karimojong* Gulu: Catholic Press
Root, Alan [see film, p. 188]
* 1964: 'The Karamojong of North-West [*sic*] Uganda' *East African Annuals* 59–64
Rottland, Franz
* 1983: 'Lexical Correspondence between Kuliak and Southern Nilotic' in Vossen and Bechhaus-Gerst 1983b:479–97
Rottland, F and Otaala, LA
   1983: 'Mid-Vowel Assimilation in Teso-Turkana' in Vossen and Bechhaus-Gerst 1983a:169–81
Rovati, G
* 1987: 'Il contributo del sistema scholastico allo sviluppo del Karamoja' in Gubert 1987
Rowland, James RJ
* 1979a: *How to grow good crops in Karamoja* Kampala: UNICEF
* 1979b: *How to grow good vegetables in Karamoja* Kampala: UNICEF
* 1981: 'Karamoja Cattle-camps Development Programme' mimeo
* 1982: 'Approaches to Karamojong Cattle People' mimeograph
* 1983: 'Jie Ritual' typescript
* 1984: 'Some information about the range of seeds for dry areas' Kotido, mimeograph
Rowland, JRJ and Wilson, JG (eds)
* 1990 'Agriculture in Karamoja' manuscript
Ruel, Malcom
   1997: *Belief, Ritual and the Securing of life: Reflexive essays on a Bantu religion* Leiden: Brill

Rupesinghe, Kumar (ed.)
* 1989: *Conflict Resolution in Uganda* London: James Currey

Sabiiti, EN
* 1990: 'The Place and Role of fire in Pasture and Rangeland Management in Uganda' in 'First Rangeland Improvement for Beef Production Workshop' Kampala: Makerere University

Salih, MA Mohamed and Ahmed, AGM (eds)
* 2001: *African Pastoralism: Conflict, institutions, and government* London: Pluto

Salih, MA Mohamed and Markakis, John
    1998: *Ethnicity and the State in Africa* Uppsala: Nordiska Afrikainstitutet

Salzman, PC
    1967: 'Political Organization among Nomadic Peoples' Proceedings', American Philosophical Society Apr
    1971: 'Comparative Studies of Nomadism and Pastoralism' *Anthropological Quarterly* Special Issue, July

Sanders, WJ and Bodenbender, BE
* 1994: 'Morphometric analysis of lumbar vertebra UMP 67-28: Implications for spinal function and phylogeny of the Miocene Moroto hominoid' *Journal of Human Evolution* 26/3:203–37

Sanderson, LP and GN
    1981: *Education, Religion and Politics in Southern Sudan 1899–1964* London: Ithaca Press

Saunderson, MH
    1969: *Some Economic Aspects of Uganda's Livestock Industry* Kampala: USAID

Schadeburg, TC and Bender, ML (eds)
* 1981: *Nilo-Saharan Proceedings*, 1st Nilo-Saharan Linguistics Colloquium, Leiden 8-10.9.80 Dordrecht/Cinnaminson: Foris Publications

Schlee, Günther
* 2003: 'Violent Settings in Rapid Change' *Africa* 73/3:333–42

Schmidt, Wilhelm
    1912–55: *Der Ursprung der Gottesidee* (12 vols) Munster: Aschendorff

Schneider, HK
    1957: 'The Subsistence Role of Cattle among the Pokot and in East Africa' *American Anthropologist* 59:278–300
    1959: 'Pakot Resistance to Change' in Bascom and Herskovits 1959:144–67
    1979: *Livestock and Equality in East Africa* Bloomington: Indiana University Press

Schneider, Harold K
    1984: 'Livestock in African Culture and Society: A Historical Perspective' in Simpson, JR and Evangelou, P (eds) 1984: *Livestock Development in Sub-Saharan Africa* Boulder, CO: Westview

Schweinfurth, G et al. (eds)
* 1888: *Emin Pasha in Central Africa* London: George Philip

Scripture Gift Mission
* 1938: *Akiteyar Nginga Apolon* London: SGM

* 1950a: '*Inyakunio Nanok*' London: SGM Illustrated Bible Leaflet 1
* 1950b: '*Akitadapet a Ikoku a Ngini Eveliyelan Ngiboro*' London: SGM Illustrated Bible Leaflet 3
* 1950c: '*Ngungu Ka Arerengu*' London: SGM Illustrated Bible Leaflet 4
* 1964a: *Ngunga Eyia Toma* London: SGM
* 1964b: *Totupunar* London: SGM
* 1965: *Potu* London: SGM

Sebeok, Thomas A (ed.)
   1987: *Encyclopedic Dictionary of Semiotics* 3 vols Berlin: Mouton de Gruyter

Seeland, Klaus
   1997: *Nature is Culture: Indigenous knowledge and socio-cultural aspects of trees and forests in non-European cultures* London: Intermediate Technology

Segal, Robert A
   1983: 'Victor Turner's theory of ritual' *Zygon* 18:327–35
   1986: 'The desociologizing of the sociology of religion' *Scottish Journal of Religious Studies* 7/15:5–28 Spr

Seligman, CG and BZ
   1932: *Pagan Tribes of the Nilotic Sudan* London: Routledge

Setiloane, Gabriel M
   1976: *The Image of God among the Sotho-Tswana* Rotterdam: Balkema

Shaw, Rosalind
   1990: 'The Invention of "African Traditional Religion"' *Religion* 20/4:339–53

Shearwood, GF
* 1921: 'Karamojo: One of Africa's Old Corners' *Natural History* 30/2:196–204

Sherif, NM
   1984: 'Nubia before Napata -3, 000 to -750' in UNESCO 1984:IV,244ff

Shinnie, Peter L
   1971a: 'The Legacy to Africa' in Harris 1971: ch15
   1971b: (ed.) *The African Iron Age* Oxford: Oxford University Press

Shorter, Aylward
* 1974: *East African Societies* London: Routledge Kegan Paul

Simon, David
   1997: 'Rethinking (Post)Modernism, post-Colonialism and Post-Traditionalism: South–North Perspectives' CEDAR Research Paper 22, Royal Holloway, University of London

Simon, VS
   1983: 'Christ came to Nubia-Kush – Christian kingdoms of Sudanese Africa 543–1504 AD' *AME Zion QR*

Simonse, Simon
* 2003: 'Leaving the Arms Crisis: Prelude to a second disarmament in Karamoja' Utrecht: Pax Christi

Simonse, Simon and Kurimoto, Eisei
* 1998: 'Introduction' in Kurimoto and Simonse 1998:1–28

Skvoretz, JV and Conviser, RH
* 1974: 'Interests and Alliances' *Man* 9/1:53–67 Mar

Smith, A Donaldson
   1900: 'An Expedition between Lake Rudolf and the Nile' *Bulletin of the*

Geographical Society of Philadelphia 2:115–38; also in *Geographical Journal* 1: 600–625

1901: 'Explorations in East Central Africa' *National Geographical* 12:42f

Smith, AJ (ed.)
* 1976: *Beef Production in Tropical Africa* Edinburgh: Centre for Tropical Veterinary Medicine

Smith, Paul D
* 1986: 'Famine in Karamoja and the Role of the Church' Diocese of Karamoja, mimeograph
* 1987: 'Background Information on Karamoja' typescript
* 1992: 'The Potential for Water Development as a Strategy for Reconciliation between the Teso and Karamojong along the North Teso–South Karamoja border, Uganda: A report prepared for Christian Engineers in Development and the Christian International Peace Service' Bangor: Centre for Arid Zone Studies, University of Wales

Smith, William Cantwell
1959: *Islam in Modern History* New York: New American Library

Smith, W Robertson
1901: *Lectures on the Religion of the Semites* London: A and C Black

Snowden, JI
1953: *Grass Communities and the Mountain Vegetation of Uganda* London: Crown Agents for Colonies

Somerset, HCA
1954: 'The Junior Secondary School Leavers Project: A Progress Report' Proceedings of the East African Institute of Social Research Conference, Part B, Kampala, Jan. 1–11

Spagnolo, L
* 1973: 'Piccolo Vocabolario della Lingua Karimojong (Italiano–Karimojong)' Moroto, mimeograph

Spear, Thomas and Waller, Richard (eds)
* 1993: *Being Maasai: Ethnicity and identity in East Africa* London: James Currey

Spencer, Paul
1973a: *Nomads in Alliance: Symbiosis and growth among the Rendille and Samburu of Kenya* Oxford: Oxford University Press
* 1973b: 'Review of Colin M Turnbull *The Mountain People*' *Man* 8/4:651f
* 1976: 'Opposing Streams and the Gerontocratic Ladder' *Man* 11/2:153–74
* 1978: 'The Jie Generation Paradox' in Baxter and Almagor 1978:133–49
* 1989: 'The Maasai Double Helix and the Theory of Dilemmas' in Maybury-Lewis and Almagor 1989:297–320
* 1990: *Anthropology and the Riddle of the Sphinx: Paradoxes of change in the life course* London: Routledge
* 1998: *The Pastoral Continuum* Oxford: Clarendon

Spiegel, Richard
* 1985: *Final Report, Animal Disease Control in Karamoja, Uganda* Kampala: FAO

Spooner, B
1971: 'Towards a Generative Model of Nomadism' *Anthropological Quarterly* 44:192–210

Stanier, MW
* 1953: 'The Blood of the Karamojong' *Uganda Journal* 17/2:172–7 Sept
Stephenson, RS
* 1980: 'Karamoja: Famine relief July–September 1980' London: International Disaster Institute
Stewart, Frank H
* 1972: 'Fundamentals of Age-Set Systems' DPhil. thesis, University of Oxford
* 1977: *Fundamentals of Age Group Systems* New York: Academic
Stonier, GW
* 1967: *Off the Rails* London: Hutchinson
Stranex, Ruth
* 1977: *Amudat Sister* London: Patmos
Sundal, Mary B
* 2002: 'Mortality and Causes of Death among Karimojong Agropastoralists of Northeast Uganda, 1940–99' MA dissertation, University of Kansas
Sutherland, Stewart, Houlden, L, Clarke, P and Hardy, F (eds)
1988: *The World's Religions* London: Routledge
Sutton, JEG
* 1974: 'The Settlement of East Africa' in Ogot 1974:70–97
* 1993: 'Becoming Maasailand' in Spear and Waller 1993:38–61

Takana, J (ed.)
1980: 'A Study of Ecological Anthropology on Pastoral and Agropastoral Peoples in Northern Kenya' Kyoto University
Tanner, RES
* 1970a: *Homicide in Uganda 1964* Uppsala: The Scandinavian Institute of African Studies
* 1970b: *Three Studies in East African Criminology* Uppsala: The Scandinavian Institute of African Studies
Taylor, John V
1963: *The Primal Vision* London: SCM
Taylor, Rhena
* 1987: *The Prisoner and Other Stories* Eastbourne: MARC
Tempels, Placide
1969: *Bantu Philosophie* Paris: Présence Africaine
Tescaroli, C
* 1979: 'The Karapokot: A waiting people' *World Mission* 30:28–33
* 1981: 'The Tragedy of Uganda's Karamoja Region' *World Mission* 32:17–21
Thelwall, R
1982: 'Linguistic Aspects of Greater Nubian History' in Ehret and Posnansky 1982:39–56
Thomas, AS
* 1943: 'The Vegetation of Karamoja District' *Journal of Ecology* 31/2:149–77 Nov
Thomas, HB and Scott, R
* 1935: *Uganda* Oxford: Oxford University Press

Tiberondwa, Ado K
* 1978: *Missionary Teachers as Agents of Colonialism* Lusaka: Neczam

Timberlake, L
* 1985: *Africa in Crisis: The causes, the cures of environmental bankruptcy* London: Earthscan

Time-Life Books (ed.)
* 1986: *East Africa* Amsterdam: Time-Life Books

Topolski, D
* 1976: *Muzungu: One Man's Africa* London: Arlington

Tornay, Serge A
* 1978: 'L'Enigma des Murle de L'Omo' *L'Ethnographie* 1:55–75
* 1979a: 'Générations, classes d'âges et superstructures: à propos de l'étude d'une ethnie du cercle karimojong' *Equipe Ecologie* 1979:307–28
* 1979b: 'Armed Conflicts in the Lower Omo Valley' in Fukui and Turton 1979: 97–117

  1979c: 'Rites de mort, rites de vie chez les Nyangatom, Ethiopie' in *Les Hommes et la Mort* Paris: Le Sycomore and Objets et Mondes, Revues du Musée de L'Homme 305–13
* 1979d: 'Médecine du corps, médecine du cosmos: L'éclipse chez les Nyangatom' in Francillon, G and Menget, P (eds) 1979: *Soleil est mort L'éclipse totale de soleil du 30 juin 1973* Nanterre: Laboratoire d'ethnologie et de sociologie comparative 201–43
* 1980a: 'Etudes Ethiopienne, Deux Visages de l'Ethnographie' *L'Homme* 20/2: 99–118
* 1980b: 'La ruine du Karamoja' *Production Pastorale et Société* 7:3–19 Aug
* 1980c: 'Generational Age-Systems and Chronology: Exploring Northern Groups of Central Paranilotes' paper at seminar on 'The archaeology and ethnohistory of the Southern Sudan and adjacent areas' 3–4.12.80 SOAS, University of London

  1981: 'The Nyangatom: an outline of their ecology and social organization' in Bender 1981:137–78
* 1982a: 'La dimension dans la démarche ethnographique' in Heber, Hugo (ed.) 1982: *Enquiête sur le terrain* Fribourg: University Press
* 1982b: 'Archéologie, ethno-histoire, ethnographie' in Mack and Robertshaw 1982:131–48
* 1983: 'Territoire et organization territoriale chez les Nyangatom' *Production Pastorale et Société* 13:103–11
* 1984-5: 'Le Principe Générationnel en Afrique Orientale' *Production Pastorale et Société* 15:87–97 Aug 17:67–72 Aug
* 1985: 'Age et génération en Afrique Orientale', *Production Pastorale et Société* 17:73–81 Aug
* 1986: 'Une Afrique Démasquée, Initiation et Sacrifice chez les Pasteurs d'Afrique Orientale' in Centlivres, Pierre and Hainard, J (eds) 1986: *Les Rites de Passage Aujourd'hui* Lausanne: L'Age d'Homme pp. 69–92
* 1987: 'Vivre en Société Générationelle' in Kellerhals, Jean and C Lalive d'Epinay (eds) 1987: *La Représentation de Soi* Department of Sociology, University of Geneva pp. 145–65

* 1989: 'Un système générationnel: les Nyangatom du sudouest de l'Ethiopie et les peuples apparentés' thèse de doctorat d'Etat, Université de Paris X, Nanterre
* 1998: 'Generational Systems on the Threshold of the Third Millennium: An Anthropological Perspective' in Kurimoto and Simonse 1998:98–120
* 2001: *Les Fusils jaunes: Générations et politique en pay nyangatom (Éthiopie)* Nanterre: Société d'Ethnologie

Tosh, John A
  1973: 'Colonial Chiefs in a Stateless Society: A case study from Northern Uganda' *Journal of African History* 14:473–90
* 1978: *Clan Leaders and Colonial Chiefs in Lango: The political history of an East African stateless society c.1800–1939* Oxford: Clarendon

Tothill, JD
* 1940: *Agriculture in Uganda* Oxford: Oxford University Press

Totty, Lawrence H, Chaundy, GH and Huntingford, GWB
* 1944: *The People and District of West Suk* Nairobi: Ndia Kuu

Tourigny, Yves
* 1979: *So Abundant a Harvest: The Catholic Church in Uganda 1879–1979* London: Darton Longman and Todd

Trappe, Paul
* 1978: 'Development from Below as an Alternative: A Case Study in Karamoja' *Social Strategies* vol. 6 Basle: Social Strategies Publishers

Trendall, AF
* 1961: 'Explanation of the Geology of Sheet 45 (Kadam)' Geological Survey, Uganda

Tricker, BJK, Taylor, WH and Bishop, WW
* 1963: 'Fossils from Karamoja' *Uganda Journal* 27/1:109–14 Mar

Trowell, M and Wachsmann, KP
* 1953: *Tribal Crafts in Uganda* Oxford: Oxford University Press

Tucker, Alfred R
* 1911: *Eighteen Years in Uganda and East Africa* London: Edward Arnold

Tucker, Archibald Norman
* 1967a: 'Erythraic elements and patternings' *African Language Review* 6:18–25
* 1967b: 'Fringe Cushitic' *SOAS Bulletin* 30/3:655–80
* 1971: 'Notes on Ik' *African Studies* 30:341–54
* 1972: 'Notes on Ik' *African Studies* 31:183–201
* 1973: 'Notes on Ik' *African Studies* 32:33–48

Tucker, AN and Bryan, MA
* 1956: *The non-Bantu Languages of North-eastern Africa* London: Oxford University Press
* 1966: *Linguistic Analyses: the non-Bantu Languages of North-eastern Africa* London: Oxford University Press

Tuma, Tom and Phares Mutibwa
* 1978: *A Century of Christianity in Uganda (1877–1977)* Kampala: Uzima

Turnbull, Colin M
  1961: *The Forest People* London: Chatto and Windus
  1965: 'The Mbuti Pygmies of the Congo' in Gibbs 1965:279–317

* 1966a: 'The Ik Mountain farmers' in Turnbull, CM (ed.) 1966: *Tradition and Change in African Tribal Life* Cleveland: World Publishing pp. 119–30
* 1966b: 'Report from Africa: A People Apart' *Natural History* 75/8:8–14 Oct 1966: (ed.) *Tradition and Change in African Tribal Life* Cleveland: World Publishing
* 1967: 'The Ik, alias Teuso' *Uganda Journal* 31/1:63–71
* 1968: 'The Importance of Flux in Two Hunting Societies' in Lee, RB and Vore, I De (eds) *Man the Hunter* Chicago: Aldine Press pp. 132–7
* 1973a: *The Mountain People* London: Jonathan Cape
* 1973b: 'Human Nature and Primal Man' *Social Research* 40/3:511–30 Aug 1973c: *Africa and Change* New York: Knopf
* 1974: 'Reply to Barth' *Current Anthropology* 15/1:103
* 1976: *Man in Africa* London: David and Charles; New York: Anchor/Doubleday

Turner, Victor
1966: 'Colour Classification in Ndembu Ritual' in Banton 1966:47–84
1969: *The Ritual Process* Ithaca: Cornell University Press
1972: 'Passages, Margins and Poverty: Religious Symbols of Communitas' *Worship* 46/7–8:393ff

Turpin, CA
* 1948: 'The Occupation of the Turkwell River Area by the the Karamojong Tribe' *Uganda Journal* 12:161–5

Turton, David
2002: 'Lip-Plates and Globalization among the Mursi' Identity and Ethnicity Seminar, ISCA, University of Oxford 8.3.02
2004: '"Lip Plates and the People who take Photographs": Uneasy encounters between Mursi and tourists in southern Ethiopia' *Anthropology Today* 20/3: 3–8

Twaddle, Michael
* 1967: 'Review of Dyson-Hudson's Karimojong Politics' *Journal of Commonwealth Political Studies* 5/3
* 1969: 'Tribalism in Eastern Uganda' in Gulliver 1969
1988: 'Decentralized violence and collaboration in early colonial Uganda' in Porter, A and Holland, R (eds) 1988: *Theory and Practice in the History of European Expansion Overseas* London: Frank Cass pp. 71–85

Tylor, EB
1903 [1871]: *Primitive Culture* London: John Murray

Uganda Census
* 2001: '1991 Census' available at http://www.undp-org/popin/softproj/pmappl/ uganda-private/sexrcoun.htm, accessed 4.6.01

Uganda Elections
* 2001: 'Uganda Elections' available at http://www.uganda-elections.com/results/ index.html, accessed 4.6.01

Uganda Human Rights Commission
* 2002: 'Civil Military Operation Centres: Karamoja, lessons learnt' Kampala: UHRC

Uganda Land Alliance
* 1997: 'Land Uses, Ownership, and Tenure Systems in Karamoja' Kampala: Uganda Land Alliance

UNCDF
* 1991: 'Integrated Development in Kotido District, Karamoja' New York: UNCDF
UNDP
* 2001a: 'Uganda Census' available at http://www.undp-org/popin/softproj/ pmappl/uganda-private/sexrcoun.htm, accessed 4.6.01
* 2001b: 'Uganda Census' available at http://www.undp-org/popin/softproj/ pmappl/uganda-private/morufeli.htm, accessed 4.6.01
UNESCO
* 1973: 'Educational Development in Uganda' Geneva, 19–27.9.73
* 1975: 'Educational Development in Uganda' Geneva, 27.8–4.9.75
* 1983: *Ugandan Education: Recovery and Reconstruction* Paris: UNESCO
* 1981–: *General History of Africa* 7 vols London: Heinemann
USAID
* 2003: '2002 Annual Report for Uganda: Informational Annexes', avaliable at www.dec.org/partners/ardb/index.cfm?fuseaction=onPage.startcountrycd=617, accessed 13.3.03
Usher-Wilson, LC
  1952: 'Dini ya Misambwa' *Uganda Journal* 16/2:125–9 Sept

Vansina, Jan
  1965: *Oral Tradition* London: Routledge, Kegan Paul
  1985: *Oral Tradition as History* Madison: University of Wisconsin Press
  1990: *Paths in the Rainforests: Toward a history of political tradition in equatorial Africa* Oxford: James Currey
  1999: 'Linguistic Evidence and Historical Reconstruction' *Journal of African History* 40/3:469–73
Veer, Peter van der (ed.)
  1996: *Conversion to Modernities: The globalization of Christianity* London: Routledge
Vigano, M
* 1987a: 'Valutazione dei progetti di intervento' in Gubert 1987
* 1987b: 'Intervention Impact in Karamoja, Uganda, 1981–1986 People's Participation in Projects' MSc dissertation, University of Reading
Vignali, F
* 1983: 'Matany Agricultural Project, Annual Report' Diocese of Moroto Social Services
Vignato, A
  1935: *Racalto di dottrini e suggerimenti per l'utilità practica del giovane missionario* Verona: Nigrizia
  1936: *Raccolta di dottrine sul sacramento del Battesimo* Verona: Nigrizia
Visser, Johannes J
  1982: 'Towards a Missionary Approach among the Pokot' Nairobi
* 1989a: 'Pökoot Religie' dissertation, University of Utrecht
* 1989b: *Pökoot Religion* Oegstgeest: Hendrik Kraemer Institut
Vollbrecht, Judith
* 1984: 'The Karimojong Woman: Decision-making and development' Moroto: Diocese of Moroto

Vossen, Rainer
* 1981: 'The Classification of Eastern Nilotic and its significance for ethnohistory' in Schadeburg and Bender 1981:41–57
* 1982: *The Eastern Nilotes* Berlin: Dietrich Reimer Verlag

Vossen, R and Bechhaus-Gerst, M (eds)
* 1983a: *Nilotic Studies* vol. I Berlin: Dietrich Reimer
* 1983b: *Nilotic Studies* vol. II Berlin: Dietrich Reimer

Wabwire, Arnest
* 1992: 'An Evaluation of the Role of NGOs in Karamoja' paper presented in the workshop on Pastoralism, Crisis and Transformation in Karamoja, 14–15.8.92, Moroto, Kampala: Centre for Basic Research, Working Paper no. 31
* 1993: 'Pastoral Crisis and Transformation: An evaluation of the role of non-governmental organizations in Karamoja' Kampala: Centre for Basic Research

Wachsmann, KP
* 1956: 'Folk Musicians in Uganda' Uganda Museum, Occasional Paper 2
  1963: 'Musicology in Uganda' *Journal of the Royal Anthropological Institute* 83: 50–57

Wainwright, GA
  1954: 'The Diffusion of -UMA as a Name for Iron' *Uganda Journal* 18:113–36

Walcot, P
* 1979: 'Cattle raiding, heroic tradition and ritual' *History of Religions* 18:326–51 May

Walker, Robert
* 2002: *Anti-pastoralism and the growth of poverty and insecurity in Karamoja: Disarmament and development dilemmas* Kampala: DfID East Africa

Wangoola, Paul
* 2000: 'The transformation of cattle rustling and conflict in North Eastern Uganda and the search for participatory solutions' Mbale: AWE, Uganda National Chapter

Watson, John M
* 1949-51: 'The Wild Mammals of Teso and Karamoja' *Uganda Journal* 13–15

Wayland, EJ
* 1931: 'Preliminary Studies of the Tribes of Karamoja' *Journal of the Royal Anthropological Institute* 61:187–230
* 1934: 'Rifts, Rivers, Rains, and Early Man in Uganda' *Journal of the Royal Anthropological Institute* 64:333–52

Wayland, EJ and Burkitt, C
* 1932: 'The Magosian Culture of Uganda' *Journal of the Royal Anthropological Institute* 62:369–90

Wayland, EJ, Brasnett, NV and Bisset, CB
* 1937: *Interim Report on Soil Erosion and Water Supplies in Uganda* Entebbe: Government Printer
* 1938: *Soil Erosion and Water Supplies in Uganda* Geological Survey of Uganda, Memoir 4, Entebbe: Government Printer

Weatherby, John M
* 1962: 'Intertribal Warfare on Mount Elgon' *Uganda Journal* 26:200–212

* 1967: 'Aspects of the Ethnography and Oral Tradition of the Sebei of Mount Elgon' MA thesis, Makerere, University of East Africa
* 1969: 'A Preliminary Note on the Sorat (Tepeth)' *Uganda Journal* 33/1:75-8
* 1972: 'The Sor in Karamoja History before c1780s' seminar paper, Department of History, Makerere University
* 1979: 'Raindrums of the Sor' in Webster 1979:317-31
* 1988: 'The Spirit Cult of the Sor in Karamoja' *Africa* 58/2:210-29

Weber, Max
    1930 [1904-5]: *The Protestant Ethic and the Spirit of Capitalism* London: George Allen and Unwin
    1949: *The Methodology of the Social Sciences* Glencoe, Illinois: Free Press
    1956: *The Sociology of Religion* London: Methuen

Webster, JB (ed.)
* 1970: 'Pioneers of Teso' *Tarikh* 3/2:47-58
* 1973: *The Iteso during the Asonya* Nairobi: East African Publishing House
* 1979: *Chronology, Migration and Drought in Inter-lacustrine Africa* London: Longman

Weinthal, Leo (ed.)
* 1923-6: *The Story of the Cape to Cairo Railway and River Route 1877-1922* 5 vols London: Pioneer

Welbourn, Frank B
* 1961: *East African Rebels* London: SCM
    1965: *Religion and Politics in Uganda* Nairobi: East African Publishing House

Welch, CP
* 1969: 'Pastoralists and Administrators in Conflict 1897-1968' MA thesis, University of East Africa, Makerere

Wellby, MS
* 1900: 'King Menelik's Dominions and the country between Lake Gallop (Rudolf) and the Nile Valley' *Geographical Journal* 16/3:292-306

Wells, Melissa
* 1984: 'We can Improve Relief Efforts, if We Try' *Ekistics* 51/309:501-6
* 1985: 'The Relief Operation in Karamoja: What was learned and what needs improvement' in Dodge and Wiebe 1985:177-82

Wendorf, Fred and Schilde, Romuald
    1994: 'Are the early Holocene cattle in the eastern Sahara domestic or wild?' *Journal of Anthropological Archaeology* 3/4

White, RF
* 1920: 'Notes on the Turkana Tribe' *Sudan Notes and Records* 3:217-22

White, Stephen K
* 1988: *The Recent Work of Jürgen Habermas* Cambridge: Cambridge University Press

Wiebe, KD
* 1984: 'Sources of Pastoral Conservatism: an Economic Analysis of Karimojong Aversion to Market Participation' Department of Anthropology, Carleton College

Wiebusch, Brandi Lynn
* 2002: 'Environmental Effects on Mixed-Longitudinal Growth in Weight of Immunized Karimojong Children' MA dissertation, University of Kansas

Wikan, Unni
  1999: 'Culture: A new concept of race' *Social Anthropology* 7:57–64
Willis, John Jamieson
* 1919: *Uganda* London: CMS
  1925: *An African Church in Building* London: CMS
Wilson, DB
* 1962: 'Malaria Surveys in the Bunyoro, Mubende and Karamoja Districts of Uganda' *East African Medical Journal* 39/10
Wilson, John G
* 1959: 'The Soils of Karamoja District, NP, Uganda' Uganda Protectorate, Department of Agriculture, Series 1: Soils 5
* 1962a: 'The Vegetation of Karamoja District, NP, Uganda' Uganda Protectorate, Department of Agriculture, Series 2: Vegetation 5
* 1962b: 'Opportunities for pasture improvement in the various ecological zones of Karamoja' *East Africa Agriculture and Forestry Journal* 27, Supplement: 47f
* 1962c: 'Soils of the Atumatak catchments' *East Africa Agriculture and Forestry Journal* 27, Supplement: 59f
* 1970a: 'Notes on the Use of Naturally Occurring Minerals in Karamoja' *Uganda Journal* 34/1:81f Mar
* 1970b: 'Preliminary Observations on the Oropom People of Karamoja' *Uganda Journal* 34/2:125–45
* 1970c: 'Recent Archaeological Finds in Karamoja District Uganda and Related Finds in Kenya' typescript
* 1972: 'The Use of Stone Hammers in the Alteration of Horn Profile and the Postulated Origin of This and Other Customs in Ancient Egypt' *Uganda Journal* 36:57–65
* 1973a: 'East Karamoja: Its potential as a National Park' *Uganda Journal* 37:19–27
* 1973b: 'Check-List of the Artifacts and Domestic Works of the Karimojong' *Uganda Journal* 37:81–93
* 1973c: 'The Addition of Talc and Asbestos to Pot Clay by Past and Present Inhabitants of Karamoja District in Uganda and Adjoining Districts of Kenya' *Man* 8:300–302
* 1985: 'Resettlement in Karamoja' in Dodge and Wiebe 1985:163–70
* 1986: 'Oxfam Kapedo Resettlement Project' Moroto: Oxfam
* 1988: 'Livestock' typescript
Wilson, JG and Bredon, RM
* 1963: 'Nutritional value of some common cattle browse and fodder plants of Karamoja' *East Africa Agriculture and Forestry Journal* 28:204–8
Wilson, JG and Napper, DM
* 1979: 'The Assessment of Vegetation Change on the Atumatak Water Catchment Experiment from 1957 to 1975' *East Africa Agriculture and Forestry Journal* 44: 198–205 Special Issue
Wilson, JG and Rowland, JRJ
* 2001: *Land and Agriculture in Karamoja* Leeds: Rowland
Wilson, PJ, Turnbull, CM *et al.*
* 1975: 'More Thoughts on the Ik and Anthropology' *Current Anthropology* 16/3: 343–58 Sept

Wilson, W
* nd: 'Teso-Karamojong English Dictionary' manuscript
Winter, JC *et al.*
* 1975: 'Der soziale Untergang der Ik (Nord Uganda)' *Internationales Afrikaforum* 12/4:344–58
Wolf, Jan-J de
    1980: 'The Diffusion of Age-Group Organization in East Africa' *Africa* 50/3: 305–10
    1983: 'Circumcision and initiation in W Kenya and E Uganda' *Anthropos* 78/3–4:369–410
Wooding, D and Barnett, R
* 1980: *Uganda Holocaust* Grand Rapids: Zondervan
World Bank
* 1985: *Uganda: Progress Towards Recovery and Prospects for Recovery* Washington, DC
Wozei, MN
* nd: 'Karamoja:a Brief Study of Barriers to Development' Institute of Public Administration
* 1977: 'Karamoja' in Young, M (ed.) 1977: *Uganda District Government and Politics 1974–7* Madison: University of Wisconsin, African Studies Program
Wright, ACA
    1940: 'The Supreme Being among the Acholi of Uganda' *Uganda Journal* 7:130–37
    1942: 'Notes on the Iteso Social Organization' *Uganda Journal* 9/2:57–80

Zwilling, Ernst Alexander
* 1965: *Wildes Karamoja: Streifzüge durch unberührtes Uganda* Mödling, Vienna: St Gabriel

D Sundry Works

Maps

* 1874: Baker 1874:I
* 1888: 'Equatorial Province' 1:3 000 000 in Schweinfurth 1888
* 1891a: Casati 1891: II
* 1891b: 'FJ Jackson's Expedition to Uganda, 1889–90' by E Gedge 1:1 000 000 Proceedings of Royal Geographical Society Apr
* 1899a: Uganda Protectorate and Territories to the North, explored by the Macdonald expedition 1897–8 London: War Office IDWO 1420
* 1899b: Uganda Protectorate and territories to North, showing products 1:1 900 800 London: War Office
* 1899c: Uganda Protectorate and territories to North, showing distribution of tribes 1:1 900 800 London:War Office
* 1899d: 'Uganda Protectorate and Territories to the North, explored by the Macdonald expedition 1897–8' in Macdonald 1899a
* 1899e: 'Uganda and adjoining territories' in Macdonald 1899b
* 1900: Map of Uganda 1":10 miles London: War Office IDWO 1429 a–d

* 1901: Report by HM Special Commissioner on the Protectorate of Uganda PP 48:595 London: HMSO
* 1902: Map of Uganda 1:633 600 London: HMSO
* 1903: 'Macdonald Expedition' 1:4 000 000 in Austin 1903
* 1904: Keane 1904:II,596
* 1905: Albert Nyanza 1:1 000 000 Africa 86 Southampton: Ordnance Survey, Geog Section General Staff 1539
* 1907: Uganda 1:125 000 London: War Office
* 1909: 'Rough Map of Usoga and Elgon Districts' in Purvis 1909
* 1917: 'Northern Territories of the Uganda Protectorate' 1:750 000 by RH Leeke *Geographical Journal* 49/3:240
* 1919: Kenya Colony 1:2 000 000 London: War Office
* 1922: Uganda, Kenya, and part of Tanganyika and Belgian Congo 1:3 000 000 Map no. 7, section 5 in Weinthal 1923–:5
* 1923: Uganda Protectorate 1:500 000 Sheet 2 A1 Entebbe: Uganda Survey Department

  1924: Anglo-Egyptian Sudan 1:250 000 Sheet 78-P Khartoum: Survey Office, Dec
* 1925: East Africa London: Philips
* 1926: 'Map Showing Southern and Western Frontiers of Abyssinia' in Darley 1926: 1

  1927: Anglo-Egyptian Sudan 1:250 000 Sheet 78-L Khartoum: Survey Office, Sept
* 1928: Uganda Protectorate 1:1 000 000 Sheet A2 Entebbe: Uganda Survey Department

  1930a: Anglo-Egyptian Sudan 1:250 000 Sheet 78-O Khartoum: Survey Office, June
* 1930b: Anglo-Egyptian Sudan 1:250 000 Sheet 86-C, Madial Khartoum: Survey Office, June

  1933: Anglo-Egyptian Sudan 1:250 000 Sheet 78-K Khartoum: Survey Office, Sept
* 1935a: Kenya Colony 1:2 000 000 London: War Office 2nd edn

  1935b: Anglo-Egyptian Sudan 1:250 000 Sheet 78-H Khartoum Survey Office, June
* 1940: 'Uganda Protectorate Communications' in Tothill 1940:522

  1941: Anglo-Egyptian Sudan 1:250 000 Sheet 78-P Khartoum: Survey Office, July
* 1943: Kenya Colony 1:2 000 000 5th edn Southampton: Ordnance Survey, Geographical Section General Staff 2871
* 1945: Anglo-Egyptian Sudan 1:250 000 Sheet 86-C Khartoum: Survey Office, Oct
* 1948: Uganda Protectorate 1:1 000 000 W and AK Johnston
* 1950: Uganda 1:50 000 Prelim, Directorate of Colonial Surveys, Teddington
* 1953: Karamoja District of NP, Uganda Protectorate 1: 500 000 A1109 Survey, Lands, and Mines Department, Uganda
* 1954–: 'Geological Survey of Uganda' Entebbe
* 1955: Gazetteer No1 British East Africa, Office of Geog Department of Interior, Washington DC

* 1957–: Uganda 1:50 000 Series Y732 Entebbe: Lands and Surveys Department; Directorate of Overseas Surveys 26/426
* 1958–: East Africa 1:250 000 Series Y503 Entebbe: Lands and Surveys Department/Nairobi: Survey of Kenya
* 1958: Southern Karamoja Water Resources by VR Dyson-Hudson, Lands and Survey Department, USD 10 cf. Dyson-Hudson, N 1958b and 1966
* 1961: Uganda 1:2 000 000 2nd edn Directorate of Overseas Surveys 986
* 1962: Atlas of Uganda Entebbe: Department of Lands and Survey
* 1963: Uganda 1:500 000 Department of Lands and Survey
* 1964: Gazetteer no.82 Uganda Office of Geography, Department of Interior, Washington,DC: Govt Printing Office
* 1965-: 'Uganda Atlas of Disease Distribution' Makerere
* 1966: 'Geology of Karamoja' Entebbe: Department of Lands and Survey
* 1967: 'Uganda, 1:2 500 000 Moroto' Uganda Geological Survey, Kampala
* 1968: 'The Uganda Vegetation Survey' 1:500 000 in Aerial Surveys and integrated studies Proceedings of the Toulouse Conference, Paris: UNESCO; cf. Langdale-Brown et al. 1964
* 1971: 'Population geography' Langlands 1971
* 1980: Kenya and Uganda 1:2 000 000 London: George Philip

Government Reports

* 1920: *Report on the Karamoja District* 1920 Chidlaw-Roberts, Capt. J
* 1939–60: *Annual Reports on the Eastern Province*
* 1947–60: *Annual Reports on the Northern Province*
* 1950: *Geographical and Tribal studies from the east African Census 1948: African population of the Uganda Protectorate* Nairobi: East African Statistical Department
* 1953–4: *Annual Report* Geological Survey Department, Entebbe
* 1958: *Karamoja District Plan* Entebbe: Government Printer
* 1958: 'The Karamojong' Background to Uganda, 193, Information Department, Entebbe
* 1959: *Karamoja District, Northern Province, district plan, 1958 revision* Entebbe: Government Printer
* 1961: *Annual Report* District Veterinary Office, Moroto
* 1961: *Report of the Uganda Relationships Commission* Chairman: Earl of Munster, Entebbe: Government Printer
* 1961: *The Economic Development of Uganda* International Bank for Reconstruction and Development
* 1963: *Report of the Committee of Inquiry into the Marketing of Cattle from Karamoja* Chairman: Dr Mahndevan, Entebbe: Government Printer
* 1965–7: 'Report on Uganda Census of Agriculture' Dept of Agriculture, Entebbe: Government Printer
* 1970: *White Paper on the Report Committee on the Marketing of Livestock, Meats, Fish, and their Products in Uganda* Entebbe: Government Press
* 1971: *Report on the 1969 Population Census* Entebbe: Government Press

* 'Annual Reports, South Karamoja Farm Institute, Nabuin' Entebbe: Department of Agriculture
* 197?–: *Annual Reports of the Veterinary Department* Entebbe: Government of Uganda
* 1990: 'Integrated OPL Workshop for Kotido District: 23rd October–4th November 1989' Mbale: Ministry of Health, Health Manpower Development Centre
* 1992: *The 1991 Population and Housing Census* Entebbe: Statistics Dept, Ministry of Finance and Economic Planning
* 1993: *Uganda National Environment Action Plan* Kampala: Ministry of Natural Resources
* 1996a: 'Karamoja Project Implementation Unit: Inception report' Kampala: Ministry of State for Karamoja
* 1996b: 'Proceedings of Workshop on Land Tenure, Natural Resources, and Wildlife in Karamoja' Kampala: Ministry of State for Karamoja
* 1996c: 'Biodiversity of Karamoja: Ground survey results and analyses' Kampala: Ministry of Natural Resources

Sound, Films and Plays

Alwyn, Rachel
* 1998: 'Gun for Sale' Television programme broadcast on 22.1.98 in the series '*Under the Sun*' London: BBC

Anon American
* 1953: 'Karamoja' Private

Bradshaw, Jeremy
* 1983: 'A Tear for Karamoja' Anglia TV

Brook, Peter
* 1975: 'Les Iks' Bouffe du Nord Theatre, Paris: Stage Play

Fanshawe, David
* 1975: 'Africa: ceremonial and folk music' Wotton-under-Edge, Glos: Savdisc, Sound Recording Libraries: 140
* 1991: 'Spirit of African Sanctus, the Original Recordings by David Fanshawe (1969–73)' Wotton-under-Edge, Glos: Savdisc, Sound Recording Libraries: 30
* 2002: 'East Africa Ceremonial and Folk Music' New York: Nonesuch CD

Friedman, David
* 1950: 'Roadshow Trailers' Vol. 1 Seattle, WA: Something Weird Video

Macdonald, JRL
* 1899: Lantern-Slides from the Juba Expedition

MacDougall, David
* 1972?: 'To Live with Herds', in RAI Film Library, Glasgow
* 1973?: 'Nawi' Ethnographic Film Program of California, in RAI Film Library, Glasgow
* 1973: 'Under the Men's Tree' Los Angeles, CA: University of California Extension Media Center, VHS Tape

Marshall Thomas, Elizabeth
* 1963: 'Dodoth Morning' Berkeley: University of California Extension Media Center, Visual Material Libraries:3

Pozner, André
* 1982: 'Jacques Prévert' Paris: Ediciones del Norte, Hanover, NH: Visual Material Libraries:7

Root, Alan
* 1971: 'The Karamojong' Anglia TV: Survival, Series: *The Vanishing Tribes of Africa*

Stockley, RJ
* 1990: Video Recording, London: CMS

Stonier, GW and P
* 1961: 'A Journey to Uganda' Private

TEAR Fund
* 1985: 'Candle in the Darkness' TEAR Fund, Teddington

Index

The Ngakaramojong vocabulary has been included here to allow it to shape and qualify the terminology. A plural form followed by 's' denotes the singular which will also be alphabetically listed. The meaning and page references will always be given against the singular and infinitive forms, if extant. Names of peoples are normally shorn of their prefixes and singular suffixes, which makes their affinities clearer. Personal and place names are located by giving their territorial section and tribe or age-class or country in brackets. The territorial sections are listed under the tribe. Scholars who have researched the Karamojong are listed. Subjects are grouped under one heading rather than listing each separately.

aate, cow 78, 86, 133, 191, 210, 218, 248f
Abac 13, 50
    Abyssinia 43, 47, 50, 64, 66, 74, 119
    Southwest Ethiopia 23, 29, 38–44, 46f, 53f, 128, 173
abar, to grow rich 167
aberu, wife, woman 81, 85, 90, 95, 100f, 110, 160, 164, 167
abokok, turtle 65
abole, gourd-stopper 49
abolokoc, wooden spoon 172
abolokoki, wide-necked gourd 49
Abrahams, RG 106, 109, 143f, 147, 161f; see also ameto
abulangatarun, smooth stones 231
abunore, to come 110
aburuc, trumpet, horn 217
abururiar, to turn upside down 171, 210
Abwor 24, 39, 46, 52f, 64, 106, 112f, 128, 142–5, 147, 161, 213
Aciya, 'Totokobok' (Pian, Karimojong) 69, 75, 158, 194
Acoli 30, 39, 47, 52f, 59, 69, 156, 167, 169, 221
    beliefs 233
    customs 132
    military 120f, 148, 200, 216
Acuka (Jie) 155
acukot, bank, valley 148
adis, sky 232, 236
adokin, to go away in anger, emigrate 193
adome, tree 182
adyak, to be ill 205

    sickness 205
aet, seed, harvest time 189, 195
Africa 3–8, 16, 18, 26, 36, 42f, 49, 58, 74, 94, 113, 131, 158, 179, 223, 256, 258f
    Horn of 38, 57
Afroasiatic 37f, 40–43, 47, 178, 235
    beliefs 224, 232
    'Hamitic' 37f, 47
    Semitic 37, 50
    customs 91, 169, 240
agaa, chameleon 179
agat, to pray antiphonally, invoke 168, 204, 249
age-class 13, 24, 30f, 55, 57, 74, 133–76, 178, 217, 252, 261
    age-section 31, 136–9, 142f, 147f, 149, 151–3, 157f, 166, 171, 177, 242, 248
    age-set 14, 43, 60, 88, 92, 104, 106–11, 116, 130f, 135–79, 184, 200f, 213, 215, 245, 261
    generation-set 14, 30f, 33, 53–6, 59f, 62f, 66, 89, 100, 107, 109, 114–16, 134–74, 182f, 187, 195, 198f, 242, 252, 259, 261
    junior 30, 60, 98, 114, 134, 140, 147, 149, 153–6, 166, 171, 173, 175, 179, 249
    senior 114, 137f, 140, 155f, 160, 166, 170–73, 177f, 246, 249, 252
    leader 138
    names 32, 137

overaging 154, 158f
   system 10, 44, 54, 98, 106, 133–76, 195, 247, 261
   underaging 154, 157
   women's 110, 159, 252
ager, to scarify
agerat, cicatrix, scarification 125f, 198
agiro, thunder 225
agogong, strength 223
agogonyar, to be strong 167
Agoro Mountains (Acoli) 47, 50f
agriculture 17, 19f, 22, 110, 210
   development and 26, 97, 123, 129, 135, 189, 257
   history of 37f, 41, 67, 70, 72, 75
   hoe 41, 110, 113, 128f, 188f
   ritual 31, 33, 129, 183f, 189, 191, 257
   significance 160
agyat, ostrich-feather headdress 216
ajong, to stop, 64
ajore, to raid 50
   raid, company of raiders or warriors 111, 116, 195f
ajukot, ointment 171
ajulot, animal sacrifice 189, 192, 195, 240
akaae, small gourd 181
akai, hut 27, 87
akaipapait, half-sister 87
akaiyeyait, coeval cousin 87
akalele, flood 225
akaleman, invoker of spirits 181, 255
akaloro, divining or ceremonial sandal 222
Akamu, Zephaniah (Ik) 73
akamuran, mother-in-law 89
akaparaparat, shiny metal nose-plate
akapil, to practise sorcery 224
   evil 223
akare, well 232
akerit, to revere 134
akero, threshing-floor, dancing ground 134, 163, 184, 189
aketunetunet, stone blade 200
akiar, to kill 110
akibem, to cast an evil eye 225
akibok, to dig 65
akibut, to contribute to blood/bridewealth 85
akicen, to curse 203
akiciket, order 236
akicolicol, to leave first 53
akicud, to remove hair, bewitch 224

akicul, to eat meat 84
akicum, to spear 105
akicun, to burn blood off spear 197
akidong, to jump in the dance 216
akidung, cut, separate 167, 175, 242, 244
akiduny, to be near 28
akidwar, to divine, predict, promise 87, 220
akidyak, to miss the target 205
akidyek, to forgive, absolve 83, 108, 205, 213
akigat, to pray antiphonally 1, 250
akijuk, anoint, smear 166, 219, 243
   to push, travel 243
akijul, to alter 189
akikarit, to be thin 60f
akiker, to revere 134
akiki, to repent 107
akikujukuj, to tie up the rain 192, 235
akikwaar, to stop raining 232
akikwang, to swim 233
akila, to be clean 166
akilal, to tie up the rains 110, 186, 192, 241, 253
akilam, to curse 203, 222
akilamilam, to divine 222
akilamakinet, curse 203
akileer, to be clear 18
akilek, to vomit 18
akileleb, to fill up 18
akilem, harvest 18
akilep, to milk 18
akilimet, stain 202
akilip, to beg, pray 78, 83, 168, 249f
akilok, to trap, hunt 42, 126, 171
akimal, to greet, court 80
akimar, to count 88
akime, to drive (livestock, people) 104
akimuj, food 86, 172, 247f
akine, goat 110
akingol, kill, slaughter 108, 187
akiniamun, to escort 89
akinup, to believe 250
akinyakun, to bring back 110
akinyal, to mix up, confuse society 110
akinyalinyalakinet, chaos 236
akinyan, to avenge 225
akinyang, crocodile 225
akinyonyo, to anoint 160
akipe, to roast 240
akipet, to stamp 217
akipyed, to curse 203, 225

akiram, to drive livestock 86, 105
akired, to stain with blood 233
akirik, to guide, surround, hunt 134
akiriket, sacred assembly; *see* assembly
  church 28, 133, 162, 166, 189
akiro, word, thing, matter 105, 186, 220
akiroga, to be about to die 179
akiru, rain 110, 191f, 225, 232, 249
akiruet, water-trough 87
akisec, to spoil, transgress, sin 188, 224, 243
akiseg, to be antisocial 243
akisegar, to avoid 243
akisil, to make peace 101, 122, 200, 224, 236
akisitakin, to accuse 224
akisub, to devise spiritually, create 186, 195
akisyon, to have mercy 108
akitac, to compensate 105
akiting, to hold hands, woo 83
akitiptowo, prostitution 80
akitocol, to feed meat to, beseech the elders 187, 193f, 205; *see also angola*; sacrament
akitolim, to cool down 202
akitopolor, to promote, promotion 141–4, 146–8, 173, 196, 252
akitub, to distinguish, discriminate 105
akitujuk, to anoint, bless 166, 243
akitwar, to herd domestic livestock 89
akiwan, to spoil, break 222
akiwat, to sprinkle 252
akiwo, stop, stand 105, 193
akiwodokin, freeing the herd(er)s, 160, 176, 182, 185, 193f, 202, 205
akiwonga, to cry out 214
akiwor, to call out the name of the beloved ox 252
akoloba, bushbuck 67
akoro, hunger, famine 94
akuj, god, spirit 33, 226f, 233f, 247
akuja, well 232
Akujů 178, 207, 219–37, 239, 242–61; *see also* pray
  Creator 33, 172, 178, 186, 194f, 232–6, 252
  death 229f
  elders 60, 115, 177f, 192, 250
  emuron 180f
  fire-maker 183
  gender of 234f

  place of 229f, 232, 236
  presence of 49, 132, 135, 166, 168, 171, 197, 207, 225, 228, 234, 236ff
  preserver 75, 80, 88, 91, 101, 108, 124, 132, 134, 153, 167, 194–203
  punisher 79, 97, 105, 188, 197–9, 230, 235
  rain 192, 198, 219, 226, 234
  revealer 90, 136, 166, 233, 243
  sky 33, 225, 228, 233, 236
  trusted 98, 168, 170, 172, 176, 187, 190f, 194, 203, 206, 219, 235f
  water 225
  wind, spirit 169, 225–8, 231–3, 243, 250
akujwanut, miracle 222
akuring, ox-fat 170
akurwor, to unlock 175, 201
Akut, Lokwaki (Kanawat, Orwakol, Jie) 93
akuta, digging-stick, ace-of-spades hoe 66, 189
akwaara, spear 67
akwaare, night 232
akwap, country, land 29, 32, 175, 186, 188, 229, 232, 235
akwar, day 232
alalak, so many 167, 252
alar, fence 27
alel, to flow 18, 225
alelyakin, to love greatly 225
alelyan, to be joyful, 18
Aleper, Apei (Kanawat, Orwakol, Jie) 93f
Aleper, Apothia (Kanawat, Orwakol, Jie) 125
Alerek, (Labwor) 1, 20, 128
alilat, resentful, envious 224
alokakinet, rainbow 225
aloket, snare, frame of headdress 171, 198
alomar, massed cattle-camp 29, 97, 115f, 196
alut, single-orificed flute 174
Alwa, Kingdom of (Sudan) 43, 49
amagwoikin, to be distorted 55
amalaat, harlot 80
amatida, home-made gun 128
amet, to possess livestock 104
ameto, enforcement, penal system 104–110, 179, 203
amojong, to grow old 167
amolitenyit, intestine 219
amomwara, horn 217
amon, funeral banquet 201

amoni, the bush, thicket 181, 200, 220, 222
amoru, stone, rock
amunyen, notch in ox's ear 125, 214
Amurkwang (Kaceri, Caicaon, Oding, Najie) 189
amuro, hind legs 145, 167, 175, 180, 219, 242, 244
    to sacrifice 162, 167, 239
amuron, healer, ritual specialist 31f, 63, 90, 162, 179, 180, 182, 188, 224, 253
amuronot, sacrifice 162, 195, 202, 240
amuros, sacrifice 174, 180, 201
angarwe, iliac gland 153, 219, 242
angola, slaughter beseeching the elders 182, 187, 194; *see also akitocol*
anok, calf-pen 50
anupit, belief, faith 251
anyamet, generation-set 142
anyarare, cow-in-milk 89
Apa-, father, master (of) 135, 179, 215; *see also* cattle, ox-name
apedor, to be able 223
    power 173
Apeitolim (Moroto, Karimojong) 122
aperit, fireplace 27f
apese, girl 92
apoka, to plant
apol, flank 242
apolon, big 225; *see also ere apolon*
    Moru Apolon (Turkana) 241
apolou, honour, quality of greatness 85
apongai, a bush 108
aporojan, to sing, recite exuberantly 219
apua, dust 201
apudor, to betrothe 84
Apule River (Karimojong) 59, 64, 66, 134, 173f
apun, funeral 201
apunor, to cut open a sacrificial victim 201, 242
Arab 43, 49, 68
aramet, hammer 214
archetypal myth 31, 49, 54, 60, 233
arikor, to capture, lead away (in chains) 88
Aring, Apainyangainyang (Jie) 173
armlets 137, 151, 210
aro, black cotton soil, 19, 252
aropar, part-payment of bridewealth 85
aroparitai, pledged, fiancée
arukan, leather strip, strap 198
aruko, to be together 85, 167

Arupan (Jie) 109
arupepe, wooden trumpet 86, 174, 194, 217
asapan, age-class, to initiate 82, 93, 135, 142f, 154, 156, 162–4, 175, 185, 246
asapanet, age-set 141, 175
asapanů, initiation, age-class system 53, 107, 126, 135f, 146, 156–62, 164, 172, 177f, 181f, 198, 261
asecit, social problem, transgression 106
asenorit, stone cairn 227
asiket, cow-dung 51
assembly 29–32, 74, 87, 105, 115, 120, 132–5, 146, 153, 155, 167f, 176, 178–80, 193f, 205f, 211, 219, 241f, 250, 252
asuka, sheet, blanket 164, 211
asukongiro, knee-joint 241
asulany, agrarian sacrifice 189
ataloupal, *see loupal*
atapapa, *see papa*
atapapaa, *see papaa*
atap, sorghum stodge 58, 87, 90, 138, 167, 172, 185, 195
Atap (subsection of Oding, Najie) 143; *see also* Ekatapit; Tap
atapar, dam 189, 231
atapitowo, prostitute 81
ateker, clan 24, 173
ateran, bride, daughter-in-law 88f
atimat, old lady 166, 252
atingat, engaged 83
atom, gun 131
atorobe, chest, bosom 180
atuko, to gather 133
atukokin, to assemble, gather, herd 86, 93
atukot, gathering, meeting 113, 133, 193
atum, great or ceremonial spear 147, 184, 241
atuman, fat 215
atwanare, to die 48, 105, 164, 201
atyonis, power, miracle 222
auryanet, resting-place, subsection 28
Awapawosit (Jie) 182
awatun, sprinkling, blessing 252
awi, cattle-camp 29, 116, 174, 193; *see also nawi*
awiyenit, spirit of the departed 228
ayeerit, spiral of hair 233

Baanga (Dodosö generation-set) 152
    (Jie age-set) 151
    (Karimojong age-section) 139, 157

Bako (EC clan) 47, 50, 53
Barber, James 11, 119, 148, 259
Bari (Sudan) 39, 46, 48–52
Baringo, Lake (Kenya) 44
BCMS 70–73
belief 6–8, 12f, 29, 77, 194, 232, 234, 237, 250, 258; *see also akinup*
  and behaviour 8, 17, 67, 236
  beliefs 29, 33, 145, 187, 237, 251
  implicit 246
Bilatuk, Pian river-unit 20, 28, 65
birth 18, 32f, 84, 90f, 99, 124, 157, 176, 219, 255, 257
blessing 136, 163, 166, 176, 185, 223, 226, 256
  Akujů 30, 33, 49, 79f, 101, 124, 134, 144, 167, 182, 186, 194f, 202, 207, 219, 228f, 235f, 239, 242f, 247–51
  elders 126, 173, 176, 187–9, 193f, 196, 228, 252, 255
  families 84f, 88–91, 252
  fathers 113, 195
  fire-maker 183f
  women 125, 170, 196
blood 42, 95, 159, 202, 261
  brotherhood 200
  diet 195, 210, 212, 233, 236, 240, 253
  -feuding 98, 119f
  spear 130, 197–200
  sacrifice 166, 172, 196, 242–5, 247
Boko (Jie age-set) 136, 149f
bon, only, alone 59
borders 4f, 16, 19, 22f, 29f, 40, 45, 47, 60, 106, 116f, 121, 182, 191, 220–23
bracelet 43, 178, 180
brands, cattle 78, 122, 124, 176, 214, 219, 240; *see also emacar*
British, 1, 35, 129
  administration 11, 109f, 115, 117, 119f, 125, 200, 227
  Christian mission 68–70
  Empire 4, 23, 30, 74f, 113, 120, 148, 173, 258
Bukusu (Luyia, Kenya) 119, 149
Bunyoro (Uganda) 47, 62
burial 38, 67, 192, 229; *see also* rites; sacraments
Bushmen 36–8, 41
  Khoisan languages 37, 41, 45, 50
Butong, Peter 109, 201

Buxton, Alfred 70–72

castration 42, 50, 214, 216f, 245
cattle 38–42, 45, 47, 60, 64, 132, 250, 252
  and *passim*; *see also aate*; milk
  beloved ox 87, 94, 104, 125, 198, 201f, 205, 213–17, 219, 241; *see also akiwor*; ox-name
  birthwealth 84, 95
  bloodwealth 84f, 97, 101, 108f, 211, 230, 240
  brand 24, 78, 122, 124, 166, 176, 214, 219, 240; *see also emacar*
  bridewealth 31, 44, 60, 78–90, 92–99, 101, 105f, 108f, 113, 132, 158–60, 164, 202, 210, 240
  -camps 31, 42, 81, 114, 116, 125, 146, 193–6, 213, 251, 252
  carrying capacity and grazing 22, 116f, 124, 132
  ceremonies 33, 130, 140f, 164ff, 185, 211, 219f, 235, 239–52
  chyme, *see also ngikujit*
  complex 4
  corral 24, 27, 32, 41, 86–90, 94, 163, 165, 169f, 183, 189, 195, 201f, 215, 249
  cow 27, 38, 41–4, 59, 78, 84, 89, 93, 95, 101, 167, 174, 189, 190f, 218, 228
  -bell 210, 214, 231
  spirit 1, 231
  disease 22, 63, 75, 84, 124, 189, 250
  dung 47, 51, 90, 201
  hides 53, 62, 67, 86f, 90, 110, 129, 170f, 174, 199f, 210, 214f
  hoof 47, 166, 210
  horn 44, 167, 202, 215f, 241
  hump 41–4, 47, 218
  identity with 62, 124, 142, 159, 210–20, 241, 247
  ox-name 171, 179, 214–16; *see also Apa-*
  ox-songs 216–19
  -raiding 8, 24, 29f, 33, 50, 67, 75, 84, 92f, 97, 99, 110, 112, 114, 116–27, 132, 179, 216, 218, 225, 260
  relationships in 78f, 99, 103, 108, 133, 194, 210f, 241
  transhumance 60, 132, 186, 193f, 210
  valuation of 215, 217f
  varieties 47

ceremonies 33f, 55, 71, 128–30, 133–48, 149, 152–67, 171–206
chaos 97, 114f, 229, 236
Cherangany Hills (Pokot) 124
Christian faith 7, 9, 14, 69, 76, 163, 187, 214f, 229, 241
　baptism 14, 69f, 73f, 123, 214, 162, 257f
　Church 57f, 68–76, 98, 100f, 123f, 134, 164, 179, 255–8
　mission 18, 43, 57, 68–74, 163, 237, 255–8; *see also* BCMS, CMS
　Monophysite 43, 49
　Protestant 123f, 129, 214, 228f, 233, 237, 251
　　Anglican 14, 70f, 181f
　　Diocese of Karamoja 73f, 123f
　　Diocese of Upper Nile 70–72
　　Roman Catholic 14, 20, 73f, 123, 178f, 201, 235, 237, 244, 246, 251, 258
　　Verona Fathers 72, 237, 258
cicatrix 48, 125f, 128, 198f
circumcision 44f, 67
clans 24, 31, 50, 53, 63, 65–8, 110, 126, 135, 144f, 173, 180, 220
　beliefs 225f
　customs 78f, 88–91, 93–5, 99, 159f, 167, 173–5, 187f, 207, 210, 228, 252
　sub-clans 31, 78, 180
Clark, Bob 71–3, 214
　Doris 71f, 84, 89, 94, 99, 133, 138, 146f, 198, 201, 215, 218, 225, 228, 242
CMS 68–71
cobra, Egyptian 203, 230f
continuity 12, 35, 60, 75, 100, 110, 114, 173, 200, 233, 259, 261
　discontinuity 74, 111
　traits 43, 125
cosmogony 232f
cosmology 7, 12, 33, 112, 114, 160, 162, 194, 229–32, 237
Creator 68, 179, 186, 195, 227, 233–5, 242, 255
Cubae (Karimojong age-section) 139, 148, 158
culture 6, 8–10, 12–20, 22, 26, 29–31, 33, 35–7, 42f, 49, 144–6, 184, 209f; *see also* ethnicity; religion
　counter- 258

　dominant or marginal 40, 44, 46, 55, 57, 63, 77, 81f, 116, 124, 133, 163, 173, 221, 231, 253, 255, 257, 260
　dynamic 68, 76, 98–101, 183, 197–9, 207, 237, 239, 251
　enculturation 9, 17, 29, 55, 66, 75, 77, 79, 101, 103, 124, 128, 131f, 159, 193f, 213–15, 218, 231, 251, 255, 259
　ineluctability 71, 73f, 103f, 108, 112, 114, 117, 127f, 132, 153, 186, 227, 237, 257–262
　material 36, 55
　new 67
　pastoralist 124, 133, 247
　sub-culture 98
　threatened 117, 123f, 129–31, 163, 256
curse 33, 82, 91, 189, 218, 222, 230, 236, 256
　Akujů 199, 232, 241, 251
　elders 65, 105, 109f, 126, 146, 149, 193–5, 197, 203, 205, 213f
　spirits 129
Cushites 37f, 45, 52
　beliefs 233f
　customs 44f
　Eastern 24, 38, 41, 52,
　　beliefs 55
　　customs 45, 50f, 54f, 135
　　languages 45, 48
　languages 38, 41, 44, 50
　Northern 40, 52
　Southern 38, 41, 52
　　beliefs 235

Daidai (Kadwoman, Orwakol, Najie) 53, 58, 67, 135, 141
Danya clan (Karimojong) 144f, 173f; *see also* Nakadanya
Dasanec 24, 38, 41, 52–5, 130; *see also* Maliri, Marille
death 9, 33, 75, 114, 160, 197–202, 235f, 240, 257
　beliefs about 170, 177f, 220f, 224f, 246–8
　deaths 69, 73, 124–30
　immortality 162, 182, 231
　mortality 91f, 109, 120, 127, 149, 155
　sentence 95, 105, 108f
dedeng, fierce 117, 196
dental evulsion 43, 126

Index

desacralization 57, 128
devil 48, 71, 224, 257
Dioki clan (Jie) 189
divination 7, 32, 180f, 188, 193, 198, 222, 224, 236, 240f, 243
  divine, 32, 50, 71, 111, 116, 180f, 243; see also emuron
  diviner 31f, 111, 179, 181, 222, 243
    haruspex 117, 166, 174, 180f, 195, 222; see also ekesiemon
divinity 7f, 49, 56, 68, 181, 225, 234f, 242, 246
Dodinga 39, 41f, 46
Dodosŏ 14, 23f, 29f, 39, 46, 63, 66, 73, 145, 257
  Ato 25, 66
  beliefs 163, 214, 218, 226, 228–30, 233
  cattle, valuation of 66, 251
  cattle-raiding 66, 99, 111, 112f, 119, 121, 199, 222, 225
  customs 84, 95, 133f, 149, 180, 199, 201, 242
  identity 153
  Meris 25, 66
  oral history 149, 152–3
  Orikituk 25, 66
dogs 42, 54; see also sacrifice, victim
Dokoi (Jie generation-set) 139, 148
Dongiro 23f, 29, 39, 41, 46, 52, 59, 62f, 246
Dopes River (Najie) 41
Dorobo (Kenya) 39, 44f, 48; see also Nilotes, Southern
dreams 9, 48, 180, 220
  dreamer 31, 166, 220, 243
  interpretation 32, 136, 188
drunkardness 29, 42, 132
Dyson-Hudson, Neville 10, 18–20, 24, 28, 48, 55, 61, 65, 106, 114f, 126, 137, 142–8, 152–5, 157–160, 167, 173–5, 202, 205f, 211, 218–21, 225f, 237, 242, 252, 261
  Rada 19, 23, 29, 85, 87, 89, 94, 99, 162, 192, 194, 224

ebilanŭ, ceremony of the wand 86, 93f
ebobore, fig tree 32, 134, 163
eboolo, narrow-mouthed gourd 49
ecenit, vengeful spirit of departed 130, 197f, 224, 251
ecology 10, 20, 33, 68, 120, 186, 206, 224, 235, 240, 242, 246, 251

ecula, birthwealth 84
eculi, kite 166
edeke, tuberculosis of the spine 220, 224
edonga, jumping dance 216f
edonge, castrated animal, eunuch 50, 164, 216f
edunyet, neighbourhood 28
edya, boy 135
edyekir, apology, beseeching 83, 93
eete, song 216, 218
egilit, small metal box 210
egogol, scrotum, bag 188
egolit, branch 27
Egypt 40–43, 47
ejamu, ox-hide 53, 86f
ejie, fight, battle 63
ejok, it is good 227f, 243
ekabeman, witch, wizard 225
ekadedengan, fierce man, battle-leader 119, 196
ekadwaran, prophet 31, 220
ekadwarun, unmarried, stubborn person 221
ekagatan, prayer-leader 167f, 235, 250
ekajon, warrior, raider 124, 154
ekal, yard 27, 78, 83, 87, 89, 92, 201, 253
ekalale, brushwood 27
ekaliye, willow-tree 107, 167; see also *lokaliye*
ekaliyet, switch, whip from *ekaliye* 108
ekamar, jumping dance 87, 216
ekamaran, jumper 216
ekameton, herder 104
ekangaran, opener of age-class 137–9, 142, 144, 148–52, 171
ekapelimen, Acacia tree 89
ekapeton, stamper in the dance 217
ekapilan, evil-doer, wizard 32, 224f
ekapolon, head of homestead, master 27, 111, 211, 248
  ka ajore, war-leader 111, 116
ekaracuna, uninitiated (derog.) 135
ekasapanan, initiand, age-mate 107, 164
ekasikout, elder 18, 13, 140, 177f
Ekatapit, agriculturalist 61, 65
ekatotoit, maternal brother 27, 78, 81
ekatubok, juror, judge 105
ekaurunan, genitor 84
ekawalet, white ostrich feather 217
ekelae, tooth, tusk 170
ekerujan, dreamer 31, 34, 220

ekeseran, spokesman, facilitator 138, 177, 193f
ekesiemon, diviner, haruspex 31, 117, 166, 222
ekeworon, fire-maker 31, 182
ekicoli, part-payment of birthwealth 84
ekicolong, stool, headrest 166
ekile, male, man, 90, 164, 225
ekimomwor, circle dance 134, 185, 194, 196, 200, 217, 252
ekinyom, seed, 202
ekios, anointing 95, 136, 159f
ekipie, spirit, 1, 33, 225f, 230f, 253, 255
ekipwor, pool 231
ekipye, spirit 1, 33, 54, 202, 225f, 230f, 253
ekiro, name 66, 214f
ekitanŭ, marriage process 86, 94, 100
ekitela, territorial section 29, 136; *see also* Lokitela-ebu
ekitoi, tree, tree-leaves, medicine 27, 31, 181, 196
ekokwa, men's open place 27
ekoliteran, green snake: *Coluber constrictor* 231
ekone, friend 167
ekor, honey-badger, ratel 67, 206; *see also* Kor
ekujwalet, headdress socket 217
ekujwana, godly 234
ekukurit, worm 172
ekutan, wedding, marriage 86, 93f, 98, 101, 157, 159
ekuwam, wind, spirit 225, 231
elamacar, perineal steak 166, 175, 219, 248
elders 26–33, 60, 63, 173–5; *see also akitocol; Akujŭ; angola*; blessing; curse; *ekasikout; esorok*; promotion
    assembly 169–71, 193–200, 202f, 219f, 240, 242
    family 97–101
    gods 260, 187–9, 247f, 250–52, 260
    judgment 97, 103–16
    representation 66f, 70f, 75, 79, 82, 134–46, 192, 219, 222, 230, 235, 245
    rule 119–23, 149, 153, 155–7, 160f, 163, 166f, 177–80, 182f, 186, 205f, 211, 214, 217, 259f
    sub-clan 87f, 95
    tradition 125f, 129f, 132, 213
elelya, spring 18, 225

elepinit, grass 18
elepit, wooden milking pail 18
elepunoit, abscess 18
eleto, suitor's deputation 84, 93
eletot, offspring
Elgon, Mount 41, 44f, 65, 71, 106, 119, 149, 155
elilat, divining spirit 224
elilya, Kuliak dance 224
eloket, trapper, hunter 126, 171, 198
elope, self, owner 66, 104, 113, 211, 216
    ka ere, head of family 27, 78
emacar, brand, clan 24, 50, 166, 173, 176; *see also* brand; clan
emal, blocked arrow for bleeding cattle, 50, 90
emanangit, bull-calf 50
ematida, complex hoe with v-shaped handle 128
emedot, clay headdress 39f
emesek, ram 87, 91, 172; *see also* ram
emoit, stranger, enemy 10, 12, 23f, 29f, 33, 49, 54, 59, 67f, 74, 85, 107–11, 115–32, 134, 140, 149, 153, 155, 181–3, 186, 200, 205, 214, 220, 224, 228, 230, 232, 235, 238, 243, 245f, 250, 256
    enemy-name 125, 130, 195–9
emojong, old man 61
emomwae, sorghum 185, 190, 195, 215, 248f
emo(ng), bullock 50, 60, 64, 105, 152, 164, 214–16, 218
emoru, mountain 43, 225
Emoru, Andrew (Pian, Karimojong) 10, 33, 55, 65, 121, 136, 229
emuria, star-grass 89
emuron, divine, ritual specialist 31f, 71, 83, 116f, 131, 162, 179–82, 186, 188f, 192, 195f, 220, 222, 224, 243, 245
emunyen, ritual clay 63, 88, 171, 174, 214; *see also* sacred
emuut, twin 91
epalal, it is wet 240
epapait, agnatic nephew 78
eparait, ancestral spirit 33, 130, 198, 228, 230
epei, one 66
epeyos, roast offering 185, 187, 196, 240
epiding, low door 27
epiripirit, whirlwind 231, 243

epit, firestick 47, 182, 194
epuot, butchery, cutting 240
epye, tree: *Terminalia spinosa* 225
ere, homestead 27, 33, 78f, 81–92, 104f, 119, 169, 183f, 201, 218, 229, 231, 241, 253, 257
　ere apolon, the great homestead 33, 229f
ereng, red 134, 233
erikot, metal chain, belt 217
eripipi, flat roof
erokit, sacred medicine 179
erono, it is bad 224, 233
　Erono, disasters of the 1890s 74, 149, 155
esapanit, initiate 171
esapat, would-be initiate 163, 171
eseket, shoulder-blade 184, 242
esigirait, cowrie-shell 65
esigiria, donkey 50, 65
eslim, AIDS 181
esokod, 179
esorokit, adult, member of the junior-generation-set 31, 154, 157, 179, 193
etaaba, rock 32, 139, 148
etaba, snuff, tobacco 90, 173f, 231
etal, tabu, custom, sacred tradition 89, 91, 93f, 103, 143f, 153, 186f, 261
etau, heart, spirit, will-to-life 128, 130, 223; *see also* will-to-life
etem, meeting place 27
eteran, bridegroom 87
Ethiopia, *see* Abac
ethnicity 4f, 16, 19, 22–4, 38, 50–53, 55, 60–68, 74, 78, 80, 110f, 114, 116, 120, 125f, 145, 184, 256
　identity 4f, 12, 23f, 29, 35, 42, 53, 60, 68, 75f, 111f, 198, 259; *see also* cattle; Dodosǒ; Jie; Karimojong; pray; Turkana
etic, work 181
etimat, headdress 171
etimu, black ostrich feather 217
etinganŭ, engagement 83
etirir, Acacia tree 89
etolim, cool, shade 202
etop, star 232
etorobe, shade, shadow 180, 202
etuleru, fur bob 198
etunganan, person 23f, 59, 144, 166, 249
etworoit, knee-bell 174, 217
European 79, 237; *see also* Western

　influence 41, 47, 73, 75, 230, 233–5
　intervention 57, 68f, 98, 117, 148
　names 14, 257
　presuppositions 4f, 16, 36, 38, 141, 162, 226f, 239, 258, 260
eutut, bullock, steer 214
evil 48, 71, 132, 135, 161, 168f, 190, 192, 197, 205, 211, 220, 223f, 249f; *see also akapil*; *karonan*
　-eye 90, 176, 185, 225
　spirit 167, 250
ewae, side 27, 32, 78, 92
eyenit, kinsman, relative

faith 33, 232, 236; *see also anupit*
　enculturation 237, 246, 251, 261
　foreign 76
　prayer of 190f, 250
　shared 29, 75, 98, 162, 187, 251
　social science 8
feathers 42, 85–7, 94f, 137, 139, 149f, 164, 171f, 174, 178, 200, 216f, 230, 233
fieldwork 7, 9, 11
　informants 8–11, 14, 54, 62, 137, 142–4, 147f, 149, 156f, 178, 250, 255, 257, 263f
　interviewing 13–15, 182f, 195, 227
finger-knife 178, 210
fire 42, 59, 89, 143, 166, 175, 193, 219, 248
　fire-maker 28, 31, 51, 67, 111, 129, 174, 176, 182–4, 188f, 194
Funj (Sudan) 48f

Gezira (Sudan) 41
ghee 42, 81, 89, 93, 136, 170, 210; *see also* milk
goats 22, 27, 40f, 44, 47, 49f, 132, 149, 155; *see also* sacrifice
　birthwealth 82, 84
　raiding 110, 121, 135
　rainmaking 188
　skins 88, 164, 180f, 198f
God 7, 42–5, 176–9, 188f, 192–5, 203–6, 224–37, 246–9, 261
　deity 7, 115, 245
　divinity 7f, 68, 181, 225f, 246
　enemies' names 220, 224, 226, 231
　gods 32f, 55, 225, 233, 239, 247
　High God 44–6, 232–4, 236, 255
　rain-god 45, 232

Gourlay, Kenneth 60, 62, 90f, 127, 189, 192,
    195f, 205, 215–18, 220, 233, 245, 252
granary 143, 184, 229
Gray, Sandra 77, 124, 126f, 210, 253
grindstones 11, 38, 89, 99
Gulliver, Philip 72, 79, 92, 94f, 106, 115,
    141, 144f, 147, 149, 153f,
    fieldwork 11, 23
guns 1, 3, 26, 54, 76, 101, 107, 109f,
    111–14, 116–120, 122–32, 211, 251
    AK-47 26, 119, 127–30, 132
    disarmament 30, 119, 122, 260

Hanbury Tracy, Algernon 148
health 17, 57, 90, 92, 129, 186–8, 203, 226,
    228, 248, 250f
    healing 31–3, 61, 71, 79, 163, 179–82,
        206, 253–5
hereditary office 67, 138, 147, 163, 177,
    179–82, 228
history 5, 11–14, 16–18, 35f
    African 5, 9, 11ff, 35f, 74f, 94, 257–61
    concept of 53, 140
    Karamojong 11, 35–75, 119, 125–7, 144,
        174
    language 13, 17f, 38
    military 111–13, 119, 126, 132
    mission 72–4
    oral 12f, 35, 47–9, 51, 55, 58, 60, 66f,
        153, 164, 171, 257
    prehistory 35f, 75
    religions 4, 57, 77, 133
    salvation 11, 30f, 49, 68, 239, 247
homicide 85, 95, 108, 110, 120, 125f, 199,
    219, 229
hunting 42, 55, 61, 126, 134, 170f
    and gathering 36, 41, 149, 155, 240
    and trapping 58, 126

ikaaya, coeval cousin 78, 87
ikale, lamb, kid 27, 50
ikoku, child 249, 252
Ikwaibong (Lotuko) 221
imesek, lamb 50
implicit 6f, 9f, 17, 32, 77, 133, 138, 144,
    184, 186f, 237, 139
Indian Ocean 26, 57
initiation 14, 31, 29, 33, 55, 59, 87, 107,
    110, 179, 195f, 214, 219, 241, 245,
    248–50; *see also asapan*; rites;
    sacrament; sacrifice,

age-class 133, 135–76, 184–7, 211
ancient 126, 198f
marriage 66, 79f, 93, 114, 159f, 163,
    213, 217
raiding 114
women's 93, 252
innovation 17, 112, 131, 136, 155, 231,
    251, 255f, 258
intensity 86, 116, 119, 121, 123f, 130, 143,
    162, 187, 209, 223, 240, 246f, 253
    dense moment 30, 32, 90, 240, 247; *see
        also* sacrament; sacred
Iriama (Pian, Karimojong) 158
Iriri (Bokora, Karimojong) 20, 113
iron 11, 36, 42, 45f, 49f, 128, 164, 178, 214
    blacksmiths 49, 58, 66, 113, 128, 145,
        175
Iron Age 11, 36, 50
iryono, black 233
isitana, habitual accuser 224
Itunga (proto-Karamojong cluster) 39–42,
    46, 48, 51–3, 58–62, 161

Jebel Moya (Sudan) 39, 43
Jie 10, 11, 14, 23f, 29ff, 39ff, 44, 46, 48,
    50ff, 105ff, 109, 115
    age-classes 134ff
    cattle, valuation of 78, 108, 210
    clans 78, 145, 220
    customs 85ff, 92, 94, 97, 129, 234, 242
    ethnic identity 111, 255ff
    military 109, 111ff, 129, 145, 154, 156,
        160, 175, 216f, 222
    naming 69, 111
    Oding 25, 58f, 63, 94,
        customs 135–8, 140–3, 147, 150f,
            166, 183, 189, 206
    old age 161
    orality 259
    Orwakol 25, 54, 58f, 60, 67
        customs 134f, 137, 140–43, 146f,
            151, 156, 164, 182, 186–8, 189,
            206, 245
    religiosity 237, 241
    settlement and expansion 58ff, 245
Jimos clan (Losilang, Orwakol, Najie) 51,
    129, 182–4
Jiye (Sudan) 23, 29, 39, 52, 63, 193
jok, sacred 224, 227, 243
jurality 104–6, 109–11, 115, 120, 133, 160,
    164, 169, 210f; *see also* curse

Kaabong town (Nadodosŏ) 20, 66, 152, 253f
Kaceri, (Caicaon, Oding, Najie) 67, 129, 136f, 183, 189, 216
Kadam, Mount 19, 41, 44, 51
kakujŭ, place of Akujŭ 229, 232, 236
Kakamongole, Pian river-unit 28
Kalenjin 39, 41, 44–6, 106; *see also* Nilotes, Southern
Kalokengel (Bokora, Karimojong) 70
Kamare, Dengel (Losilang, Orwakol, Jie) 183
Kamion (Timu) 41; *see also* Ik
Kanawat (subsection of Orwakol, Najie) 69, 74, 137, 182f, 257
Kanimuget River (Najie) 231
kapel, spotted 53, 89, 122, 131, 224
Kapeta Valley (Nadodoso) 30
Kapoeta (Toposa, Sudan) 46f, 63
Karabokol (Oding, Najie) 63, 184
Karamoja 1, 10–12, 18–26, 37, 64, 213f, 258 and *passim*
  borders 19, 30, 182
  Initiative for Sustainable peace (KISP) 123, 146, 174, 189
  maps 21, 25
  'problem' 123, 209
  Seeds Scheme 135, 189
  settlement 36–53, 67f
Karamojong 23, 25, 213f, 258, 260, and *passim*
  cluster 23, 29, 58, 62, 140
  cradlelands 29, 59, 134, 145, 164, 170, 201
Karimojong 10, 19, 24f, 28, 46, 52, 54f
  beliefs 115, 145, 185, 229, 237, 245, 251
  Bokora 24f, 28, 70, 127, 145f, 174
    cattle-raiding 107, 112, 121–4, 217, 225
  cattle, valuation of 210f, 215, 218
  clans 65, 144
  customs 80, 84, 86, 88, 92, 97, 106, 125, 128f, 134, 137–48, 149, 154f, 160, 163f, 168, 173f, 178, 180, 187, 199, 240f
  formation 58–67
  identity 23f, 29–31, 59, 146, 153, 198, 257, 259
  Kaala 24f, 59, 194
  language 39, 45
  Leeso 24f, 173

Maseniko 24f, 28, 44, 64f, 101, 112, 116, 127, 145, 173f, 215, 218
  cattle-raiding 121f, 124, 131
  military 111–15, 117, 120–22, 126f, 131, 225
Mogos 19, 24f, 53–5, 58–61, 63–6, 175, 182
Mosingo 24f, 28, 65, 173f
Muno 24f, 44, 60
myth 60f, 63
oral history 44, 46, 48, 51, 54, 156
Osowa 24f
peace 121
Pei 24f, 54, 60, 65, 113, 173, 175, 217
Pian 10, 14, 20, 24f, 28, 33, 44, 145f, 148
  cattle-raiding 112, 121f, 124, 200
  customs 82, 97, 107f, 156–8, 173f, 194f, 225
Tome 19f, 24f, 28, 70–73, 146, 159, 214
  cattle-raiding 122, 124
  customs 168, 213
karonan, bad 190, 223, 248
karanoni, *see karonan*
Katakwi District (Teso) 122
Kenya 19, 23, 29, 41, 44, 46, 53, 65, 70f, 112, 116, 119, 121, 125, 199, 259
  Kapenguria 65
  Kitale 155
  Mombasa 70
  Mount Kenya 22, 62, 258
  Nairobi 121, 200
  Nasokol 65
  Trans-Nzoia 149
Khartoum 38, 40, 42
Kidepo River 45
  Valley 48, 51
  Valley National Park 121
kidyama, up, north 232, 236, 243
Kitosh (*see* Bukusu) 149
Kok (Jie generation-set) 59, 150
Kopus (Nadodosŏ) 66, 95, 153
  River (Najie) 191
Kor (section of Toposa) 63; *see also* ekor
Koria (Abwor generation-set) 142f
Korio (Tap clan) 53, 63
  (Jie age-section) 144, 149f, 152, 166
Koten Hill 19, 48, 53–5, 58–60, 62–7, 134, 182
Kotiang subsection (Orwakol, Najie) 63, 135, 141, 147, 182f

Kotido town (Najie) 11, 20 22f, 65, 81, 105f, 113, 116, 121f, 134, 144, 147, 167, 181, 188f, 192, 196, 216, 221, 233
District 258, 105, 1332
Kucila (Karimojong age-set) 157
Kuliak 39, 40f, 44f, 50, 52, 66, 188, 224
Ik 39, 41f, 45, 48–50, 52, 112
Nyangiya 39, 41f, 44, 52, 66
Sor 39, 41, 44, 51, 112, 231
Kumam (Teso) 49, 53, 149, 169
Kumi District (Teso) 122
kupoi, ilmenite 233
Kush, Kingdom of 42f
Kwangai (Dodosŏ generation-set) 149f
(Karimojong generation-set) 139
Kwei (Jie age-section) 136f, 149f

Labwor 30, 58, 63f, 69, 106, 128, 156, 161, 216
Lamphear, John 10f, 182, 206, 259
age-system 106f, 141–4, 146f, 150f, 156, 162, 178, 237
informants 11, 62, 74, 93, 112, 141, 164, 173, 177, 181, 226, 234, 257
nomenclature 22–4, 38
oral history 13, 51, 53–5, 60–64, 74, 111
periodization 112
warfare 111–29, 131, 200
Lango 30, 38f, 64f, 106
beliefs 233
Christian mission 69
famine refuge 59
military 117, 122, 132
oral history 46, 49–53
language 12f, 17f, 26, 29, 37–47, 50f, 53, 63, 66, 209f, 215, 227
African 12, 37f
phylum 12, 37–40, 45
Laparanat famine 59f, 65, 67
law 9, 58, 81f, 100, 103, 131f, 159
alien 76, 104, 117, 120
customary 5, 97, 100, 103–10, 116; *see also* jurality
marriage 90
outlaw 107–10, 205, 211, 224
Lep clan (Jie) 182
Lip clan, (Karimojong) 24, 51, 65, 144, 173f
lip-plugs 40, 43f, 137
Lira (Lango) 50, 69

Lobal clan (Karimojong) 65, 173
lobunat, clan marriage ceremony 88
Lobunei (Karimojong) 73
loburia, clan marriage ceremony 88
lobwo, marriage ceremony 88
Locap, Rufus (Jie) 79, 82, 85–7 89, 91, 94, 98f
Locat, Pian river-unit 28
Locukut 148; *see also* Hanbury Tracy
Lodio, Michael 141f, 147
Lodoc (Losilang, Orwakol, Jie) 49, 128
Loduk, Aporkamali (Pian, Karimojong) 158f
Lodul (Jie) 182
lodunga, harp, lyre 216
Lodunge, lunar month in February-March 187
Loingolem (Panyangara, Orwakol, Jie) 181
lokaliye, switch, wand from *ekaliye* 89, 166f, 249
Lokatap Rock 58, 189; *see also* Atap
Lokero, Locia (Duman, Oding, Jie) 94
lokidor, clan marriage ceremony in corral 88
lokinyom, that of the seeds, final memorial ceremony 47, 201
Lokitela-ebu, (Kanawat subsection, Orwakol, Najie) 109, 164, 168
Lokol (Kanawat, Orwakol, Jie) 93f, 97, 157f
Lokol, Apalomongole (Pian, Karimojong) 146
Lokong, Israel (Kanawat, Orwakol, Jie) 69f, 74, 180, 257
Sarah 70, 229
Lokumro (Nadodosŏ) 153
Lokwakenya, Timos (Pian, Karimojong) 100
Lokwangiryang, Teko (Oding, Jie) 94–6
Loluk, Adia 74
Lolukwangit (Najie) 191
lomalol, clan marriage ceremony 88
lomari, ceremony for counting bridewealth 88
Lomaruk, lunar month in March-April 189
Lomej (Nadodosŏ) 41
Lomiluk (Lotuko) 221
Lomongin, Peter (Pian Karimojong) 74, 158f
Lomotin (Dodosŏ) 180
Lomuleu, Epuriapua (Losilang, Orwakol, Jie) 183

Index

Longaren (Kanawat, Orwakol, Jie) 203
Longiro River (Najie) 54, 61–3, 141
Longok, Erisa (Losilang, Orwakol, Jie) 222
    Paulo (Caicaon, Oding, Jie) 109
Longoli, Aquilino (Caicaon, Oding, Jie) 99, 121
Longora (Maseniiko, Jie) 131
Lonyili, Mount (Mening) 50, 221
Looi (Losilang, Orwakol, Najie) 61, 184, 188
Lopei (Pei, Karimojong) 113
Lopore (Dodosŏ) 230; *see also* Pore
Lopul, Daniel (Tome, Karimojong) 159
Loram, Timos (Pian, Karimojong) 158
lore, home 163, 202, 204; *see also* ere
Lorec, John (Pian, Karimojong) 129
Loriang (Panyangara, Orwakol, Jie) 111f, 131, 147, 155f, 217
Lorike, (Pian, Karimojong) 111
Lorocom (Maseniko, Karimojong) 106, 119
Lorukude, Rufus (Karimojong) 3
Losilang (subsection of Orwakol, Jie) 59, 73, 137, 167, 182f, 188, 222; *see also* Silang
Losuban, lunar month in July-August 185f, 195, 206
Lotakipi swamp (Turkana) 37, 46
Lotisan water-hole (Turkana) 53, 58
Lotome (Tome, Karimojong) 18f, 70–73, 146, 159, 214
Lotuko (Sudan) 11, 39, 221
Loumo (Pian, Karimojong) 10
loupal, Egyptian cobra: *Naja haje* 231
Loutan (Kanawat, Orwakol, Jie) 203
Lowok, Yakobo (Bokora, Karmojong) 111, 129
Loyoro (Orikituk, Nadodosŏ) 30, 59, 63, 66, 134
Lwo (Uganda) 50f, 53, 58, 67f, 182, 216, 224, 255; *see also* Nilotes, Western
    clans 49, 51, 67
    language 51, 64, 106, 128

Maasai 39, 40, 46, 48, 62, 126, 179, 237
Macdonald, JRL 'Bilic' (promoted from Major to Lt Col. after his expedition) 13, 38, 45, 148, 149, 237
Maliri, *see* Dasanec
Maniman (Akinyo) River 65, 70, 148
    camp 148
Marille, *see* Dasanec

marriage 14, 33, 79–101, 185, 198f, 206f;
    see also sexuality
    adultery 80, 95, 97, 104, 108, 159
    anointing 79, 94f, 136, 154f, 159f
    barrenness 27, 90–92, 197, 202
    changes 97–101, 251
    church 100
    courtship 79, 82–4, 216
    divorce 95, 97, 101, 108, 158, 219
    exogamy 66, 68, 78f, 99, 145
    intermarriage 10, 66, 74, 126, 200
    polygyny 92, 95, 97–100, 113
    process 79f, 86, 91–3, 98, 168
    social status 79, 82, 94, 159, 217
Marshall Thomas, Elizabeth 120, 133, 162, 180, 196, 198, 210, 218, 221f, 224, 230–33, 258
Matany (Bokora, Karimojong) 20
    Hill 65
    RC mission hospital 107
memory 6, 12–14, 17, 35, 49, 53f, 62f, 66f, 103, 119, 125, 127, 133, 142, 144–8, 149, 163, 171, 228, 250
Mening 59, 128
Meri-emong, Pian subsection 28
    Dodosŏ age-section 152, 215
Meroë 42f
milk 38, 42, 44, 47, 50, 67, 84, 87–90, 101, 138, 143, 187, 193, 202, 211, 231, 240, 245; *see also* ghee
millet 38
    bulrush 40, 42, 47, 181, 255
    finger 42f, 47
Mirio (Karimojong generation-set) 137–9, 146
Miro (Lango) 51, 63, 65f
Mirzeler, Mustafa 46, 48f, 54, 61f, 77, 91, 111–17, 122f, 127–30, 183f, 189, 234, 245, 258
Monia (section of Turkana) 63f
Moroto, Mount 19, 24, 51, 65, 188, 226, 228, 231
    Town 10, 19f, 26, 69, 73, 105, 105, 122f, 243
Moru (Karimojong generation-set) 137–9, 146, 148–52, 157, 249
Moru a Nayece (Turkana) 62
Moru a Siger (Turkana) 64f
Moru Apolon (Turkana) 240; *see* Moru a Siger
Moru Ewur (Losilang, Orwakol, Najie) 70

Moru Linga (Bokora, Karimojong) 70
Moruita (Pian, Karimojong) 20, 64
Morungole (Nadodosŏ) 41; *see also* Ik
Mosingo (Toposa section) 63 ; *see also* Karimojong
mountains 19, 22, 44, 47, 50f, 57, 62, 119
   age-class names 137, 139, 151, 152
   spirit 32f, 188, 221, 225f, 229, 231, 233
Mugeto (Jie generation-set) 140–43, 146f, 149f, 157, 166, 170, 173
Murle (Ethiopia) 39, 49
Murya (Dodosŏ generation-set) 149f
   (Jie age-section) 150
Muslim 14, 18, 49

Nacam, Alifayo (Caicaon, Oding, Jie) 93, 136, 141, 142, 156, 183, 189, 201
Nacere 7
najaluntet, girls' share (of beer) 87
Nakadanya (Mogos, Karimojong) 59, 123, 134, 145f, 149, 152–3, 173–6, 240; *see also* Danya
Nakapelimoru (subsection of Orwakol, Najie) 53, 59, 137, 167, 182, 240
Nakapor (Losilang, Orwakol, Jie) 183
nakiruet, trough-full 87
nakujŭ, heaven 229, 236
Nakwaki (Caicaon, Oding, Jie) 156
Nakwakwa (Nadodosŏ) 153
Nakwapua (Najie) 28
Namalu, (Pian, Karimojong) 20, 53, 108, 113, 122, 135, 146, 195, 197
Namoja (Oding, Najie) 135, 141f
Namuya (Losilang, Orwakol, Najie) 1, 7
Nandi (Kalenjin) 39, 44–6, 232
Naokot River (Najie) 191
Napak, Mount (Sor) 46
Napeikisina 48f
Naporit (Kanawat, Orwakol, Jie) 93
Natoo River (Karimojong) 60
nawi, at the cattle-camp 114; *see also awi*
Nayece 61–3
Nayen (Orwakol, Najie) 134, 141, 173, 184; *see also* Yen
ngaatuk, cattle, cows, *see aate*
ngaberu, see aberu
ngabulangataruk, see abulangatarun
ngaburucu, see aburucu
ngaetin, see aet
ngageran, see agerat
ngagwe, sorghum beer 185

ngakaae, see akaae
ngakaipapai, see akaipapait
ngakaiyeyai, see ikaaya
ngakalemak, see akaleman
ngakile, milk 18
ngakimak, see akimat 252
ngakimuj, see akimuj
ngakipi, water 225, 230, 248
ngakiro, see akiro
ngakoloro, see akoloro
ngakookes, pebbles for a gourd 176
ngakujo, see akuj
ngakutae, see akuta
ngalepito, flying termites 18
ngalepon, dairy herd 18
ngaloketa, see aloket
ngalomarin, see alomar
ngaluto, see alut
ngamitidai, see amatida
ngamoliteny, see amolitenyit
ngamomwar, see amomwara
ngamon, see amoni
ngamoru, see amoru
ngamunyen, see amunyen
ngamurok, see amuron
nganokin, milking-pens 27
nganya, grass 225
ngaokot, blood 166, 245
ngaropar, see aropar
ngarukanes, see arukan
ngarupepe, see arupepe
ngasapan, see asapan
ngasike, see asiket
ngasinge, beer dregs 51
ngasuban, ceremony, feast 176, 184–6, 195
ngasukai, see asuka
ngatekerin, see ateker
ngatomonitomon, one hundred 48
Ngatunyo (Dodosŏ generation-set) 152
   (Jie age-section) 142, 149f
   (Karimojong generation-set) 139, 146
ngatyoniso, see atyonis
ngawiyenito, see awiyenit
ngawiyoi, see awi 193
ngican, problems, trouble 130, 197f, 251
ngicen, see ecenit
ngidulae, granaries 27
ngidwe, see ikoku
ngidyain, see edya
ngigilita, see egilit
ngijamu, see ejamu

ngijie, fighters 111
ngikadwarunak, *see ekadwarun*
ngikaitotoi, *see ekatotoit*
ngikaiyeyai, *see ikaaya*
ngikajok, *see ekajon*
ngikalia (Ngajie), *see ekal*
ngikalyo (Ngakarimojong), *see ekal*
ngikangarak, *see ekangarak*
ngikapilak, *see ekapilan*
ngikaracuna, *see ekaracuna*
ngikasapanak, *see ekasapanan*
ngikasikou, *see ekasikout*
Ngikatap, *see* Ekatapit
ngikatubok, *see ekatubok*
ngikawaleta, *see ekawalet*
ngikerep, spirits of madness 181, 221, 253
ngikeworok, *see ekeworon*
ngikial, *see ekelae*
ngikoliterak, *see ekoliteran*
ngikone, *see ekone*
ngikujit, chyme 95, 109, 166f, 219, 243, 247; *see also* sacred
ngikujwaleta, *ekujwalet*
ngikukur, *see ekukurit*
ngililae, *see elilat*
ngilok, *see eloket*
ngiloupal, *see loupal*
ngimatidoi, *see ematido*
Ngiminito (Pian, Karimojong) 21f
clan 51
ngimoe, *see emoit*
ngimomwa, *see emomwae*
ngimongin, *see emong*
ngimoru, *see emoru*
ngimurok, *see emuron*
ngimuu, *see emuut*
ngipara, *see eparait*
ngipeyos, *see peyos*
ngipian, *see ekipye*
ngirerya, *see ere* 27f
ngisigira, *see esigirait*
ngisigirya, *see esigiria*
ngisorok, *see esorok*
ngitaaba, *see etaaba*
ngitain, *see etau*
ngitalia, (Ngajie), *see etal*
ngitalyo (Ngakarimojong), *see etal*
ngitim, *see etimat*
ngitunga, *see etunganan*
ngitworoi, *see etworoit*
ngiyeneta, *see eyenet*

Ngora (Teso) 62, 70
Niger-Congo 12f, 37
Bantu 7, 13, 37f, 46f
beliefs 234
Nile, River 19, 38, 40, 43, 45–7, 51, 55, 68, 70
Upper Nile 38; *see also* Christian faith
West Nile 70
Nilo-Hamitic 38; *see also* Afroasiatic
Paranilotic 23, 38
Nilo-Saharan 12, 38–40, 43, 52
beliefs 234
customs 13, 40
languages 13, 18, 37, 39f, 45, 61, 66
Nilotes 42–6, 49, 52, 183
cradleland 42, 55
customs 42–4, 47, 55, 101, 126, 136, 187, 210
Eastern 26, 43, 45, 52, 55–8, 182
languages 39f, 42–5, 62, 125, 135, 224
cradleland 46ff, 62
customs 45, 54, 88, 173, 47f, 188, 197
languages 18, 39, 47f, 50, 224, 227, 232, 234
Southern 10, 43–55, 125, 145, 234
languages 39, 48, 50, 227
Western 43, 47f, 52, 55, 58, 62
beliefs 227, 232f
customs 88, 91, 182, 188, 200, 225, 227
languages 39, 224f, 229, 234
Novelli, Bruno 22, 24, 54, 83, 105, 112, 117, 125, 128, 137f, 245, 148, 173, 188f, 229, 237, 242, 245
Nubia 39f, 42f
nudity 49, 71, 73, 112
numerals 42, 65, 84, 86–8, 93, 143, 174f, 185f, 206, 210, 219
Nyakwai 14, 24, 46, 65, 145, 175
Nyamdere famine 54, 59, 62
Nyanga (subsection of Pian, Karimojong) 28
Nyangatom, *see* Dongiro

Ober (EC clan) 47, 50
offering 185, 192, 206, 219, 240–43
Omo River (Ethiopia) 36, 50, 63
orality 6, 10f, 17, 257
Oromo (EC) 47f, 50, 52, 55, 64; *see also* Rom, Mount

Oropoi (Turkana) 44, 246
Oropom 39, 44–6, 48, 51f, 54, 64f, 67, 71
   beliefs 145, 224
Osowa (Jie age-section) 142f, 149f, 152, 173
Owa (Karimojong generation-set) 138f
   (Dodosŏ generation-set) 152

Palajamů (first Turkana generation-set) 53f, 62, 149
Panyangara (subsection of Orwakol, Jie) 28, 113, 121, 167, 181
papa, father, maternal uncle 78, 84, 135, 171, 179, 228, 234
papaa, forefather, ancestor 136, 170, 228
pastoralism 8, 26, 31, 38, 41, 43, 49, 51, 53, 56–60, 65, 68, 75–7, 104, 117, 125–7, 145, 162, 175, 182, 214, 229
   new 56f, 126
   nomadic 4, 29, 75, 77, 99, 119f, 124, 133, 209, 251, 256
   values 4, 162, 211
Pazzaglia, Augusto 23f, 28, 62–5, 105, 108, 130, 134, 138, 141, 185–7, 225, 252
Pei (Karimojong section), *see* Karimojong
Pianyanya, (Pian river-unit) 28
Poet (Tap clan) 46, 53, 66–8,
Pokot 39, 44ff, 54, 226
   clans 64
   enemies 10, 195
   peace 200
   violence 111, 113, 119ff, 149
politics 17, 101, 111–17, 133–6, 211, 227;
     see also age-class; *akiriket*;
     pastoralism; pray; state; traditional;
     Uganda
   acephalous 57, 75, 112, 123
   community 103, 110, 126f, 130, 138, 179, 245
   democracy 75, 259
   gerontocracy 67, 98, 100, 106, 109, 134, 138, 148, 171–4, 211, 251, 259, 261
   Karamojong 18, 20, 23–6, 29, 31–3, 54, 63, 65, 114–16, 124, 145f, 252
   religion 141, 145f, 162f, 167, 177, 183, 186f, 193, 195, 199f, 207, 210, 216, 252
   validity 8, 31, 61, 131, 177, 237, 261
   Western 5, 123, 125, 131
Pore 39, 52–4, 188

clan (Jie) 203
pray 78, 95, 167–70, 186–98, 201–4, 247–51; *see also* faith
   Akujů 48, 88, 91, 108, 115, 132, 178, 180, 192, 207, 219f, 225–9, 235f, 239, 243, 245, 247f, 250, 255, 261
   Christian 70
   identity 29f, 167
   politics 31f, 135, 140, 143, 173, 186, 198
   well-being 31, 88, 117, 127, 131, 134f, 175, 184, 189, 199, 214, 261
   preternatural 33, 162, 177, 181, 203, 214, 223
   promotion 29, 32f, 55, 133, 138, 140f, 143, 145–8, 149, 154–9, 173–6, 179, 182, 184, 187, 242; *see also akitopolor*, rites; sacraments
prophecy 9, 31, 125, 149, 173, 190, 220f, 243
prophets 125, 181, 221
Pulkol, David (Maseniko, Karimojong) 10, 113

rain 11, 63, 75, 110, 169, 181–4, 232
   rainfall 19–22, 37, 51, 103, 142, 186, 188, 194
   rain-making 17, 28, 67, 172, 174, 188–95, 200, 214, 221
   rain-stone 221, 240
   significance 42, 45, 47, 68, 202, 225–35, 240
   to tie up the, *see akilal*
ram 50, 87, 91, 93, 95, 107, 109, 143, 172, 201
rape 97, 104f, 108
religion 3–14, 17f, 23, 35, 68, 223, 237 and *passim*; *see also* politics
   encounter 57, 74–6, 182, 214
   traditional African 3–14, 18, 31–3, 57, 74, 77, 132, 209f, 256–8
   traditional Karamojong *passim* 17f, 57, 74f, 133, 194, 198, 221, 226–37, 239f, 247, 250f, 258–61
   women's 251–6
Rengen (Jie), *see* Oding, Yen
Rengidwat, Pian river-unit 28, 65
Riama clan (Karimojong) 51, 53, 65
Ribor clan (Karimojong) 65, 144f, 173f
Rift Valley 19, 23, 44–6, 48

ritual 6–8, 17, 23f, 28f, 59, 120, 177, 187, 219f
 divination 222f
 organization 55, 66, 100, 110, 114f, 133, 136, 138, 140f, 143, 145f, 154, 156, 162
 potency 186–94, 237
 prayer 220
 rites
  agrarian 33, 130
  body 43, 48, 61, 196
  fire-making 67, 182
  funerary 200–202, 228
  healing 243, 255
  homicide 126, 197–9
  initiation 136, 162–72
  marriage and birth 79–95
  peacemaking 123, 127
  promotion 175
  restorative 202–6
 sacred 210, 239f
 specialists 179–83
 transgression 186, 228, 235
rivers 19, 22, 28, 36f, 40f, 45, 50
 threat 30, 47, 54, 68, 75
 spirit 33, 174, 191f, 199, 202, 230–32, 240, 249
rock 1, 37, 41, 47, 61, 137, 141, 175, 188f, 221, 223, 226–8, 235, 240, 249
Ro (Nilotes) 52, 58, 60–68, 75, 134, 179, 210
Rom, Mount (Yen) 50f, 53, 64, 67, 134; see also Oromo
Rowland, Jim 17, 20, 88, 91, 130, 188f, 197–200, 202, 226, 236, 240, 250, 257
Rub (Kuliak) 41
Rupa (Maseniko, Karimojong) 44, 54

Sabawot, see Sapiny
sacral 32f, 190, 194
 desacralization 128–31
sacrament 184–207, 236f, 252
 sacramental ceremonies 32f
 sacramentality 11f, 30, 206f, 230, 239
 sacraments 29
  absolution 203–6, 213
  beseeching 19, 93, 187f, 205; see also *akitocol*; *angola*
  cooling down 202f
  freeing the cattle 29, 193f; see also *akiwodokin*
 funerary and memorial services 200–202
 harvest festival 194f
 initiation 187, 219
 killing the sacred 206
 peace-making 199f
 promotion 187, 242
 rain-making 188–93; see also rain
 receiving an enemy-name 197–9
 war sacrifices 195–7, 217
sacred 30, 131, 184f, 200, 209f, 227f, 231, 239–42, 246, 260
 animals 95, 206
 assembly 31
 ceremonies 101, 134, 162, 167, 184f, 239, 245
 chyme 95, 166f, 219, 243
 clay 59, 63, 88, 149, 153, 171, 174, 181, 184, 187, 193f, 196, 214
 colour 61
 duty 79
 groves 28, 32, 61, 123, 134f, 141, 143, 163, 170, 173, 183f, 187–9, 193f, 196, 199, 205, 213, 220, 240f, 247; see also Amurkwang; Lodukanit; Lokatap; Lokitoipeta; Lokumro; Lolukwangit; Lomos; Looi; Nakadanya; Nakwakwa; Nakwapua; Namoja, Nayen
 meat 174, 180, 219, 242
 medicine 179
 mountains 124
 numbers 174, 185
 people 179, 181, 246
 places 134, 184, 230, 241
 plants 89, 242f
 social institutions 95, 134, 171, 174
 soil 189, 243
 spear 174
 spirit 246f
 water 174, 187
sacrifice 1, 7, 28f, 31–3, 134, 162, 239ff, 258f
 sacrificial ceremony for 133, 179–207, 211–36
  birth 90f, 219
  death 153, 200–202, 215
  fire-making 183
  homicide 125, 130, 198f

initiation 162–175
  marriage 88, 91–3, 219
  peace 121, 199f
  rain 188–92, 231f
  repentance and absolution 107, 193, 203–6, 213, 219
  restoration 202f, 206, 230f
  seasons 134f, 187, 189, 193–5, 206
  war 117, 131, 195–7, 258
 ancient 48, 50
 enemies 186, 232
 gender 253–5
 meanings 239–52
 victim 88, 137, 166, 222, 247
  bullock 93, 104f, 110, 219
  cow 95; see also cattle
  dog 121, 181, 192
  donkey 188
  goat 91, 110, 130, 135, 153, 164, 180, 187, 197f, 202, 219, 231, 242
  human 188, 246
  ram 91, 93, 95, 109, 172, 187, 242; see also ram
Samburû 39, 48, 62, 119, 153
Sapiny 39, 44, 45, 64f, 115, 119, 200, 225, 227
  cattle-raiding 119
Sebei, see Sapiny
sections, territorial 23f, 28f, 31, 54, 58, 60, 63, 67, 110, 114, 120, 140, 145–7, 199f; see also ekitela
  customs 167f, 174f, 187, 189, 195, 219, 250
  subsections 28, 136, 143, 180, 182, 184, 187, 189, 194, 206, 250
Ser(a) clan 51, 67, 220
sexuality 79–81, 200, 216, 218, 233f
  prostitution 77, 80f
  sexual relations 79–81, 94f, 97f, 105, 146, 159, 163, 198, 200, 221
sheep 22, 27, 41, 44, 47, 68, 132, 149, 155, 201; see also emesek; ram, sacrifice
  mothers 82, 93
  raiding 121
Shilluk (Sudan) 39, 48; see also Nilotes, Western
Siger (clan) 64f
Silang (Tap) 59; see also Losilang
SIM 70f
Sirikwa 39, 45f

smallpox 149, 175
soils 20, 62, 69, 129f
  black cotton 70, 251f; see also aro
  erosion 17, 20, 22
  significance 188f, 232
Somali 45, 48, 52
sorcery 110, 162, 192,
  sorcerer 202, 224f
sorghum 40, 42, 51, 81, 87f, 90f, 94f, 116, 135, 163, 169, 183; see also ajulot; atap; ngagwe; ngimomwa
  pests 134, 221
  Seredo 128f
  valuation 185, 189f, 192, 195, 249, 252
Soroti (Teso) 49, 69, 122, 129
spear 1, 107, 120, 125, 128–31, 221
  -blooding 130, 197
  bury the 128
  -cleansing 130, 190, 197
  ox 31, 94, 105, 138, 142, 147, 159, 163f, 166, 177, 196, 219, 241
  ram 172
  symbolic 67, 94, 145, 169, 175, 241
Spencer, Paul 23, 98, 153, 155f, 158, 259
spirit 55, 130, 172, 182, 201f, 223–34, 246f; see also ekipye
  ancestral 91, 129, 192, 202, 229f
  angry, avenging 73, 91, 94, 130, 167, 189, 197f, 202, 224, 231, 248, 250, 253
  departed 33, 128f, 197, 201, 228–30
  divine 219, 225–7, 233f, 239, 243, 247
  human 28, 67, 229, 247; see also will-to-life
  madness 181, 221, 253
  nature- 1, 3, 7, 32, 41, 192, 225–8, 233, 240, 253
  -religion 253–5
  water-sprite 68, 230–32, 253, 255
  -world 220, 227, 230f
spiritual 30, 63, 163, 185, 209, 223f, 227; see also sacred
  causation 1, 32, 107, 131, 202, 223, 251
  conversion 69, 72, 104, 162
  creation 32, 68, 168, 172, 176, 194, 202, 219, 223, 225f, 228, 230f, 240f, 243
  danger 33, 197, 199, 223
  force 30, 116, 163, 197f, 223, 225, 234, 253; see also will-to-life
  heart 42, 129

peace 89, 176, 223
people 161, 178f, 180
place 32
presence 30
sociality 101, 213
validation 131
stars 63, 225, 230, 232f
state 73–5, 116–23, 237, 258
  colonial 5, 12, 122
  institutions 107, 112–14
  justice 104f, 127, 198
  nation- 16, 23, 72
  pre-colonial 43f
Stone Age 11, 37, 41
Sudan 19, 23, 29, 40f, 43f, 46f, 49, 53, 70, 116, 199, 221
Sudanic 234
  Central 39f, 46
  Eastern 39–42, 49, 52
  beliefs 230, 234
Swahili 119
  language 18, 80, 198

Taaba (Karimojong age-section) 139, 148
Taaruk (Pian subsection) 28
tabu 167, 179, 181, 186
  body 49, 79, 91, 95, 97, 125
  food 166, 242
  gender 143, 225
  place 32, 146
  restoration after breaking 33
  totem 206
Tanzania 26, 41, 44f, 53, 70, 112
Tap (agricultural people) 51–3, 58f, 63–7, 75, 134, 167, 182f, 189, 210
Tepes, *see* Sor
territoriality 17, 22f, 26–31, 44, 57, 78, 103, 162 210f; *see also* sections, territorial
territory 30, 45, 60, 64, 148, 156f, 194, 210, 218, 228, 232
Teso 14, 30, 44, 46, 52f, 62, 129
  beliefs 220, 224
  Christian mission 69
  famine refuge 65, 75, 155
  Katakwi 122
  Kumam 49, 53, 149, 169
  military 117, 122, 126, 171, 198
  oral history 40
Teuso, *see* Ik
theft 28, 42, 108, 203, 228
Tiang clan (Najie) 51, 94

Timu Forest (Ik) 45
Titi (Tap) 66f
Tome (Dodosǒ generation-set) 152
  (Jie generation-set) 136–8, 140–43, 147, 149, 150–51, 157, 170–73, 183
  (Karimojong section), *see* Karimojong
tomon, ten 48
topojo, a tree 108
Toposa 23f, 29, 39, 48, 52, 59, 61, 63, 66, 70, 193, 199
  beliefs 232
Toror, Mount 19, 45, 50, 128f, 192, 225f
torture 113, 260
trade 16, 23, 65, 97, 123, 126, 210f, 260
  cattle 210f
  cowrie-shells 65
  guns 116, 128, 131, 210
  markets 116
  skins 42, 131
tradition 1–14, 17f, 26–30, 35, 71f, 77–80, 88, 93f, 133, 195, 259–61
  disappearing 26, 115, 124, 251, 258 260
  invented 3–5, 8, 10, 13, 16, 22–4, 26, 38, 54, 109, 111, 145, 237, 259, 261
  oral 41, 46–53, 62–7, 74–6, 103, 106, 128, 133, 142, 144, 143–6, 174–6, 182, 237
  sacred 171, 186, 200
traditional 98–101
  agriculture 129
  army 111f, 117, 119f, 123, 126f, 154f, 171, 198
  culture 114, 117, 123, 186, 259f
  economy 202, 260
  law 103, 106, 108
  marriage 132, 216
  medicine 90, 181, 255
  mentality 135, 210, 214f, 223–61
  music and dance 91, 215–18
  police 107–10
  politics 12, 119, 123, 131, 183, 259
  societies 3, 131, 172–4, 177–9, 259–61
traditionalism 129, 161f, 189f, 213, 228, 257, 260f
tribe 14, 22–4, 26, 28f, 55, 62f, 71, 78, 107, 110, 141, 145, 149, 153–5, 171, 174, 182, 193, 197, 216, 219, 229, 237, 245, 250

Tunga (proto-EN apart from the Bari) 39, 46, 48, 52; *see also* Itunga; Nilotes, Eastern
Turkana 11, 19, 23f, 29–31, 37–41, 44, 48, 51f, 54, 193
   beliefs 226, 234, 246
   cattle-raiding 61, 112–14, 116, 119f, 128, 136, 214
   cattle, valuation of 210
   customs 59, 161, 179, 186f, 199f
   formation 6–9
   identity 259
   oral history 48, 53, 62, 149
Turkana, Lake 37–46, 50f, 54f
Turkwel River 44, 65, 149

Uganda 14, 18–20, 23, 46f, 62, 65, 68–72, 75f, 100, 111f, 124, 132f
   attitudes to Karamojong 26, 126, 198f, 217
   Baganda 4f, 121, 125
   Entebbe 181
   Government of 72, 100, 107, 117, 120–22, 209
   Karamojong and Uganda 75–7, 252, 256f, 258
   north(east) 50, 53, 58, 119, 128, 227
   President of 108, 113, 120, 122, 124f, 132, 197, 260
   radio 97, 100, 195, 260
   UPDF 30, 121f, 128, 191
Upe 54, 120, 131; *see also* Pokot
urine 42, 211

Verona Fathers (Comboni Missionaries) 72, 124, 137, 237, 258
Victoria, Lake 37, 125
violence 26, 66, 75f, 103, 109, 112, 117, 119–27, 235, 245
   escalation 125, 127f, 130
   non-violence 173

war 23, 29, 31, 54, 67, 69, 101, 112f, 115, 125, 127f, 136, 182–4, 195f, 199–201, 211, 217, 231
   -leader 31, 111, 115, 131, 195f
   military 12, 17, 30f, 33, 43, 45, 75, 97, 100f, 106, 111–13, 116f, 119–23, 125f, 131, 133f, 155f, 197f, 211, 215
   warlord 111, 113, 115–17, 119, 121

warrior 43, 66, 97, 100f, 107, 109, 113f, 116f, 119, 121f, 124–8, 130, 132, 146, 148, 149, 154, 159, 183, 189, 193, 196, 199, 205, 213, 217, 247, 257
Wayland, Edward 19, 22, 24, 62, 64, 82, 125, 145, 175, 199, 216, 226–8, 234
Western 126, 133; *see also* European; politics
   education 5, 14, 69–4, 79f, 82, 97, 100f, 124, 186, 211, 213f, 216, 257
   influence 112
   intervention 57, 68f, 70f, 73, 90, 98, 117, 148, 213
   presuppositions 6–8, 12, 18, 58, 113, 125, 131, 185, 187, 209, 222f, 235, 258
will-to-life 32, 223; *see also etau*
   life-force 130, 166, 197
witchcraft 31, 71, 90f, 162, 179, 224, 257
   accusations 187, 202f, 225, 253, 257
   witch 32, 73, 79, 225, 230, 255; *see also ekabeman; ekapilan*
wizard 32, 71, 179; *see also ekabeman; ekapilan*
women 14, 27f; *see also* age-class; blessing; initiation; marriage; Nacere; Napeikisina; Nayece; religion
   brewers 189
   casualties 120, 125, 127
   concubines 80
   cultivators and landowners 188, 110, 131, 188
   decoration 86, 233
   foreign 71
   gender distinctiveness 31f, 44, 79, 109, 116f, 124f, 135, 159f, 181f, 198, 201, 223, 234, 242, 256, 260f
   home 27
   informants 14
   nudity 49
   praying 32, 48, 250
   ritual 65, 75, 87, 85–95, 110, 143, 148, 164, 166, 171–6, 185f, 195f, 201, 251–5
   social actors 5, 81f, 92, 98–101, 124, 131, 160f, 182, 192, 196, 206, 217, 229, 234, 256
   social value 101, 108, 129, 199, 215, 256

wrist-knife 43, 210

Yen (WN clan) 46, 53, 134, 141, 210

Zulia, Mount (Ik) 53

For Product Safety Concerns and Information please contact our EU
representative GPSR@taylorandfrancis.com
Taylor & Francis Verlag GmbH, Kaufingerstraße 24, 80331 München, Germany

www.ingramcontent.com/pod-product-compliance
Lightning Source LLC
Chambersburg PA
CBHW071233290426
44108CB00013B/1393